Ronald W. Clark's widely-praised biographies include lives of Einstein, Bertrand Russell, the Huxleys, and J. B. S. Haldane. Born in 1916, he served as a War Correspondent with the Canadian Army in the Second World War, landing in Normandy on D-Day and covering the fighting until the end of hostilities. He subsequently reported many of the most famous War Crimes trials. Later he wrote two well-known works on science and war, *The Birth of the Bomb* and *The Rise of the Boffins*. For these, and for his life of Sir Henry Tizard, he was given access to much hitherto inaccessible material and interviewed many of the scientists who have worked with the Services. His latest work on the subject is the recently-published *The Greatest Power on Earth*.

His ability to describe scientific work excitingly but accurately is well exercised in *Freud: The Man and the Cause*. It uses much previously unknown material and has been described by Stuart Hampshire as 'an admirably balanced biography'; by Anthony Storr as 'a notable success'; by R. D. Laing as 'a masterly biography'; and by Richard Holmes in *The Times* as making 'the whole story of the Psychoanalytic movement intensely interesting and exciting'.

Ronald Clark is also a distinguished historian of mountaineering and has written extensively on the subject during the last 30 years. He divides his time between London and Wiltshire.

RONALD W. CLARK

Freud

The Man and The Cause

PALADIN
GRAFTON BOOKS
A Division of the Collins Publishing Group

LONDON GLASGOW
TORONTO SYDNEY AUCKLAND

Paladin
Grafton Books
A Division of the Collins Publishing Group
8 Grafton Street, London W1X 3LA

Published in Paladin Books 1982
Reprinted 1987

First published in Great Britain by
Jonathan Cape Ltd/Weidenfeld & Nicholson Ltd 1980

Copyright © E. M. Partners A. G. 1980

ISBN 0-586-08395-2

Printed and bound in Great Britain by
Collins, Glasgow

Set in Baskerville

Acknowledgments

My first thanks are to Prince Masud Khan and Mark Paterson, of Sigmund Freud Copyrights Ltd., who have generously allowed me to use published and unpublished copyright material which they control. I am grateful also to Mrs. Pat Marsden, of Sigmund Freud Copyrights Ltd., for extensive help in consulting the Freud archives over the years.

I also wish to thank the Institute of Psycho-Analysis, which has enabled me to consult the papers of the late Ernest Jones as well as other material. I am especially grateful to Prince Masud Khan, John Jarrett, Dr. Dennis Duncan and Miss Jill Duncan.

Those whom I wish to thank for permission to use other copyright material include Mrs. Balint-Edwards (letters of Dr. Michael Balint); Charles Biederman (letter to Ernest Jones); Dr. Med. M. Bleuler (letters of Dr. Eugen Bleuler); Clark University (letter from Dr. Stanley Hall); Dr. Helene Deutsch (unpublished MS of Dr. Felix Deutsch); Mrs. Katherine Jones (letters of Dr. Ernest Jones.

While the opinions in the book, and responsibility for facts given, are entirely my own unless the reverse is made clear, I am most grateful for help and advice from Professor Henri F. Ellenberger; Dr. Alexander Grinstein; Dr. Paul Kline; Professor William A. Koelsch and Miss Suzanne Hamel; Dr. Zigmond M. Lebensohn; Dr. J. D. W. Pearce; Dr. Charles Rycroft; Professor Richard Slobodin.

ACKNOWLEDGMENTS

Others I wish to thank include the Adirondack Museum, Blue Mountain Lake (Craig Gilhorn); Vincent Brome; George Edinger; the Francis A. Countway Library of Medicine, Boston (Richard Wolf); the Jewish National and University Library, Jerusalem (Dr. M. Nadav); John Rylands University Library of Manchester (Miss Glenise A. Matheson); Dr. Otakar Kucera; Leo Baeck Institute, New York; the Library of Congress, Washington (John C. Broderick and Dr. Ronald Wilkinson); National Archives and Records Service, Washington (Ronald E. Swerczek); National Archives and Records Service, Hyde Park (Donald B. Schewe); Nový Jičín District Archivist, Czechoslovakia; Opava Chief Archivist, Státníoblastni Archiv v, Czechoslovakia; Professor Paul Roazen; Dr. Helene Schur; Metropolitan Library, Toronto (Ms. Margery Allen); Rayner Unwin; the Wiener Library; the Weizmann Archives, Rehovot.

R. W. C.

Contents

CONTENTS

THE FREUDIAN AGE

Illustrations

PICTURE CREDITS

The author and publishers would like to thank the following for permission to reproduce copyright material in the illustrations:

Adirondack Museum, New York; Basic Books Inc., New York (photo by Edmund Engelman); Bildarchiv Preussicher Kulturbesitz, Berlin; Institut für Geschichte der Medizin der Universität Wien; Österreichischer Nationalbibliothek, Wien; all other photographs supplied by Sigmund Freud Copyrights.

A
FREUDIAN
BEGINNING

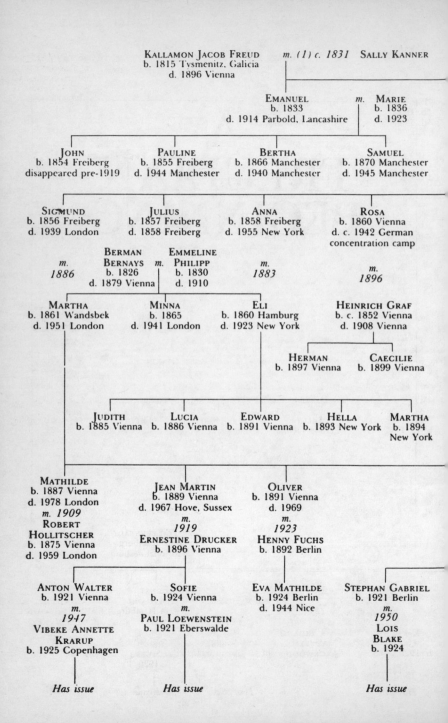

KALLAMON JACOB FREUD *m. (1) c. 1831* SALLY KANNER
b. 1815 Tysmenitz, Galicia
d. 1896 Vienna

EMANUEL *m.* MARIE
b. 1833 b. 1836
d. 1914 Parbold, Lancashire d. 1923

JOHN PAULINE BERTHA SAMUEL
b. 1854 Freiberg b. 1855 Freiberg b. 1866 Manchester b. 1870 Manchester
disappeared pre-1919 d. 1944 Manchester d. 1940 Manchester d. 1945 Manchester

SIGMUND JULIUS ANNA ROSA
b. 1856 Freiberg b. 1857 Freiberg b. 1858 Freiberg b. 1860 Vienna
d. 1939 London d. 1858 Freiberg d. 1955 New York d. c. 1942 German
concentration camp

m. BERMAN EMMELINE *m.*
1886 BERNAYS *m.* PHILIPP *1883* *m.*
b. 1826 b. 1830 *1896*
d. 1879 Vienna d. 1910

MARTHA MINNA ELI HEINRICH GRAF
b. 1861 Wandsbek b. 1865 b. 1860 Hamburg b. c. 1852 Vienna
d. 1951 London d. 1941 London d. 1923 New York d. 1908 Vienna

HERMAN CAECILIE
b. 1897 Vienna b. 1899 Vienna

JUDITH LUCIA EDWARD HELLA MARTHA
b. 1885 Vienna b. 1886 Vienna b. 1891 Vienna b. 1893 New York b. 1894
New York

MATHILDE JEAN MARTIN OLIVER
b. 1887 Vienna b. 1889 Vienna b. 1891 Vienna
d. 1978 London d. 1967 Hove, Sussex d. 1969
m. 1909 *m.* *m.*
ROBERT *1919* *1923*
HOLLITSCHER ERNESTINE DRUCKER HENNY FUCHS
b. 1875 Vienna b. 1896 Vienna b. 1892 Berlin
d. 1959 London

ANTON WALTER SOFIE EVA MATHILDE STEPHAN GABRIEL
b. 1921 Vienna b. 1924 Vienna b. 1924 Berlin b. 1921 Berlin
m. *m.* d. 1944 Nice *m.*
1947 PAUL LOEWENSTEIN *1950*
VIBEKE ANNETTE b. 1921 Eberswalde LOIS
KRARUP BLAKE
b. 1925 Copenhagen b. 1924

Has issue *Has issue* *Has issue*

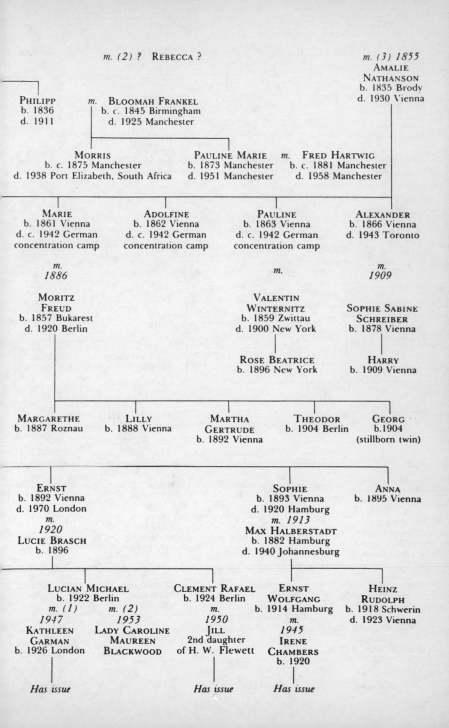

m. (2) ? REBECCA ?

m. (3) 1855
AMALIE
NATHANSON
b. 1835 Brody
d. 1930 Vienna

PHILIPP
b. 1836
d. 1911

m.   BLOOMAH FRANKEL
b. c. 1845 Birmingham
d. 1925 Manchester

MORRIS
b. c. 1875 Manchester
d. 1938 Port Elizabeth, South Africa

PAULINE MARIE   m.   FRED HARTWIG
b. 1873 Manchester   b. c. 1881 Manchester
d. 1951 Manchester   d. 1958 Manchester

MARIE
b. 1861 Vienna
d. c. 1942 German
concentration camp

ADOLFINE
b. 1862 Vienna
d. c. 1942 German
concentration camp

PAULINE
b. 1863 Vienna
d. c. 1942 German
concentration camp

ALEXANDER
b. 1866 Vienna
d. 1943 Toronto

m.
1886

MORITZ
FREUD
b. 1857 Bukarest
d. 1920 Berlin

m.

VALENTIN
WINTERNITZ
b. 1859 Zwittau
d. 1900 New York

m.
1909

SOPHIE SABINE
SCHREIBER
b. 1878 Vienna

ROSE BEATRICE
b. 1896 New York

HARRY
b. 1909 Vienna

MARGARETHE
b. 1887 Roznau

LILLY
b. 1888 Vienna

MARTHA
GERTRUDE
b. 1892 Vienna

THEODOR
b. 1904 Berlin

GEORG
b.1904
(stillborn twin)

ERNST
b. 1892 Vienna
d. 1970 London
m.
1920
LUCIE BRASCH
b. 1896

SOPHIE
b. 1893 Vienna
d. 1920 Hamburg
m. 1913
MAX HALBERSTADT
b. 1882 Hamburg
d. 1940 Johannesburg

ANNA
b. 1895 Vienna

LUCIAN MICHAEL
b. 1922 Berlin
m. (1)   m. (2)
1947   1953
KATHLEEN   LADY CAROLINE
GARMAN   MAUREEN
b. 1926 London BLACKWOOD

CLEMENT RAFAEL
b. 1924 Berlin
m.
1950
JILL
2nd daughter
of H. W. Flewett

ERNST
WOLFGANG
b. 1914 Hamburg
m.
1945
IRENE
CHAMBERS
b. 1920

HEINZ
RUDOLPH
b. 1918 Schwerin
d. 1923 Vienna

Has issue

Has issue

Has issue

1

Jewish Boyhood

. . . if a man has been his mother's undisputed darling he retains throughout life the triumphant feeling, the confidence in success, which not seldom brings actual success along with it.

FREUD, "A Childhood Recollection" from *Dichtung und Wahrheit*

Sigismund Freud was born on May 6, 1856, in the Moravian town of Freiberg, in a small second-floor room that was the family's only home until 1859. In this one room of No. 117 Schlossergasse there lived Kallamon Jacob Freud,* his wife Amalie, their son Sigismund, a second son who died a few months after birth, and then a daughter. In the only other room on the floor lived the family of Johann Zajic, a locksmith who occupied the ground floor as a workshop and whose ancestors had lived in the building for generations.

The boy born in these humble circumstances was to revolutionize man's view of his own mind and of the control over it which he can exercise. Declaring that unconscious motives lie below much mental disease, he was to develop a theory which maintained that similar factors govern many events in the everyday lives of ordinary people. The belief that a link exists between the mentally abnormal and the mentally sound would, when Freud set up in practice, have in itself been enough to make him the target for distortion and abuse. Yet it was also to be the essence of his ideas not only that repressed sexual feelings or experiences lie behind much mental disease but that from earliest childhood sex plays an

---

*The names of Freud's parents, like those of other Jews of the same time and country, are spelled in a number of ways, even appearing differently in a single official document. Those used here are the generally accepted Anglicized spellings.

important if usually unrecognized part in life, claims which brought condemnation not only from church, society and state, but from many members of the medical profession.

Much of Freud's work, like that of most successful pioneers, had become incorporated into the accepted order of things even before his death. Some of it has since been reduced in importance, some of it discarded; and over the manner in which his fundamental ideas have been developed and exploited, bitter dispute still rages. To devoted followers, his theories raised him to the level of Galileo, Darwin and Einstein; yet Sir Peter Medawar, a Nobel Prize-winner for Medicine, in a methodological criticism of the foundations of psychoanalysis as practiced by many of Freud's successors, has called its theories "one of the saddest and strangest of all landmarks in the history of twentieth-century thought." The differences in assessment have proliferated during the forty years that have passed since Freud's death, and have been deepened on both sides by claims often put forward with a vigor more usually reserved for theology or politics than for science or medicine. Only around Darwin has the intellectual battle raged so fiercely, and with so little quarter being asked for or given by either side. Over it, as unmoved by the beatification of followers as by the diatribes of opponents, there has remained the figure of Freud himself—dispassionate, rock-steady and, in public at least, utterly self-confident.

Prominent in the debate about theories which have for almost eighty years divided ideas about the mind into pre-Freudian and post-Freudian is the argument about how far these theories were molded by the circumstances of Freud's early life and his determination to struggle upward against adversities which, if sometimes overestimated, were nevertheless very real.

Certainly it is difficult to isolate the claustrophobic family intimacies of his early surroundings from his psychic development, and more than a century after his birth his own doctor noted that the "family's cramped living quarters . . . must have meant that during those three formative years [he] was subjected to perceptions of the kind he later described as traumatic." To these circumstances of his early years there was added the unusual composition of the family. Jacob Freud, aged forty when his son Sigismund was born, already had two grown sons by an earlier marriage: Emanuel, born in 1832, and Philipp, born in 1836. Sigismund's twenty-year-old mother was as young as, or younger than, her stepsons, who lived nearby. His father was old enough to be his grandfather, his mother young enough to be his sister, while his boyhood playmates were his nephew John, a year younger than himself, and his niece Pauline, of roughly the same age.

Hovering in the background, there may also have been the ghost of Rebecca, the woman listed as Jacob Freud's wife in the register of Jews made in Freiberg in 1852 by the Catholic authorities: the woman who was neither Sally Kanner, the mother of Emanuel and Philipp, nor Amalie, mother of the Sigismund who later saw the mother-child relationship as a key to psychic development. The theme of the "two mothers" was to be a backbone of his controversial speculation on Leonardo da Vinci, and it is ironic that only after Freud's death should the figure of Rebecca, apparently the first of his stepbrothers' two stepmothers, add a further complexity to an already complex family history.

Rebecca was disinterred from the Freiberg records in the 1960s. The initial discovery has been amplified by more than one researcher, and during the last two decades much fresh light has been thrown on Freud's earliest years. Uncertainties remain, but today it is possible to be confident of one thing: Freud's infant years in Freiberg are likely to have been far more influential on the birth and growth of psychoanalysis than has previously been admitted.

The family into which he was born had a history similar to that of many European Jews. Jacob Freud's ancestors had settled centuries earlier in the Rhineland; had been driven into the Baltic States by anti-Semitic persecutions; and had only in the nineteenth century drifted south into Galicia, a country once in Poland, then in the Austro-Hungarian Empire and today a part of the Soviet Ukraine. Jacob had been born in 1815 in Tysmenica, where Jews made up half the population of 6,000, a town surrounded by villages and hamlets that were strongholds of Jewish rabbinic and Hasidic learning. Little is known about his life until 1840, when the Freud family split up. One branch moved south to Roumania; the other traveled some 200 miles west into Moravia. Jacob's maternal grandfather, Abraham Sisskind Hoffman, settled in Freiberg. Jacob, together with other members of the family that may have included his father and one or more of his brothers, settled in Klogsdorf, a hamlet separated from Freiberg by the river Lubina. But Jacob's first wife, Sally Kanner, appears to have remained in Tysmenica with their two sons, Emanuel and Philipp.

Freiberg, which reverted to its former name of Příbor when Czechoslovakia was carved out of the Austro-Hungarian Empire after the end of the First World War, lies in the foothills of the Carpathians, 150 miles northeast of Vienna, and a dozen miles from today's frontier with Poland. Bisected by the Vienna–Cracow road, now the E7 highway, its houses straggle along the banks of the river Lubina or stand on the steep westward-facing slopes which rise from it. A few miles away to the west lay Heinzedorf—now Hyncica—the birthplace of Gregor Mendel, the monk who laid the foundations for the study of genetics. In 1856 the town's activities were centered on the main square, where terraces of arcaded houses were dominated by the church of Maria Geburt with its ten altars. Of Freiberg's 5,000 inhabitants, some 4,000 were Catholic, about 100 Protestant. The Jews numbered about 100, were mainly of German extraction and, with the rise of Czech nationalism in the 1840s, suffered from a local attitude that tended to be both anti-Semitic and anti-German. It is true that most of them rubbed along well enough with their neighbors in the free-and-easy atmosphere of the small market town, yet they still remained the potential scapegoat for whatever misfortunes arrived.

Four years after the Freuds had moved to Moravia, Sisskind Hoffman, who like his grandson Jacob was registered as a Galician wandering Jew, applied for permission to take Jacob into partnership. "As is known," went his application to the magistrate,

I deal in cloth, wool, honey, suet [tallow], etc. and have been for several years partly in Freiberg and partly in the surrounding area. I intend to settle in Freiberg . . .

I am sixty-nine years old and cannot myself handle the demands of business, so have taken my grandson Kallman [Jacob] Freud as partner. He will direct other affairs while I conduct the buying and selling in Freiberg. I have therefore secured for myself and my grandson K. Freud a traveling passport from the government of Lemberg, valid for one year.

I therefore ask the honorable magistrate to grant both of us tolerance in Freiberg for the duration of the passport, that is, until May 1845.

The head of the clothmakers guild, asked for advice, reported that Sisskind Hoffman and his grandson Kallamon [Jacob] Freud were both honorable and good men. Local trade was increased by their residence, and it was therefore proposed that their application be granted. Not only was this done but the permit was regularly extended, and in 1848 the local Council went so far as to comment on the benefit which Jacob Freud and other traders from Galicia were bringing to the town.

The joint business appears to have prospered for some years, and before the end of 1852 Jacob's two sons, Emanuel and Philipp, now aged about twenty and sixteen, joined him in Freiberg. Not only does the local register of Jews for that year list his wife as a thirty-two-year-old Rebecca, but a Freiberg document has been quoted for the fact that the two sons came to Freiberg with this second wife.

Nothing has come to light about the death of Sally Kanner, presumably in Tysmenica. Rebecca disappears from the records as mysteriously as she arrived, and it has been assumed that she died before Jacob Freud married his third wife, Amalie Nathanson, Sigismund Freud's mother, in Vienna in 1855. However, an official search of the State Archive at the regional center of Opava has failed to produce any evidence of Rebecca's death. There are other alternatives, as Professor Renée Gicklhorn has pointed out. "Maybe," she has written, "Rebecca was repudiated because she had no child, a fact which authorizes an Orthodox Jew to break up a marriage and to consider himself free to marry again. But he would have been obliged to mention before the magistrate in Vienna the fact that he had divorced his second wife before marrying Amalie Nathanson—a fact he kept silent about." Whatever the truth about Rebecca, the founder of psychoanalysis made no reference to her in any published family history, or in any correspondence made available by his descendants.

There appear to be three possibilities. The first is that the records are incorrect. Statements made during this period to the Catholic authorities by the Jews have been questioned before, and it is true that in the relevant Freud entry at least one age appears to be wrongly given. Nevertheless, in view of the evidence the case against Rebecca as a wife appears to be slim, although it cannot be entirely ruled out. The second possibility is that she was successfully, but for reasons unknown, kept a secret from Sigismund Freud. Yet Sigismund's mother spent from 1856 until 1859 in the small town of 5,000 inhabitants where Jacob had been registered with his wife Rebecca. It seems unlikely that Amalie would not know of the fact—at least from the neighbors—and equally unlikely that she would have successfully kept the truth from her much-loved son until her death at the age of ninety-five. In addition, if Sigismund was kept in ignorance, both Emanuel and Philipp must also have failed to mention to him the stepmother who appears to have brought them to Freiberg.

The third alternative is that the young Freud acquired some knowledge of his father's affairs but repressed it, for the whole of his life, respecting the family taboo out of filial loyalty and keeping its knowledge secret even from his wife Martha, who always spoke of Jacob Freud as having been married twice, not thrice. This third possibility, if correct, would, according to Freud's own beliefs, have significantly affected the development of his own mental life, and it would be ingenuous to believe that it would not have affected the course of psychoanalysis.

His early family environment—even without any later need to deal with a family taboo—was of a kind to leave its mark. Yet—or perhaps it should be "so"—Freud himself was always anxious to discount the effect of personal experience on psychoanalysis.

Many of his followers have taken the same line, his brilliant youngest daughter Anna suggesting that too much could be made of her father's neurosis, and other Freudians disapproving of the suggestion "that because Freud had a certain neurotic symptom, therefore he pronounced a certain theory." Yet at many critical moments in his life the evidence, though circumstantial, is too strong to be ignored. Thirty years after Freud had developed his theory of the unconscious, Werner Heisenberg, the world-famous German physicist, was showing that in the physical world, at the subatomic level, the mere act of observing inevitably affected what was being observed. Freud, the neurologist who had shown that man's intellect was at the mercy of his unconscious, worked, on the psychic level, within comparably limiting parameters of experimental experience: in the world of the mind the mental background of the observer inevitably—if unconsciously—affected the significance of what was observed.

Of Jacob Freud's life for the three years following 1852 virtually nothing is known, and it is only in 1855 that he again appears in the records. On July 29 he was married in Vienna to Amalie Nathanson, describing himself on the certificate as a widower since 1852.

The bride, a beautiful girl who at nineteen was roughly half Jacob's age, also came from Galicia, where in the town of Brody a tombstone recalled her ancestor Samuel Charmaz as prince, leader, chief, rabbinical scholar. The daughter of a business agent, she was, in 1855, living with her parents in Vienna. Though the marriage to Jacob was performed by an exponent of Reform Judaism, the bride, if not the groom, retained her strictly Orthodox practices. And to her, Sigismund Freud—or "Sigmund" as he was later called—was to owe much of the Jewish mysticism that would surface occasionally in his writings.

The status of Jacob Freud and his young wife when their first son was born in 1856 remains obscure. While it was not then unusual for minor traders in such towns as Freiberg to live in a single room of a house whose dimensions were only some 30 feet by 30 feet, it is clear that Jacob was hardly a mill owner as he has been described, and his son's reminiscences of a family which was originally well-to-do must be taken with caution.

Shortly after Freud's birth his father recorded the event in the family Bible in these words: "My son Shlomo Sigismund, may he live, was born on Tuesday, Rosh Hodesh Iyar (5)616, 6:30 P.M. on May 6, (1)856 and was circumcised on Tuesday, the 8th day of the month of Iyar, on May 13, (1)856. The *mohel* [circumciser] was Reb Shimshon Frankel of Ostrau [Moravská Ostrava], godparents were

Reb Lippe and his sister Mirel Hurwitz, children of the rabbi of Czernowitz. The *sandek* [the man who holds the infant on his knees during circumcision] was Reb Shmuel Samueli . . ." Schlomo had been the name of Jacob Freud's father, who had died only a few weeks before the birth of his grandson, and it has been speculated, not too implausibly, that Jacob had great expectations of the child of his beautiful young wife. The German name Sigismund had its association with *Sieg*, or "victory."

The boy had been born in a caul—traditionally a sign of good fortune—and so covered with black hair that his mother called him a little blackamoor. Not much more is known about his birth or, indeed, about the next few years of his life. As might be expected, unconfirmable stories abound, notably that of the woman—midwife or shopkeeper according to source—who at the birth announced that Amalie had brought a great man into the world. Forty years on, Freud himself, by then quite sure of his destiny, could write: "Prophecies of this kind must be very common: there are so many mothers filled with happy expectations and so many old peasant women and others of the kind who make up for the loss of their power to control things in the present world by concentrating it on the future. Nor can the prophetess have lost anything by her words." Yet the words had stuck, and after quoting them he was to ask: "Could this have been the source of my thirst for grandeur?"

Almost all the details of Freud's early years come from his own recollections and reconstructions near the turn of the century. They were recovered, and built up, while carrying out his self-analysis following the death of his father and are described in the letters to his colleague Wilhelm Fliess, which have been published only in censored form; in a paper on "Screen Memories" purporting to give the first-person reminiscences of a patient but now known to be autobiographical; in *The Interpretation of Dreams*, where he wrote that the dreams were recorded after "taking the edge off some of my indiscretions by omissions and substitutions"; and in the autobiographical paragraphs of *The Psychopathology of Everyday Life*, which was published in 1901. His *An Autobiographical Study* is almost exclusively a record of his professional life.

It is not surprising that the autobiographical material dealing with Freud's earlier years is often contradictory in detail. It is not even surprising that he should give two versions and three interpretations of some memories; recollections, given over the years and mutually confirmatory in detail, are, after all, often suspicious rather than otherwise. The omissions and substitutions of *The Interpretation of Dreams* may have been used to bend arguments; it is more likely that discrepancies between reminiscence and fact are those to be expected from any man groping back into the past. Yet as Max Schur, Freud's doctor of the 1930s who tried to correlate fact and reminiscence, has pointed out: "The actuarial data . . . point to certain inaccuracies in Freud's reconstruction of early childhood memories, which he [Freud] derived mainly from the interpretation of his own dreams during his self-analysis." His recollections in middle age of his earliest years should therefore be viewed with care as evidence of what may actually have happened.

Among the events that took place in Freud's youth was his entry into his parents' bedroom from curiosity, after which he was ordered out by an irate father; date uncertain, since it conflicts with the single room of No. 117 Schlossergasse. He recalled how on another occasion, after he had been reprimanded by Jacob for wetting his bed, he had consoled his father by promising to buy him a new bed in Neu Titschein, the main town of the area. In "Screen Memories" he wrote: "But what should have made most impression on me was an injury to my face which caused a considerable loss of blood and for which I had to have some stitches put in by a surgeon. I can still feel the scar resulting from this accident, but I know of no recollection which points to it, either directly or indirectly. It is true that I may perhaps have been under two years at the time."

These recollections, correct or not, appear less important in retrospect than others, which Freud believed played a significant part in his later development. He was convinced that he ". . . welcomed [his] one-year younger brother (who died within a few months) with ill wishes and real infantile jealousy, and that his death left the germ of guilt in me. I have long known," he continued at the age of forty-one, "that my companion in crime between the ages of one and two was a nephew of mine who is a year older than I am and now lives in Manchester; he visited us in Vienna when I was fourteen. We seem occasionally to have treated my niece, who was a year younger, shockingly. My nephew and younger brother determined not only the neurotic side of all my friendships but also their depth."

One example of cruelty was recalled in some detail. "I see a rectangular, rather steeply sloping piece of meadow-land, green and thickly-grown," he wrote;

in the green there are a great number of yellow flowers—evidently common dandelions. At the top end of the meadow there is a cottage and in front of the cottage door two women are standing, chatting busily, a peasant-woman with a handkerchief on her head and a children's nurse. Three children are playing in the grass. One of them is myself (between the age of two and three); the two others are my boy cousin, who is a year older than me, and his sister, who is almost exactly the same age as I am. We are picking the yellow flowers and each of us is holding a bunch of flowers we have already picked. The little girl has the best bunch; and, as though by mutual agreement, we—the two boys—fall on her and snatch away her flowers. She runs up the meadow in tears and as a consolation the peasant-woman gives her a big piece of black bread.

More important, as it was later to appear, although more open to controversy, was his recollection of the woman he recalled as an aged and ugly nurse, but who is now known beyond reasonable doubt to have been Monika Zajic, a maid-servant who worked for his half-brother Emanuel's wife and also for his mother.

The memory of the nurse was to lie concealed in Freud's unconscious until almost the turn of the century, but two other influences of his first years in Freiberg were more obvious for much of his life. One was that of the rolling forests that stretched down from the Carpathians to within half a mile of his home. As an infant, he regularly went into their depths with his father, and there quickly grew up the strong feeling for wild natural scenery which, as he recollected in adult life, filled a need both intellectual and aesthetic. When he was taken with his family from Freiberg, at the age of three, the change of environment hurt—even in Vienna where the woods half enclose the capital. "I never felt really comfortable in the town," he was later to write. "I believe now that I was never free from a longing for the beautiful woods near our home. . . ."

Judging from Freud's own words, it is possible that this yearning for the deeply enclosing Moravian pine forests was a response to one of the phobias in his neurotic make-up. Years later, seen to hesitate when crossing a wide street, he turned to his companion and said, "You see, there is a survival of my old agoraphobia which troubled me much in younger years." Significantly, it has been pointed out that "The common symptom of agoraphobia . . . is usually linked with the persistence of childhood dependency, fear of abandonment by the mother, and also with fears of the patient's own sexuality and aggression. The presenting symptom of being frightened to cross an open space or street unaccompanied is only the peak of the iceberg."

The other influence, as fundamental as the physical environment in Freud's upbringing, was the psychological impact of the family's Jewishness, as much a part of life as sunrise and sunset. Jacob's essentially happy-go-lucky and comparatively questioning attitude to the religion of his people was more than offset by Amalie's orthodoxy; and the young Freud, increasingly critical as he was of the Jewish—and any other—religion, grew up with a feeling for his race second only in importance to the cause of psychoanalysis. "My parents were Jews," he always stressed, "and I have remained a Jew myself."

His loyalty was by no means inevitable, as during his youth and manhood the life of the ghetto slowly disappeared from Europe. As it did so, more and more Jews took the road of baptism, the "admission ticket to European civilization" as Heine called it, and an insurance compared with the danger of retaining the Jewish faith. Freud's colleague of the early 1900s, Alfred Adler, was to be baptized. So was Fritz Haber, the German chemist whose revolutionary method of producing ammonia helped the Fatherland during the First World War—and who found that baptism did not save him from being forced to flee from Germany when Hitler came to power.

Freud trod the harder road. Acutely sensitive to the slightest hint of anti-Semitism, he formed very few friendships with Gentiles. To the end of his life he did not wish to accept royalties from any of his works translated into Hebrew or Yiddish; Jewish mysticism was never far below the level of his conscious thoughts, and at times he felt that the shade of the biblical Joseph, whose interpretation of dreams had brought him prominence in Pharaoh's kingdom, was walking by his side. Important among the historical figures with whom he was to identify, and whose past tended to guide his present, were Hannibal, who had exhorted his armies toward the gates of Rome, and Moses, who led the Chosen People into the Promised Land. Deeply conscious of his separation from many fellow Europeans by an unbridgeable chasm, Freud knew the dangers and was to devote much time, and many schemes, to warding off the charge that psychoanalysis was a Jewish creation. Without the need for this defense, its history might well have been different.

His pride of race had early qualified his respect for Jacob Freud, whom his instinct wished to regard as the unblemished patriarch. The father had recalled to his son the occasion, apparently in Galicia, when he had been walking in the street wearing a new fur cap. "A Christian came up to me," he said, "and with a single blow knocked off my cap into the mud and shouted: 'Jew! get off the pavement!' " Asked what had happened next, Jacob replied: "I went into the roadway and picked up my cap." At the age of forty-three Freud still remembered how he had contrasted the situation with the scene in which Hannibal's father made his son swear to take vengeance on the Romans.

Freud's reaction, and his recording of the incident many years afterward in *The Interpretation of Dreams,* is significant for at least one reason and possibly for two. His shame for his father—if he remembered correctly—emphasizes the gulf between a generation brought up within the ghetto atmosphere of a Europe where Jews were treated as a race apart, and the succeeding generation to whom assimilation, even if not personally acceptable, was a fact of life. It raises, moreover, the possibility that even the most sacred of Freud's beliefs owed more to personal experience than is usually admitted. As Henri Ellenberger has pointed out, the incident with its emotional swing against the father may well help to explain the genesis of the Oedipus complex.

Four years after Jacob Freud had brought his new bride to Freiberg, three years after the birth of his youngest son, the entire Freud family—Jacob, his wife and children and his two elder sons, together with Emanuel's family—left the town. The reason for the move, which brought the young Freud from an Austro-Hungarian province to the bustling capital of Vienna, is by no means certain. It has been suggested that the upheaval was a result of the war between Austria and Italy that broke out early in 1859, and it is certainly true that Jacob and his family are said to have gone first to Leipzig in Germany and to have returned to Hapsburg soil soon after the end of the war, while his sons of military age remained outside the Empire. Nevertheless, a move to avoid conscription, which would hardly have affected forty-four-year-old Jacob, is rather implausible. A more usually accepted explanation is the age-old role of the Jew as scapegoat; yet from the records it seems likely that this played little part in the move. A statement from the burgomaster of the district of Freiberg in which the Freuds' home lay—possibly made when residence permits were being renewed—stated that Jacob and his wife had a good reputation with nothing against them ever having been recorded. And their close Jewish friends, the Flüss family, who had also come to Freiberg from Tysmenica, not only remained in the town but survived and prospered, eventually becoming textile suppliers to the Emperor.

More important than anti-Semitism was the industrialization of the late 1850s, which badly affected the less forward-looking elements in the wool trade, and the fact that the new railway line by-passed Freiberg. It is now known, moreover, that Freud wrote only thirteen years later of a crisis that led to the family's move and that it was the unfavorable turn that their business had taken which caused his stepbrothers to emigrate. Jacob Freud may well have believed that the struggle for survival might be less exacting and more in accordance with his easygoing ways if he sought the security of a big city. Yet, from the admittedly scanty evidence it seems to have been the stepbrothers who provided the main reasons for the translation of Jacob and his wife and children from the provinces to Vienna. It has even been speculated that one reason for the parting of the ways, with Emanuel and Philipp crossing the Channel to Britain while Jacob and his family remained on the Continent, was Jacob's anxiety to put as much distance as possible between his young wife and his equally young son Philipp. No facts have so far surfaced to support the speculation.

Emanuel and Philipp settled in Manchester, where both were soon running prosperous businesses. Jacob, with his wife Amalie and their two children Sigismund and Anna, left Freiberg in 1859 and had by 1860 settled in Vienna. Nothing is known of the family's fortunes in this limbo, although in middle age Freud said that his father had first stayed for a while in Leipzig. At least one of Freud's sons did not believe this was so, and Freud himself did not mention Leipzig in *An Autobiographical Study.* In 1859, Freud recollected years later, the journey from Freiberg—whether to Leipzig or elsewhere—began with a coach ride to the nearest railway station, followed by a train journey through a station identified by Freud as Breslau. Here the blazing gas lamps, possibly the first that the three-year-old boy had seen, seemed to him like souls burning in Hell.

He was in no doubt that the change from the forested countryside of Moravia to the townscapes of big cities was a change for the worse. When a plaque was being unveiled at his birthplace more than seventy years later, he wrote to the burgomaster that, overlaid, but ". . . deeply buried within me there still lives the happy child of Freiberg, the first-born son of a youthful mother, who received his first indelible impressions from this air, from this soil." But it was not only the recollections of Freiberg itself which were to linger at the back of Freud's mind for the rest of his life. For the relatives he had known there during his early childhood—Philipp, Emanuel, Pauline and John, all of whom settled in England—he maintained an affection that went far beyond the family feelings of a typically tight-knit Jewish family. Almost seventy years after the move from Freiberg he could write to Emanuel's younger son Samuel Freud of his grief that he was not to see his English relatives again, "the living ones no more than the dear deceased and remembered."

Jacob Freud and his family came to Vienna in 1860 shortly before the birth of another daughter, Rosa. The city was the capital of an empire that stretched from the Rhine in the west to the Dneister in the east, from the Po Valley of what is now the Italian plain to the outliers of the Carpathians, a conglomerate of races and nationalities for whom there were published newspapers in German, Hungarian, Polish, Ruthenian, Czech, Slovak, Serbo-Croatian, Slovene, Roumanian and Italian. The polyglot atmosphere increased during the following years as emigrants from the provinces sought to make or restore their fortunes in the capital. In 1860 the city's population was under 500,000; within two decades it had risen to more than 700,000.

As the Freuds settled into their humble apartment in the Weissgärberstrasse, the city was in a state of transition. The massive fortifications, which since the sixteenth century had protected Vienna, were now being demolished, and in their place there was already taking shape the magnificent Ringstrasse, nearly 200 feet wide and providing a series of splendid boulevards which buttoned the inner city back against the Danube. Along it there were to rise— even though the ghetto still remained, and legal restraints on the Jews were not completely to be lifted for another seven years—the magnificent *palais* of such Jewish bankers as Eduard Tedesco and Friedrich Schey, and the great home of Fritz Wertheim. Later came the pseudo-Gothic Rathaus, the Imperial Opera House and numerous imposing government buildings. The Empire was indeed at the height of its ebullient self-confidence; Franz Joseph was to rule for another half-century. But these were to be fifty years of national decline during which the Austrians and Hungarians were excluded from Germany, forced from Venezia and finally pushed into becoming a junior partner to the dominating Prussians to the north. Freud's youth was to be spent in a country where, it was sometimes claimed, the situation was "always desperate but never serious."

For a while the family fortunes also sank, and he was later to write of the move from Freiberg: "long and difficult years followed, of which, as it seems to me, nothing was worth remembering." It is significant that Jacob does not appear to be listed in either the Vienna Trade Register or the Trade Tax Register since, as Professor Gicklhorn has commented after an exhaustive investigation, this apparently rules out not only his existence as a wool merchant but as any sort of trader. Freud was later to say that the family lived in very limited circumstances; and his son Martin, who was only about ten when Jacob Freud died but who presumably gleaned much from his grandmother, has described his grandfather as the typical Micawberish figure, always waiting for something to turn up. Of his father, Freud once said to his bride-to-be: "When he isn't exactly grouchy, which alas is very often the case, he is the greatest optimist of all us young people."

Of Jacob Freud's brothers even less is known. Freud says of his Uncle Joseph that he was concerned with an infringement of the law that turned Jacob's hair gray. The infringement, according to

Ernest Jones, Freud's official biographer, was only a minor offense settled by payment of a fine, but Professor Gicklhorn has shown that it was in fact the handling of forged bank notes, for which Joseph was sentenced to ten years in prison.

During the next few years, as Amalie Freud produced three·more daughters and another son—Marie in 1861, Adolfine in 1862, Pauline in 1863 and Alexander in 1866—the family moved first to Pillersdorfgasse, then to the Pfeffergasse on the outskirts of the Leopoldstadt, the mainly Jewish quarter where Napoleon's Marshal Masséna had made his headquarters after helping to capture the city in 1809. In the 1860s the short narrow street led into comparatively open country, and only a short distance away a wooded area joined the meadows and parks of the Prater. But as far as Freud was concerned, not even the Wienerwald made up for the pine forests of Moravia.

The Freud's third apartment was larger than their earlier homes and included two living rooms, three bedrooms and a small chamber separated from the rest of the apartment. There were other signs that Jacob was now, by one means or another, less hard up. When Sigismund entered the local *Gymnasium,* following a short spell of home teaching and some terms at a private school, his father continued to pay the routine fees even though his son quickly reached the head of the class, an achievement that exempted Jacob from the need to pay. Freud remembered the family as having one of the first new, and expensive, oil lamps in the district. A young sister was for a while given piano lessons, and Jacob Freud employed a local artist to paint portraits of his children. One hint of where the money came from is given by Jacob's eldest daughter Anna, who wrote of her father having business interests in England. Sons Emanuel and Philipp, known to have made a success of their emigration, probably helped to ease their father through financial hard times. Sigmund Freud later did the same.

Of the first years in Vienna, Freud had few memories. There was a time when he had deliberately urinated in his parents' bedroom. The alleged exhibition reportedly brought from his father the pronouncement that he would never amount to anything, a remark which crops up regularly in childhoods of the famous. He remembered his mother telling him that humans were made of earth and would return to earth, then trying to prove her point by rubbing her hands together and showing him the dark pieces of epidermis. There was also the occasion when, he recollected, his father gave him and his sister a book that described a journey through Persia and contained colored plates. The children's job was to destroy it.

"Not easy to justify from the educational point of view!" Freud wrote. "I had been five years old at the time and my sister not yet three; and the picture of the two of us blissfully pulling the book to pieces (leaf by leaf like an *artichoke,* I found myself saying) was almost the only plastic memory that I retained from that period of my life."

Sigismund was nine when he passed the examination that allowed him to join the Leopoldstadter Communal Realgymnasium. This was the official name of the school, although in the late 1870s, when an extension was made into the Sperlgasse, it became colloquially known as the Sperlgymnasium. And it was here that the forecast of future greatness first looked as though it might be realized. Freud stayed at the top of his class until he graduated at the age of seventeen.

Education was along strictly classical lines. The rigorous grounding in Latin and Greek opened his eyes to the ancient world, aroused an interest in archaeological discovery that never left him and gave him the ability to express the most complex ideas in simple prose with an ease so many of his supporters and followers were to lack. But there was more to it than that, for at the *Gymnasium* there opened up the "first understandings of a civilization that had vanished. At least for me," Freud wrote, "they later became a never excelled comfort in the struggle for life."

He also learned French and English and in his spare time taught himself the rudiments of Spanish and Italian. Interest in natural science may have been aroused by a copy of *History of Animal Life,* awarded as a school prize when he was eleven. He certainly brought home plant and flower specimens collected during solitary wanderings in the woods surrounding the city; poor substitutes as these were for the forests around Freiberg, they were better than nothing.

Despite Freud's later suggestions that he had a bitterly unhappy childhood, he appears to have enjoyed life at the *Gymnasium.* The teachers, he has written, "called up our fiercest opposition and forced us to complete submission; we peered into their little weaknesses, and took pride in their excellences, their knowledge and their justice. At bottom we felt a great affection for them if they gave us any ground for it, though I cannot tell how many of them were aware of this. But it cannot be denied that our position in regard to them was a quite remarkable one and one which may well have had its inconvenience for those concerned. We were from the very first equally inclined to love and to hate them, to criticize and respect them. Psychoanalysis has given the name of 'ambivalence' to this readiness to contradictory attitudes, and it has no difficulty in pointing to the source of the ambivalent feelings of such a kind."

From the reminiscences of his sister Anna, which describe the boys her brother brought back home as study-mates rather than playmates, it is clear that Freud as a youth was earnest, studious and dedicated to success, even though he as yet had little idea of what he wanted to succeed at. When thirteen or fourteen, an age when most youths would have been receiving presents of a very different kind, he was given the complete works of Ludwig Börne, the German political journalist then known for his social awareness. At least one essay by Börne (*"Die Kunst in drei Tagen ein Original-Schriftsteller zu werden"* ["The Art of Becoming an Original Writer in Three Days"]), read and long remembered, appears to have influenced his later thinking.

In spite of these signs of the soberly ambitious student, Freud was attracted, as were most boys his age, to military adventures, an attraction hardly requiring his later *apologia* that the ideal was traceable back to his childhood. For better or for worse, boys as a rule enjoy playing soldiers, and Freud was no exception. One of the first books that he read was Thiers' history of the Consulate and Empire, and years later he recalled how he had stuck labels on the backs of his wooden infantrymen and then written on them the names of Napoleon's marshals. Napoleon himself was an early hero. So was Masséna, and so was Alexander the Great, whose exploits he knew by heart.

Freud was ten when war broke out between Prussia and Austria. "At the North Station in Vienna," his sister later recalled,

> long trains arrived bringing wounded soldiers to the city hospitals and my father would go there, taking Sigmund with him, to see them taken from the trains to hay-filled carts which bore them to the hospitals. Sigi was greatly impressed by the plight of the wounded. He begged my mother to let him have all her old linen so that from it he could make "Charpie," which was then used instead of medicated cotton. We girls made "Charpie" in our schools and Sigmund begged his teachers to organize "Charpie" groups in his boys' high school as well.

The military interest continued, and four years later, on the outbreak of the Franco-Prussian war, Freud pinned to his desk a map of the battle areas on which he marked out the lines with colored flags. "While he did this," his sister Anna has said, "he lectured to me and to my sister Rosa about the war in general and the importance of the various moves of the combatants."

Freud frequently lectured his sisters. His position as his mother's first-born and favorite gave him a privileged place in the home which he was not reluctant to exploit. To his mother he was "my golden Sigi," the youth of which so much was expected, and it was accepted that the home should be run very largely for his convenience, particularly after he had graduated from the Sperl-gymnasium *summa cum laude*. The benefits of being mother's chosen one were considerable, and he was later to remark "that if a man has been his mother's undisputed darling he retains throughout life the triumphant feeling, the confidence in success, which not seldom brings actual success along with it."

In the larger apartment to which the family had moved as offspring accumulated, the others had candles in their bedrooms. Sigismund had the oil lamp. And after his sister Anna had begun piano lessons, he complained of the noise, to good effect. "He appealed to my mother to remove the piano if she did not wish him to leave the house altogether," Anna wrote. "The piano disappeared and with it all opportunities for his sisters to become musicians." In addition, the brother exercised what the sister described as definite control over her reading. "If I had a book that seemed to him improper for a girl of my age, he would say: 'Anna, it is too early to read that book now.'"

The running of the house in Sigismund's interest extended even to the meals. He did not join the family for the evening supper but ate it alone in the long narrow chamber that was his own domain and where he worked and lived until, in his middle twenties, he joined the General City Hospital. "All through the years of his school and university life," his sister remembered, "the only thing that changed in this room was the increasing number of crowded bookcases added to the writing desk, bed, chairs and shelf which furnished it."

Freud's attitude to his family in general and to his sisters in particular was an early indication of belief in his own destiny. "I seem to remember that through the whole of this time," he later wrote, "there ran a premonition of a task ahead, till it found open expression in my school-leaving essay as a wish that I might during the course of my life contribute something to our human knowledge." Like Shaw's artist who "will let his wife starve, his children go barefoot, his mother drudge for his living at seventy, sooner than work at anything but his art," Freud kept at the head of his priorities fitness for the task to which he knew he would be called.

Just what that task would be remained uncertain as in the summer of 1872 he considered the final year's work for the *Matura*, the examination which had to be passed before he could progress from *Gymnasium* to university. First, however, he was to go through an emotional experience whose full significance has only recently come to light, and a change of heart in professional ambition without which psychoanalysis might never have been born.

2

Ambitious Youth

A well-respected man could, with the support of the press and the rich, work miracles in alleviating physical ills if he were scientist enough to try new methods of treatment.

FREUD, in a letter to Eduard Silberstein

At the age of sixteen Freud was an exceptionally personable youth. To the thick dark hair and penetrating dark eyes there was added an air of assurance that today could hardly escape the adjective "charismatic." His reputation for being a bookworm, his obvious seriousness when approached, and his transparent dedication to the more sober side of life may have tended to qualify any friendships that he formed with the other sex. Yet the almost total absence of references to women in the autobiographical parts of his writings still suggests either that the man who revealed the unexpected significance of sex in much of mental illness was singularly sexless himself, or that his periodic destruction of personal documents had an ulterior if humanly understandable motive. The truth appears to be rather more complicated.

The lack of information on Freud's private life during adolescence—in fact, until the meeting with his future wife in 1882 at the age of twenty-six—is partly due to the natural ravages of time. In addition, his forced emigration from Vienna after the Germans arrived in 1938 made it necessary to destroy papers which could not easily be brought out. But much earlier phases of destruction, when Freud appears to have burned correspondence indiscriminately, have until recently meant that relatively little was known of his youth.

The situation has been compounded by the actions of his descendants and admirers. Many surviving letters have been embargoed until the year 2000. An important series to his friend Wilhelm Fliess has been published only in bowdlerized form, and it is now known that the excisions radically affect the significance of some censored letters. The reason for such cutting may well be a reaction to the virulent attacks made on Freud and psychoanalysis in his lifetime; but its effect has been to arouse suspicion that the personal Freudian cupboard is as full of skeletons as a graveyard. Only time seems likely to disperse it and counteract the disservice of Freud's friends.

By chance, two groups of letters that have come to light in the last decade not only cover Freud's adolescence but, specifically, the occasion of his first love. And they help solve the riddle of what Ernest Jones called his "extremely strong motives for concealing some important phase of his development—perhaps even from himself."

The smaller group of letters was addressed to Emil Flüss, one of the family of three sons and two daughters of Ignatz Flüss, head of a Freiberg family that survived the recession of 1859. The Freud–Flüss letters had an exciting history, being brought from Vienna to London after the Nazis had occupied Austria. One letter only was printed, in 1941 in the German-language *Imago,* then published in London, and was quoted in 1953 by Ernest Jones who regretfully noted that it was the sole survivor.

A correction came sixteen years later when Prince Masud Khan, archivist and librarian of the Institute of Psycho-Analysis in London, discovered an envelope of faded and almost unreadable letters which had come into the Institute's hands. X-rayed, enlarged and eventually deciphered, they were found to contain Freud's account of his return to Freiberg in the summer of 1872.

The second, and much more important, group of letters was written to Eduard Silberstein, a young Roumanian who had studied in the same class as Freud at the Sperlgymnasium. "We were friends," Freud wrote,

at a time when one sees friendship not as a diversion but as a part of life. When we were not at school we spent all the day with each other. We learned Spanish together, we had our own mythology and code names which we took from a conversation of the great Cervantes. We had found in our Spanish reader a facetious philosophical dialogue between two dogs lying comfortably outside a hospital door, and we adopted their names. In our talks and letters, he was called Berganza and I Cipion, and I often addressed him in letters as Querido Berganza and signed myself tu fidel Cipion, perro en el hospital de Sevilla. We founded a peculiar learned association, the

Academia Espanola Castellana, collected an extensive humorous literature that can be found among my old papers, shared our frugal
dinners and never got bored in one another's company.

At the height of their friendship, Freud wrote:

I really believe we shall never part, though we became friends from
free choice, we are so attached to each other as if nature would have
made us blood relations. I think we are so far gone that we live in
one another the whole person as he is, not only, as it was earlier, his
good features. I am afraid that even if, through an unworthy deed,
you should appear tomorrow completely different from the image I
had conceived of you, I still could not cease to wish you well.

Throughout the 1870s Freud opened his heart to Silberstein in
letters discussing his work, his plans for the future, a visit to England, the books he was reading, and a wide range of subjects
which ran from his first views about women to his opinions on the
philosopher Brentano whose lectures he was attending. Eventually
he began to feel that he had written too much. As early as 1875
he was considering the destruction of the "Academia Espanola"
archives and by September 1877 had finally made up his mind,
writing to Silberstein, "I suggest that we decide upon a nice winter
evening and that we then burn the archives in a solemn auto-da-
fé." This decision, made at the age of twenty-one, long before he
had embarked upon his life's work, at least helps to lay one ghost.
In the first years of the twentieth century, after Freud had begun
to emphasize the importance of experiences in childhood and early
youth, he again destroyed many of his papers. An assumption can
easily be drawn: that "the man feeling his way towards these new
revelations must have considered it necessary to obstruct possible
attempts at psychoanalysis of his own development by his colleagues, adherents and opponents." But eagerness to erase the
record had in fact begun long before.

The earliest of the important Silberstein letters describes the
summer holiday which Freud spent in Freiberg during 1872 with
two colleagues from the Sperlgymnasium. All three stayed with the
prosperous Flüss family, with whom the Freuds had kept in touch
since leaving Moravia thirteen years previously. Seeing the town
where he had been born, he told his fiancée a decade later, had
made him "feel sentimental," and he had fallen in love with Gisela
Flüss, the younger of the two Flüss daughters, then aged fifteen.
The incident could be written off as unimportant but for three

things: Freud's life-long determination to expunge it from his memory; the virulence with which he responded to the news of Gisela's marriage; and his revelation to Silberstein that there had in fact been another *"Leidenschaft"* (passion or strong emotion), and that he had "translated esteem for the mother into friendship for the daughter." Ernest Jones, who did not see the Silberstein letters but who intuitively felt that some mystery remained unresolved, speculated eighty years later that Freud had strong motives for concealing an important phase of his development, and added: "I would venture to surmise it was his deep love for his mother." Certainly Freud was a devoted son. But nowhere does he express for his mother the adulation reserved for Frau Flüss.

He appears to have referred to his feelings for Gisela on only four occasions throughout his life. The last was twenty-seven years after the encounter, when in "Screen Memories," ostensibly describing the experiences of a patient, he recalled incidents in his own life. "It was my first calf-love and sufficiently intense, but I kept it completely secret . . . ," he wrote there. "A strange thing. For when I see her now from time to time—she happens to have married someone here—she is quite exceptionally indifferent to me. Yet I can remember quite well for what a long time afterward I was affected by the yellow color of the dress she was wearing when we first met, whenever I saw the same color anywhere else."

By the end of the 1870s the Flüss family had moved to Vienna. They maintained their friendship with the Freuds, and were also known to the family of Martha Bernays, to whom Freud was to become engaged. And to Martha he related the affair in a few dismissive lines: "Did I ever tell you that Gisela was my first love when I was but sixteen years old?" he wrote. "No? Well, then you can have a good laugh at me, firstly on account of my taste and also because I never spoke a meaningful, much less an amiable word to the child."

These throwaway lines were for long believed to contain all that Freud directly wrote of the incident, and Jones commented on "the quite extraordinary precautions [Freud] took to conceal a most innocent and momentary emotion of love in his adolescence. His wife was the only person on earth to know anything of that side of his life, and she was the only person to whom he related the Gisela incident in question."

This is not so. In September 1872 Freud gave two accounts, one to Gisela's brother Emil and one to Silberstein. To Emil he banteringly described Gisela as "Ichthyoesaura," derived from the Greek for fluvial creatures and a natural enough name for a Flüss. "But if you want me to entertain you with reports about Ichthyoesaura, let me tell you that there was more irony, yes, mockery, than seriousness in this whole flirtation," he wrote. "You were never present at a meeting of the 'Spanish Academy.' But had you heard how the poor creature was torn to shreds, you would have had a different picture of 'our' relationship to her. Any detailed description would have to be prefaced by Goethe's line: 'A fairy tale . . . it was once upon a time.' "

"Torn to shreds" is hardly the right phrase. In fact, a very different impression is given in Freud's account to Silberstein. He wrote a daily diary of the visit to Freiberg "which I keep only for you and from which you will hear more than you actually ought to know," as he put it. But on September 4 Silberstein was informed that he would now hear everything. "Gisela's beauty," he was told, "is wild, I would say Thracian. Her aquiline nose, the long black hair, the tight-lipped mouth she has from her mother, the dark-brown color of her face and the sometimes indifferent expressions from her father."

But by this time Gisela had gone, apparently back to school, but not before playing a joke on Freud which, he admitted, annoyed him for a long time. "I was very sad saying good-bye and went to the Hochwald, my small paradise, where I spent a most pleasant hour," he went on. "I have now calmed all my surging thoughts and only flinch slightly if her mother mentions the name of Gisela at mealtimes. The attachment appeared like a beautiful spring day, only my nonsensical 'Hamlet-dom,' my shyness in thoughts, prevented me from conversing with pleasure and delight with the half-naïve, half-cultured girl. I will explain to you in detail the difference between my attachment and another *Leidenschaft,*' but now let me only add that I did not get into a dilemma between ideal and reality, and that I am unable to make fun of Gisela."

So far this differs only in detail from Freud's later recollections incorporated in "Screen Memories." Friendship was to be expanded by reminiscence into love, and the joke that had discomfited him was to be pushed down into the unconscious by repression, which certainly worked as forcefully in Freud as in anyone else. Whether the fifteen-year-old had been making fun of Freud's serious manner, or whether the daughter of the successful Flüss family tended to look down her nose at the poor Freuds is not important.

But Freud now went on to describe to Silberstein his other "passion"—Frau Flüss, the mother of Gisela. She had, it is clear, treated him as a favorite son when one day he had drunk himself into unconsciousness in the hope of curing an aching tooth. He wrote Silberstein:

I was raving the whole day and after having tried every remedy in vain I drank spirits to stop the pain. I was down at Emil's at the dyeing shops. [Frau Flüss] knew little of my not feeling well. I fell asleep soon or, rather, fell down unconscious. Emil had me carried upstairs, the severe shock on an empty stomach contributed. I had to vomit violently but the toothache stopped, as I hoped it would. Now, neither the hangover nor the vomiting had been my intention but when it happened [Frau Flüss] cared for me as for her own child. The doctor was called. I slept all night and got up the next morning healthy and without toothache. She asked me how I had slept. I answered "badly." I had not closed an eye. That's what I felt. She said, laughingly, "I came up to you twice in the night and you never noticed." I was ashamed.

However, Freud's "passion" for Frau Flüss was something more than reaction to kindly mothering; though not sexual passion, it was a feeling within the dictionary definition of "vehement, commanding, or overpowering emotion." While describing Giseia's beauty, he also stated that he had

deviated from the subject dear to me; it seems that I have translated esteem for the mother into friendship for the daughter. I am, or consider myself to be, a sharp observer. My life in a numerous family circle where so many characters developed, has sharpened my eyes and I am full of admiration for this woman, none of whose children can completely come up to her. Can you imagine that this woman from a bourgeois family, where early life was passed in fairly poor conditions, has managed to acquire a culture of which a nineteen-year-old *Salondämchen* need not be ashamed. She has read a lot, including classical authors, and what she has not read she has heard of and can talk about. There is hardly a branch of knowledge which is too remote from her and she even has a correct appreciation of those basic subjects which are really beyond her. At the same time she admits clearly that it is possible in Freiberg to forget everything and learn nothing. Yes, she is even knowledgeable about politics, takes part in all the events of this little town and I think it is she who pushes the family into the stream of things.

But after what I've said don't take her for an unsuccessful bluestocking. I have seen myself that she takes as much a part in the running of the business as Herr Flüss, that all the people in the factory obey this woman as they obey him, and I am fully convinced that she knows how to command just as well as anyone, even more strictly. You should also see how she has brought up her seven children and how she is still bringing them up; how they obey her, the older ones more than the younger ones, how no concern of any of the children ceases to be hers. None of her children has a point of view which excludes hers. Superiority I have never observed.

Other mothers—and why hide the fact that ours are among them; we shall not stop loving them any the less for it—only look after the physical needs of their sons. Their spiritual development has been taken out of their hands. Frau Flüss knows no sphere that is beyond her influence. But you should also see the love with which the children are attached to their parents and the willingness with which their servants obey her. I cannot blame her for the fact that she loves Gisela most of all. She is the first daughter to receive a really thorough education and she was treated like a guest in the house. I have never seen her [Frau Flüss] in a bad mood, or, rather, have never seen her vent her bad mood on an innocent person. She punishes the children with her looks, and by withholding little favors. She affects their sense of honor rather than their behinds.

After this paean of praise, Freud adds that Frau Flüss is an amiable hostess, hospitable beyond bounds, and that it is impossible for him to merit all the friendliness and kindness with which she treats him. "She obviously recognizes that I always need encouragement to speak or to help myself, and she never fails to give it," he goes on. "This is where her dominion over me shows; as she guides me, so I speak, so I present myself. I shall retain a beautiful memory of a good and noble human being and will show myself grateful in my own way by making you the confidant of my esteem. She was never beautiful but her eyes must always, as now, have sparkled with intelligence and fire . . . Enough of this. You see how words flow out of my heart and the letters out of my pen."

Freud returned to Vienna in mid-September, sending Emil a long account of the journey and adding as a postscript to a second letter: "My regards to your esteemed mother. . . ."

No other record of Freud's reactions to Frau Flüss appears to have survived, and it would be unwise to make too much of what the young boy described as "passion." The "crushes" of sixteen-year-olds for older women are not all that unusual. Yet the exceptional care which he afterward took to dissimulate when describing his feelings for Gisela, now known to be a reversion of his feelings for her mother, suggest that the influence of Frau Flüss may have unconsciously lasted on.

After the family had moved to Vienna a few years later, the two Flüss daughters renewed their friendship with Freud's sisters. He responded with restrained sarcasm, telling Silberstein early in 1875 that his sisters were attending dancing lessons and adding: "Evidently not without the Flüsses; what, anyway, could happen without the Flüsses? They are the pattern which my lady sisters endeavour to follow. So if they attend dancing lessons it will be together with G. and S. Flüss. If you will come here, you will have the pleasure (which cannot be expressed in words or, at least, very feebly and vaguely so) to 'touch' Gisela, for which I have neither enough incentive nor opportunity."

Later in the year the girl married, an event that Freud celebrated by enclosing with a letter to Silberstein a poem which was accurately described as "nothing but a derision, a scoffing." Freud, relates a later owner of the poem, "considers as 'Antidiluvian' the life of the newly established, commonplace home, where the man 'is devoted to the study of the art of making money' and the woman 'is restricted to household duties.' Most of the attacks are obviously directed against the bride and dire envy fills the lines in which the snug appearance of the bride is described, and the groom's anticipation of its delights."

More than a third of a century later, when the name "Gisela" was mentioned during a psychoanalytic session with a patient, Freud felt it necessary to put three exclamation marks after the name written in his notes. But the apparent absence of any reference to Frau Flüss in Freud's correspondence or reminiscences should be noted, together with his view that "the theory of repression is the cornerstone on which the whole structure of psychoanalysis rests."

After his return to Vienna in September 1872, Freud settled down for a year's hard haul to the *Matura*. His choice of career was the law, mainly because it opened the door to a political career, one of the very few fields in which it might be possible for a Jew to exercise influence, a prospect which had grown brighter with the coming to power of the middle-class "Bürger" government. His father had brought home portraits of some of its members whom he obviously held in respect. They included a number of Jews, and to the young Freud it now seemed that every Jewish schoolboy had the chance of receiving a minister's portfolio.

Two other influences, one important, the other trivial, had pulled him in the same direction. The first was his schoolboy friendship with Heinrich Braun, later the socialist politician. The two youths had become close companions, and it was under Braun's influence that Freud planned to study law on entering the university. Secondly, there was the evening when he and his parents were sitting in the Prater. Told to bring to their table an itinerant poet who was offering to compose a verse on any subject named, Freud was rewarded by a few lines in which it was predicted that he would one day become a member of the government.

However, in the first half of 1873 he changed his mind. The reason, he later wrote, was that he had attended a lecture at which a brief fragment, "On Nature," ostensibly written by Goethe, had been read, and that this had induced him to matriculate in the school of medicine.

"On Nature" is now believed to have been inspired, and possibly actually written, by the Swiss theologian Georg Christoph Tobler who in 1781 had spent six months in Weimar. Tobler became a close friend of Goethe who in 1828, four years before his death, wrote that the essay had been sent to him a short time previously by the Duchess Anna Amalia, and added, "it is written by a well-known hand, of which I was accustomed to avail myself in my affairs, in the year 1780, or thereabouts. I do not exactly remember having written these reflections, but they very well agree with the ideas which had at that time become developed in my mind." Such was the accident which brought the essay into Goethe's collected works and then into a Viennese lecture room where it was to divert Freud away from the law and toward the path he was to follow for the rest of his life.

"Nature! We are surrounded and embraced by her," it began; "powerless to separate ourselves from her, and powerless to penetrate beyond her.

"Without asking, or warning, she snatches us up into her circling dance, and whirls us on until we are tired, and drop from her arms.

"She is ever shaping new forms: what is, has never yet been; what has been, comes not again. Everything is new, and yet nought but the old.

"We live in her midst and know her not. She is incessantly speaking to us, but betrays not her secret. We constantly act upon her and yet have no power over her . . ."

This was heady stuff for a young man of seventeen, but it appears that the effect on Freud was not quite as sudden as he recalled years later. On March 17, 1873 he revealed to Emil Flüss, not yet moved from Freiberg: "As for me, I can report what is perhaps the most important bit of news in my miserable life . . . But the matter is as yet undecided." Only six weeks afterward did he give the news, in words somewhat suggesting those of "On Nature," that he had made up his mind to abandon the law as a career. "I have decided," he told Flüss, "to be a Natural Scientist and herewith release you from the promise to let me conduct all your law suits. It is no longer needed. I shall gain insight into the age-old dossiers of Nature, perhaps even eavesdrop on her eternal processes, and share my findings with anyone who wants to learn. As you can see, the secret is not so frightful; it was fearful only because it was altogether too insignificant."

The switch from law to natural science has been interpreted as a move away from power over men toward power over nature, and it has been suggested that the change may have been caused by a delayed reaction to Freud's experiences in Freiberg the previous year. If so, Frau Flüss certainly has her niche in history. Yet it would be unwise to ignore totally the possibility that influences more mundane than either Frau Flüss or "On Nature" played their part. Were the Freud family finances able to guide even "golden Sigi" through the gates into legal affluence? Was the cut-and-thrust of legal debate genuinely attractive? And if the prize of ministerial status eluded him, was the courtroom the place where he could best exercise the leadership to which he was sure he would be called?

When it came to the final decision science was, after all, just as likely a field in which to win his spurs. Perhaps he might even, like Darwin whose views were the controversial talk of the time, evolve a theory to change the world. Indeed, that he would do so some day, somehow, in some field, was a belief that never entirely deserted him. Freud could complain as heartily as any man, and more heartily than most, at the ignorance of those who refused to take him at his own assessment. What he wanted was not merely recognition but unqualified recognition, and at regular intervals throughout his life he would maintain that his work would be ignored, that his name would be forgotten, and that if anyone reaped rewards it would be those who followed him. Yet at times the complaints have an almost spurious air. Freud never doubted that he had been chosen for great things, that his mantle of leadership was tailor-made, and that while Moses had been picked to lead his people into the promised land, Sigismund Freud had a comparable destiny ahead of him. As he now forsook the path that led through the courts to the cabinet office, he was not yet certain what that destiny was to be; but it would extort sacrifices—from himself and from those who would have the privilege to serve under him.

The decision, however, was the abandonment of law for science in general rather than for medicine, and he was to write of this period: "Neither at that time, nor indeed in my later life, did I feel any particular predilection for the career of a doctor." The youth who was to become one of the world's best-known doctors was a reluctant physician.

But before university, the *Matura* had to be passed. While this was unlikely to present any problem to a young man regularly at the top of the class, there was in the summer of 1873 one main distraction which hampered concentration during the final run-up to the examination room. This was the International Exhibition, housed in an enormous building with a central rotunda 312 feet in diameter that was among the wonders of its day. Opened on May

1 by the Emperor with a flanking escort of European royalty, the Exhibition was to be unlucky. For on May 1, to be remembered as "Black Friday," a series of financial crashes brought about the collapse of both the Berlin and the Vienna stock exchanges. If this was not enough to throw a shadow over the Exhibition, the disasters were almost immediately followed by a cholera outbreak in Vienna which soon led to a major exodus of visitors. Reaction to the financial collapse was inevitable: Jewish capitalism, Jewish love of money, were claimed to be the root of the trouble, and the flames of anti-Semitism were soon burning a little more brightly. Freud's decision, that science or medicine offered better prospects of success than law, seemed to be confirmed.

However, the Exhibition remained a potentially disruptive magnet. "[It] does not suit me a bit," Freud wrote to Emil Flüss. "It adds to my laziness and provides me with a thousand excuses to exculpate myself before my tender conscience! I fear, through curiosity, I'll fail the *Matura,* and through my sense of duty miss the World Exhibition." This was not to be the case, and by the middle of the following month he had paid more than one visit. "Interesting, but it didn't bowl me over," was his verdict. "Many things that seemed to please other people didn't appeal to me because I am neither this nor that, not really anything completely. Actually, the only things that fascinated me were the works of art and general effects . . . When my 'martyr' (this is what we call the *Matura* among ourselves) is over, I intend to go there every day."

The examination was held in mid-June, and to Emil Flüss, Freud gave a long account of how he had fared.

In Latin we were given a passage from Virgil which I happened to have read on my own account some time ago. This misled me into doing the work quickly and in half the time allotted for it, thus forfeiting the *exc*[ellent]. So it went to someone else, I myself coming second with *good.* The German-Latin translation seemed very simple but in this simplicity lay the difficulty. We took only a third of the time for it. Consequently it miscarried ignominiously. Result: *Satisfactory.* Two others managed to get *good.* The Greek paper, consisting of a 33-verse-long passage from *Oedipus Rex,* came off better: *good.* The only one. This passage, too, I had read for myself and made no secret of it. The maths. paper which we approached with fear and trembling, was a complete success. I wrote *good* because I don't know yet exactly how it has been marked. Finally, my German essay was stamped with an *excellent.* It was a very ethical theme: "On the Considerations in the Choice of a Profession," and I wrote more or less the same as I wrote you two weeks ago, without you acknowledging it with an *exc*[ellent]. At the same time my professor told me—and he is the first person who ventured to tell me this—that I had what Herder so neatly calls a distinctly personal style, i.e. a style at once correct and characteristic. I was duly surprised at this amazing fact and hasten to spread the news of this happy event abroad as far and wide as possible—the first of its kind. To you, for instance, who, I am sure, have until now not been aware that you are exchanging letters with a German stylist. So now I would counsel you, as a friend, not as one with a vested interest—preserve them—bind them together—guard them well—you never know.

There had been little doubt of the young Freud's success among his friends and, unknown to him, the choice of Sophocles' *Oedipus* by the examiner meant that the authorities too had little doubt. Only students expected to gain the highest marks in the *Matura* were given Greek tragedy to translate; those expected to do less well were given Plato, and so on down the scale.

Having passed the *Matura* with flying colors, Freud registered in the University of Vienna's medical department in the autumn of 1873, a step that allowed him to keep his options open, since the department trained not only men who were to become physicians but also those who planned to spend their lives in research. "As to the first year at the university," he wrote to Silberstein,

I shall spend it entirely in studying humanistic subjects, which have nothing at all to do with my future profession, but which will not be useless to me. So, if you want to become a physician, you will still be able to catch up and make your first cut on the human corpse in my company. However, if you are going to be a diplomat, nobody will ever catch up with you, not even history. To this end, I am joining in the first year the faculty of philosophy. Accordingly, if anybody asks me (or asks you about me) what I intend to do, refrain from giving a definite reply and say merely—Oh, a scientist, a professor, something like that.

He himself refrained from being too definite for quite a while. After three years of varied, if not exactly chaotic, studies—which meant that it took him eight years to graduate rather than the normal five—he turned to research; only when the prospects here looked too bleak to support marriage did he concentrate on medicine. "I have no knowledge of having had any craving in my early childhood to help suffering humanity," he once admitted.

The impression that his record gives of restlessly probing for some subject which could command his full attention, of searching for some field where he could make his mark and then sweep on to success, is one feature which distinguishes him from other students. Another was his apparent lack of interest in women. In most other ways, as his letters to Silberstein reveal, he was the model of iconoclastic youth, ribald about the Emperor and his fine trappings, contemptuous of established religion—the Adriatic, he notes, "perhaps as a true Italian, hates the Pope, the priests and Sundays"—the typical young idealist whose left-wing enthusiasms are often modified into conservatism.

Any doubts that he might have retained about the wisdom of jettisoning a future in law and politics were to be quickly swept away. At the gymnasium he had begun to understand for the first time what it meant to belong to an alien race. Now, at the university, he found the tide of anti-Semitism rising higher. But the situation did have its useful lessons. At an early age, he records, "I was made familiar with the fate of being in the Opposition and of being put under the ban of the 'compact majority.' The foundations were thus laid for a certain degree of independence of judgment."

No one should underestimate the long-term effects on Freud of this ever-present glowering background of racial prejudice. It strengthened his resolve to succeed and it strengthened his Jewishness; yet during his student days he rarely felt himself inhibited. He belonged to the *Leseverein der deutschen Studenten*, a German nationalist group later disbanded through government pressure on account of its anti-Austrian leanings, and here he could show an arrogant disregard for the accepted rules. When the young Viktor Adler, the future Social Democrat leader, revealed in debate that he had once tended swine in his youth, the admission drew the comment from Freud that since he now knew that the speaker had tended swine in his youth, he was no longer surprised at the tone of his speeches. A general uproar ensued and Freud was called upon to withdraw his remark. He refused. But the man he had insulted let the affair drop.

His verdicts on the all-mighty were no less outspoken. After the Emperor had opened the great Exhibition, Freud had sent his own deflating account to Emil Flüss:

Should you, in 20 or 30 years from now, read somewhere an account written in Byzantian court style to the effect that—"The 1st of May, 1873, was one of the most beautiful days our northern climate has ever known. The proverbial luck of His Majesty Kaiser Franz Joseph I did not fail him on this solemn occasion, as usual. The regal figure drove past the happily cheering multitude in an open carriage flanked by the highest ranking princes of his time, etc. etc."—don't believe it but take my word for it that the 1st of May was a day of well-nigh Siberian cold, with a most democratic rain drenching roads and meads, that His Majesty looks about as regal as our (for he is mine too) *Bürstenbinder* [street sweeper], that the foreign princes seem to be made up exclusively of mustachios and medals and, finally, that no one, with the exception of a few street urchins who sat in the trees, broke into shouts of joy at the sight of the Apostolic Highnesses, while His Majesty's humble and obedient subjects took cover under their umbrellas and hardly raised their hats.

Similar scathing observations went to Silberstein the following year when Vienna celebrated the coming-of-age of Prince Rudolph of Hapsburg, the Emperor's heir who fifteen years later was to die by his own hand at Mayerling. "The exalted chick," Freud wrote,

is, despite his 16 years of age, only very sparsely feathered and is being carefully kept away from attempts at independent flight. Nevertheless, such days are memorable as they bring out—the otherwise hardly noticed fact—that a crown prince is older by one year every 365 days. Several journals which I read because they wrote of this event behave with quite stupid surprise and deliver themselves —I don't know whether gratis or against payment—of much unbelievable nonsense. One of these journals regrets that the Prince will now have to give up his youthful illusions, and will have to concentrate his thoughts and care on the future ruling of a great empire, as if monarchs, like shirt collars and philosophers, were not among the most useless things in the world.

His politics were spelled out the following year when he testified to Silberstein: "I am indeed a Republican but only insofar as I consider a Republic the only reasonable, in fact the only self-evident, form for a State. However, from this idea to the practical proposal of establishing a Republic . . . I should like to know whether your Social Democrats are of an equally revolutionary mind in philosophy and religion?" As for the Romanoffs, they were as detestable in Freud's eyes as the Communists were to be half a century later: "Those crazy rulers, bad citizens and incapable soldiers, those apes, I cannot sufficiently express my hatred against them. But I console myself with the fact that they are digging their own graves."

References to philosophy occur with some regularity in Freud's long descriptions to Silberstein of his life and work at the university. The subject was no longer compulsory for medical students but in his third semester—the winter term of 1874-5—he added a course given by Franz Brentano to a curriculum that by this time included anatomy, dissection and chemistry, general biology and Darwinism, microscopy, mineralogy, the physiology of voice and speech, magnetism, electricity and heat, and the theory of magnetic forces. Philosophy had attracted him for some time, and had possibly influenced an early essay which he had sent to Silberstein, and whose apparent loss he was soon deploring. "It was a little essay," he wrote, "a Biblical study but with modern ideas included. It was the sort of thing I could not write again and I'm as proud of it as of my nose or my *Matura*. It really would have refreshed you and I can hardly appreciate that it was written indoors. It is such a sensitive piece, Biblically naïve and forceful, both melancholy and happy, and it's the very Devil that it's been lost."

The course with Brentano was to have more than passing significance. The philosopher's major work, *Psychologie vom empirischen Standpunkt* ("Psychology from the Empirical Standpoint"), included two long discussions of the unconscious which, while denying its existence, traced the idea back to Thomas Aquinas. It seems almost inevitable, therefore, that Freud first began serious study of the subject he was to make particularly his own during the four consecutive terms of his philosophy course. Certainly his regard for Brentano steadily increased as he and a colleague, Josef Paneth, worked their way into the subject.

"I should be very sorry if you, studying law, entirely neglected philosophy while I, the godless empirically minded man of medicine, attended two philosophy courses with Paneth and read Feuerbach," he wrote to Silberstein. "One of the courses—lo and behold—just listen, you will be surprised—deals with the existence of God, and Professor Brentano, who lectures on it, is a marvelous person. Scientist and philosopher though he is, he deems it necessary to support with his expositions this airy existence of a divinity."

A few months later Freud was able to report that he and Paneth had established closer contact with Brentano. "We sent him a letter containing some objections, then he invited us to his house and refuted our statements," he wrote on March 7. "After having sent him another letter with some objections, we were again called to him. I shall personally tell you more about this peculiar, and in many respects, ideal man, a believer in God, a teleologist, a Darwinist and altogether a darned clever fellow, a genius in fact. For the moment I will say only this: that under Brentano's influence I have decided to take my Ph.D. in philosophy and zoology."

The young man on whom philosophy was by this time exercising such influence was an assiduous student. He belonged, as he described it, to that group of human beings who can be found for the largest part of the day between two pieces of furniture, one formed vertically, the chair, and one extending horizontally, the table, and who the social historians agree are the basis of all civilization because they can justify their claim to be sedentary. Because this position does not demand the same things of all parts of the body, the nobler ones stick out above the horizontal table for a considerable way, and I am henceforth forced to do two things to occupy them: read and write. What I write is mathematics and what I read is paper. Thus, and not with the sentimental "words, words," Hamlet ought to have answered Polonius when the latter worried about how the Prince whiled away his time. To be paper is the common property and also the common destiny of all books.

The books which I read deserve this destiny so little that they might as well be engraved on metal were this not so expensive. These are the lectures by Helmholtz, Carlyle's *Sartor Resartus,* and Aristotle's *Ethica Nicomachaea.* It is superfluous to talk about the first and the last because in short words I cannot give you an idea of their essence. Carlyle's *Sartor Resartus* deserves to be advertised. (I must arrange a separate cabinet in my apartment.) The book is introduced in the manner of Jean Paul [Johann Paul Friedrich Richter, one of Germany's greatest humorists, usually known by his pen name of Jean Paul] and at times shows Jean Paul's spirit. However, on the whole it is definitely English and derides us brooding Germans. A German professor, Diogenes Teufelsdröckh, at the University of Don't-Know-Where, Professor of the science of things in general, has written a "Philosophy of Clothes." This is sent to the author (Carlyle) with the request to publish an English translation thereof. The latter complies with the demand insofar as he translates at least some extracts of this peculiar literary effort, whose author appears to assume various features—to be simultaneously Faust and Mephistopheles, a satirist and a philosopher. However, under all these funny names there is great wisdom and the multi-colored scraps of folly cover the open wounds of humanity and of the hero. What is said about the philosophy of clothes is partly in the form of a parody, partly as a witty opinion which starts from the assumption that clothes are a representation of the apparent and physical, behind which the spiritual shamefully hides.

It was not only Carlyle whom Freud enjoyed, and his comments on lighter reading are significant. He disagreed with those who denied any value to Dumas's *La Dame aux Camélias* on account of its subject matter, adding: "I do not say, as some aesthetes do, that everything considered immoral according to bourgeois or Mosaic law is also unpoetic. Gottfried's *Tristan and Isolde* brilliantly refutes that idea. Indeed it is quite possible that poetry, supported by passion, can idealize and lend an aspect of beauty to things 'immoral'—or rather those which society deems unpermissible."

. . .

Yet whatever his preoccupation with philosophy, however great the discussion on literature and morals, Freud's leaning toward science steadily increased. "I have decided," he wrote to Silberstein in the summer of 1874, "and my father has approved of the idea, to spend the winter semester in Berlin to attend the lectures of Du Bois-Reymond, Helmholtz and Virchow, circumstances permitting. I am as glad as a child and could not bear the thought of giving up the project." The choice of two physiologists and a pathologist was good enough indication of the way Freud's thoughts were moving. But there was one disadvantage in the scheme. "Should I be [in Berlin] in the winter," he pointed out, "I could hardly guarantee that I would not remain there for the summer semester as well. However, advantageous though it may be for the members of the Academia Espanola to see the 'world' in some of its largest 'habitations,' the A. E. will have to continue in its seclusion for another semester."

The plan was eventually abandoned, presumably because circumstances, possibly financial, ruled it out. But the move toward medical research was speeded up by a journey to England that Freud made the following summer. It had been proposed two years earlier, probably as the traditional special treat arranged by the head of a family whose son had succeeded in the *Matura*. But here also circumstances had intervened and it was not until 1875 that Freud found himself in the city of Manchester, where his two half-brothers had settled some sixteen years earlier.

Before he left Vienna for England, a change had taken place in the signature with which he ended his regular letters to Silberstein. Until now it had been "Sigismund." But on June 28, ending what was one of his last letters before leaving Austria for the visit to his half-brothers, he signed himself "Sigmund," the name he was to use for the rest of his life. In the Freud family Bible his name had been written "Sigismund" in Hebrew although "Sigmund" in the German translation, while at school he had been known as Sigismund until about 1870. It has been suggested that the change which he gradually adopted in the 1870s was merely the adoption of German rather than Slav usage; but "Sigismund" was Vienna's favorite name for abuse in anti-Semitic jokes.

It is not known whether he was most influenced in England by his half-brothers, by life in Manchester or by some particular incident that he never recorded. But by the time he returned he had decided to devote his life to medical research. The evidence for this has until recently been only that of his sister Anna. Writing in old age, she recalled: "It was in England that Sigmund resolved to study medicine on his return to Vienna, and so informed my father. Not satisfied with this decision, father stated his objections, claiming that Sigmund was much too soft-hearted for the task. But Sigmund's mind was made up, though at first he planned to do only research. 'I want to help people who suffer,' was his reply." This evidence is supported by Freud himself in a revealing letter to Silberstein, written some forty-eight hours after arriving back home. "The day before yesterday," he began,

I returned in the morning to dear old Vienna after my seven and a half weeks of travels. I used the first two days to slough off my English habits and am now sitting in my comfortable little room with all my treasures stowed away and my mind calmed down. I am sitting in the light of my poor eye-destroying paraffin [kerosene] lamp (in England every beggar has a gas lamp), in order to answer your letter which arrived in Manchester while I was preparing for my journey home. . . .

You will certainly want to know about my relatives in England and about my relationship with them. I do not think that I have told you much about them. They are two brothers on my father's side from my father's first marriage, twenty and twenty-two years older than me; the first, Emanuel, married from early youth; the younger one, Philip, married for 2 1/2 years. Originally they lived with us in Freiberg where the three oldest children of my elder brother were born. The unfavorable turn which their business took there caused them to move to England which they have not left since 1859. They are now held in good esteem, not because of their fortune, for they are not rich, but because of their personal character. They are shop-keepers, merchants who have a shop; the elder sells cloth, the younger jewelry—in the sense which this word seems to have in England. My two sisters-in-law are both jolly women, one of them is an Englishwoman [Bloomah Freud, née Frankel, from Birmingham] which makes my conversation with her extremely pleasant. Of the persons of our family whose uncle I can call myself, you know John already; he is an Englishman in every sense with a knowledge of languages and technical matters greater than that of most business people. Unknown to you, as well as to me until recently, are two amiable nieces, Pauline aged nineteen and Bertha aged seventeen years, and a fifteen-year-old boy with the name of Sam[1], which I think in England has been fashionable since Pickwick, and generally called a "sharp and deep" chap. I find less to blame than to praise in my relations and much to praise warmly. And my partisan position as brother and uncle, and the cordial reception which I have been given, does not prevent me from being a judge and critic. There is nothing special I have to record regarding England, although I must say straight out that I would rather live there than here in spite of fog and rain, drunkenness and conservatism. Many peculiarities of the English character and country, which might be unbearable to other continentals, agree with my attitude very well. Perhaps, dear friend, after the conclusion of my studies a favorable wind may blow me to England for practical work. To make a confession to you: in addition to the theoretical ideal of my earlier years I have now acquired a practical one. Last year, if asked what was my greatest wish, I would have answered: a laboratory and free time, or a ship on the ocean with all the instruments needed by a scientist; now I am doubtful whether I would not rather say a large hospital and plenty of money in order to restrict some of the evils which befall our bodies, or to remove them from the world. If, therefore, I wanted to influence many people rather than a small number of readers and co-scientists, then England would be the right country for such a purpose. A well-respected man could, with the support of the press and the rich, work miracles in alleviating physical ills if he were scientist enough to try new methods of treatment. All these are as yet unclear thoughts. I will stop here.

London, Sheffield, Birmingham, Oxford and so forth—what you would expect of someone who travels for pleasure—I have not seen. I have been flattered with the hope that I would see England again next year or in two years. In order to move the poet in you, think! I have seen the sea, the holy Thalassus. I have followed the waves of the high tide as they leapt the land, growlingly, and I have collected crabs and starfish on the beach!!

I have brought very few books back with me; but the acquaintance which I have made with English scientific books will always keep me, in my studies, on the side of the English for whom I now have an extremely favorable prejudice: Tyndall, Huxley, Lyle, Darwin, Thomson, Lockyer and others.

I am more distrustful than ever about philosophy. . . .

Freud apparently impressed his English relations as much as England had impressed him. "You have given us great pleasure by sending us Sigmund," his stepbrother Emanuel wrote to the family in Vienna. "He is a splendid specimen of a fine human being, and if I had the pen of a Dickens, I could well make a hero of him . . . All your descriptions of him have been worthless; only now, since he is with us, do we see him as he really is."

Freud's Anglophile strain remained strong, even though he was to make only one more visit to Britain before settling in the country after the Nazi occupation of Austria in 1938. Indeed, this may have lain behind the habit, which he exhibited for the rest of his life, of dropping an occasional English phrase into his letters. Written in the style which was to bring tributes from such masters as Thomas Mann, they would without warning include colloquialisms such as "fall flat" or "ups and downs" before continuing in polished German.

Yet however warm the affection Freud retained for England it was more than balanced by that for Vienna. On the surface his feelings for the capital were very different. He was to write from Berlin to his fiancée that he would worry about nothing until he saw "with [his] own eyes the detestable tower of St. Stephen's," Vienna's 450-foot landmark. Fourteen years later he wrote to a correspondent: "I hate Vienna with a positively personal hatred, and, just the contrary of the giant Antaeus, I draw fresh strength whenever I remove my feet from the soil of the city which is my home." Vienna, he could proclaim, "is Vienna, that is to say, extremely revolting," and after fame had arrived he would be told by a colleague that she was about to visit him "in the Vienna you like so little."

Some of this curmudgeonly reaction to one of the great capitals of Europe, set in its diadem of surrounding hills, was a sign of what has been called the characteristic affectation of hating Vienna, so typical of the Viennese. However, there was more to it than that. Vienna was the scene of his hard personal struggle, the city where he always felt himself honored less than justice demanded. It was the city where Karl Kraus, satirist and critic, attacking Freud in the columns of *Die Fackel* ("The Torch"), had described psychoanalysis as the illness that pretended to be its own cure. And its university had, to the bitter end, shied away from giving him what was no doubt his professional due. One result was that Freud, genius that he was, could nevertheless claim that Vienna was a city in which, after fifty years' residence, he had never met a new idea; yet this, within his own experience, had been the city of Mach, Schlick, Carnap and Wittgenstein, as well as of Franz Kafka and Gustav Mahler, a city where the intellectual ferment bubbled even more vigorously than in the Zurich which had harbored during much the same period Lenin and Einstein, Rosa Luxemburg and James Joyce.

It seems probable, however, that Freud's dislike was neither deep-seated nor real. "And my own feeling," his son Martin has written, "is that sometimes my father hated Vienna, and that sometimes he loved the old city, and that, in a general sense, he was devoted." The devotion was illustrated after the end of the First World War when Freud was visited by Ernst Lothar. "Like you," Freud told him, "I have an indomitable affection for Vienna and Austria, but, unlike you, I know her abyss." Then he took from the drawer a paper on which was written: "Austro-Hungary is no more. I do not want to live anywhere else. Emigration is out of the question. I will continue to live with this torso and will imagine that it is the whole." Turning to Lothar he said: "You are right. This is a country about which one is irritated to death and yet where one would like to end one's life." In the early 1930s, as anti-Semitism grew in Germany with the rise of Hitler and threatened to spread out beyond her frontiers, there was increasing incentive to leave. Yet Freud clung on tenaciously, left in 1938 only with great reluctance, and on arrival in London wrote to his friend Max Eitingon: "The feeling of triumph on being liberated is too strongly mixed with sorrow, for in spite of everything I still greatly loved the prison from which I have been released."

In 1875 he was certainly glad to be back in Vienna and quickly started revising his plans for the coming autumn. Although he continued his course with Brentano, more time was to be spent on physiology, anatomy and the practical zoology which he studied in Carl Claus's Institute of Comparative Anatomy. And it was Claus, who only two years previously had arrived in Vienna from Göttingen, full of ambitious plans to modernize the Institute, who in March 1876 gave Freud the first original research he was to tackle.

Two years earlier, the Polish scientist Dr. Simone de Syrski had reported a solution to one of biology's oldest and most puzzling problems. "No one," as Freud himself subsequently wrote, "ever [had] found a mature male eel—no one [had] yet seen the testes of the eel, in spite of innumerable efforts throughout the centuries." Dr. Syrski, however, had located a small lobed organ which appeared to be the elusive one, and Claus now set Freud the task of checking the Pole's observations. Much of the work was done during two sessions at the Zoological Experimental Station which Claus had just set up in Trieste. He had acquired funds for sending bright students there twice a year, and the fact that Freud was singled out for two spells suggests that Claus had a high opinion of his abilities.

From Trieste, Freud sent Silberstein a lengthy account of the difficulties involved in dissecting four hundred eels and examining them microscopically. However, it is clear that he enjoyed Trieste, his first experience of the "soft South." He noted the beauty of Italian women but was, he owned, able only to appreciate them from afar. "Physiologically I only know that they like walking," he added; and, concerning anatomical investigations, "it is unfortunately forbidden to dissect humans."

He returned to Vienna in September with the raw material for his first scientific paper, presented by Claus to the Academy of Science in March 1877. On the face of it, he had done well. The paper, "always self-assured—at places even cocky," as it has been described, confirmed Syrski's statements. Claus, there is every reason to believe, was pleased with his student. Yet only a few months later, Freud had deserted him to work as a research student in Ernst Brücke's Institute of Physiology. The move was to be significant not only for his personal fortunes but for the basic ideas which he assimilated from Brücke's teaching.

The man under whose stern influence he was glad to remain for the next six years had three decades earlier been a prominent member of the Berlin group led by Helmholtz and Du Bois-Reymond, two of the three whose lectures Freud had wished to attend in Berlin. Du Bois-Reymond had encapsulated the leading belief of the group when he had written: "Brücke and I pledged a solemn oath to put into effect this truth: 'No forces other than the common physical and chemical ones are active in the organism. In those cases which cannot at the time be explained by these forces, one has either to find the specific way or form of their action by using the physical-mathematical method or to assume new forces equal in dignity to the chemical-physical forces inherent in matter, reducible to the force of attraction and repulsion.' " This belief was strengthened a few years later when Helmholtz expanded into biology the concept of the conservation of matter, and it lay at the root of Brücke's teaching. The effect on Freud was twofold. It led him to believe that effect must follow cause in mental as well as physical fields, and thus drove him toward his first fundamental concept: that the physical symptoms of the hysteric were not random and meaningless but the direct result of undiscovered causes. Secondly, it led him for a while to assume that mental as well as physical processes were dependent on particulate entities whose actions could be described in terms of physical and chemical forces. The idea proved incapable of development but it nevertheless remained at the back of his mind; to the end of his life Freud continued to hope that his theories about the nature of the mind would one day be capable of description in physiological terms.

Ernst Brücke, who was to have such influence on his young student, was an exceptional man who commanded affection and respect in roughly equal proportions. Short, with red hair, piercing blue eyes and a rather enigmatic smile, Brücke—"our ambassador to the Far East," as his Berlin colleagues called him after his move to Vienna—was regarded by Freud as the greatest authority he had ever met, and in Brücke's laboratory he spent some of the happiest years of his life. In some ways, Brücke, stern yet benevolent, calm and unflappable, with the confident air of a scientific entrepreneur that disguised his real genius, was a model for the man his assistant was to become. "One morning," Freud has said after admitting that he was sometimes late for work, "he turned up punctually at the hour of opening and awaited my arrival. His words were brief and to the point. But it was not they that mattered. What overwhelmed me were the terrible blue eyes with which he looked at me and by which I was reduced to nothing . . . No one who can remember the great man's eyes, which retained their striking beauty even in his old age, and who has ever seen him in anger, will find it difficult to picture the young sinner's emotions."

The most likely reason for Freud's move from Claus to Brücke was the attraction of the Helmholtz school of which Brücke was such an ardent member. It is also possible that he was reacting against the inevitable messiness of much zoological work. Years later his fastidiousness was to assert itself even in his psychoanalytic work when he discovered, on a visit to Jung in Zurich, that there were patients very different from the upper-class ladies of Vienna who had for years been his patients. And the student who, as his sister has written, could not bear the sight of blood, may well have found the dissection of four hundred eels a singularly unattractive task.

However, given the knowledge of the unconscious and its workings that Freud has brought into the light of day, given also the neurosis-encouraging conditions of his early upbringing, there is another explanation, put forward by the psychoanalyst Siegfried Bernfeld, which cannot be entirely discounted. Claus was some twenty years older than Freud, roughly the same age as Freud's half-brother Philipp; Brücke, Bernfeld has pointed out, was about forty years older, a contemporary of Freud's father. "From Freud's self-analysis," Bernfeld says,

> we know that in his early childhood in Freiberg he concentrated all his love, admiration and trust on his father, and had shifted his distrust and rebellious and hostile attitude to the brother, yet without ceasing to love him. The young man accepted guidance and criticism from the old Brücke as he had admiringly and with awe looked up to his father in those early childhood years in Freiberg. Toward the younger Claus he may have felt that same mixture of love and hostility, of admiration and distrust, which had colored his relationship to his half-brother.

Whatever the actual amalgam of reasons for the move to Brücke's Institute, Freud never regretted it, and he later recalled:

"At length in Ernst Brücke's physiological laboratory, I found rest and full satisfaction—and men, too, whom I could respect and take as my models."

It was in Brücke's laboratory that Freud first met Josef Breuer, the doctor who, as he was to state, "brought psychoanalysis into being." Fourteen years older than Freud, Breuer had since 1871 built up a flourishing private practice in Vienna, and was at the height of his powers when the two men met in the late 1870s. One of the city's most sought-after physicians, he did not limit his interests to medicine, and was as comfortably at home in discussion of music, painting and literature as among the details of his profession. Kindly, compassionate, he lived a life suggesting that his acknowledged duty was that of helping lame dogs over stiles.

Breuer's cultural interests attracted Freud, who was later to drop references to Shakespeare or Kipling into his letters, boast that he regularly enjoyed the Munich humorous magazine *Simplicissimus* and would jump up to interrupt a colleague's argument by reaching for *Faust* and exclaiming, "Let's see what old Goethe has to say about it." Freud and Breuer took to each other, and for the next fifteen years grew more closely together, Freud drawing what he could from the older man's experience, Breuer kept mentally alert by the younger man to whom no task was too difficult to tackle, no idea too extraordinary to investigate. Their friendship, and eventual collaboration, was to have an outcome which neither could have imagined as their acquaintanceship ripened to friendship and their friendship matured to professional admiration.

Brücke's laboratory was still extremely primitive when Freud joined it. The Institute was housed in the basement and ground floor of an ancient building once used for making guns; the accommodation was an auditorium, two small adjoining offices and a number of small cubicles, some unlit, which served for experiments. Heating of chemicals had to be done over a spirit lamp, and the only water available came from a well, from which it was drawn by the caretaker each morning. Here, in the most unsophisticated conditions, Brücke helped to lay the foundations for Vienna's future success as a medical center. And here Freud was to set out on the path that led him, via the study of nerve cells, through nervous diseases, to the neuroses in particular and finally to analysis of the mind.

His first work was investigation of the large nerve cells, which had recently been discovered by Reissner, in the spinal cord of the *Ammocoetes (Petromyzon Planeri)*, the larval form of the brook lamprey. It was an investigation that turned out to be of more than merely biological interest, since it was relevant to the controversy still bitterly raging about the assumption of Darwin's *The Origin of Species* that the higher animals were but developments of the lower. If this were so, then the nervous system might show that the human mind had a mechanism more complicated than that of the lower orders of life but one which was nevertheless built of similar basic units. Thus Freud now began, if involuntarily, looking for answers, as one writer has implied, which would throw light "on the nature of man, the existence of God and the aim of life." Within a few weeks he had discovered that the posterior nerves originated in some of the Reissner cells. On Brücke's instigation he quickly put together a preliminary report, carried out a further and more thorough investigation, and in a second report showed conclusively that the nervous systems of the lower animals had evolved gradually into those of the higher without perceptible demarcation.

His next work was along similar lines. This time it was the nerve cells of the crayfish whose structure he investigated, using a new and difficult technique to examine the live tissues microscopically. In both researches he was describing work that bore directly not only on the controversies aroused by Darwin but on the riddle of nerve action and its mechanism, a subject already beginning to attract him. "My demon," he wrote to Silberstein,

> drove me to visit Stricker's laboratory during the holidays. [Salomon Stricker, the experimental pathologist.] I was well received there and was provided with good working projects. I am now involved in microscopic studies of the nerves of salivary glands, and I am sure I am on to something. Not so sure, though, whether I shall publish a paper, the subject being very rewarding and highly popular. Somebody might easily precede me in publication, as I am not yet able to foresee when I will have any results. From next month I shall start experimenting with salivary secretions in dogs.

The remark about publication was significant. If there was a likelihood that he would not be first in the field, then Freud would switch to something else. Understandable when progress at the start of a career was largely dependent on publication, it was nevertheless an early indication of the determination to make his mark. During the following year, and in 1880, he extended his researches to the nervous system of the fresh-water crab, work which brought him to the verge of seeing that the anatomical and functional unit of the nervous system was the individual cell plus its extension. But this discovery was to be left to Wilhelm von Waldeyer in 1884.

He now had to face a one-year spell of compulsory military service, the first of two which all able-bodied Austrians had to perform. For medical students the year was boring rather than arduous. Their duties consisted of standing in at military hospitals, and between duty hours they continued to live at home. Nevertheless, Freud, following eight successive periods of absence without leave, found himself under military arrest on his twenty-fourth birthday, May 6, 1880.

However, at least some of this conscript year was turned to good advantage. His earlier enthusiasm for Brentano now bore fruit, and he was commissioned to translate into German a volume of John Stuart Mill. Theodor Gomperz, professor of history in the university and a well-known figure in Viennese society, was editing a collected German edition. Eduard Wessel, a translator preparing to start on the twelfth volume, had died suddenly and Gomperz mentioned to Brentano that he was looking for a substitute. "Brentano . . . named my name," Freud wrote years later, and throughout the autumn and winter of 1880 his tedium with military service was relieved by at least one intellectual task. His method was to read a section, consider with book closed how a German writer would have expressed the same thoughts, and put them down in German.

With one exception, Freud enjoyed Mill. Adopting the attitude of the nineteenth-century Teuton, he could never take seriously the philosopher's acceptance of the equality of women. His views had been firmly expressed five years previously when he took Silberstein to task for carrying on a minor affair with a sixteen-year-old girl. "A thinking man is his own legislator and confessor, and obtains his own absolution," Silberstein was primly told; "but the woman, let alone the girl, does not have the measure of ethics in herself. She can only act if she keeps within the limits of morality, following what society has established as fitting. She is never forgiven if she has revolted against morality, possibly rightly so."

Now, translating Mill, he refused to consider the idea that a married woman could earn as much as her husband. In this respect, he was later to tell his fiancée, "I adhere to the old ways, to my longing for my Martha as she is, and she herself will not want it different; legislation and custom have to grant to women many rights kept from them, but the position of woman cannot be other than what it is: to be an adored sweetheart in youth, and a beloved wife in maturity."

But the beloved wife had also to be attentive and obedient. "A few weeks ago, while we were at table in a hotel at a mountain resort in the Tyrol," he wrote some fourteen years after his marriage, "I was very much annoyed because I thought my wife was not being sufficiently reserved toward some people sitting near us whose acquaintance I had no desire at all to make. I asked her to concern herself more with me than with these strangers."

There was a good deal of condescension in some of Freud's other *pronunciamentos* on the subject. "Woman, whom culture has burdened with a heavier load (especially in propagation)," he was to claim in criticizing a colleague's paper, "ought to be judged with tolerance and forbearance in areas where she has lagged behind man." The belief remained unchanged. Half a century later he was to proclaim that "women must be regarded as having little sense of justice . . . as weaker in their social interests [than men] and as having less capacity for sublimating their instincts . . ." And lest there be any doubt about the matter, he reiterated his views to an American visitor who asked whether it would not be better if both partners in a marriage were equal. "That is a practical impossibility," Freud replied. "There must be inequality, and the superiority of the man is the lesser of two evils."

Freud's anti-feminist attitude, for which he has repeatedly been under heavy fire from the women's liberation movements, accurately reflected the received opinions of nineteenth-century Europe in general and especially of nineteenth-century Vienna. His failure to change with the times was no doubt partly the result of a nature which, outside his own special field, was innately conservative. Yet there was another factor. Later, when his ideas might have been expected to broaden out, they were reinforced by one item in his developing picture of the female psyche: penis envy. According to Freud, this accounted for the fact "that envy and jealousy play an even greater part in the mental life of women than of men." Once this was taken as gospel, much else followed—even to the point where "superiority of the man is the lesser of two evils."

Freud's translation of Mill was a pleasant and profitable sideline during this year of military training. There were a number of leaves, and during one of them he returned once more to Freiberg. Here, out of professional interest he watched the local doctor treating his patients. Each one, he reported, described his symptoms, such as backache, stomach troubles or pains. "The doctor then examined him and, after satisfying himself as to what was the matter, called out the diagnosis, which was the same in every case. He translated the word to me; it meant approximately 'bewitched.' I asked in astonishment whether the peasants made no objection to his verdict being the same with every patient. 'Oh, no!' he replied, 'they are very pleased with it: it is what they expected. Each of them, as he went back to his place in the row, showed the others by looks and gestures that I was a fellow who understood things.' " Freud, relating the story years later, after his former colleague Alfred Adler had deserted him, compared the Freiberg treatment to Adler's system of "Individual Psychology."

On his return from military service to university life he at last decided to sit for his medical degree. Despite the zealous wish to help people, expressed after his visit to England, he had shown no particular enthusiasm for a doctor's life. Indeed, as he admitted, he was "decidedly negligent" in pursuing his medical studies. He had probed into various fields of medical research without settling down seriously in any one of them. And from the evidence that has survived, admittedly fragmentary, it appears that his aim was not so much to make his mark in some chosen area as to make it wherever opportunity offered a promising reward. He never doubted that he had a mission; he still did not quite know what it was.

However, there were good reasons for becoming medically qualified. Most of the scientists whom he admired had taken their M.D. even though they had rarely if ever practiced. There was, moreover, his personal reputation to think of: his acquaintances regarded him as a loafer and doubted whether he would get through.

Freud got through, but he seems to have been lucky. The oral examination he described to his friend Carl Koller: "I no longer believe in earthly justice, for I can now obediently announce to you that I did not fail . . . ," he wrote. He had doubts about the outcome, being especially worried by the subject of pharmacology. Then he plucked up courage. "After a short collapse I went forth to the battlefield determined to defend my life in every possible way and to keep unrestrainedly quiet in pharmacology," he told Koller. "The nearness of battle exerted its usual stimulating effect on me. I was lively, bold, and confident. From Sigmund [Dr. Karl Sigmund Ritter von Ilanor, professor of dermatology and syphilology at the university] I got an 'Excellent' in no time for a clinical presentation of measles. Now came the Schlemil historicus ["unlucky fellow," apparently Freud's nickname for one of the examiners]. With his usual lack of skill he questioned me on one subject only, brain hemorrhages. We had a lively debate. I could hardly use the most commonplace abstractum without his saying, 'This is not correct, this is a phrase,' etc. I replied, 'I did not speak without thinking.' 'Think it over again and you will understand it yourself,' he said." The following day he told his friend the full results: "Excellent" in pathological anatomy, general pathology, gastroenterology, and "Satisfactory" in four other subjects. "In pharmacology," he went on, "it may be announced that I did not miss a single question, but I could not avoid giving the impression of having learned nothing, as it always took me a long time before I could compose the right answer."

He was equally fortunate in the three written examinations. The first, in chemistry, botany and zoology, was held by his friend Ernst von Fleischl-Marxow. This was fortunate. Freud had little aptitude for chemistry; when it came to botany he failed to identify a simple flower. However, he somehow earned an "Excellent." In the afternoon it was only a "Satisfactory" in forensic medicine, thus leaving the final result resting on the third examination, which was held some months later. But he appears to have spent little of the available time in preparation, relying instead on his photographic memory. It was sufficient.

Later, in the spring of 1881, he received the degree at the impressive ceremony held in the Old University. His family was present; so was Richard Flüss, one of Gisela's three brothers, as well as Frau Flüss and her husband.

3

Determined Doctor

I have allotted the various parts of the body in the manner of a Commander in Chief.

FREUD, in a letter to Martha Bernays

Freud's graduation as a doctor at first made little difference to his life or his prospects. In May 1881 he was promoted to the rank of Demonstrator in Brücke's Institute, and at the same time began part-time work on gas analysis in Carl Ludwig's Chemical Institute. But the future looked as unsettled as ever. He was hard-pressed financially, kept afloat partly by loans from better-off friends. He still believed that somewhere in medical research a great opportunity was waiting to be seized, a technique or process whose value he alone would be able to see and to develop for the good of the world and of Sigmund Freud. To others he was a pleasant but sober young man who appeared to have missed the bus.

A transformation took place in the summer of 1882, after he had finished his earlier researches on the crayfish and was carrying on routine work in the Institute. Freud's own account, given in his brief autobiography, is beguilingly misleading. "The turning point," he says, "came in 1882, when my teacher, for whom I felt the highest possible esteem, corrected my father's generous improvidence by strongly advising me, in view of my bad financial position, to abandon my theoretical career. I followed his advice, left the physiological laboratory and entered the General Hospital."

The vital point that he omitted was that he had fallen in love, realized that research was unlikely to provide an income on which he could marry, and had reluctantly begun to acquire the two or three years' experience necessary for either a viable hospital appointment or for setting up his own practice. Potential genius had at last been pricked into action by a spur no stronger than a normal biological impulse.

In the spring of 1882 he was still living at home, returning from the Institute each evening and invariably giving the family only a brief greeting before retiring to his long, narrow study. Even when he later moved into hospital quarters and came home only at weekends, he would still make for the study with any friends who accompanied him. "One would have imagined," his eldest sister later regretted, "that the presence in the house of five young women would have had some attraction for these young men, but they seemed less interested in entertainment than in scientific discussion with our learned brother, and disappeared into his room with scarcely a glance at any of us!"

Freud appears to have adopted the same attitude toward his sisters' friends, and his reaction one evening in April 1882 was unexpected. Arriving home, he found a young girl chatting with the other members of the family and peeling an apple. Instead of making straight for his room he joined them.

The visitor was Martha Bernays, the twenty-one-year-old daughter of a family of German Jews who had moved to Vienna in 1869. Her father, Berman Bernays, had died in 1879, and the position as head of the family had been taken by his son, Eli, who acted as counselor and adviser to his two sisters, Martha and Minna. The Bernays were a distinguished family, Martha's grandfather having been chief rabbi of Hamburg during the 1840s. Berman Bernays had been a merchant. His widow and children were in the 1880s apparently more prosperous than the Freuds, and although the two families were on visiting terms, it seems that they had only recently become so.

Martha Bernays was slim and self-assured, with long dark hair tightly drawn back from a narrow face. She combined a strong will with, after her marriage, unquestioning obedience to her husband, inwardly disagreeing with him on both religion and psychoanalysis, yet remaining circumspectly silent. She had already rejected at least one suitor but quickly succumbed to the protestations of a young Freud for whom the evening encounter awoke love at first sight.

Freud's decision to marry Martha Bernays as soon as practicable was one of those unpremeditated acts whose justification he gave to a friend years later. "When making a decision of minor importance," he said, "I have always found it advantageous to consider all the pros and cons. In vital matters, however, such as the choice of a mate or a profession, the decision should come from the unconscious, from somewhere within ourselves. In the important decisions of our personal life, we should be governed, I think, by the deep inner needs of our nature." Martha was more cautious. Nevertheless, the couple became engaged on June 17, without the knowledge of either family and on the eve of Martha's departure from Vienna for a ten-week holiday with relatives in Wandsbek, on the outskirts of Hamburg. Freud followed in July, spending ten days in Wandsbek and meeting his fiancée surreptitiously.

His marriage to Martha Bernays, which did not take place until 1886, after four years of almost unrelieved separation, can be cited in support of the saying that behind every great man there stands a woman. As the mistress of his home she was to run the house strictly to his professional demands; in her attitude to the cause, the establishment of psychoanalysis, she dutifully concealed disbelief, only rarely allowing herself such irreverences as her remark to one visitor: "Do you really think one can employ psychoanalysis with children? I must admit that if I did not realize how seriously my husband takes his treatments, I should think that psychoanalysis is a form of pornography!" She produced the family of which he was so greatly fond, and she remained without demur the obedient wife that he, to the end of his days, saw as the destined role of any successful woman.

Between his Freiberg holiday in 1872 and his meeting with Martha a decade later, Freud would seem to have lived a life of comparatively monastic seclusion. Just how monastic is not clear. Ernest Jones states of Freud's relations with women that "any physical experiences were probably few and far between," while Freud himself wrote to the American, James Jackson Putnam, saying, "I stand for a much freer sexual life. However, I have made little use of such freedom, except in so far as I was convinced of what was permissible for me in this area."

Nevertheless, Freud's lifelong, and generally successful, efforts to draw a veil over his emotional life and its sexual outlets probably has an explanation at variance with the one which might naturally be inferred. At the age of forty-one he wrote to his friend-confessor, Wilhelm Fliess: ". . . sexual excitation is of no more use to a person like me." His ignorance of women and their ways was obvious and self-confessed, and when asked in old age to fill in a questionnaire on the essence of love beyond the realm of sex, he replied: "Up to the present I have not yet found the courage to make any broad statements on the essence of love, and I think that our knowledge is not sufficient." Prepossessing, and on the face of it very attractive to women, Freud gave no one the impression of having more than a professional interest in the opposite sex. Indeed, to the percipient French poetess Comtesse Anna de Noailles he fell far short of expectations. "I never saw her more disappointed than after their short conversation," wrote her friend Maryse Choisy. " 'Surely,' she exclaimed, '*he* never wrote his "sexy" books. What a terrible man! I am sure he has never been unfaithful to his wife. It's quite abnormal and scandalous!' "

Only one question has been raised regarding Freud's steady faithfulness to his wife. It concerns his sister-in-law Minna, who in 1895 came to live in the Freud household for a few months and prolonged her stay for the rest of her life. Freud was certainly to say that it was Minna Bernays, as well as his friend Wilhelm Fliess, who sustained his faith in himself when he was developing psychoanalysis in the face of determined opposition. Certainly Minna Bernays had an understanding of, and sympathy for, psychoanalysis far greater than that of her sister. Freud occasionally went on summer holidays with his sister-in-law while Martha joined them later on, and some observers have found it difficult to believe that the relationship was entirely Platonic.

The only so-called evidence to the contrary that even the most bitter of Freud's opponents has been able to provide is a remark reported to have been made by Carl Jung, apparently in the 1950s, about his first meeting with the Freud family in 1907. According to this, the thirty-two-year-old Jung was approached by both Martha and Minna, who separately spoke of Freud's passion for his sister-in-law. The story sounds decidedly unlikely, as does the even less substantiated suggestion that Freud's emphasis on sex in his work was a reflection of his own voracious longings. Maybe he was an unsublimated randy young man who grew into an unsublimated randy old man, but there is not a tatter of evidence for this, and the known context of his life makes it distinctly improbable. Were it not for the secrecy with which his papers have long been shrouded —almost certainly a reflex action to the attacks made on his theories during his lifetime—the idea would long ago have died a natural death.

Although Freud's devotion to his wife was lifelong, their engagement was at times stormy, and occasionally in danger of foundering on the rocks of his possessiveness. Martha had her admirers as well as her family friends, and her fiancé was almost equally jealous of both, an attitude which, it has been suggested, was to affect the psychoanalytic view of the artist. Two admirers were Fritz Wahle, a painter, and Max Meyer, a composer, and Freud revealed his reactions to them when he wrote: "I think there is a general enmity between artists and those engaged in the details of scientific work. We know that they possess in their art a master key to open with ease all female hearts, whereas we stand helpless at the strange design of the lock and have first to torment ourselves to discover a suitable key to it."

This early feeling of inferiority illustrates how Freud's theories and beliefs could be motivated by his own personal experiences. "Here," the artist Charles Biederman has written,

> I think we have a situation that developed into unconscious material which was to impose its influence upon Freud's formulation of the role of the artist and his art, namely, the artist is one unable to face reality and turns to a world of fantasy. This fantasy manages to give the artist the satisfaction in life that reality would have denied him. Fortunately, those who use art seem to have a desire and propensity for precisely the artist's particular personal fantasy needs. This in turn happily solves the artist's problems—women, fame, etc.
>
> The scientist, however, unlike the artist, is wholly compelled to face reality; in fact, that act is his very life blood, just as fantasy is for the artist. So we have another one of Freud's famous "pairs of opposites" . . .

Martha Bernays' admirers were not alone in being subjected to Freud's criticism. In arguments with her brother Eli, who before the end of 1882 had become engaged to Freud's eldest sister Anna, Freud insisted that Martha should take his side rather than her brother's. And of Emmeline Bernays, Martha's mother, he complacently wrote: "I can foresee more than one opportunity of making myself disagreeable to her and I don't intend to avoid them." When Martha stood up for her mother, Freud's reaction was unequivocal: Frau Bernays was "the enemy of our love."

Those overdramatic but no doubt effective words seem to have reflected Freud's early antipathetic attitude to the Bernays family in general. When it came to his own relatives he was devoted, and his hundreds of letters in the Library of Congress reveal, as one example, how anxious he was for the Freud umbrella to cover not only his in-laws but, in the case of second marriages after a death, those whom he regarded as honorary members of the family. Yet these feelings extended only with caution to the Bernays.

However, such caution had not yet matured when he put into operation the plans which would eventually enable him to marry Martha. He worked quickly. Engaged in mid-June, he only a month later joined the Vienna General Hospital. Here he was to spend the next three years of his life, sitting for much of the time at a desk above which there hung a plaque bearing the warning attributed to St. Augustine: *"En cas de doute, abstiens-toi"* ("In case of doubt, don't"). During that time, marriage with Martha was the aim of all hope and ambition, and in furtherance of that aim he eagerly sought about for any ideas, any process, any discovery that would speed his climb up the ladder and ease the way either to a more important hospital appointment or to the prospect of success in private practice.

The General Hospital was a good place for such an ambitious man. Stretching across 25 acres of the city, its wards usually sheltered more than 3,000 patients, who came not only from the capital itself but from the farthest parts of the Empire and even from Asia and Africa. Cases which elsewhere might be seen only once in a lifetime were frequent here, and for a doctor with great ideas there were few better places in Europe in which to gain experience. Yet conditions in the hospital were appalling. There was only limited gaslighting, so that during the winter months patients spent a good deal of time in the dark. Operations were sometimes carried out by candlelight, and even the wards that accommodated lung cases were filled with clouds of dust during the daily cleaning. But here, defying the conditions, a handful of doctors had built up, and were now consolidating, the great reputation of Viennese medicine.

For the first two months Freud worked in the surgical wards, but finding this very tiring and not to his liking—hatred of the sight of blood presumably playing its part—applied for a post as assistant to Hermann Nothnagel, recently arrived from Germany to take charge of the division of internal medicine. A man with a reputation for hard work—"whoever needs more than five hours of sleep should not study medicine" was one of his maxims—Nothnagel was a formidable figure. "A germanic caveman," was Freud's report to Martha. "Completely fair hair, head, cheeks, neck, eyebrows, all covered with hair and hardly any difference in color between skin and hair. Two enormous warts, one on the cheek and one on the bridge of the nose; no great beauty, but certainly unusual."

Freud had brought to his interview with Nothnagel copies of his own published papers and a letter of introduction from Professor Theodor H. Meynert, head of the hospital's psychiatric department. One of the greatest brain anatomists in Europe, Meynert was a formidable man in both build and temper, his huge head with forked beard giving him a Mephistophelian air. His strong views on hypnotism were to transform him, within a few years, from an admirer of Freud into a dedicated enemy.

Nothnagel was impressed both by Freud's papers and by the

note from Meynert; a week later the young man was assigned to Nothnagel's department. Here he stayed for six and a half months until, in May 1883, he joined Meynert's department of psychiatry, serving two months in the male wards, then three in the female. There followed a few months in the department of dermatology; then he moved to the department of nervous diseases where he stayed until leaving the hospital in the summer of 1885.

Some while before Freud at last steered himself into neurology, he had been given a fresh incentive to hurry on until marriage became possible. This was the removal of the Bernays family from Vienna back to Wandsbek, a move which he opposed with great vigor and outspoken condemnation of his future mother-in-law's plans. Her projected move, he complained to Minna, who had by now become engaged to his friend Ignaz Schönberg, was "at the behest of some extraordinary whim, oblivious of the fact that by doing so she would be separating you and Schönberg, Martha and myself for years to come. This certainly isn't very nobleminded, nor is it downright wicked; it is simply the claim of age, the lack of consideration of energetic old age . . ." There was much more along the same lines, a passionate pleading that the breadth of Germany should not be put between him and his betrothed.

Nevertheless, the Bernays moved and the separation increased Freud's need for a discovery, or at least for observations that would justify more scientific papers, those passports to the success that was never far from his mind. "It is hard to find material for publication," he complained to Martha in January 1884, "and it infuriates me to see how everyone is making straight for the unexploited legacy of nervous diseases." But it was not run-of-the-mill stuff for which he was looking. "A man must get himself talked about," he declared. And after a lecture to hospital colleagues he lamented that "now comes the worry about holding one's own, finding something new to make the world sit up and bring not only recognition from the few but also attract the many, the well-paying public." Surely something would one day present itself, something unexpected, startling and strange enough to bring marriage nearer, a hope further stimulated when, in October 1883, his eldest sister, Anna, married Martha's brother, Eli Bernays.

An indication of his attitude is shown in a letter to Martha in the autumn of 1883:

Strange creatures are billeted in my brain. Cases, theories, diagnostics, formulas, have moved into brain accommodations, most of which have been standing empty, the whole of medicine is becoming familiar and fluid to me, here bacteria live, sometimes turning green, sometimes blue, there come the remedies for cholera, all of which make good reading but are probably useless. Loudest of all is the cry: Tuberculosis! Is it contagious? Is it acquired? Where does it come from? Is Master Koch of Berlin right in saying that he has discovered the bacillus responsible for it?

For some months he pinned his hopes on a new process he had devised for hardening and staining sections of the brain for microscopic examination. At times he was optimistic, usually taking care to add a qualification to Martha: ". . . don't be disappointed if I write again that it doesn't work; discovery requires patience and time and luck; if something is to succeed it always has to start like this . . ." Brücke, after witnessing a demonstration of the staining process, remarked encouragingly, "I see your methods alone will make you famous yet," and in March 1884 the method was described in the *Centralblatt für die medizinischen Wissenschaften.* But when Freud's friend Ernst von Fleischl-Marxow advised him to spend the next seven years developing it, Freud replied that he would starve long before then. Breuer, inspecting the process, sagely remarked, "Now that you have the weapon, I wish you a happy war," thereby inducing Freud to tell Martha that if he won the war, then "the years of waiting for my darling would be shortened."

When Freud saw success in the distance he gathered friends to help, operating in a way that foreshadowed the Vienna Psychoanalytical Society of two decades later. Each of the friends was persuaded to use the new staining process for a different purpose, one for the brain, another for the skin, another for the bladder. "So," he concluded to Martha, "I have allotted the various parts of the body in the manner of a Commander in Chief."

The first trials were encouraging. Freud described his method in another Viennese medical journal as well as in a paper for *Brain: A Journal of Neurology,* and requests for translation were soon coming in from other countries. However, it eventually became clear that success depended too much on the skill of the operator; Freud's idea failed to gain support, and nothing came of his hopes.

The five months in Meynert's department of psychiatry was the only experience of that branch of medicine Freud was to gain in the General Hospital. Some later commentators believe this was fortunate. "Had he started with the psychiatry of his time," his American translator, A. A. Brill was to note, "he would surely have become discouraged and he might have returned to his original intention of studying jurisprudence."

Toward the end of the five months Freud went to Breuer for

advice. Should he concentrate on becoming a specialist, he asked, or should he aim at general practice? He obviously preferred specialization; but he realized that this would tie him to Vienna, whereas the opportunities in general practice would be more numerous, the chances of getting married that much greater. Breuer's advice was not to make a final decision yet, to specialize in whatever really attracted him, but to accept the fact that he might eventually have to work as an ordinary practitioner.

The following day Freud applied for a transfer to the department of nervous diseases. He joined it on the first day of 1884, and a week after starting work he was able to report: "Today I put my case histories in order at last and started on the study of a nervous case; thus begins a new era!" Before the end of the month he was finishing what he described as his first clinical publication, and early in February he lectured to the Psychiatric Club. "Just imagine your timid lover, confronted by the severe Meynert and an assembly of psychiatrists and several colleagues, trying to draw attention to one of his earlier works, the very one which had been overlooked by Prof. Kupfer [Dr. Karl Wilhelm von Kupfer, professor of anatomy at the University of Vienna]."

It did not take him long to find his feet, and a few months later he felt confident enough to write: ". . . in one field of science I am independent enough to make contributions without any further contacts or assistance, by which I mean my knowledge of the nervous system." Within little more than a year he was lecturing to visiting doctors, particularly on the *medulla oblongata* (the hind brain, excluding the cerebellum), which had become one of his specialities. His research on it was to provide the material for his *Dozentur* dissertation in 1885 and was also the subject of three papers, two minor and one more important. The last, abstracted for the *Journal of Nervous and Mental Disease* by M. Allen Starr, then a fellow worker at the same laboratory table, was to introduce Freud's name to the United States.

He soon made his mark in the department of nervous diseases, and after two doctors had been dispatched to cope with a cholera epidemic on the Austrian frontier, was made temporary superintendent, a post which gave him full responsibility for 106 patients, two nurses and three doctors.

While Freud now found himself moving toward the subject in which he instinctively felt his future lay, it was not instinct alone that was at work. There was also what he admitted to be his "eye to pecuniary considerations." At that time there were, he has written, "few specialists in that branch of medicine in Vienna, the material for its study was distributed over a number of different departments of the hospital, there was no satisfactory opportunity

of learning the subject, and one was forced to be one's own teacher
. . . In the distance shone the great name of Charcot [Dr. Jean-
Martin Charcot of the Salpêtrière, Paris]; so I formed a plan of first
obtaining an appointment as university lecturer [*Dozent*] on nervous diseases in Vienna and of then going to Paris to continue my
studies."

But before encountering Charcot, one of the most famous doctors of the day, his attention was to be diverted and his hopes
raised once again. There was, indeed, reason enough for him to
pursue anything that offered the chance of fame, and the money
that he took for granted would go with it. His hospital salary was
little more than a pittance, and he augmented it by abstracting for
a medical journal. He coached a few pupils. And he even, under
the convention of the time, was allowed to take the occasional
private patient, sent to him by well-wishers such as Brücke. Yet all
this barely sufficed to keep him above the poverty line. He was still
largely dependent on loans from colleagues: Josef Paneth and
Ernst von Fleischl-Marxow who both had private means, and Josef
Breuer with whom he was running up a steadily growing debt.
Freud would have been less than human had he not pursued what
he saw as a great opportunity.

"I am also toying now," he wrote to Martha, "with a project and
a hope which I will tell you about; perhaps nothing will come of
this, either. It is a therapeutic experiment. I have been reading
about cocaine. . . ."

Freud's interest had been aroused by reports of an experiment
carried out during the German Army's spring maneuvers. A Dr.
Theodor Aschenbrandt had treated exhausted troops with cocaine, a stimulant made from the leaves of the coca plant. Although
used by the Indians of South America, where the shrub grows
profusely, cocaine had been virtually ignored in Europe until Sir
Robert Christison, the Scots physician and toxicologist, had—
shortly before his death in 1882 at the age of eighty-five—testified
to its use as a stimulant during his vigorous last years when he
could "walk, run, or climb mountains better than any of his contemporaries." Aschenbrandt, one of the first to experiment seriously with the drug, found that "Bavarian soldiers, weary as a
result of hardships and debilitating illnesses, were nevertheless
capable, after taking coca, of participating in maneuvers and marches."

Freud read Aschenbrandt's account of his investigations in the
Deutsche Medizinische Wochenschrift and decided that the little-known
drug might be exploited for other uses. "I have now ordered some
of it," he wrote to Martha,

and for obvious reasons am going to try it out on cases of heart disease, then on nervous exhaustion, particularly in the awful condition following withdrawal of morphine (as in the case of Dr. Fleischl [-Marxow]). There may be any number of other people experimenting on it already, perhaps it won't work. But I am certainly going to try it and, as you know, if one tries something often enough and goes on wanting it, one day it may succeed. We need no more than one stroke of luck of this kind to consider setting up house. But, my little woman, do not be too convinced that it will come off this time. As you know, an explorer's temperament requires two basic qualities: optimism in attempt, criticism in work.

Before the end of the month he had personally confirmed Dr. Aschenbrandt's results:

> I first took 0.05 gram of *cocaïnum muriaticum* in a 1% water solution when I was slightly out of sorts due to fatigue. The solution is rather viscous, slightly opalescent, and with an unusual aromatic smell. At first the taste is bitter but this then changes to a series of very nice aromatic flavors . . . A few minutes after taking the cocaine one suddenly feels light and exhilarated. The lips and palate feel first furry and then warm, and if one drinks cold water it feels warm to the lips but cold to the throat. But on some occasions the main feeling is a rather pleasant coolness in mouth and throat.

After the first few personal experiences, Freud began to administer cocaine to friends, colleagues and patients, and repeated the experiments on himself. "We would take the alkaloid internally by mouth," said Carl Koller, "and after the proper lapse of time for its getting into the circulation we would conduct experiments on our muscular strength, fatigue and the like (measured by the dynamometer)." But the effect of the drug continued to be obvious, even without laboratory measurements, as Freud graphically explained when he wrote to Martha on June 2, 1884:

> Woe to you, my Princess, when I come. I will kiss you quite red and feed you till you are plump. And if you are forward, you shall see who is the stronger, a gentle little girl who doesn't eat enough or a big wild man *who has cocaine in his body.* In my last severe depression I took coca again and a small dose lifted me to the heights in a wonderful fashion. I am just now busy collecting the literature for a song of praise to this magical substance.

He had also noticed that the cocaine, when taken orally, produced a numbness in the tongue. He remembered this loss of feeling when, standing with Carl Koller and a group of colleagues in a courtyard of the hospital one day, he saw a friend who was obviously in great pain. "I said to him," Freud later related, " 'I think I can help you,' and we all went to my room where I applied a few drops of a medicine which made the pain disappear instantly. I explained to my friends that this drug was the extract of a South American plant, the coca, which seemed to have powerful qualities for relieving pain and about which I was preparing a publication."

In addition to experimenting, Freud was meanwhile reading up all he could about cocaine. He incorporated the results in "Über Coca," a paper published in the July 1884 issue of the *Centralblatt für die gesamte Therapie*. The paper began with an account of the history of coca among primitive peoples and its introduction to Europe. It went on to document its effect on animals, and on the human body, and then described the results of Freud's own experiments. He concluded from these that the most important use of cocaine would be as a stimulant "where the main aim is to increase the body's physical capacity for a short period and keep some strength in reserve for coming demands." It could also be of use to cure digestive disorders. "Time after time," he reported, "I have brought this kind of relief to my colleagues; and twice I have noted how nausea following gastronomic excesses has quickly responded to cocaine. I have also learned to spare myself stomach troubles by adding a small amount of cocaine to salicylate of soda." It could also be of use to ease anemia and asthma. It was an aphrodisiac and it could also, Freud averred, help in the treatment of morphine and alcohol addiction, this claim being based largely on reports in the *Detroit Therapeutic Gazette*. The advocacy of cocaine as a treatment for morphine addiction was to be unfortunate, and it has even been claimed that "the recollection that American publications had led him to one of the most painful episodes in his career may have contributed to Freud's critical view of America."

He concluded his paper with the comment that the anesthetizing properties of cocaine made it suitable for other, unspecified, applications. Then, the paper finished, he began to prepare for a long-awaited journey to Martha in Wandsbek. He had not seen her for a year, and as he left Vienna at the beginning of September the thought of the visit drove everything else from his mind. Apparently it even drove out the memory of a meeting earlier in the summer with his friend Dr. Leopold Königstein, *Privatdozent* for ophthalmology at the university, to whom Freud had specifically mentioned that the anesthetizing power of cocaine might be used in the treatment of various eye diseases. According to an account which Freud himself gave many years later, he actually handed Königstein a sample and suggested that he use it in an operation.

Königstein took the sample to a druggist who was told to prepare a clear solution; but the druggist used too much alcohol, the experiment was not a success and Königstein then went on holiday. His departure from Vienna was followed by a visit to Freud by Carl Koller who saw a specimen of cocaine on Freud's desk and noticed the anesthetizing effect of the substance on his fingers. Koller went home and prepared his own solution. But by this time Freud, too, had left Vienna and was already with Martha in Wandsbek.

Freud's account, recollected some thirty years later, infers that he was more generous than might have been expected in handing over to others the great secret which he hoped might bring marriage nearer. Whatever the series of chances which led to Koller's experiments, the outcome has been documented. "He stepped into Professor Stricker's laboratory," says J. Gärtner, "drew a small flask in which there was a trace of white powder from his pocket, and addressed me, Professor Stricker's assistant, in approximately the following words: 'I hope, indeed I expect, that this powder will anesthetize the eye.' 'We'll find out about that right away,' I replied."

Experiments on a frog suggested that the claim was right. "Now it was necessary to go one step further and to repeat the experiment upon a human being," Koller has written. "We trickled the solution under the upraised lids of each other's eyes. Then we put a mirror before us, took a pin in hand, and tried to touch the cornea with its head. Almost simultaneously we could joyously assure ourselves, 'I can't feel a thing.' We could make a dent in the cornea without the slightest awareness of the touch, let alone any unpleasant sensation or reaction. With that the discovery of local anesthesia was completed."

Koller now hastily prepared a short note for a convention of German ophthalmologists to be held in Heidelberg on September 15. He himself could not afford to make the journey and his note was entrusted to a Dr. Josef Brettauer of Trieste, who read it at the convention. The reception was spectacular, and within a few weeks the fact that cocaine could be used as an anesthetic was being demonstrated experimentally in laboratories throughout Europe. Assured of fame, Koller next prepared a longer paper which was read on October 17 to the Physicians Society of Vienna. "Cocaine was brought into the foreground of discussion for us Viennese physicians," he said, "by the thorough compilation and interesting therapeutic paper of my colleague at the General Hospital, Dr. Sigmund Freud."

This was acknowledgment, and in the circumstances nothing more was needed. Freud had indeed brought cocaine to notice, but it was another who had shown its possibilities as an anesthetic. But he had "not been thorough enough to pursue the matter further," he himself somewhat bitterly regretted in 1899. It was the journey to Wandsbek which had prevented him from taking the next and crucial steps, and he was fully aware of the fact, writing two decades later, "but I bore my fiancée no grudge for the omission at the time."

In the 1880s, however, Freud was still the man who with his "Über Coca" had opened various medical possibilities. The monograph was translated into English before the end of 1884 and, with additions and supplements, published as a booklet in Austria early in 1885. In March he lectured to the Psychiatric Association on the effects of the drug and while warning that its use in psychiatric cases was still to be proven, praised it for other purposes. Also, and damagingly as it was to turn out, he said of the treatment of morphine addicts, ". . . I should unhesitatingly advise cocaine being administered in subcutaneous injections of 0.03–0.05 grms. per dose in such withdrawal cures and without minding an accumulation of the doses," a recommendation that was later to be seriously held against him.

Freud himself was to continue taking cocaine for another year or more without any side effects. Its use as a local anesthetic steadily developed. But it slowly became apparent that addiction was a danger comparable to other drug addictions, and inevitably there began an anti-cocaine crusade. Prominent among the critics was Dr. Albrecht Erlenmayer, who said in May 1886 that he counted himself lucky in not having recommended its use in the morphine-withdrawal cure. Later he described it as "the third scourge of humanity"—the first two being alcohol and morphine—and Freud came under increasing attack. He defended himself as best he could, declaring that he had never advised injection of cocaine but only the taking of doses orally—at best a Freudian slip which was repeated later when he omitted from his bibliography the damaging lecture to the Psychiatric Association. He had, in fact, been unlucky. When he set up his practice in 1886 he at first tended to be remembered in some medical circles not as the doctor who had discovered the anesthetizing value of cocaine but as the man who had let loose the third scourge.

While the storm over cocaine was still brewing, Freud had become a university *Dozent,* won a traveling grant which enabled him to pay the longed-for visit to Charcot at the Salpêtrière in Paris, and decided that he would take the plunge—resign from the General Hospital before the journey to France, and on his return set up in private practice.

Early in 1885 Nothnagel had agreed that Freud should apply for an appointment as *Dozent*. The procedure was formal and to Freud must have seemed interminable. First, a committee consisting of Meynert, Brücke and Nothnagel was set up to consider his application. A report which its members made to the faculty at the end of February concluded: "Dr. Freud is a man with a good general education, of quiet and serious character, an excellent worker in the field of neuro-anatomy, of fine dexterity, clear vision, comprehensive knowledge of the literature and a cautious method of deduction, with the gift for well-organized written expression. His findings enjoy recognition and confirmation, his style of lecturing is transparent and secure. In him the qualities of a scientific researcher and of a well-qualified teacher are so well united that the Committee submits the suggestion that the Honorable College resolve on his admission to the further habilitation tests." In view of such a eulogy it is surprising that even one member of the faculty should disagree with the other twenty-one who voted for acceptance of Freud's application.

It was only the first hurdle cleared; but it was the most difficult one, and surmounting it may have encouraged Freud to embark on an orgy of destruction. In April he told Martha that he had carried out an intention which some "as yet unborn and unfortunate people" would one day resent. They, he went on, were his biographers. "I have destroyed all my notes of the past fourteen years," he continued, "as well as letters, scientific excerpts and the manuscripts of my papers. . . . I couldn't have matured or died without worrying about who would get hold of those old papers. . . . As for the biographers, let them worry, we have no desire to make it too easy for them. Each one of them will be right in his opinion of 'The Development of the Hero,' and I am already looking forward to seeing them go astray." Two things are notable: first, Freud's confidence that the future would want to know about him; secondly, his obsession to wipe the slate clean, as though a future *Dozent* might not wish to acknowledge, or even remember, some of the ideas he had once contemplated.

Plausible as the belief may be that Freud was wishing to hide youthful errors—and "worrying about who would get hold of those old papers" reinforces the belief—it seems more likely that on this occasion his action merely illustrated one side of his ambivalent attitude to self-explanation. "Freud was a confessor . . . ," it has been stated by one close colleague, "but at the same time he kept certain personal secrets to himself. He was a self-revealer and a self-concealer. In a certain passage he writes of the 'discretion which one owes also to oneself.'

"This discretion was rarely breached. It was as if he felt he had to keep personal things to himself, even from those of us who were his most loyal students. In his old age he sometimes spoke to one or another of us almost casually of a fragment of his own life he had never mentioned before, as if he had suddenly tired of his secrecy."

Freud himself put his views on the subject to at least two biographers. To his former colleague Fritz Wittels he observed: "It seems to me that the public has no concern with my personality, and can learn nothing from an account of it, so long as my case (for manifold reasons) cannot be expounded without any reserves whatever." And when Arnold Zweig proposed writing Freud's life he was firmly rebutted. "Anyone turning biographer commits himself to lies, to concealment, to hypocrisy, to flattery, and even to hiding his own lack of understanding, for biographical truth is not to be had, and even if it were it couldn't be used," he was told.

"Truth is unobtainable; humanity does not deserve it, and incidentally wasn't our Prince Hamlet right when he asked whether anyone would escape a whipping if he got what he deserved?" There was, of course, something in this; but, as Freud shrewdly realized, "biographical truth" is certainly more difficult to reach when the subject has, from his early years, been "looking forward to seeing [his biographers] go astray."

At the time of the 1885 destruction, Freud had another three months to wait for the oral examination, at which it was necessary to arrive in top hat, white gloves and morning suit. After this came the final test of a public lecture. Freud survived the oral examination and then spoke in public on "The Medullary Tracts of the Brain." After the lecture had been duly accepted as satisfactory, the faculty recommended in July that he should be appointed a *Privatdozent* in neuropathology. In August he reported to the police so that a check could be made on his character, and in September, some nine months after he had made his formal application, the Ministry ratified his appointment. From then on, although unable to attend faculty meetings, he was authorized to lecture, to hold classes and generally to let the world know that he had moved a rung up the ladder.

Freud's success with the all-important traveling grant did not take as long, although the outcome seemed to be even more uncertain. The grant, a university travel scholarship which had been founded twenty years earlier, was awarded by a different faculty each year, and in 1885 it was the turn of the medical faculty. It was competed for by junior *Sekundärärzte*, was for 600 gulden, and the winner, to be chosen by faculty members, was given six months' leave of absence. Freud applied early in March 1885, and after May 1, the final date for entry, began heavy lobbying. He had, he discovered, only two rivals, and it is an illustration of current conditions that when one of them withdrew, Freud felt that his chance of success had receded. The two other men were Gentiles and might have been expected to split the "opposition" vote; now all this would presumably go to one man. But when the faculty met at the end of May, its members could arrive at no decision, and a subcommittee was set up to consider the matter once again.

While the traveling grant was being discussed, a minor enough affair for the faculty but one on which Freud believed, rightly as it turned out, that his whole future hung, he was invited to act as a relief doctor at a private mental hospital in Oberdöbling, on the outskirts of Vienna. Permission was granted by the General Hospital, and he took up his duties on June 7. The following day he described the hospital in a long letter to Martha. It was, apparently, an unusual place in which to work. The elderly director made a point of choosing only pretty girls as housemaids, while all the patients—counts, countesses, barons, and two Highnesses, including a son of Napoleon's Marie Louise—were rich. "You cannot imagine how dilapidated these princes and counts look," Martha was told, "although they are not actually feeble-minded, rather a mixture of feeble-minded and eccentric." Nevertheless, Freud had to wear a silk hat and white gloves on his rounds. But despite the attractions of the place, Oberdöbling was not for him. One could, he told Martha, live an idyllic life there with wife and child "if it weren't for the lack of the challenging and stimulating element of the struggle for existence."

This was soon to come. On June 19 Freud learned that he had won the travel grant, by thirteen votes to eight, and as a result would soon be able to visit Martha in Wandsbek before traveling to Paris. "Oh, how wonderful it will be!" he wrote exultantly to her. "I am coming with money and staying a long time and bringing something beautiful for you and then go on to Paris and become a great scholar and then come back to Vienna with a huge, enormous halo, and then we will soon get married, and I will cure all the incurable nervous cases and through you I shall be healthy and I will go on kissing you till you are strong and gay and happy."

He then, after three weeks with the feeble-minded and eccentric, returned to the General Hospital and prepared for the future. There was no need for him to claim the six months' leave of absence that went with the award, for he now resigned from his post and on the last day of the month left the hospital. He sought an interview with Moritz Benedikt, professor of neurology in the university, and received a letter of introduction to Charcot. All was now ready. Before him there lay a journey to Martha; then, in October, Paris and the Salpêtrière.

4

Paris

In the distance there shone the great name of Charcot.

FREUD, *An Autobiographical Study*

Freud left Vienna late in August 1885 on what was to be the most important journey of his life. First there was to be six weeks in Wandsbek, a holiday made in circumstances different from those of his surreptitious visit three years earlier. By this time he was something more than the newly graduated doctor of 1882, the man of twenty-six who had not yet decided where he was going. If no sign of genius yet glimmered through, he appeared at least to have the makings of a successful professional man. Martha indeed might have done better for herself. Her fiancé's determined agnosticism, and his scorn of the Jewish observances that ran so strongly in the Bernays' intellectual bloodstream, made the coming marriage a cause for regret among some members of the family. But the ability to charm, which was later to become an asset in professional work, had already come to Freud's aid, and by August 1885 he had made his peace with Frau Bernays. The six weeks in Wandsbek passed pleasantly and all too quickly. On October 11 he set out for Paris and the great adventure of sitting at the feet of Jean-Martin Charcot.

He broke his journey first in Cologne, then in Brussels, which he described in a long letter to Martha. "I walked through the whole town, passing from the Boulevard du Nord to the Boul. du Sud, and deviating wherever there might be something beautiful," he wrote. "The proper discoveries I made only when I came upon a steep hill where there was a building so massive and with such magnificent columns as one imagines an Assyrian Royal Palace to have had, or as one finds in the Doré illustrations. I really took it for the Royal Palace, especially since a crown-like cupola rose above it. But there was no guard, no life there, and the building was evidently not finished; over the portals there was a lion bearing the Ten Commandments. It was the Palace of Justice, and from the edge of the hill one had the grandest view of the town lying below. . . ." From there he traversed the rest of the city, taking in *en route* a quick two-franc lunch which "had to last till I got to Paris the next day."

Arrived in the French capital on October 13, he booked in at the Hôtel de la Paix, midway between the Panthéon and the Sorbonne, found a letter from Martha awaiting him and replied by return. He was bewildered by his impressions of the French capital, missed her very much and wished that she were with him. But he would write every other day—more often to begin with.

He spent the next few days acclimatizing, sought about for cheaper accommodation and in the evenings went to the theater, in the hope of improving his French. He also made a number of long sightseeing walks through the Place de la Concorde. "Imagine," he wrote to Martha, "a genuine obelisk, scribbled all over with the most beautiful birds' heads, little seated men and other hieroglyphs, at least 3000 years older than the vulgar crowd around it, built in honor of a king whose name today only a few people can read and who, but for this monument, might be forgotten." And he visited the Louvre, attracted above all by the past, whose relics he was later to collect with such zeal, and reporting to Martha that he had seen there "a few wonderful things, ancient gods represented over and over again. . . . I just had time for a fleeting glance at the Assyrian and Egyptian rooms, which I must visit again several times. There were Assyrian kings—tall as trees and holding lions for lap dogs in their arms, winged human animals with beautifully dressed hair, cuneiform inscriptions as clear as if they had been done yesterday, and then Egyptian bas-reliefs decorated in fiery colors, veritable colossi of kings, real sphinxes, a dreamlike world."

On October 19, having got his bearings, he arrived at the Salpê-trière. But he forgot to take with him the introduction from Benedikt that he had obtained before leaving Vienna and decided to wait until the following day before presenting himself to Charcot. He was feeling homesick for Vienna, love-sick for Martha, and extremely depressed. "Apart from some subjective and scientific profit," he wrote after his abortive visit, "I expect so little from my stay here that in this respect I cannot be disappointed."

Within twenty-four hours all had changed. On the twentieth he entered the gates of the Salpêtrière, the start of four months that were to change his life.

Until the reformation of the Salpêtrière under Charcot, the treatment of the insane throughout the Continent, as well as in Britain and the United States, had differed in degree rather than in kind from the treatment of Hogarth's day. Patients, securely chained, had been exhibited to the public like wild beasts. Possession by the Devil was considered a main cause of the mouthings and frothings, the wild gestures and cries, that marked the worst afflicted. Incarceration within secure walls was seen as the only treatment for those who, unlike the common criminal, could not even be argued with. Most medical men, dedicated to the cure of the potentially curable, left the custody of the mad to those, almost as unfortunate, who could be hired as jailers. Into this dark area of unconcern a few men had throughout the nineteenth century entered with the hope if not of curing, then at least of understanding. Prominent among them was Jean-Martin Charcot, by the 1880s the leading figure in the rambling conglomeration of buildings and squares and gardens known as the Salpêtrière.

Originally an arsenal for the storage of saltpeter, a curious parallel to Brücke's Viennese Institute for Physiology, which had also been an arsenal, the Salpêtrière had been built in the reign of Louis XIII; had become first an asylum for beggars, prostitutes and the insane; and then, in addition, the largest of the Parisian poorhouses for women. By the second half of the nineteenth century it housed between 4,000 and 5,000, under conditions that still had little of the hospital and much of the horrific lunatic asylum. But Charcot had begun a transformation. Appointed chief physician to the Establishment Department, he had added teaching and training units as well as laboratories, had taken over a special ward for epileptics and hysterics, and had by 1885 turned the institution into one of Europe's most famous centers of neurological research.

When Freud arrived at the Salpêtrière the daily consultation with outpatients was being held, and he watched as Pierre Marie, Charcot's second-in-command, examined the patients before a number of visiting doctors. At ten o'clock Charcot himself arrived. By 1885 he was one of the most famous doctors of his age, and more than one description has been given of his commanding presence. Few are better than that of Axel Munthe, whose account in *The Story of San Michele* helps to explain both Charcot's influence on Freud and the importance of Charcot's support which Freud was to receive. "Short of stature," Munthe recorded, with the chest of an athlete and the neck of a bull, he was a most imposing man to look at. A white, clean shaven face, a low forehead, cold penetrating eyes, an aquiline nose, sensitive cruel lips, the mask of a Roman Emperor. When he was angry, the flash in his eyes was terrible like lightning; nobody who has ever faced those eyes is likely to forget them. His voice was imperative, hard, often sarcastic. The grip of his small, flabby hand was unpleasant. . . . Among his assistants he had his favorites whom he often pushed forward to privileged positions far above their merits. A word of recommendation from Charcot was enough to decide the result of any examination or concours, in fact, he ruled supreme over the whole faculty of medicine.

His demonstrations leaned toward the dramatic. The dais from which he addressed his audience was usually surrounded by drawings or photographs, and when giving a lesson on patients with palsy he rarely failed to ornament their coiffures with long plumes. These not only interested his audience but succeeded, by the variety of their oscillations, in helping his students understand the different movements he was demonstrating. Charcot himself was not averse to the histrionic gesture; at times, and particularly when demonstrating, his right arm would move horizontally across his body and find a resting place between the buttons of his smart frock coat. The Napoleon of medicine looked out commandingly over his parade of students.

When all the outpatients had been seen on the morning of the twentieth, Charcot called Freud forward, noted Benedikt's signature on the introduction and invited the visitor to accompany him on his morning tour of the hospital. Everything, Martha was informed that evening, went off better than expected. Pierre Marie ensured that he would have the necessary material on which to start work, and Charcot himself wrote to a colleague, asking for a supply of children's brains, needed for Freud's study of the secondary atrophies and degenerations that follow disease.

Until this first visit Freud had wondered whether he should not, after all, have chosen Berlin for research rather than Paris; he would then have been able to leave the German capital every Saturday evening and spend Sunday with Martha. But the mood quickly changed, and on returning to his room that evening he concluded his happy account to Wandsbek with a single passing regret, for the plight of his relatives in Vienna. "But my stay here is going to be well worth it, this I can see clearly," he said. "If I didn't have to think of the misery at home, I would feel quite all right. But I am so old and so weak or so wicked that I cannot deny myself a thing. I eat my fill and I smoke and I cannot do anything but—be sorry. Whenever I think of them it upsets me, but this doesn't do them any good."

The regular letters from Martha demanded a strict account of his doings, which was not at all to his liking, and he often strove to put the Bernays family in its place. Thus in a long letter written in October he demanded that she "must stop abusing me and getting things wrong. I am around Paris," he continued, "quite alone, have so far seen nothing but a little of the Louvre, a couple of grave-diggers in the Pantheon, and the streets along which I have to walk; and in Paris there are so many people, houses, museums, theaters, gardens and churches and all the rest, and you complain that I am immoderate and upsetting myself with sightseeing. . . . When we are married you must trust me and not believe that the Bernays family alone runs the whole world. Besides, I was so little annoyed at the time, and still less so now when I am half-lying on a sofa, in a most excellent humor, writing to my darling, that you will hardly believe it. However, it is so; I am only a little annoyed with you about the injustice." There was, in fact, comparatively little time for sightseeing, although on the platform of Notre Dame, Freud found a refuge after his own heart as he clambered about there between the monsters and the devils.

On Mondays he attended the public lectures at which Charcot demonstrated his patients. On Tuesdays he watched the more interesting of the outpatients brought for examination and discussion by the hospital's assistants; on Wednesdays there were the ophthalmological examinations carried out under Charcot on his rounds of the wards, when Freud saw and examined the patients and listened to Charcot's verdicts on them.

From the start he was deeply impressed by what he saw at the Salpêtrière. As early as November he wrote to Martha that he thought he was changing a great deal:

> I will tell you in detail what is affecting me. Charcot, who is one of the greatest physicians and a man whose common sense borders on genius, is simply wrecking all my aims and opinions. I sometimes come out of his lectures as from out of Notre Dame, with an entirely new idea about perfection. But he exhausts me; when I come away from him I no longer have any desire to work at my own silly things; it is three whole days since I have done any work, and I have no feelings of guilt. My brain is sated as after an evening in the theater. Whether the seed will ever bear any fruit, I don't know; but what I do know is that no other human being has ever affected me in the same way.

Here was a first hint of the change which was about to take place in Freud's main interest. Despite the help that he had been given by everyone at the Salpêtrière, he had decided by the first days of December to give up work in the laboratory. He was in fact to return to it briefly during the first weeks of the following year, and in a long letter to Martha said that he would be taking up anatomical work when he returned to Vienna. The continuation of his interest was to be shown not only by his monograph, *On Aphasia*, a masterpiece neglected for many years but later recognized for what it was and still studied today; there was also to be a long article on cerebral paralysis in children, contributed to Nothnagel's handbook ("Die infantile Cerebrallähmung" in *Spezielle Pathologie und Therapie*) in 1897, and which was described nearly forty years later as still the most thorough study ever written of cerebral paralysis in children. Nevertheless, Freud had been observing Charcot for only a week or so before his concentration on the physiological began to be rivaled by a growing interest in the psychological. Not for the first time, but now with fresh eagerness, as though sniffing a great challenge in the air, he began to speculate on the links between the physical manifestations of disease and their possible mental causes.

At the time, he maintained that the pathological laboratory "was not at all adapted to the reception of an extraneous worker," and it is certainly possible that conditions did not come up to his expectations. It is possible, too, that a German-speaking Jew found himself ill at ease in a country that bitterly remembered its defeat in the Franco-Prussian war and that was to sentence Dreyfus only a few years later. Other reasons may have played their part. Freud himself admitted that he did not attract people immediately, while the prickliness that came from his self-confidence may have made the extraneous worker not too welcome. There were also his feelings about certain types of work. Almost a decade later he nearly fainted during an operation, and there are other indications, small but cumulative, that his highly developed sense of the fastidious may have inhibited him in carrying out some fairly routine medical tasks. There was also the constant tug of war between scientific investigation, which offered poor financial rewards, and clinical work, which gave a man better chances of earning an income sufficient to marry on and bring up a family. Now, walking the wards with Charcot, he had sensed that it might be possible to combine both, in a field even more exciting than neurology: to build up a successful specialist practice and at the same time "to understand something of the riddles of the world in which we live and perhaps even to contribute something to their solution."

. . .

The riddle that now drew his attention was that of the neuroses in general and of hysteria in particular. In 1885 neuroses were still believed to be solely the result of functional disturbances of the nervous system. It was thought that they could show themselves in almost any combination of symptoms and that these symptoms could not be anatomically localized. Until this could be done, if it ever could be done, most doctors devoted little time to the subject, and many regarded it as a hardly respectable field for investigation. As for hysteria, some still followed the Greek belief that the cause was a malfunctioning of the uterus, or *hysteron,* and that the disease must thus be restricted to women, particularly those of a more excitable, or "hysterical" nature—even though Charles Lepois had as early as the seventeenth century maintained that the cause of hysteria lay in the brain and that men as well as women must therefore be susceptible. The stigmata of hysteria were, indeed, reported in men from time to time, and throughout the eighteenth and nineteenth centuries their numbers increased. Nevertheless, the earlier belief died hard.

Then came Charcot, already equipped with a masterly knowledge of what caused many organic diseases. He set about unraveling the mysteries of hysteria with the methods he had developed to an art: the careful, laborious observation of as many cases as possible, and analysis of all the symptoms which they exhibited. "He used to look again and again at the things he did not understand, to deepen his impression of them day by day, till suddenly an understanding of them dawned on him," says Freud. "In his mind's eye the apparent chaos presented by the continual repetition of the same symptoms then gave way to order: the new nosological pictures emerged, characterized by the constant combination of certain groups of symptoms."

With hysteria, Charcot soon discovered that its various manifestations could be classified into different groups, each conforming to its own laws, and that the various stages of hysterical attack could be identified. As Freud was to describe it: "In a series of researches he . . . succeeded in proving the presence of regularity and law where the inadequate or half-hearted clinical observations of other people saw only malingering or a puzzling lack of conformity to rule."

This was not all. Hysteria, Charcot found, was more common among men than had previously been supposed, but it was no more common among "excitable" nationalities than among the phlegmatic. Investigating phenomena popularly considered to be the prerogative of French actresses, he was delighted to find a case of hysteria in a German grenadier. When it came to causes, he believed that while a chance accident causing psychological damage might be the initiating cause of hysteria, its development only followed where there had been an hereditary deterioration of the brain. Freud was later to remark that neurotics often came from families in which there was a record of other neurotics, although he did not believe that this necessarily proved the importance of heredity; it might, he argued, be merely that the neurotic behavior of one member of a family acted as an environmental stimulus to another member. Nurture rather than nature might still be a part of the trouble.

Whatever qualifications later had to be made to the importance Charcot gave to heredity, he took at the Salpêtrière what Freud was to call the step which "assured him for all time . . . the fame of having been the first to explain hysteria," the step which was to lead Freud himself toward his life's work. Charcot found that some among his nonhysterical patients would exhibit the paralyses, tremors and other symptoms of the hysteric if the idea of such exhibition was implanted in their minds under hypnosis. Thus at least some physical symptoms were indisputably shown to be due not to tissue changes, to lesions or to other physical causes but solely to workings of the mind. It was under Charcot, therefore, that Freud was able to glimpse a new link between mental cause and physical effect.

His initial excitement at what he saw in the Salpêtrière was balanced by other factors, and early in December he even appears to have contemplated cutting short his stay in Paris. Certainly he confided to Martha in mid-December how a French friend had warned him "that this would not be the moment to leave Charcot, when one has just begun to establish a contact with him." Homesickness may have played a part in this passing thought of retreat. "As you realize," he wrote to his future sister-in-law Minna, "my heart is German provincial and it hasn't accompanied me here; which raises the question whether I should not return to fetch it." Yet Freud was now in his thirtieth year. Even though he was alone in a foreign capital, living among people whose language he spoke only with difficulty, the feeling for his family in Vienna or for Martha in Wandsbek does not satisfactorily account for what must be interpreted as a sudden backing away from the work he was observing in the Salpêtrière. One theory is that the basically Puritan Freud reacted strongly against the more extravagant of Charcot's demonstrations. Many revealed the sexual basis of certain cases of hysteria, and it is not entirely implausible that Freud, whose personal rectitude was to be a strong armor in the battles of the future, was, in Paris, momentarily inclined to avoid the whole subject, whatever its scientific interest.

If such considerations did indeed cross his mind, they were soon disposed of, and before the middle of December he had linked himself to Charcot's star by an ingenious move that he saw as a useful aid to his future career. With the help of the friend who had advised him to remain in Paris, he wrote to Charcot, asking if he might translate into German the volume of Charcot's lectures that had appeared in French. As proof of his German style he cited his translation of John Stuart Mill.

Two days later he was able to report success, telling Martha that Charcot had agreed not only to the translation of the one volume but also of another that had not yet been published even in French. It was, he told her, very gratifying: "It is bound to make me known to doctors and patients in Germany and is well worth the expense of a few weeks and several hundred Gulden, not to mention the few hundred Gulden it will bring in." And by the time he left Paris for a week's Christmas visit to Wandsbek, he could report that all the details had been fixed.

Freud returned to Paris on the last day of December, solaced by his week with Martha, excited by the increasing interest that Charcot appeared to be taking in him and, in these circumstances, able to enjoy the French capital. Indeed, within a few weeks he was to be writing: "What a magic city this Paris is!" And shortly before he finally left for home: "I couldn't help thinking what an ass I am to be leaving Paris now that spring is coming, Notre Dame looking so beautiful in the sunlight, and I have only to say one word to Charcot and I can do whatever I like with the patients. But I feel neither courageous nor reckless enough to stay any longer." The real reason for his return to Vienna was given some months later to Koller. "You are right in thinking that Paris meant the beginning of a new existence for me," he said. "I found Charcot there, a teacher such as I had always imagined. I learned to observe clinically as much as I am able to and I brought back with me a lot of information. I only committed the folly of not having enough money to last for more than five months."

Early in the New Year there came an incident which emphasizes Freud's determination to make his mark. In January he met L. Darkschewitsch (Liweri Osipowitsch von Darkschewitsch), a young Russian neurologist attending the Salpêtrière. It was Darkschewitsch who a few years earlier had translated into Russian Freud's paper on the staining method; and the two men naturally enough began to talk shop. Freud spoke of a discovery on brain anatomy which he had made in Vienna but had not published, as he believed that more work would first be required. The Russian then pulled out his own notes on the subject and added that he had mentioned the work to a colleague who was planning to discuss it in a paper. Freud, very humanly concerned with priority, had other ideas. "No, dear friend," he said, "we will publish that together—and, what's more, at once. I have brought several slides along, you have any amount of them; we will study them together, then you make a drawing, I will do the text and then we will get it off together."

The work, a by-product of his researches on the *medulla oblongata*, took three days. Freud was to write one more paper on the *medulla oblongata* and was to make a number of contributions to neurology while working, part-time, in Vienna's first public Institute for Children's Diseases after his return from Paris. He was to write several articles on brain anatomy and his first important monograph, published in 1891, *On Aphasia.* Yet it is clear that from early in 1886 any doubts about the future had been resolved and that from now on he was dedicated to psychopathology. Here, though he may not yet have realized it fully, was the unexplored territory he was seeking.

Once it was decided that he should translate Charcot's two volumes of papers, Freud was quietly brought into a new social circle by way of the splendid Tuesday evening receptions held for the smart world of Paris at Charcot's home on the Boulevard Saint-Germain. As he prepared for the first of these ordeals, he was nervous enough to fortify himself with cocaine. "My appearance was immaculate except that I had replaced the unfortunate ready-made white tie with one of the beautiful black ones from Hamburg," he reported to Martha. "This was my tail coat's first appearance; I had bought myself a new shirt and white gloves, as the washable pair are no longer very nice; I had my hair set and my rather wild beard trimmed in the French style; altogether I spent 14 francs on the evening. As a result I looked very fine and made a favorable impression on myself." He drank his beer and coffee, "smoked like a chimney, and felt very much at ease without the slightest mishap occurring." And at one moment during the evening he became, as he called it, the center of attention. "These were my achievements," he proudly reported, "(or rather the achievements of cocaine) which left me very satisfied."

Freud's Paris letters to Martha, which continued almost daily until he left the city in March 1886, give a revealing portrait of the man who for the first time found himself immersed in the life of a sophisticated capital very different from Vienna. What stands out from them is his intense anxiety to be noticed, to be a success, and his delight when visitors to the Salpêtrière were found to have heard of his papers on cocaine. There is also a growing sense of his own ability, changing rapidly from confidence to the arrogance which allowed him to tell Martha that "given favorable conditions I could achieve more than Nothnagel, to whom I consider myself superior." All this runs beside the growing influence being exercised by Charcot, the man beginning to convince Freud that for him the field for study was the human mind.

By this time he had begun to show a remarkably well-developed knowledge of human nature and the problems with which it can be faced. His comments on colleagues, visitors and friends are uninhibited, and a letter to his future sister-in-law, written after his return from the Christmas visit to Wandsbek, suggests an appreciable awareness of the ways of the world.

Freud's friend Ignaz Schönberg had become engaged to Minna Bernays; had developed tuberculosis and become a patient of Freud. When he realized that his disease was incurable he broke off the engagement. Schönberg died in February 1886, and relations between his family and the Bernays, already bad, quickly worsened. After his death, Minna Bernays wrote to Freud, asking whether he thought Martha and she should make a gesture of friendship to the Schönbergs and ask for a memento. Freud advised against the idea. "You may as well be prepared within a few weeks or months to hear the whole family saying (and believing) that either your love or my medical treatment or Mama's relationship was the cause of his illness," he warned. "Human beings are always glad when for some irrevocable event they can find a reason which is not entirely impersonal but tinged with some kind of emotion."

Less than a month later he was on his way back to Vienna, a journey made via Berlin where, at Adolf Baginsky's clinic, he continued his research on the mental abnormalities of children. "As long as their brains are free of disease, these little creatures are really charming and so touching when they suffer," he noted to Martha. "I think I would find my way about in a children's practice in no time." But as far as Berlin was concerned, he was hardly enthusiastic. "Although I have already been here for a week I haven't seen anything of the city, except for a few streets through which I walk every day," he wrote to his sister Rosa. "I want to make an effort next week and go to the aquarium. I am still very lonely here, and in the evenings, when I can't work, I'm bored stiff. The city doesn't really make any impression on me. Slightly more lively and a little less attractive than Vienna. Life much cheaper, and the people work hard for their living; many police and many soldiers."

Back in Vienna he now concentrated on Charcot's work, on the extraordinary sights which he had witnessed at the Salpêtrière, and on their implications. He was nearly thirty. Despite his varied experience in the General Hospital, he had so far had only minimal contact with psychiatry, and at first glance it must have seemed that he had singularly little background for the work on which he was to embark. This was not so.

Whatever his critics might say, and they were to say much, Freud's delvings into the obscurities of mental disease were to be forays made by a man already equipped with physiological knowledge of the first order. The importance of this has rarely been better emphasized than in a note for the *Schweizer Archiv für Neurologie und Psychiatrie* at the time of Freud's eightieth birthday. "[He] had, as it were, started from the ranks, as a private, yet from the beginning he carried the Commander's baton in his knapsack," it said. "From his first investigation on the structure of the spinal ganglia and the spinal cord of the most primitive vertebrates; from his observations on the finer structure of the elements of the nervous system; his cerebro-anatomical studies, he gradually advanced to the recognition of the most complicated clinical affections. Not until then did he venture upon the complex problems of brain pathology, such as the teachings on aphasia, passing at the very last to the investigation of the functional neuroses. His thorough anatomical and clinical neurological training served as a guarantee that also in the tackling of this last and most difficult problem, he would remain on a solid biological basis and therefore not be led too far astray."

He was to need all this ballast of conventional training, and more, during the years that now lay ahead.

THE MAKING OF A LEADER

5

Early Days in Practice

I am not basically interested in therapy and I usually find that I am engaged—in any particular case—with the theoretical problems with which I happen to be interested at the time.

FREUD, quoted by Abram Kardiner, "Freud—The Man I Knew, The Scientist and His Influence"

Freud had left Vienna as a budding neurologist, anxious to learn in the Salpêtrière all that could be learned about the anatomy of the nervous system; he returned with his interest in the subject somewhat evaporated. In its place there had grown up, under the influence of Charcot's theatrical demonstrations, a determination to concentrate, instead, on the problems of the mind in general and the problems of hysteria in particular. The student of structural neurology was becoming the proponent of dynamic psychiatry.

Freud was no doubt a benevolent revolutionary, a doctor in the great tradition of men in advance of their times. Yet as he prepared to set up in practice, the study of the mind was undergoing a transformation which had begun almost a century earlier, a transformation which did at least make his task less difficult than it would have been during the 1820s or 1840s. At the start of the nineteenth century the links between psychology and philosophy were still strong. By the 1880s they had become weakened as biology had advanced and as experimental and mathematical methods began to give a scientific rigor to a subject that had previously lacked it. The change was particularly noticeable in the study and treatment of the mentally ill. At the end of the eighteenth century the way had been opened up by Philippe Pinel, who had courageously maintained that the poor creatures crowding the asylums were ill rather than wicked and that disease rather than demonic possession was the cause of their troubles. The change, epitomized three quarters of a century later by Charcot in the Salpêtrière, had also taken place in England, where the efforts of William Tuke had been supported by the Society of Friends, and in the United States under the influence of Dorothea Dix: reformers typical of the small band of lay enthusiasts with whose encouragement doctors slowly began to classify mental diseases, the first step toward finding a cure for them.

During the first half of the nineteenth century, experiment, microscopy and staining techniques opened the way to accurate mapping of the distribution of sensory and motor nerves; and, as the workings of the nervous system began to be understood, physiological laboratories—particularly on the Continent of Europe—produced the first outlines of an experimental psychology. Men thus started to investigate the links between mind and matter with a new interest. What, after all, was the connection between the sensations experienced by a living human being and the physical entities which could be found after death in dissection of the brain? The barriers separating psychology and physiology still remained, but they were lower than before.

In 1879 Wilhelm Wundt, professor of philosophy in Leipzig, founded the world's first psychological laboratory. Stanley Hall set up his own at Johns Hopkins in 1883, and in the same year Emil Kraepelin produced the first classification of mental disorders. These developments inevitably encouraged a new attitude toward the mentally ill. Those with minor neurotic troubles no longer had to throw themselves on the mercy of lay advisers, religious or otherwise, and hope that they would be received sympathetically; those whose mental abnormalities approached insanity had less fear of incarceration. Yet this more responsible treatment of the unfortunates living on the borderline between eccentricity and madness was, despite the advances made earlier in the century, largely one of degree, and had barely started to affect the treatment of hysterics.

"[The typical doctor]," Freud said in the United States years later, when describing the European attitude of the 1880s, "cannot understand hysteria, and in the face of it he is himself a layman. This is not a pleasant situation for anyone who as a rule sets much store by his knowledge. So it comes about that hysterical patients forfeit his sympathy. He regards them as people who are transgressing the laws of his science—like heretics in the eyes of the orthodox. He attributes every kind of wickedness to them, accuses them of exaggeration, of deliberate deceit, of malingering. And he punishes them by withdrawing his interest from them." Freud, seeing an understanding of hysteria as a key which might unlock the riddles of the mind, was to take a very different attitude in the practice he was now about to start in Vienna.

First, however, he had to prepare a report for the faculty on what he had seen in Paris and Berlin. He set to work at once and within less than three weeks had signed a twelve-page account. In it he bluntly stated that after studying under Meynert he found himself unable to learn anything essentially new in a German university. After this opening he went on to emphasize the difference between the German school epitomized by Meynert and that led by Charcot. "The French school of neuropathology," he noted, ". . . seemed to me to promise something unfamiliar and characteristic in its mode of working, and moreover to have embarked on new fields of neuropathology, which have not been similarly approached by scientific workers in Germany and Austria."

Alone, this would hardly have endeared him to the doctors of the Vienna school. But some findings of the French on hypnotism and hysteria, he went on, "had been met in our countries with more doubt than recognition and belief; and the French workers, and above all Charcot, were obliged to submit to the charge of lacking in critical faculty or at least of being inclined to study rare and strange material and to dramatize their working-up of that material." Freud therefore "gladly seized the opportunity which was thus offered of forming a judgment upon facts based on my own experience."

This smart critique of his masters out of the way, Sigmund Freud, M.D., Lecturer in Neuropathology at the University of Vienna, opened his practice. His rooms were at Rathausstrasse 7; the day on which he announced himself as ready to see patients, Easter Sunday. It was a curious date on which to start: a public holiday with businesses and offices closed, and even the city's emergency medical services pared down for the occasion. Christmas Day would alone have been a more unusual date for a doctor to meet his first patients. The explanation, it has been suggested, was Freud's smoldering dislike of the Catholic Church—"my true enemy," as he was later to describe it. If the timing was in fact a gesture by a young man anxious to tilt against any windmills in sight, the motive was probably unconscious, with a more obvious reason for the date that has never come to light.

Freud's prospects were hardly good. Thirty was a late age at which to launch himself into private practice, and he had little capital to carry him across periods of misfortune. He had, moreover, come to medical practice by a roundabout route. He had dabbled with pharmacological products, with medical translation, with children's diseases; if anywhere he had shown a spark of genius, that spark had never set the tinder alight. And although he intended to specialize in nervous illnesses, a field which he rightly considered could be profitably exploited in Vienna, he was soon leaning toward methods that would arouse mistrust among medical colleagues and suspicion among potential patients.

There was also the effect of his Jewishness, a subject on which it is possible to cite conflicting evidence. Anti-Semitism had continued to grow after the financial crisis of 1873, and there had been anti-Jewish riots in Pressburg (today Bratislava), 40 miles east of Vienna, only a few years before Freud set up in practice. The Archduchess Maria Theresa had begun to support at least one anti-Semitic newspaper, while in Vienna itself the anti-Semitic agitator Franz Holubek had declaimed, "The Jews are no longer our fellow citizens but have become our masters, oppressors and tormentors." Yet if this augured badly for a young Jew on the lowest rung of the professional ladder, there were compensations. At the time of the 1873 crash the Jews in Vienna had numbered about 70,000; by 1890 the figure had increased to 118,000 and by the turn of the century had reached 147,000. This alone gave Freud a constantly growing area of potential support, while it has been remarked that the faculty of medicine in the University of Vienna was particularly rich in Jewish professors. Whatever the strength of anti-Semitism, it could still be overcome by men of ability.

As important as the influence of anti-Semitism was another factor which might have been damaging to Freud's prospects. Following his visit to England in 1875, he had decided on a medical career; he had wanted to help people who suffered, and there is no doubt that some vocationary ideal remained to the end of his life. But the switch of interests which had taken place in Paris was to establish a complementary balance. He now wanted to know how the mind worked, and the search for that knowledge ran parallel to relief of suffering; sometimes it ran ahead. "In [Freud's] personality," wrote Theodor Reik, one of his most devoted followers, "the particular impulse which would incline a man toward being a healer was not so strongly developed as his impulse to knowledge. He had nothing of the *furor therapeuticus* that so many doctors manifest."

Freud himself agreed. "I am not basically interested in therapy," he once wrote, "and I usually find that I am engaged—in any particular case—with the theoretical problems with which I happen to be interested at the time." Pity was always creeping in, but it was not the only spur which drove him on, as he inferred more than forty years after he had set up in practice. "I have told you," he said in the "New Introductory Lectures" of 1932, "that psychoanalysis began as a method of treatment; but I did not want to commend it to your interest as a method of treatment but on account of the truths it contains, on account of the information it gives us about what concerns human beings most of all—their own nature—and on account of the connections it discloses between the most different of their activities." Thus when Freud set out to cure his first patients in the Rathausstrasse, the healer was in pursuit of knowledge as well as cure.

To start with, he was thinking of only a two-month trial period in the city. If that failed, as he seems half to have expected, he might emigrate to the United States. "We both of us had nothing," he later recalled of himself and Martha, "or more precisely, I had a large and impoverished family, and [Martha] a small inheritance of roughly 3,000 fl. from her Uncle Jacob. . . ." Apart from emigration to America, he considered joining the Freud family in England, or moving to one of the smaller towns in Austria. Vienna itself held out no particular attractions, and few of his colleagues would have thought it likely that the ambitious doctor of thirty would be practicing in the capital for more than half a century.

Freud had comparable doubts. Writing to Martha about his resources as he set up in practice, he said, "In a few weeks the money —which I still haven't touched—will have come to an end, and then we shall see whether I can go on living in Vienna. I would like to think that the next birthday will be just as you describe it, that you will be waking me up with a kiss and I won't be waiting for a letter from you. I really no longer care where this will be, whether here or in America, Australia or anywhere else. But I don't want to be much longer without you. I can put up with any amount of worry and hard work, but no longer alone. And between ourselves, I have very little hope of being able to make my way in Vienna." His nervous anxiety for success caused his hopes to rise as precipitously and as unaccountably as they fell. "In spite of everything my position here is a strong one, as I can see from several indications," he wrote a week after seeing very little hope.

The first auguries were far from auspicious. In May he lectured to the Physiological Club on hypnotism, and announced to Martha that he would be doing the same thing before the Psychiatric Club and the Medical Association later in the month. "So," he warned her, "the battle of Vienna is in full swing." More than one battle was in fact being fought, and those who now criticized Freud's advocacy of hypnotism soon had another weapon to hand. Before the end of May a second paper by Albrecht Erlenmayer repeated his earlier warning against the dangers of cocaine and strongly criticized Freud personally.

But it was support for hypnotism that made most enemies, as

Freud soon realized. On his return to Vienna he had been offered the facilities of Meynert's clinic. But once it became obvious that Freud did not rule out the use of hypnotism, Meynert changed tack. Freud, he plainly indicated, would no longer be welcome.

This was the start of a guerilla war between the two men that continued sporadically until Meynert's death in 1892. In 1888, writing a preface to a German translation of *"De la suggestion et de ses applications à la thérapeutique"* ("Suggestive Therapeutics" in the English translation) by the famous French hypnotist Hippolyte Bernheim, Freud went as far as he dared. "Because the attitude of all my friends demanded it," he wrote of the preface, "I had to be moderate in my criticism of Meynert, who in his usual impudent-malicious manner had delivered himself authoritatively on a subject of which he knew nothing. Even so, they think I have gone too far. I have belled the cat." For his part, Meynert added a footnote to a paper on Charcot's theories of traumatic paralyses, remarking that Freud's opinions were more dogmatic than scientific and indeed contradicted Charcot's teachings. Freud replied in a review of August Forel's *Hypnotism,* knowing well that most readers would identify his target:

> It is difficult for most people to suppose that a scientist who has had great experience in certain regions of neuropathology, and has given proof of much acumen, should have no qualification for being quoted as an authority on other problems; and respect for greatness, particularly for intellectual greatness, is certainly among the best characteristics of human nature. But it should yield to respect for the facts.

It was in this uneasy climate that Freud, at loggerheads with received opinion, began to build up his practice. Of the first few months, most of what is known comes from the reports sent to Martha in Wandsbek. As might be expected, he had a variety of patients, by no means all of them the cases of nervous illness in which he was particularly interested. But at least by the autumn his concentration on hysteria was clear. "If you want to give me something I need urgently," he wrote to Carl Koller on October 13, "let it be a perimeter [an instrument for measuring the field of vision], since as a clinician I depend more than anything else on the study of hysteria and one cannot publish anything nowadays without a perimeter."

Despite this specialization he was glad to have more run-of-the-mill patients: they did, after all, supply the safety net if his work with the neuroses in general and hysteria in particular failed to pay dividends. A professor's wife came with an attack of sciatica. Two police officials visited him twice a week for some ailment which he does not record. There was also an American physician with a nervous complaint who greatly interested Freud. "His case," he revealed to Martha, "is complicated by his relationship with his beautiful and interesting wife with whom I also have to deal and on whose account I am going to see Prof. [Rudolf] Chrobak [professor of gynaecology at the University of Vienna] tomorrow. I am too tired to describe to you in detail all the delicate aspects." In the same letter he gave an early hint of the weakness for superstition, which he was never able entirely to shake off. "It seemed weird to me," he wrote in describing two visits of the American wife, "that on both the occasions . . . your photo, which has otherwise never budged, fell off the writing table. I don't like such hints, and if a warning were needed—but none is needed."

On some days his waiting room was full of patients, although he noted to Martha that there were not many paying ones. At times he appears to be desperately hard up, as when he writes: "Here I am counting every Gulden and I am called to go and see a distant acquaintance in the Stadtgutgasse, no remuneration of course, and two hours out of the day gone, for I cannot afford a cab. Today the same. When I get home I find an urgent message to go and see the man again. This time of course I am obliged to take a cab, and what I have saved in suppers during the past three days has to be spent on it." Yet to Carl Koller he gave a distinctly brighter picture: "However, it went better with me than I expected," he reported. "I shall not analyze whether this was due to Breuer's help, or to Charcot's name, or because I was a novelty. In three and a half months I earned 1100 fl. and said to myself that I could marry if matters continued to improve."

During the summer, as he began to find his feet, prepared for the second half of his compulsory military service that was due in August, and continued to hope that marriage would soon be possible, the new practice was not his only preoccupation. In June and July he finished the translation of Charcot's lectures begun in Paris, a task that brought him a leather-bound set of the doctor's own works with the dedication: *A Monsieur le Docteur Freud, excellents souvenirs de la Salpêtrière.* In July he completed the paper on work carried out in Meynert's laboratory the previous year and also took up a part-time appointment as head of the newly organized neurological outpatient clinic of the Viennese Children's Hospital.

By this time Martha had received another legacy, and the young couple had been encouraged to set a date for their wedding. It was to take place in September, and it was therefore a shock when

Freud learned that his army service would run on into the first week of that month. Nevertheless, he refused to postpone the long-awaited event, much to the horror of his future mother-in-law who condemned his determination as recklessness.

On August 11 Freud reported for military service and was posted as Regimental Chief Physician for the concentration of troops in Moravia. During the following maneuvers he was promoted from lieutenant to captain; afterward served as Battalion Head Physician; and seems to have carried out his duties to the satisfaction of everyone. He enjoyed "great confidence among military and civilians," stated his military report. His qualities of mind and character were "Honest, firm character, cheerful." Conduct toward his superiors was "Obedient and open, moreover modest"; toward equals "Friendly"; and toward subordinates "Benevolent and exerting a good influence." His off-duty conduct was given as "Very decent and modest, pleasant manners."

All this, which adds up to a good bedside manner, suggests that Freud was more than adept at concealing his personal views about military service, which surfaced in a letter to Breuer. "An officer is a miserable creature," he wrote; "he envies his equals, he bullies his subordinates, and is afraid of the higher-ups; the higher up he is himself, the more he is afraid. I deeply dislike having my value written on my collar, as though I were a sample of some material. And yet the system has its loopholes. It wasn't until recently when the commanding officer from Brünn arrived here and paid a visit to the swimming bath that I learned to my surprise that bathing trunks show no signs of rank."

Freud returned to Vienna at the end of the maneuvers, on September 10, changed into civilian clothes and shortly afterward left for Wandsbek. But he was still dogged by financial misfortune; his army pay had been only half that expected, and he was forced to write to Minna Bernays for the fare.

As the wedding was to be in Germany, Freud had hoped that only a civil ceremony would be needed. But at the last minute Martha pointed out that while that would be sufficient for Germany, Austrian law demanded a religious wedding as well; if they failed to have one, they would not be married when they settled in Vienna. He was therefore faced with the complications of Jewish wedding ceremonies. He detested them but was, perhaps grudgingly, coached for the ordeal by Elias Philipp, the bride's uncle, who as an Orthodox Jew took a poor view of her groom's attitude to Jewish customs. The civil ceremony took place in Wandsbek Town Hall on September 13; the religious ceremony the following day, Freud making the bridegroom's responses in Hebrew. The couple then left for a two-week honeymoon that took them to Lübeck and Travemünde on the Baltic coast; on to Berlin, Dresden and Brünn; and finally to Vienna, where they arrived on October 1.

The home to which Freud brought his wife was an apartment in the Kaiserliches Stiftungshaus, the building—known also as the House of Atonement—erected on the site of the Ring-Theater, which had burned down with great loss of life in December 1881, a death toll largely attributed to official negligence. Rents from the new building went to Viennese charities, but for some while after its completion, superstition hampered lettings. "It was hard to get tenants for the apartment house where so many people had lost their lives," Freud's sister Anna wrote years later. "My brother, far from sharing the general superstition, did not hesitate to establish himself there with his young wife, and his example quickly encouraged others." So much so that when the Freud's first child was born the following year, the Imperial Chancery sent a letter congratulating the father of the first baby to be born in the building. Legend, operating through Anna Freud Bernays' recollections, adds to the letter a vase from the Royal Porcelain Workshops.

Upon arriving at the Stiftungshaus in October, the young couple found that the apartment was not yet ready. They were forced to stay for a few nights in a nearby hotel, and it was for long a family joke that Freud's "Freud aus Wien" in the Register, written in nearly indecipherable hand, was taken for "Freud aus Asien."

The young couple had to face various problems during their first weeks of married life. One was lack of money, and on Freud's first day of practice in his new home there were not enough chairs to accommodate all the patients. Martha had to borrow more from the porter's flat in the basement. However, within a few weeks Freud was able to tell Carl Koller, "My little wife, helped by her dowry and wedding presents, has created a charming home which, however, looks too modest for the noble and splendid rooms of Master Schmidt [Stadtbaumeister F.V. Schmidt, the architect of the building]." There is no doubt that they were happy. But there were a few minor problems, one being Freud's dislike of some Jewish ways. "I remember very well her telling me," one of Martha's cousins later wrote, "how not being allowed to light the Sabbath lights on the first Friday night after her marriage was one of the more upsetting experiences of her life."

Freud had barely settled into his new quarters when he addressed the Imperial Society of Physicians of Vienna on what he had learned from Charcot and the work in the Salpêtrière. It had at first been planned that he should lecture in June, but more important matters forced the Society to postpone the event until after the summer recess, and it was only on October 15 that he presented his paper, "On Male Hysteria," to an audience that included Vienna's leading neurologists.

A considerable mythology has grown up around the occasion, much of it due to Freud's assertions, repeated over decades, that he was treated badly; in fact, his reception was cool rather than cantankerous. One point is that Freud represented the opposition. It could be forgiven that in his formal report on his sponsored visit to the Salpêtrière he had praised the virtues of Charcot and the French school. Here, however, he was doing something rather different and something which had about it a touch of professional high treason.

To understand why this was so it is necessary to appreciate current medical feeling about the contentious subject of hysteria. Under dispute there were two aspects of differing importance. A few doctors continued to maintain that it was an exclusively female complaint, even though Pierre Briquet had decisively proved this to be incorrect twenty years previously. Briquet had demonstrated, by analyzing hysterics in the Paris hospitals, that while male cases were rare among upper-class patients, among the lower classes they outnumbered female hysterics. Five years before Freud addressed the Society, Moritz Rosenthal, professor of nervous diseases in Vienna, had in fact published a paper giving Briquet's statistics, while the *Index Catalogue* of the Surgeon-General's Library in Washington, available in the Society, listed more than a hundred references under the specific heading "Hysteria in the Male." Nevertheless, a few die-hards still protested that hysteria was created by a malfunctioning of the uterus, and that one conclusion must inevitably be drawn from that.

Yet if the case for male hysteria had virtually been won by 1886, there was another issue on which opinion was still divided. It had for long been held that hysteria had a physiological basis that was to a greater or lesser extent hereditary. Slowly, however, there had grown a belief that the triggering cause could be a traumatic event in which the patient had undergone a frightening experience. Many examples of "traumatic hysteria" were being traced back to accidents on the railways, then rapidly being extended throughout Europe, and the phrase "railway hysteria" was coined. It immediately became important to discover more about hysteria, since if it could be shown that such cases were in fact only brought into the open by accidents, then this would affect legal claims for damages. By the time Freud addressed the Society in October 1886, the main controversy about hysteria had thus begun to center on the question of psychic origins, a concept accepted by many British doctors, supported by Charcot, but hotly disputed in Germany and Austria. It was in these circumstances that Freud elected to read his paper.

He began by relating his experiences in Paris and went on to describe a case of hysteria involving paralysis of an arm that followed a patient's fall from scaffolding. Although the text of his address has not survived, it is obvious from reports in the medical press that the case was presented as one of indisputably traumatic male hysteria in which the results were due to psychic shock and not to physical injury.

The reaction of the Society was critical mainly because Freud had used as his illustration not a case of his own but, as it were, a second-hand case from someone else. One of the strictest rules of the Society was that speakers must present new material, and Charcot's patient failed to fill the bill.

It has been claimed that at the end of the meeting Freud was challenged by Professor Meynert to present before the Society some cases of his own that would support his paper. There is no record of such a challenge in the reports; but Freud did eventually find a patient, and it can be assumed that in conversation after the meeting, Meynert had informally asked him to do so.

A footnote to the evening, which Freud was to remember with considerable bitterness, was added years later by Rudolf von Urban, the founder of the Vienna Hospital at Cottage, a suburb of the city, and a man who had great plans for cooperation with Freud after the First World War. "Everyone in that room knew that the highly emotional Meynert was subject to attacks of aphasia with palsy of the right arm," he has written. "This was his defensive reason for finding an anatomical basis for hysteria, and probably his incentive for mapping cerebral localizations generally. When the young Freud opened up on the existence of hysteria in males also, Meynert felt uncomfortable. Meynert's wild youth and unstable personality were proverbial; as a young man he had been repeatedly drunk and locked up by his grandfather, the police surgeon. It is possible that Freud on this occasion was easing himself of an *animus,* which was grasped by the astute Meynert, whose retort when he challenged Freud to find male hysteria in his clinic was the psychological equivalent of saying, 'I challenge you to find it in *me.*' "

On November 26 Freud appeared before the Society once again. "Gentlemen," he began,

when on October 15 I had the honor of claiming your attention to
a short report on Charcot's recent work in the field of male hysteria,
I was challenged by my respected teacher, Hofrat Professor Meynert,
to present before the Society some cases in which the somatic indications of hysteria—the "hysterical stigmata" by which Charcot charac-
terizes this neurosis—could be observed in a clearly marked form. I
am meeting this challenge today—insufficiently, it is true, but so far
as the clinical material at my disposal permits—by presenting before
you a hysterical man, who exhibits the symptoms of hemi-anesthesia
[anesthesia down one side of the body] to what may almost be described as the highest degree. Before beginning my demonstration,
I will merely remark that I am far from thinking that what I am
showing you is a rare or peculiar case. On the contrary, I regard it
as a very ordinary case of frequent occurrence, though one which
may often be overlooked.

His patient was a twenty-nine-year-old engraver, brought to him
for confirmatory diagnosis by a colleague. And on this occasion
Freud showed, apparently to the satisfaction of the audience, that
the hysterical symptoms could be traced back to an accident in
boyhood. "This time," he somewhat grudgingly admitted, "I was
applauded, but no further interest was taken in me. . . . As I was
soon afterwards excluded from the laboratory of cerebral anatomy
and for terms on end had nowhere to deliver my lectures, I withdrew from academic life and ceased to attend the learned societies.
It is a whole generation since I have visited the *Gesellschaft der
Aerzte.*"

Ernest Jones observes, in a kindly phrase, that Freud here gives
an ambiguous impression. Indeed, this is so. On February 16,
1887, less than three months after the demonstration, Freud's
candidacy to the Society was submitted by seven prominent members. He was elected on March 18, 1887, and did not cease to be
a member until he left Vienna for England more than half a century
later.

Yet if the formal position was different from what Freud implied,
the memory of that October evening, when the medical opinion of
Vienna had put the young man in his place, rankled for decades.
Some forty years later he found that a learned journal he required
could only be obtained from the Society. His colleague Theodor
Reik suggested that if Freud wrote a note, he would collect the
journal. Freud forgot to do so. Asked a second time, he once again
forgot. Finally he confessed. "I couldn't bring myself to do it. My
resistance was too strong."

It was not only the Viennese who were less than enthusiastic
about Sigmund Freud, whom they had already seen as ardently

taking up an attitude toward hysteria about which they were cautious. The French might have been flattered that he had, as it were, espoused their cause. Any chance of this disappeared with the rise of Pierre Janet, the French psychologist and neurologist with whom Freud was to fight a guerilla war virtually to the end of his life. Janet, born in Paris in 1859, had reached psychology by a route very similar to Freud's. He had, it is true, first studied philosophy but had then progressed through hypnotism and medical training to the study of hysteria. Before working in the Salpêtrière from 1890 onward he had published a number of case histories and, following the publication of Freud's work during the last years of the century, a bitter argument about priority developed between the two men. Each was to accuse the other of plagiarism—a subject better considered at a later point in Freud's story—and each died convinced of his own innocence. It seems likely that both were right.

All this lay in the future, however, and whether the attitude of the Society in Vienna in 1886 was justified reaction to an overzealous young man in a hurry or a typical attempt by older men to fend off acceptance of new ideas, their attitude did little to help Freud in his early years of struggle.

What did help was the friendship he formed, when his practice was still barely on its feet, with the man who for some years was to exercise over him a Svengali-like influence. He was Wilhelm Fliess, a young Berlin physician who had been advised by Josef Breuer to attend the occasional lectures that Freud was giving in the university as *Dozent*. The two men met for the first time in November 1887. Shortly afterward Freud wrote to Fliess, by this time back in Berlin. After mentioning a patient who had been treated by Fliess in the German capital and who had later come to Vienna, Freud added, ". . . but I must start with the confession that I hope to remain in contact with you, and that you left a deep impression on me, which might lead easily to my telling you frankly in what class of men I place you."

The letter was to be the first of some hundreds that passed between the two men, a correspondence unique in the light it throws on the early years of psychoanalysis and on a strange and even now not completely explained friendship. Interest in the letters themselves is compounded by Freud's anxiety that they should never be read by others, by the curious train of events that ensured the survival of his side of the correspondence and by the efforts, so far successful, made after his death to ensure publication only in a censored version.

Preserved by Fliess's widow, Freud's letters to Fliess were put on sale by a Berlin bookseller after Frau Fliess's death in the 1930s and were bought by one of Freud's pupils and friends, Princess Marie Bonaparte, who feared for their safety. Her fears were justified. Freud unsuccessfully tried to buy them from her, confiding, "Our correspondence was of the most intimate nature, as you can surmise. It would have been most painful to have it fall into the hands of strangers . . . I don't want any of them to become known to so-called posterity." As it happened, the Nazis might well have discovered them, an eventuality circumvented by their deposit in the Danish Legation in Paris, where they remained for most of the Second World War. After the liberation of the city in 1944, five years after Freud's death, the letters were brought to Britain— according to one story, after being wrapped in waterproof coverings and attached to buoyancy bags to ensure their survival if the ship were sunk.

Freud's efforts to prevent publication are not entirely accounted for by the reserve of a man who spent most of his life probing the secrets of others and who wished his own to be kept from the common gaze. It is true that in 1885 he had destroyed a mass of private papers and that he did the same early in the twentieth century. But his worry in old age about the impact of the letters written to Fliess half a century earlier was of a different order and can be explained on either, or both, of two counts. To Fliess he had been outspokenly critical of his old friend Breuer, and outspoken in terms apparently as revealing of Freud as of Breuer; moreover he had described the false starts and mistakes that had inevitably fogged the emergence of psychoanalysis. Despite claims to the contrary, Freud was usually ready to admit errors and to emphasize that the early days of psychoanalysis had been a fumbling in the dark, but even in the portions of the Fliess letters so far published he is seen to have been remarkably outspoken.

It seems unlikely that the correspondence contains material of a darker nature and any suspicion that it does is aroused only by the way in which it has been treated. When a selection appeared in 1950 under the title *The Origins of Psycho-Analysis,* the three editors affirmed that the letters contained "nothing sensational." They did in fact throw much light on Freud's thinking during the crucial last five years of the nineteenth century, and it is possible that "nothing sensational" was a reflex defense action justified by what the editors had seen but not published. Of the 284 letters and drafts available, only 168 were quoted, while of the 153 letters quoted, 119 were published with cuts, some of which have since been revealed as considerable and significant.

"The selection was made," the editors stated, "on the principle of making public everything relating to the writer's scientific work and scientific interests and everything bearing on the social and political conditions in which psychoanalysis originated; and of omitting or abbreviating everything publication of which would be inconsistent with professional or personal confidence." However, any innocent assumption that this apparently laudable aim had been carried out without affecting Freud's image was shattered in 1966. In that year Freud's former physician, Dr. Max Schur, who had seen a complete set of the letters, or of photostats, used them in an extraordinary forty-page paper on "Some Additional 'Day Residues' of 'The Specimen Dream of Psycho-Analysis.' " This showed that in the 1890s Freud had gone to what has rightly been called "almost unbelievable lengths to rationalize his faith in the scientific judgment of his indispensable authority-figure at the time, Wilhelm Fliess." Of even greater importance, the paper showed that Freud had given, for the "specimen dream" of his great book on dream interpretation, an explanation that is now seen to be transparently incomplete. The Freud–Fliess letters give a detailed personal background to the birth and early growth of a new therapy, but until they are all made available, uncensored, it is impossible to know how many qualifications to the story have been omitted for reasons which are considered, quite possibly without justification, as embarrassing to Freud.

The emotional links between Freud and Fliess, which Freud admitted had homosexual undertones, have at least one perfectly reasonable explanation. Soon after their first meeting each man realized that the other was investigating new and controversial ideas. Both were Jews, and thus each found it possible to discuss with the other, without chance of ridicule, ideas which in the Vienna of the 1880s could be denigrated as Jewish, just as Einstein's relativity was to be denigrated as Jewish physics in the Berlin of the 1930s. What could be more natural than that there should be an exchange of problems, speculations, doubts and hopes? What more natural than that occasionally—as when Freud describes his colleague as "an even greater visionary than I"— their correspondence should suggest a two-member mutual admiration society?

At first glance there might seem little reason for Freud to have taken Fliess seriously as he struggled to build up his practice during the later 1880s. The theory that the Berliner was developing, and about which Freud remained overcredulous for an overlong time, was that much of human life was governed by a periodicity which rested not only on the female menstrual period of twenty-eight days but also on a male periodicity of twenty-three days.

There eventually came a time when Fliess found it difficult to explain enough of life's events with these two simple numbers, but this little difficulty was, for a while at least, overcome by the use of four numbers. Not only twenty-three and twenty-eight, but also five (twenty-eight minus twenty-three) and fifty-one (twenty-eight plus twenty-three) were invoked. Some of the ideas by which Fliess set so much store have even now not been entirely demolished, and it would be surprising if enthusiasts could not dredge up occasional items of apparently supporting evidence. Nevertheless, however excellent a practicing physician Fliess may have been, his ideas—occult numerological determinism as they have been called —have a great deal in common with the numerology of the Great Pyramid.

How seriously, it must be asked, did Sigmund Freud, of impressive mental stature whatever view is held of his theories, really take such a farrago of nonsense? Part of the answer is given by Ernest Jones who years later asked him how Fliess found it possible to apply his twenty-three–twenty-eight days periodicity theory. Freud looked quizzical and replied, "That wouldn't have bothered Fliess. He was an expert mathematician, and by multiplying twenty-three and twenty-eight by the difference between them and adding or subtracting the results, or by even more complicated arithmetic, he would always arrive at the number he wanted."

Freud was often skeptical, and not only of Fliess's numerology. Walking over the Hirschbuhl to Berchtesgaden with him one summer, Freud signed the register at the inn for both of them, describing his companion as "universal specialist from Berlin." There is a touch of the same attitude in his reply to a letter from Fliess one summer. "If you have really solved the problem of conception," he concludes, "the only thing left for you to do is to make up your mind what kind of marble you prefer. For me your discovery is a few months too late, but it may come in useful next year." Nevertheless, Freud for long found it impossible to shake off the legacy of Fliess's numerology; as late as 1920 he merely qualified its ideas with the admission that "doubts must be cast upon the rigidity of Fliess's formulas, or at least upon whether the laws laid down by him are the sole determining factors."

But from the early days of the friendship there was one way in which Freud saw that Fliess might be able to help him. To the end of his life he remained basically loyal to the ideas of Helmholtz and Brücke with their fundamental assumption that if only the key could be found, mental processes could be linked to measurable entities such as those of chemistry and physics. "The relationship between the chain of physiological events in the nervous system and the mental processes is probably not one of cause and effect," he wrote in 1891. "The former do not cease when the latter set in; they tend to continue, but, from a certain moment, a mental phenomena corresponds to each part of the chain, or to several parts. The psychic is, therefore, a process parallel to the physiological, 'a dependent concomitant.' " The linkage was a mystery. But who could better help solve that mystery than a practicing physician with considerable biological knowledge, a flourishing practice and an imaginative grasp, as it appeared, of the whole field of medicine; a physician, moreover, who hoped to establish biology on a firm physical-mathematical foundation? Thus from the start of the friendship Freud was eagerly hoping that Fliess would help him find the link, and almost a decade after their first meeting he is writing, "Anxiety, chemical factors, etc.—perhaps you may supply me with solid ground on which I shall be able to give up explaining things psychologically and start finding a firm basis in physiology!" More than two years later he writes: "I am not in the least in disagreement with you, and have no desire at all to leave the psychology hanging in the air with no organic basis. But, beyond a feeling of conviction (that there must be such a basis), I have nothing, either theoretical or therapeutic, to work on, and so I must behave as if I were confronted by psychological factors only. I have no idea yet why I cannot yet fit together (the psychological and the organic)."

As well as the hope that Fliess could help in linking the physiological and the psychological, there was also the moral support of which Freud was in such need as he struggled both to build up a practice and to investigate how the human mind worked. "When I talked to you, and saw that you thought something of me, I actually started thinking something of myself," he wrote in the summer of 1890, "and the picture of confident energy which you offered was not without its effect." On another occasion: "People like you should not die out, my dear friend; we others need the like of you too much." It was natural that the strong professional links should merge into deep friendship and as natural that on the first birthday of Fliess's son Robert that "Uncle Doktor," as Freud was known, should include with his present a note to Frau Fliess saying that it showed "that I partake of your ambitions for the little man, as you already know from my love for the big one."

It was understanding, stimulation and support that really mattered during the first decade of Freud's practice, the years when he slowly but steadily began to treat an increasing number of patients by methods that at best were controversial and at worst were anathema to the medical establishment. His methods were not yet those of psychoanalysis but the foundations on which psychoanalysis developed. The evolution was gradual, utilizing a multiplicity of small developments and improvements, each of which made the treatment of a new patient slightly different from that of the one before. But the end product was as different from his exploratory methods of the late 1880s as *Homo sapiens* was different from the animal that learned, only after many millennia, to stand up on two feet.

In the earliest days of his practice Freud used for the treatment of nervous troubles methods that were non-conventional rather than controversial. One was electrotherapy, evolved by Wilhelm Heinrich Erb, the German who did much to turn neurology into a separate discipline. In Erb's treatment, electrodes were applied to parts of the body and a mild electric current used to produce a tingling sensation or a muscle jerk. Another method was a development of electrotherapy known as the Weir Mitchell system after its American originator, which consisted of a combination of rest in bed, isolation, feeding-up, massage and electrotherapy, all given in a strictly regulated manner.

Freud had at least some initial success with electrotherapy, judging from the account of a Viennese bookseller who later told two psychoanalysts, Siegfried and Suzanne Bernfeld, that as a boy of fourteen he had been run down by a taxicab on the Ringstrasse and developed hysterical fits from the shock. Freud cured him after a few weeks' faradic treatment, "and he had always remembered his kindness and wonderful eyes."

Despite such apparent successes, Freud soon began to drop the variants of electrotherapy that in Erb's textbook were claimed to provide methods of treating almost any symptom of nervous disease. He turned elsewhere, and during the last days of 1887 plunged into hypnotism, which soon appeared to give him a certain measure of success. As a student he had attended a public exhibition given by Carl Hansen, whose dramatic stage performances had encouraged numerous doctors throughout Europe to experiment with hypnotism. Freud had noted that one of the volunteers demonstrated by Hansen had become deathly pale at the onset of cataleptic rigidity and had remained so as long as the catalepsis lasted. This firmly convinced him of the genuineness of hypnotism. His conviction had been strengthened as he watched Charcot sending women into trances and inducing the symptoms of hysteria virtually at will. Nevertheless, most medical men considered hypnotism almost as a form of black magic, and its status is illustrated by the jibe of Professor Julius von Wagner-Jauregg, later professor of psychiatry at the University of Vienna: with hypnotism, "you never know who is pulling the other fellow's leg."

However, Freud did not totally abandon the Weir Mitchell system when he began using hypnotism, and on occasion used a combination of both as a psychotherapeutic aid. "This gives me the advantage," he explained, "of being able on the one hand to avoid the very disturbing introduction of new psychical impressions during a psychotherapy, and on the other hand to remove the boredom of a rest cure, in which the patients not infrequently fall into the habit of daydreaming." A third possibility was ruled out for reasons which he gave later when he was famous: "My therapeutic arsenal contained only two weapons, electrotherapy and hypnotism, for prescribing a visit to a hydropathic establishment after a single consultation was an inadequate source of income."

Freud's use of hypnotism at first followed that of Charcot in the Salpêtrière; he would put a patient into a trance and then suggest to him that a specific symptom would disappear when he returned to normal consciousness. Fairly soon, however, he was using another and radically different method which was to be all-important for the evolution of his work. In it the process of suggesting that a symptom would disappear was abandoned; instead, the patient was asked to recall when the symptom first appeared and, in as much detail as possible, the circumstances in which it had appeared.

This method—the pebble that started the avalanche—was the direct result of a case which had been treated by Josef Breuer at the beginning of the 1880s; so direct that when, years later, Freud lectured at Clark University in the United States, he began by bluntly announcing: "If it is a merit to have brought psychoanalysis into being, that merit is not mine. I had no share in its earliest beginnings. I was a student and working for my final examinations at the time when another Viennese physician, Dr. Josef Breuer first (in 1880–2) made use of this procedure on a girl who was suffering from hysteria."

6

Prospecting the Unconscious

. . . a lengthy medical conversation on moral insanity and nervous diseases and strange case-histories . . .

FREUD, in a letter to Martha Bernays

Dr. Breuer's patient whom Freud cited at Clark University was "Anna O.," the case-book disguise for Bertha Pappenheim. If Freud's generous acknowledgment rendered more to Breuer than is justified—Freud himself was later to qualify it—Anna O. was indisputably the pointer who directed him toward the path he was to follow. As Breuer was to write, the treatment of Anna O. became "the germ cell of the whole of psychoanalysis."

It is not surprising that the case from which so much was to grow has been subjected to the most detailed scrutiny. More remarkable is the change in the informed view which has taken place over the years. Breuer, writing from incomplete notes of thirteen or fourteen years earlier, first told the story of Anna O. publicly in the second chapter of *Studies on Hysteria*, written with Freud and published in 1895. Freud himself gave different accounts to Carl Jung, to Stefan Zweig and to his colleague and biographer, Ernest Jones. And years after Freud's death, Dr. Henri Ellenberger of the University of Montreal, tenaciously pursuing the search for the truth about Anna O., discovered two important new documents, one written by Breuer when the patient had left him in 1882, thirteen years before the *Studies on Hysteria* account. These put beyond doubt Ellenberger's conclusion that "the patient had not been cured. Indeed, the famed 'prototype of a cathartic cure' was neither a cure nor a catharsis."

Bertha Pappenheim was the daughter of a wealthy Jewish merchant in Vienna whose family was known to the Bernays. In her early twenties she developed an extraordinary range of neurotic symptoms, which were treated by Breuer. Following this, she devoted herself to social work among the Jews, traveled extensively throughout Europe, died unmarried in 1936 at the age of seventy-seven, and was in 1954 honored in West Germany by the issue of a stamp bearing her portrait.

Freud first heard of her from Breuer in November 1882, but it was only on July 12 of the following year, the hottest, most excruciating day of the whole season, as he described it in a letter to Martha, that Breuer really appears to have unburdened himself to his young colleague. Freud, exhausted by work in the hospital, called on Breuer late in the evening and was first encouraged to get into the bathtub for a refreshing dip. Both men then sat down to supper in their shirt-sleeves. The meal finished, there came, Freud told Martha, "a lengthy medical conversation on moral insanity and nervous diseases and strange case histories—your friend Bertha Pappenheim also cropped up. . . ." Judging from Freud's later disclosures, the phrase "cropped up" was a considerable understatement. Breuer, he afterward said, read him parts of the case history and apparently did so on a number of subsequent occasions. So impressed was his listener that in Paris, two years later, he tried to discuss the case with Charcot, but had the feeling that the great man was not interested. Back in Vienna, however, he turned again to Breuer and asked him for further details.

The story was a remarkable one. While nursing her father in his fatal illness, Bertha Pappenheim had in 1880 developed paralysis in three limbs, a convergent squint, severe disturbances of vision, inability to eat and a serious cough. She also showed signs of dual personality, one normal, the other that of a naughty child. "There were extremely rapid changes of mood leading to excessive but quite temporary high spirits," Breuer wrote, "and at other times severe anxiety, stubborn opposition to every therapeutic effort and frightening hallucinations of black snakes, which was how she saw her hair, ribbons and similar things. At the same time she kept on telling herself not to be so silly: what she was seeing was really only her hair, etc. At moments when her mind was quite clear she would complain of the profound darkness in her head, of not being able to think, of becoming blind and deaf, of having two selves, a real one and an evil one which forced her to behave badly, and so on."

Eventually her father died, her symptoms became worse, and a consultant—now known to have been Richard von Krafft-Ebing, professor of psychiatry at the University of Vienna—was brought in. As with all strangers, Breuer wrote, "she completely ignored

[him] while I demonstrated all her peculiarities to him. 'That's like an examination,' she said, laughing, when I got her to read a French text aloud in English. The other physician intervened in the conversation and tried to attract her attention, but in vain. It was a genuine 'negative hallucination' of the kind which has since so often been produced experimentally. In the end he succeeded in breaking through it by blowing smoke [from a scrap of paper] in her face."

Some days later Bertha Pappenheim was moved away from Vienna; "against her will" in Breuer's 1895 version, "without deceit, but by force," according to his 1882 account. Eventually she returned to Vienna where there was an occurrence which, Breuer wrote, greatly surprised him. It was the height of the summer, but for some inexplicable reason the patient had found it impossible to drink. "She would take up the glass of water she longed for, but as soon as it touched her lips she would push it away like someone suffering from hydrophobia. As she did this, she was obviously in an *absence* for a couple of seconds. She lived only on fruit, such as melons, etc., so as to lessen her tormenting thirst. This had lasted for some six weeks, when one day during hypnosis she grumbled about her English lady-companion, whom she did not care for, and went on to describe, with every sign of disgust, how she had once gone into that lady's room and how her little dog—horrid creature!—had drunk out of a glass there. The patient had said nothing, as she had wanted to be polite. After giving further energetic expression to the anger she had held back, she asked for something to drink, drank a large quantity of water without any difficulty and woke from her hypnosis with the glass at her lips; and thereupon the disturbance vanished, never to return."

Both the patient and Breuer apparently realized the significance of the episode. According to Freud's version as relayed by Jones, the patient appreciated what had happened, and treated her other symptoms the same way—by what she called the "talking cure" or "chimney-sweeping." Breuer, almost certainly with justification, gives more credit to himself and less to the patient:

She took a great step forward when the first of her chronic symptoms disappeared in the same way—the contracture of her right leg, which, it is true, had already diminished a great deal. These findings —that in the case of this patient the hysterical phenomena disappeared as soon as the event which had given rise to them was reproduced in her hypnosis—made it possible to arrive at a therapeutic technical procedure which left nothing to be desired in its logical consistency and systematic application. Each individual symptom in this complicated case was taken separately in hand; all the occasions on which it had appeared were described in reverse order, starting before the time when the patient became bedridden and going back to the event which had led to its first appearance. When this had been described the symptom was permanently removed.

However, for reasons which he was never anxious to stress, Breuer did not follow up the implication of his observations and habitually played down his own importance in the affair. "My merit," he subsequently wrote, "lay essentially in my having recognized what an uncommonly instructive and scientifically important case chance had brought me for investigation, in my having persevered in observing it attentively and accurately, and my not having allowed any preconceived opinions to interfere with the simple observation of the important data."

His choice of name for the process shows the way in which even more enlightened doctors still linked the problems of the mind with the purely physiological concepts on which their training had been based. Many diseases were thought to be caused by poisoning of the blood by waste substances collecting in the bowel, and the cure frequently consisted of purging or catharsis. In Breuer's view Anna O.'s cure had been brought about by purging her mind of the memories disturbing it; "catharsis" the process therefore became, a word appropriated by the psychiatrists from the physicians.

Bertha Pappenheim's illness went through four stages and, not unnaturally, there are discrepancies between Breuer's account written when his treatment ceased in June 1882 and that written thirteen years later from his notes. The earlier version puts more stress on the girl's family difficulties, mainly with mother and brother, and gives additional details of the various neurotic symptoms which were removed by the "talking cure." But neither report substantiates the nature of the patient's illness. Here Dr. Ellenberger has said what is probably the last word, with his proposal that the case was similar to one of the great "magnetic diseases" of the early nineteenth century, that group of mysterious illnesses which included somnambulism, deep lethargy and catalepsy. "This would mean," he has written, "that the illness was a creation of the mythopetic unconscious of the patient with the unaware encouragement and collaboration of the therapist. . . . Anna O's illness was the desperate struggle of an unsatisfied young woman who found no outlets for her physical and mental energies, nor for her idealistic strivings."

Enough facts are now available, moreover, to assess the contradictory reports of the alleged cure. Breuer, describing the termination of the treatment in June 1882, stated that the patient was then "free from the innumerable disturbances which she had previously exhibited. After this she left Vienna and traveled for a while; but it was a considerable time before she regained her mental balance entirely. Since then she has enjoyed complete health."

Freud's version was given in a letter to Stefan Zweig in 1932 and, apparently with trimmings, to Ernest Jones. "On the evening of the day when all her symptoms had been disposed of, he was summoned to the patient again, found her confused and writhing in abdominal cramps," he told Zweig. "Asked what was wrong with her, she replied: 'Now Dr. B[reuer]'s child is coming!' " Breuer failed to realize that this pseudocyesis (phantom birth) might have thrown fresh light on what was really wrong with his patient. "Seized by conventional horror," Freud continued, "he took flight and abandoned the patient to a colleague. For months afterward she struggled to regain her health in a sanatorium."

Jones adds dramatic detail to both sides of the announcement "Dr. Breuer's child is coming":

> It would seem that Breuer had developed what we should nowadays call a strong countertransference to his interesting patient. At all events he was so engrossed that his wife became bored at listening to no other topic, and before long jealous. She did not display this openly, but became unhappy and morose. It was long before Breuer, with his thoughts elsewhere, divined the meaning of her state of mind. It provoked a violent reaction in him, perhaps compounded of love and guilt, and he decided to bring the treatment to an end.

The patient, according to this account, had apparently improved considerably by the time she was told of the decision and appears to have taken it calmly. However, later on the same June day Breuer was recalled to face an anguished Bertha. "Though profoundly shocked," Jones writes of Breuer's reaction, "he managed to calm her down by hypnotizing her, and then fled the house in a cold sweat. The next day he and his wife left for Venice to spend a second honeymoon, which resulted in the conception of a daughter. . . ." But, as Dr. Ellenberger has pointed out, Breuer's last child was born on March 11, 1882, some three months earlier; this means that at least part of the Freud–Zweig story is wrong and that the Freud–Jones story is "fraught with impossibilities."

Yet, on the future of Bertha Pappenheim the Freud–Jones version is basically correct, if wrong in detail. "The poor patient did not fare so well as one might gather from Breuer's published account," this goes. "Relapses took place, and she was removed to an institution in Gross Enzersdorf. A year after discontinuing the treatment, Breuer confided to Freud that she was quite unhinged and that he wished she would die and so be released from her suffering. She improved, however, and gave up morphia." A few years later, in 1887, Martha related how Anna O. sometimes visited her. She was then well during the daylight hours but suffered from hallucinations in the evenings.

Freud's version was indeed correct. Breuer's claim that at the end of her treatment—in Vienna, judging by the story in *Studies on Hysteria*—Bertha Pappenheim was "free from the innumerable disturbances which she had previously exhibited," and that "she left Vienna and traveled for a while," is decidedly misleading, despite his admission that "it was a considerable time before she regained her mental balance entirely."

It is now known that within a month of her last session with Breuer she had become a patient at the Bellevue Sanatorium, Kreuzlingen, on the shores of Lake Constance, and that she remained a patient there, a severe morphinist, until the end of October. With her went a report on her case written by Breuer. A further report, on the evolution of her illness in Kreuzlingen, also unearthed by the indefatigable Dr. Ellenberger, revealed moreover that while there she exhibited "hysterical features," made "disparaging judgments against the effectiveness of science in regard to her sufferings," and showed a "lack of insight into the severity of her nervous condition." And on leaving Bellevue she was still requiring heavy morphine sedation.

Judging by Bertha Pappenheim's later record as a social worker, this condition must have been considerably ameliorated at a later date or, at least, ceased to worry her. But her cure, such as it was, appears to have had little direct connection with Breuer's treatment. Freud's observations tend to be ambivalent, and one of his last reads more like evidence of his deep-seated Victorian attitude to women than of a verdict on therapy. "In spite of her recovery," he wrote, "in a certain respect she has remained cut off from life; she remained healthy and efficient, but avoided the normal course of a woman's life." What he meant was that she had remained a spinster.

However, the dubious record of the Anna O. case does not affect its significance in the history of psychoanalysis. Freud's insight had perceived in Breuer's removal of at least some symptoms under hypnosis a clue to a potentially important new method of therapy. Nevertheless, he would not so easily have been able to investigate this new possibility had it not been for Breuer's reactions to his patient. It is true that years later Breuer told August Forel that Anna O. had shown "that a fairly severe case of hysteria can develop, flourish, and be resolved without having a sexual basis." Despite this, it now seems clear that he was fully aware of the sexual undertones and had decided that no more such cases were for him.

Another reason for his decision was the length of time that the treatment demanded; hours had to be spent daily, not for weeks but for months, and Breuer decided that his practice could not stand the strain. "It was impossible," he subsequently wrote,

> for a "general practitioner" [an English phrase in his German letter] to treat a case of that kind without bringing his activities and mode of life completely to an end. I vowed at the time that I would *not* go through such an ordeal again. When cases came to me, therefore, which I thought would benefit much from analytic treatment, but which I could not treat myself, I referred them to Dr. Freud. . . . These cases, their course, their treatment, and whatever contributions to theory arose from them, were naturally constantly discussed between us. In this way our theoretical views grew up—not, of course, without divergencies, but nevertheless in work that was so much carried out in common that it is really hard to say what came from the one and what from the other.

Thus to Freud there was directed during his early years in practice a small but constant trickle of the patients whom Breuer considered too dangerous or too time-consuming to handle. Even had he wished, Freud could hardly have afforded to refuse them. He was still so hard up that at one point he had to pawn his gold watch, and it has been claimed that his wedding present to Martha—her gold wrist watch—would have followed but for the help of her sister Minna.

The patients passed on by Breuer were in no sense a typical cross section of the Viennese, and it is interesting that psychoanalysis, an investigative instrument that was to throw light on the workings of the normal as well as the abnormal mind, should have come into being during the treatment of a relatively small number of unrepresentative neurotic patients drawn mostly, as Breuer and Freud later put it, from "an educated and literate social class."

One of Freud's first tasks as he began to deal with them was to discover whether or not Anna O. had been an exceptional case. "I began, with Breuer's constant co-operation," he later wrote, "to make close observations of a fairly large number of hysterical patients and to examine them from this point of view; and I found that the behavior of this first patient had in fact been typical and that the inferences which were justified by that case could be carried over to a considerable number of hysterical patients, if not to all."

The inferences began with the assumption that the physical symptoms of hysteria were directly related to unpleasant experiences in the past. In the case of normal people, the natural reaction was that of "letting off steam," or "crying one's eyes out." As one of the early commentators on Freud's method noted: "The benefit of tears in emotional shock—*she must weep or she will die*—comes just midway between the benefit of auricular confession and the benefit of getting out a good crop of measles." In the case of the hysteric, however, there was no immediate reaction, due to the unacceptability of certain wishes evolved by the experience. Instead, all recollection of the traumatic event was thrust from the conscious mind into the unconscious, festering there until, by a process called conversion, it eventually made its way to the surface as one of the physical symptoms of hysteria. If, however, the reverse process could be accomplished—if the unconscious and, therefore, forgotten memory could be brought back into consciousness— then the discharge that should have taken place earlier would do its ameliorating work; the safety valve would be opened, the pressure would be released, and the physical symptom would disappear. At first Freud believed that this process alone had a therapeutic effect, a view which began to change as he appreciated that the patient's understanding of the treatment, and of the significance behind what had been repressed, also played its part.

For some time he continued to use hypnosis as a tool for inducing the patient to bring to the surface the past that she could not recollect in normal waking life. In the summer of 1889 he traveled to Nancy to study the methods of Hippolyte Bernheim and Auguste Liébeault, then among Europe's leading hypnotists, and even persuaded one of his patients to follow him. Freud had been unable to achieve any permanent cure with her, and Bernheim also failed. "He frankly admitted to me," Freud later wrote, "that his great therapeutic successes by means of suggestion were only achieved in his hospital practice and not with his private patients."

The implications of this admission were important. Bernheim was saying, in effect, that the hospital patients, poorer and less educated, could be hypnotized more easily than his bettereducated private patients. But, if this were so, it would reinforce Freud's suspicion that there might be a way, more efficient than the constant repetition of suggestions under hypnosis, of inducing a patient to reach back to long-past traumatic events. Might it not, he ruminated, be possible to recover the memory of forgotten events in the normal waking state?

With this idea lodged safely at the back of his mind, he returned to Vienna, traveling as far as Paris with Bernheim and Liébeault, and attending there both the Congress of Physiological Psychology, held under the presidency of Charcot, and the First International Congress of Experimental and Therapeutic Hypnotism. He left the city on the evening of August 9 and thus missed a paper read the following day by two French doctors, Henri Bourru and Ferdinand Burot, in which they described a technique almost identical with that used in Breuer's treatment of Anna O.

In Nancy, Freud had heard Dr. Liébeault lament, "If only we had the means of putting every patient into a state of somnambulism, hypnotic therapy would be the most powerful of all," and for a while he continued to hope that he could eventually develop such a technique. But he soon discovered that his powers were limited and that if he could not produce somnambulism in three attempts, then he would never do so. Years later one of his American disciples, A. A. Brill, explained how he, too, found that the hypnotism he had once practiced did not always work. "The hypnotist," he said, ". . . plays the role of the drill sergeant, who shouts commands which he expects the patient to obey. If everything follows his scheme of operation, he can obtain temporary results. But this does not always follow. I shall never forget my feelings when, after a prolonged suggestive preparation, I finally said emphatically to the young girl on the couch, 'Now you are asleep.' She looked up and quietly said, 'No, doctor, I am not asleep.' My omnipotence of thought was suddenly deflated."

Although he had comparable reverses, Freud carried on with hypnotism, partly because he saw it as the only practicable method. At the end of the 1880s he still appears to have been making therapeutic suggestions to his patients under hypnotism rather than directly questioning them about the origin of their symptoms. More than forty years later he claimed that from the start he had used hypnotism in both ways, but it seems likely that here his memory was at fault. The truth of course is that, as in many other corners of psychoanalysis, the question at issue is one of emphasis rather than of hard fact, and emphasis is even more vulnerable than fact to the blurring effect of recollection. Yet even though firm dates are uncertain, it is clear that by the end of the 1880s Freud was already moving across the border separating Breuer's technique from the practice of psychoanalysis.

He was now on the verge of great things. But the creator of a revolutionary new branch of psychology still clung on to other medical interests, was still a struggling Jewish doctor with penurious relations to support, with a steadily increasing family and with prospects of fame and fortune that still looked as distant as ever. This was the man who within a few years was to provoke controversies that made his disagreement with the Imperial Society of Physicians look like a storm in a teacup.

He had not yet given up his interest in cerebral anatomy, a field in which he had become an acknowledged expert, and where he remained while delving into the problems of his hysterics; not only because, like most experts, he enjoyed displaying his expertise but because work in this area could still provide a financial safety net if the venture into hysteria failed. His position was confirmed by his major treatise, *On Aphasia,* whose proofs he began passing soon after his return from Nancy.

In the 1880s, aphasia, the complex of neurological disorders which include an involuntary garbling of speech and an inability to understand the speech of others, was attributed primarily to damage affecting certain lobes of the brain. Yet this rough-and-ready explanation failed to account for the multiple varieties of the illness, and attempts to develop the primary explanation merely compounded the difficulties. In *On Aphasia* Freud tackled the subject from a new angle, offered a functional explanation of the varying symptoms and produced what he always considered the most valuable of all his neurological writings. Until its publication at least two kinds of aphasia were considered as definitely the result of lesions in specific parts of the brain. It was further considered likely that this concept would eventually be extended to cover not only all forms of aphasia but also other aspects of behavior, controlled as these were thought to be by identifiable areas of the cerebral cortex. Freud now suggested that in aphasia the linking of a symptom with a specific part of the brain was accompanied by functional peculiarities of the speech apparatus. In particular, he believed that when injury lowered the efficiency of the apparatus, that apparatus reacted by moving to more primitive ways of functioning, a physiological example of the principle of regression as this was later to appear in psychoanalytical theory. There were other indications of Freud's belief in hitherto undiscussed relationships between mind and matter, the psychological and the physiological, and at least one commentator has called *On Aphasia* the first Freudian book. Nevertheless, almost half a century later Freud refused to have it included in his collected works on the ground that it belonged to his neurological rather than his analytical phase.

On Aphasia was dedicated "in friendship and respect" to Breuer. But, wrote Freud, the breach with his old friend and helper was already widening. "Breuer's reception of [the book]," he informed his sister-in-law, "was such a strange one; he hardly thanked me for it, was very embarrassed, made only derogatory comments on it, couldn't recollect any of its good points, and in the end tried to soften the blow by saying that it was very well written. I believe his thoughts were miles away."

Breuer's attitude may have been a reaction to Freud's view of the links between physiology and psychology. More probably it was a reaction to what the older man considered the iconoclastic way in which the younger one dealt with contemporary views. After listing on his first page "the best brains of German and foreign neurology" who had studied the subject, Freud went on: "I shall endeavor to demonstrate that the theory of aphasia jointly built up by the above-mentioned writers, contains two assumptions which might profitably be revised." The revision, moreover, was carried out without mincing words. "I have," Freud himself admitted to Fliess, "been very cheeky in [On Aphasia], and have crossed swords with your friend Wernicke, as well as with Lichtheim and Grashey, and have even scratched the high-and-mighty idol Meynert." Published in 1891, On Aphasia was ignored throughout the decade by most of the medical reviews. However, publication did mark progress. On the occasion of Sigmund's thirty-fifth birthday earlier in the year, Jacob Freud wrote in the family Bible a verse on his son's success.

My darling Son Shlomo,
At the age of seven the spirit of the Lord began to move you
And spoke to you: Go read the books I have written
And there will break open to you the fountains of wisdom,
    knowledge and understanding.
The Book of Books is the well that the sages digged
And [in which] the lawgivers taught knowledge and justice.
The vision of the Almighty you saw, you heard, and you ventured.
You ascended and rode upon the wings of the spirit.
From then on that book was hidden like the Broken Tablets
In an Ark with me.
On the day you attained your thirty-fifth birthday
I bound it in a new leather binding
And named it "Spring up, O well—sing ye unto it"
And dedicated it to your name and for a remembrance of love.
From your father, who loves you an eternal love
Jacob son of Rabbi Shlomo Freud.

In the capital city of Vienna, on the 29th of Nisan
                                    (5)651, May 6, (1)891

Jacob was by this time in his mid-seventies, and his financial situation—no doubt part of the misery at home to which Freud had referred while in Paris—can be judged by Freud's words to Fliess only a few years later: that Alexander, his brother, "shares with me responsibility for two old people and so many women and children. . . ."

Freud paid a filial visit to his parents' home every Sunday. "It was not a pious household," his niece Judith Bernays Heller has said,

> but I do remember one Seder [the festival meal celebrating the Jewish Passover holiday] at which I, as the youngest at the table, had to make the responses to the reading of the song about the sacrifice of the kid; I was greatly impressed by the way my grandfather recited the ritual, and the fact that he knew it by heart amazed me. I liked, too, to hear the stories he would tell about my Mother, who, as eldest daughter, seemed to have been his pet; he held her up to me as an example to follow.
> But what I think struck me most about [him] was how, in the midst of this rather emotional household, with its three young women who sometimes did not get on well with one another, and their mother who was usually troubled and anxious—probably with financial worries—he remained quiet and imperturbable, not indifferent but not disturbed, never out of temper and never raising his voice.

Although Freud did his share in supporting this ménage, his own position remained precarious. He never fell back to the near-penury of his first days in practice; but keeping up the appearance of a successful doctor was still an effort that strained his resources and he was still grateful for financial aid from colleagues; still embarrassingly unable to pay back Breuer.

One reason for the constant battle to make both ends meet was his growing family. His first child Mathilde, born in 1887 and named after Breuer's wife, had been followed in 1889 by Jean Martin, named after Charcot. Two years later came Oliver, named after Cromwell, one of Freud's heroes, and the next year Ernst, named after Professor Brücke. Two more children were to follow: Sophie, born in 1893 and named after the niece of his old schoolmaster, Professor Hammerschlag; and Anna, born in 1895, named after the professor's daughter.

The large family typified Freud's position as a normal nineteenth-century paterfamilias. So did the loving interest in the children which creeps out from between the lines of letters to professional colleagues. "My little Mathilde is thriving, and causes us much amusement," he notes before recording an argument at the

Medical Society. Life, he relates between reports of his financial problems, "goes on tolerably well here, and our pretensions are constantly abating. When our little Mathilde chuckles we think it the most beautiful thing that could happen to us, and otherwise we are not ambitious and not very industrious." And he tells, with obvious pleasure, of the noisy children's party of twenty for Mathilde's birthday.

The home was becoming seriously overcrowded, and in 1891 he took the bold step of moving to larger quarters. The change was a mixture of premeditation and chance. He and Martha first drew up a list of essential requirements which included the number of rooms they needed, ease of access for patients and closeness to schools. Then they began to look about, at first without success.

At this date Freud was hiring a carriage to visit patients. One afternoon, his round done, he dismissed it and began to walk, apparently at random, through the streets of the central city. Then, unexpectedly, he found himself outside a building in which an apartment was to let. He suddenly felt a great attraction toward the house, went in; inspected the available apartment, decided that it suited the family's needs and without more ado signed the lease.

He returned home and told Martha that he had found their ideal quarters, Berggasse 19, and that evening took her there. Martha was apparently appalled. The neighborhood was a poor one, the stairs inside the building were dark, steep and of stone, and the accommodation was barely sufficient. But she did not protest. She realized that her husband had not only signed the lease but had set his heart on the place. The reason was an interesting one: 19 Berggasse had been the home of Viktor Adler, the future Social Democrat leader with whom Freud had argued as a student, and the house to which his friend Braun, Adler's brother-in-law, had once taken him while at the university.

Freud and his family lost no time in moving in. At first they occupied only one apartment; but a year or so later, when three more rooms became vacant, Freud rented them for use as a consulting suite.

Shortly after Anna's birth Minna Bernays, who after the death of her fiancé had been companion-governess to friends in Brünn, arrived for a stay of several months. She stayed for more than forty years. "Though she never really assumed the full responsibility of directing the large household with its six children," Freud's niece Judith Heller has written, "she shared it with my Aunt Martha who set the tone, gave the orders, held the reins. All the purchasing for the family was done jointly by the two sisters, and they always accompanied each other on shopping expeditions." Also in the building there lived for a time Freud's sister Rosa; when she moved in 1908 Freud took over her apartment.

In this home, close to the university and the General Hospital, Freud was to live from 1891 to 1938, found a cause, lead it, and in the process become one of the most controversial figures of the twentieth century.

7

The Birth of Psychoanalysis

They regard me rather as a monomaniac, while I have the distinct feeling that I have touched on one of the great secrets of nature.

FREUD, in a letter to Wilhelm Fliess

The decade that started with Freud's move into Berggasse 19 was to be the most important in his life. When it began he and his practice had survived, but only just. *On Aphasia* failed to attract the attention it deserved, and the reputation he was beginning to acquire in his own speciality was qualified by his use of hypnotism, still distrusted by many medical men. Ten years later it was acknowledged, although deplored, that he was developing a new method of therapy for treating the mentally abnormal, while within the medical establishment he was on the verge of securing at least a toehold. He himself was by no means satisfied, considering his work unappreciated and looking toward a future in which he expected only his successors to reap the rewards. There was something in this, although not as much as he imagined. By the start of the twentieth century Freud was ready to move out into battle.

The improvement in prospects, although not yet in fortune, was the result of his dogged exploration of the human mind with the help of the unconscious, a technique which he claimed could ameliorate, or in some cases remove, the symptoms of mental illness, much as radioisotopes were half a century later to be used for removing the growths of physical disease. The unconscious itself was no newcomer to the scene, but its use as a therapeutic instrument was an innovation, almost inadvertently discovered by Breuer, then developed by Freud, for the treatment of neurotics. Before the twentieth century had got into its stride, the same instrument was beginning to transform not only the therapy of the mentally ill but man's view of his everyday actions and of the springs of creativity in literature and art.

Some fifteen centuries earlier St. Augustine had speculated in his "Confessions" on the fact that potential recollections would sometimes be beyond memory but would at others thrust themselves forward into consciousness from some unknown reservoir. The implications of this mystery were discussed for more than a millennium as mystics, theologians and philosophers tried to fathom what obstinately appeared to be unfathomable. Freud himself once told his friend Theodor Reik that the sixteenth-century scientist and philosopher Paracelsus had advanced a theory of neurotic therapy very like psychoanalysis, in which a strengthening of the ego was seen as a counterpoint to the instinctual forces morbidly expressed in neurosis. "Just what he himself understood by it, I don't know," Freud admitted, "but there is no doubt about its correctness." Leibniz, with his idea of the *limen,* or threshold of perception, carried the investigation a little further. Johann Friedrich Herbart, who put forward such fundamental concepts as repression and the pleasure principle, proposed a model in which strong conscious perceptions thrust weaker perceptions below the threshold into the unconscious, and began to give the mind an almost quantitative framework. And from the late 1860s Wilhelm Griesinger was directing more attention to the unconscious than to the conscious in his formulation of psychiatry.

By contrast, the nature philosophers of the early nineteenth century concentrated on the more speculative aspects of the subject, as did Garth Wilkinson, a noted Swedenborgian who, although a physician, confined his new method of releasing the unconscious to literary and religious aims. Yet Carl Gustav Carus, with the opening words of his *Psyche*—"The key to the knowledge of the nature of conscious life of the soul lies in the realm of the unconscious"—said in general terms what Freud was to say specifically half a century later, while Eduard von Hartmann's *Philosophy of the Unconscious* began a stratification of the subterranean mind that was, in some respects at least, to be taken up by Jung forty years afterward.

Hartmann's book was no little-known dissertation for specialists. By 1882 it had gone into nine editions in Germany, had been published in France and in another two years was to be published in England. "Around 1870," says the British philosopher Lancelot Law Whyte in his survey of the unconscious before Freud, "the 'unconscious' was not merely topical for professionals, it was already fashionable talk for those who wished to display their culture. The German writer von Spielhagen [Friedrich Spielhagen], in a period novel written about 1890, describes the atmosphere in a salon in Berlin in the 1870s, when two topics dominated the conversation: Wagner and Von Hartmann, the music and the philosophy of the unconscious, Tristan and instinct." In 1883, moreover, Theodor Lipps, whose works were known to Freud, had written: "We maintain not merely the existence of unconscious processes beside the conscious ones; we postulate further that unconscious processes are the basis of conscious ones and accompany them."

As the emphasis changed from the unconscious in perception to the unconscious in memory, the subject tended to encourage the eccentric, and the English writer Samuel Butler, having claimed that memory and habit were transmitted unconsciously from generation to generation, finally maintained, in *Unconscious Memory,* that memory was a property of matter itself and that each atom retained a memory of certain antecedents. Investigations in Britain into such intractable problems, perhaps encouraged by the success of the physicists preparing in the 1890s for the nuclear revolution, varied widely in approach. F.W.H. Myers, who was to praise Freud's first writings on hysteria and who called the unconscious the "subliminal self," was before the end of the century trying, with the pioneer Society for Psychical Research, to demonstrate that the disembodied psyche could exist beyond the physical body. By contrast, Henry Maudsley, who as early as 1867 had maintained that the most important part of mental action was unconscious mental activity, believed that not even consciousness, let alone unconsciousness, was a necessary accompaniment to mind at all.

There were also literary predecessors, those who had subscribed to the view that the unconscious was an important motivation in human affairs. Freud knew of Sterne's Tristram Shandy and his: "The body and the mind are as a jerkin and its lining, rumple the one, and you rumple the other," and once said that Hardy's Tess knew all about psychoanalysis. He was, moreover, always willing to admit that Shakespeare, Goethe and Dostoyevsky "had come closer to the fundamental truths of psychoanalysis than had the physicians." Creative writers, he always emphasized, "are valuable allies and their evidence is to be prized highly, for they are apt to know a whole host of things between heaven and earth of which our philosophy has not yet let us dream. In their knowledge of the mind they are far in advance of us everyday people, for they draw upon sources which we have not yet opened up for science." Even while Freud had been struggling during his first months of practice, Edouard Dujardin had written the first "stream-of-consciousness" novel, *Les Lauriers sont coupés*. The interior monologue, Dujardin later said, was "the direct introduction of the reader into the interior life of the character, without any interventions in the way of explanations or comments by the author, and, like all monologues, was neither heard nor spoken."

Yet although the unconscious had a long history, no one before Freud had pronounced so positively that it was the undiscovered country into which man tried to banish those memories he wished to ignore; that in many cases the banished memories came to the surface transformed into the stigmata of hysteria, into dreams, or even into what came to be known as the "Freudian slips" of everyday life; and, most important of all, that the pulling back of these memories from the unconscious into the conscious could have a vital therapeutic effect. At the start, very few believed that this was so. "I am pretty well alone here in tackling the neuroses," Freud wrote to Fliess in 1894. "They regard me rather as a monomaniac, while I have the distinct feeling that I have touched on one of the great secrets of nature."

For Freud, raised in the belief that all physical events could ultimately be conceived in terms of measurable forces, his theory was a natural development. For if even the most bizarre physical event had its cause not in chance but in a preceding set of circumstances—a comforting belief which could be held of the physical world until the physicist-philosophers of the 1920s made it, with the quantum theory as an aid, at the best implausible and at the worst untenable—might not the same apply to mental events? Yet if this was a logical development, it was also a bold one and typical of Freud's willingness to take great intellectual gambles. If some were to be unwarranted, others—including the basic assumption of psychoanalysis—were eventually to bring the rewards due to genius.

The great and unexpected importance of the unconscious was confirmed only slowly, and at times Freud had doubts about the wisdom of having specialized. However, there were certain inherent advantages in treating patients with nervous diseases of a not-too-acute kind. In the nature of things, those who came for treatment tended to be comparatively well-to-do, while the time-consuming nature of the treatment, a distinct disadvantage to a man like Breuer, busy and in constant demand, worked the other way with Freud. Desperately anxious for patients, and by no means unhappy when they could provide him with a source of income over long periods, he could hardly be expected to put length of treatment on the debit side of the ledger.

Freud began to give up hypnotism in the treatment of patients during the 1890s, reluctantly and only under a variety of pressures: the most important may well have been the fact that he himself was not a particularly successful hypnotist. In addition, it was becoming apparent that hypnosis tended to mask certain reactions of the patient which could be helpful to the physician in his treatment. It has also been suggested that hypnosis itself had sexual implications and a sexual stimulation for the patient that made Freud uncomfortable. Finally, he may have had another, possibly unconscious, motive. By the last decade of the nineteenth century, hypnotism had begun to escape from its music-hall wrappings. Bernheim, Liébeault, Charcot and Breuer were only four of the established medical men using it. Freud, if he had continued with hypnotism, would have been just one more practitioner, a role hardly suited to his ambitions.

Yet his faith in the efficacy of hypnotism did not evaporate completely, and years later, discussing a German doctor's use of it in the treatment of shell-shock cases, he said: "I myself would reach back for the hypnotic method if faced with similar case material and for certain psychoses." Even in the 1890s he was daunted by the prospect of inserting useful therapeutic suggestions into the patient's mind without the use of hypnotism, let alone of tracing back symptoms to initial causes. "At first, I must confess, this seemed a senseless and hopeless undertaking," he later admitted. "I was set the task of learning from the patient something that I did not know and that he did not know himself. How could one hope to elicit it?" He was, however, encouraged by the recollection of a case in Nancy in which Bernheim had induced a woman under hypnotism to believe that he was no longer present and had then tried to draw her attention to his presence. Bernheim failed, and even after the patient had been awakened she had continued to deny that he had been present. "But he did not accept this," Freud later wrote. "He insisted that she could remember everything and laid his hand on her forehead to help her to recall it. And lo and behold! she ended by describing everything that she had ostensibly not perceived during her somnambulism and ostensibly not remembered in her waking state."

That experiment, Freud wrote, served as his model when he began to give up hypnotism. "I decided," he said,

to start from the assumption that my patients knew everything that was of any pathogenic significance and that it was only a question of obliging them to communicate it. Thus when I reached a point at which, after asking a patient some question such as: "How long have you had this symptom?" or: "What was its origin?," I was met with the answer: "I really don't know," I proceeded as follows. I placed my hand on the patient's forehead or took her head between my hands and said: "You will think of it under the pressure of my hand. At the moment at which I relax my pressure you will see something in front of you or something will come into your head. Catch hold of it. It will be what we are looking for.—Well, what have you seen or what has occurred to you?"

The advantage of the pressure technique, Freud explained, was that he was able to "dissociate the patient's attention from his conscious searching and reflecting—from everything, in short, on which he can employ his will—in the same sort of way in which this is effected by staring into a crystal ball, and so on. . . ."

The method was not always successful. But many results confirmed what had already been demonstrated by Bertha Pappenheim under hypnosis: the importance of the unconscious, "what one does not know but which nevertheless is actively at work." So, as Freud wrote years later, "I abandoned hypnotism, only retaining my practice of requiring the patient to lie upon a sofa while I sat behind him, seeing him, but not being seen myself."

The practice of seeing but not being seen was later to give rise to a good deal of slightly lunatic speculation. One writer has pointed out that the Israelites were not allowed to stare at Moses while he blessed them, and that in Africa and Asia "the mothers of the nomadic tribes carry their infants attached to their backs, so that the babies never see mama face-to-face." Although the writer knocked down the Aunt Sallies she had set up, she nevertheless created the suggestion of some mystic significance at work. A far more practical explanation later came from one of Freud's most famous patients, "the Wolf-Man." Freud had told him that in his early days as an analyst he had sat at the opposite end of the couch so that he and the patient could look at each other. "One female patient," the Wolf-Man went on, "exploiting this situation, made all possible—or rather all impossible—attempts to seduce him. To rule out anything similar, once and for all, Freud moved from his earlier position to the opposite end of the couch." The truth was much less exciting. However poker-faced the listening analyst might be, his attitude and his reaction to the disclosures of his patient might, face-to-face, well be noted, and might quite as easily affect the revelations on which so much depended.

The investigative usefulness of the method increased as Freud continued, during the early 1890s, to urge and to question without the use of hypnotism. Then, unexpectedly one of his patients reproved him for interrupting her flow of thought. He took the hint and, following what he termed an obscure intuition, told her to continue talking—to talk, moreover, about whatever came into her head, however irrelevant it might appear to be. The method, followed with other patients, produced a stream of apparently unconnected recollections and thoughts which Freud found he could put to good therapeutic use.

"Free association," as this was to be called, in fact had an ancestry. In the early 1820s the German writer Ludwig Börne had ended an essay on "The Art of Becoming an Original Writer in Three Days" with the words: "Take a few sheets of paper and for three days in succession write down, without any falsification or hypocrisy, everything that comes into your head. Write what you think of yourself, of your women, of the Turkish war, of Goethe, of the Funk criminal case, of the Last Judgement, of those senior to you in authority—and when the three days are over you will be amazed at what novel and startling thoughts have welled up in you. That is the art of becoming an original writer in three days." Freud, given Börne's works as a boy, had read them avidly, and years later remembered some of them clearly, although not what he called the "cryptomnesic" one. "When I read this one again I was amazed to see how much in it agrees practically word for word with things I have always maintained and thought. [Börne] could well have been the real source of my originality."

There may also have been another source quite as important. As early as 1879 Francis Galton, the British anthropologist, devised a technique later known as the "word association test." After a long series of experiments he concluded that the mind was "apparently always engaged in mumbling over its old stores, and if any one of these is wholly neglected for a while, it is apt to be forgotten, perhaps irrecoverably." Later he concluded a paper in the July 1879 issue of *Brain* with the statement: "Perhaps the strongest of the impressions left by these experiments regards the multifariousness of the work done by the mind in a state of half-unconsciousness, and the valid reason they afford for believing in the existence of still deeper strata of mental operations, sunk wholly below the level of consciousness, which may account for such mental phenomena as cannot otherwise be explained." Galton's biographer D. W. Forrest points out that Freud makes explicit reference to papers by the neurologist Hughlings Jackson in the January and October issues of *Brain*. Freud subscribed to the journal and Forrest reasonably assumes that he probably read Galton's paper. "It is perhaps unimportant whether Freud's subsequent adoption in the 1890s of the free association technique really sprang from his availing himself of Galton's discovery," he suggests. "What is of greater significance today is the way in which Freud put the discovery to work as the therapeutic tool of psychoanalysis."

When free association was used in the consulting room the results were certainly surprising and, to a man as steeped as Freud in deterministic philosophy, very gratifying. For it did seem to confirm that the deterministic laws governing the chemical and physical processes were replicated in the mental world: that neurotic symptoms could be traced back to specific causes.

Yet the method had to be used with care, and the results had to be interpreted with discrimination. It left much opportunity for honest mistake and this, combined with the confident dogmatism that sometimes marked Freud's pronouncements, made it vulnerable to attack. Thus even when psychoanalysis had years later gained a reputable following, a by no means overcritical commentator in the United States could write:

> For example, my use . . . of the expression "Freudian principles" seems an obvious enough act on my part, given the context; but let me apply the method of "free association" to these words, as Freud would have me do if there were anything suspicious about them. I then get, starting from "Freudian," first the name "Freud" itself, then the German *"Freude,"* meaning "joy," then a phrase in Wagner's Siegfried, *"froh und freudig,"* which reminds me instantly of Nietzsche and his "blonde beast," who ruthlessly gets what he wants. Next I get the Greek word *"Epis," "hubris,"* meaning again a ruthless getting what you want, and then the English derivative "hybrid," which brings to mind irregular sexual relations—enough said! Again, when I start my train of associations with the word "principles," I immediately get Machiavelli's "Prince," and land once more in ruthlessness. The juxtaposition of two such *meaningful* words as "Freudian" and "principles" is thus extremely suspicious, and leads to the conclusion that my choice of words was not dictated simply by a desire to express my overt meaning, but that the Unconscious in me was thus giving expression to a deep-seated wish, repressed by forces of circumstances, for a career of unbridled lust . . .

This may be considered an example, not to be taken too seriously, of an energetic anti-Freudian on the attack. Nevertheless, the danger was outlined many years later by Joseph Wortis, whom Freud had taken into analysis. "So far as analytic procedure is concerned, I did not find that letting the subject find his own associations was always observed," was his verdict. "I would often give a whole series of associations to a dream symbol, for example, and he would wait until he found an association which would fit into his scheme of interpretation and pick it up like a detective at a line-up who waits until he sees his man. I am not saying that this procedure is invalid—in the long run it is probably necessary—but I wish to make the point that the procedure is far from foolproof and lends itself easily to pseudoscientific conclusions on an arbitrary basis. A successful piece of analytic insight will continue to require the old-fashioned wisdom that good novelists have had for centuries. Freud had the insight, but I'm not so sure that the procedure he developed allowed him to successfully communicate it to others." This was profoundly true. Freud knew, and often stressed, the limitations of the technique which he had evolved.

There was, moreover, one aspect of the process which might have irked him. For if the mind obeyed deterministic laws, what then became of free will? Freud settled this problem to his own satisfaction by pointing out that even when the unconscious had become conscious, and even when an analysis could be considered successful, the patient did not automatically recover. "After such an analysis the patient has been placed in a position in which he can get well; before analysis this was not possible. But whether or not he really will get well depends on his wish to recover, on his will," he said. The comparison, he suggested, was with the purchase of a railway ticket. The ticket made the journey possible; the decision to travel or not to travel still rested with the individual.

During the early 1890s he continued to develop his technique, discussing it with Breuer who in some cases worked jointly with him. Although he progressively abandoned hypnotism, the dates at which he introduced the pressure technique and free association are uncertain, and the evidence in some cases is contradictory. The explanation is probably simple enough. Freud now had three methods of probing the unconscious, and it would have been surprising if he had not found that their usefulness varied with different patients. It is only certain that the technique of free association was eventually seen as more important than the other two; even here, however, a case can be made out for a re-emphasis on the use of the pressure technique during 1896–7, when Freud was formulating his ill-fated seduction theory.

Slowly, however, the process of what was to become psychoanalysis settled down to a regular routine. The patient talked about whatever she wished to talk about—her life story, the history of her illness or recollections of her childhood. Freud usually opened with the reminder that he had to know as much as possible about the patient and then went on:

One thing more, before you begin. Your talk with me must differ in one respect from an ordinary conversation. Whereas usually you rightly try to keep the threads of your story together and to exclude all intruding associations and side issues, so as not to wander too far from the point, here you must proceed differently. You will notice that as you relate things various ideas will occur to you which you feel inclined to put aside with certain criticisms and objections. You will be tempted to say to yourself: "This or that has no connection here, or it is quite unimportant, or it is nonsensical, so it cannot be necessary to mention it." Never give in to these objections, but mention it even if you feel a disinclination against it, or indeed just because of this. Later on you will perceive and learn to understand the reason for this injunction, which is really the only one that you have to follow. So say whatever goes through your mind. Act as if you were sitting at the window of a railway train and describing to someone behind you the changing views you see outside. Finally, never forget that you have promised absolute honesty, and never leave anything unsaid because for any reason it is unpleasant to say it.

In old age he was to give a striking example of how unequivocally he believed in these principles. Eva Rosenfeld, under training with him, had learned of the seriousness of the cancer that was eventually to kill him; but she tried, unsuccessfully, to conceal her knowledge when under analysis. "We have only one aim and only one loyalty, to psychoanalysis," she was reprovingly told by Freud. "If you break this rule [that the patient should, without exception, say whatever comes into her head] you injure something much more important than any consideration you owe to me."

The adoption of the technique of free association, which lies at the heart of psychoanalysis, has been cited as supporting evidence of its much-argued connection with Judaism. Thus Ernest Simon, in a detailed discussion on Freud's Jewish beliefs, first quotes him as saying: "If we write the dream down and compare it with all the associations which it produces, we are likely to find that they have multiplied the length of the text of the dream many times." The relation between an "inner core" and its wider interpretations, Simon then goes on, "brings to mind the characteristic form of the traditional Jewish book, such as the Mishna and the Gemara, and also Maimonides' *Mishne Tora,* despite this author's desire to write a straightforward treatise free of any burden of interpretation and commentaries."

However strong the link between the Talmudic way of thought and the technique of psychoanalysis as Freud developed it in the 1890s, the new therapy certainly involved a relationship between doctor and patient which was entirely new to the medical profession and one whose nearest counterpart was that between the priest and the layman during confession. Freud found that when patients were encouraged to talk with complete freedom, they did indeed reveal not only their hopes and fears but details of their current and earlier sexual lives that could be, and often were, pornographic, scatological, or both.

It was soon appreciated that analysis and interpretation of the material brought forth was a complicated and difficult matter, and that certain problems were inevitable. Among the first was what seemed to be a built-in resistance to the process of drawing material from the unconscious into the conscious. This varied in intensity from patient to patient, but was almost always present. At first, resistance appeared to make the doctor's task more difficult. In due course, however, Freud discovered that the subjects about which resistance was strongest were frequently those of the greatest significance; thus the resistance, once identified, could yield essential clues to those events in the patient's past that were the cause of the trouble.

There also came to light the process known now as "transference." Freud noted that many of his patients, talking on without inhibition as they followed the practice of free association, no longer spoke as patient to doctor but as patient to mother or father. In other words, they were transferring to the analyst feelings and ideas that reflected their earlier relationships with their parents. While transference was at first another complicating factor, Freud eventually saw how this, like resistance, could often give helpful clues to the unremembered past. Indeed, he was eventually to believe that every conflict had to be fought out in the sphere of transference. However, if this were so, there was a price to be paid: countertransference, or the analyst's attitude to his patient, an attitude which could destroy the strictly objective approach that Freud always considered essential. One method of countering this was for the analyst to be analyzed before setting up in practice, thus enabling him to recognize his own vulnerability in advance.

It was not only that many of the feelings transferred by the patient onto the analyst "moved back," as Freud explained, "from the scene which we were trying to elucidate to earlier experiences, and compelled the analysis, which was supposed to correct the present, to occupy itself with the past." The regression led back still further, at first only to puberty, then to childhood. "It appeared," he continued, "that psychoanalysis could explain nothing belonging to the present without referring back to something past; indeed, that every pathogenic experience implied a previous experience which, though not in itself pathogenic, had yet endowed the later one with its pathogenic quality. . . ." For Freud the process had a parallel with some of the work on which he had been engaged before coming under Charcot's influence. Once he had been physically sectioning human brains to investigate brain lesions; now he was cross-sectioning the patient's emotional condition as he traced her history back to the traumatic past.

The problems were revealed only slowly, and the methods of dealing with them were evolved along lines that could be called either empirical or hit-or-miss. Freud described the situation with typical clarity many years later. "At first," he wrote,

> the analyzing physician could do no more than discover the unconscious material that was concealed from the patient, put it together and, at the right moment, communicate it to him. Psychoanalysis was then first and foremost an art of interpreting. Since this did not solve the therapeutic problem, a further aim quickly came in view: to oblige the patient to confirm the analyst's construction from his own memory. In that endeavor the chief emphasis lay upon the patient's resistances: the art consisted now in uncovering these as quickly as possible, in pointing them out to the patient and in inducing him by human influence—this was where suggestion operating as "transference" played its part—to abandon his resistances.

Prizing up long-forgotten memories from the unconscious with the help of free association would have been a delicate enough job whatever the root of the trouble. It was made more difficult by accumulating evidence not only that sexual problems played a greater part in the cause of hysteria than most investigators had previously suspected but that they appeared to have a similar role in many other neuroses. Most were in fact now seen by Freud as consequences of an arrested or faulty development of the libido, a word by which at this stage he meant the energy of the sexual instincts. And he now seized on this diagnosis with a resolution that was to make him famous in some medical circles, notorious in others, and was to end his collaboration with Breuer.

In later years Freud maintained that he gave to the word "sexuality" a far wider meaning than that of common usage. "This extension is justified genetically," he wrote in 1910; "we reckon as belonging to 'sexual life' all expressions of tender feeling, which spring from the source of primitive sexual feelings, even when those feelings have become inhibited in regard to their original sexual aim or have exchanged this aim for another which is no longer sexual. For this reason we prefer to speak of *psychosexuality*, thus laying stress on the point that the mental factor should not be overlooked or underestimated. We use the word sexuality in the same comprehensive sense as that in which the German language uses the word *lieben* [to love]." No doubt. But this meaning is distinctly more embracing than that in the examples which Freud claimed had set him on the right path, or in most of those which he described in his writings.

The first glimmerings of the truth, he later wrote, came to him as he was musing over three statements he had heard from his superiors. At one of Charcot's evening receptions, he wrote:

> I happened to be standing near the great teacher at a moment when he appeared to be telling Brouardel [P.C.H. Brouardel, professor of forensic medicine in Paris] a very interesting story about something that had happened during his day's work. I hardly heard the beginning, but gradually my attention was seized by what he was talking of: a young married couple from a distant country in the East—the woman a severe sufferer, the man either impotent or exceedingly awkward. *"Tâchez donc,"* I heard Charcot repeating, *"je vous assure, vous y arriverez."* Brouardel, who spoke less loudly, must have expressed his astonishment that symptoms like the wife's could have been produced by such circumstances. For Charcot suddenly broke out with great animation: *"Mais, dans des cas pareils c'est toujours la chose génitale, toujours—toujours—toujours";* and he crossed his arms over his stomach, hugging himself and jumping up and down on his toes several times in his own characteristically lively way. I know that for a moment I was almost paralyzed with amazement and said to myself: "Well, but if he knows that, why does he never say so?"

The second statement, he recalled, was when Breuer had said, apparently in reference to the case of an hysteric, and the difficulty in discovering the facts: "These things are always *secrets d'alcôve!*" —secrets of the bedchamber. The third statement was by Chrobak who had remarked of one patient that the only realistic hope of cure lay in prescribing regular doses of a normal penis—possibly the case of the American physician which had the "delicate aspects" Freud did not pass on to his fiancée.

Freud's explanation is hardly sufficient. None of the three examples testifies to more than the effects of frustrated sexual satisfaction, a point that is unlikely to have escaped his notice by the time he had reached his thirties. The facts suggest, rather, that Freud was driven to his conclusion about the importance of sexuality, tentative at first, hardening later, by a multitude of small details noted in his patients. It was, moreover, a conclusion which Freud himself, a man of almost Puritan beliefs, found acutely discomforting; indeed, it is possible to believe that his innate primness helped him to give to sex in the etiology of the neuroses not only the importance it deserved but also an additional emphasis.

A good deal has been written, and as much denied, about the influence of contemporary Viennese life on the significance that Freud gave to sexuality in the theories he developed in the 1890s. He himself always denied that there was any influence at all, maintaining that if the Viennese were, as sometimes claimed, more sexually libertarian than the population of other great cities, this itself would make any abnormal concentration on sexual problems there less likely. The persistence with which they were found by him to be the root cause of mental illness would, ran his argument, be expected in the Calvinist, Puritan, Protestant centers rather than in Catholic Vienna where, he concluded, there was less embarrassment about sexual relationships than in other European cities.

While this may have been true, the mere statement tends to put an illusory gloss on the city that was to be Freud's home for more than three quarters of a century. It was not all "Blue Danube" and "Merry Widow." Neither was it only the world of Hugo von Hofmannsthal and Arthur Schnitzler. Music and the arts, whose importance in the city had probably reached a peak three quarters of the way through the nineteenth century, continued to be heard and experienced; but almost exactly from the year when Freud began to consolidate his practice, a new sound was heard in the air and a fresh sight seen in the streets. On May Day 1890, Freud's last year in the Stiftungshaus, Vienna witnessed its first workers' march. Organized by a new party founded by Freud's old friend Viktor Adler, himself serving one of his regular brief prison sentences, it numbered tens of thousands—workers, wives and children— calling for an eight-hour day. The *Neue Freie Presse,* by no means an alarmist newspaper, noted: "Soldiers are standing by, the doors of houses are being closed, in people's apartments food supplies are prepared as though for an impending siege, the shops are deserted." Shopkeepers pulled down their shutters, and it was with an air of surprised relief that the Viennese went to bed that night in the knowledge that nothing serious had happened.

Yet the May Day march of 1890 was a sign of things to come. The Vienna of "Congress Dances"—if it had ever existed—survived only in artificial form, a public relations façade behind which the problems of the coming century began to mount, very much as they did elsewhere. There was, perhaps, only one feature of the prosperous middle- and upper-class Viennese society, which supplied Freud with most of his patients, that was different from its equivalent in other European capitals. This was the polyglot composition of the Empire and the ever-present need to form its disparate units into more viable groups. The economic imperative was stressed more than once by Karl Kraus, that most famous of all Viennese polemical journalists, at first supporter of Freud and then relentless opponent of psychoanalysis. "Kraus," it has been written,

> saw that the actual root of [hysteria], so common among bourgeois Wienerinnen, lay in the business character of bourgeois marriage. Marriages designed to create financial dynasties, regardless of the personal fulfillment of the partners, guaranteed frustration, especially for women in so strait-laced a society. For the husbands, incompatibility meant recourse to prostitutes, or to affairs of the sort that Schnitzler was so adept at re-creating in his stories and plays. For the wives, the problem was more complicated, since it was instilled in them early on that only lascivious, depraved women could actually desire or enjoy sexual gratification. No wonder if, when they discovered that sex was pleasant after all, they came to think of themselves in those terms; extramarital sex, which was a challenging game for the husbands, necessarily generated deep-seated feelings of guilt in the wives.

However significant this fact may have been, there was certainly another which made those of Freud's Viennese patients with guilt complexes more likely to discuss them than would have been the case elsewhere. In 1886 Krafft-Ebing had published his *Psychopathia Sexualis*, a book which was an immense success, was frequently brought out in new and revised editions, and which made the previously undiscussable, if not a subject of dinner-party conversation, at least fit to talk about to a doctor. It is, therefore, less remarkable than is sometimes supposed that Freud's patients were prepared to discuss their most intimate problems.

Nevertheless, Freud himself has often stated that they needed encouragement before describing gross disturbances of their *vita sexualis*, and it is difficult entirely to dissociate his persistent attempts to "follow his hunch"—whether or not this arose from unconscious personal motives—from the evidence he collected. "The more I set about looking for such disturbances—bearing in mind the fact that everyone hides the truth in matters of sex—and the more skillful I became at pursuing my enquiries in the face of a preliminary denial," he has written, "the more regularly was I able to discover pathogenic factors in sexual life. . . ." Some years later, speaking on the future prospects of psychoanalytic therapy, he described his treatment as "made up of two parts—what the physician infers and tells the patient, and the patient's working-over of what he has heard. The mechanism of our assistance is easy to understand: we give the patient the conscious anticipatory idea (the idea of what he may expect to find) and he then finds the repressed unconscious idea in himself on the basis of its similarity to the anticipatory one."

Freud's statements about the reception of such techniques are contradictory. Years later he claimed: "I unhesitatingly sacrificed my growing popularity as a doctor, and the increase in attendance during my consulting hours, by making a systematic enquiry into the sexual factors involved in the causation of my patients' neuroses. . . ." Nearer the event, in 1893, he had seen things very differently. "The sexual business attracts people," he wrote; "they all go away impressed and convinced, after exclaiming: 'No one has ever asked me that before!' "

However much Freud's own accounts differ on certain points, they do agree on one vital matter: that he saw it as part of his technique to draw out sexual details from his patients. This is not to suggest that the details were sometimes deliberately elaborated or embroidered into untruths under the persistent questioning of a persistent doctor; even a confession made under the heaviest interrogation is not necessarily false. There is also the evidence of Breuer, with whom Freud was still discussing his cases. The prominent place of sexuality in their joint *Studies on Hysteria,* Breuer said, "arose from no inclination towards the subject but from the findings—to a large extent most unexpected—of our medical experience. . . . I confess that the plunging into sexuality in theory and practice is not to my taste. But what have my taste and my feeling about what is seemly and what is unseemly to do with the question of what is true?" Breuer clearly had even less liking than Freud for what was being revealed by the cases he passed on to his colleague, and for the implications they discussed in detail. But while Breuer was to back away, partly from personal feeling, partly from a reluctance to risk endangering a flourishing practice, Freud saw the potential for new discoveries as the great chance he had been awaiting so long.

Many of his patients were women, many were to some degree mentally unstable and many appear—from the scanty evidence available—to have been sexually repressed. In these circumstances it is not only the prurient who have asked from time to time what happened on the couch at No. 19 Berggasse. The answer is, almost certainly, little if anything. Freud has himself recalled the occasion when a patient impetuously threw her arms round his neck; his salvation from further embarrassment was the apparently fortuitous entry of a maid—a somewhat incongruous story since one must assume that psychoanalytic sessions were not usually interrupted by servants. A male patient has written that Freud told him of one seduction attempt—but rather gilds the tale by claiming that this was the start of Freud's sitting behind the couch rather than at its foot. Beyond that, silence.

Now, it is obvious that Freud himself would be unlikely to spread any suggestions of improper conduct. Like the government official who is asked whether he is a spy for the enemy, the answer will be "No" whatever the state of play. Yet there is one factor here that is important: the atmosphere of criticism in which he operated throughout his professional life. It is inconceivable that his opponents would not have exploited the slightest suggestion of professional or moral misdemeanor, and equally inconceivable that had such existed it could have remained unknown. Yet while the moral turpitude allegedly encouraged by psychoanalysis was to be a constant preoccupation of the critics, Freud himself was never to be the object of serious attack.

In the first publication outlining the methods which he had begun to use, "On the Psychical Mechanism of Hysterical Phenomena: Preliminary Communication," signed jointly by Breuer and Freud, and published in the *Neurologisches Centralblatt* in January 1893, the role of sexuality was not spelled out. The paper followed the treatment of a Frau Cäcilie M. whose physical symptoms, notably acute facial neuralgia, pains, spasms and hallucinations, were revealed to have psychic causes. The symptoms were dissipated when the causes were discovered and recalled by her. In spite of the comparative innocuousness of the case history, Freud reported "a long battle with my collaborator" before Breuer agreed to publication, and even Freud himself may have had reservations, although of a different kind. The paper was begun in June 1892 but not published until after the death in that year of both Brücke and Meynert, Freud's scientific mentors and champions of the organic view of all disease. Only with their passing, it has been suggested with some plausibility, was Freud willing to put on public record his belief in psychic causation.

The "Preliminary Communication" reported that as the result of a chance observation—the Anna O. case—the authors had been able to investigate many cases of hysteria by a new method, and had often found that the cause was not an obviously identifiable traumatic event but one which had apparently been totally forgotten. The paper used the word "repressed" for the first time as meaning the pushing into the unconscious of an unpleasant memory that the patient wished to forget, and after explaining that hysterical symptoms could be removed by bringing those memories back into consciousness, described the process by which the cure operated:

It brings to an end the operative force of the idea which was not abreacted [discharged as emotion] in the first instance, by allowing its strangulated affect to find a way out through speech; and it subjects it to associative correction by introducing it into normal consciousness (under light hypnosis) or by removing it through the physician's suggestions, as is done in somnambulism accompanied by amnesia.

The paper was noted in Austria and Germany, and in France where Pierre Janet wrote that he was "happy to see that the results of my findings, already old, have recently been confirmed by two German authors, Breuer and Freud." But, as was to happen with a number of Freud's early publications, the kindest words came from England. In the medical journal *Brain* the distinguished British doctor J. Michell Clarke described in a lengthy paper on hysteria and neurasthenia how Breuer and Freud had stressed the need for arousing in the patient's mind the memory of the occasions on which hysterical symptoms first appeared. "Then," he went on, "the connection between the latter and the symptoms present at the time of examination comes out in the clearest and most convincing manner. Observations made in this way are worthy of record, both from the theoretical and practical points of view." The "Preliminary Communication" was also noticed by F. W. H. Myers, a founder-member of Britain's Society for Psychical Research, who in an address on "The Subliminal Consciousness," later published in the Society's *Proceedings,* observed that he had only one thing to add to Breuer and Freud: "That extraordinary potency of subliminal action, which they frankly present as insoluble by pure physiology, is part and parcel of my scheme of man: and its occasional appearance in this form is to me but the natural concomitant of its habitual and inevitable residence within us; in readiness—if we can contrive to summon it—to subserve our highest needs."

Two years after the "Preliminary Communication" there came *Studies on Hysteria,* a volume dealing with Breuer and Freud's joint work, and the real introduction of psychoanalysis to the world. The book began with the "Preliminary Communication" and was followed by five case histories; the first, that of Anna O., written by Breuer, and the four others by Freud. Then came six chapters on the theory of hysteria written by Breuer and a concluding chapter on the psychotherapy of hysteria by Freud.

Certain questions immediately spring to mind regarding the women chosen to illustrate the new techniques that Freud was building on Breuer's experience with Anna O. Who were they? Why were they chosen from among those whom Freud had treated in some eight years of practice? And were they typical of those whom it might be possible to help with his new ideas?

A great deal had come to light about Bertha Pappenheim, the "Anna O." of the first case history, even before Professor Ellenberger unearthed more information in the 1970s. But mystery continues to surround all but one of the four patients whom Freud describes in *Studies on Hysteria:* Frau Emmy von N. She was Fanny Moser, born Fanny Sulzer-Wart in 1848, and at the time of her visit to Freud reported to be the richest woman in Europe. The daugher of a wealthy family from the Swiss town of Winterthur, she had in 1870 married a Swiss widower, Heinrich Moser, who had amassed a vast fortune from business enterprises throughout Europe and Asia. Herr Moser was sixty-five at the time of his marriage, his bride twenty-three. He died four years later, and when it was discovered that he had left his entire estate to his widow, the children of his first wife maintained that he had been poisoned by his second. Disinterment of the body, and an autopsy, cleared the accused.

It was fifteen years later that Fanny Moser, suffering from a variety of tics, illusions and other symptoms of hysteria, arrived in Vienna for treatment by Josef Breuer. After six weeks she was passed on to Freud, "his chief assistant" according to one of her daughters; seven weeks later she returned, much improved, to one of her estates in Switzerland where Freud later visited her. But the following year Frau Moser was back in Vienna for a further two-month treatment, and Freud himself was to admit in *Studies:* "The therapeutic success on the whole was considerable; but it was not a lasting one. The patient's tendency to fall ill in a similar way under the impact of fresh traumas was not got rid of."

Virtually nothing is known of the other three women: "Fräulein Elisabeth von R."; an English governess in Vienna disguised under the name of "Miss Lucy R."; and "Katharina," a peasant girl in the Tyrol with whom Freud had had a single short talk. Fräulein Elisabeth was given an aristocratic "von" and a personal background of large family estates which, according to a descendant, fitted the environment of her early life but disguised her real, Jewish, middle-class milieu. The editors of the Standard Edition of Freud's works assume that not only names and places but also chronologies have been changed in order to prevent identification of the patients, and it is difficult to decide what weight should be given to the evidence cited.

The case histories selected were certainly not chosen to illustrate the unfailing success of the new technique. Of Anna O. even Breuer at his most optimistic could claim only that she had recovered her mental balance a considerable time after the treatment had ended. Frau Moser's recovery was not lasting. Miss Lucy R., the governess, did recover once she had been forced to admit that she had fallen in love with her employer, but the effect on Katharina is unknown, since Freud never saw her again. Elisabeth von R. did finally recover, although on the evidence presented, it would be difficult to maintain that recovery was a result of the treatment.

However, there was one very understandable reason for the selection of these particular cases, since, as reported, most of them did carry one stage further the technique of what was to become psychoanalysis. The spontaneous discovery of the cathartic method was the essential feature of the Anna O. case. Emmy von N. insisted on talking about whatever she wanted; her talk often led on to unrequested pathogenic reminiscences and was thus an early, if not the first, demonstration of free association. Neither Miss Lucy R. nor Elisabeth von R. could be hypnotized. So with one Freud initiated the pressure technique; with the other, largely as a result of that technique, he discovered the need for overcoming repression.

Breuer had consented to publication of the case histories only after persistent persuasion from Freud, and a hint of the reason for his reluctance is given in the preface where, after explaining that some of the most instructive material had to be omitted for fear of patients being identified, the authors continue:

> This of course applies especially to all those cases in which sexual and marital relations play an important aetiological part. Thus it comes about that we are only able to produce very incomplete evidence in favor of our view that sexuality seems to play a principal part in the pathogenesis of hysteria as a source of psychical traumas and as a motive for "defense"—that is, for repressing ideas from consciousness. It is precisely observations of a markedly sexual nature that we have been obliged to leave unpublished.

It was, as both Breuer and Freud knew, just the different weight which each man gave to this factor in neurosis that was already leading them down divergent paths. Yet nowhere in the book does Freud state his later belief that a sexual etiology is invariably present in cases of hysteria. And by contrast it is Breuer who insists that "the sexual instinct is undoubtedly the most powerful source of persisting increases of excitation (and consequently of neuroses)." Thus the views of the two men on the importance to be granted to sexuality were less far apart than is sometimes assumed.

It was on the future application of their discovery that they were divided, a difference in outlook accounted for by their characters and their respective positions in the medical hierarchy. Breuer, the established medical practitioner, believed that if he followed up his theories, they might arouse distrust among many of his patients. Freud, concentrating on the hysterics, certain that he was at last on the trail that would lead to fame, discounted such caution. He had no built-in reluctance to *épater les bourgeois* and he believed that he had, indeed, "touched on one of the great secrets of nature."

He was, moreover, desperately anxious to stake his claim to this secret before anyone else did so. In writing to Fliess about a collection of essays by Paul Julius Möbius, the German psychologist, he commented "they are important on the subject of hysteria. His is the best mind among the neurologists; fortunately he is not on the track of sexuality." Pierre Janet was considered an even greater danger, and Freud reported that he had picked up a recent book of Janet's "with a beating heart, and laid it down again with my pulse returned to normal. He has no inkling of the clue. . . ."

The remark is significant in view of the acrimonious argument about priorities that was to rumble on for so long between Freud and Janet. It is true that Janet had published a number of case histories between 1886 and 1893, and that Breuer and Freud had referred to his work both in the "Preliminary Communication" and in *Studies on Hysteria.* But it can be claimed with some plausibility that Janet only began to understand the deeper roots of hysteria after Breuer and Freud's publications of the 1890s.

Janet's views were, not unnaturally, rather different. Freud, he was to maintain,

changed first of all the terms I was using; what I had called psychological analysis he called psychoanalysis; what I had called psychological system, in order to designate that totality of facts of consciousness and movement, whether of members or of viscera, whose association constitutes the traumatic memory, he called complex; he considered a repression what I considered a restriction of consciousness; what I referred to as a psychological dissociation, or as a moral fumigation, he baptized with the name of catharsis. But above all he transformed a clinical observation and a therapeutic treatment with a definite and limited field of use into an enormous system of medical philosophy.

Janet no doubt considered that final sentence as a condemnation. Yet it is one of the points to be made for Freud that while the idea of the unconscious was very much alive during the 1890s, he alone used the evidence not only from his own work but from that of his contemporaries, and with the sum total constructed a new method of mental diagnosis and treatment. As *The Times* of London was to write of Einstein's General Theory of Relativity, the genius of its originator consisted "in taking up the uninterpreted experiments and scattered suggestions of his predecessors, and welding them into a comprehensive scheme. . . ."

While Breuer and Freud had agreed, some time before publication of *Studies on Hysteria,* that cooperation was no longer possible, the reception of the book no doubt reinforced Breuer's view that continuing to work with Freud would do him little but harm. For in two ways their jointly produced book went farther than Krafft-Ebing's *Psychopathia Sexualis* which, despite its popularity among curious laymen, dealt primarily with discussion of sexual details by medical men among medical men. *Studies on Hysteria,* on the other hand, advocated the most intimate doctor-patient discussions. *Psychopathia Sexualis,* moreover, dealt largely with perversions of the more obviously ill or deranged; Breuer and Freud, describing hysterics at a lower level of illness, at least inferred, if they did no more, that troubles due to unsuspected sexual problems might be far more common than was generally admitted.

The question of patient-doctor discussion was taken up by the German neurologist Adolf von Strümpell, writing in the *Deutsche Zeitschrift für Nervenheilkunde.* The therapeutic procedure outlined by Breuer and Freud, he said, "requires a penetrating investigation, often extending into the most minute details, of the patient's private affairs and experiences. I do not know whether such fathoming of the most intimate private affairs can in all circumstances be considered legitimate, even on the part of the most high-principled physician. When sexual relations are concerned I consider it particularly questionable." To all except the pathologically sensitive this might have seemed a fairly expressed matter of personal opinion. But Strümpell's review was, in Freud's words at the time, a disgraceful notice. However, thirty years on he was, he said, "able to laugh at the lack of comprehension which his criticism showed, but Breuer felt hurt and grew discouraged."

The *Neue Freie Presse* described the book as "nothing but the kind of psychology used by poets" but Freud was able to consider this as a "very sensitive article." As with the "Preliminary Communication," criticisms by Freud's own countrymen were counterbalanced by those of the English. F. W. H. Myers, who had earlier described the "Preliminary Communication" to the Society for Psychical Research, now discussed *Studies* in an address to the Society on "Hysteria and Genius." Michell Clarke gave it a set-piece review in *Brain* and was cautiously welcoming. But he muted his praise with the reminder that what Anna O. had called the talking cure had "been long recognized in the Roman Church, by the institution of confession." And he must somewhat have deflated Freud with his remark that it was "interesting to note a return, in part at least, to the old theory of the origin of hysteria in sexual disorders. . . ."

Freud himself claimed years later that he had been able to elaborate and test his therapeutic method "only on severe, indeed on the severest cases; at first my material consisted entirely of patients who had tried everything else without success, and had spent long years in sanatoria. I have scarcely been able to bring together sufficient material to enable me to say how my method works with those slighter, episodic cases which we see recovering under all kinds of influences and even spontaneously. Psychoanalytic therapy was created through and for the treatment of patients permanently unfit for existence, and its triumph has been that it had made a satisfactorily large number of these permanently *fit* for existence." Yet the cases reported in *Studies* seem to have been those of patients whose troubles were due to lack of motivated work, and were slight rather than so severe as to render the victims unfit for existence.

In this respect it should be remembered that Freud's success in alleviating his patients' nervous troubles was not solely the result of his dredging of the unconscious and his exploitation of the fact, known to able men for generations, that confession is good for the soul. What he was able to add to the stimulated remembrance of things past was a specialized knowledge of the human nervous system and the experience of a general practitioner. Beneath the new techniques and the jargon that was to follow, there lay a foundation of worldly wise common sense.

At this stage Breuer and Freud were cautious in the claims they made for their new method. What they did maintain, and in specific terms, was that some patients' physical symptoms, as well as their recollection or otherwise of past events, and their responses to them, were conditioned by motives of which they were not consciously aware. As a basis for psychoanalysis this has for long been accepted as beyond doubt, although the importance of the sexual factor has been qualified and the atypical nature of the patients described in *Studies* has laid open to attack some of the generalizations that the authors drew. Nevertheless, more than one theory which helped change the world has had beginnings less plausible and less supported by evidence.

The same is not necessarily true of the large number of theories and speculations erected on this foundation, sometimes in a rather uncertain way, sometimes by Freud himself, sometimes by his followers. Their growth over the years has encouraged the skepticism of psychoanalysis, epitomized by Sir Karl Popper in his evaluation of the theories of Freud and of Alfred Adler, the first of the Freudian defectors. These theories, notes Popper, were, "simply non-testable, irrefutable. There was no conceivable human behavior which could contradict them. This does not mean that Freud and Adler were not seeing certain things correctly: I personally do not doubt that much of what they say is of considerable importance, and may well play its part one day in a psychological science which is testable. But it does mean that those 'clinical observations,' which analysts naïvely believe confirm their theory, cannot do this any more than the daily confirmations which astrologers find in their practice." To this criticism, potentially more damaging than the high-pitched screams of "scandalous" which greeted Freud's emphasis on sex, analysts have reasonably replied that it is impossible satisfactorily to apply the strict evidential criteria of physics or chemistry to the delicate nuances of the mental condition. Yet the very fact that great difficulties lie in the way of substantiating results makes it less easy to support the sometimes grandiose claims made for psychoanalysis as a science.

Publication of *Studies on Hysteria,* which was to sell little more than 600 copies within the next decade, confirmed both Freud's and Breuer's belief that they could no longer work together. Even by the summer of 1894 Freud had been able to write: "I actually spend the whole day thinking about nothing but the neuroses, but since my scientific contact with Breuer has ended I have been thrown back on myself alone, which is why it goes so slowly." Now, with the critics reinforcing Breuer's suspicions that he had made a mistake in getting too closely involved with this young man Freud, the possibility of reconciling their interests was finally ruled out.

There was, however, a reason for their inability to agree that went deeper than the differing importance each gave to sexual problems. Both men were seeking the underlying causes of the neuroses, and the question they had to answer was that asked by Freud years later in his autobiography: When is it that a mental process becomes pathogenic? Breuer's explanation was physiological. Freud's was psychological; as it has been said, he "postulated not molecules and motion but intention and purpose." Breuer, despite the cases he had witnessed or heard about from Freud since his treatment of Bertha Pappenheim, was still reluctant to abandon totally the belief in physiological causation with which he had grown up. Beneath this, and beneath his almost embarrassed distaste for discussing the role of sexuality, there lay the difference of emphasis between the older man, unwilling to dispense too quickly with accepted ideas, and the young man, anxious to embrace the new. The not-so-uncommon situation was here complicated by the fact that Breuer had done so much to help Freud, not only by professional support but by regular financial loans. Freud was anxious to repay his debts but still unable to do so.

The exact date of their rupture is unknown; but Rudolf von Urban, describing the incident that guided him toward psychoanalysis and the founding of his sanatorium in Vienna, has maintained that the two men were on good terms after the Easter of 1895. "I was walking home from my fencing school through the Liechtensteinstrasse in Vienna," he has written,

> when I came upon a very humorous situation. A wagon loaded with pigs stood before a butcher's shop. One pig escaped but after a hilarious pursuit was captured by a bystander. The problem of forcing the pig into the butcher's shop drew a large crowd. The more the pig was forced toward the shop, the more stubborn it became, and retreated in the opposite direction. The traffic on this busy street was completely disrupted. Even a policeman was unable to help. I took it upon myself to approach the butcher, who was by then completely exhausted, and said, "Do you not see that the pig goes opposite to the way you want him to go? Why don't you turn him round and pull him toward the street, then I believe he will naturally back into the shop."
>
> The butcher looked at me with astonishment, scratched his head and then followed my advice. As the crowd melted away, two gentlemen approached me; one of them said, "Why do you think the pig acted contrary to what you expected of him?" My answer was: "Because his instinct warned him not to trust man, for in the end man will kill him, and the pig is right." "You are a perspicacious boy," the stranger said. "What do you want to become?" "A Catholic priest." "Why not a psychologist? Since you know the mind of a pig, as you have so ably demonstrated, I believe you can also handle human beings . . ."

Von Urban walked on with the two men who stopped at Berggasse No. 19. One was Freud, the other Breuer.

In the immediate aftermath of the final break, which must have occurred shortly after the meeting with Von Urban, Freud was bitter. Hanna Breuer has recorded how her father, walking in Vienna, saw Freud approaching and appeared to forget the broken relationship. "Instinctively, he opened his arms," she has written. "Freud passed, professing not to see him."

Ernest Jones has written that "Breuer, so it would appear, had certain characteristics which were particularly antipathetic to Freud's nature. One was a weakness in his personality that made it hard for him ever to take a definite stand on any question. The other was a pettifogging kind of censoriousness which would induce him to mar any appreciation or praise by searching out a small point open to criticism—an attitude very alien to Freud's open-hearted and generous spirit." Whether this spirit was shown in Freud's stronger criticisms of Breuer is uncertain since Jones apparently disagreed with Voltaire's "One owes respect to the living; but to the dead one owes nothing but the truth." He reported only Freud's milder opinions and said that the rest "need not be reproduced."

For his part, Breuer stuck to his guns. A decade later Ludwig Binswanger, a psychoanalyst from Zurich, called on Breuer when visiting Vienna and asked how he now regarded Freud. "His look of downright pity and superiority, as well as the wave of his hand," Binswanger wrote, "a dismissal in the full sense of the word, left not the slightest doubt that in his opinion Freud had gone scientifically astray to such an extent that he could no longer be taken seriously, and hence it was better not to talk about him."

8

Splendid Isolation: Disaster

It was a beautiful, heroic, period; the splendid isolation was not
devoid of advantages and charm.

FREUD,
On the History of the Psycho-Analytic Movement

Freud's rift with Breuer was accompanied by another change of
stance as he began to feel more confident of himself. Between
1886, when he had returned to Vienna as Charcot's devoted pupil,
and the publication of *Studies*, he had slowly but steadily fallen
away from Charcot's ideas. In 1889 he was raising his first objections to the Frenchman's views on the nature of hysteria, and in
1893 he was even more openly critical in a paper on hysterical
paralyses. It is true that his obituary of "The Master of the Salpêtrière," who died in 1893, was eulogistic; but by the following year
he was beginning to reject Charcot's teaching on the importance
of heredity in neurosis. Soon he was identifying four neuroses—
hysteria, obsession, anxiety neurosis and neurasthenia, each with
a different sexual etiology; and by 1896 he was confident that all
resulted from unconscious sexual events in childhood. As an etiological factor, Charcot's heredity had disappeared.

From 1895 on, Freud was on his own. For some years before his
death in 1892, Meynert had decided that it was safer to keep Freud
at arm's length. So did many others who worked with him in the
university. Even Krafft-Ebing, although not personally antagonistic, saw a great difference between his studies and those of a physician who deliberately encouraged his patients to discuss sexual
problems. Now that the link with Breuer was finally broken, Freud
entered a period of what, echoing Lord Goschen, he was later to
call "splendid isolation"—another example of his lifelong habit of

interspersing German with the untranslatable English phrase. This one had been used when the British Empire's isolation in Europe was felt more than the splendor, and it was the isolation which Freud remembered as he looked back in 1913. "At that time," he wrote of 1896, "I had reached the peak of loneliness, had lost all my old friends and hadn't acquired any new ones; no one paid any attention to me, and the only thing that kept me going was a bit of defiance and the beginning of *The Interpretation of Dreams.*" A few years later he underlined his position at the end of the century when he told a Swiss friend, "What personal pleasure is to be derived from analysis I obtained during the time when I was alone, and since others have joined me it has given me more pain than pleasure. The way people accept and distort it has not changed the opinion I formed of them when they nonunderstandingly rejected it. An incurable breach must have come into existence at that time between me and other men."

Yet by this time he had already made the seminal discoveries that were to divide man's understanding of himself into ante-Freud and post-Freud: that human actions were more governed by unconscious motives than had previously been thought possible by more than a small number of men through the centuries; that repressed tendencies, pushed from the conscious mind and battened down in the unconscious, played a great and unsuspected role in human life; that neuroses were not the result of small, so-called functional changes in brain tissue but the outcome of complicated mental processes and of strong emotional conflicts; and that knowledge of these facts could enable a doctor to understand mental disease and in suitable cases even cure it.

As this basis of psychoanalysis became firmer during the mid-1890s, Freud realized that in the aftermath of his break with Breuer, the only exception to his isolation was his friendship with Fliess. The distance between Vienna and Berlin limited the meetings of the two men to "Congresses" held at irregular intervals but their correspondence, which since 1888 had been lengthy, detailed and intimate, now became even more so.

Freud had grown emotionally dependent on Fliess, the one man to whom he could confide his ideas without fear of ridicule, and dependence was reinforced by the medical connection. Although Breuer had been his family doctor, Freud had for some while leaned heavily on the advice of Fliess, particularly in dealing with a heart condition that had first shown itself in 1893 and which at times had appeared to threaten not only his health but his life. Smoking, which he would give up only intermittently and only after the most urgent warnings, was almost certainly a contributory cause, but it would be unwise to ignore completely the effects of the controversy which began in 1893 as he urged Breuer to publish the "Preliminary Communication," and ended with the final break two years later.

Freud had for long been an inveterate cigar smoker but it was not until the summer of 1893 that Fliess, alarmed by his friend's report of cardiac symptoms, began a relentless but only intermittently successful campaign against the habit. In mid-October Freud promised to give it up. A month later he found the effort too much and asked Fliess whether he really considered it "such a great boon to live a great many years in misery?" He gave up again at the end of March 1894 and could, he said, watch others smoking without envy. However, within days his cardiac oppression, as he called it, was worse than ever. His condition may well have been the result of giving up smoking. Freud himself always regarded the cigar as essential to work, and the doctor of his later years seriously asked whether he would ever have been able to achieve the results he did without "the specific pharmacological effect of nicotine."

In April 1894 Freud consulted Breuer. But he was already discontented and was soon complaining that his old friend was not seeing him for as much as two weeks at a stretch. The one consolation was that Breuer believed the trouble might be a nontoxic heart condition; this would be affected only slightly by smoking—a diagnosis which Freud was far more ready to accept than Fliess's view that nicotine addiction was the real cause. Before the end of June he was smoking again, reporting the fact to Fliess and justifying his decision on the grounds that he had seen heart conditions similar to his own in patients who had never smoked, and that he himself, back on cigars, was able to work properly once more. Fliess responded with a peremptory demand for abstinence. Freud obeyed for eight days, slipped back to one cigar a week and then, on a further demand from Fliess, again gave up smoking completely. This time his resolution lasted for more than a year, and it was only in the summer of 1895 that he told Fliess he had succumbed once more.

The cardiac symptoms gradually disappeared and they did not reappear for years, although Freud continued his daily quota of cigars to the end of his life. Even Dr. Schur was unable to identify the symptoms with any certainty. Nevertheless, "I am inclined to the opinion," he has said, "that between late 1893 and 1896 Freud suffered from attacks of paroxysmal tachycardia, with anginal pain and signs of left ventricular failure; that these attacks reached their peak during April 1894, at which point he suffered an organic myocardial lesion, most likely a coronary thrombosis in a small artery, or perhaps a post-infectious myocarditis, with temporarily increased nicotine sensitivity."

But that phase was now over. Freud's cardiac symptoms had gone. He had broken with Breuer. He was now convinced that he could see ahead the job that had to be done, the mission to be fulfilled. All that remained was to do it.

On the face of it, the task must have seemed as difficult as any in the annals of medicine, the coming battles as hopeless as any in the records of war. Freud was a Jew in an anti-Semitic environment. He had little money but a growing family and a reputation for arguing with authority. He had, it is true, a nucleus of well-to-do patients, but many of them had been sent to him by Breuer, a patron with whom he had seen fit to differ and from whom he could expect no more support. He was, moreover, intent on forcing down the throats of a reluctant public a theory of mental disease that he knew would offend the medical establishment and the nearly omnipotent Catholic authorities.

One reason for his survival was the tenacity born of ambition; another was the spur of opposition. But yet another reason, not always appreciated, was that the general climate of the times, and the particular climate of medical opinion, was more favorable to new ideas than was readily apparent.

Beneath the surface, society itself was beginning to break out of the mold which had contained it for so long. In Europe it was not only *"la belle époque"* but also the *"fin de siècle,"* and the Austro-Hungarian Empire under its aged Franz Joseph was showing signs of coming apart. Throughout Austria the virtues of middle-class liberalism were already being challenged by the working class, while in Vienna, where Jew and Gentile had for the last quarter century been moving toward mutual toleration, moderation was soon to receive a body blow; Karl Lueger, the anti-Semite who had already proposed that Jews should be crammed into ships to be sunk with all on board, became mayor of the city. The scent of battles ahead, the premonition that great changes were coming, in science as well as in politics, made it possible to discuss new ideas and to give them the chance of survival. And despite all the attacks made on it, psychoanalysis did survive.

In the medical world, moreover, ideas were on the move. In science, ideas can demonstrably be seen to wait upon technological advance. The electric light had only become practicable with the development of equipment for producing high vacuums; the Wright brothers needed the gasoline engine to transform flight from dream to reality. The jet engine, utilizing an idea as old as the early Greeks, remained a chimera until the coming of titanium alloys. Radio demanded the vacuum tube, and the atomic bomb demanded isotope separation. In much the same way, the medical advances made during the last third of the nineteenth century were now leading to a deeper and more understanding discussion of the problems of the mind. The first International Congress of Psychology had been held in Paris in 1889. In 1890 there had come William James's *The Principles of Psychology* and, significantly for Freud's future, Frazer's *The Golden Bough* with its deep probings into the birth and growth of human institutions. Within a couple of years Henry Havelock Ellis, an unknown Englishman, was working on *Man and Woman,* a popular forerunner of his massive *Studies in the Psychology of Sex.*

The repercussions of a new interest in the mind and how it worked were, moreover, being felt beyond the medical world. In Norway, Ibsen had conscripted psychology in his attack on the pillars of society. In Paris, Marcel Proust with his *A la Recherche du Temps Perdu* was summoning up from unconscious memory the material for his resplendent masterpiece. In America, William James, who had daringly left physiology for psychology, was applying the new science to religion while his brother Henry, cozily settling down in southern England, was already exploring with novelist's insight the border country that lies between dream and reality. The signs were more propitious than Freud in Vienna may have appreciated, and in England the psychiatrist T. S. Clouston even prophesied that a man might be coming who would soon bring about "an enormous extension of our definite knowledge in regard to the relationship of mind and brain."

Freud was in his fortieth year when *Studies on Hysteria* appeared —almost at that crucial age after which, it is often speculated, no scientist ever achieves much that is worthwhile. Yet 1895 was to mark the beginning of an extraordinary five years of activity. While still at work on the final stages of *Studies* he had, for the first time, fully analyzed one of his own dreams, an operation of the utmost importance to his future work, so much so that he later asked jokingly whether at the place where he had slept there might not one day be erected a tablet bearing the words: "In this house on July 24th, 1895, the secret of Dreams was revealed to Dr. Sigmund Freud." Later in the year he wrote, in a few weeks, an elegant paper in which he tried to describe psychical processes in terms of quantifiable forces, an attempt in which he only just failed to outline the neurone theory put forward by Wilhelm von Waldeyer the following year, and describing the nervous system in terms of neurones, the word used for the individual cell and its extensions. In 1897 he began the searing task of self-analysis, a process speeded up by the death of his father, and in the same period he perpetrated what he called his "first great error." This was the formulation of the seduction theory which, disaster though it was, led on to the Oedipus complex, which he was soon to see as the main clue to psychic development. And he ended the last year of the century with the publication of *The Interpretation of Dreams,* usually considered his most influential book.

Yet throughout the second half of the 1890s, while relentlessly following the path he had first glimpsed at the Salpêtrière, Freud continued to build up a practice which by the turn of the century was giving him at least a modified security he had barely hoped for fifteen years earlier. The practice was the essential background to all his other activities and alone enabled him to keep financially afloat, support his family and justify the devotion of whatever spare hours he could find to the more important business of developing his theories. Its success was fluctuating rather than regular. But if there were downward trends in the graph of prosperity, the impression given is that each upward surge usually rose a little higher than its predecessor.

At the end of 1895 things were going well, and he could record that he was dealing daily with six to eight analytical cases—"most beautiful things, all sorts of new material." He worked nine to eleven hours a day with his patients and then, at eleven at night, settled down at his desk to write. In the last month of the year he could say triumphantly to Fliess, "I have trouble in fitting everything in, and I can pick and choose and begin to dictate my fees. I am getting confident in the diagnosis and treatment of the two neuroses, and I think the town is gradually beginning to realize that something is to be had from me."

Within six months the story was different, and he found it less agreeable "that this year for the first time my consulting room is empty, that I see no new faces for weeks on end, that I get no new cases for treatment, and that not one of the old ones is finished yet. . . ." Within the year his fortunes had radically changed once again, and he was able to start paying Dr. Breuer part of the 2,300 florins which he still owed. Within another twelve months things appeared to be going even better. There was a flood of patients, and he was handling ten or eleven therapeutic sessions every working day.

This was almost as much as he could do, since he was also continuing his regular university lecturing, a task which did not give him particular pleasure. "It had been a hot summer afternoon," he wrote in explaining the background to one of his dreams, and during the evening I had delivered my lecture on the connection between hysteria and the perversions, and everything I had had to say displeased me intensely and seemed to me completely devoid of any value. I was tired and felt no trace of enjoyment in my difficult work; I longed to be away from all this grubbing about in human dirt and to be able to enjoy my children and afterwards visit the beauties of Italy. In this mood I went from the lecture room to a café, where I had a modest snack in the open air, since I had no appetite for food.

There were times when his lectures at the university did not even claim his full interest. They were, he wrote, "attended by an audience of eleven, who sit there with pencil and paper and hear damnably little that is positive. I play the part of neuropathological researcher before them and comment on Beard [G. M. Beard, author of *American Nervousness, its Causes and Consequences* and *Sexual Neuraesthenia (Nervous Exhaustion), its Hygiene, Causes, Symptoms and Treatment*], but my interest is elsewhere."

Early in 1899 he was again complaining of overwork, and in July, before moving out of the city for three months like the rest of the academic world, he could claim that on the whole it had been a triumphant year. Yet the perpetual insecurity of the man on his own, lacking the safety net of a university chair, emerges from two letters to Fliess written after he had returned in the autumn. Even if the practice picked up, he said in one of them, he would not be able to cover his expenses for the year; in fact he was considering attaching himself to a hydropathic establishment and, apparently, giving up private practice. A few weeks earlier he had given Fliess an inkling of his constant financial nervousness and uncertainty. "A thing I remember from my boyhood is that when wild horses on the pampas have once been lassoed, they retain a certain nervousness for life. In the same way I once knew helpless poverty and have a constant fear of it. You will see that my style will improve and my ideas be better when this town affords me a prosperous livelihood." Within six months it seemed that it might be doing so, and he could gaily report: "It is my busy time now, 70 to 80 florins a day, about 500 a week. . . ."

While the majority of the patients who climbed the stairs of No. 19 Berggasse suffered from purely nervous troubles which could be treated without calling on outside help, there were exceptions. Among them was "Irma," known to the Freuds socially, and the subject of the most famous dream—one of his own—that Freud ever interpreted.

During the summer of 1895 he was staying with his family for the holiday months at Schloss Belle Vue, an ornate house standing in large grounds on the hills outside Vienna. Once a center where dances, concerts and parties were held, it was by 1895 a pleasant family hotel. Here, on the night of July 23–24, Freud dreamed what was to become known as "the dream of Irma's injection."

His interest in dreams was partly a result of his use of free association, since he found that many patients described their dreams as though they were part and parcel of their conscious daytime thoughts, a plain hint that he should consider them as important as other intelligible phenomena. Thus he was driven to assume that dreams were not meaningless, as most men maintained them to be, but clues to events which a patient had repressed into the unconscious. He now began to realize that this was so, and years later could still recall how he had found dream analysis "a sheet-anchor during those difficult times when the unrecognized facts of the neuroses used to confuse my inexperienced judgment. Whenever I began to have doubts of the correctness of my wavering conclusions, the successful transformation of a senseless and muddled dream into a logical and intelligible mental process in the dreamer would renew my confidence of being on the right track."

However, confidence came only after he had begun to submit the dreams of patients, as well as his own, to detailed interpretation, a process first carried out at the Belle Vue. The dream here has been the subject of much exegesis by writers who have analyzed Freud's analysis and then examined in great detail every aspect of the dream on which so much has been built. There are, however, two curious exceptions. In his three-volume life of Freud, Ernest Jones merely says that July 24, 1895, was an historical moment and refers to the remark about the marble tablet which Freud had suggested might be affixed to the walls of the Belle Vue. Jones does not go into the incident in any sort of detail. Since Freud used the episode as the main example of his major book, this appears odd. Even more odd is the fact that although Freud was in regular correspondence with Fliess at this period, the only references to the dream in the book of Freud's letters to Fliess are Freud's reference to the marble tablet and a single paragraph in his "Project for a Scientific Psychology." Surprise at the silence in these two publications is heightened when it is realized, as it is today, that Fliess himself was dramatically involved in the event of which the dream was one repercussion.

The story, as later told by Freud in *The Interpretation of Dreams*, is that during the summer of 1895 he had been treating Irma, a young woman who was a friend of the family. Her hysterical anxiety had been partially relieved, but there were other, somatic, symptoms. Freud had then proposed a course of action that she had refused to carry out, and the treatment had been broken off for the duration of the holidays. On July 23 Freud was visited at the Belle Vue by a junior colleague who had been staying with the patient and her parents in the country and who told Freud that the girl was "better, but not quite well." Freud detected a note of criticism and later in the evening wrote out the patient's case history, "with the idea of giving it to Dr. M. (a common friend who was at that time the leading figure in our circle) in order to justify myself."

Martha Freud's birthday came a few days later, and she had recently told her husband that Irma would be among the friends coming to visit her on that day. The case of Irma was thus occupying at least some of Freud's thoughts as he went to bed that night. The dream followed. As noted down by Freud on waking the following morning, it went thus:

A large hall—numerous guests, whom we were receiving.—Among them was Irma. I at once took her on one side, as though to answer her letter and to reproach her for not having accepted my "solution" yet. I said to her: "If you still get pains, it's really only your fault." She replied: "If you only knew what pains I've got now in my throat and stomach and abdomen—it's choking me."—I was alarmed and looked at her. She looked pale and puffy. I thought to myself that after all I must be missing some organic trouble. I took her to the window and looked down her throat, and she showed signs of recalcitrance, like women with artificial dentures. I thought to myself that there was really no need for her to do that.—She then opened her mouth properly and on the right I found a big white patch; at another place I saw extensive whitish gray scabs upon some remarkable curly structures which were evidently modeled on the turbinal bones of the nose.—I at once called in Dr. M., and he repeated the examination and confirmed it . . . Dr. M. looked quite different from usual; he was very pale, he walked with a limp and his chin was clean-shaven . . . My friend Otto was now standing beside her as well, and my friend Leopold was percussing her through her bodice and saying: "She has a dull area low down on the left." He also indicated that a portion of the skin on the left shoulder was infiltrated. (I noticed this, just as he did, in spite of her dress) . . . M. said: "There's no doubt it's an infection, but no matter; dysentery will supervene and the toxin will be eliminated" . . . We were directly aware, too, of the origin of the infection. Not long before, when she was feeling unwell, my friend Otto had given her an injection of a preparation of propyl, propyls . . . propionic acid . . . trimethylamin (and I saw before me the formula for this printed in heavy type) . . . Injections of that sort

ought not to be made so thoughtlessly . . . And probably the syringe
had not been clean.

In his interpretation Freud was able to link virtually every item
in the dream with events that had recently taken place or had been
discussed. Not all were directly concerned with Irma; thus, with the
apparent inconsequence of dreams, an earlier examination of a
good-looking governess which had revealed her false teeth surfaced in the dream as Freud taking Irma to the window to look
down her throat. The white patch and gray scabs also had clearly
identifiable links with waking experiences, and Freud had no doubt
about the conclusions at which he finally arrived. "The dream
acquitted me of the responsibility for Irma's condition by showing
that it was due to other factors—it produced a whole series of
reasons," he wrote. "The dream represented a particular state of
affairs as I should have wished it to be. *Thus its content was the
fulfillment of a wish and its motive was a wish.*" As for Fliess, he was
the friend who in real life had introduced trimethylamin to Freud
a short while before.

Yet the events which led to the dream throw a very different light
on the affair. They were revealed in 1966 when Dr. Max Schur
utilized censored portions of the Freud–Fliess correspondence in
a paper on the Irma dream. They reveal that Fliess, far from being
merely the introducer to Freud of trimethylamin, had been consulted by Freud soon after he had begun to treat "Irma"—real
name Emma—for hysteria. Her somatic symptoms were, as in the
dream, concerned with nose and throat, and it was natural that
Fliess, a nose and throat specialist, should be called in. He traveled
down from Berlin, recommended surgery, apparently on the turbi-
nate bone and on the sinuses, and himself carried out the operation either later in February or early in March. He returned to
Berlin a few days afterward.

On March 4 Freud wrote to Fliess. The censored version of the
letter printed in *The Origins of Psycho-Analysis* makes no reference to
Emma. The letter did, however, contain an opening 150-word
paragraph in which Freud reported on her condition. She had
suffered a massive hemorrhage, and Freud had called in Dr. Gersuny, a prominent Viennese surgeon. "I would be grateful for your
expert opinion," Freud added. "I am not happy about another
operation on this girl."

Fliess appears to have answered the letter by return. Freud replied to him on March 8 with a report which, he said, would
"probably upset you as much as it has upset me; but I hope that
you will recover from the shock as fast as I have." He had, he went

on, been awakened early in the morning with the news that Emma was having another hemorrhage. Dr. Gersuny was unable to attend until the evening, and Freud had called in another physician, Dr. M.

Attending the patient, Dr. M.

suddenly pulled out something resembling a thread. Before we realized what was happening, a good half meter of gauze had been withdrawn from the cavity. Immediately there was a flow of blood, the girl turned white, her eyes bulged and her pulse almost stopped. At once he packed the cavity with fresh iodoform gauze and the bleeding stopped. It had continued for about half a minute, but it was long enough to make unrecognizable the poor creature who by this time was lying quite flat. Then something else happened. Just as the foreign body was removed, and as the whole thing became clear and I was faced with the sight of the patient, I felt sick. When the packing was completed I fled to the adjoining room, drank a bottle of water, and felt rather miserable. The brave Frau Doktor [a phrase by which Freud presumably refers to a nursing sister] then brought me a small glass of cognac and I felt better.

Freud returned to the patient. She had, he discovered, not lost consciousness during the huge hemorrhage and greeted him with what he called a patronizing remark: "This is the strong sex."

In spite of Freud's constitutional dislike of the sight of blood, it was not this, he assured Fliess, which had overwhelmed him. Instead, he explained, it was the fact that *"we had misjudged her. She had not been in the least abnormal. . . ."* The trouble had been what Schur, somewhat unnervingly, has called "one of the not too uncommon surgical 'parapraxes' " (the word Freud was later to use for "Freudian slips"—faulty actions or verbal expressions caused by unconscious wishes). Fliess had, on finishing the operation, left a half meter of gauze in the wound. Had Freud been of less tough material, he might have echoed Browning's "never glad confident morning again."

In his 800-word letter Freud entirely exonerated Fliess. "Of course no one blames you at all, and why should they," he added consolingly. In a letter nearly three weeks later he was able to add that Emma was doing well—"a very nice reasonable girl who does not hold either of us to blame for the affair; in fact she speaks of you with great respect." And after another three weeks, when Emma had recovered from a relapse and was at last on the road to recovery, Freud was able to reassure his friend that for him "you will always remain the healer, the kind of man into whose hands a man trustingly places his life and the lives of his family."

Freud's wish to exculpate himself from blame for the patient's treatment, the wish which he interpreted as the motivation for the dream, was in fact dominated by the wish to exculpate Fliess. Any doubt about this is removed by four other letters, written by Freud a year and more later. In the first he says that he now has an explanation of Emma's hemorrhage that will give Fliess satisfaction. Ten days later he follows this up: "You were correct, as I shall prove to you. Her hemorrhages were hysterical, brought on by desire, probably at a menstrual period. . . ." A further three weeks on he asserted that the patient was in fact a hemophiliac and went on to reinforce his earlier claim that her hemorrhage after the operation was of a sexual origin.

Finally there came a letter dated January 17, 1897. In it Freud discussed the links between the symptoms of hysterics and the medieval theory of possession by the Devil. Then, in two sentences cut from the version published in *The Origins of Psycho-Analysis,* he continues: "Emma has a scene [in mind] where the *Diabolus* sticks pins into her finger and puts a piece of candy on each drop of blood. As far as the blood is concerned, you are altogether innocent!" As Schur says: "Meaning the hemorrhage. Now Fliess has been completely vindicated, even of having left the iodoform strip in the wound!"

Freud's efforts to exonerate Fliess from an error that had so nearly proved fatal are explicable enough. Fliess was still the ideal confidant for the ideas surging through Freud's brain; he was still the man on whom Freud was emotionally dependent. But there is one more important point. After giving, in 1900, his interpretation of the Irma dream, Freud concludes: "I will not pretend that I have completely uncovered the meaning of this dream or that its interpretation is without a gap."

Attempts to fill this gap have been made by many enthusiastic dream-interpreters who have been ignorant of, or who have chosen to ignore, the facts given in the previously censored portions of the Freud–Fliess correspondence. Their proposals have been of varying plausibility, and since Freud admits to being incomplete in his own interpretation of his own dreams they are, as Karl Popper has commented more generally of psychoanalytic theories, "simply non-testable, irrefutable." Sexual undertones can of course be discovered in the dream, and the close family and friendly relationships of identifiable characters make it easy to use the dream as the foundation for a Schnitzler-like Viennese drama. More important is the question raised by the hitherto unrevealed portions of the Freud–Fliess correspondence: by the time that Freud wrote *The Interpretation of Dreams,* had he realized that the specimen dream was linked with the exculpation of Fliess rather than of himself? If so, his interpretation has a deliberately created gap of Grand Canyon proportions; if not, the choice of the Irma dream as a reliable specimen of dream interpretation appears unfortunate.

As Emma recovered throughout the summer of 1895 from Fliess's negligence, Freud was deep in a fresh task. So far he had been concerned mainly with malfunctioning minds, with the reasons for their disorder and with the ways in which the mental machinery could be induced to work properly again. Yet his glimpses of the causes producing neurotic symptoms showed him only a portion of the human mind. It was as if an engineer, faced with an unfamiliar machine that did not work properly, had removed a small inspection plate, had discovered how to repair some cogs that were failing to mesh, yet had in spite of his success learned very little about the machine as a whole. Freud was determined to understand how the mind worked, in health as well as in sickness; only then would he be able to see the problems of his neurotics in their true perspective. But the mind has few inspection plates, and it was therefore necessary for him to conceive for it a model whose operations would account for the facts he had observed.

Early in the spring he had begun worrying out how this could be done, and before the end of April was deep in what he called the "Psychology for Neurologists," noting to Fliess that he had "never been so intensely preoccupied by anything." He was trying, he recorded the following month, "to see how the theory of mental functioning takes shape if quantitative considerations, a sort of economics of nerve force, are introduced into it; and secondly, to extract from psychopathology what may be of benefit to normal psychology." He had, he said, "devoted every free minute to such work; the hours of the night from eleven to two have been occupied with imaginings, transpositions, and guesses, only abandoned when I arrived at some absurdity, or had so truly and seriously overworked that I had no interest left for the day's medical work." The next month he was more optimistic but worried about being too hopeful, as he makes clear to Fliess when he writes: "Saying anything now would be like sending a six-months female embryo to a ball."

His enthusiasm waxed and waned, and in high summer he almost cast the project aside. "This psychology," he wrote in August, "is really an incubus—skittles and mushroom-hunting are certainly much healthier pastimes. All I was trying to do was to explain defense, but I found myself explaining something from the very heart of nature. I found myself wrestling with the problems of quality, sleep, memory—in short, the whole of psychology. Now I want to hear no more of it."

It seemed that the project had finally been abandoned, and so it might have been had not Freud visited Fliess in Berlin during September. The reason for the visit was a minor operation on Freud's ethmoidal bone. But the two men discussed Freud's ideas, and his excitement was once again aroused; so much so that he could not wait until he reached Vienna. In a long letter written after he had reached home, then gone on to join his family at Belle Vue, he told Fliess of the rail journey back from Berlin. "Shortly before Teschen," he said, "I opened my suitcase and took out some paper because I was too lazy to read and it was too early to sleep, and I thought I would write down the first draft of 'Psychology' as well as I could in the circumstances."

The intention of the project, began the first of the four and a half penciled pages written on the train, "is to furnish a psychology that shall be a natural science: that is, to represent psychical processes as quantitatively determinate states of specifiable material particles, thus making those processes perspicuous and free from contradiction." The particles postulated were neurones of three kinds. The phi neurones received excitation from outside the body but, being regulated by the principle of inertia, did not retain it. The psi neurones were excited either by the phi neurones or by internal stimuli such as appetite and instinct but, being ruled by the principle of constancy, retained some of the stimulation and were thus responsible for memory. The difference between these two kinds of sensory neurones, each kind forming its own neuronic system, lay in the presence or absence in each system of what Freud called "contact-barriers" between the individual neurones—the synapses described by Charles Sherrington a few years later. Thirdly, there were the omega neurones, stimulated either by the phi neurones, or by the body, and different from the other two in that they transformed quantity into quality and provided the basis of perception.

From these basic constituents, described in the language of physics and cerebral physiology rather than that of psychology, Freud erected in "The Project"—as "Psychology for Neurologists" was later to be known—the framework of a complex machine whose workings could explain in physiological terms almost any psychological state. "The Project" provided not only an explanation of memory but also of the process by which psychic energy could be accumulated and thus made available for certain specific actions that memory said were necessary; and it contained many ideas later to be developed within the framework of psychoanalysis, notably the primary and secondary processes to be elaborated in *The Interpretation of Dreams.*

The work was finished in October. Freud sent the manuscript to Fliess, writing exultantly: "Everything fell into place, the cogs meshed, the thing really seemed to be a machine which in a moment would run of itself."

His satisfaction was short-lived. A month later he had gone from the crest to the trough and was telling Fliess that he did not understand the state of mind in which he had "concocted" the scheme. "I cannot conceive how I came to inflict it on you," he went on. "I think you are too polite; it seems to me to have been a kind of aberration." So great was his disappointment that he left "The Project" in Fliess's hands. His own copy—if he kept one, as he almost certainly did—does not appear to have survived, and the world knows of "The Project" only through the far-sightedness of Princess Marie Bonaparte who in the 1930s saved it, with the Fliess correspondence, from Freud's desire for destruction.

He was reluctant to abandon the central idea of "The Project," and years later still clung to the hope that it would be possible to represent systems of neurones as psychical paths in terms of organic elements of the nervous system. Two decades later he was reluctantly admitting that no progress had yet been made. "We are taken a step further—we do not know how much—by the discovery of the unequal importance of the different parts of the brain and their special relations to particular parts of the body and to particular mental activities," he wrote in "The Unconscious." "But every attempt to go on from there to discover a localization of mental processes, every endeavor to think of ideas as stored up in nerve cells and of excitations as traveling along nerve fibers, has miscarried completely."

The failure caused Freud genuine regret, a fact that should be stressed as he is seen first improvising what he hoped would be a bridge between physiology and psychology and then abandoning the project. It is true that after his experience at the Salpêtrière he had increasingly swung toward the interpretation of much illness in purely psychological terms, and his fame was to rest on that interpretation. But throughout the first decades of the twentieth century fresh light was thrown by a host of disparate discoveries on the possible causes of mental illness. The rediscovery of Mendel's laws and the chromosomal theory of inheritance that followed; the effects of hormones—including those of the sex hormones whose existence had by then been suggested by Freud; the mechanism of the nervous impulse and the potentials of chemotherapy; all these were to produce, before his death, more sophisticated instruments that could be used either to help discover the etiology of mental illness or to cure it.

With some qualifications, Freud welcomed such additions to the medical armory. After saying, in 1928, that the chief defect of psychoanalysis lay "in the fact that the quantities of energy that we mobilize through the analysis are not always of the order of magnitude of those warring with each other in the neurotic conflict," he went on: "As a still hazy future possibility we may hope that endocrinology will provide us with the means of influencing this quantitative factor, in which event analysis will retain the merit of having shown the way to this organic therapy." Three years later he congratulated a correspondent who was "not among those who place psychoanalysis in opposition to endocrinology, as though psychic processes could be explained directly by glandular functions, or as though the understanding of psychic mechanism could replace the knowledge of the underlying chemical process."

All this was of course but an indication of the hope that his theories about the real nature of the human mind could eventually be explained in physiological terms. But the gap between hope and fulfillment created its own penalty. "One great enigma that has always hung over the Freudian unconscious," it has been pointed out, "is that no one, not even its author, seemed to know quite what should be its proper ontological status. Freud himself, being no metaphysician, was perhaps understandably evasive on the point. On the one hand he always insisted (after his first false start) that any theory of the unconscious must be formulated in purely psychological terms; on the other hand he never said anything to contradict the belief, implicit in the materialist tradition in which he had grown up, that if only we knew enough, the activities of the unconscious would be regarded as functions of the nervous system."

In "The Project" Freud had also begun to develop his theory that sexual problems lay at the root of the neuroses. Of the major cases described in *Studies,* only that of Anna O. appeared to be devoid of sexual content, and even at the time of the book's publication Freud may have suspected that Breuer had been less than frank in the information he had passed on. It would have been unreasonable for him to believe that Vienna was more sex-conscious than London or Paris, Berlin or the world in general, and no more than human for him to believe that his practice, where patients were encouraged to discuss their sexual problems with unusual freedom, reflected a fair cross section of the middle- or upper-class population.

In "The Project" he had begun to outline what he believed was the specific cause of trouble. "Note," he said in the letter he sent with it to Fliess, "that among other things I suspect the following: that hysteria is conditioned by a primary sexual experience (before puberty) accompanied by revulsion and fright; and that obsessional neurosis is conditioned by the same accompanied by pleasure." After sending Fliess the manuscript, he hardened up this idea which removed sexual traumas from adult life, where the layman could readily conceive their existence, however much they might embarrass him, to a childhood in which most people still found it difficult to imagine any place for sexuality at all. "Have I revealed the great clinical secret to you, either in writing or by word of mouth?" he asked. "Hysteria is the consequence of a presexual *sexual shock.* Obsessional neurosis is the consequence of presexual *sexual pleasure* later transformed into guilt."

By the end of the year he had become even more convinced, by stories related to him by patients, of the importance of sexual experiences undergone during childhood. He bluntly called them infantile seductions, adding later: "Foremost among those guilty of abuses like these, with their momentous consequences, are nursemaids, governesses and domestic servants." Teachers were also involved, as were siblings who had already been seduced by an adult, while the age at which the seduction took place—or, more accurately, the age at which the memory of it was thrust back into the subconscious—tended to determine the type of neurosis produced.

At the end of 1895 Freud still shared his belief only with Fliess. Early in 1896, however, he completed the first of three papers in which he outlined it in some detail. All were written within a few months and with a certainty which contrasts strongly with the more cautious approach of *Studies on Hysteria.* This time, Freud appears to have felt, he had at last struck the vein which would make him famous; if he had discovered the great clinical secret, he intended to hedge it round with as few qualifications as possible.

The first of the three papers was "Heredity and the Aetiology of the Neuroses," written for the *Revue Neurologique,* addressed mainly to pupils of Charcot and bringing to their attention "some objections to the aetiological theory of the neuroses which was handed on to us by our teacher." In this, Freud dropped the phrase "psychological analysis," used for the first time the term "psychoanalysis," and outlined his new classification of the neuroses. They all, he maintained, had one common source: *"the subject's sexual life, whether they lie in a disorder of his contemporary sexual life or in important events in his past life."* The idea, he admitted, was not entirely new, although doctors had rarely investigated those causes unless the patient had raised them. "What gives its distinctive character to my line of approach," he went on, "is that I elevate these sexual influences to the rank of specific causes, that I recognize their action in every case of neurosis, and finally that I trace a regular parallelism, a proof of a special aetiological relation between the nature of the sexual influence and the pathological species of the neurosis."

This, he continued, could be one of two kinds. There were *actual neuroses*, brought about by current sexual problems and divided into neurasthenia, caused by excessive masturbation, and anxiety neurosis, caused by frustrated sexual stimulation; and *psychoneuroses* which were caused by sexual abuse by an adult in childhood. The latter developed into hysteria in the case of passively suffered abuse and into obsessional neurosis if the child's role had been more active. "I am quite sure," Freud added, apparently as much in hope as in anger, "that this theory will call up a storm of contradictions from contemporary physicians."

The second paper, "Further Remarks on the Neuro-Psychoses of Defense," gave more details of the cases on which he based his theory. However, it was in a lecture to the Society of Psychiatry and Neurology in Vienna, and forming the basis of the third paper, that Freud most firmly nailed his colors to the mast. The lecture, "The Aetiology of Hysteria," had a critical reception; it was later published as a paper, largely in defiance.

Krafft-Ebing, the society's president, was in the chair, and there is every indication that Freud took more than normal care in preparing the paper for what he saw as a particulary important occasion. From his first words—"Gentlemen, When we set out to form an opinion about the causation of a pathological state such as hysteria. . . ."—he did his best to convince the audience that whatever views they might have of him, or of his work, he was a practicing physician like themselves. He led them, and he led them well, particularly when he came to his method of investigation. Why not consider it, he argued, as similar to the method used by an explorer discovering a ruined city. The explorer could question the nearest inhabitants or he could invoke their help in clearing away the rubbish and uncovering the buried remains. "If his work is crowned with success, the discoveries are self-explanatory," he went on; "the ruined walls are part of the ramparts of a palace or a treasure house; the fragments of columns can be filled out into a temple; the numerous inscriptions, which, by good luck, may be bilingual, reveal an alphabet and a language, and, when they have been deciphered and translated, yield undreamed-of information about the events of the remote past, to commemorate which the monuments were built. *Saxa loquuntur!"*

Stones talk; so, he continued, could the uncovered memories of childhood. What these memories revealed he now described, to the mixed disbelief and disgruntlement of his listeners: childhood seduction by adults ranging from nursemaids to parents, a catalogue of incidents which had been forced on his notice by what his patients had told him on the couch. Although some of his audience were impressed by his presentation—and by his archaeological parallel, so reminiscent of Schliemann's recent excavations of Troy—the theory of infant seduction was nevertheless more than they were willing to consider. Krafft-Ebing appears to have summed up the feeling of the meeting with his damning comment: "It sounds like a scientific fairy tale."

Freud had a winning manner, a natural control of his audience that the academics of any country might envy, and the reaction may have been due as much to the exciting presentation of his theory as to its content; his crime not so much that of wild speculation as speaking in terms which might be understandable to laymen as well as to doctors. Yet the president's "scientific fairy tale" was not so very different from the verdict that Freud himself was to give to Fliess on his own theory eighteen months later: "I no longer believe in my *neurotica.*" As he was later to admit, the "aetiology broke down under the weight of its own improbability and contradiction."

In April 1896, however, he was indignant that he had, as he wrote, been given "an icy reception from the asses. . . . And this after one has demonstrated to them the solution to a more than thousand-year-old problem—a 'source of the Nile'!" Even so, it was Krafft-Ebing, chairman of the despised "asses," who supported Freud's application for the title of Professor Extraordinarius the following year.

In the United States Freud received rough handling. The *Alienist and Neurologist,* stating that "The Aetiology of Hysteria" had appeared in the *Wiener Klinische Rundschau,* said that it was referring to the fact "only to condemn the absurdity of such wildly conjectural, unproved and unprovable conclusions . . . Hysteria, whatever its exciting causes . . . over sexual, grief, disappointment, or other psycho-neural sources of depression and exhausting excitation, is usually bad neuropathic endowment, dormant at birth but ready—prepared like the lucifer match—for flame when rightly struck. Herr Sigmund Freud should try again." Later it returned to the attack on what it called "Sigmund Freud's Foolish Conclusion," explaining that it had reported him only "as a curiosity of the absurd lengths to which medical men will go in their conclusions, either when seeking medical notoriety or when they take leave of their reason."

Freud continued to press on with his theory, and with an intensity which showed as much enthusiasm as scientific objectivity. It has been claimed that by this time he had a high investment in the seduction theory, that he indulged in an "aggressive pursuit of evidence to substantiate" it, and that "once generalized, the hypothesis was essentially forced on fresh case materials although it did not fit at least some patients. . . ." He continued to keep Fliess posted with supporting evidence, and early in 1897 identified signs of a psychoneurosis in his own sister. And looking back to this period in the autumn, he admitted that "in every case the father, not excluding my own, had to be blamed as a pervert." But in the letter as published in *The Origins of Psycho-Analysis*, the "not excluding my own" was censored out.

Throughout 1896 and the first half of 1897 Freud continued to collect from his patients more information that confirmed his seduction theory. It has been suggested that confirmation was closely linked with the use of the pressure technique. Freud certainly mentioned the technique in a letter to Fliess on October 28, 1895, and subsequently remarked that the "error into which I fell for a while, and which might well have had fatal consequences for the whole of my work," was made under the influence of the technical procedure which he used at that time. It is not at all clear when he finally abandoned the technique, although it was probably after the turn of the century; but he appears to have used it first in the autumn of 1892 on Fräulein Elisabeth von R., whose treatment was described in *Studies*, and any extensive use in 1896 and 1897 would seem to have been a merely temporary revival of a technique that he was, in general, tending to abandon.

"Associations which were not deemed adequate to explain the symptoms were rejected," the analyst Alexander Schusdek has pointed out. "The patients may have received some cues from the therapist. In some cases they were warned about the scenes which would emerge. These they reproduced under 'the strongest compulsion of the treatment' with uniformity in detail, until the frequency with which fathers were accused of perversions aroused suspicion. Under such circumstances it is difficult to distinguish between the relative contribution made by the patients' memories and phantasies, and the therapist's expectations."

Indeed, it seems possible that Freud might have continued to believe in the seduction theory had it not been for two things: the death of his father in the autumn of 1896 and his own self-analysis to which he turned so much energy after that death.

In June 1896, he warned Fliess that his father, aged eighty, was ill in Baden, and when he met his colleague later in the summer it must have been clear to Fliess that Jacob Freud was unlikely to recover. Late in October he heard the news. "The old man died on the night of the twenty-third, and we buried him yesterday," Freud wrote on the twenty-sixth. "He bore himself bravely up to the end, like the remarkable man he was. . . . It all happened in my critical period, and I am really down over it. . . ." Almost a quarter of a century later he declared of his father's death: "It revolutionized my soul."

Within little more than a week, the feelings that made his self-analysis so necessary were coming to the surface. "By one of the obscure routes behind the official consciousness the old man's death affected me deeply," he wrote on November 2, 1896. "I valued him highly and understood him very well indeed, and with his peculiar mixture of deep wisdom and imaginative light-heartedness he meant a great deal in my life. By the time he died his life had long been over, but at a death the whole past stirs within one.

"I feel now as if I had been torn up by the roots."

Meanwhile, throughout the winter of 1896 and the spring of 1897, he clung on to the seduction theory. "Not long ago," he wrote to Fliess on May 31, "I dreamt that I was feeling over-affectionately towards Mathilde"—his eldest daughter, aged nine —"but her name was 'Hella' and then I saw the word 'Hella' in heavy type before me. . . . The dream of course fulfills my wish to pin down a father as the originator of neurosis and put an end to my persistent doubts."

Early the following month Martha, the six children and Minna all traveled for the summer holidays to Aussee, the mountain resort in the Salzkammergut. For a few weeks Freud worked on alone in Vienna. He joined the family early in August, soon tormented with grave doubts about his theory of the neuroses, doubts which appear to have grown as during the first weeks of September he toured northern Italy with Martha, visiting Siena, Perugia, Assisi, Ancona and the famous towers of San Gimignano.

Freud may first have begun to realize that his seduction theory was collapsing about him while alone in Vienna. The disenchantment may have started in the mountains, as he took his normally strenuous walks, not yet consciously certain of the unpleasant truth that would soon be brought to the surface. But the day after he and Martha returned to Vienna he confided his story to Fliess, ruefully admitting that the complex theory he had painstakingly constructed was without proper foundation. "Let me tell you straight away the great secret which has been slowly dawning on me in recent months," he said. "I no longer believe in my *neurotica.*"

There were a number of reasons for the conclusion to which he had been reluctantly drawn. One was that in many cases where he had taken infantile seduction to be the cause of neurosis, he had been unable to bring his analysis to a satisfactory finish. Another, he had to admit, was that "it was hardly credible that perverted acts against children were so general." Yet a further suspicion was raised by his realization that in the unconscious, fact was indistinguishable from emotionally charged fiction.

But the real destruction of the theory was made inevitable by one fact with which Freud was inescapably faced in the aftermath of his father's death the previous year. The suspicions about his father, he now realized, had been groundless: Jacob Freud's assumed molestation or seduction was no more than the figment of Freud's own imagination. The realization that this was so destroyed the last of his defenses. If he himself had been wrong, how much more likely was it that the seduction stories of many patients—the individual timbers which he had used as the scaffolding of his theory —had also been fiction.

Many, but not all. Explaining his error years later, Freud affirmed that his material at the time "happened by chance to include a disproportionately large number of cases in which sexual seduction by an adult or by older children played the chief part in the history of the patient's childhood. I thus overestimated the frequency of such events (though in other respects they were not open to doubt)." The seduction stories were of the kind, Ernest Jones has admitted, which "the vast majority of physicians would have doubted at once and regarded as one more example of the unreliability of hysterics and their tendency to fabulation. . . ."; the explanation, Freud's "well-recognized difficulty in forming an accurate estimate of personal character."

Eventually, Freud was reluctantly forced to face up to the situation. "I was at last obliged to recognize that these scenes of seduction had never taken place, and that they were only phantasies which my patients had made up or which I myself had perhaps forced on them. . . ."

Freud's honest but damaging words, "which I myself had perhaps forced on them," were followed by a qualification: "I do not believe even now that I forced the seduction-phantasies on my patients, that I 'suggested' them." Even so, it must be taken with other statements bearing on the critics' claim of oversuggestion.

In *Studies,* Freud had written: "We need not be afraid, therefore, of telling the patient what we think his next connection of thought is going to be. It will do no harm," an attitude whose dangers had been pointed out by Dr. Michell Clarke who had noted in *Brain* that patients might be "liable to make statements in accordance with the slightest suggestion given to them by the investigator." And in the more general question of the sexual etiology of the neuroses, Freud was to argue that the psychoanalyst might "boldly demand confirmation of our suspicions from the patient. We must not be led astray by initial denials. If we keep firmly to what we have inferred, we shall in the end conquer every resistance by emphasizing the unshakeable nature of our convictions."

The attitude could, furthermore, be defended in terms of therapy, as when Freud wrote: "Quite often we do not succeed in bringing the patient to recollect what has been repressed. Instead of that, if the analysis is carried out correctly, we produce in him an assured conviction of the truth of the construction which achieves the same therapeutic result as a recaptured memory." Thus the patient could be cured if he believed what the analyst told him rather than what he recollected, and it has been remarked: "We do not know how many patients . . . were convinced, on the strength of Freud's convictions, that they had been seduced." Krafft-Ebing's "scientific fairy tale" had not been too inaccurate a description, but another eight years were to pass before Freud publicly admitted his mistake.

Looking back, he was in no doubt of the error he had made. "Analysis had led back to these infantile sexual traumas by the right path, and yet they were not true," he admitted. "The firm ground of reality was gone. At that time I would gladly have given up the whole work. . . . Perhaps I persevered only because I no longer had any choice and could not then begin again at anything else." A decade later, in 1907, he still regarded himself privately as having been "made uncertain by that first great error." And another five years on he could still write of his first error, vividly confessing to a correspondent that he was now keeping his eyes "open every step of the way."

At the time, his feelings were more qualified. He had thought that the seduction theory had given him the key to the neuroses and now that it had been found no key at all, he certainly had regrets. "The hope of eternal fame was so beautiful, and so was that of certain wealth, complete independence, travel and removing the children from the sphere of the worries which spoiled my own youth," he wrote to Fliess. After the gold-staining method, after cocaine, now the theory of infantile seduction! Life was really too hard. Yet Freud was not totally dismayed. "It is curious that I feel not in the least disgraced, though the occasion might seem to require it," he confessed. "Certainly I shall not tell it in Gath, or publish it in the streets of Askelon, in the land of the Philistines —but between ourselves I have a feeling more of triumph than of defeat (which cannot be right)."

His ambivalence toward what many men would have considered an unqualified disaster was no doubt the result of his feeling that his mistake, as he wrote more than a quarter of a century later, had been no more than to give to "the aetiological factor of seduction a significance and universality which it does not possess." Some seductions had in fact taken place and in these cases did have etiological importance, even though they were too infrequent to support a theory. The error had just escaped being lethal.

The sequel to the collapse of the seduction theory has been condemned by Freud's detractors as a sleight-of-hand and praised by his supporters as an example of intellectual genius. On balance, and despite the qualifications that the sequel demands today, the second view is more easily supportable. Freud realized that if the seductions were not real but imagined, this raised even more intractable questions. For he still firmly believed in determinism: that in the mental world, as in the physical, everything had a cause which could be discovered if one searched for it long enough and diligently enough. Thus the fictitious seductions had not been imagined by chance but for some reason which had to be uncovered. Here Freud, looking back on his professional experience with neurotics, remembered that with many of them, genuinely felt fears had turned out to be the expression of unconscious wishes. Could the imagined stories of seduction, he asked himself, therefore represent both an unsuspected sexuality in very young children and a sexual desire for a parent, the memory of which had been lost to the adult mind by its suppression into the unconscious? As Freud put it, had the facts-turned-fantasy been imagined in order "to cover up the auto-erotic activity of the first years of childhood, to embellish it and raise it to a higher plane"? Was it possible that if the adults had not lusted after the children, the children had lusted after the adults? He began to believe so, and "from behind the phantasies, the whole range of a child's sexual life came to light."

9

Splendid Isolation: Recovery

> We shall not be shipwrecked. Instead of the passage we are seeking, we may find oceans, to be fully explored by those who come after us; but if we are not prematurely capsized, if our constitutions can stand it, we shall make it. *Nous y arriverons.* Give me another ten years and I shall finish the neuroses and the new psychology. . . .
>
> FREUD, in a letter to Wilhelm Fliess

During 1897, as Freud contemplated the ruins of the seduction theory, he carried on with the self-analysis that he had begun many months earlier. This operation, which marked a turning point in the solution of his own mental problems, was linked with the destruction of the seduction theory and with the creation of its replacement. It was therefore of fundamental importance not only to Freud's own development but to that of psychoanalysis, two processes which are here even more than normally intertwined.

Freud himself is vague about the details. Thus in August 1897, while on holiday, he told Fliess: "The chief patient I am busy with is myself." Yet three months later he is telling Fliess that his self-analysis only began after the holiday. The contradiction is explained by the fact that both the abandonment of the seduction theory and Freud's self-analysis were developing processes which took place during overlapping periods. Neither could be measured with mathematical precision, or accurately compared. To expect such treatment in the, at times, rather casual correspondence of two friends merits the comment on a great Alpine controversy which split the mountaineering world at the turn of the century: "We are all human. And who on earth in those early days ever expected the minute criticism to which nowadays . . . matters are, in the fierce light of completed knowledge, exposed? God help all those early authors. . . ."

Freud's self-analysis continued in a modified form for the rest of his life and was in any case not of a sort easily confined within the straitjacket of verifiable description. In fact, his best account of the process was given some sixteen years later when he wrote: "I soon saw the necessity of carrying out a self-analysis, and this I did with the help of a series of my own dreams which led me back through all the events of my childhood; and I am still of the opinion today that this kind of analysis may suffice for anyone who is a good dreamer and not too abnormal." However, he was also to admit that self-analysis could never be entirely satisfactory and that in it "the danger of incompleteness is particularly great."

It is necessary to remember that throughout 1897 Freud was suffering from overwork and was anxious about the fate of the seduction theory. At the same time, he was holding a mental inquest on his relations with his father over the preceding forty years. He knew that he suffered from a number of neurotic traits, not the least being a superstitious foreboding about the date of his own death, encouraged by the mumbo-jumbo of Fliess's numerology, which could make almost any date appear ominous. His self-analysis was therefore not only an attempt to apply to himself the therapeutic methods he was using on his patients but, on another level, the necessary process of pulling himself together that many men—and women—carry out about the age of forty. In Freud's case the outcome was to be so significant that it is not too much of an exaggeration to claim, as it has been claimed, that throughout 1897 he survived a creative illness.

From Freud's accounts it is not at all clear which of the events he records as part of his self-analysis are specific recollections, which are dreams and which are interpretations of dreams. Yet he did make some effort, by questioning his mother, to obtain confirmation of what might be confirmable, and it is ironic that he himself was later to warn about the danger of taking just such a course. Stories freely remembered by children, he said, could as a rule be considered authentic. "So it may seem tempting to take the easy course of filling up the gaps in a patient's memory by making enquiries from the older members of his family," he went on; "but I cannot advise too strongly against such a technique. Any stories that may be told by relatives in reply to enquiries and requests are at the mercy of every critical misgiving that can come into play."

Dr. Schur has added his own explanation of the discrepancies between establishable facts and Freud's reconstructions of them during his self-analysis. Some, he has written;

sound partly contradictory and partly reminiscent of the "deductions" conveyed to [him] by his hysterical patients as actual memories. We must remember that Freud had reported only two weeks earlier about his realization that his patients must have confused memories with fantasies. The realization of the basic importance of fantasies and their universal character was only gradually emerging in Freud's thinking. It is therefore entirely plausible that *he* was one of the first patients who provided him with material for this distinction.

Yet whatever the accuracy of Freud's reconstruction of his past, it contained a key which enabled him to find emotional peace and, at the same time, to open the door on to what he was to claim as his "supreme achievement, a discovery fit to rank beside that of electricity and the wheel."

On October 3 he reported to Fliess the first of the conclusions he was drawing from his mélange of dream and recollection: ". . . that my 'primary originator' [of neurosis] was an ugly, elderly but clever woman who told me a great deal about God and hell, and gave me a high opinion of my own capacities; that later (between the ages of two and two-and-a-half) libido towards *matrem* was aroused; the occasion must have been the journey with her from Leipzig to Vienna, during which we spent a night together and I must have had the opportunity of seeing her *nudam* . . . and that I welcomed my one-year-younger brother (who died within a few months) with ill wishes and real infantile jealousy, and that his death left the germ of guilt in me." The remembrances were soon supplemented by others: that the "clever woman" had been a nurse who had been "my instructress in sexual matters, and chided me for being clumsy and not being able to do anything"; and that she had unaccountably disappeared. For a forty-one-year-old remembering what happened at the age of two and a half, the "must have" is no doubt a necessary qualification, but it does suggest that the personal foundations on which Freud was to build so much should be regarded with caution.

At this stage Freud questioned his mother about life in Freiberg forty years earlier, obviously hoping that she would confirm his recollections and reconstructions. She did not fail to do so, telling him that the elderly nurse had been discovered stealing money; that Philipp Freud had reported her to the police and that she had been sent to prison for ten months. There were other events apparently described by his mother, such as the birth and death of his younger brother, and the birth of his younger sister, which Freud was able to fit satisfactorily into the dream interpretations he used for his self-analysis. But, apparently, no reference to "nudam." There are *lacunae* or discrepancies which make it unwise to regard these interpretations as leading very accurately back to the details of Freud's life forty years earlier. He was at least two and a half when Freiberg was left, apparently for Leipzig; that city was presumably left for Vienna up to a year later, and in view of the family's poor circumstances it is highly unlikely that he had not been exposed much earlier to his mother's nudity and to comparable stimulation. In addition, the Freiberg records have revealed that the "ugly, elderly but clever woman" was beyond all but a vestigial doubt Monika Zajic, a maid who worked for the family of Freud's half-brother Emanuel. There is no specific discrepancy between the "maid" and the "ugly, elderly" nurse, but certainly a hint that the fit between fact and interpreted reminiscence may have been less than perfect.

Yet this is important only on one level. And there appears little doubt that Freud's self-analysis, whatever the correctness of his recollections and interpretations, did remove the worst of his mental worries. Whether these recollections were of what had taken place, or of what he thought had taken place, no one can say with any certainty, since his evidence was hardly more reliable than that which had supported the seduction theory. Yet he sincerely believed that he had stumbled across the great explanation of mental development and, like a mountaineer with only a suspect hold in sight, had to make use of what was available.

On October 15 Freud reported to Fliess what was to be the most important outcome of his self-analysis:

I have found love of the mother and jealousy of the father in my own case too, and now believe it to be a general phenomenon of early childhood, even if it does not always occur so early as in children who have been made hysterics. . . . If that is the case, the gripping power of *Oedipus Rex,* in spite of all the rational objections to the inexorable fate that the story presupposes, becomes intelligible, and one can understand why later fate dramas were such failures. Our feelings rise against any arbitrary, individual fate such as shown in the *Ahnfrau* [*Die Ahnfrau* ("Ancestress"), a play by Franz Grillparzer] etc., but the Greek myth seizes on a compulsion which everyone recognizes because he has felt traces of it in himself. Every member of the audience was once a budding Oedipus in phantasy, and this dream-fulfilment played out in reality causes everyone to recoil in horror, with the full measure of repression which separates his infantile from his present state.

The theory developed from the Greek story, which had been part of his *Matura* examination twenty-four years previously, would help explain the stories of childhood seduction which Freud had taken for fact and which in most cases now had to be accepted as fantasies. Moreover, it was, if one looked around long enough, possible to discover supporting evidence from other sources. "The idea has passed through my head," Freud went on, "that the same thing may lie at the root of *Hamlet.*" If the Prince had been hesitant to avenge his father—an interpretation popular in Europe at the end of the nineteenth century—this might, Freud suggested, be explicable if Hamlet himself had thought of parricide because of passion for his mother. Shakespeare himself, moreover, might have been impelled to write the play by an unconscious understanding of the hero following the death of his own father. It was an intriguing and potentially very useful idea. Indeed, as Norman N. Holland has suggested in his massive *Psychoanalysis and Shakespeare*, perhaps "it is not so much that Freud brought the Oedipus complex to 'Hamlet' as that 'Hamlet' brought the Oedipus complex to Freud."

Three years later Freud publicly outlined his Oedipus theory in *The Interpretation of Dreams*. The destiny of King Oedipus, he said, "moves us only because it might have been ours—because the oracle laid the same curse upon us before our birth as upon him. It is the fate of all of us, perhaps, to direct our first sexual impulse towards our mother and our first hatred and our first murderous wish against our father."

Here Freud still retained a cautious "perhaps" in suggesting that all humans were affected by the group of unconscious ideas he was to make famous. The qualification was dropped as the theory developed, and before the end of his life he was stating that "if psychoanalysis could boast of no other achievement than the discovery of the repressed Oedipus complex, that alone would give a claim to be included among the precious new acquisitions of mankind."

Freud's idea, based at first on his own dream-reconstructions and recollections remembered during self-analysis, was that a boy's physical and emotional dependence on his mother during the first years of infancy is superseded by something stronger at the age of about four or five. "He wishes to possess her physically in such ways as he divined from his observations and intuitions about sexual life . . . his early awakened masculinity seeks to take his father's place with her. . . . His father now becomes a rival who stands in his way and whom he would like to get rid of." At this stage, castration anxiety appears on the scene, the fear that he will be mutilated as a result of the new feelings which he is unable to understand. "You will of course object that after all that is not a real danger," Freud once told an audience. "Our boys are not castrated because they are in love with their mothers during the phase of the Oedipus complex. But the matter cannot be dismissed so simply. Above all, it is not a question of whether castration is really carried out; what is decisive is that the danger is one that threatens from outside and that the child believes in it. He has some ground for this, for people threaten him often enough with cutting off his penis during the phallic phase, at the time of his early masturbation, and hints at that punishment must regularly find a phylogenetic reinforcement in him." Here Freud was drawing on views of the origins of human society incorporated in his controversial *Totem and Taboo*, as he went on to illustrate. "It is our suspicion that during the human family's primeval period castration used actually to be carried out by a jealous and cruel father upon growing boys, and that circumcision, which so frequently plays a part in puberty rites among primitive peoples, is a clearly recognizable relic of it."

Freud's parallel theory for girls, the Electra complex, was based on the assumption that they, too, began life with mother as the principal focus of interest and love. With the discovery that the male possessed a penis, affection swung to father from mother, who was unconsciously blamed for such lack of equipment.

According to Freud, the way in which children of both sexes dealt with those situations affected the rest of their lives, since the grown child had to face the task of mastering the repressed complexes of earlier years and of achieving an emotional detachment from both parents. There was here a strong analogy with the differing responses to the other traumatic situations which could produce neuroses. Reaction could come to the surface where its dissipation would result in a normal life; or, alternatively, a repression of the reaction into the unconscious could result, years later, in symptoms of abnormality. In neurotics, detachment was not accomplished at all . . . "In this sense the Oedipus complex may justly be regarded as the nucleus of the neuroses."

He did not specifically and publicly name the complex until 1910, in his paper, "A Special Type of Object-Choice." But during the first years of the twentieth century he did continue to develop the idea, which in its final stage could be responsible not only— when inadequately dealt with—for neurosis but for a long succession of features which form part of the psyche.

As he grew older, Freud hardened his views and increasingly saw the Oedipus complex as the center post of the entire structure of psychoanalysis. When it came to discussion, his attitude was distinctly subjective. Thus when the Vienna Psychoanalytical Society discussed the Infantile Oedipus Complex years later, Freud opened the proceedings "by remarking that the point is to demonstrate the presence in the child of the Oedipus complex"—not, as might have been expected of a self-styled scientific body, to consider whether or not it was present. When, moreover, the debate was continued some weeks later, he found that the complex in the case history under discussion was "obvious enough," and went on: "It is our task to establish that the behavior has only sexual motives." Even the least critical observer might wonder why the task was not to investigate rather than to establish.

Most of Freud's followers for long agreed with him on the cardinal importance of the Oedipus complex. Yet there were those who, while believing that there was objective evidence to confirm its existence, felt that Freud had given it too much importance, had stressed a ubiquitousness where none existed, or had interpreted a mainly biological phenomenon in largely psychic terms. Thus David Eder, who was to play an important role during the early years of psychoanalysis in Britain, was, he wrote, "inclined to regard this relationship in a rather different light [from Freud]. Though in the phantasies or dreams of the adult, one gets evidence of this love toward the mother and rivalry toward the father, this is rather to be viewed as symbolic of a desire to return to the infantile dependence upon the mother and the undisputed claim to her whole care and tenderness, the rivalry toward the father symbolizing the resentment at the interference with this relationship."

Another, and more serious, criticism is that Freud assumed each member of the human race to have a psychic development the same as his own. But in the eyes of his followers this was a sign of genius rather than a reckless assumption, a view with which many were to take issue. One who did so was the anthropologist Bronislaw Malinowski, whose studies of the matriarchal society of the Trobriand Islanders led him to question the universal application of Freud's theory. For this he was taken to task by Jones, who summarized the differences between Malinowski and himself in a single sentence. "In other words," he wrote, "the one set of thinkers would regard the Oedipus complex as the product of a particular social and family organization, whereas the other set would regard it as the fundamental and universal motor, of which the different social organizations are by-products."

Contemporary research, devised to confirm or refute Freud's theories with respectable scientific machinery, has had only qualified success with the Oedipus complex. To many devout Freudians it is still the Ark of the Covenant, and for them any suggestion that its effects should be differently interpreted has at least a touch of heresy. At the other end of the spectrum is the contention of the psychologist R. R. Sears that the whole idea is a grotesquerie of Freud's imagination. Between these two extremes—with the vested interests of psychoanalysis on one hand and, on the other, the critics whose objectiveness is undermined by distaste for sexual revelation—there does remain an honest disagreement.

The truth seems to lie in the judgment given after a lengthy and detailed analysis carried out in the 1970s. "Freud's persuasive sweep in presenting the Oedipal theory," say Fisher and Greenberg after a fifty-page discussion of tests, trials and experiments,

> creates the impression that it is a unified entity. However . . . it embraces a number of large behavioral areas. It covers almost every major aspect of the entire socialization process beyond the age of three. There is no one experiment or even series of experiments that can check out the validity of such a theory *as a totality*. One must necessarily investigate it in manageable chunks. This means that when one assembles the pertinent empirical findings, they fall into clumps; the grand design of the original theory is not brightly visible. The empirical bits and pieces lack the glamour of the theory as an apparently unified structure. What we have found in our search is that parts of the Oedipal theory are directly or indirectly well affirmed and others distinctly contradicted.

In fact, although attraction between a child and the parent of opposite sex is indeed strong at the appearance of the Oedipus complex, a boy's eventual identification with his father is more likely to be the result of admiring his father than of fear of castration. Homosexuality, as Freud suggested, does appear most likely to arise in families having an affectionate mother and a harsh father. Yet his view that sexual life is virtually nonexistent between the Oedipus period and the onset of puberty appears simply to be wrong.

Dissection of the Oedipus complex, some parts of which still remain plausible under the closest inspection while others invite refutation, has brought a re-valuation of what Freud regarded as the cornerstone of his whole system of beliefs. Three quarters of a century later an investigator, trying to discover whether objective evidence supported the theory, sums up an experiment as showing "in one case that boys and girls do have sexual feelings toward the opposite sex parent of which they are largely unaware. In the other example the study of dream content indicates that the Oedipal situation is a source of psychological conflict in that it regularly appears in dreams. This, therefore, is an example of where the objective evidence so far confirms the Freudian theory but suggests that Freud may have attached too much importance to it."

A similar verdict was given by the late D. W. Winnicott, one of Britain's leading child psychiatrists and a former president of the British Psycho-Analytical Society. "Direct observation," he wrote, "does not confirm the degree of importance given to the Oedipus complex by the psychoanalyst. Nevertheless, the psychoanalyst must stick to his guns, because in analysis he regularly finds it, and regularly finds it to be important. . . ." But the "fact seems to be that the full Oedipus situation is but seldom enacted openly in real life."

Modern thought thus tends to remove Freud's famous complex from the center of psychoanalysis. It remains as one of his theoretical expositions, rather curiously described by Ernest Jones as "responses to his own intellectual needs rather than assertions of general validity." But it was just Freud's constant assertion of general validity that stuck in the throats of some critics. "The real sin which [he] has committed," said one writer to the *British Medical Journal*, "is: that when he found that a certain phenomenon occurred sometimes, he said it occurred always. What we want to know is the proportion of times in which it occurs."

For those who found it difficult to take the theory at its face value, but who had respect for Freud himself, there was at least the escape route taken by the Danish scholar Georg Brandes, whom Freud met in Vienna in 1925. "I am only a literary man, but you are a natural scientist and discoverer," Brandes said. "However, there is one thing I must say to you: I never had any sexual feelings toward my mother." Freud reassured him: "But there is no need at all for you to have known them; to grown-up people those are unconscious feelings." Brandes was relieved, pressing Freud's hand as he replied: "Oh! so *that's* what you think!"

In 1897 controversy about the subject, at that date described only in letters to Fliess, still lay some years ahead, although Freud could already imagine in advance the hostile reception it would get. His imagination was correct, as he was to find when he outlined his concept, first in *The Interpretation of Dreams*, then in *Three Essays on the Theory of Sexuality* * and later in *Totem and Taboo*.

*Freud's *Drei Abhandlungen zur Sexualtheorie* was first published in English under the title *Three Contributions to the Sexual Theory*, later as *Three Contributions to the Theory of Sex* and finally as *Three Essays on the Theory of Sexuality*.

Meanwhile he pressed on with his self-analysis and, at the same time, with his investigation of what he saw as the importance of dreams. What he did not do, rather surprisingly, was publicly to renounce the seduction theory. He had admitted his error to Fliess in the most uncompromising terms, yet he continued to make no mention of it in his writings. The Viennese medical establishment was thus allowed to go on believing that the theory, the discovery as important as finding the "source of the Nile," still played a key part in Freud's beliefs about the etiology of the neuroses. Not until 1905, in his *Three Essays on the Theory of Sexuality,* did he publicly abandon it, and even then in such an ambiguous way that the psychiatrist Emil Kraepelin showed four years later in the eighth edition of his textbook that he believed Freud still adhered to the theory. For eight years he thus allowed himself to carry the burden of a "fairy tale" in which even he no longer believed. Without it, the opposition about which he felt so keenly might well have been less.

Freud's failure publicly to admit his first "great error" can be explained by his formulation of the Oedipus complex so soon afterward, by the special importance he attached to sexuality itself, and by his constitutional reluctance to give an inch on such sacred ground. He believed sexuality to hold the key to the neuroses. He was impatient of society's unwillingness to face unpleasant truths and contemptuous of its hypocrisy, which cloaked the subject in Vienna as in Victorian Britain, Calvinist Switzerland or the God-fearing homes of New England. In the mind of society, as in Newton's physics, every force produces its counterforce, and the reaction of the 1890s to Freud's concept of infantile sexuality was particularly strong. Yet the effect was merely to increase his reluctance to admit the error until the time was ready for slipping the Oedipus complex into the gap and thus leaving undiminished the importance of sexuality. When he spoke of this importance, Carl Jung was to write after his first meeting with Freud only a few years later, "his tone became urgent, almost anxious, and all signs of his normally critical and sceptical manner vanished. A strange, deeply moved expression came over his face, the cause of which I was at a loss to understand. I had a strong intuition that for him sexuality was a sort of numinosum [divine presence]." Jung is by no means an impartial witness, but there is little reason to doubt his report of Freud's statement in 1910. "I can still recall vividly how [he] said to me, 'My dear Jung, promise me never to abandon the sexual theory. That is the most essential thing of all. You see, we must make a dogma of it, an unshakable bulwark!'"

The belief that the neuroses were directly connected with infantile sexuality—at first by the subsequently abandoned seduction theory, later through inadequate handling of the Oedipus complex —had by the last years of the century been steadily reinforced in Freud's mind by another: that in excavating the hidden causes of neuroses the interpretation of dreams was a tool of unexpected value. He himself dreamed regularly and vividly, and soon after becoming engaged had written to Martha, "I have such unruly dreams. I never dream about matters that have occupied me during the day, only of such themes as were touched on once in the course of the day and then broken off." He was already recording his dreams in a notebook but apparently decided to burn it in one of his destructive orgies, probably that referred to in his letter to Martha before their marriage.

There was also the influence of Theodor Gomperz, who had commissioned his translation of a volume of Mill. It appears to have been soon after this that Freud, as he later wrote, "heard from [Gomperz] the first remarks about the role played by dreams in the psychic life of primitive men—something that has preoccupied me so intensively ever since."

Freud has described a part of his own dream-analysis in a foot-note to *Studies on Hysteria.* "For several weeks," he wrote there,

I found myself obliged to exchange my usual bed for a harder one, in which I had more numerous or more vivid dreams, or in which, it may be, I was unable to reach the normal depth of sleep. In the first quarter of an hour after waking I remembered all the dreams I had had during the night, and I took the trouble to write them down and try to solve them. I succeeded in tracing all these dreams back to two factors: (1) to the necessity for working out any ideas which I had only dwelt upon cursorily during the day—which had only been touched upon and not finally dealt with; and (2) to the compulsion to link together any ideas that might be present in the same state of consciousness. The senseless and contradictory character of the dreams could be traced back to the uncontrolled ascendancy of this latter factor.

Once again he was to emphasize that he had not been seeking what he found, but had discovered it through the pressure of external evidence. "My desire for knowledge," he later wrote, "had not at the start been directed towards understanding dreams. I do not know of any outside influence which drew my interest to them or inspired me with any helpful expectations." But his conviction that dreams were something more than a meaningless jumble of inexplicable sleeping experiences had been encouraged by his detailed analysis of the Irma dream, and reinforced when he used the method in his own self-analysis. The idea was not entirely new. Friedrich Leopold von Hardenberg, known as Novalis, had a century earlier maintained that dreams comprised more than streams of disconnected nonsense. Gotthilf Heinrich von Schubert's *Die Symbolik des Traumes* had not only anticipated some of Freud's theories but had asserted that the dreams carried out, among other functions, that of wish fulfilment. More prophetically, John Hughlings Jackson, the English physician, had pronounced: "Find out all about dreams and you will have found out all about insanity." There had been many other men who had investigated the phenomena during the nineteenth century, and Freud was indeed to begin *The Interpretation of Dreams* with a 30,000-word survey of "The Scientific Literature dealing with the Problems of Dreams."

Thus there was justification for the energy that he had devoted, early in his practice, to collecting the dreams of his patients, of his colleagues and of himself. The climax had come with the dream of Irma's injection, which he was to record as the "specimen dream." "When, after passing through a narrow defile, we suddenly emerge upon a piece of high ground, where the path divides and the finest prospects open up on every side," he then went on,

> we may pause for a moment and consider in which direction we shall first turn our steps. Such is the case with us, now that we have surmounted the first interpretation of a dream. We find ourselves in the full daylight of a sudden discovery. Dreams are not to be likened to the unregulated sounds that rise from a musical instrument struck by the blow of some external force instead of by a player's hand; they are not meaningless, they are not absurd; they do not imply that one portion of our store of ideas is asleep, while another portion is beginning to wake. On the contrary, they are psychical phenomena of complete validity—fulfilments of wishes; they can be inserted into the chain of intelligible waking mental acts; they are constructed by a highly complicated activity of the mind.

Freud was to claim later that the huge book he now had in the making was finished in all essentials within six months of the specimen dream. This was possibly true of the theoretical framework, and Freud was certainly confident enough to lecture on the subject to the Jüdisch-Akademische Lesehalle in May 1896. However, he was later to state that after the book was published he realized it to have been a "portion of my own self-analysis, my reaction to my father's death—that is to say, to the most important event, the most poignant loss, of a man's life." Even so, it was not apparently until the autumn of 1897, a year after Jacob Freud's death, that he seriously began putting his material into shape. In December he gave two lectures on dreams to the B'nai B'rith [the Jewish society in Vienna] and reported an enthusiastic reception.

Early in 1898 he felt convinced that his investigation was important enough to warrant tidying up for publication as a full-scale book, and in February he told Fliess: "I am deep in the dream book, writing it fluently and smiling at all the matter for 'head-shaking' it contains in the way of indiscretions and audacities." He wanted, he said, to get his own ideas into shape before making a thorough study of the literature of the subject. Then he would make such insertions or revisions as were necessary. He worked hard but by the autumn was going through a bad patch. "The dream book is irremediably at a standstill," he told Fliess. "I lack any incentive to prepare it for publication, and the gap in the psychology, and the other gap left by the thoroughly analyzed example, are both obstacles to finishing it that I cannot overcome yet. Apart from that, I am completely isolated, and have even given up my lectures this year, in order not to have to talk about things I do not understand. . . ." But he labored on for a reason that he set down to Fliess. "I have decided . . . ," he wrote, "that I cannot afford to keep to myself the finest—and probably the only lasting —discovery that I have made."

As each chapter progressed through several drafts, it was sent to Fliess, who on occasion acted as censor. "I am reasonable enough to recognise that I need your critical help," Freud wrote on June 9, 1898,

> since I myself have lost the feeling of shame required of an author. So this dream is condemned. However, now that sentence has been passed, I would like to shed a tear for it. I confess that I regret its absence and that I cannot hope to find a better one as a substitute. You must know that a beautiful dream and no indiscretion do not go together. At least write me to which topic you took exception, and where you feared an attack by a malicious critic. Was it my anxiety, or Martha, or the *Dalles* [a Jewish word for poverty, frequently used colloquially by Viennese Jews] or my being without a fatherland? (Please let me know) so I can omit the topic you designate in a substitute dream, because I can have dreams like that to order. . . .

Later he again referred to censorship by Fliess. "The gap made by the big dream you took out is to be filled by a small collection —(innocent and absurd dreams, calculations and speeches in dreams, affects in dreams)," he wrote. "Real revision will only be required for the last, psychological chapter. . . ."

The big dream that Fliess had taken out does not appear to have been the Irma dream that had been brought about by Fliess's incompetence, since this was to be included and interpreted with the ingenious, if unconscious, transmogrification of Fliess's role; however, the possibility cannot be excluded that Freud had originally included it in a rather different form. Since he was vague about the fate of Fliess's letters to him—"I don't know till this very day whether I destroyed them, or only hid them ingeniously," he wrote in 1937—and since Freud's letters to Fliess have been published only in bowdlerized form, the riddle of this part of the Fliess censorship remains.

Throughout the summer of 1899, as the family was spending its holiday at Riemerlehen, a farmhouse on the outskirts of Berchtesgaden, Freud's zeal increased. "I work at finishing off the dreams in a big, quiet ground-floor room with a view of the mountains," he told Fliess. "My grubby old gods, of whom you think so little," he went on in a reference to his collection of statuettes and ornaments, "take part in the work as paperweights. . . ." At times, remembered his youngest daughter, Anna, when he was interrupted by being called to a meal he walked as if in a trance, oblivious of his surroundings, and years later Martin Freud wrote of his father's absorption in the book: "It was unusual for him to discuss his work in the family circle; but this was something of an exception. We had all been told about it, and he even encouraged us to tell him of our dreams, something we did with enthusiasm. He even explained to us in simple language what could be understood of dreams, their origin and meaning." In August, Freud was able to report to Fliess: "Next month I shall begin the last, philosophical chapter. I dread it; it means doing some more reading."

In November 1899—although dated 1900—*The Interpretation of Dreams* was published in Leipzig and Vienna. As motto, Freud chose Virgil's lines from *Aeneid* VII, 312: *"Flectere si nequeo superos, Acheronta movebo."* The words in Freud's translation meaning, "If I cannot move Heaven, I will stir up the underworld," were not taken direct from Virgil but from *Der italienische Krieg und die Aufgabe Preussens,* by Ferdinand Lassalle, founder of the German Democratic Movement, a copy of which Freud had taken with him on his holidays in the summer. Lassalle had presumably used the quotation in a sociological rather than a psychological context. Freud used it to emphasize how the repressed dream-wish stirred up the mental underworld of the unconscious.

The Interpretation of Dreams, its author declared, was "my own dung-heap, my own seedling and a *nova species mihi (sic!).*" It did, moreover, expand analysis from being merely a method of treatment into a psychology of the unconscious, and of its importance he had no doubt. "Insight such as this," he wrote, "falls to one's lot but once in a lifetime." The material that revealed this insight had been subject to limitations beyond that of Wilhelm Fliess's *diktat.* "The only dreams open to my choice were my own and those of my patients undergoing psychoanalytic treatment," he wrote in his preface to the first edition,

> but I was precluded from using the latter material by the fact that in its case the dream-processes were subject to an undesirable compli-cation owing to the added presence of neurotic features. But if I were to report my own dreams, it inevitably followed that I should have to reveal to the public gaze more of the intimacies of my mental life than I liked, or than is normally necessary for any writer who is a man of science and not a poet. Such was the painful but unavoidable necessity; and I have submitted to it rather than totally abandon the possibility of giving the evidence for my psychological findings. Nat-urally, however, I have been unable to resist the temptation of taking the edge off some of my indiscretions by omissions and substitutes. But whenever this has happened, the value of my instances has been very definitely diminished.

It is impossible to state with certainty how seriously the value of Freud's examples was diminished, although it is now known that he gave the dream of Irma's injection an interpretation that was, at its most charitable assessment, only partly correct. Of another example he wrote: "I might pursue the intricate trains of thought further along these lines and explain fully the part of the dream which I have not analyzed; but I must desist at this point because the personal sacrifice demanded would be too great." And in a brief, popular account, "On Dreams," he admitted that in report-ing one interpretation he had broken off his account because "there were some [thoughts] among them which I should prefer to conceal from strangers and which I could not communicate to other people without doing serious mischief in important direc-tions."

Years later, after Freud had been challenged by André Breton, one of the founders of surrealism, to explain the fact that "sexual preoccupations apparently play no role in his personal dreams, whereas they contribute quite preponderantly to the working out of the other dreams (mainly of hysterics) which he [Freud] submits to us," he elaborated on his position. "I believe that if I have not analyzed my own dreams as extensively as those of others," he wrote, "the cause is only rarely timidity with regard to the sexual. The fact is, much more frequently, that it would have required me regularly to discover the secret source of the whole series of dreams in my relations to my father, recently deceased. I maintain that I was in the right to set limits to the inevitable exhibition (as well of an infantile tendency since surmounted)."

It was perhaps this self-censorship which drove Freud to use so many of his patients' dreams, despite his realization that they "were subject to an undesirable complication owing to the added presence of neurotic features." The catalogue of dreams which forms an appendix to the book does in fact contain dreams of many patients. It seems unlikely that none of them was undergoing psychoanalytic treatment at the time.

However, examples of his own dreams, or of his patients, formed only part of Freud's massive work. After surveying the existing literature on the subject and analyzing the dream of Irma's injection as a specimen, he went on to outline a theory which accounted for the Wonderland quality of dreams, and then proposed how their meaning might be interpreted. Basically his assumption was that every dream represented a wish fulfillment which rose into dream consciousness, while the barriers holding back the contents of the unconscious were lowered during sleep. What surfaced during the dream was, however, merely the manifest content of material that had been transformed by a process of dream-work from what Freud described as the "latent" material. There were various components of dream-work, each of which helped to give dreams their bizarre and irrational character which, until the coming of Freud, had seemed to need no explanation.

Processes in the dream-work identified by him included condensation, displacement and symbolism, and even some of his critics were forced to admit that these gave, for the first time, reasonable explanations of dream characteristics that had until then been inexplicable. Condensation consisted of a bunching together or fusion of elements which were kept separate in waking life but could during the process of dreaming overlie each other, like the separate images with which Sir Francis Galton had built up photographic portraits. By displacement, a central feature of a dream's latent content—or the affects, or feelings, aroused by it—could be moved on to other and possibly trivial features. These two processes alone did much to account for the ability of the dream to transmute the familiar features of waking life into a surrealist extravaganza. There were others of minor importance and, in addition, the introduction into the manifest dream of certain symbols each of which, Freud maintained, could be linked to specific unconscious wishes.

Further, he developed the concept of two different kinds of

mental process which he had briefly outlined in "The Project." A difference in the physiological outcome of the stimuli which triggered off thought was already well-known; that is, the difference between the reflex action, when the response is uninhibited and virtually instantaneous with the stimulus, and the response which comes after consideration by the brain. What Freud now did was roughly to equate these two methods of functioning with what he called the primary and the secondary processes. The first was the activity of the unconscious mind, motivated by the instincts, uninhibited by logic or reason, a ruthless process striving only toward satisfaction. The secondary process was by contrast reined in by common sense, and it was in the interrelationship of these two processes during sleep, when the transformations of dream-work were allowed to take place, that Freud saw his working explanation of dreams. Just as important was the parallel which he saw between the workings of the unconscious and the conscious in his hysterical patients and the dream-mechanism of normal men and women. The tenets of psychoanalysis, it was becoming steadily more clear to him, could be applied to the human mind in health as well as in sickness.

Interpreting a dream demanded first dealing with the additions and omissions with which the dreamer unconsciously distorted his account; then a searching back, largely by the method of free association, for the features of the latent material. While this could consist of repressed sexual feelings, there were dreams which Freud himself agreed could be caused by more mundane factors. Indeed, he went so far as to claim that he could dream one dream experimentally whenever he wished. All he had to do was eat anchovies or olives during the evening. He would then wake up thirsty, but not until he had dreamed of drinking great gulps of fresh water.

Freud's insistence that all dreams had a cause, whether it was a sexual trauma in youth or a surfeit of anchovies, was in line with folk memory since the days of the Old Testament, when it had been taken for granted that the dreams of Pharaoh and his servants were significant. The idea had been ridiculed by educated men, a point which Freud noted when he claimed that an ancient and stubbornly retained popular belief was nearer to the truth than was modern science. Such a statement would have made any author unpopular in orthodox medical circles, even had he not been the exponent of a new and greatly suspect therapy. But Freud had entitled the book *Die Traumdeutung*. Quite properly translated as "The Interpretation of Dreams," "*Traumdeutung*" was nevertheless the word used to describe the popular fairground interpretation of dreams by fortunetellers.

The book apparently sold only 351 copies during the first six years following publication. The number sounds ludicrous. Yet perspective is gained by noting that earlier in the century John Murray had printed only with misgiving a cautious 1,250 copies of another book that helped change man's view of himself: Darwin's *The Origin of Species*. The fact that Freud was almost completely unknown outside the small circle of Viennese mental specialists no doubt limited interest in *The Interpretation of Dreams*. That he was a Jew did not help. Neither, for that matter, did his style. "Somewhere inside me there is a feeling for form, an appreciation of beauty as a kind of perfection," he wrote to Fliess while correcting proofs; "and the tortuous sentences of the dream-book, with its high-flown, indirect phraseology, its squinting at the point, has sorely offended one of my ideals. And I do not think I am going far wrong if I interpret this lack of form as a sign of deficient mastery of the material." On the latter point he was too self-critical. Yet there were parts of the book that did need specialist insight before they could be fully understood, and even James Strachey, the distinguished translator of Freud's works, has noted, "It is no exaggeration to say that much of the seventh chapter . . . has only become fully intelligible since the publication of 'The Project.'"

Yet *The Interpretation of Dreams* was rightly considered by Freud as the most significant of all his works, and it was no doubt the extreme importance he attached to it which so distorted his view of its reception. To Fliess he wrote bitterly that "not a leaf has stirred to show that the interpretation of dreams meant anything to anyone. . . . I was stupid enough to be intoxicated with the hope that it meant a step toward freedom and prosperity. The book's reception, and the silence since, have once more destroyed any budding relationship with my environment. . . ." The same line was continued by Ernest Jones, who, after briefly glossing over a few of the notices that did appear, remarked in his biography, "Seldom has an important book produced no echo whatever."

In fact, the book was widely noted, although in the nature of things reviews in the specialist journals were spread over many months. But William Stern acknowledged in the *Zeitschrift für Psychologie und Physiologie der Sinnesorgane* that the book included "many details of a highly stimulative value, fine observations and theoretical outlooks, and above all, an extraordinarily rich material of very accurately recorded dreams." W. Weygandt wrote in the *Zentralblatt für Nervenheilkunde* that Freud had gone "farther in effort toward the analysis of dreams than anyone has hitherto tried," and there were many similarly appreciative reviews. Two researchers have shown that *The Interpretation of Dreams* was in fact initially noticed in at least eleven journals, to a total length of 7,500 words. It is true that the book sold very few copies during the years immediately after publication. Yet it would be ingenuous to equate sales with reviews, and even Freud himself had to admit, after Fliess had told him of a dozen readers in Berlin, "I have readers here too; the time is not yet ripe for followers. There is too much that is new and incredible, and too little strict proof."

He was unlucky in that one of the first published notices, that in the Viennese daily *Die Zeit,* was by a writer who gave what has been described as "an ironic and malicious journalistic distortion" of Freud's ideas. "[The review] is unflattering, uncommonly lacking in understanding and—most annoying of all—is to be continued in the next number," Freud protested to Fliess. His pride was hurt, and after reading the second installment he complained that it not only failed to show understanding, "but unfortunately also no respect," a pompous response from an author who well knew he would have to fight an uphill battle for acceptance of his ideas. In this area of the popular press *Die Zeit*'s report was, in any case, counterbalanced by others. The Viennese *Fremdenblatt* described the book as extremely ingenious and interesting, and the *Arbeiter Zeitung* praised it. So much for Freud's forecast to Fliess—"I do not believe I shall get a review here. We are terribly far ahead of our time."

One review in a Viennese weekly, which found the book abstruse and unscientific, was to have unexpected repercussions. It was read by Wilhelm Stekel, a young psychiatrist then practicing in the city, and himself a writer as well as a doctor. Stekel mistrusted reviews and decided to call upon Freud. "He lent me his new book," Stekel has recalled. "I was enraptured. I wrote a long paper in two parts in the *Neues Wiener Tageblatt* and emphasized the importance of this book which was inaugurating a new science of dream interpretation. . . . Freud was much pleased and dedicated a volume to me, with the words, 'With best thanks to my colleague Stekel for his appreciation.'" The friendship was to dissolve in anger a dozen years later.

Freud pulled all available strings in an attempt to get the book noticed, sending a copy to Theodor Herzl, literary editor of the *Neue Freie Presse,* whose reporting of the Dreyfus case from Paris he had followed closely. With it went a note asking the father of Zionism to "retain this book in any case as a sign of the high esteem in which I—like so many others—hold the poet and the fighter for the human rights of our people." He does not appear to have known Herzl personally, although Hans Herzl, the Zionist's son, is reported to have sought Freud's advice on his personal troubles some while before committing suicide.

The strength of Freud's interest in Zionism at the time is uncertain, but according to a distant relative, Dr. Joseph Freud, he referred to Herzl in a university lecture in 1905 or 1907, saying that the Zionist leader had appeared to him in a dream. "An appearance filled with glory, with a dark yet pale countenance, adorned with an attractive black beard, and with eyes which expressed infinite grief," the doctor observed of Freud's description of Herzl. "The apparition attempted to persuade Freud of the need of immediate action, if the Jewish people was to be saved. These words astonished him by their logic and their pent-up emotion."

For a while Freud was annoyed by critics who pointed out what he himself called comic mistakes in *The Interpretation of Dreams;* he had referred to Schiller's birthplace as Marburg instead of Marbach, and to Hannibal's father as Hasdrubel instead of Hamilcar. By the middle of 1900 he seems to have convinced himself that the book would disappear without trace.

Yet it was not only to Wilhelm Stekel that the book had come as a revelation. Alfred Adler noted, "This man has something to say to us!" while Hanns Sachs described his first opening of *Die Traumdeutung* as his moment of destiny—"like meeting the 'femme fatale,' only with a decidedly more favorable result." But in medical circles, as well as among the general public, interest continued slight and acceptance slow, and not until 1909, after psychoanalysis had begun to make its mark, was a second edition needed. Freud even then still felt it necessary to write in a new preface: "My psychiatric colleagues seem to have taken no trouble to overcome the initial bewilderment created by my new approach to dreams." Two years later, as a third German edition appeared, *Die Traumdeutung* received a major accolade from Havelock Ellis, who in *The World of Dreams* said that Freud's book had been written "by one of the profoundest of living investigators into the obscure depths of the human soul. Even if one rejects Freud's methods as unsatisfactory, and his facts as unproved, the work of one so bold and so sincere cannot fail to be helpful and stimulating in the highest degree. If it is not the truth, it will at least help us to reach the truth." The rub here was that by 1911 Freud and his followers were tending to claim that they had reached the truth itself.

In subsequent editions Freud added new material and—in contrast to conventional claims made against him—continued to revise his theories, at least in points of detail. Nevertheless, criticism continued, and as late as 1921 he found it necessary to write in the preface to the sixth edition: "If its earlier function was to offer some information on the nature of dreams, now it has the no less important duty of dealing with the obstinate misunderstandings to which that information is subject." Criticism centered on two things. One was the absolute nature of his claims. His first sentence had stated: "In the pages that follow I shall bring forward proof that there is a psychological technique which makes it possible to interpret dreams . . ." The word "proof" was unfortunate and may have played a part in persuading the reviewer of the English-language edition in *The Nation* to object that the psychologist must see in the book "the building of a huge structure upon a very slim and unstable foundation" and that the author portrayed himself in it "as one whose scientific judgment cannot be trusted, [which] must lead even his most enthusiastic followers to question whether they are not overestimating the value of his work in other directions." A second point was raised by W. H. R. Rivers, the English psychiatrist who not only accepted much of Freud's dream-theory but who during the First World War was among the first to use dream-interpretation in the psychological rehabilitation of war-wounded. One of Freud's rules was that only the analyst, studying the dream as a whole, could decide whether a given element in it was to be interpreted in one fashion or in its opposite. "Such a method," wrote Rivers, "would reduce any other science to an absurdity, and doubts must be raised whether psychology can have methods of its own which would make it necessary to separate it from all other sciences and put it in a distinct category."

The points are valid. Nevertheless, it is difficult not to believe that even when Rivers was writing in the early 1920s, some residue of the early feelings about Freud's attitude to sexuality still colored opinion. This certainly comes through in the preface to Rivers' own book on dreams, written by G. Elliot Smith, who, after saying that Rivers' attitude modifies Freud, adds, "Not only does it prune from the method of the psychoanalytic school of dream-interpretation most of the repulsive excrescences that have brought upon it so much odium, but it introduces for the first time principles of logic and consistency and a closer connection with reality."

Almost eighty years after the publication of *The Interpretation of Dreams*, less importance is paid to the "repulsive excrescences" and more to the genuine modifications which have altered some of its conclusions. The manifest content has been claimed to be as important as the latent; the belief that all dreams are examples of wish fulfillment, modified by Freud himself in 1920, has been shown as oversimplistic; and symbolization is now realized to have

SPLENDID ISOLATION: RECOVERY [185]

an application less universal than Freud imagined. More fundamental is the remark of Bertrand Russell in *Human Knowledge: Its Scope and Limits.* "To attempt—as Freud did—to make a science of dreams is a mistake," he has declared; "we cannot know what a man dreams, but only what he says he dreams. What he says he dreams is part of physics, since the saying consists of movements of lips and tongue and throat; but it is a wanton assumption to suppose that what he says in professing to relate his dream expresses an actual experience."

Freud's own feelings have been rather ambivalent. In 1933 he admitted that the associations in which dream-thoughts are contained often came to a stop "precisely before the genuine dream-thought: it has only come near to it and has only had contact with it through allusions." He then went on: "At that point we intervene on our own; we fill in the hints, draw undeniable conclusions, and give explicit utterance to what the patient has only touched on in his associations. This sounds as though we allowed our ingenuity and caprice to play with the material put at our disposal by the dreamer and as though we misused it in order to interpret *into* his utterances what cannot be interpreted *from* them. Nor is it easy to show the legitimacy of our procedure in an abstract description of it." As two basically sympathetic analysts have said, ". . . just beneath his reassuring bravado, Freud's uncertainties about the dream-interpretative procedure come through clearly."

The one point about which Freud rarely had doubts was the failure of his work to gain the attention it deserved. Many years after its publication he claimed that in most of the literature dealing with the subject it had still not been even mentioned; "it has, of course," he went on, "received the least attention from the so-called 'research workers on dreams,' who have thus afforded a brilliant example of the aversion to learning anything new so characteristic of the scientist. . . . If there were such a thing in science as the right of revenge, I, in my turn, should be justified in ignoring the literature which has appeared since the publication of this book."

Even during the early days of 1900, as he scanned the first newspaper reports, Freud was pessimistic about the future. "The new century—the most interesting thing about which for us is, I dare say, that it contains the dates of our death—has brought me nothing but a stupid review," he complained to Fliess. "I do not count on recognition, at any rate in my lifetime."

COMMANDER
IN
CHIEF

10

Founding the Cause

We possess the truth. I am as sure of it as fifteen years ago.

FREUD, in a letter to Sandor Ferenczi

Despite Freud's pessimism, he had by the first months of the new century completed the foundations on which he was to build the multiroomed establishment of psychoanalysis. They consisted of an acknowledgment that the unconscious played a more important part in the motivation of human conduct than had previously been admitted; that much mental illness could be traced back to unsuspected traumatic events, often of a sexual nature and often occurring at a childhood age where all had been thought of as innocence and bliss; and that such illnesses could sometimes be alleviated or even cured by a new and revolutionary form of dialogue between patient and physician. In addition, there was the wider base provided by *The Interpretation of Dreams,* in which he had not only maintained that dreams could offer clues to the behavior of the neurotic but had demonstrated that his theories of the unconscious were as applicable to the healthy as to the mentally ill.

The next few years were to witness a transformation. As Freud elaborated ideas only lightly touched upon in "The Project" and other earlier papers, the practice of psychoanalysis developed; what had begun as an understanding of, and sometimes a cure for, hysteria was found to be applicable to obsessions, phobias and a host of minor mental troubles that barely warranted the word neurosis. This widening of the field had its dangers, of which not even Freud himself seems to have been fully aware. Usually cautious, and anxious to stress the limitations of what psychoanalysis could do, he was not entirely able to prevent its exploitation by supporters as a miracle-working "cure-all."

But it was not only the uses of psychoanalysis for medical purposes that increased during the first years of the twentieth century. At the same time it began to emerge from the consulting room into the investigation of anthropology, history and biography, so that years later "educators, pediatricians, sociologists and anthropologists, surgeons and criminologists [were all] to believe that if psychoanalytic theory was correct, this had important implications for their own work." Simultaneously with its extension into different areas went its institutionalization, first into a small society in Vienna, then into an international organization.

The expansion and then consolidation of the psychoanalytic empire was matched near the turn of the century by other events which were radically to change the world as it was then known. The discovery of X-rays by Wilhelm Röntgen, in the year which witnessed the publication of *Studies on Hysteria,* had led on to the confirmation of radioactivity by Antoine Becquerel the following year, to the Curies' work on radium and, a few years later, to the concept of the nuclear atom and all that that was to foreshadow. In 1900 Max Planck, walking in the Berlin woods, had confided to his son, "Today I have made a discovery as important as that of Newton": the quantum theory, which was to revolutionize physics. In the same year Mendel's laws of inheritance were rediscovered, simultaneously but independently, by Karl Correns, Hugo de Vries, and Erich von Tschermak, and the science of genetics, with its opportunities and dangers, began to emerge. In literature, in music and in art there were equally disturbing new movements and ideas, and if they can be considered as no more than items in a continuing process of evolution, they yet appeared in remarkable numbers during the 1900s. Most had one thing in common with Freud's beliefs about the wellsprings of the mind: they were looked upon usually with suspicion and frequently with contempt by all except the pioneers themselves. Thus Freud and his followers had more in common with the leading spirits of the age than they may have realized.

Opposition to psychoanalysis was nevertheless more determined and less compromising than the conservative forces that fought rear-guard actions in science and art and literature. In general the opposition sprang from the emphasis that Freud put on sexuality, from the seduction theory in which he no longer believed but which he was late in publicly renouncing, and from his theory that the sexual awareness of children began during their very early years, an idea that to many minds was a horrifying travesty of the truth. The strength of the hostility was exemplified by the man who accosted him in the street and attacked him with: "Let me tell you what a dirty-minded filthy old man you are." Freud, inured to attack, smiled and turned away. He was well aware of the situation and would later say that people treated him like a freshly painted wall: they never dared to touch him. He believed that silence was often the best defense and once wrote: "I know that my work is odious to most people. So long as I behave perfectly correctly, my opponents are at a loss. If I once start doing the same as they do, they will regain their confidence that my work is no better than theirs. . . ."

Max Graf, the Viennese musicologist who was to become a close friend, has described the attitude in the capital at the turn of the century when he and Freud first met. "In those days when one mentioned Freud's name in a Viennese gathering, everyone would begin to laugh, as if someone had told a joke," he wrote. "Freud was the queer fellow who wrote a book about dreams and who imagined himself an interpreter of dreams. More than that, he was the man who saw sex in everything. It was considered bad taste to bring up Freud's name in the presence of ladies. They would blush when his name was mentioned. Those who were less sensitive spoke of Freud with a laugh, as if they were telling a dirty story. . . ."

In medical circles he was not ignored, as he was often to maintain, but dismissed as someone who could not be taken seriously. Thus it was typical that when the Viennese Medical Society acted out a parody of Molière's *Le Malade imaginaire* at one of its parties, the quack doctor was made to say, "If the patient loved his mother it is the reason for this neurosis of his; and if he hated her, it is the reason for the same neurosis. Whatever the disease, the cause is always the same. And whatever the cause, the disease is always the same. And so is the cure: twenty one-hour sessions at fifty kronen each."

Freud himself had few inhibitions when explaining to his friends what this attitude meant to his practice. Thus to Rudolf von Urban he recounted over dinner one evening how he had been called by an anxious mother to advise on her son. "She listened outside the door to the conversation," Von Urban later wrote, "and when she heard Freud speaking about sex matters with her son, she stormed into the room, cursed [him] and was so threatening that [he] had to run in haste from the house, not even having time to put on his overcoat."

Yet although it was dislike of sexual outspokenness—encouraged by moral, social and religious taboos—that fueled popular animosity, there was a more fundamental reason for opposition. Centuries earlier Copernicus had displaced the earth from the center of the universe and begun to show it as it is known to be today: a speck on the perimeter of a vast system which itself is but a speck in a vast system of similar specks. As Freud was growing up, Darwin had taken man one more rung down the ladder of his own self-importance, demonstrating that far from being the result of special creation he was but the latest example of a long line of evolving creatures whose ancestry led back to the simplest living organisms. What still remained was man's immortal mind, his own shining sword to use as his intellect thought fit, for better or for worse. And so it remained until Freud appeared with his concept of the primary and secondary mental processes, and his belief that the first not only dominates the second in dreams and disease but even subtly affects the everyday life of normal men and women. "Psychoanalytic teaching," as it has been said, "shifted the balance of power in the human psyche from the secondary to the primary, and thus undermined the orthodox belief of western man, established since Greek times, in the priority of reason." Therefore it was to be expected, as Freud once said to his friend Ludwig Binswanger, that "there is nothing which man, according to his organization, is less able to accept than psychoanalysis." The result was that he faced the new century assured of an uphill struggle in which he would have to fight not only the conservatism of medical colleagues but the instinctive if unformulated distrust of the layman.

The apparent dethroning of the intellect strengthened the other suspicions with which Freud and his ideas were viewed, and during the early 1900s his position had something in common with that of William Harvey more than 250 years earlier. In 1628 Harvey's slender book describing the circulation of the blood had, by its dramatically different picture of a single functioning organism, undermined Galen's conception of the human body as a collection of only loosely connected organs. For his pains Harvey was called "the Circulator," a nickname for the quacks who hawked medicines at fairgrounds. Medical men wrote learned volumes ridiculing his ideas, and his practice declined. Freud was in much the same situation as he began to do for the mind what Harvey had done for the body, demonstrating that consciousness and overt behavior were only items in a dynamic system that included the unconscious. There was, moreover, one other similarity between the two men and their work which made it as easy to ridicule Freud as it had been to ridicule Harvey: the unconscious operations of the mind were as far beyond scientific inspection and demonstration as was the circulation of the blood in the seventeenth century.

Freud was not unduly worried. "They may abuse my doctrines by day," he would say, "but I am sure they dream of them by night."

In spite of the opposition, whose strength and tenacity should certainly not be underestimated, Freud continued to attract patients, particularly those who had failed to find a cure elsewhere and who came to No. 19 as a last resort. Among them was the German conductor Bruno Walter, then making his name at the Vienna Opera, who developed in his right arm what medical science called professional cramp but which he feared was incipient paralysis. "I went from one prominent doctor to another," he has written. "Each one confirmed the presence of psychogenic elements in my malady. I submitted to any number of treatments, from mud baths to magnetism, and finally decided to call on Professor Sigmund Freud, resigned to submit to months of soul searching."

The interview went quite contrary to Walter's expectations. He had thought that Freud would be "professionally interested in a possible connection between my actual physical affliction and a wrong I had suffered more than a year before." Instead, Freud asked whether Walter had ever been to Sicily. He had not. "In short," says Walter, "I was to leave that very evening, forget all about my arm and the Opera, and do nothing for a few weeks but use my eyes." He did as instructed.

On his return, with the arm apparently very little better, he was told to start conducting again, and the following conversation took place:

Walter: But I can't move my arm.
Freud: Try it, at any rate.
Walter: And what if I should have to stop?
Freud: You won't have to stop.
Walter: Can I take upon myself the responsibility of possibly upsetting a performance?
Freud: I'll take the responsibility.

He again took up his baton. He began a series of sessions with Freud, and, "by dint of much effort and confidence, by learning and forgetting," he has written, "I finally succeeded in finding my way back to my profession. Only then did I become aware that in my thoughts I had already abandoned it during the preceding weeks."

Walter's friend, the composer Gustav Mahler, a Jew who had

become a Catholic, also came to Freud as a last resort. His relationship with his wife Alma was the trouble, although his biographer believes that it is "not firmly established whether Mahler saw Freud because he wanted to understand himself better, in order to alleviate his guilt feelings concerning his attitude toward Alma or simply to encounter Freud intellectually." Mahler was racked by indecision and on three occasions telegraphed Freud for an appointment, then canceled it at the last minute. Finally, in 1910 he traveled to Holland, where Freud was spending one of his rare holidays away from the mountains. "I analyzed Mahler for an afternoon in Leyden," Freud told Theodor Reik. "If I may believe reports, I achieved much with him at that time. . . . [During] a highly interesting expedition through his life history, we discovered his personal conditions for love, especially his Holy Mary complex [mother fixation]. I had much opportunity to admire the capability for psychological understanding of this man of genius."

In spite of the respect of the famous whom Freud was beginning to attract, opposition continued to increase; indeed, it was to be expected that every fresh sign of success should encourage the enemy to extend a battle which Freud was now fighting within a context unlike that of his earlier struggles. His efforts to probe the mysteries of the mind, aroused in the Salpêtrière by Charcot, had been encouraged not only by the desire to expand human knowledge but by the hope of financial success. The gold-staining method had failed, and the rewards for cocaine had gone elsewhere, but there would be no mistake over the use of the unconscious as a new means of therapy. Then, during the period of mounting tension with Breuer, his interest in the riddles he was investigating began to change. It would be totally wrong to suggest that his ambition decreased; indeed, it had been augmented, but augmented by the belief that he alone could successfully explore the unconscious. The dedication to a vocation, which he had found difficult to feel as a doctor, began to aid his work as a psychoanalyst.

Now, during the early 1900s, this amalgam of ambition and dedication was to be fused into something even tougher and more demanding. Within a few years Freud was to free himself from the influence of Fliess. He was to make a longed-for visit to Rome. And he was to return from that visit determined to gain a chair in the university, using whatever methods were necessary. At the end there emerged a new equation: Sigmund Freud equals psychoanalysis, the new method, technique, or even science, which he had discovered.

All this took place against the background of a life made up for years of nine unbroken months of work in Vienna and three months of relaxation, the greater part usually spent in the Alps. Freud was now in his late forties, a paterfamilias with a wife and six children to support. His position at the university was still only that of *Dozent*. *Studies,* written with Breuer, had, like his own *On Aphasia* and *The Interpretation of Dreams,* created no more than a few ripples which had quickly died away, while among the medical profession in Vienna he was still regarded with the familiar suspicion and distaste. As his friend Hanns Sachs was to write of Martha: "The attitude of friends and acquaintances in general was that of pity for the poor woman whose husband, formerly a clever scientist, had turned out to be a rather disgusting freak."

Financially he was still hard-pressed. Support of elderly relatives, demands of a growing family and the uncertainties of a practice which for long continued to hover between success and notoriety combined to make life more worrying and more hazardous than his well-groomed exterior suggested. "The truth," his son Martin has written, "is that my father's respectable address and the smart carriage and pair he used hid the poverty of a man who, with his wife, found it difficult to make both ends meet."

Nevertheless, it was to Freud that many members of the family automatically looked, not only for cash as was the case in later years but for advice. Thus in 1900 Eli Bernays, already prosperous and flourishing in New York, presented Freud with a nineteen-page request for help in deciding what should happen to Freud's sister Pauline who had emigrated to the United States some years earlier. Her husband had died, and Freud was asked to adjudicate on what would be best for her: to remain in America or to return to her husband's family in Berlin. Eli would provide money for the journey and for support until she had re-established herself; but Freud was given the task of sounding out the relatives, proposing alternative arrangements if necessary and then reporting back without delay by telegram. The incident, trivial in itself, which was to end with Pauline returning to Berlin, was an augury of events to come. Throughout the following years Freud became increasingly recognized as the father-confessor of a steadily growing family circle, a human postbox to whom everyone retailed the news and who then passed it on in a stream of letters to which Martha, or Minna, or sometimes both, added their own postscripts.

This intense interfamilial activity was complemented by a personal life so unruffled that it is reminiscent of George Eliot's comment that "the happiest women, like the happiest nations, have no history." Martha, organizing No. 19 entirely for Freud's personal convenience, directing the servants with a "great kindliness and deep humanity, which never tolerated the idea that the life of a human being shall be subordinated to the welfare of the furniture," remained discreetly in the background. So did Minna, who shared with her sister the tasks of bringing up the children, keeping the household machinery running without hitch and ensuring that Sigmund Freud's wishes were carried out, if possible, even before they were expressed.

His pleasures were simple and inexpensive, as much from choice as from necessity. On Saturday evenings he would join a few friends in a local café for a session of taroc, the Viennese card game. On Sundays there would be walks with the children in the woods surrounding the city, and every other Tuesday he would spend the evening with the B'nai B'rith, the Jewish society in which he found refuge from the unappreciative outer world. "I felt," he told the organization years later, "as though I were despised and universally shunned. In my loneliness I was seized with a longing to find a circle of picked men of high character who would receive me in a friendly spirit in spite of my temerity. Your society was pointed out to me as the place where such men were to be found."

At times he found it difficult not to be depressed. "After the exaltation and feverish activity in which I finished the dreams last summer," he wrote in March 1900,

> I was stupid enough to be intoxicated with the hope that it meant a step toward freedom and prosperity. The book's reception, and the silence since, have once more destroyed any budding relationship with my environment. My second iron in the fire is my daily work, the prospect of reaching an end somewhere, solving many doubts, and then knowing what to think of the therapeutic outlook. . . . In my spare time I take care to avoid thinking. I abandon myself to my phantasies, play chess, read English novels; everything serious is banned. For months past I have not written down a line of anything I have learned or suspected. When my work is over I live like a pleasure-seeking Philistine. You know how limited my pleasures are. I must not smoke heavy cigars, alcohol does not mean anything to me, I have finished with begetting children, and I am cut off from contact with people. So I vegetate harmlessly, carefully diverting my attention from the contents of my daily work. Under this régime I keep cheerful and can deal with my eight victims and tormentors.

The cheerfulness usually carried him on to the start of the three-month summer holiday, which habitually began with the family spending the first four or five weeks in the Eastern Alps. He would then set off alone to meet friends, or travel further afield with his brother Alexander. During these breaks, he once wrote, he would not go back to the grindstone "for the sake of any patient known or unknown. . . ."

The annual holiday followed a pattern which changed only slightly over the years. Martha and the children would leave Vienna in advance for a cottage already rented in one of the more picturesque parts of the Alps. Freud would follow later, arrangements often being made by Alexander so that his brother could travel in comfort and in solitary state. His arrival, always the highlight of the summer holiday according to his eldest son, Martin, marked the start of rambles, scrambles, mushroom-hunting and the search for flowers.

These pursuits were enjoyed in an Alpine landscape uncluttered by funiculars, chair-lifts or the trappings of tourist resorts, a landscape not so different from that which only a century earlier had seen the first ascent of the Gross Glockner, the highest peak in the Austrian Alps, by the Bishop of Gurk. Freud showed that he was by no means the townsman turned pseudo-countryman, dependent on others in a different habitat and helpless in emergency. Martin remembered his father's reaction to the torrential floods that swept the Aussee district one year, washing away mountain tracks, cutting off villages and endangering supplies. "When father came down from his room one morning shouldering his biggest knapsack and dressed in the Norfolk jacket, knickerbockers, thick stockings and boots he used for forest expeditions, we were surprised," he has written. "No plans had been made for a family expedition; but when we were told that he was about to begin a foraging expedition over the mountain road, in the hope of finding villages not affected by the flooding and with shops open, we decided that he was the most efficient, the wisest and most knowledgeable hero in the world."

He was also a connoisseur of scenery with an eye for the niceties of a great view, and embedded deep within his psyche there was a compelling need for intimate contact with nature. The need had to be regularly assuaged. "At about this time of year," he wrote one June, "I acquire a notable similarity to Columbus. Like him, I long for land"—the German word also meaning "country." The longing stands out clearly from his correspondence, and it lasted all his life. In his late seventies, already eaten into by cancer, and staying in the Alps on one of his last visits, he impressed his doctor by an "enthusiastic appreciation of nature, of flowers, a meadow, the view of the mountains. It was obvious that all the suffering did not substantially impair his capacity for such enjoyment." Later still, able only to reach the suburbs of Vienna, his eye was as sharp as ever when he wrote to Arnold Zweig: "I am sitting in my room in Grinzing, in front of me the glorious garden with its fresh green and reddish brown leaves (copper beech) and I note that the snow-storm with which May came in has stopped (or paused), and that a cold sun dominates the climate."

In the 1890s lack of money had sometimes restricted the family to the Belle Vue, where he had experienced the dream of Irma's injection, and in April 1898 he had written despondently: "I should love to go to our lovely Italy again this year, but earnings have been very bad. I must economize . . ." Yet even from the Belle Vue he could write that "the evenings and mornings are delightful; the scent of acacia and jasmine has succeeded that of lilac and laburnum, the wild roses are in bloom, and everything, as even I notice, seems suddenly to have burst out."

But it was the mountains that he most enjoyed. "The first climb of the season is not easy," he wrote to the family from Waidbruck, in the south Tyrol, where he was staying with Alexander, "but the new boots proved a great success. I feel so at home in them I might have been born in them. So long as the people in the Fürichgasse sell boots like this they may so far as I am concerned stick their tongues out at their customers before and after the deal."

The limitations imposed by his heart during the 1890s had been a cause of constant nagging regret. "I have given up [mountain] climbing 'with a heavy heart,' " he had written to Fliess, ". . . how meaningful colloquial usage is!" But eventually he had seemed to be fighting his way back. "Monday morning I climbed the Rax with my brother-in-law H. as in the good old days," he was able to write. "3 1/2 hours going up, 2 1/2 coming down. Only, the Rax has gotten much higher since I climbed it the last time, at least 500 meters. My heart took it splendidly."

All this was essential to his *Weltanschauung,* in which enjoyment of fine scenery was an essential to human life. What really pleased him was the "delightful solitude—mountain, forest, flowers, water, castles, monastery, and not one human being," as he wrote. "Yes-terday," he recorded at the age of fifty-three, "after dragging my weary bones to a mountain slope, where nature achieves such a magnificent effect with the simplest props, white rock, red fields of Alpine roses, a patch of snow, a waterfall, and lots of green, I hardly knew myself."

Freud did not climb in the modern meaning of the word, but he walked and scrambled strenuously, had gone up to the 6,000-foot Raxalp three times in some weeks—once meeting the Katharina of *Studies on Hysteria* on the way—and when forced by circumstances to take a holiday in Holland could not think of anything much to do on a flat beach. There is, moreover, some indication that he might have developed as a genuine mountaineer—like his son Ernst—had he seriously taken to the sport in his youth. In 1891, when visiting Schladming, he traversed the Dachstein from south to north, climbing alone. The direct route up the south face of the 9,830-foot mountain, the second highest of the northern lime-stone Alps, was described by the Baedeker of the period as fit for "proficients" but only when accompanied by a guide. Fixed wire ropes and stanchions had to be negotiated, and while only just a rock climb in the mountaineer's sense of the phrase, the ascent demanded freedom from vertigo and strength of wind and limb.

However, as Martin has written: "Although father loved climb-ing and had a flair for it, it would not be true to say that he was a good mountaineer: he started too late in life, too late to appreci-ate what might be called the rigor of the game; and he showed the faults of all eager beginners, notably that optimistic attitude of mind towards snow-bridges, towards hidden crevasses in glaciers, to exposed ravines upon which rocks can crash and towards shrubs growing out from steep rock faces."

Second only to mountains as a holiday attraction there were the mushrooms that feature so often in his letters. At Berchtesgaden he and his children collected them daily. At Aussee he recorded finding "a wonderful wood full of ferns and mushrooms," while his report on Reichenhall, visited on a carriage outing from Thumsee, says that he had lost his heart to the place, with its "Alpine roses coming right down to the roadway, a little green lake, magnificent woods all around, as well as strawberries, flowers and (we hope) mushrooms." Although all the family was trained in the tricks of mushroom hunting, Freud himself usually found the best. When he had discovered a perfect specimen, Martin Freud remembered, "he would run to it and fling his hat over it before giving a shrill signal on the flat silver whistle he carried in his waistcoat pocket to summon his platoon. We would all rush towards the sound of the whistle, and only when the concentration was complete would father remove the hat and allow us to inspect and admire the spoil."

The obsession lasted. During the First World War he and his family spent one holiday in the Tatra mountains along which there today runs the Polish–Czech frontier. Here there grew *Herrenpilze*, among the most tasty of all mushrooms, and here Freud instituted a competition, with finders of the best and the second-best speci-mens winning twenty and ten heller respectively. But, his friend Hanns Sachs reported, only one member of the family ever won the money: Freud himself always got both prizes.

· · ·

Strenuous days in the open air were only part of the three-month summer break. Although he resolutely kept his practice at arm's length throughout the holiday, Freud did not isolate himself from his psychoanalytic colleagues or from the fight for recognition. The changed environment, the break from normal routines, enabled him to stand back from the details of his work, to think, and he was able to write to a friend about Berchtesgaden: "Literary work there is nothing but a pleasure in comparison with the hard professional grind." Even in the loneliest Alpine hamlet he ensured that letters would be delivered promptly, and one of the first tasks after arrival was to make special arrangements with the local postman.

The weeks in the mountains were usually followed by sightseeing tours, often to Italy. There were exceptions, and Martin Freud has told of the family's visit to Lovrana, the small Adriatic port then within the Austro-Hungarian Empire. "Father and Uncle Alexander naturally went further out from the shore than we children were permitted to go," he has written, "and when, as sometimes happened, they refused to come ashore even for lunch, so much did they enjoy every minute in that warm salt water, a waiter would wade or swim out to them balancing a tray with refreshments and even cigars and matches."

The three-month summer break was a very necessary counterpart to the previous nine months of concentrated effort. It helped to keep Freud in balance as he began slowly to convince first one, then another of his Viennese colleagues that there might, after all, be something in what were still regarded as extraordinary ideas. Then, as he felt that the time for the next move forward was approaching, as his sense of mission strengthened, he turned with determination toward Rome.

His desire to visit the city had for long been obsessional, and he himself had described it to Fliess as deeply neurotic. More mundanely, he also described it as connected with his schoolboy hero worship of Hannibal, a motivation to which he returned in *The Interpretation of Dreams,* although admitting there that "the wish to go to Rome had become in my dream life a cloak and symbol for a number of other passionate wishes." Certainly the city featured in many of his dreams; certainly Hannibal, the Carthaginian who epitomized the struggle for supremacy between the Semitic and the Aryan races, was one of the leaders whose example was rarely forgotten, and it is significant that in 1897, approaching Rome, Freud felt able to turn back at Lake Trasimeno, where the Carthaginian had won his devastating victory.

The natural wish to follow in the footsteps of a boyhood hero was in Freud's case intensified by his fascination with the past, aroused in the Sperlgymnasium and fed during the following years by the discoveries of what had been a new golden age of archaeology. Emanuel Loewy, professor of archaeology in Rome, was a friend who always visited Freud on his annual trips to Vienna, keeping him up until three in the morning with his talks about Rome. By the autumn of 1898 Freud was confiding to Fliess that his longing for the city whose topography he was diligently studying was becoming more and more acute. There were recurrent plans, all abandoned for a variety of reasons, to meet Fliess in Rome, and in August 1899 Freud had reflected: "Learning the eternal laws of life in the Eternal City would be no bad combination."

It was not so much the persistence of his ambition to make the visit as his failure to gratify it for so long that raises a psychological question mark. He no doubt had to watch his money, but the visit is unlikely to have been postponed so often for this reason alone, while his statement in *The Interpretation of Dreams* that "at the season of the year when it is possible for me to travel, residence in Rome must be avoided for reasons of health," cannot be taken too seriously. Once he had been, he returned many times, invariably during the season previously ruled out "for reasons of health."

Various explanations have been given for his attachment to Rome. One of the more ingenious, although totally unlikely, hoists Freud on his own theories by arguing that repressed wishes can be the opposite of their manifestations. Father Peter J. R. Dempsey says that "if we take [Freud] on his own principles, a dream that the Pope was dead could signify a repressed wish, for instance, to go to Rome. But the phrase 'to go to Rome,' which occurs so often in Freud's conscious and unconscious life, is highly ambiguous. It could mean to visit ancient imperial Rome, with its wealth of archaeological treasures, and Freud, in spite of the Punic Wars, loved and admired the old Empire. It could signify a desire to see the modern Italian Rome. But it is also sometimes used of those who go to Rome, as the administrative center of the Catholic Church, of those who go over to Rome, who become Catholics." The argument is further embroidered by Maryse Choisy, who submits that Freud consciously considered Catholicism "as synonymous with intolerance, suppression, anti-Semitism, as well as with power and protectiveness." What more natural, she suggests, than that an attachment should unconsciously arise.

This explanation, like many other vague speculations about Freud's motives which have flourished over the years, is of course unverifiable. His ambition to visit one of Europe's great capitals—

an ambition whose absence would have been remarkable in any literate man—his lifelong interest in the military career of Hannibal and in the wonders of the Ancient World, all drew him to Rome. What held him back was not solely worry about danger to his health or even shortage of cash. His trouble appears to have been that of many middle-aged men who put off the great treat of their lives until what they hope will be the most propitious moment. As he was to explain to Fliess, he had intended to reserve his first visit to Rome for the time when he had made his mark in the world; he probably knew.

He had hoped that *The Interpretation of Dreams* would bring him fame, and throughout 1900 depression over the book's reception persuaded him that he should still hold back. He felt the same during the first months of 1901. Then a change began to take place. He was forty-five. He knew within his bones that his ideas would survive. He would wait no longer. Leaving his family in Thumsee at the end of August, he traveled with Alexander, breaking his journey in Trent and arriving in Rome on September 2 for a twelve-day stay in which he made the tourist rounds, tossed the traditional coin into the Trevi fountain, spent one day in Tivoli and another in the Alban hills, and returned to Vienna, regretting that he had not made the journey earlier.

He was to make six more visits. On the second, the following year, again traveling with his brother, he went also to Venice and Naples, climbed Vesuvius and explored Pompeii. Two years later, after what was becoming a regular pilgrimage, the two men sailed from Brindisi to Greece, into whose ancient history Freud was already beginning to probe for signs of the unconscious at work. On the same vessel was Professor Dörpfeld, who only a few years earlier had helped Heinrich G. Schliemann discover the historical Troy; but Freud, gazing on the great man with awe, was too shy to approach him.

When in 1901 he returned to Vienna from his first and therapeutic visit to the Eternal City, he decided that the time had come to raise his professional status. He wanted the money to visit Rome again. He wanted to care for his family. He wanted the security of a better position. He decided to press his case for a professorial chair in the university and to use all the influence, to pull all the available strings. To "break with my strict scruples and take appropriate steps, as others do after all," was the way he put it to Fliess.

A professorial appointment would give distinct advantages, academic and social. However, Freud's prospects were not good. It has usually been accepted that his Jewishness was a major handicap, and although it seems likely that this factor has been exaggerated, it certainly did exist. His reputation as the man who insisted that a root of hysteria was the seduction of children by adults, a statement not yet publicly withdrawn, did not help. Neither did *The Interpretation of Dreams.* Yet by the time that he began to lobby seriously for a professorial chair, Freud had already staked out a claim that lifted his views on the importance of the unconscious out of abnormal psychology into the realm of everyday life. To some limited extent the dream book had done this, although the fact that dreams formed part of most people's normal lives was offset by the fairground implications of its title and by its emphasis on sex.

More important in demonstrating the wider applications of his theories was a lengthy two-part paper which had been published in the July and August 1901 issues of *Monatsschrift für Psychiatrie und Neurologie.* To be expanded later into *The Psychopathology of Everyday Life,* it linked unconscious motivations to the day-to-day events of ordinary life. It finally struck down the barrier separating the normal from the pathological and, however questionable some of the examples it cited, showed the unconscious to be a factor in the lives of the healthy as well as of the sick. The "Freudian slip," with which the book was so largely concerned, had come to stay.

The idea was not new. Karl Kraus filled the odd corner of some issues of the iconoclastic *Die Fackel* with misprints claimed to show that the typesetter had unconsciously revealed a writer's real thoughts. Goethe had years earlier maintained that while some of the slips made by his secretary had an overt explanation, others were due to unconscious motives; and more than one psychologist had by the 1900s begun to investigate slips of the tongue. Freud's achievement was more ambitious: the description of a machinery whose workings accounted for all manner of human errors, both oral and written.

The first sections of his paper analyzed a number of events covered by "parapraxes," a word produced as a fresh translation of the German *Fehlleistung* or "blunder." "By parapraxes, then," Freud wrote, "I understand the occurrence in healthy and normal people of such events as forgetting words and names that are normally familiar to one, forgetting what one intends to do, making slips of the tongue and pen, misreading, mislaying things and being unable to find them, losing things, making mistakes against one's better knowledge, and certain habitual gestures and movements. . . ."

His first suspicion that slips of this kind were not attributable to chance had come a few years earlier when he was, as he told Fliess, getting bored at Aussee. He had, he said, been trying to remember the name of a poet which he believed ended in "au," perhaps Lindau or Feldau. He could think of the first name, Julius, but the surname escaped him until, after a short period of self-analysis, he realized that it was Mosen. He wrote that he was "able to prove . . . that [he] had repressed the name Mosen because of certain associations." Today, using his methods, one must ask if they concerned Frau Moser, the richest woman in Europe. Furthermore, he went on, material from his childhood had played a part in the repression, while the substitute names that occurred to him had arisen from both groups of material.

The following month he told Fliess that he had explained another example, and this time went into details. In a train from Ragusa to a town in Herzegovina he had asked a fellow-traveler whether he had ever seen the magnificent frescoes in Orvieto Cathedral. About to name the artist, he found himself thinking of Botticelli or Boltraffio, but knew that neither name was correct. Only later was he told that the artist was Signorelli, a name as well known to him as either of the other two.

His explanation for the lapse of memory was that just before the subject of Orvieto cropped up there had been talk of the customs of the Turks in Bosnia and Herzegovina. He knew how great a value they put on sexual enjoyment but did not wish to discuss this with a stranger. The subject was therefore repressed into the unconscious where, Freud's explanation went on, it joined his memories of a patient in the Tyrolean village of Trafoi who had recently committed suicide on account of a sexual disorder. The "Signor" of Signorelli was linked through the German "Herr" with Freud's suppressed story of the Turks and was suppressed as well. The second syllable, "elli," made with the unsuppressed "Bo" of Bosnia the name of Botticelli, while in the second instance the "Bo" was linked with the suppressed "Trafoi" to produce Boltraffio. "How," Freud asked Fliess, in describing his first efforts to explain the parapraxis, "can I make this seem credible to anyone?" Shortly afterward he attempted to do so in his paper for the *Monatsschrift für Psychiatrie und Neurologie.*

The Signorelli example was rather too complicated to be easily convincing to laymen. Freud, in *The Psychopathology of Everyday Life,* therefore illustrated with many simpler examples the theory that "when someone makes a slip of the tongue it is not chance, nor difficulty in articulation either, nor similarity in sound that is responsible; but that in every case a disturbing group of ideas—a complex—can be brought to light which alters the meaning of the intended speech under the guise of an apparent slip of the tongue." Mental slips were thus the end product of a chain of events, each related to its predecessor as certainly as the successive stages of a chemical transformation or the interactions of Newtonian physics. To that extent, Freud himself admitted, the theory "contributed towards circumscribing the field of mental free will." But this chain of unsuspected events existing in the unconscious could only be uncovered by analysis.

Once the possibility had been established of linking such slips with concealed motives analysts lost no time in looking for links. A. A. Brill, who was to translate *The Psychopathology of Everyday Life* into English, has described the mood of the search for parapraxes that enlivened the psychoanalytic world during the first decade of the century:

> We made no scruples, for instance, of asking a man at table why he did not use his spoon in the proper way, or why he did such and such a thing in such and such a manner. It was impossible for one to show any degree of hesitation or make some abrupt pause in speaking without at once being called to account. We had to keep ourselves well in hand, ever ready and alert, for there was no telling when and where there would be a new attack. We had to explain why we whistled or hummed some particular tune or why we made some slip in talking or some mistake in writing. But we were glad to do this if for no other reason than to learn to face the truth.

While many of Freud's statements about parapraxes were accepted, critics pointed out that some slips could be explained more simply. In reviewing the book in the *Journal of Mental Science*, Havelock Ellis had reservations as well as praise. "I go to a locked drawer and automatically select from the bunch the wrong key," he wrote. "There is a reason for that wrong selection. But the reason is not, as Freud might be inclined to suppose, any secret emotion or desire, sexual or other; the wrong key I have automatically selected simply happens to be the key that I have lately most frequently required—that is to say my action has been determined by the general tendency of nervous action to flow in the direction of least resistance, in the channel formed by habit."

There was the case cited by Freud in which a father told the registrar that the name of his new-born daughter was Hanna but was then reminded that he already had a daughter of that name. To Freud, the slip was an indication that the father preferred his first-born and had not wanted the second. But critics pointed out that a father, having by habit answered "Hanna" when the name of his daughter was asked for, might naturally do the same in any circumstances and without any suppressed motives at all.

But did the theory in fact rule out simple explanations? Freud himself seems uncertain. At the end of the first chapter of the book he says: "We shall, I think, have stated the facts of the case with sufficient caution if we affirm: *By the side of simple cases where proper names are forgotten there is a type of forgetting which is motivated by repression.*" But elsewhere he appears to have forgotten the "simple cases," contending that "all" cases of forgetting have their origin in repression. Subsequent editions failed to clear up the contradiction. In 1907 he reverts to the "all" theory and writes: "The view of 'slips of the tongue' which is advocated here can meet the test even in the most trivial examples. I have repeatedly been able to show that the most insignificant and obvious errors in speaking have their meaning and can be explained in the same way as the more striking instances." Later still, while asserting that the "Freudian slip" could not occur by chance, he admitted that the same could not be said of other parapraxes.

The theory of repression is an obvious explanation for many of the examples which Freud gives. When the German member of the Reichstag, asking for "unreserved" loyalty to the Kaiser, used the word *"rückgratlos"* (spineless) instead of *"rückhaltlos"* (unreserved) he revealed the servility he was trying to hide. The Jew who has become a Christian convert betrays himself when, visiting a Christian family, he tells his children to go into the garden but calls them *"Juden"* instead of *"Jungen."*

These examples, and many others, supply ample evidence for the way in which the unconscious can move beneath the surface of everyday life, and it is a misfortune that Freud should have attempted to buttress his argument with so many illustrations that prove little more than his ingenuity. One of the most famous has been dealt with at length by Sebastiano Timpanaro in his long and detailed analysis of parapraxes. As a Marxist with an axe to keep sharp, Timpanaro cannot be considered an impartial critic; nevertheless his remarks are pertinent. Freud explains in his book how a companion, a young Austrian Jew whom he had met on holiday, and who was deploring the position of Jews in Austria-Hungary, tried to quote the line Virgil put into the mouth of Dido, abandoned by Aeneas and on the point of suicide—*"Exoriar(e) aliquis nostris ex ossibus ultor"* ("Let someone [*aliquis*] arise from my bones as an avenger!"). But his memory was imperfect and he said *"Exoriar(e) ex nostris ossibus ultor,"* omitting the word *"aliquis"* and inverting the words *"nostris ex."* Challenged to give a reason for the slip, Freud produced a lengthy chain of links to show that it had been caused by his companion's worry that he might have made a young Italian woman pregnant.

Timpanaro first offers a simple linguistic reason for the slip. It is not necessarily the correct reason and he does not claim that it is. But he does go on to suggest that Freud's "reason" could have resulted from almost any other misquotation of the lines. Let us suppose, he says, that instead of forgetting the word *"aliquis"* Freud's companion had slipped up on *"exoriare,"* "arise." Timpanaro continues:

> He would have had no difficulty in connecting the idea of "arising" with that of "birth" (*exoriare* can have both meanings): the birth, alas, of a child—so feared by him. Next let us suppose that he forgot *"nostris":* the Latin adjective *noster* would have brought to mind the Catholic *Pater noster* (we have seen that even though Freud and his interlocutor were both Jewish, much use was made in the "authentic" episode of associations between ideas taken from the Catholic religion), and he could easily connect God the Father with the saints, and—passing from saint to saint—eventually with San Gennaro [San Gennaro, or St. Januarius, the saint martyred in A.D. 305. Phials of his blood, kept in the crypt of Naples cathedral, are claimed to liquefy miraculously on certain days of each year] and the feared failure of the woman to menstruate; or more directly, the thought of the Father in heaven would have aroused in the young man his fear of soon becoming a father on this earth. Now let us suppose he forgot *"ossibus":* bones are typical relics of Catholic saints, and having once reached the thought of relics of various kinds, the way was again wide open to San Gennaro; or the well-educated young man's mind might have connected *os* "bone" with *os* "mouth" (pronounced with a long ō), and thence with the passionate kisses between himself and the woman, and with all the compromising events that followed the kisses (perhaps Freud would at this point have added one of those polyglot digressions he loved so much, on the euphemistic use of the verb *baiser* in French)

Thus far, Timpanaro appeared to have done a successful hatchet job. But there was one more possibility left, and to this he now turned:

> Finally, what if he forgot *"ultor"*? In this case several itineraries were possible. *Ultor* does not sound too different from *Eltern* ("parents" in German), and this word would have led our young man back to the painful thought of himself and the woman as parents of the child that was perhaps already conceived. Or else the wish-threat (recalling the devotees of San Gennaro) that the woman's menstrual flow must begin shortly, . . . could have become embodied in the *Ultimatum,* which is again phonetically not far from *ultor.* Or thirdly, the concept of "vendetta," expressed by the word *ultor,* could have led

the young man to think of the ill-fated St. Simon, associated with all the plans for revenge which the Catholics had calumniously attributed to the Jews in order to have a pretext for their own vendetta against them—and hence with the infanticide-abortion temptation we noted above.

Whether or not any or all of these solutions are less plausible than Freud's depends largely on faith, but use of Occam's razor suggests a purely linguistic slip as more likely. More important, Timpanaro's exegesis underlines the fact that the majority of Freud's examples, whether right or wrong, defy any imaginable refutation. So much is this so that doubt has been thrown on the very existence of the *"aliquis"* incident itself. "The question can indeed now pose itself, rather more seriously," one critic has argued, "whether the episode . . . ever really took place. May it not have been supplied by that imaginative faculty which Freud was obliged to conceal by presenting his gospel less as the evangelistic fictions of a Jewish Liberator than as the scientific discoveries of a properly 'neutral' Herr Professor?"

In spite of the skepticism aroused by Freud's more extravagant examples, the existence of the Freudian slip, with all its implications for the importance of the unconscious, had been put on record by the time he decided to take practical steps toward acquiring a professorship. The way in which he went about it is revealing both of the university system in the Empire and of Freud's determination to get what he rightly considered his due.

In 1897, with twelve years as a *Privatdozent* behind him, Freud had been told by Nothnagel that his name was being put forward for an appointment as associate professor. His supporters included Krafft-Ebing, but the Ministry of Education failed to ratify the university's recommendation. It failed to do so the following year, and again in 1899. In 1900 Freud's was the only name put forward, but the Ministry once more did not accept it. It has been claimed, with some plausibility, that a change in the university regulations, which ruled out the promotion of a *Dozent* with Freud's particular qualifications, was responsible for the rebuff. This may technically be so. But few regulations are invulnerable given the will of those administering them, and it is difficult not to believe that while a Jew might have been approved, and a man who saw sex at the root of most things might be approved, the combination of both was too much for the authorities.

Now, in 1901, Freud called on his old teacher, Sigmund Ritter von Exner. He gained little support, was told of prejudice higher up, and was advised to seek what was guardedly called "counterin-fluence." He first turned to Frau Elise Gomperz, one of his pa-tients; her husband, for whom he had translated the volume of John Stuart Mill twenty years earlier, had useful connections in the government. Frau Gomperz visited the Minister of Education, Wil-helm Freiherr von Hartel, a man sometimes accused of anti-Semit-ism; the Minister politely denied all knowledge of earlier applica-tions on Freud's behalf, recommended that a fresh application be made, and effectively brought the situation back to square one. Nothnagel and Krafft-Ebing once again proposed Freud's name; once again, nothing happened.

However, Freud, when aroused, had a bulldog ability to cling on, and another of his patients, Frau Marie Ferstel, now became in-volved. Some details are missing and appear to have been cut from the published version of Freud's account to Fliess. But it is known that Frau Ferstel, the wife of a diplomat, lost no time in striking up a friendship with the Minister. The Modern Gallery was about to be opened in Vienna under Von Hartel's control, and legend has it that Freud was granted his professorship in return for Ar-nold Böcklin's "Burgruine," a picture which, it has been said, Frau Ferstel took some months to coax from her aunt. In fact, according to Freud, the price of professorship was a work by Emil Orlik—presumably an alternative from Frau Ferstel—and Freud believed that "if a certain Böcklin had been in her possession instead of in that of her aunt . . . I should have been appointed three months earlier."

Eventually Frau Ferstel arrived in the consulting room with the news that papers approving the appointment had finally been signed by the Emperor. "Congratulations and bouquets," Freud wrote to Fliess, "keep pouring in, as if the role of sexuality had been suddenly recognized by His Majesty, the interpretation of dreams confirmed by the Council of Ministers, and the necessity of the psychoanalytic therapy of hysteria carried by a two-thirds majority in Parliament." Even so, the appointment was only that of professor extraordinarius. Freud could now use the socially and professionally valuable title; but he still had neither the rights nor the duties of a member of the faculty, and more than twenty years were to pass before the university rather shamefacedly made him professor ordinarius. Even then it failed to give him a seat on the faculty.

The appointment in 1902 involved thanking the Emperor dur-ing a special audience at which Freud had to wear his one military medal, but when the time came the medal could not be found. "His friend Professor Herzig lent his own," Ernst Freud has written, "but at the same time warned him with the words: 'You will see. The moment you enter the room the old gentleman will find out and will ask you: is this not Herzig's medal.' " However, the audience appears to have gone off without incident.

But was the reason for the long delay really dislike of Freud's emphasis on sexuality? Was it only anti-Semitism? These questions cannot be answered with an unqualified "yes."

In Vienna there were many Jews on the university's medical faculty who had mapped the most eccentric byways of sexuality. The explanation of Freud's long wait thus seems to demand some factor other than his Jewishness and his development of an unpopular theory. It has been suggested that the authorities felt he was devoting too much time to his practice and too little to university affairs. In view of his lowly position as *Dozent* the supposition seems unlikely, and a more probable contributory reason can best be explained in peculiarly Anglo-Saxon terms. Freud does not appear to have been a particularly "clubbable" man. He tended to keep himself to himself, and he was unable to dissimulate with the minor small-talk that oiled the machinery of day-to-day acceptance for many lesser scientific figures and even for a few of the great ones. Perhaps he was too serious too often, saw his destiny hanging too ominously above him or the figure of the Biblical Joseph too often beckoning from ahead. Perhaps he could never entirely reconcile himself to the sophisticated climate of medical Vienna, and thus remained to the university the German provincial as he had described himself to Minna when in Paris two decades earlier. It was an honorable enough category in which to belong, but in the last years of Imperial Vienna it must have been a factor making it more difficult for members of the club to overlook sexuality and Jewishness.

Although in 1902 he had at last received the title that increased his status, enabled him to raise his fees and, most important of all, made him a more formidable figure in the fight for "the cause," Freud's position was little changed as far as university life was concerned. As *Dozent* he had been allowed to lecture as he wished, and these lectures now continued much as before. He had a convincing presence and the knack of presenting difficult matters simply, in terms which his audience could understand. Many, coming to see the scandalizer who was now a professor, and expecting to hear a catalogue of crankeries, were first surprised, then charmed, by his air of sweet reasonableness.

On Saturday evenings he would arrive in the old psychiatric clinic of the General Hospital for a two-hour performance without notes. His black hair had a frizzle of distinction, his small beard was smartly trimmed and his lustrous dark-brown eyes surveyed his audience with kindness as well as scrutiny. "His method of exposition," says Fritz Wittels, the Viennese doctor who was soon to be one of Freud's supporters, "was that of the German humanist, lightened by a conversational tone which he had probably acquired in Paris. No pomposity and no mannerisms. There was a certain contrast between matter and style. Amiably, almost enticingly, he dealt with the representatives of traditional psychology, reminding us of the way in which Hauff's Satan genially appeals to his victim Hasentreffer [in Wilhelm Hauff's *Memoiren des Satans*] with the words: 'Come along over here; it doesn't hurt a bit!' "

Freud always spoke extemporaneously, drawing on experience and requiring before the lecture only a short walk during which he would organize the material in his mind. He appreciated how strange his ideas appeared to many audiences and would sometimes recall the scene in *Hamlet* in which the King's ghost cries "Swear" from within the bowels of the earth. After Horatio has declaimed, "O day and night, but this is wondrous strange!" Hamlet replies, "And therefore as a stranger give it welcome." With the scene thus set, Freud would continue: "So I, too, shall ask you first to give welcome to the things that here rise so strangely from the tomb of the past."

The telling example was always ready to hand. Explaining the psychoanalytic approach to neurosis, he would show a postcard of a half-wit trying to blow out an electric light as though it were a candle. "If you attack the symptom directly," he would point out, "you act in the same way as this man. You must look for the switch." There was also the occasion when one lecture turned into a seminar and a newcomer was describing an association experiment: "For instance," he said, "the experimenter says 'Horse' and the subject reacts with 'Library' [*Pferd-Bibliothek*]." Here Freud interrupted. "If I am not mistaken," he said, "you are a former cavalry officer and have written a book on the psychology of the horse?" The newcomer assented—as the visitor to Sherlock Holmes's Baker Street rooms might have assented that he was, indeed, a left-handed chimney sweep born in France of English parents. "Then," said Freud in the true Holmes manner, "you have unintentionally given the best proof of the strict determination of associations. With the example which you chose at random you have presented yourself and your field of interest to the audience."

While that audience consisted mainly of men and women studying at the university, some unexpected listeners were caught in Freud's net, as indeed they had been when he had lectured as a

Dozent. One of them was the American anarchist Emma Goldman, who while in Europe during the late 1890s had taken a midwifery course at Vienna's Allgemeines Krankenhaus and used the opportunity to attend a number of Freud's lectures. "His simplicity and earnestness and the brilliance of his mind combined to give one the feeling of being let out of a dark cellar into broad daylight," she wrote of Freud years later. "For the first time I grasped the full significance of sex repression and its effect on human thought and action. He helped me to understand myself, my own needs; and I also realized that only people of depraved minds could impugn the motives or find 'impure' so great and fine a personality as Freud."

But there were not many Emma Goldmans. Freud only slowly became more than the obscure professor who claimed that his views about the unconscious mind were applicable to the dreams of the healthy as well as the mentally sick, and even to the events of everyday life. Lecturing in the university, he would remind his listeners of the battle in Ariosto's *Orlando Furioso* where the giant had his head struck off but still went on fighting. "We cannot help thinking," he argued, "that the old psychology has been killed by my dream doctrine, but the old psychology is quite unaware of the fact and goes on teaching as usual." And as late as December 12, 1904, speaking on psychotherapy to the College of Physicians, he could say: "To many physicians, even today, psychotherapy seems to be a product of modern mysticism and, compared with our physico-chemical remedies which are applied on the basis of physiological knowledge, appears positively unscientific and unworthy of the attention of a serious investigator." If anything lifted Freud from the rut it was the notoriety which he had gained in professional circles and the reputation he was accorded among the *cognoscenti* that a good deal in his work was only good for a snigger. Beyond a very small circle he was still not taken too seriously.

Yet the situation was changing, largely due to his relentless determination to gain acceptance for his theories and to propagate their gospel among the most influential audiences that could be found. "I am actually not at all a man of science, not an observer, not an experimenter, not a thinker," he had once confessed to Fliess. "I am by temperament nothing but a *conquistador,* an adventurer, if you want to translate this term—with all the inquisitiveness, daring and tenacity characteristic of such a man." One must not take the first denials too seriously, but it is certainly true that as he settled down to his professorship, enjoying the new status it conferred, free of the neurosis of Rome, the *conquistador* began to emerge.

One of the first indications that a force was being prepared for battle came with the formation of the Wednesday Society, as it was first called. Wilhelm Stekel, the general practitioner in Vienna who in 1900 had visited Freud after the publication of *The Interpretation of Dreams,* had become one of his most dedicated followers, using the techniques of psychoanalysis, writing about them in the Viennese papers and later stating: "I was the apostle of Freud who was my Christ!" In the autumn of 1902 Stekel suggested to Freud that a small discussion group should be started. Freud seized the idea enthusiastically and without delay sent invitations to Max Kahane and Rudolf Reitler, two doctors who had been attending his lectures, and to Alfred Adler, an ophthalmologist who had recently turned to the study of mental disorders and was to become the family doctor of Freud's brother Alexander.

Together with Stekel, the three men soon afterward came to No. 19 for what was to be the first of regular Wednesday evening meetings. "On the first night," Stekel has written, "we spoke about the psychological implications of smoking. There was complete harmony among the five, no dissonances; we were like pioneers in a newly discovered land, and Freud was the leader. A spark seemed to jump from one mind to the other, and every evening was like a revelation. We were so enthralled by these meetings that we decided new members could be added to our circle only by unanimous consent." No records of the meetings were kept until, in 1906, the group became the Vienna Psychoanalytical Society. Four years later, after the International Psycho-Analytical Association had been formed, the Society became its Vienna branch and meetings were in future held in a room belonging to the College of Physicians. Even so, Freud contrived to keep affairs as informal as possible. "Once a year," Hanns Sachs, a later member, has written, "we had a business meeting which Freud opened by saying 'Today we must play high-school fraternity,' or words to that effect. Then the treasurer would read some figures and would state that the Society was not in debt. After that someone would move a vote of approbation and propose the re-election of the *Vorstand* [Executive Steering Committee], which was duly voted, whereupon the scientific work was resumed."

The Society's main use to Freud was as a sounding board. Two decades earlier Breuer had served the purpose. After the break with Breuer, Fliess had taken his place. These men had been Freud's confidants during the conception and birth of psychoanalysis. Now, as the child began to grow, and with the Fliess friendship about to be ruptured, there arose the need for others with whom the cross-fertilization of ideas could take place. Fritz Wittels, who was to join the Society a few years after its inception, has noted how Freud "had driven an adit deep into the mental life, and . . . needed collaborators who would line the walls of the tunnel with glazed bricks."

Membership of the Wednesday Society, which quickly grew to more than twenty, although less than a dozen men attended regularly, was not limited to those practicing Freud's methods, nor even to members of the medical profession. This was natural, since only a few of those who practiced psychoanalysis in Vienna during the first years of the century were qualified doctors. From the start the Wednesday Society did, indeed, attract many who would never practice at all. David Bach, music critic of the *Wiener Arbeiter Zeitung,* the capital's Social Democratic daily newspaper, often attended. So did Herman Bahr, leader of the modern artists in Berlin; and the musicologist Max Graf, a friend of Freud who on one occasion read to the Society a paper on the part played by psychology in Wagner's *The Flying Dutchman.* Hugo Heller, the publisher; educators; and journalists with what would now be called left-wing views, all appeared, as did Surgeon Major General Edwin Hollerung of the Austro-Hungarian Army.

Soon after the foundation of the Society, Adler introduced to Freud the young man who was to be his unfailing support for the next two decades. He was Otto Rank, a man who had started life by working in a glass-blower's factory. Having fallen ill, he was taken to Adler who discovered him to be one of the few in Vienna who had read Freud's books and papers. Rank, a quiet, spectacled youth with a look of a particularly discreet owl, was drawn into Freud's circle in 1905 at the age of twenty-one. At first Freud's secretary, he soon became proofreader, research worker and pupil, eventually becoming so indispensable as to be regarded almost as an adopted son. In fact he was later to claim that Freud had wanted him "to marry his [youngest] daughter, to be his heir, and continue his work."

Other recruits were Hanns Sachs, who had attended Freud's university lectures, and Sandor Ferenczi, a neurologist from Budapest who had started to practice psychoanalysis after reading *The Interpretation of Dreams.* Ferenczi, with pince-nez precariously perched on his nose, and lips perpetually curved upward in a gentle smile, visited Freud in January 1908 after explaining that he was to give a series of lectures to the Budapest Medical Association. "Now," he wrote,

I am more than ever in need of thorough instruction, since I am going to represent the whole complex of your discoveries before a

medical audience which is in part wholly ignorant and in part errone-
ously informed on the subject. While doing so I intend to bear your
axiom in mind that in order to do justice to the truth one must take
one's audience into consideration; I shall, therefore, first discuss
only quite obvious, easily understandable facts which will consequently be convincing. In any case the task is very difficult and I
should only do harm to the cause by a sudden tactless assault, and
I mean to behave at any rate as a master of restraint.

Ferenczi greatly impressed Freud, rapidly became one of his closest friends, and was to remain his first lieutenant until, in 1933, a
widening rift between the two men was closed by Ferenczi's death.

Different as the members of the Society were in their backgrounds and personalities, say the editors of the Society's minutes,
they "were held together by their common discontent with the
conditions that prevailed in psychiatry, education and other fields
dealing with the human mind." These subjects also, as distinct
from the treatment of the mentally sick, they soon regarded as
their affair. "They knew," the editors have written, "that man is a
social being as well as a biological entity. They recognized that the
relations of man with his environment are expressed not only in
his behavior but also in works of art and literature, in religion and
in social institutions. Therefore, they found it necessary to concern
themselves not only with the sick human being but also with literature, religion, philosophy, anthropology, sociology, and so forth."

A high percentage of Wednesday Society members were Jews,
a fact which was soon to cause Freud some misgiving. One reason
for their predominance, it has often been suggested, was that Jews
found it easier to bear the semi-ostracism which interest in psychoanalysis brought, since it was merely an intensification of the
treatment to which they were accustomed. Opinions of the Society
differed. Ernest Jones, the most devoted of all Freud's British
followers, took a critical view of its members. "I was not highly
impressed with the assembly. It seemed an unworthy accompaniment to Freud's genius," he once wrote, "but in the Vienna of
those days, so full of prejudice against him, it was hard to secure
a pupil with a reputation to lose, so he had to take what he could
get." The words are somewhat partial. It is true that no member
approached Freud's caliber. Yet Jones's view that all were merely
second-raters is affected by one fact: that many members of the
Wednesday Society were to abandon at least parts of the Freudian
gospel which Jones held sacred. Adler left with nine supporters in
1911; Stekel followed later, as did others, including even Otto
Rank, who had become the most trusted of all Freud's followers.

Certainly Jones was correct in emphasizing that from the early days Freud towered above the rest. He also ruled over them. He ruled not only because he was the man who had started it all but because he was now emerging as a born leader, confident of himself and taking up the role to which he believed he had been called. Like most born leaders, he could be both compassionate and cunning, far-sighted and narrow-minded, struck by flashes of intuitive insight that merited the word genius yet capable of damaging errors of judgment. Few of these characteristics, or their effects, appeared to worry him seriously. He naturally lamented the tribulations which he sometimes brought on himself; nevertheless, they did give the useful impression that he was, after all, a human being on a level with the rest of this band of brothers. Freud himself knew better. Years later, giving a public lecture, he looked down from the platform to see sitting in the front row Otto Rank, Ernest Jones, Hanns Sachs and Sandor Ferenczi. He made a graceful bow in their direction and addressed them with the words: *"Un parterre des rois* [A row of kings]." An honor, no doubt, but it was Napoleon's description at the Congress of Erfurt of the assorted princes he had summoned to impress the Russian Czar Alexander I.

"We foregathered in Freud's waiting room," Fritz Wittels has written of the Society's meetings,

> and sat round a long table. The door leading into the study was open and through the doorway we had a glimpse of walls lined with well-filled bookshelves. . . .
>
> Freud took the chair. We had all supped before coming, but at Freud's we were refreshed with black coffee and cigars. The chairman smoked like a furnace. Proceedings usually began with the reading of a paper, which did not necessarily bear strictly on psychoanalysis. Discussion followed, and all were expected to participate. The order in which we spoke during the discussion was decided by lot; Rank, who acted as secretary, arranged the drawing of the lots. The impression in my mind today is that Freud always spoke last.

As winder-up he could be critical, and often was, remarking at the end of a dissertation on chess: "This is the kind of paper that will bring psychoanalysis into disrepute. You cannot reduce everything to the Oedipus complex. Stop!" He was rigorously moral in his judgments, and after a discussion one evening over the psychological factors behind a case of malpractice concerning an analyst, sharply brought the argument to a conclusion. "This may all very well be so," he said, "but malpractice is none the better morally for having psychological origins." With younger members he was apt to keep his criticisms discreetly guarded. When one recruit was speaking at length on generalized ways of treating scientific questions, instead of dealing with the problem at hand, Freud slipped a sheet of paper to his neighbor. On it he had written: "Does reading menus fill your stomach?" However, everyone had to take part in the discussions, and when new members were reluctant to speak, Freud would urge them on with the words: "We won't be divided into an Upper House that does all the talking and a Lower House that plays the part of a passive listener."

He himself followed everything with the most careful attention. "When a speaker's remarks aroused his particular interest or when he was trying to make his own point especially clear," one member has recalled, "he would lift his head and look intensely, with extreme concentration, at a point in space, as if he were seeing something there."

When the meeting was over, Freud would accompany some members part of the way home, often stopping at a nearby café where discussion would be continued. His son Martin would meanwhile be inspecting the room where the meeting had been held, noting that beside each chair there was an ashtray, some of them items from Freud's collection of Chinese jade, and usually finding the place so thick with smoke that he could hardly understand how human beings could have survived in it.

Ostensibly the Wednesday Society was not dissimilar from the groups of like-minded scientists and researchers that have often gathered around leading figures propagating new and unpopular ideas. Yet there was in fact a subtle difference, which was to harden and crystallize throughout the years as the comparatively humble body evolved through the Vienna Psychoanalytical Society into a branch of the International Psycho-Analytical Association. Max Graf, who while sympathetic to psychoanalysis could look at it objectively, has vividly described the atmosphere in which the members of the Society met. "There was," he has said,

> an atmosphere of the foundation of a religion in that room. Freud himself was its new prophet who made the theretofore prevailing methods of psychological investigation appear superficial. Freud's pupils—all inspired and convinced—were his apostles. . . . However, after the first dreamy period and the unquestioning faith of the first group of apostles, the time came when the church was founded. Freud began to organize his church with great energy. He was serious and strict in the demands he made of his pupils; he permitted no deviations from his orthodox teaching. Subjectively, Freud was of course right, for that which he worked out with so much energy and

sequence, and which was as yet to be defended against the opposition of the world, could not be rendered inept by hesitations, weakening, and tasteless ornamentations. Good-hearted and considerate though he was in private life, Freud was hard and relentless in the presentation of his ideas. When the question of his science came up, he would break with his most intimate and reliable friends. . . .

Comparison with a religion was something for which Freud had little taste. Comparison with the military was different. He spoke of his comrades-in-arms and of desertions from the cause, a more emotive word than "movement." Military inflections give to some of his correspondence with supporters a whiff of battle order, as though his youthful war games had not been entirely forgotten. And when he later chose a "Crown Prince" to succeed him, the traditional military appointments of the Crown Prince in some European monarchies should not be forgotten. Writing to James Putnam, one of his first American supporters, Freud remarked that Putnam's name would "enlist many partisans," a word more redolent of battle than of science. His followers for some time took the same view, and Stekel claimed in the first issue of the *Zentralblatt für Psychoanalyse:* "We can say with pride that our teaching, which is the teaching of Freud, is daily gaining more supporters and marches forward continuously. . . . We feel in these days like brothers of an order which demands from each single one sacrifices in the service of all. . . ."

During the next few years Freud increasingly saw himself as the embattled leader to whom, in the heart of the fight, exceptional loyalty had to be paid. Those who had supported him formed as much a band of brothers as Prince Harry's on St. Crispin's Day, and those who remained supporters throughout the battles quickly assumed the mantle of Nelson's captains. It was not an abnormal development, but it tended to make Freud's followers different from those questioning, critical adherents who throughout the same years were debating with Thomson in Cambridge whether Rutherford's theories of the atom could possibly be true or discussing with Einstein in Zurich his extraordinary theory of relativity. The spirit of open enquiry, of following investigations wherever they might lead, whatever the consequences, was certainly an avowed principle of Freud himself and of those he gathered round him. But any changes of belief had to be incorporated by him into the received version before they could be considered elsewhere. Moreover, whatever Freud maintained in public, his flexibility was slight. "We possess the truth," he wrote unequivocally to Ferenczi in May 1913; "I am as sure of it as fifteen years ago." His "convictions of the truth of his theories was so complete," it has been pointed out, "that he did not admit contradiction. This was called intolerance by his opponents and passion for truth by his followers."

Those who modified their original beliefs, or who even felt that parts of psychoanalytical theory were unacceptable, could hardly be regarded as scientists holding unorthodox views: "traitors" seemed a far more suitable word, and the annals of psychoanalysis are littered with examples of high-minded virulence. Jung, who was later to be cast into outer darkness, wrote of a lapsed supporter that "Everyone here"—Zurich, that is,—"is staggered by the incredible megalomania of this miserable pen-pusher." Freud himself reserved most of his bitterness for Jung's defection but could nevertheless use scathing terms for other comrades who had dared to disagree. Thus Morton Prince, the American, was "really . . . an arrogant ass, who would be conspicuous even in our menagerie." Magnus Hirschfeld, who had left the ranks, was "No great loss . . . a flabby, unappetizing fellow, absolutely incapable of learning anything." As for Adler, the first of the defectors—"highly intelligent . . . but . . . paranoid," according to Freud—he was merely the leader of "the Adlerian buffoons."

As the belief that those who were not with him were either fools or traitors, or possibly both, was gaining ground, there came Freud's final break with Fliess. Each man's need for the other had already grown less, and the friendship would have disintegrated slowly had it not disappeared more quickly beneath a torrent of recrimination.

Their relationship had passed through three phases, each of which had gradually merged into the next. The links between the two men had been strong from their first meeting in 1887 until the summer of 1895. The episode which had then led to the dream of Irma's injection had not consciously weakened them, and Freud's self-analysis, his formulation of the Oedipus complex and his completion of *The Interpretation of Dreams*, which had all taken place during the next few years, did nothing to reduce his reliance on Fliess. But then Fliess seemed to be reaching the plateau of his career. Freud, despite his pessimistic protestations, was glimpsing great things ahead.

However, the earlier devotion lingered on, exemplified by his reaction to criticism of a new book by Fliess on the alleged relationship between the nose and the female sex organs. This carried the periodic theory farther than even Fliess had previously dared carry it. The periods—twenty-eight days for women and twenty-three days for men—"can no more be created anew than can energy, and their rhythm survives as long as organized beings reproduce themselves sexually." Nor was that all. "These rhythms," Fliess maintained, "are not restricted to mankind, but extend into the animal world and probably throughout the organic world. The wonderful accuracy with which the period of twenty-three, or, as the case may be, twenty-eight whole days is observed permits one to suspect a deeper connection between astronomical relations and the creation of organisms."

To take this extravagance at its face value, without demanding details of the wonderful accuracy, was to strain loyalty. Freud remained loyal. When the *Wiener Klinische Rundschau,* a journal on whose board he sat, published a scathing review, Freud wrote protestingly to the editor. Not receiving a reply, he resigned from the board in protest at what he described to Fliess as "a sample of that type of insolence which is characteristic of absolute ignorance." The phrase, illustrating how bewitched Freud still was with Fliess's biological numerology, was significantly omitted when the letters were first published.

Freud's adherence to at least some of Fliess's fantasies died hard. Part of his tenacity was rooted in a Jewish upbringing in which certain numbers were "good" while others were "bad." The number seventeen, for instance, could stand for "constancy" and Freud and Martha had not only become engaged on the seventeenth of the month but for years regarded it as a lucky number. And as late as 1909 he was writing to Jung about the date of his death with the words: "You will see in this another confirmation of the specifically Jewish nature of my mysticism."

At times he revealed an undertone of doubt. But skeptical questionings were rare. Years later he was still seriously justifying his worries about a new telephone number acquired back in 1899. He had then been aged forty-three. The new number was 14362. "Thus it was plausible to suppose," he stated, "that the other figures signified the end of my life, hence sixty-one or sixty-two," an apparent gullibility which later led his physician to write, "Freud cannot be characterized as an obsessional neurotic, but his preoccupation with the prospective date of his death had the character of an obsessive trait." This was certainly true. When Freud visited Athens with his brother Alexander in 1904 he still believed that he would die between the ages of sixty-one and sixty-two. It was, he wrote in 1909, "really uncanny how often the number 61 or 60 in connection with 1 or 2 kept cropping up in all sorts of numbered objects, especially those connected with transportation. This I conscientiously noted." And if neither sixty-one nor sixty-two was present, the numbers would be contrived without much effort. In Athens, Freud was given room number thirty-one. It could, he commented, "with fatalistic licence . . . be regarded as half of sixty-one or sixty-two."

Even a decade later, almost twenty years after he had finally severed his links with Fliess, he was still unable totally to break away from his former friend's numerical mysticism. "According to the large conception of Wilhelm Fliess" he wrote in *Beyond the Pleasure Principle*, "all the phenomena of life exhibited by organism —and also, no doubt, their death—are linked with the completion of fixed periods, which express the dependence of two kinds of living substance (one male and the other female) upon the solar year. When we see, however, how easily and how extensively the influence of external forces is able to modify the date of the appearance of vital phenomena (especially in the plant world)—to precipitate or hold them back—doubts must be cast upon the rigidity of Fliess's formulas or at least upon whether the laws laid down by him are the sole determining factors." So if the mumbojumbo of numerology was no longer the sole determining factor, it was, in Freud's view, still apparently one of them.

His residual belief in periodicity was expressed some twenty years after the men had met for the last time, ending the second stage of their relationship and paving the way for the third: three years during which they corresponded sporadically but realized increasingly that each was now seeking independence.

The final meeting was in 1900, on the Achensee, a dark-blue lake lying above the Inn Valley, northwest of Innsbruck. As might be expected, both men gave their own versions of what happened. According to Freud, complaining to Fliess a year later, the latter had taken sides against him and told him "that 'the thought-reader merely reads his own thoughts into other people,' which deprives my work of all its value." The allegation was probably common enough in Berlin by this time, and Fliess may well have repeated it. However, his own story of the meeting reveals that his obsession with the periodic theory played at least a part in the break. "On that occasion," he wrote,

Freud showed a violence toward me which was at first unintelligible to me. The reason was that in a discussion of Freud's observations of his patients I claimed that periodic processes were unquestionably at work in the psyche, as elsewhere; and maintained in particular that they had an effect on those psychopathic phenomena on the analysis of which Freud was engaged for therapeutic purposes. Hence neither sudden deteriorations nor sudden improvements were to be attributed to the analysis and its influence alone. I supported my view with my own observations. During the rest of the discussion I thought I detected a personal animosity against me on Freud's part which sprang from envy. Freud had earlier said to me in Vienna: "It's just as well we're friends. Otherwise I should burst with envy if I heard that anyone was making such discoveries in Berlin!" In my astonishment I told my wife about this exclamation at the time, as well as our friend, Frau Hofkapellmeister Schalk, *née* Hopfen, who was then in Vienna and will gladly confirm it.

Writing when his relationship with Freud had finally dissolved in anger, Fliess seems to have been making the most of a poor case. The final break came in 1903 over a question not merely of priority but of honesty. On priority Freud was liberal in theory if touchy in practice, and might have been expected to act with the utmost propriety. Yet even Ernest Jones has been forced to admit that the case was "perhaps the only occasion in Freud's life when he was for a moment not completely straightforward." The subject under dispute was bisexuality, acrimoniously discussed by the two men some years previously. Fliess had as early as the 1890s put forward the idea that traces of both sexes were to be found in all men and women, and had mulled it over with Freud during their evening walks in Breslau in 1897. Freud had then refused to accept it but after a few months' thought had come round, writing in January 1898: "The facts of the matter seem to me to be as follows: I seized eagerly on your notion of bisexuality, which I regard as the most significant for my subject since that of defense." By the following year he was quite won over. However, during their last meeting on the Achensee he had suddenly brought up the idea of bisexuality as something new and denied any previous discussion of the subject with Fliess.

It was against this background that in the summer of 1901 Freud, writing to Fliess, regretting that they had "drawn somewhat apart from each other," then upbraiding his colleague for his claim that "the thought-reader merely reads his own thoughts into other people," made a surprising announcement:

And now for the most important thing of all. My next book, so far as I can see, will be called *Bisexuality in Man;* it will tackle the root of the problem and say the last word which it will be granted to me to say on the subject—the last and the deepest. . . . The idea itself is yours. You remember my saying to you years ago, when you were still a nose specialist and surgeon, that the solution lay in sexuality. Years later you corrected me and said bisexuality, and I see that you are right. So perhaps I shall have to borrow still more from you, and perhaps I shall be compelled in honesty to ask you to add your signature to the book to mine; this would mean an expansion of the anatomical-biological part, which in my hands alone would be very meager. I should make my aim the mental aspect of bisexuality and the explanation of the neurotic side. That, then, is the next project, which I hope will satisfactorily unite us again in scientific matters.

Fliess objected and Freud replied somewhat disingenuously: "I certainly had no intention of doing anything but get to grips, as my contribution to the theory of bisexuality, with the thesis that repression and the neuroses, and thus the independence of the unconscious, presupposes bisexuality." This may have been true, but the letter announcing *Bisexuality in Man*—a book that Freud never wrote—suggested something rather different.

Two years later Fliess was himself completing a book dealing with the subject. His thesis was that the bisexuality of the cell was the supreme arbiter of all living matter, and while bisexuality itself was a fairly common subject of medical debate, this extension of it, which he had discussed with Freud, had not so far been seriously proposed by anyone. Fliess was therefore surprised when in the summer of 1903 Dr. Otto Weininger, a young Viennese, published *Geschlecht und Charakter (Sex and Character)* in which the importance of the cell's bisexuality was emphasized. Within a year Weininger —"a sick genius, and greatly misguided about what I was teaching," according to Freud—had carried out a fragmentary self-analysis and, according to Wittels, it was this "glimpse into his unconscious which drove him to suicide." In 1903 Fliess thought it suspicious that Weininger was reported to be a close friend of a Dr. Hermann Swoboda, since Swoboda was understood to be a pupil of Freud. He was in fact a patient. Only an abnormally unsuspicious man would have failed to write to Freud as Fliess wrote, asking what he had to say about the situation.

At first Freud tried to dissimulate, replying that he had merely mentioned the idea of bisexuality to Swoboda who had passed it on to Weininger—and Weininger could, in any case, have got the idea from a number of other sources. "That's all I know about the matter," he concluded. The reply was not enough to satisfy Fliess, who pointed out that the bisexuality of the cell had not, in fact, been suggested elsewhere. Forced into a corner, Freud now admitted that in passing on the information he must, unconsciously of course, have been influenced by a wish to undermine Fliess's claim to originality. And in a tactless end to the letter he regretted that Fliess should write to him about such a trivial matter—an adjective which Fliess no doubt thought inappropriate for what he considered an important biological discovery.

In 1906 there came a sequel. Fliess published *Der Ablauf des Lebens: Grundlegung zur exakten Biologie (The Course of Life: A Foundation for an Exact Biological Study)* and a Berlin journalist, A. R. Pfennig, published—allegedly on the prompting of Fliess—a pamphlet entitled *Wilhelm Fliess und seine Nachentdecker: O. Weininger und H. Swoboda (Wilhelm Fliess and His Echoers: O. Weininger and H. Swoboda).* "It is not our task to criticize the way that Professor Freud made use of his friendship for Fliess," Pfennig wrote. "It is enough that after disputing that Swoboda was his pupil and maintaining his careful silence on the main point at issue—that is, his knowledge of Weininger's work before publication—his confession has a character which can only be called—cynical."

The rupture of the friendship with Fliess has inevitably aroused Freud's critics to ask whether he suffered from a capacity to forget inconvenient conversations, whether he found it hard to acknowledge originality in others, and whether some of his relationships with men were of a very passionate nature. Freud himself has admitted to there being homosexual overtones to his relationship with Fliess; yet the admission has all the signs of being a red herring, produced with the unconscious aim of diverting attention from the motivation behind more than one of his close friendships: the aid they could give to the cause. Fliess had been of considerable potential use when Freud was trying to explain psychology in physiological terms. Carl Jung was to be seen as a non-Jewish political counterweight as psychoanalysis grew into an international movement, while Sandor Ferenczi, the Hungarian who became one of Freud's closest confidants, was an invaluable right-hand man. As for Ernest Jones, working as devotedly for Freud as T. H. Huxley, "Darwin's bulldog," had worked for Charles Darwin, few men were to be of more value to the cause. Such friendships were no doubt of a "passionate nature"; but the passion appears to have been overwhelmingly a passion for the triumphant advance of psychoanalysis. Beside that, very little else mattered.

By 1906 the relationship with Fliess had dissolved in bitterness, and Freud turned for support to Karl Kraus, the editor of *Die Fackel.* Founded by Kraus seven years earlier, the paper had already built up a reputation for attacking the Austrian establishment in general and the *Neue Freie Presse* in particular. Freud's early view of *Die Fackel* had been shown in 1904 when he left in the journal's office a visiting card on which he had written: "A reader, who is rarely your follower, wishes to compliment you on your perceptiveness, your courage, and your ability to see what is significant concealed in what is insignificant, as shown in your article about Hervay [presumably Marie Jean Léon, Marquis d'Hervey de Saint-Denys, author of "Les rêves et les moyens de les diriger," Paris 1867]."

Kraus quoted Freud the following year when protesting against proposed anti-homosexual legislation, and Freud began a letter to him on January 1, 1906, with the words: "That I find my name repeatedly mentioned in the *Fackel* is caused presumably by the fact that your aims and opinions partially coincide with mine. On the basis of this impersonal relationship, I am taking the liberty of drawing your attention to an incident whose further developments will probably create a considerable stir among the contributors to your journal." He then went on to complain that Weininger and Swoboda had been "accused of the most flagrant plagiarism and abused in the cruelest fashion." This may well have been fair enough, since both men appear to have been the unconscious victims of Freud's indiscretion. The same can hardly be said of his protestation to Kraus that the statement that he had passed on Fliess's information was an "absurd slander."

Correspondence between Freud and Kraus continued during the year, but for some reason the meeting that Freud sought never took place. It was, moreover, during 1907 and 1908 that Kraus's attitude to Freud and to psychoanalysis underwent a decisive change. This was mainly due to the strong views which Kraus held on the subject. Yet it is possible that those views may first have begun to form as he deliberated on the circumstances when Freud was "for a moment not completely straightforward," and had in fact decided that Fliess had had the better of the argument.

11

Early Skirmishes

Our Aryan comrades are really completely indispensable to us, otherwise psychoanalysis would succumb to anti-Semitism.

FREUD, in a letter to Karl Abraham

As the meetings of the Wednesday Society, reported every Sunday in the *Neues Wiener Tagblatt* by Wilhelm Stekel, began to attract attention, Freud's belief that he had discovered the subterranean motives of conduct was subsumed into a fervor compounded of dedication and an almost divine mission in life. From the Jewish doctor convinced that he had found the key to human behavior, the decent man anxious to ameliorate some of the miseries of the world, there emerged the leader determined to guide the human race toward the promised land. From now on Freud was to lead a growing band of supporters, sometimes deviously, sometimes unsuccessfully, but always with the unqualified determination to support the cause. However much his mission was to be confounded by his own enthusiasm, impeded by heretics and muddied by charlatans, it was not an ambition of which any man need be ashamed.

Freud's three main publications in 1905 contributed to the cause in different ways. The first was an ingenious attempt to describe, as the title put it, *Wit and Its Relation to the Unconscious,* a book which like *The Psychopathology of Everyday Life* revealed the relationships between day-to-day affairs and the unconscious, and thus made the basic tenets of psychoanalysis less difficult for the layman to accept. The second was a case history, withheld for five years for fear that publication would bring a charge of professional indiscretion and finally made public because of the light it threw on dream analysis. The third was *Three Essays on the Theory of Sexuality* in which

Freud brought to fruition the results of his earlier researches on the neuroses, described a coherent theory of infantile sexuality and completed the main structure of belief for which he was to be bitterly attacked for the rest of his life.

Years earlier he had noticed the frequency with which his patients had described jokes, many arising from a play on words, which they had experienced in dreams. The jokes intrigued Freud for several reasons. There was his slightly ironic sense of humor, titillated by the absurdities of life. There was his general interest in Jewish humor and his specific interest in Jewish anecdotes of deep significance. But there was also another reason, since it appeared that dream-jokes sprang from the unconscious and Freud wished to consider their links, if any, with the jokes of everyday waking life. "It is certainly true that the dreamer is too ingenious and amusing, but it is not my fault, and I cannot be reproached with it," he had admitted to Fliess. "All dreamers are insufferably witty, and they have to be, because they are under pressure, and the direct way is barred to them. If you think so, I shall insert a remark to that effect somewhere [in *The Interpretation of Dreams*]. The ostensible wit of all unconscious processes is closely connected with the theory of jokes and humor."

He continued to speculate, further stimulated by Theodor Lipps's *Komik und Humor*. He began to read Rabelais, Cervantes, Molière, Lichtenberg, Mark Twain and Spitzer, among many other writers, specifically to note examples of their wit, and started to work his way through collections of jokes and folklore stories. "I . . . found," he recalled, "that their essence lay in the technical methods employed in them, and that these were the same as the means used in the 'dream-work' . . . This led to an economic enquiry into the origin of the high degree of pleasure obtained from hearing a joke. And to this the answer was that it was due to the momentary suspension of the expenditure of energy upon maintaining repression, owing to the attraction exercised by the offer of a bonus of pleasure *(fore-pleasure)*."

Freud kept the growing manuscript on one table in his study and that of *Three Essays on the Theory of Sexuality* on another, working on each as the spirit moved him. Both were published in the summer of 1905, the joke book appearing under the title *Der Witz und seine Beziehung zum Unbewussten*, finally being translated as *Jokes*—rather than *Wit*—*and their Relation to the Unconscious.* The book divided jokes into various categories, including those involving condensation, application of material in different ways, and the introduction of double meaning. Thus it might be expected to invite the criticism of being a typically Teutonic attempt to explain what was understood instinctively. It is, however, one of the most readable of all Freud's attempts to explain nonmedical features of everyday life in terms of the unconscious; moreover, the seemingly laborious classification is justified by similarities between jokes and dreams, which include condensation, displacement, the dream's use of absurdity and contradiction, and representation through the opposite. "Such a far-reaching agreement as found between the means of wit-work and those of dream-work can scarcely be accidental," he noted.

Freud's own sense of humor regularly bursts through, and it is difficult to read the explanations without grasping at least an outline of the reasons for laughter. The primarily Jewish and German jokes of the original are replaced in the English-language edition by many from American sources, introduced by A. A. Brill, Freud's translator, who found it necessary to exclude certain German examples when it was impossible to translate effectively from one language to another. Condensation is illustrated by Sainte-Beuve's description of Flaubert's *Salammbô* as "Carthaginoiserie," and by a poor man's description of how he was treated by a Rothschild "as if I were his equal, quite *famillionaire.*" Brill once introduced as a play on words the quip that "Hood once remarked that he had to be a lively Hood for a livelihood," while as an example of double meaning, Charles Mathews the actor, asked what his trainee-architect son was to do for a living, is quoted as answering: "Why, he is going to draw houses like his father."

Jokes and their Relation to the Unconscious was well reviewed in the popular Viennese *Die Zeit* but almost completely ignored in medical and psychological journals. It was seven years before the first printing of little more than a thousand copies had been sold, and for all practical purposes the book passed without notice. The reverse was the case with Freud's other two publications of 1905, his *Fragment of an Analysis of a Case of Hysteria* and *Three Essays on the Theory of Sexuality.* The first laid him open to the damaging accusation of having breached medical confidence; the second appeared to compound the various crimes for which the critics had for so long been denouncing him.

Some five years earlier Freud had carried out the analysis of an eighteen-year-old girl, identified merely as "Dora," who had broken off her treatment at the end of eleven weeks. He wrote up the case history and finished it by January 1901, writing to Fliess on the twenty-fifth, "It is a fragment of an analysis of a hysteria, in which the interpretations are grouped round two dreams, so it is really a continuation of the dream book. It also contains resolutions of hysterical symptoms and glimpses of the sexual-organic foundation of the whole. All the same it is the subtlest thing I have so far written and will put people off even more than usual. But one does one's duty and does not write just for the day alone." He added that the paper had been accepted by the joint editors of the *Monatsschrift für Psychiatrie und Neurologie*, but four months later reported that he had not made up his mind about publication. Soon afterward the position was that it would "meet the gaze of an astonished public in the autumn"; but once again Freud appears to have changed his mind, and it was not until 1905 that the paper was at last published.

The passage of more than four years may well have made him feel that accusations of breaching medical confidence were by now weakened. Moreover, he had two strong reasons for pressing on with publication. "In the first place," he wrote, "I wished to supplement my book on the interpretation of dreams by showing how an art, which would otherwise be useless, can be turned to account for the discovery of the hidden and repressed parts of mental life . . . In the second place, I wished to stimulate interest in a whole group of phenomena of which science is still in complete ignorance today because they can only be brought to light by the use of this particular method."

There were also other inducements. The Wednesday Society was meeting regularly. Interest was growing. His position was stronger. Freud was always the man to challenge boldly whenever opportunity offered, and the case of Dora, incorporating almost every feature for which he had been attacked, presented an irresistible opportunity. He agreed in his prefatory remarks that while he had been accused of giving no information about the patients of *Studies on Hysteria,* in this case he would "be accused of giving information about my patients which ought not to be given. I can only hope that in both cases the critics will be the same, and that they will merely have shifted the pretext for their reproaches; if so, I can resign in advance any possibility of ever removing their objections." If his opponents expected to be shocked, he would give them no half-measures. Moreover, judging by his account at a meeting of the Vienna Psychoanalytical Society a few years later, he had worked hard on the Dora paper in order to make it an illustration of how psychoanalysis was carried on. In a discussion on the best way of propagating his ideas he then agreed, in the words of the Society's minutes, "that case histories that are not worked over are completely indigestible. A scrupulous but 'artistic' presentation, such as that of Dora's history, is the only acceptable possibility."

The story was an almost inexplicable one for Freud to record at a length of about 50,000 words, since the treatment had been broken off by the patient, and only the most dubious claims could be made that it had been effective. It had begun in October 1900, when a wealthy businessman whom Freud had treated a few years earlier brought his daughter to No. 19 Berggasse. Dora had been afflicted with shortness of breath, long bouts of coughing, and fainting, and shortly before arriving in Vienna had written a suicide note which her father had not taken very seriously. All these symptoms were considered to be signs of neurosis, and, under Freud's questioning, reasons for neurosis were certainly revealed; so many, in fact, that as he himself admitted, the case read more like fiction than fact. But, he wrote to Fliess after the first week, "the case has opened smoothly to my collection of picklocks."

"Dora" was the daughter of an unhappily married couple who were close friends with a similar pair, called, by Freud, Herr and Frau K. Frau K. had become the mistress of Dora's father; Herr K. had unsuccessfully attempted to seduce Dora. There was what Ernest Jones has called "a warm, but platonic, homosexual relationship" between Frau K. and Dora, and the situation was still further complicated by the fact that although Dora had rebuffed Herr K., she did have a suppressed sexual desire not only for him but also for her father as well as for Frau K.

The details were drawn from the patient following Freud's interpretation of two dreams and his discussion with the girl of the most intimate details of the group's sexual relations and the various perversions that appeared to have taken place. It was this which Freud knew he would have to explain away, since, as he wrote at the start of the paper, "sexual questions will be discussed with all possible frankness, the organs and functions of sexual life will be called by their proper names, and the pure-minded reader can convince himself from my description that I have not hesitated to converse upon such subjects in such language even with a young woman."

The case history of Dora, sometimes described as Freud's most famous patient, brought considerably more obloquy than the case itself would now seem to warrant, since the patient's identity was suitably disguised. It also included a passage which was often to be used to stick a dagger into the ribs of psychoanalysis. Freud says that at one point in the analysis his expectations

were by no means disappointed when this explanation of mine was met by Dora with a most emphatic negative. The "No" uttered by a patient after a repressed thought has been presented to his conscious perception for the first time does no more than register the existence of a repression and its severity; it acts, as it were, as a gauge of the repression's strength. If this "No," instead of being regarded as the expression of an impartial judgment (of which, indeed, the patient is incapable), is ignored, and if work is continued, the first evidence soon begins to appear that in such a case "No" signifies the desired "Yes."

This may at times be true. But should what the analyst believes to be reaction to a repressed thought be in fact nothing of the kind, then the reaction may still be a "No," the only difference being the tone of voice in which the word is uttered.

The Dora paper did apparently show that Freud, by interpreting two dreams, was able to reveal the existence of a labyrinthine complex of sexual motives previously unsuspected by the girl herself. But her ending of the analysis after eleven weeks, on the face of it a move to spite Freud personally, appears to have been quite as much a protest against what he was telling her.

Freud's beliefs in the sexual basis of neurosis, some of which he had utilized in an effort to solve Dora's problems, were elaborated in *Three Essays on the Theory of Sexuality,* also published in 1905. It was a short, eighty-six-page book in which he drew together his various findings since the 1880s and presented them as a coherent theory of the libido's development. Over the years he added, deleted, and developed the text to an extent only equaled by his revisions to *The Interpretation of Dreams,* even though its basic structure remained unchanged.

The three essays dealt with "The Sexual Aberrations," "Infantile Sexuality" and "Transformations of Puberty," and in each Freud included material which affronted contemporary ideas as much by his dry unemotional approach as by the subject matter. Thus in a long account of the genesis of the perversions, ranging from homosexuality to fetishism, he took the view that just as there was no dividing line between sanity and insanity but an almost infinite series of gradual steps, so could "normal" behavior be regarded as merging into eccentricities which themselves finally merged into perversions. The disturbing implication that the seeds of the unmentionable lay concealed in the psyche of even the most respectable was inescapably spelled out in the closing sentences of the first essay. "The conclusion," Freud argued,

now presents itself to us that there is indeed something innate lying behind the perversions but that it is something innate in *everyone,* though as a disposition it may vary in its intensity and may be in-

creased by the influences of actual life. What is in question are the
innate constitutional roots of the sexual instinct. In one class of cases
(the perversions) these roots may grow into the actual vehicles of
sexual activity; in others they may be submitted to an insufficient
suppression (repression) and thus be able in a roundabout way to
attract a considerable proportion of sexual energy to themselves as
symptoms; while in the most favorable cases, which lie between these
two extremes, they may by means of effective restriction and other
kinds of modification bring about what is known as normal sexual
life.

That homosexuality frequently followed an upbringing in which
a child grew overattached to its mother—an item in Freudian theory that tends to be supported by modern evidence—was a new
idea particularly vulnerable to attack, while the mere discussion of
the perversions in a clinical rather than critical climate raised opposition of a virulence which sounds strange three quarters of a
century later. At the end of the first essay, moreover, Freud compounded his crime by stating that his theory of the perversions
would "only be demonstrable in *children*, even though in them it
is only with modest degrees of intensity that any of the instincts can
emerge. A formula begins to take shape which lays it down that the
sexuality of neurotics has remained in, or been brought back to,
an infantile state. Thus our interest turns to the sexual life of
children, and we will now proceed to trace the play of influences
which govern the evolution of infantile sexuality till its outcome in
perversion, neurosis or normal sexual life."

Evidence of infantile sexuality had usually been regarded as
evidence of abnormality. Freud unceremoniously demolished the
idea, maintaining that sexuality was present virtually from birth
and that where it was not recognized the reason was lack of observation, inability to interpret the evidence, or a mixture of both
increased by distaste. There had always been, as has been said, "a
difficulty in the way of regarding children as angels, for angels have
no excreta; but people put up with that little peculiarity in children.
Still, they find it atrocious that anyone should describe 'innocent'
children as utterly immoral libertines. That is how they summarized Freud's discovery, for in the view of our traditional educa-
tionalists, 'innocent' and 'sexual' are incompatible terms."

One exception to the prevailing view that sexuality began
with puberty had already been put forward in 1902 by Sanford
Bell in the *American Journal of Psychology* where, in "A Preliminary Study of the Emotion of Love between the Sexes," he had
noted that "The emotion of sex-love . . . does not make its ap-

pearance for the first time at the period of adolescence, as has been thought." But Bell did not follow up the idea, at least not in the thoroughgoing way that Freud was now to develop it. There were, Freud maintained, three successive kinds of infantile sexuality, the first being oral activity in which pleasure was derived from taking food from the mother's breast. Later there was anal activity in which pleasure was derived from control of the feces, followed by the phallic stage at which the incestuous wishes of the Oedipus complex came to the fore. There then came a latent period which continued until the age of puberty. In the *Three Essays* Freud did not clearly divide these differing activities into specific stages, although he was later to do so, estimating that the anal stage began at about the age of two and that the phallic stage took over a year or two later.

He was subsequently to carry forward the theory of the developing sexual instincts in two ways. First, he maintained that the satisfactory expression, repression or sublimation of these different forms of libido governed the personality of the grown adult. Secondly, he maintained that there was a correlation between arrested development at any particular stage and the specific mental disorders that would follow; thus arrest in the early oral stage could be correlated with schizophrenia, in the late oral stage with melancholia, in the early anal stage with paranoia, the late anal stage with obsessional neurosis, and in the phallic stage with hysteria.

These theories have had diverse fortunes. A good deal of evidence has tended to substantiate the general conclusion of a threefold division of sexuality up to the age of four or five, and the psychic consequences of arrested development. Less demonstrable has been the theory that satisfactory expression, repression or sublimation of early instincts governs the personality of the adult. One contemporary judgment given after an in-depth assessment of many surveys says: "In brief, therefore, it must be concluded that Freudian psychosexual theory, as it relates personality syndromes to infantile experiences and repressed pregenital erotism, receives almost no support. On the other hand, methodological problems are more than sufficient to account for such failures." A verdict which the Scots would give simply as "not proven."

The *Three Essays* also included Freud's first public qualification of the seduction theory, although it was so carefully worded that it made a very different impact on the reader from the "first great error" which he had admitted in his private letters. "In the foreground," he says, we find the effects of seduction, which treats a child as a sexual object prematurely and teaches him, in highly emotional circumstances, how to obtain satisfaction from his genital zones, a satisfaction which he is then usually obliged to repeat again and again by masturbation. An influence of this kind may originate either from adults or from other children. I cannot admit that in my paper on "The Aetiology of Hysteria" I exaggerated the frequency or importance of that influence, though I did not then know that persons who remain normal may have had the same experiences in their childhood, and though I consequently overrated the importance of seduction in comparison with the factors of sexual constitution and development.

Freud's third essay, dealing with the transformations and problems of puberty, developed his views on the chemical basis of sexuality and at the same time emphasized how much depended on the experiences of childhood. On the first of these subjects he was in advance of his time, proposing the existence of the sex glands, which were to be discovered some years later. As to the experiences of childhood, it was here that Freud's words caused most offense, spelling out, even more clearly than in *The Interpretation of Dreams,* what he meant by the Oedipus complex: "Among these [infantile] tendencies the first place is taken with uniform frequency by the child's sexual impulses towards his parents, which are as a rule already differentiated owing to the attraction of the opposite sex—the son being drawn towards his mother and the daughter towards her father."

It was the spelling out that brought down on Freud's head the wrath of the uneducated and the more rigidly conservative. But it should be emphasized that the *Three Essays* were welcomed in some quarters, and that the impression of universal condemnation later given by some of Freud's adherents cannot really be justified. Laudatory comments came from very different sources. Thus Karl Kraus's *Die Fackel,* not yet gone over to the attack on psychoanalysis, was enthusiastic. The book was compared favorably with August Forel's recently published *The Sexual Question* and a review-essay by Otto Soyka went so far as to declare, "Forel stands as far below the level of science in the area of sex as Freud stands above it." There were other enthusiastic notices in Vienna, where the *Wiener Klinische Rundschau* devoted the entire two pages of its review section to the book, and also in Berlin. In Britain the *British Medical Journal* gave it nearly a page of praise, concluding: "Certainly no one can read these essays without an inward acknowledgment of the author's acumen, courage and endless patience in the pursuit of truth; nor, having read them, fail to realize more clearly the need for fuller knowledge and more careful guidance of the gradual unfolding of the sexual life."

The foundation of Freud's theory of sexuality outlined in the *Three Essays* was the hitherto unadmitted sexuality of children; but the evidence came largely from the retrospective stories of adults. As he wrote,

> even a psychoanalyst may confess to the wish for a more direct and less roundabout proof of these fundamental theorems. Surely there must be a possibility of observing in children at first hand and in all the freshness of life the sexual impulses and wishes which we dig out so laboriously in adults from among their own debris—especially as it is also our belief that they are the common property of all men, a part of the human constitution, and merely exaggerated or distorted in the case of neurotics.

And now a remarkable stroke of good fortune came to his aid. During 1906 he began to receive reports of "Little Hans," the young son of his friend Max Graf. Throughout the next two years, as it became clear that the boy was sexually precocious, Hans developed a phobia about horses. He was both mentally and physically healthy, but his fear that he would be bitten by a horse was so great as to keep him indoors in an age when the motorcar had barely arrived in the streets of Vienna and horses were to be numbered by the thousand.

From the details of the boy's development and the parents' handling of his sexual awakening, Freud assumed that the phobia was directly linked to repression. Working almost entirely through the boy's father, he was able to dissipate the phobia; but in addition he was able to record, in his account of the case, evidence which he saw as confirming, for the first time from a child, many of the points he had already made in the *Three Essays*.

Publication of "Analysis of a Phobia in a Five-Year-Old Boy" laid Freud open to two charges, the first being that he had merely found what he was looking for. This tended to be supported by his own statement that Hans had to "be told many things that he could not say himself, that he had to be presented with thoughts which he had so far shown no signs of possessing, and that his attention had to be turned in the direction from which his father was expecting something to come."

The second charge was that the boy's future had been ruined, that he had been a victim of psychoanalysis, and that he had been "robbed of his innocence." That this was far from the truth became obvious in the spring of 1922 when a strapping youth of nineteen appeared at No. 19 Berggasse and introduced himself as "Little Hans." "He declared that he was perfectly well, and suffered from no trouble or inhibitions," Freud was able to record.

"Not only had he come through his puberty without any damage, but his emotional life had successfully undergone one of the severest of ordeals." His parents had been divorced and both had married again; yet despite what could have been a traumatic experience, Little Hans had weathered the storm and succeeded in remaining on good terms with both of them. He was, moreover, about to embark on what was to be a successful career as an opera director in New York, Philadelphia and Zurich.

The story of Little Hans became one of Freud's most famous case histories, and for more than half a century it was praised unstintingly by psychoanalysts, Carl Jung going so far as to call it "indeed the first true insight into the psychology of the child." Only in 1960 did a paper in the *Journal of Nervous and Mental Disease* present a totally different view. Dealing almost line by line with Freud's account, it devastatingly criticized many of the claims made in the paper, and concluded "that it does not provide anything resembling direct proof of psychoanalytic theorems."

However, by the end of 1905 Freud's fame, as well as his notoriety, was steadily if slowly growing, and in England, in the United States and in Switzerland he was soon to have a small group of supporters.

In England they were to be centered around Ernest Jones, the twenty-six-year-old Welshman then working in London's University College Hospital. A spare, sharp-featured man who allowed himself only two hobbies, chess and figure skating, Jones's entire medical career was to be characterized by a phenomenal capacity for work and an unswerving devotion to a cause: psychoanalysis. He had become aware of it in 1905 when reading reviews of Freud's papers. So impressed was he that together with his brother-in-law, Wilfred Trotter, he began to learn German so that they could read Freud in the original.

By 1906 Jones was using Freud's methods, but, as on later occasions, he was to be remarkably unlucky. "I well remember the first patient with whom I practiced the new therapy, surely the first person to be analyzed outside of German-speaking countries," he has written. "She was the sister of a surgical colleague, and suffered from a conversion hysteria. One upshot of the analysis was that she decided to divorce her husband, a well-known New York neurologist, on grounds of cruelty. Presently, when I lived in America, he formed the habit of following me from one congress to another in order to exercise his very considerable powers of vituperation, and on one particular occasion Dr. Putnam of Harvard, already a good friend, magnanimously traveled a thousand miles to support me; between us we got on very well."

James Jackson Putnam, who was to become Freud's most influential supporter in the United States, had in the first issue of the *Journal of Abnormal Psychology* published the first clinical test of psychoanalysis in an English-speaking country but had inferred that Freud's claims were exaggerated, though stimulating. A similar attitude still prevailed in France and Germany, although the general rejection of psychoanalysis in Germany was qualified by men such as Hermann Oppenheim and Leopold Löwenfeld. As Hannah S. Decker has shown in "The Medical Reception of Psychoanalysis in Germany, 1894–1907: Three Brief Studies," the picture was not quite as black as Freud and his friends painted it. His attitude, she has pointed out, "was based on the illogical expectation that the entire medical world would immediately recognize the truths he had uncovered. Because it did not do so, he felt 'isolated' and wrote about it in all his accounts of psychoanalysis; his version has often been accepted without further investigation."

Outside Germany and Austria there was, moreover, an important exception to what was admittedly the general skepticism. In the Burghölzli, the huge labyrinthine building standing on the hills to the east of Zurich, built in 1860 as cantonal asylum as well as psychiatric clinic for the city's university, and by 1906 housing some 3,000 patients in all stages of insanity, psychoanalysis was actually being practiced.

In 1900 Carl Jung, a twenty-five-year-old Swiss doctor, had become assistant staff physician to the Burghölzli's director, Eugen Bleuler. One of the few who had read Freud's *The Interpretation of Dreams,* apparently on Bleuler's recommendation, Jung considered it to be a masterpiece, even though later saying, "When I first read Freud's writings it was the same with me as with everybody else: I could only strew the pages with question marks." Jung quoted Freud in his paper "On the Psychology and Pathology of So-Called Occult Phenomena" in 1902, and under his influence psychoanalysis began to be used in the treatment of patients at the Burghölzli, although only tentatively and with many reservations on the part of Bleuler.

The encouragement of psychoanalysis in Switzerland did more than extend the area in which Freud's ideas might take root. It allowed them to be applied to a far wider cross section of human beings than was ever likely to be treated by a small handful of Viennese doctors in private practice. It is not entirely correct to maintain that Freud himself dealt only with well-to-do patients, most of them women, whose ample spare time gave them much opportunity for indulging in minor mental illnesses. Nevertheless they were certainly in another class from the army of poverty-stricken cases, often uncontrollable, sometimes raving, with which Bleuler and his staff had to deal at the Burghölzli, living with them week in week out, as keepers as well as doctors, somewhat comparable in this way to Charcot in the Salpêtrière. "How in the world," asked Freud when Jung once demonstrated a case to him in Zurich, "were you able to bear spending hours and days with this phenomenally ugly female?" It was something, Jung replied, that had never occurred to him. "In a way," he later wrote, "I regarded the woman as a pleasant old creature because she had such lovely delusions and said such interesting things. And after all, even in her insanity, the human being emerged from a cloud of grotesque nonsense."

Contact with Zurich was in the very nature of things thus likely to take the psychoanalysis of Vienna out into a less rarefied atmosphere, into an environment where its assumptions could be more closely examined. From the start, Jung was both interested and questioning. Although a good many of his later statements contain wisdom after the event, there is no reason to doubt his version of the position he claimed to have taken up from the first. His concentrated interest in Freud dated from 1905, he stated years later. "My scientific conscience did not allow me, on the one hand, to let what is good in Freud go by the board, and, on the other, to countenance the absurd position which the human psyche occupies in his theory," he added. "I suspected at once that this partly diabolical sexual theory would turn people's heads and I have sacrificed my scientific career in doing all I can to combat this absolute devaluation of the psyche."

In April 1906 Jung followed up his personal interest by sending Freud a copy of his newly published *Diagnostic Association Studies*. The word-association tests that the studies described used a series of stimuli—words which were read out to the patient who responded with the first word that came into his head. The time-lag in the response was measured by stopwatch. Jung had quickly discovered that while reaction to words lacking any emotional association was rapid, the reverse was true with certain other words; the patient hesitated, made no response at all or showed some other sign of disturbance even though he did not realize he was doing so. Typically, a man who reacted in this way to the words "bottle," "knife," "beat," "lance" and "pointed" was found, as Jung had suspected, to have served a prison sentence for knifing a man in a brawl. The association tests gave strong independent confirmation that material could be repressed down into the unconscious as maintained by Freud, who had bought a copy of

Jung's book on publication and now replied cordially to him. Jung's most recent paper, "Psychoanalysis and Association Experiments," he said, confirmed "that everything I have said about the hitherto unexplored fields of our discipline is true. I am confident that you will often be in a position to back me up, but I shall also gladly accept correction."

The opportunity for backing up came in the autumn and, in view of what was to happen within the next few years, is particularly instructive. Gustav Aschaffenburg, a German professor of psychiatry and neurology, attacked Freud's *Fragment of an Analysis of a Case of Hysteria*—the Dora case history—at a congress of neurologists and psychiatrists in Baden-Baden. When Jung came to his aid with "Freud's Theory of Hysteria: A Reply to Aschaffenburg," Freud was grateful. The "Reply" has sometimes been used as evidence of Jung's early and unquestioned devotion to Freud, yet he opened by calling Aschaffenburg's statement "on the whole [a] very moderate and cautious criticism of Freud's theory of hysteria." Moreover, in this, his first public comment on the sexual basis of Freud's theory, Jung introduced a small seed of qualification. He agreed that sexuality was a far more basic and widespread drive than Freud's opponents were willing to admit. However, he went on, what about Freud's particular view that all hysteria was reducible to sexuality? "Freud," he continued,

> has not examined all the hysterias there are. His proposition is therefore subject to the general limitation which applies to empirical axioms. He has simply found his view confirmed in the cases observed by him, which constitute an infinitely small fraction of all cases of hysteria. It is even conceivable that there are several forms of hysteria which Freud has not yet observed at all. Finally, it is also possible that Freud's material, under the constellation of his writings, has become somewhat one-sided.
>
> We may therefore modify his dictum, with the consent of the author, as follows: An indefinitely large number of cases of hysteria derive from sexual roots.

His "with the consent of the author" was slightly misleading since Jung, writing to Freud in October, described his views as a standpoint with which Freud "may not be entirely in agreement." He was right, although what was to become a wide chasm between the two men was at this stage only a hair-crack. At least, so it appeared. But Jung had in fact highlighted a weakness later to be seized upon by many of Freud's opponents: his practice of generalizing widely from the evidence or, as was stated of his later excur-

sions into the analysis of literature and art, of "building explanations of complex phenomena on a single datum."

Nevertheless, Freud's theories had taken root in Zurich, and in
January 1907 he was visited by Max Eitingon, a young member of
Bleuler's staff who wished to consult him on a particularly difficult
case—"the first emissary to reach the lonely man" as Freud was to
call him. Early the following month there came Jung himself, together with his wife and Ludwig Binswanger, a young pupil who
a year earlier had published a paper supporting Freud's views.
"The day after our arrival," Binswanger has recalled,

> Freud questioned Jung and me about our dreams. I do not recall
> Jung's dream, but I do recall Freud's interpretation of it, namely, that
> Jung wished to dethrone him and take his place. I myself dreamed
> of the entrance to his house at No. 19 Berggasse, which was then
> being remodeled, and of the old chandelier swathed in a shabby
> covering to protect it from the plastering. Freud's interpretation of
> this dream, which I found rather unconvincing—he recalled it thirty
> years later when my wife and I visited him on the occasion of his
> eightieth birthday—was that it indicated a wish to marry his oldest
> daughter but, at the same time, contained the repudiation of this
> wish, since it actually said that—I remember Freud's words—"You
> won't marry into a house with such a shabby chandelier."

Jung has given his own account of the first meeting with Freud,
by any standards an historic occasion. On one side Jung, tall and
upright, clean-shaven and with a bullethead of close-cropped hair;
except for his gold-rimmed spectacles the very model of a Nordic
Siegfried and, as Martin Freud put it, "holding himself more like
a soldier than a man of science and medicine"; on the other, Freud,
twenty years older, already the leader of a cause, looking for volunteers, anxious to recruit an army for battle.

"We met at one o'clock in the afternoon and talked virtually
without a pause for thirteen hours," Jung later wrote. "Freud was
the first man of real importance I had encountered; in my experience up to that time, no one else could compare with him. There
was nothing the least trivial in his attitude. I found him extremely
intelligent, shrewd, and altogether remarkable. And yet my first
impressions of him remained somewhat tangled; I could not make
him out."

He had, moreover, certain reservations. "We talked about everything," he recalled. "But I could not swallow his so-called science
positivism, his merely rational view of the psyche and his material-
istic point of view." There were other qualifications which he
claims to have remembered many years later. "Above all," he

wrote in *Memories, Dreams, Reflections*, "Freud's attitude towards the spirit seemed to me highly questionable. Wherever, in a person or in a work of art, an expression of spirituality (in the intellectual, not the supernatural sense) came to light, he suspected it, and insinuated that it was repressed sexuality." This, Jung maintained, would if followed to its logical conclusion create a farce of culture, which would be no more than a morbid consequence of repressed sexuality. "Yes," Freud agreed, "so it is, and that is just a curse of fate against which we are powerless to contend."

Jung continued to dilute the importance that Freud gave to sexuality and, looking back on the relationship that developed between the two men, the remarkable thing is Freud's early failure to note how fundamental was the difference between Jung's views and his own. It might have been apparent even after Jung had defended him against Aschaffenburg once again at the first International Congress for Psychiatry, Psychology and the Assistance to the Insane, held in Amsterdam later in 1907. Freud had turned down an invitation. "Apparently a duel was planned between Janet and myself," he told Jung, "but I detest gladiatorial fights in front of the noble rabble and cannot easily bring myself to put my findings to the vote of an indifferent crowd." It was an odd reaction from a man usually eager for battle, possibly explained by a commonsense realization that the occasion was one in which a subordinate could win his spurs. Just before the event he sent Jung an encouraging letter. "Whether you have been or will be lucky or unlucky, I do not know; but now of all times I wish I were with you," he said before describing his long struggle for recognition and the years of waiting before a voice answered his. "That voice was yours," he added; "for I know now that Bleuler also came to me through you."

As it happened, Jung bungled things badly in Amsterdam. "Unfortunately," says Ernest Jones, who was also present, "he made the mistake of not timing his paper and also of refusing to obey the chairman's repeated signals to finish. Ultimately, he was compelled to, whereupon with a flushed angry face he strode out of the room. I remember the unfortunate impression his behavior made on the impatient and already prejudiced audience, so that there could be no doubt about the issue of the debate." Even discounting Jones's allergy to Jung, it seems likely that Freud himself would have done better. Jung's paper on "The Freudian Theory of Hysteria" was itself almost apologetic in places. Speaking of sexual symbolism, he pointed out that there were "uncommonly far-reaching and significant analogies between the Freudian symbolisms and the symbols of poetic fantasy in individuals and in whole nations. The Freudian symbol and its interpretation is therefore nothing unheard of, it is merely something unusual for us psychiatrists." Again, in the foreword to *The Psychology of Dementia Praecox,* the book which in the same year brought him into prominence, Jung actually set out his differences with Freud, saying that he could not ascribe such importance as did Freud to concepts of infantile sexual trauma, or agree to place sexuality itself so firmly in the foreground.

Since Freud had for more than a decade been emphasizing the importance of infantile sexuality, his persistent encouragement of Jung might at first seem strange. Yet however much he might have wondered about Jung's intentions, the cause came first; and as long as he could retain Jung's support, any potential danger was more than counterbalanced. The Swiss in the Burghölzli might, he believed, be ready not only to extend the use of psychoanalysis there but also to form a group comparable to what was now the Vienna Psychoanalytical Society; once this had been done, other groups could no doubt be set up in other countries to help spread the gospel yet farther. Perhaps more important, Freud had already seen in Jung the young man capable of taking over as commander in chief in the years ahead. "I now realize," he had written in the spring of 1907, "that I am as replaceable as everyone else and that I could hope for no one better than yourself, as I have come to know you, to continue and complete my work."

There was another reason for his attitude. Psychoanalysis had to overcome not only the opposition aroused by its emphasis on sex but also the antagonism evoked by its creator being a Jew. Freud himself had ambivalent feelings about the fact that during its first few years converts were almost exclusively Jewish. Later, when psychoanalysis had become established, he could say: "I don't know whether you're right in thinking that psychoanalysis is a direct product of the Jewish spirit, but if it were I wouldn't feel ashamed." In the early years the situation was very different and more dangerous.

In fact there was, as Edmund Wilson has written, a natural reason why such a disturbing new movement should have had a Jewish conception. After pointing out that nobody but a Jew such as Marx could have fought so uncompromisingly for the victory of the dispossessed classes, he continued:

The great Jewish minds of these first generations that had been liberated from the closed Judaic world, still remembered the mediaeval captivity, and they were likely to present themselves as champions of other social groups or doctrines which had not been freed or vindicated yet. . . . So Einstein became preoccupied with the few unemphasized anomalies in the well-operating system of Newton and made them the cornerstone that the builder had rejected on which to build a new system that should shake the authority of the old. So Lassalle took up the cause of feminism at a time when German women were largely at the mercy of their fathers and their husbands; and so Proust transferred from a persecuted race to the artist and the homosexual, both that race's tragic fate in society and its inner conviction of moral superiority. [And so did Freud see] the vital importance of those sexual impulses that civilization had outlawed or that puritanism had tried to suppress, and forced psychiatric science to take account of them.

Most of Bleuler's staff was non-Jewish. Jung himself was the apotheosis of Aryan manhood, and it was not surprising that Freud should welcome the Swiss in general and Jung in particular, not only for their ideological support but for their immunity from attack on racialist grounds. "Our Aryan comrades," he was to write, "are really completely indispensable to us, otherwise psychoanalysis would succumb to anti-Semitism." It is ironic that less than a decade later, when Jung had left the Freudian circle to start his own school, Freud should complain bitterly of Jung's "anti-semitic condescension towards me."

Yet his foresight was justified by events. Sixty years after his fear that psychoanalysis might become a predominantly Jewish movement, and open to attack on that ground, researchers investigated psychotherapy in New York, Chicago and Los Angeles. "In brief," says a comment on their report, "analysts were predominantly upwardly mobile, politically liberal Jewish men who traced their origins to eastern European countries and who grew up in large metropolitan areas. They also tended to be either second generation Americans or foreign born (25 percent of the analysts indicated they were born in other countries). By examining age in relation to other factors, it was discovered that rather than broadening their base, analysts are becoming increasingly recruited from the ranks of Jews with eastern European ethnic ties. In short, psychoanalysis is becoming even more homogeneous with regard to the cultural identities of its practitioners."

In 1907, when Freud realized that the Burghölzli might contain a nucleus of adherents as enthusiastic as those in the Vienna Psychoanalytical Society, it was at last becoming practicable to consider organized support in other countries. He believed that "once the English have become acquainted with our ideas they will never let them go," but had less confidence in the French. His judgment of the Germans was perceptive if cynical: "I don't believe that

Germany will show any sympathy for our work until some bigwig has solemnly given his stamp of approval. The simplest way might be to arouse the interest of Kaiser Wilhelm—who of course understands everything. Have you any connections in those quarters?" he asked Jung. "I haven't."

The United States was still an unknown quantity and it was with some surprise, therefore, that Freud learned, early in 1908, that a young man at the Burghölzli was anxious to translate his works for publication in North America. "The interest [there] is very great at present," Jung told him, "so it wouldn't be a bad speculation."

The young man was Abraham A. Brill. He had left his birthplace in Austria at the age of fifteen and settled in the United States where he began training as a psychiatrist during the first years of the century. In 1905 he visited the Vienna clinics and after leaving had been asked by a young Austrian, "Why don't you come to Vienna and take courses with Freud?" But Brill had never heard of Freud. "I expressed my opinion that he could not be famous enough to go to for courses," he has written. " 'Oh,' [his companion] said, 'he must be somebody; else he would not have so many opponents.' "

Two years later, working in the Hospice de Bicêtre in Paris and disappointed at being unable to learn more about psychoneuroses, Brill received a letter from his psychiatric mentor, Dr. Frederick Peterson, clinical professor of psychiatry at Columbia University. Why, Peterson suggested, did he not go to the Burghölzli. "They are doing the Freud work there," he said, "and I think you will like it." That was, Brill went on, "the third time in my life I had heard the name of Freud, concerning whom I knew nothing; and although Peterson's remark, 'I think you will like it,' provoked in me some uncertainty, I decided to follow his suggestions." He found the Burghölzli inspiring. "Under the wise guidance of Bleuler and the aggressive inspiration of Jung, his *Sekundärarzt* [chief assistant], everybody worked assiduously to test Freud's theories, and as I was soon appointed as a regular assistant in the clinic, I worked heart and soul in the pioneer work of testing and applying the Freudian mechanisms to psychiatry." He also began to translate into English Jung's *Über die Psychologie der Dementia praecox* (*The Psychology of Dementia Praecox*).

The next step was toward Freud, and after a visit to Vienna it was agreed that he should translate Freud's first books into English. "The magnitude of this task I hardly appreciated at the time," he has recalled. "I was instigated by a strong obsessive sort of drive, which absorbed all my leisure time for over ten years. I made no effort to produce literary excellencies; I was only interested in conveying these new ideas into comprehensible English." The results were none too happy. Freud's most influential supporter in the United States, James Putnam, described the translations as "atrocious 'English' (if one must call it such)," while Freud himself admitted that they were "conscientious rather than beautiful."

Brill's admitted failings should be considered against the larger problem already faced by Freud in describing his work. He had been forced to use the existing vocabulary, and to make it yield the subtle nuances and insights he wished to communicate, he had found it necessary to extend, and sometimes to distort, the current and accepted meaning of words. It was probably inevitable, but led naturally to what was almost a new language made out of old words. This was less off-putting than the multisyllabled jargon that eventually transformed much psychoanalytical writing into medical gobbledegook; but it did make Brill's job of translation extremely difficult.

It is true that in some cases the phrases which he introduced and which have long passed into the psychoanalytic vocabulary are confusingly misleading. Notable among them was the use of "free association" for the German *freier Einfall. Einfall* means sudden idea, brain wave or inspiration, not association, and while the individual ideas brought out by "free association" can be termed "free," the links between them are not free but, according to Freud, closely linked by the workings of the unconscious. But Brill had closely studied Jung's association experiments and "free association" was perhaps to be expected. *Angst* had probably, for better or for worse, to be translated as "anxiety," despite the fact that the English word has a range of meaning different from that of its German counterpart. There were also the *aktuell* neuroses, which for Freud meant the symptoms of current disturbances of sexual functioning—the German *aktuell* meaning "contemporary," or "of the present time." "Actual" neuroses, the phrase used by Brill, did not suggest the same thing.

As psychoanalysis thus began to make its way into the English language, the first dissensions among the newly established fraternity gradually appeared, within the Vienna Psychoanalytical Society as well as between it and the Zurich group. Freud's attitude to these early troubles was wise, firm and as conciliatory as possible to both sides. Here, as in some later confrontations between those holding different views on a subject about which no one yet knew very much, he combined a judicial air with a benign humanity. Only later, when disputes touched him personally, when his own role as the Delphic oracle of the movement was at stake, did he present a different picture: that of the commander in chief who struck at the first hint of defection with relentless determination and the technique of an accomplished politician.

The first suggestion of trouble arose within the Vienna group itself. As early as September 22, 1907, Freud had sent members a circular letter. "I wish to inform you," it said, "that I propose at the beginning of this new working year to dissolve the little Society which has been accustomed to meet every Wednesday at my home and immediately afterward to call it to life again." Members who disagreed with one another were thus enabled to retire from the movement without argument.

However, during the first months of the new working year, which began in the autumn, what had initially been no more than natural disagreements among pioneers discussing new routes across unexplored territory began to crystallize into something more disturbing. No details of the ways in which members expressed themselves during these arguments have survived, but the minutes of the Society, published only after the lapse of more than half a century, suggest that exchanges were sometimes bitter.

On February 5, 1908, Alfred Adler proposed that the practice of picking names out of an urn to decide the order of speaking should be abolished, together with the obligation on everyone to say something at every meeting. The rule had been adopted to prevent a few members from monopolizing the discussion and also to encourage a measure of self-discipline. However, some of those attending, wishing neither to break the rule nor to speak, solved the problem by leaving the meetings early, while a memorandum read when the proposal was discussed a week later noted that "the obligation to speak may easily tempt those who have nothing better to say to indulge in personal invective." A compromise saved the situation. The urn was retained but the requirement to speak was abolished.

The word "invective" had not been used lightly. At the February 5 meeting Isidor Sadger proposed that: "Personal invectives and attacks should immediately be suppressed by the Chairman who shall be given the authority to do so." Freud delicately brushed the idea aside, saying that he found it difficult to reprimand anyone. "If the situation is such that the gentlemen cannot stand each other, that no one expresses his true scientific opinion, etc., then he cannot help but close down [shop]," the minutes reported. "He has hoped—and is still hoping—that a deeper psychological understanding would overcome the difficulties in personal contacts. He would make use of the authority offered to him in Motion 5 only when some people were disturbing the speaker by their conversation."

It is clear from another proposal, made for the abolition of "intellectual communism," that many early members were no less anxious than other men to ensure that their own professional successes were not confused with those of their colleagues. They were hardly to be condemned. It is true that to Darwin, Rutherford, Einstein, as well as to other scientists of that caliber, the word "priority" would have seemed both vulgar and unnecessary—as it occasionally did to Freud. But no member of the Vienna Psychoanalytical Society, except possibly Freud himself, could be claimed as a Darwin or a Rutherford, let alone an Einstein. Their achievements tended to be additions to the new building Freud was erecting rather than separate constructions of their own, and each man must have felt a strong urge to ensure that his name was clearly seen on the brick he had laid. In such a situation it was easy for the line between "mine" and "his" to become almost invisible, and the admission that it at times disappeared completely came from Stekel. According to the minutes, he had "considered it his duty to spread the Professor's ideas; if in doing so he has occasionally slipped, he says a *pater peccavi:* it will not happen again; he will give up this type of journalism, and will try to avoid giving rise to friction."

The apology was made after Federn had proposed that no idea presented to the Society should be used without the consent of its author. Otherwise, he went on, members would feel inhibited in discussing their views. Freud disagreed. He believed it was a matter of personal tact, which could never be regulated by rules, and that any member could always indicate how he wished his ideas to be treated. As for himself, he concluded, he personally waived all rights in anything that he said. The matter was finally resolved with what sounded like a sensible compromise: "Every intellectual property set forth in this circle," it was proposed, "may be used as long as it has not explicitly been claimed by the author as his property." The resolution was carried unanimously.

By this time plans were going ahead for a Congress of all professionals interested in psychoanalysis, which Jung had proposed should be held in the spring of 1908. Freud had outlined the idea to members in December 1907, and early the following January a formal circular of invitation was drawn up. "From many quarters the followers of Freud's teachings have expressed a desire for an annual meeting which would afford them an opportunity to discuss their practical experiences and to exchange ideas," it said. "Since Freud's followers, though few in numbers at present, are scattered all over Europe, it has been suggested that our first meeting should take place immediately after this year's 3rd Congress for Experimental Psychology in Frankfurt (22–25 April)."

Jung became chief of staff for the enterprise. "I remember," recalled Ernest Jones who visited him in Zurich early in 1908, "vainly protesting against his wish to call it a Congress for Freudian Psychology, a term which offended my ideas of objectivity in scientific work." Freud himself was meanwhile trying to avoid the role of chairman, stressing to Jung that it would "make a better impression abroad if [Bleuler], the oldest and most authoritative of my supporters, should take the lead in the movement in my favor." Jung, feeling certain that Bleuler would refuse, did not ask him. The meeting therefore took place without a chairman, although there was no doubt that Freud's was the dominating presence.

The Congress was held on April 27 in Salzburg, a city conveniently midway between Vienna and Zurich. A total of forty-two men attended, more than half of them from Austria. The Swiss contingent numbered six, the German five. Sandor Ferenczi and F. Stein arrived from Hungary; Brill represented the Americans; and from Britain there came Ernest Jones and his brother-in-law Wilfred Trotter, soon to be one of England's leading surgeons. Jones was introduced by Jung to Freud who remarked that he saw by the shape of Jones's head that he could not be English but must be Welsh. "It astonished me," Jones has said, "first because it is uncommon for anyone on the Continent to know of the existence of my native country, and then because I had suspected my dolichocephalic skull might as well be Teutonic as Keltic." Only years later did he learn that Jung had told Freud in advance what his nationality was.

Work started at eight in the morning in the Hotel Bristol, time was set aside for a brisk walk in the afternoon, and further papers were read either before or after dinner. The keynote speech was given by Freud, who spoke on what was to become his internationally known case of the Rat Man. This was a lawyer, aged twenty-nine, well-known in Vienna, who had come to Freud the previous autumn complaining of obsessions from which he had suffered since childhood and which had grown worse during the previous four years. "The chief features of his disorder," Freud has written, "were *fears* that something might happen to two people of whom he was very fond—his father and a lady whom he admired. Besides this he was aware of *compulsive impulses*—such as an impulse, for instance, to cut his throat with a razor; and further he produced *prohibitions,* sometimes in connection with quite unimportant things." The obsessions had really become serious, Freud soon discovered, as a result of two incidents which had taken place during army maneuvers earlier in the year. One was the recounting to the patient by a fellow officer of an Eastern punishment in which a pot containing live rats was strapped to a man's buttocks. The second incident involved the loss of the patient's glasses and the part played by the same fellow officer in the arrival of a replacement.

Freud extracted elaborate descriptions of both incidents from the patient and set them down in his published account of the case before adding: "It would not surprise me to hear that at this point the reader had ceased to be able to follow. For even the detailed account which the patient gave me of the external events of these days and of his reactions to them was full of self-contradictions and sounded hopelessly confused." But much as a detective unravels a tangled skein of evidence, Freud untangled his patient's confusions. The process, and the interpretation of what lay behind it all, intrigued his listeners. "Delivered without any notes, it began at eight o'clock," Jones has written of the occasion, "and at eleven he offered to bring it to a close. We had all been so enthralled, however, at the fascinating exposition that we begged him to go on, and he did so for another hour. I had never before been so oblivious to the passage of time." The patient was still in analysis and was to remain so until the following September, a year after the treatment had begun. But by then Freud had traced the obsessions back to infant sexual experiences. The patient appeared to have been cured and the case was finished.

At Salzburg Jones himself spoke on "Rationalization in Everyday Life," Jung on "Dementia Praecox" and Adler on "Sadism in Life and in Neurosis." With the exception of Freud, each speaker was allowed half an hour, followed by a period for questions which were continued during afternoon walks in the winding streets of Salzburg. Before the Congress ended, an international organization was discussed, and it was decided to start a Yearbook (*Jahrbuch für psychoanalytische und psychopathologische Forschungen*) under the direction of Freud and Bleuler, with Jung as editor. The decision caused a repressed disgruntlement among the Viennese who felt themselves being kept off the higher ground that was now emerging.

Even before the Salzburg Congress the chances of the Viennese and the Swiss working amicably together seemed slight. Jones had been told by Jung in Zurich that "Freud had no followers of any weight in Vienna, and that he was surrounded there by a 'degenerate and Bohemian crowd' who did him little credit." Now, in Salzburg, Jones began asking himself whether Jung's account was more than simple anti-Semitism. He decided that it was. In Jones's view the Viennese were by no means first-class, a view that cannot be accounted for entirely by the contrast between Freud and even the best of his Viennese followers. To this difference there was added not only the Jew–Gentile problem but the difference in outlook between the Viennese and the Swiss. Freud always ridiculed the criticism that psychoanalysis was biased toward sexuality on account of the alleged semilibertine habits of the Viennese, maintaining that they were no different from the rest of Europeans, and that in any case the Swiss were not straight-laced. It is difficult to know whether he really believed this argument or used it merely for tactical reasons, but his records contain innumerable cases which fit almost unnoticed into the Viennese scene but would have been scandalous eccentricities in the land of Calvin.

If those at the Salzburg Congress believed that psychoanalysis was now preparing to sweep all before it they might have been warned by one example. Wilfred Trotter had one of the best brains of his time. His most famous book, *The Instincts of the Herd in Peace and War,* was to show him open to new and, in fact, even revolutionary ideas. But his behavior at Salzburg was an example of the conservative reaction that Freud and his followers were frequently to meet in the future. Trotter did not attend the session at which Freud spoke, giving his poor German as an excuse. And when one of the company made a facetious remark at dinner, he turned to Jones and said in English: "I console myself with the thought that I can cut a leg off, and no one else here can."

Nevertheless, the Congress was a success. Furthermore, as Freud made clear to Jung shortly afterward, it had enabled the two men to resolve a hint of difference which had sprung up between them. "So you too are pleased with our meeting . . . ," he wrote. "It refreshed me a good deal and left me with a pleasant aftertaste. I was glad to find you so flourishing and every suspicion of resentment melted away when I saw you again and understood you."

But a price had to be paid for Jung's support, notably the opposition which his touchiness aroused in other members of the movement. This was demonstrated after the Salzburg Congress when Jung protested that Karl Abraham had failed in his paper to give credit to work carried out by the Swiss. A young German Jew from Bremen, Abraham had gone to the Burghölzli in 1904. Three years later he resigned, visited Freud in Vienna and then settled in Berlin, where he became Germany's first full-time practicing psychoanalyst.

As the future founder of the Berlin Psychoanalytical Society, Abraham had started a Freudian Association as early as October 1907, reporting to Freud that "No less than twenty doctors appeared at the second meeting . . .; some came quite a long distance from hospitals in the country. There is therefore no lack of interest. . . ." A few months later he was reporting a lively Freudian discussion at a party for doctors and their wives held by Professor Hugo Liepmann, a Berlin neurologist. "In the course of the battle," wrote Abraham, ". . . I defended the wish-fulfillment theory of dementia praecox in one room, my wife in the other room had to defend the theory of repression. Otherwise there is little opportunity for propaganda. . . ." Nevertheless, Abraham continued to battle for the cause, admitting that when he spoke to the Berliner Gesellschaft für Psychiatrie und Nervenkrankheiten (Berlin Society for Psychiatry and Nervous Illnesses) he had not mentioned Freud's name too often since "it acts like a red rag to a bull," but then adding that he "might advance in the second half of the winter with heavier artillery."

To Abraham, who was "becoming more and more convinced that a paper can be useful to our cause only if the author unreservedly identifies himself with our findings," Freud revealed something of his tactics. On being asked whether he would attend the next Congress of the Gesellschaft Deutscher Nervenärzte (Society of German Nerve Specialists) in Vienna, he replied:

> Unless the most improbable changes take place in the meantime, I shall not myself attend the Congress in Vienna, and shall also prevent my hotheads from taking an active part. If you wish to attend and speak, that is a different matter. You possess the necessary self-control and detachment. But you will not derive much pleasure from it, and I shall not grant my dear Viennese the pleasure of a battle in which we should be shouted down. On the other hand, our absence will annoy them, and that suits me. . . .

Freud could control his Viennese more easily than he could control either the independent Abraham or the Swiss, who from the first were allies whose support needed constant attention. All his tact was therefore needed when after Salzburg Jung protested about the omission from Abraham's paper—on "Psychosexual Differences between Dementia Praecox and Hysteria"—of the expected acknowledgments to himself and Bleuler. This was a touchy subject. Dementia praecox, or "early insanity," was the name which had during the last years of the nineteenth century been given by Emil Kraepelin to a large group of mental illnesses. Their causes and the possibility of cure were, in the early 1900s, the subject of considerable discussion by psychiatrists, notably Eugen Bleuler who in 1911 coined the word *schizophrenia,* or "splitting of the mind," to describe a range of mental illnesses smaller than Kraepelin's but all characterized by disintegration of the patient's emotional stability. Jung believed that the troubles generally covered by the phrase "dementia praecox" were produced by a toxin which brought about an organic condition of the brain. This was different from Abraham's view, or Freud's for that matter. Yet each man working in this particular field did owe something to his colleagues, and each no doubt felt that in such a situation it was essential that the niceties of acknowledgment should be meticulously observed.

Freud, acting as mediator, told Abraham that he was unwilling to allow dissension. "There are still so few of us that disagreements, based perhaps on personal 'complexes,' ought to be excluded among us." There was, moreover, a special reason for wishing to keep Jung within the fold, since he, as Freud went on, "as a Christian and a pastor's son finds his way to me only against great inner resistances. His association with us is the more valuable for that. I nearly said that it was only by his appearance on the scene that psychoanalysis escaped the danger of becoming a Jewish national affair."

On this occasion Abraham came quickly to heel, writing an apologetic note to Jung and admitting to Freud that he had deleted from his Salzburg address a sentence from the manuscript which would have gratified Bleuler and Jung. "I deceived myself momentarily by a cover-motive, that of saving time, while the true reason lay in my animosity against Bleuler and Jung."

Freud succeeded in averting the potential crisis, noting to Abraham afterward,

> I nurse a suspicion that the suppressed anti-Semitism of the Swiss that spares me is deflected in reinforced form upon you. But I think that we as Jews, if we wish to join in, must develop a bit of masochism, be ready to suffer some wrong. Otherwise there is no hitting it off. Rest assured that, if my name were Oberhüber, in spite of everything my innovations would have met with far less resistance. . . .

Toward the end of the summer he at last managed to fit in a longed-for visit to England, traveling first to Southport on the northwest coast, where his half-brother Emanuel was now living in semiretirement. Emanuel had come to England almost half a century earlier and was now in his seventies; but according to Freud, who on arrival sent a "Best Wishes from Southport" card to his daughter Mathilde, Emanuel looked "much younger than when he came here"—words in English that he added to his greetings in German. After an enjoyable brief spell in London he returned to Vienna by way of Zurich, where he spent three days in Jung's quarters in the Burghölzli. They had, he reported to Abraham, spent up to eight hours a day walking and talking. Jung, moreover, had for the time being suppressed heretical views of his own, had "overcome his vacillation, adheres unreservedly to the cause, and also will continue to work energetically on the dementia praecox question on our lines. That is highly gratifying to me, and I hope it will be pleasing to you also."

Before traveling to Zurich, Freud had outlined to Jung the place that he was expected to occupy in what was a steadily, if slowly, growing movement. "My selfish purpose, which I frankly confess, is to persuade you to continue and complete my work by applying to psychoses what I have begun with neuroses," he wrote. "With your strong and independent character, with your Germanic blood which enables you to command the sympathies of the public more readily than I, you seem better fitted than anyone else I know to carry out this mission. Besides, I'm fond of you; but I have learned to subordinate that factor."

Thus encouraged, Jung readily accepted the mantle of chief of staff to a commander in chief busily preparing for the battles ahead. Freud knew well that in spite of the growing interest in psychoanalysis aroused by the Salzburg Congress opposition would continue and might intensify. "No, the dawn is not yet," he wrote to Jung a few months later. "We must carefully tend our little lamp, for the night will be long."

Nevertheless, psychoanalysis was no longer restricted to a small Viennese group. With Abraham working hard for the cause in Berlin, Ernest Jones an eager recruit about to publicize the message in North America, Ferenczi an outpost in Hungary, and the cantonal Burghölzli progressively adopting the therapy, it had the makings of an international movement. It was, moreover, already starting to show the characteristic of success breeding success, and it now began to draw in men who a year earlier might have given Freud's ideas less serious attention. Among them was an unexpected recruit, Pfarrer Oskar Pfister, a quiet resolute Swiss whose bushy mustachios gave him an uncanny resemblance to the Kaiser. His speciality was pastoral work among young people, and after publication of his paper *Wahnvorstellung und Schüler Selbstmord* ("Fantasy and Schoolboy Suicide"), his friend Carl Jung recommended that he send Freud a copy.

"It's really too nice of him—a Protestant clergyman—" Freud

acknowledged to Jung, "though rather upsetting to me to see PA enlisted in the fight against 'sin.' " He was, however, in no two minds about Pfister's usefulness and in thanking him recorded his satisfaction "that our psychiatric work has been taken up by a minister of religion who has access to the minds of so many young and healthy individuals."

Pfister, the first educational specialist to concern himself with psychoanalysis, soon produced a second paper with which Freud opened a discussion at the Vienna Psychoanalytical Society. Between the two men there grew up a friendship which was to survive both Freud's determined attacks on religion and Pfister's equally determined defense. In April 1909 Pfister visited the Freud family in Vienna for the first time, Freud's son Oliver playing truant from school to guide the visitor round the Prater. It was the first of many meetings, and Anna Freud remembered how in "the totally non-religious Freud household Pfister, in his clerical garb and with the manners and behavior of a pastor, was like a visitor from another planet."

Pfister had already begun to use in his daily work the clues to mental disturbances he had picked up from his layman's reading of Freud. Now, with the interchange of correspondence, he started to use on a more formal basis the techniques of psychoanalysis, slowly building the foundations of a psychologically oriented system of education and pastoral work. But Pfister's pastoral contacts with young people were extensive, and there seems little doubt that Freud accepted from him suggestions for child analysis. The influence was even wider, as Freud was to admit when he wrote, "I am very much struck by the fact that it never occurred to me how extraordinarily helpful the psychoanalytic method might be in pastoral work, but that is surely accounted for by the remoteness from me, as a wicked pagan, of the whole system of ideas."

Pfister had a way with young people, and Freud's eldest son long remembered the occasion when, as a student, he arrived home after being knifed in an anti-Semitic brawl. Pfister was dining with the family. "I apologised for my appearance," Martin Freud recalled years later, "and father threw me a sympathetic glance. The clergyman, however, got up and approached me to shake hands warmly, congratulating me on being wounded in so just and noble a cause. This sympathy and kindliness from a dignified leader of the Christian Church heartened me considerably, making me feel less like a battered ruffian."

To Pfister, the intelligent outsider, Freud wrote with a disarming frankness that revealed the inner strength of his beliefs. "If only," he wrote, "one could get the better people to realize that all our theories are based on experience (there is no reason, so far as I am concerned, why they should not try to interpret it differently) and not just fabricated out of thin air or thought up over the writing desk. But the latter is what they all really assume, and it throws a remarkable light on their own methods of work." The value of what psychoanalysts wrote, he stressed on another occasion, was that it contained nothing accepted on authority alone, but only "what can be stated as the direct outcome of our own troublesome labors." Yet there was also, more openly to Pfister than to most other laymen, the arrogant assertion that psychoanalysis was above argument. "Public debate of psychoanalysis is hardly possible," Freud maintained; "one does not share common ground, and against the lurking effects nothing can be done. Psychoanalysis is a deep-going movement, and public debates are bound to be as useless as the theological disputations of the time of the Reformation."

However, by the time he was pressing his own almost theological beliefs on Pfister, the Salzburg meeting had helped to bring about another major step forward in the movement's progress. Freud was invited to lecture in the United States.

12

A Sortie to America

... the audience is now at our mercy, under obligation to applaud
whatever we bring them.

FREUD, in a letter to C. G. Jung

Jung's assertion in January 1908, made when Brill was asking to
translate Freud's works, that interest in psychoanalysis in America
was very great, was something of an enthusiastic exaggeration.
Interest was certainly increasing, but so was opposition. In New
England and in the cities along the East Coast, where many of
America's important medical schools had grown up, the Puritan
ethic was still strong. The importance given to sex in Freud's
theories—an emphasis regarded in the more sophisticated parts of
Europe as in bad taste rather than wrong—therefore tended in
many parts of the United States to be considered not only incorrect
but perverse. Years later Weir Mitchell, whose rest cure Freud had
prescribed for his patients during his early days in practice, was
still happy to describe Freud's writings by the single word "filth."
However, there was another side to the coin. Medical practitioners in the United States lacked, on the whole, the built-in resistance
to new ideas which was often a feature of their counterparts in
Europe, dedicated as they were to their centuries-old traditions
and closely knit societies. The Americans' readiness to experiment
was later shown in their reception of insulin therapy, chemotherapy, electroshock therapy, psychosurgery and other treatments for
the psychoses. Originating in Europe, the new techniques were
seized upon in the United States, improved, modified and adapted
for mass use. Such open-mindedness helped to counterbalance the
instinctive gut reaction to Freud; the result was that although his

theories came under the usual barrage of attack, they invariably aroused a few staunch defenders within the medical establishment. A subsidiary reason may have been that Freud's name had already been heard of in the United States through his monograph on aphasia and his work on the cerebral palsies of children; however much his critics might pour scorn on some of his ideas, they had to admit that as a nerve specialist he had already carved out a niche for himself. This made it at least marginally more difficult to write him off as a crank who should not be taken seriously.

In addition, there was within organized American psychiatry an underlying acknowledgment of much which lay at the heart of Freud's theories. The admission that there was a degree of basic truth in some of his pronouncements went back at least to Samuel White, one of the men who had helped found the American Psychiatric Society. "From the cradle to the grave," he had said in an address on insanity in 1844, "man's life will be found a series of antecedents and consequents, having a direct bearing on his physical and moral powers. To investigate the human mind we must trace its history from its infant development, through manhood, to decrepitude. It is by the study of the entire man that we are to learn the deviations from the healthy standard, prostrating those energies and mental endowments." Some doctors had even dared to say what Freud was later condemned for saying, as when A. J. Ingersoll claimed in his book *In Health,* published in 1877, that "hysteria is frequently caused by the voluntary suppression of the sexual life."

But it was not doctors alone who, long before Freud, were saying in general terms what he was later to say specifically. More than one American writer in the mid- and later nineteenth century had shown an almost uncanny appreciation of what were to become the fundamental beliefs of psychoanalysis. In *The Scarlet Letter* Nathaniel Hawthorne described how the Calvinist minister, Arthur Dimmesdale, was treated by his friendly physician who "strove to go deep into his patient's bosom, delving among his principles, prying into his recollections, and probing everything with a cautious touch, like a treasure-seeker in a dark cavern." Few secrets escape such an approach, Hawthorne continued, and eventually, "at some inevitable moment, will the soul of the sufferer be dissolved, and flow forth in a dark, but transparent stream, bringing all its mysteries into the daylight." Twenty years later Oliver Wendell Holmes, addressing the Phi Beta Kappa Society at Harvard, went further. "The more we examine the mechanism of thought, the more we shall see that the automatic, unconscious action of the mind enters largely into all its processes. Our definite ideas are stepping stones; how we get from one to the other, we do not know: something carries us; we do not take the step."

By the 1890s the vague idea of using the unconscious as a therapeutic tool was beginning to seep from this largely literary area into the medical hinterland occupied by the psychologists and the psychiatrists. In 1894 William James reviewed Breuer and Freud's "Preliminary Communication" in the first issue of the *Psychological Review*. Although describing it primarily as "an independent corroboration of Janet's views," he acknowledged it as an important paper and noted how Breuer and Freud used hypnotism to work out repressed unconscious memories, which he described in an apt phrase as "thorns in the spirit." The following year, 1895, Bronislaw Onuf, a neurologist in the New York State hospital system, wrote an abstract of Freud's "The Neuro-Psychoses of Defense" for the *Journal of Nervous and Mental Disease*, the first of a series in which he openly supported psychoanalysis. Perhaps more important was a lecture, also in 1895, given by Robert T. Edes, a distinguished doctor, before the Massachusetts Medical Society. In explaining "nervous invalidism" under the title "The New England Invalid," Edes dealt with *Studies on Hysteria* and advised that it would sometimes be better for a patient to scream, as she often says she wants to, instead of restraining her feelings for propriety's sake, and developing a neuralgia or paralysis or an attack of "nervous prostration." The following year Dr. Morton Prince founded the *Journal of Abnormal Psychology* in Boston and in its first volume introduced the word "psychoanalysis" to America.

By the turn of the century William James had apparently been fully converted by *Studies on Hysteria* and in his Gifford Lectures of 1901–2, published as *The Varieties of Religious Experience: A Study in Human Nature*, gave his accolade in the following words:

> In the wonderful explorations by Binet, Janet, Breuer, Freud, Mason, Prince, and others, of the subliminal consciousness of patients with hysteria, we have revealed to us whole systems of underground life, in the shape of memories of a painful sort which lead to a parasitic existence, buried outside of the primary fields of consciousness, and making irruptions thereinto with hallucinations, pains, convulsions, paralyses of feeling and of motion, and the whole procession of symptoms of hysteric disease of body and of mind. Alter or abolish by suggestion these subconscious memories, and the patient immediately gets well.

Two points should be noted. James was lumping together a variety of very different "explorations" in much the same way as, a few years later, the term "psychoanalysis" was to be used in the United States to describe a number of techniques, some of which had little if anything to do with Freud. Secondly, there was the somewhat optimistic assertion that "the patient immediately gets well," a claim that would have been made by few psychoanalysts even in their most ambitious moments. But James could see at least something of the future. "In the relief of certain hysterias," he said when giving the Lowell Lectures in 1906, "by handling the buried idea, whether as in Freud or in Janet, we see a portent of the possible usefulness of these new discoveries. The awful become relatively trivial."

Counterbalancing such opinions there was the opposition. It was epitomized by C. R. Hughes, editor of *The Alienist and Neurologist*, a devoted enemy of Freud who had condemned Freud's paper on the etiology of hysteria. But one point should be remembered: Freud had not then publicly disclaimed his seduction theory, his "first great error." Here, as he was to confess to Wilhelm Fliess, and eventually to the rest of the world, he had been wrong and the rest of the world had been right.

While the supporters and critics of Freud's theories were airing their opinions during the first years of the twentieth century, a few men were cautiously beginning to experiment with the revolutionary ideas which had found their way across the Atlantic from Vienna. One was James Jackson Putnam. An established Boston physician and professor of neurology at Harvard, Putnam had studied under Charcot in Paris, under Meynert in Vienna and under Hughlings Jackson in London. He was to be described by Harvard's President Lowell as "a man of science, eminent in his field, a philosopher and a saint," and he had begun to investigate psychoanalysis despite the warnings of his wife. She had, his daughter later wrote, "reacted with tragic bitterness, feeling that he had been mistakenly lured into a false path which would ruin his professional standing." In 1904 he had treated two female hysterics and one male in the Massachusetts General Hospital. The tentative conclusion he drew was "not that the 'psychoanalytic' method is useless, for I believe the contrary to be the case, but that it is difficult of application and often less necessary than one might think."

Even qualified support from a man of such professional and social standing made it much harder to dismiss psychoanalysis with a sneer. Putnam's interest, moreover, had been secured before 1906, the first of four years which were to be crucial for the acceptance of psychoanalysis in the United States. By this time various psychoanalytic techniques were being used at Bloomingdale Hospital in White Plains, New York, although a history of the hospital adds the somewhat confusing rider that it was probably not Freudian psychoanalysis. Almost simultaneously, interest in psychoanalysis was increased—ironically, in view of future developments—first by discussion of Jung's association tests and later by *The Psychology of Dementia Praecox*, in which Jung showed that Freud's theory could be demonstrated in what was to become known as schizophrenia as well as in the neuroses.

In 1908 Brill returned from Europe to the United States, and the opening of his practice in New York as America's first full-time practicing psychoanalyst was a measure of the impact made on him by Freud. In the same year there appeared on the North American scene the Freudian proselyte without whose efforts the fate of psychoanalysis in America and Canada would have been very different. The newcomer was the Ernest Jones to whom Freud had been introduced at Salzburg. For the next half century Jones was to be the loyal standard-bearer of the movement, devoted to Freud and with a belief in "the cause" even more unqualified than that of Freud himself. There was good enough reason. "To me it is clear," he wrote to Freud after the First World War, "that I owe my career, my livelihood, my position, and my capacity of happiness in marriage—in short, everything—to you and the work you have done."

Jones arrived in Toronto to take charge of the university's psychiatric clinic late in 1908. Within a few months he had made contact with Brill in New York and proposed that they start contributing to the *Journal of Abnormal Psychology*. "I heartily agree with you and wish you had already done it," Freud replied to Jones on hearing of the plan. "It might be the best way to introduce my teaching to your countrymen [*sic*], perhaps much more efficacious than a translation of my papers. . . ."

A month later Jones was able to report that he had arranged visits to Boston and New York. However, he added a warning:

. . . I am not very hopeful of the present wave of interest, for the Americans are a peculiar nation with habits of their own. They show curiosity, but rarely true interest (it is the difference between the itch of the neurasthenic and the desire of a normal lover). Their attitude toward progress is deplorable. They want to hear of the "latest" method of treatment, with one eye dead on the Almighty Dollar, and think only of the credit, or "kudos" as they call it, it will bring them. Many eulogistic articles have been written on Freud's psychotherapy of late, but they are absurdly superficial, and I am afraid they will strongly condemn it as soon as they hear of its sexual basis and realize what it means. The most we can hope for is a few practical converts who can be won over and spread their experience. However we must do what we can to pave the way for the future. I published my Salzburg paper in Prince's journal in August, and from the letters I received about it it seems to have found favor. I am very eager to keep our movement scientific, for that will very greatly increase its "respectability" & power of obtaining a hearing. I am going always to dissociate myself from all these quack Xtian Science, & Emmanuel Church movements, for it is almost hopeless to convert these religious fanatics on a large scale, and also their pandering to the popular brings anyone associated with them into discredit in scientific circles. . . .

There followed, during the next few months, a series of letters in which Freud was kept closely informed not only of the prevailing opinion in the United States but of the support, or lack of it, he might expect from various members of its psychiatric community. Early in February 1909 Jones was able to report that he had made his first foray. The reception had been mixed. He had spoken to the American Therapeutic Congress in New Haven, Connecticut, where he had been unsympathetically received. "I well remember," he later wrote, "the shiver that went through the audience when I said that Freud had sometimes treated a patient daily for as long as three years, though a member admitted to me afterward that he knew of neurotics he would be proud to be able to cure in that time."

But in Boston things went better. Here Morton Prince had arranged a special meeting at which Jones spoke on Freud's theories. "William James couldn't come," Jones reported,

but all the others were there, sixteen of them, Prof. Munsterberg, Prof. Putnam (psychology and neurology respectively at Harvard), Prof. Dearborn (physiology) . . . I had to address them and then expound or answer questions for four hours. I think such personal work often does much more than writing, for one can instantly correct misunderstandings & false ideas that come up. I seemed to be a great success, judging from the complimentary congratulations I had. They were sympathetically inclined & very interested, especially in the sexual part. One must not hope too much however from it, for they are the only people in America at all interested in psychotherapy & even they are so concerned in money-making as to do practically no original work or observations. The main difficulty was their colossal ignorance. So far I have not met *one* man in America, except of course Brill, who has even *read* the *Traumdeutung.* Even Sides [Boris Sidis], who has worked at dreams for six years, and who has nearly

completed a big book on the subject, hasn't read it, though he tells
me he is "going to."

However, Putnam was "a delightful old man, meek, humble,
learned, well-read, idealistic but easily swayed in all directions."
The main problems for psychoanalysis in the United States,
Jones went on,

> are peculiar to the Anglo-Saxon race, & one must know nicely the
> kinds of currents and prejudices in order to combat them most
> successfully. I am sure it is important to aim first at the recognized
> people & not to popularize too soon. There is so much vulgarization
> & exploitation of everything here, that one has a strong weapon in
> insisting on the exact scientific side of the subject, & that is what I
> mean to do. Also I want to be generally recognized in neurology &
> psychology on [sic] other fields, so that one's influence will be greater
> & one will be more readily listened to. A man who writes always on
> the same thing is apt to be regarded here as a crank, because to the
> superficial American every subject is easily exhausted except for
> cranks, & if the subject is sexual he is simply tabooed as a sexual
> neurasthenic. Hence I shall dilute my sex articles with articles on
> other subjects alternately.

In spite of this slightly pessimistic account of the prospects in
February 1909, negotiations had already begun for Freud's visit to
the United States later in the year. The originator had been Stanley
Hall, "the Darwin of the Mind," as he has grandiloquently been
called. The ambivalent nature of Hall's character is suggested by
the fact that although a founder of the American Psychological
Association, he openly described his life as "a series of fads or
crazes." His weakness has been delicately described by William A.
Koelsch who once noted that Hall was "a publicist for research, a
synthesizer and teacher of great stimulating power, but the more
careful paths of disciplined scholarship tended to be left as a task
for others."

Hall had in 1904 given a series of lectures on sex at Clark
University in Worcester, Massachusetts, over which he had pre-
sided since its opening in 1889. Although he had excluded women
from these particular lectures and finally abandoned the series
because "too many outsiders got in and even listened surreptitiously at the door," he reacted less critically than many Americans
to Freud's emphasis on the subject. In *Adolescence,* the book that
made him famous and virtually introduced that word to the English
language, Hall mentioned Freud a number of times and even forecast that his theories would be of fundamental importance to the

psychology of art and religion. Luckily for Freud, psychoanalysis had by 1909 become the latest of Hall's "fads or crazes."

At Clark University's Decennial Celebration in 1899, August Forel had lectured on "Hypnotism and Cerebral Activity," and in the last weeks of 1908 Hall wrote to Freud. "Although I have not the honor of your personal acquaintance," he said, "I have for many years been profoundly interested in your work, which I have studied with diligence, and also in that of your followers." Would Freud, he went on, visit them during their twenty-year celebrations to be held in July and give from four to six lectures. "Janet, who has visited this country and given a similar course of public lectures, has had a profound influence in turning the attention of our leading and especially our younger students of abnormal psychology from the exclusively somatic and neurological to a more psychological basis," he continued. "We believe that a concise statement of your own results and point of view would now be exceedingly opportune, and perhaps in some sense mark an epoch in the history of these studies in this country."

Freud refused. The reason was that he normally worked until the end of July, and to stop sooner would mean the loss of several thousand kronen. Clark University was offering to contribute only $400 toward his travel expenses and, as he pointed out to Jung, he was "not wealthy enough to spend five times that much to give the Americans an impetus. (That's boasting; two-and-a-half to three times as much!)"

However, in February 1909, Hall wrote again, telling Freud that the celebrations were being postponed until September, that the travel allowance had been increased to $750 and that he was now able to add the promise of an honorary degree. Freud accepted the renewed offer without delay. "I must admit that this has thrilled me more than anything else that has happened in the last few years— except perhaps for the appearance of the *Jahrbuch*—and that I have been thinking of nothing else," he wrote to Jung. And to Abraham he observed: "Perhaps it will annoy some people in Berlin as well as in Vienna. That cannot do any harm."

In April he told Hall that he intended to sail from Trieste, and apologized for the fact that this might make him arrive a few days late. Shortly afterward he was informed that news of his coming visit had leaked out and that applications to attend his lectures were already coming in. "I have some misgivings as to whether I can answer the expectations," replied an unexpectedly modest Freud. Hall had no doubts, and on August 9 invited the visitor to be his house guest, adding that there was already "a wide and deep interest in your coming to this country, and you will have the very best experts within a wide radius."

By now Jung had also been invited. This, Freud noted to Pfister, "changes my whole feeling about the trip and makes it important. I am very curious to see what will come of it all." To Jung he wrote with the air of a father congratulating a successful son. "Such a beginning will take you far," he said, "and a certain amount of favor on the part of men and fate is a very good thing for one who aspires to perform great deeds." Jung was to be allowed three lectures, Freud a maximum of six, and into these they had somehow to pack the real essence of the complicated and revolutionary ideas of almost two decades. However, as Freud consoled Jung, "the invitation is the main thing . . . the audience is now at our mercy, under obligation to applaud whatever we bring them."

Freud was well aware of the importance of his first series of lectures to an English-speaking audience and was determined to guard, as far as possible, against any mishaps. Principally for this reason, it appears, he proposed that Ferenczi should accompany Jung and himself. Ferenczi agreed. He was to give Freud invaluable support.

It was eventually arranged that the three men should sail from Bremen on August 21. Freud soon realized that he would be hardpressed during the last few weeks before leaving; in particular, as he wrote to Jung, there was his account of the Rat Man case to be completed. "I am finding it very difficult," he confided; "it is almost beyond my powers of presentation; the paper will probably be intelligible to no one outside our immediate circle. How bungled our reproductions are, how wretchedly we dissect the great art works of psychic nature!"

Even so, he could not resist the opportunity of taking on one more case before sailing, and early in July informed Jung that he might have to visit Salonica on a consultation trip. "But I have asked for so much money for the five days that the need for me will probably vanish," he added. "It's not even a case for [psychoanalysis]."

The trip appears to have fallen through, and on August 20 Freud traveled to Bremen where Jung and Ferenczi were awaiting him. Before they left the following day on the *George Washington* there was a strange incident for which various explanations have been given. Freud was host at a luncheon party for his two colleagues, and during the meal, conversation turned to the mummified corpses of prehistoric man still being found in North Germany. This appeared to be Jung's subject, and he continued to expound on it until Freud protested and asked if Jung wanted his death.

Jung called this a funny interpretation. Thereupon Freud fainted.

"Afterward," Jung subsequently wrote, "he said to me that he was convinced that all this chatter about corpses meant I had death wishes toward him. I was more than surprised by this interpretation. I was alarmed by the intensity of his fantasies—so strong that, obviously, they could cause him to faint." But Freud had at the start of the meal persuaded Jung to renounce his teetotalism for a glass of wine, and the fainting fit has been interpreted as a psychic penalty for this minor triumph. Freud himself, who seems to have fainted rather easily when contradicted, later commented of a similar occasion: "[It] was surely provoked by psychogenic elements, which received strong somatic reinforcements (a week of troubles, a sleepless night, the equivalent of a migraine, the day's tasks). I have had several such attacks; in each case there were similar contributory causes, often a bit of alcohol for which I have no tolerance."

On the *George Washington* Freud apparently discovered to his delight that his cabin steward was reading *The Psychopathology of Everyday Life.* The three travelers whiled away the eight-day crossing by analyzing each other's dreams. Freud's, according to the account which Jung gave to Ernest Jones soon afterward, "seemed to be mostly concerned with cares for the future of his family and of his work." Later, however, Jung produced a more dramatic account:

> Freud had a dream—I would not think it right to air the problem it involved. I interpreted it as best I could, but added that a great deal more could be said about it if he would supply me with some additional details from his private life. Freud's response to these words was a curious look—a look of the utmost suspicion. Then he said: "But I cannot risk my authority!" At that moment he lost it altogether. That sentence burned itself into my memory; and in it the end of our relationship was already foreshadowed. Freud was placing personal authority above truth. . . .

Jung, perhaps, should not be taken too literally. Yet within the next few years the value that Freud put on authority was to become manifest.

They approached New York on the evening of August 27. As the ship nosed into upper New York Bay, Freud turned to Jung with the words, "Won't they get a surprise when they hear what we have to say to them!" "How ambitious you are," Jung replied, to which Freud rather indignantly retorted, "Me? I'm the most humble of men, and the only man who isn't ambitious." Jung, unwilling to be beaten, answered, "That's a big thing—to be the only one."

On shore they were met by Brill. Jones arrived from Toronto two days later, and the five men then spent a week sightseeing. Before it was over the rich American food, about which Freud maintained an obstinate lifelong grudge, had induced them to fast every third day. At the Metropolitan Museum of Art he studied the Greek antiquities and in Tiffany's was unable to resist buying a Chinese jade bowl for his collection. They visited Coney Island— "a magnified Prater." They dined at Hammerstein's Roof Garden and visited Columbia University. And in a Manhattan cinema Freud and Ferenczi saw their first moving pictures. On the thirtieth, Freud wrote to Hall announcing his arrival in the United States and two days later received the invitation to be Hall's house guest, forwarded from Vienna where it had missed him. He accepted, hoped that he would not be too much trouble, and explained that since his English was still poor he would be obliged at Worcester to "transfer the difficulty to the side of the hearers and talk in my native tongue."

On the evening of Saturday, September 4, Brill put the four men on the overnight steamer to Fall River, the next leg of their journey to Worcester. Here they were met by Stanley Hall and his wife, "plump, jolly, good-natured and extremely ugly," as Jung described her. The Halls' sumptuous home gave the visitors their first hint of the lavishness that could be experienced in America. "The house," Jung wrote to his wife, "is furnished in an incredibly amusing fashion, everything roomy and comfortable. There is a splendid studio filled with thousands of books, and boxes of cigars everywhere. Two pitch-black Negroes in dinner jackets, the extreme of grotesque solemnity, perform as servants. Carpets everywhere, all the doors open, even the bathroom door and the front door; people going in and out all over the place; all the windows extend down to the floor . . ." If these wonders were not enough, there were boxes of cigars even in what were then still called the lavatories.

The celebratory lectures, to be held in or around the factorylike Jonas Clark Hall, named after the Worcester industrialist who had founded the university, covered a good deal of ground. Mathematics, physics, chemistry, biology, history and education were all represented, while fourteen lectures on various aspects of psychology included five by Freud and three by Jung.

Freud's first lecture was to be given on Tuesday, September 7, but until almost the last moment he had little idea of what he was to talk about. For a man who had "been thinking of nothing else" once he had accepted the invitation, the lack of preparation was extraordinary. The previous June, when he and Jung had first considered their lectures, they had decided to discuss them while crossing the Atlantic. But on the ship, preoccupation with each other's dreams appears to have taken up most of the time, and on arrival at Worcester Freud felt inclined to restrict the lectures to dreams alone. On Jones's advice he decided to spread the net wider. Even so, the lectures were improvised on what was a remarkably *ad hoc* basis, in which Ferenczi played an important role. "In the morning, before the time had come for my lecture to begin, we would walk together in front of the university building and I would ask him to suggest what I should talk about that day," Freud has written. "He thereupon gave me a sketch of what, half an hour later, I improvised in my lecture. In this way he had a share in the origin of the *Five Lectures.*"

They were given on five successive mornings. The first was the occasion which really mattered. "In Europe," Freud was to write, "I felt as though I were despised; but over [in Worcester] I found myself received by the foremost men as an equal. As I stepped on to the platform . . . it seemed like the realization of some incredible daydream; psychoanalysis was no longer a product of delusion, it had become a valuable part of reality."

Lack of preparation paid dividends, for at virtually the last moment he decided to give a straightforward, relatively nontechnical account of how psychoanalysis had developed. It was not only well received in Worcester; even today, after psychoanalysis has evolved from the simple ideas of its early days into a maze of differing and sometimes competing beliefs and theories, the Clark University lectures still contain an excellent outline of the subject.

Freud began with what was, in the light of his future attitude, a remarkable statement. "If it is a merit to have brought psychoanalysis into being," he said, "that merit is not mine. I had no share in its earliest beginnings. I was a student and working for my final examinations at the time when another Viennese physician, Dr. Josef Breuer, first (in 1880–1882) made use of this procedure on a girl who was suffering from hysteria." There followed an elegant account of how Breuer had dealt with Bertha Pappenheim, although Freud made no mention of the doubts about the case which he by this time entertained. Next came one or two examples drawn from his own practice and then the much-quoted conclusion that *"our hysterical patients suffer from reminiscences."*

Always good at analogies, he explained the significance of the phrase by using as examples the carved gothic column at Charing Cross in London which commemorates the death of Queen Eleanor in the thirteenth century, and the Monument, a mile or so away in the city, built after the Great Fire of 1666. What, he asked his audience, would one think of contemporary Londoners who became melancholy about Queen Eleanor's death as they passed the Cross, or who shed tears before the Monument? "Yet every single hysteric and neurotic behaves like these two unpractical Londoners," he went on. "Not only do they remember painful experiences of the remote past, but they still cling to them emotionally; they cannot get free of the past and for its sake they neglect what is real and immediate." And he ended the first lecture on a humble note. His account, he said, might not have been particularly clear, and Breuer's explanation was incomplete; but it might well be that it was "not possible to make them much clearer—which shows that we still have a long way to go in our knowledge of the subject." As for explanations, "complete theories do not fall ready-made from the sky."

During the second lecture Freud explained how he had developed Breuer's method by dropping hypnotism. He went on to describe repression and resistance and gave his audience an account of the way in which Breuer's technique had grown into psychoanalysis, illustrating his story with the case of Elisabeth von R. from *Studies on Hysteria*. In the third lecture he introduced the technique of free association and explained that the study of jokes, and of everyday parapraxes, led to a better understanding of unconscious motives. He also revealed why he had not yet dealt at length with dream-interpretation. "I was held back," he said, "by a purely subjective and seemingly secondary motive. It seemed to me almost indecent in a country which is devoted to practical aims to make my appearance as a 'dream-interpreter,' before you could possibly know the importance that can attach to that antiquated and derided art. The interpretation of dreams is in fact the royal road to a knowledge of the unconscious; it is the securest foundation of psychoanalysis and the field in which every worker must acquire his convictions and seek his training." After this preamble he gave a brief account of the part that dream-interpretation played, was heavily sarcastic about those who condemned psychoanalysis while knowing nothing about it, and noted that his opponents no doubt included those who "would not reject the results of a microscopic examination because it could not be confirmed on the anatomical preparation with the naked eye, but who would first form a judgment on the matter themselves with the help of a microscope." The "arrogance of consciousness," he concluded, was one factor which made it so difficult for ordinary people to understand the reality of the unconscious.

Only in the fourth lecture did he come to the delicate question of sex in general and of infantile sexuality in particular. He began by reiterating that the sexual etiology of the neuroses was not something that he had been looking for but something forced upon him by evidence which he could not ignore. So, too, with infantile sexuality. Here he was able to play a trump card. For was it not Dr. Sanford Bell, himself a Fellow of Clark University, who had dealt with infantile sexuality in the *American Journal of Psychology* three years before Freud had published his *Three Essays*? Bell, Freud continued, had said "exactly what I have just told you." Moreover, Bell's concept of infantile sexuality outlined in "A Preliminary Study of the Emotion of Love between the Sexes" had been supported by no fewer than 2,500 positive observations in the course of fifteen years, among them 800 of his own. Having laid the ghost that he was propounding an un-American idea, Freud then gave a brief account of the conclusions he had arrived at in the *Three Essays* and ended by emphasizing that discussion of sexual life and the psychosexual development of children had not led too far away from the problem of curing nervous disorders. "You can, if you like," he ended, "regard psychoanalytic treatment as no more than a prolongation of education for the purpose of overcoming the residues of childhood."

His final lecture was a neat rounding-up, blaming a good deal on civilization, which made reality unsatisfying and thereby encouraged phantasy. Those with artistic gifts could sublimate their phantasies into artistic creations rather than into the symptoms of the neurotic. "The neuroses have no psychical content that is peculiar to them and that might not equally be found in healthy people." After a quick look at transference, Freud suggested that there were three possible results of successful psychoanalysis. Once the repressed unconscious had been brought to the surface it could be mastered with success. It could, secondly, be sublimated for different and more useful purposes. And, thirdly, "a certain portion of the repressed libidinal impulses" could be enjoyed once they had been brought up into consciousness. "I must thank you for your invitation," he concluded, "and for the attention with which you have listened to me."

He was over the hump; he had given an honest account yet he had, he correctly estimated, shocked a minimum number of his listeners.

On the evening of September 10 Freud and Jung were both awarded doctorates in an event that included "a tremendous amount of ceremony and fancy dress, with all sorts of red and black gowns and gold-tasselled square caps . . ." Freud's citation ran as follows: "Sigmund Freud of the University of Vienna, founder of a school of pedagogy already rich in new methods and achievements, leader today among students of the psychology of sex, and of psychotherapy and analysis, doctor of laws." He was visibly moved by the occasion, noting in his brief speech of acceptance and thanks: "This is the first official recognition of our endeavors."

Their reception had been better than expected, and Jung wrote triumphantly to his wife, "We are gaining ground here, and our following is growing slowly but surely. . . . I was greatly surprised, since I had prepared myself for opposition." From beyond Worcester, it is true, there came the expected criticism but it is difficult to know how well it reflected informed opinion. An accusation by the dean of the University of Toronto that "an ordinary reader would gather that Freud advocates free love, removal of all restraints and a relapse into savagery," was described by Jones as "by no means atypical"; yet to James Strachey, editing Freud in the 1960s, it was just this remark by which the current of opinion could be judged.

All the lectures at the celebrations had been public, and Freud had attracted a varied bag of listeners. Among unexpected visitors was Emma Goldman, who had attended his lectures in Vienna— and had once run an ice-cream parlor in Worcester with two other anarchists. On the psychiatrists and other potential converts, he had made a considerable impression, not least on Putnam who after the Worcester meeting appears to have abandoned most of his doubts. "I cannot pretend to have verified as yet all the many inferences and conclusions of Freud and his companions . . . ," he subsequently wrote. "But I have learned to believe fully in the theory and in the value of their methods of analysis and of treatment, and I am the more ready to accept their views for having made the personal acquaintance of the three men [Freud, Jung and Ferenczi] . . . and for having found them so kindly, unassuming, tolerant, earnest and sincere."

There was also William James who explained to the psychologist Théodore Flournoy that he had gone to Worcester "for one day in order to see what Freud was like." He was already fatally ill and greatly impressed Freud during a walk they took together. "I shall never forget one little scene . . . ," Freud wrote. "He stopped suddenly, handed me a bag he was carrying and asked me to walk on, saying that he would catch me up as soon as he had got through an attack of *angina pectoris* which was just coming on. He died of that disease a year later; and I have always wished that I might be as fearless as he was in the face of approaching death."

James still retained his sense of the ridiculous. Stanley Hall had asked him to bring the results of extrasensory perception experiments with a well-known psychic investigator, and both Freud and Jung were present when he arrived. He announced that he had brought some papers in which they might be interested. "And he put his hand to his breast pocket," Jung recalled, "and drew out a parcel which to our delight proved to be a wad of dollar bills. Considering Stanley Hall's great services for the increase and the welfare of Clark University and his rather critical remarks as to James's pursuits, it looked to us a particularly happy rejoinder. James excused himself profusely. Then he produced the real papers from the other pocket."

There is some doubt about James's feelings at Worcester. Ernest Jones has stated that "with his arm around my shoulder," James left Worcester with a message of encouragement, saying, "The future of psychology belongs to your work." James himself implies that his views were more qualified. "I strongly suspect Freud, with his dream theory, of being a regular *halluciné*," he wrote to Professor Mary Calkin a few days later. "But I hope that he and his disciples will push it to its limits as undoubtedly it covers some facts and will add to our understanding of 'functional' psychology, which is the real psychology." Shortly afterward he wrote to Théodore Flournoy. "I hope," he said, "that Freud and his pupils will push their ideas to their utmost limits, so that we may learn what they are. They can't fail to throw light on human nature; but I confess that he made on me personally the impression of a man obsessed with fixed ideas. I can make nothing in my own case with his dream theories and obviously 'symbolism' is a most dangerous method." According to Brill, "William James was impressed, but he was too old and weak to take any attitude about these new doctrines"; while it has also been suggested "that James's well-known affinity for a pluralistic universe was offended by Freud's seeming explanation of human behavior by one cause alone."

Whatever James's personal view, there is no doubt that Freud's sortie had been successful. It is true that few university presidents other than Hall would have risked their reputation by inviting him. It is notable that neither Yale nor Harvard issued even an informal invitation and that Freud had visited Columbia as an ordinary sightseer. Nevertheless, after September 1909 the situation began slowly to change, the result not only of the impact made by Freud on his audience but of the press reports which now introduced him and his work to a lay public.

The newspaper coverage of his lectures, and its possible influence on the spread of his theories in the United States, has been carefully analyzed by Ward Cromer and Paula Anderson, and shows considerable contrast. Of the two Worcester papers, the *Gazette* gave space to Dr. William Stern from Breslau, who spoke on "Individual Psychology"; to H. S. Jennings' lectures on the behavior of lower organisms; and to Leo Burgerstein's lectures on "The Main Problems of Schoolroom Sanitation and School Work" —merely reporting of Freud that he "spoke of his works on the psychology of everyday life, of dreams, and of sex," and that he "discussed his studies in the psychology of the future." The Worcester *Telegram* gave him more attention although somewhat ambiguously reporting that he "developed his method of psychic analysis, which is described as a sort of third degree administered with certain appliances and in certain ways, in which he finds out the general direction in which the cause of sickness is sought." On the Sunday following the ceremonies it announced with acclamation, "Conference Brings Savants together: Long-haired Type Hard to Discover: Men with Bulging Brains have Time for Occasional Smiles."

The most influential newspaper reports were made by the Boston *Transcript* which noted that Dr. Franz Boas, the celebrated anthropologist, had given up his place to Freud for the latter's first morning lecture, and that Boas and his friends were "enthusiastic over the sacrifice." On subsequent days the paper gave reasonably informed summaries of the lectures and maintained interest by publishing on September 11 a lengthy interview with Freud by Adelbert Albrecht, a reporter who claimed to have had a long acquaintance with Freud's writings and who was certainly an admirer.

"One sees at a glance that he is a man of great refinement, of intellect, and of many-sided education," Albrecht wrote. "His sharp, yet kind, clear eyes suggest at once the doctor. His high forehead with the large bumps of observation and his beautiful, energetic hands are very striking. He speaks clearly, weighing his words carefully, but unfortunately never of himself. Again and again he emphasizes the merits of his colleagues. . . . It is with great difficulty that he can be persuaded to talk about his method of psychotherapy which he calls the analytical." Albrecht seems to have reported Freud's statements accurately and to have interposed only the minimum of explanation needed for their understanding by a lay public. The result was the best newspaper description of psychoanalysis to appear for some years, certainly in the United States and possibly anywhere in the world.

Other coverage was spotty. The Boston *Daily Advertiser* reported that Dr. Ed. Freud *(sic)* had given five lectures on "The Psychology of Everyday Life." The *Boston Medical and Surgical Journal* complimented Freud on his clarity of exposition and noted that his statements "certainly gave his hearers much food for thought, however they might differ from him in details of interpretation." For *The Nation* of September 23 Stanley Hall gave an account of what Freud was trying to achieve.

"Because the newspaper coverage was limited," Cromer and Anderson conclude, "it is questionable as to how important a part they played in spreading Freud's ideas in America. It is likely that they did succeed in arousing curiosity, at least among readers in the Boston area.

"The overall absence of criticism and in many cases the outright praise suggests that possibly America was ready to receive Freud's ideas and was willing to discuss them. The attitude of all the newspapers was one of respect for Freud as a scientist and scholar, as well as respect for his ideas as being important enough to be worthy of public discussion."

What is unquestionable is Freud's consolidation of the bridgehead that had been prepared for him by Ernest Jones. If there was a doubt, it was about Jones himself, in whom Freud noted signs of lapsing while at Worcester. Recalling the occasion later, and reminding Jones of his affection and of his appreciation for all that he had done for psychoanalysis, he continued: "I remember the first time when I got aware of this, my attitude toward you; it was a bad one; when you left Worcester after a time of dark inconsistencies from your side, and I had to face the idea that you were going away to become a stranger to us. Then I felt it ought not to be so, and I could not show it otherwise than by accompanying you to the train and shaking hands before you went away."

Freud and his party were not due to sail for Europe until September 21, and during the week left to them they visited Niagara Falls and James Putnam's camp in the Adirondacks. Before leaving Vienna, Freud had spoken of his ambition to see the Falls, and on the conducted tour the spectacle fully came up to expectations. There was one aggravating incident. In the Cave of the Winds, where it is possible to step up to the spray-drenched railing and see the frightening splendor of the rushing water from a dramatic angle, the guide held other visitors back as Freud came forward. "Let the old fellow go first," he said. Freud, aged fifty-three, was not amused. Nevertheless, he remained in a holiday mood, sending a tourist postcard to his daughter Sophie from the American side of the Falls, then crossing over into Canada where the party sent a "Kindest Regards" card to Mrs. Brill signed by "Abe, Freud, Ferenczi and Jung."

From Niagara they moved on to the Adirondacks where a party of about forty was to gather. Putnam's camp was at the foot of Giant Mountain in Keene Valley, New York, set up in the mid-1870s by himself and fellow physicians from Boston. Log cabins had been built in a clearing through which a fast-flowing stream ran; some had been elaborately furnished, and the visitors lived in an unusual combination of luxury and austerity.

For September 16 the Putnam Camp Log Book recorded that "Dr. James Putnam arrived from Boston—Louisa Richardson and Miss Annie Putnam and three foreign doctors came over from Lake Placid (on the 15th)." There was some confusion about the nationality of the visitors, and Freud the Austrian, Jung the Swiss and Ferenczi the Hungarian found their cabin decorated in the colors of Imperial Germany.

Freud had been writing to Martha regularly—remembering to send her a good wishes cable on Rosh Hashanah, the Jewish New Year—and on the evening of his arrival at the camp sat down and described his impressions to the family.

It is four weeks today that I set out on my travels, and this is likely to be the last letter to arrive before I myself arrive.

Of all the things that I have experienced in America this is probably the strangest: a camp, you must realize, in a wilderness in the woods, set on an Alpine meadow, as it might be on the Loser [a mountain near Alt Aussee]. On three sides stones, moss, groups of trees and uneven ground merge into densely wooded slopes. The camp is a group of roughly made log cabins each of which, as one discovers, has its own name. One is the "Stoop," a parlor containing library, piano, desks and card tables. Another is the "Hall of the Knights," full of old interesting objects, with a fireplace in the center of the room and benches along the walls as in a peasant's dining room. The rest of the cabins consist of living quarters. Ours, with just three rooms, is called "Chatterbox." Everything, rough but natural in character, seems artificial in a way, yet looks right. Mixing bowls do service as wash basins, mugs as drinking glasses, because nothing is lacking—everything is available in one form or another. We have found special books dealing with camping and containing detailed instructions about how to use such primitive appliances.

Our reception at 2:30 consisted of an invitation to go for a walk on the nearby mountain, where we were able to appreciate the utter wilderness of such an American countryside. We went along rough tracks, and down slopes where even my antlers and hooves were not adequate [Freud had been jokingly warned that excursions through such wild country were only possible with the aid of antlers].

Fortunately it is raining today. There are many squirrels and porcupines in these woods; the latter are invisible so far. Even black bears are seen in the winter.

After supper that evening one visitor accompanied Jung on the piano as he sang German songs. Two others taught Freud and Ferenczi a board game. The Putnams spoke German, and everyone relaxed and enjoyed themselves. Freud himself suffered only two inconveniences. One was some internal trouble that has been variously diagnosed as appendicitis and as gastroenteritis. The other was lack of a barber to trim his beard, a refinement which he sorely missed since all he could do was comb his hair. "Fortunately," he observed in his letter home, "there is the greatest informality in dress, or at least so it seems."

There later came the incident of the porcupine. When discussing the Clark University lectures before leaving Europe, Freud had said that when faced with a difficult task, such as speaking to a foreign audience, "it was helpful to provide a lightning conductor for one's emotions by deflecting one's attention on to a subsidiary goal." So, before leaving Europe he maintained that he was going to America in the hope of catching sight of a wild porcupine *and* to give some lectures.

His hosts at the Putnam camp were willing to help, and two visitors who knew the area well were assigned to accompany him. "They started the climb up a rather gentle hill," says a relative of one, "and had not gone very far before they were greeted by the smell of carrion. As they proceeded, the stench grew steadily stronger, so much so that Mrs. Wearn suggested that they turn and go downwind. Freud refused. They continued and at last came upon a bloated porcupine, long dead. Freud approached it, cautiously stuck his staff into it, then turned and announced, 'It's dead.' "

There seems to have been no time for a further search, and Freud's ambition was therefore only half, and rather miserably, fulfilled. However, there was a minor consolation when, before he left, the Putnams presented him with a small porcupine paperweight made of metal. It was to sit on his desk for the rest of his life.

The party now returned to New York for the start of the eight-day voyage back to Bremen. On board the *Kaiser Wilhelm der Grosse* Freud wrote a discursive six-page letter to his daughter Mathilde, remarking that the whole trip had been highly interesting, "very meaningful for our work," and a great success; but he was very glad that he did not have to live in America. In New York, he explained, he had visited his sister Anna, but his prospering brother-in-law Eli had been away in Canada on business. He went on with a chronicle of family news which she would get before he arrived back in Vienna, since he would be posting the letter when the ship called at Cherbourg. And then, with the comment that he wouldn't be sorry to be back, he added four words in English: "East, West; Home Best."

From Bremen, where they arrived after surviving a stormy crossing that had sent most other passengers to their cabins, Jung went straight to Zurich while Freud and Ferenczi broke their homeward journeys in Berlin. Here Freud was induced by his companion to visit with him a Frau Seidler, locally known as a soothsayer able to read letters while blindfolded. Ferenczi had for a long time been inclined to accept the paranormal and this, together with Jung's somewhat similar views, had brought Freud to a path he was reluctant to follow. In this case he was skeptical of the lady's performance but admitted that she appeared to possess a gift for reading other people's thoughts.

The compromise was typical of the attitude which Freud adopted to the paranormal in general and to telepathy in particular. If it is possible to trace a line of evolution in his changing stance, it is one of decreasing skepticism. Early in 1909, after Jung had attributed to occult sources the creaks in a bookcase in No. 19 Berggasse, Freud had found that they were the normal creaks of timber and had remarked to Jung, "I confront the despiritualized furniture as the poet confronted undeified Nature after the gods of Greece had passed away." Two years later, when Jung had written of his wish to lead a crusade into the field of mysticism, apparently with Ferenczi, Freud noted, "I can see that you two are not to be held back. At least go forward in collaboration with each other; it is a dangerous expedition and I cannot accompany you." Yet a month later he could tell Jung, "In matters of occultism I have grown humble since the great lesson Ferenczi's experiences gave me. I promise to believe anything that can be made to look reasonable." And a decade later, when refusing to become co-editor of an American journal dealing with the occult, he could write, "I am not one of those who dismiss a priori the study of so-called occult psychic phenomena as unscientific, discreditable or even as dangerous. If I were at the beginning rather than at the end of a scientific career, as I am today, I might possibly choose just this field of research, in spite of all difficulties."

Freud's predilection for the paranormal, like his weakness for Wilhelm Fliess's mystic numerology, has its parallels. At the turn of the century the devoted followers of spiritualism in Britain included, among others, Sir William Barrett, Sir William Crookes, Sir Oliver Lodge and Sir George Stokes, all among the most distinguished scientists of their day. In the case of Freud, his rational sense found the so-called evidence difficult to credit, and his experience of the world had taught him how inviting a field this was to the charlatan and the confidence-trickster. Nevertheless he might well have begun to investigate the occult on an experimental basis but for one thing: "the cause." Freud surmised, no doubt correctly, that the existence of any link between the founding fathers of psychoanalysis and investigation of the paranormal would hamper acceptance of psychoanalysis. When he began to have second thoughts, resistance was stiffened by Jones and it was at least partly due to Jones's advice that Fere..czi was some years later dissuaded by Freud from presenting a lecture on his telepathic experiments to a Congress of the International Psycho-Analytical Association. "By it," warned Freud, "you would be throwing a bomb into the psychoanalytical house which would be certain to explode. Surely we agree in not wanting to hasten this perhaps unavoidable disturbance in our development."

All of this lay in the future as Freud arrived back in Vienna on October 2, 1909, rightly satisfied with the success of his mission. Psychoanalysis, he now realized, would no longer be ignored in the United States. Opposition, whether or not accurately reflected in the Toronto dean's condemnation, had certainly been less than expected. This may have been due to Ernest Jones's preparatory work, yet not until after the Worcester lectures were the fortunes of "the cause"—as Putnam was also soon to call it—safely over the American watershed.

Early in 1910 Jones read a paper on psychoanalysis before the American Psychological Association—one which induced a lady psychologist to remark that while Austrians might have egocentric dreams she was sure no Americans did—and a few months later became a founder-member of the American Psychopathological Association. The following year Brill founded the New York Psychoanalytic Society and, simultaneously, Jones founded the American Psychoanalytic Association for analysts scattered elsewhere throughout the United States. As psychoanalysis thus began to gain ground, it was Putnam, with a reputation which put him above the fray, who provided the weighty ballast of professional support. In May 1910 he spoke before the American Neurological Association in Washington; in November of the following year to the Harvard Society of New York; and in June 1914 to the Section on Nervous and Mental Diseases of the American Medical Association. These were only the more important of a series of occasions on which, if at times critical on points of detail, he saw to it that Freud received the attentive hearing from the medical profession that he had failed to receive in Europe.

Freud was quick to appreciate the dangers as well as the opportunities of American interest. Jones crossed the Atlantic to visit him in the summer of 1910 and was soon afterward telling Putnam of Freud's plans for forming in the United States a branch of the International Association which had been founded earlier in the year at Nuremberg. "[He] produced the following argument which had struck me forcibly in America," Jones wrote. "We are so likely to have the work damaged by amateurs and charlatans that it becomes necessary to protect our interests by enrolling those with some proper knowledge of the subject in a rather official Verein [society], which would therefore be *some kind* of guarantee in a general way that the members knew what they were talking or writing about." The following month Jones reinforced the argument, telling Putnam that he strongly felt the need of "some such formal move to counteract the numerous amateurs who are already beginning to spring up and who will do the cause much harm. . . ."

Fear of what might happen in the United States was a reflection of Freud's dislike of America, which was to color his opinions for life. At one level the reasons were trivial. He had been upset internally for much of the visit and put this down to what he regarded as the barbarian style of American cooking and eating. He was critical of the pace and brashness of New York, a reaction not unknown among Europeans even today and quite understandable in an inhabitant of Franz Joseph's Vienna. To Sachs he was to say: "America is the most grandiose experiment the world has seen, but, I am afraid, it is not going to be a success"; and to Jones: "Yes, America is gigantic, but a gigantic mistake."

The antipathy lasted. His sister Anna returned to Vienna from America almost every year, and in the Freud household the phrase *"Echt Amerikanisch"*—real or typically American—became, through what they learned of American life from Anna, synonymous with the superficial or the flashy. At times Freud's dislike went even further, and after describing his nephew in America as "an honest boy when I knew him," he felt forced to add, "I know not how far he has become Americanized." And more than two decades after his brief single visit to the United States, he could write, in discussing an essay on Mary Baker Eddy, "the mad and wicked side . . . is not sufficiently brought out, nor is the unspeakable grimness of the American background."

His repulsion was based on something deeper but not necessarily more rational than the memories of strange food and the bustle of Manhattan. "He foresaw the coming storm," Fritz Wittels wrote in 1924, "the 'Freud craze' which rages today, not only in the States, but in all English-speaking lands. He also realized that

those who became affected with this craze would preserve little
more of his life's work than the name and the most elementary
connections. . . ."

Freud's anti-Americanism certainly became an obsession, possibly reinforced by the number of medical practitioners in the
United States who were to move over into Jung's camp after the
two men had become bitter enemies. During the 1920s, when he
became financially dependent on Americans who came to him
either for training or for treatment, his condemnation of almost
everything American surfaced to an alarming degree. By 1930 he
had seen a representative cross section, from all parts of the States.
Many he found difficult to understand, remonstrating to one, "You
should talk more clearly. I think that way of talking is an expression
of the general American laxity in social relations." And elsewhere
he wrote: "Quite particularly often we find in American physicians
and writers a very insufficient familiarity with psychoanalysis, so
that they know only its terms and a few catch words. . . . And these
same men lump psychoanalysis with other systems of thought,
which may have developed out of it but are incompatible with it
today. Or they make a hotchpotch out of psychoanalysis and other
elements and quote this procedure as evidence of their *broad-
mindedness,* whereas it only proves their *lack of judgment.*" (Words
italicized are in English in the original.)

Stanley Hall's invitation was to have repercussions more unlikely
than he could have imagined.

13

First Defections

Rather tired after battle and victory. I hereby inform you that yesterday I forced the whole Adler gang (six of them) to resign from the
Society. I was harsh but I don't think unfair.

FREUD, in a letter to C. G. Jung

Freud returned to Vienna justifiably believing that he had successfully launched psychoanalysis in the New World. His success in
Worcester had, moreover, made him feel that things were stirring
elsewhere. "One of the most agreeable phantasies," he wrote to
Pfister as soon as he had settled into his home again,

> is that without our knowing it decent people are finding their way to
> our ideas and aspirations and then suddenly popping up all over the
> place. That is what happened in the case of Stanley Hall. Who would
> have imagined that over in America, an hour's train journey from
> Boston, a worthy old gentleman was sitting and waiting impatiently
> for the Year Book [the publication decided upon at Salzburg], read-
> ing and understanding everything, and then, as he himself put it,
> ringing the bell for us?

But Freud was under no illusion as to where the main battle
would have to be fought. Four years later, commenting on the fact
that in the United States the staffs of mental hospitals had begun
to show as much interest in psychoanalysis as independent consult-
ants, he pointed out "that precisely for this reason the ancient
centers of culture, where the greatest resistance has been displayed, must be the scene of the decisive struggle over psychoanalysis." The struggle was to be a long one although, on his return
from America, he could rightly feel that interest, as well as opposi-

tion, was steadily growing. He had reported to Brill earlier in the year that there was an increasing demand for his books, though he felt it necessary to add, "I often fear that when the triumph will come, I will be at the end of my vigor and health, but I immediately repel these dark thoughts. To die in harness is my resolution."

The autumn of 1909 therefore found Freud ready to consolidate the gains which he correctly felt had been won during the previous eighteen months. He was now in his mid-fifties, at the height of his powers, and it is necessary to ask how successful he was, not as an investigator of the way in which the mind worked but as a doctor curing sick patients. The evidence is remarkably slight. Throughout a long life Freud himself described in detail only a handful of cases—the four of *Studies on Hysteria*, Dora, Little Hans, a female homosexual, the Wolf-Man and the Rat Man—and it has been remarked that among them the Rat Man was one of the few who showed a genuine cure which could be attributed to psychoanalysis. "Indeed," it has recently been pointed out by Seymour Fisher and Roger P. Greenberg in their acute analysis of Freud's results, "we must conclude that Freud never presented any data, in statistical or case study form, that demonstrated that his treatment was of benefit to a significant number of the patients he himself saw."

Although this is by no means the whole story, Freud might well have agreed. "I have many limitations as an analyst," he said. "In the first place, I get tired of people. Secondly, I am not basically interested in therapy, and I usually find that I am engaged—in any particular case—with the theoretical problems with which I happen to be interested at the time." And then he added, "I am also too patriarchal to be a good analyst." His self-deprecatory remarks should not be taken too seriously. He knew that he was good and in the cause of fairness would always bend over backwards to emphasize imperfections of which he was well aware. Yet a psychoanalyst as good as the Swiss Raymond de Saussure could write: "Since [Freud] had not been analyzed himself, he tended to commit two kinds of errors. First, he had practiced suggestion too long not to have been materially affected by it. When he was persuaded of the truth of something, he had considerable difficulty in waiting until this verity became clear to his patient. Freud wanted to convince him immediately. Because of that he talked too much."

Freud's impatience was that of many men with first-class minds, perpetually irritated at the need to wait while the others caught up. "This impatience," his doctor Max Schur was later to explain, "revealed itself in small mannerisms, in small gestures with which he seemed to hasten the end of the sentence to which he was listening. Acutely sensitive to stupidity and lack of logic, he yet had to endure the stubborn resistance of the patient's neurotic mind."

But patients continued to come, and to come for treatment that was lengthy and expensive even though it appeared to involve nothing more than a quiet remembrance of things past. Steadily, Freud's use of the material trawled up from the unconscious became more complex; additional attention had to be given to the resistances encountered, more care taken to deal with the transference of feelings from patient to analyst and with the countertransference that had to be avoided. Yet such was the simplicity of the system that, in Freud's words, it did not require the use of any special aids. In general, he even advised psychoanalysts not to take notes in the presence of the patient, the only exceptions being "dates, the text of dreams, or single incidents of a noteworthy kind which can easily be detached from their context to serve an independent purpose as examples."

Those who climbed the stairs of No. 19 Berggasse came, certainly in the early days and to a lesser extent later on, from a comparatively small circle within which the benefits or otherwise of the hourly sessions on the couch would be discussed. If, in the days of *Studies on Hysteria,* psychoanalysis could be accused of being launched on an unsubstantiated prospectus, that censure became more difficult to maintain as Freud's practice continued to flourish. This does something to sustain the thesis that psychoanalysis is not an operation to be judged by the statistical criteria of the physical sciences. Faith, it is said, can move mountains, and in some comparable way psychoanalysis could sometimes remove neuroses. Yet this explanation, which would help to deflect criticism, has little in common with Freud's own definition of psychoanalysis: "the name (1) of a procedure for investigation of mental processes which are almost inaccessible in any other way, (2) of a method (based upon that investigation) for the treatment of neurotic disorders, and (3) of a collection of psychological information obtained along these lines, which is gradually being accumulated into a new scientific discipline."

Nevertheless, "the cause" continued not only to survive but to prosper. It flourished under Freud's skillful command, exercised from a headquarters which during the previous two decades had changed surprisingly little. His rooms in No. 19 were still furnished in the comfortable but no-longer-fashionable style of the 1880s, and only one of them showed any imprint of an individual personality. This was his study, and even here the furniture had changed little throughout the decades; the walls, however, were by now covered almost from floor to ceiling either by tightly filled bookshelves or by glass cabinets which housed his steadily growing collection of antiques.

There was also, prominently featured on one wall, an engraving of Brouillet's famous painting which shows Charcot demonstrating a case of "grand hysteria" to a distinguished audience. Anna would often ask her father what was wrong with the woman who appeared to be fainting, and he would always give the same reply: that the lady was *"zu fest geschnürt* [too tightly laced]," which was very silly of her.

The Charcot picture stood out, an isolated illustration of drama in a fundamentally undramatic environment. "Nothing appealed less to [Freud] than ostentatiousness," Sachs has written, "and instead of adapting himself to the Viennese manner of dramatization, he withdrew from it more and more till he became practically invisible." There were other characteristics of the Freud family which tended to set it apart from the run of middle-class Viennese. Both Martha and her sister Minna continued to speak in the pure German of their Hamburg upbringing, and to Sachs "the household gave an impression of extraterritoriality, like an island that is easily accessible from the mainland, but still an island."

In the study a large sheet of paper always lay on the writing desk, and on it Freud noted, under the date of each day, on the left the letters he had received and on the right those he had sent. Only rarely did a letter go unanswered for more than twenty-four hours. Virtually all were replied to by Freud himself, in longhand, with a large fountain pen equipped with the broadest available nib, although after the First World War Anna was to take over more and more of the secretarial work.

He hated the telephone. One reason was that he preferred to look a man straight in the eyes when being spoken to. It was then more easy to detect a lie. "Father, aware of this power when looking at a person," wrote Martin, "felt he had lost it when looking at a dead telephone mouthpiece." His dislike of the mechanical explains his reaction to photographers who, as his fame increased, frequently asked him to sit for them. He disliked being photographed, but the portraits would go round the world, providing propaganda for the cause, and he therefore "sat" more often than he wished. On these occasions, his son has remembered, he would put on his photographic face, "rather a stern, serious face which did not for a moment reflect his kindly and friendly nature, not severe and reserved, as the world must regard him if they judge him by posed photographs." Nevertheless, it was no bad expression for a leader.

Across the corridor at No. 19, domestic life was organized by Martha solely to aid the smooth running of her husband's professional life. For him, anything less would have been unthinkable. The man to whom Mill's views on the status of women were nonsensical took it for granted that his wife would follow at least the last two thirds of the *Kirche, Küche und Kinder* philosophy. Martha did. Bridling at a suggestion that she would ever be nervous in running the house, she once replied, "Nervous? I couldn't afford to be nervous. Everything in the household has to run smoothly. Otherwise, how could my husband do his work?"

The *Kinder* fitted well into a family life that exhibited a placid normality in striking contrast to the lives of Freud's patients. "A spirit of congeniality and freedom pervaded the atmosphere of his home," Brill has written. "It may be trite to state that the master who traced all our good and evil qualities back to early childhood knew how to bring up his children properly. This is not always the case even in the best psychoanalytic families, but in Freud's home one sensed a certain relationship, a sort of subdued freedom, between parents and children, which I have seen nowhere else." Moreover, the freedom worked. Few fathers of Freud's intellectual stature have brought up six children as unstressed and as stable as his three sons and three daughters. Mathilde, the eldest of the daughters, had been married in 1909 to Robert Hollitscher on the day that Freud's brother had also married in Vienna. Sophie was to marry the Hamburg photographer Max Halberstadt four years later. The three sons were all to marry in the aftermath of the First World War.

The routine at No. 19 was regular and almost unbreakable. Freud rose at seven, and was then attended by his barber who trimmed his beard and hair. He breakfasted and was ready by eight for the first of the day's fifty-five-minute consultations, which continued, with a five-minute interval between each, until lunch at one o'clock. There followed a break during which he would take a brisk walk, often replenishing his stock of cigars, of which he was still smoking a steady twenty a day. Work would start again at three and continue until nine or later, the evening meal being followed by another brisk walk and then retirement to the study for writing or answering correspondence. To end the day in lonely isolation was essential. Freud, like a famous field marshal of the Second World War, believed that the wise commander was "well advised to withdraw to his tent or caravan [trailer] after dinner at night and have time for quiet thoughts and reflection."

On Sunday there was a visit to Freud's mother for luncheon. With equal regularity she came with her daughters to the Sunday-evening meal at No. 19, where the family sat down beneath the portrait of Martha's distinguished grandfather, Hakham Isaac Bernays of Hamburg. On Sundays, also, there might be visits from professional colleagues or walks with the children. All went according to plan. Order, discipline, enabled Freud with exemplary regularity to fill Kipling's unforgiving minute "With sixty seconds' worth of distance run." Few homes have been less like that of a revolutionary who was to change the world.

Such concentration—on his patients, on the developing themes of psychoanalysis, on spreading the gospel abroad—was fully needed. Although Freud was correct in regarding the American sortie as an important breakthrough, although the time was in fact propitious for the extension of psychoanalysis to the international scene that he was about to organize, opposition to what he stood for was in many quarters still implacable.

Although Freud's name was spoken of respectfully in some departments of physics and chemistry, among psychologists it tended to be followed by the verdict: "Oh, he's crazy!" However, this was the least that he had to suffer. "You have probably heard that there exists something called 'psychoanalysis,' " the famous brain anatomist Nissl told one audience in 1910. "It is enough to call this pornography, and we will now proceed to the discussion of general paralysis." A few months later Professor Wilhelm Weygandt, attending a congress of German neurologists and psychiatrists in Hamburg, responded to a mention of Freud's theories by banging his fist on the table and objecting, "This is not a topic for discussion at a scientific meeting; it is a matter for the police." In Berlin the same year Professor Hermann Oppenheim, a leading German neurologist, told a meeting of directors of psychiatric establishments that Freud's writings should be boycotted in any respectable establishment of the kind they were running. "The discussion," Abraham told Freud, "mainly consisted of a number of directors of sanatoria getting up and solemnly declaring that they did not practice psychoanalysis."

In later years Freud, and most of his supporters, could afford to look back with comparative equanimity. "The situation," he once said, "recalled what was actually put in practice in the Middle Ages when an evil-doer, or even a mere political opponent, was put in the pillory and given over to maltreatment by the mob." However, there is more than a hint, in what Freud and some of his supporters wrote during these embattled years, that opposition was not, after all, entirely unwelcome. Abraham, reporting on a Berlin meeting, says, "Only Raimann from Vienna stood out, proposing that, since Freud was evading a discussion, the enemy should be sought out in his own camp (sic!) and every failure of psychoanalytic treatment should be publicized. Boycott and denunciation. I find the unpleasant signs are mounting up in a most gratifying way."

Freud himself also shows at times what could superficially be considered an almost perverse pleasure at the way in which the attack on psychoanalysis was so often made in purely sexual terms. It was partly, no doubt, his astute realization that opinion was changing, that the unmentionable of today would become the commonplace of tomorrow. Yet Freud was too intelligent not to be aware that the enemy, in building up a great wash of horrified protest against sexual frankness, was misdirecting its energies. The greater the concentration on the sexual factor, the less the attention directed to an objective investigation of what psychoanalysis was achieving. The need for such investigation was brought out with exceptional clarity by Bernard Hart, later to become an early member of the British Psycho-Analytical Society. Writing in the British *Journal of Mental Science* in 1910, Hart said:

> Genuine criticism of Freud's work hardly exists—we are badly in need of it. That which has been attempted has generally foundered upon one of two rocks. Many critics have totally failed to realize that Freud's views deal largely with conceptual constructions. They have imagined that his complexes and unconscious mental processes were phenomena on the plane of sensations and perceptions and have asked how their existence can possibly be demonstrated. This is comparable to asking a *Mendelian* to produce his recessives and dominants for general inspection. It is surely obvious that Freud's conceptions can only be established or disproved by the process of applying them and determining whether or not they suffice to explain the phenomena observed, and to predict the occurrence of future phenomena. Other critics—the majority—confuse the categories in the most lamentable manner. They attack Freud on the really astounding ground that his theories are ethically objectionable, that it would not be desirable for such things to be true, and that therefore they are not true. On the other hand, certain of Freud's followers are, perhaps, too enthusiastic, and tend to convert his school into something dangerously like a religious sect. . . . The need of the moment is—not the enthusiasm of the disciple who builds the construction ever higher, not the undiscriminating attack of the *a priori* opponent—but the cold criticism of the impartial investigator, who will examine the foundation with every care, and estimate the justification with which each stone has been laid upon another.

As psychoanalysis, now confidently launched outside Austria, began to attract such serious scrutiny, the Vienna Psychoanalytical Society was joined by a remarkable recruit. He was Victor Tausk, a thirty-year-old former lawyer, former writer, former journalist, who had come to Vienna the previous year to study medicine at the university. Tausk soon showed that he had at last found his *métier*. A month after first appearing at the Society he read a paper on

"Theory of Knowledge and Psychoanalysis." His contributions to
the evening discussions began to show an almost alarming
precocity, and it was soon clear that despite the vacillations of his
earlier years he had the potential of a first-class analyst. But by
1911 he was one of the three members, the others being Stekel and
Sadger, who according to Ernest Jones were giving Freud trouble.
Put bluntly, he was daring to question the master.

But it was not only among analysts that there was beginning the
natural questioning of those moving into unmapped territory,
where few landmarks were discernible and the way forward was
uncertain. In the aftermath of the visit to America there was also
trouble from Karl Kraus, of whom Freud had once held great
hopes. During 1907 and 1908 his *Die Fackel* had started to criticize
psychoanalysis, satirizing Freud's method of dream-interpretation
and the first attempts of psychoanalysts to dissect the operations
of authors and artists. "By all means," Kraus wrote in reporting on
a "pathography" of August Strindberg, "we should concede more
to the psychiatrist than he concedes to genius. Let us admit once
and for all that all poets are mad; perhaps that will spare us from
the spectacle of psychiatrists proving this in each and every case
separately."

Kraus was a journalist with eyes always open for suitable targets,
and he would probably have continued his attacks even had Fritz
Wittels not read a paper to the Vienna Psychoanalytical Society on
"The *Fackel*-Neurosis." But the glee with which he and his journal
ever afterward pursued psychoanalysis owes much to what was,
judged even by psychoanalytic criteria, an exceedingly unfortunate
exercise.

The only account of Wittels' paper, read to the Society on January 12, 1910, is that given in the minutes. It begins, in the English
of the published version: "The speaker takes off from the question
of the purpose with which we undertake pathographies of artists;
he sees as the reason for our doing so the fact that we wish to find
out how art and neurosis are related, and how the one passes over
into the other."

Wittels then went on to relate how Kraus had begun work on the
Neue Freie Presse, left it to found *Die Fackel*, and had thereafter
consistently attacked the *Presse*. Totally failing to understand that
this was nothing more than the natural progress of a young and
ambitious journalist, Wittels described it as a symptom of Kraus's
Oedipal frustration with his father: "The *Presse* is the father's
organ, which corrupts the whole world; the *Fackel*, on the other
hand, is but a small organ, which is, however, capable of destroying
the big organ. . . . The *Presse* is the father's organ, which the little

one does not have; the father is superior to the son, inasmuch as he can read. . . ." Any doubt that remained in Wittels' mind was apparently removed by the fact that Kraus's father was called Jacob, the Hebrew for "blessed"; this was the equivalent to the Latin *"benedictus,"* the root of "Benedikt"; and one of the two owners of the *Neue Freie Presse* was Moritz Benedikt. The enemies of psychoanalysis could afford to sit back and wait.

It is clear, even from the English of the published minutes, that "The *Fackel*-Neurosis" was too much for many dedicated followers of Freud. Carl Furtmüller, a schoolteacher who was to resign from the Society the following year with Alfred Adler, seems to have represented the general feeling of the meeting which had listened to this rigmarole. "Furtmüller," say the minutes, "would like to put forward a general comment. He cannot help seeing a danger in Wittels' paper. The question is whether analysis is to be considered a structure of dogmas or a method of working. In today's paper it was rather the first conception that held sway; the result, therefore, is not very convincing and a good deal was neglected; all of which has actually led us in a certain sense to a misunderstanding of this man. A man like Kraus cannot find a place on the *Presse,* even without a neurosis."

The Society's meetings were regularly reported by Stekel, but even had this not been so, the news of Wittels' paper would obviously have become known, and early in April *Die Fackel* launched a counterattack. At the Society's meeting on the fourteenth, Adler, believing that silence was the best course, advised members to make no comment. Freud felt the same and added "the further admonition to avoid in private conversation, too, making any remarks about this matter. For the Vienna Psychoanalytical Society, 'The Kraus Affair' does not exist."

While Freud was thus hoping that thought-control would erase all signs of Wittels' pathetic pathography, there came to him the young man who was later to emerge as possibly his best-known patient. He was the twenty-three-year-old Russian now known to a half century of analysts as "the Wolf-Man," the central figure in one of Freud's rare published case histories and one of the few psychoanalytic patients whose lives have been followed in some detail into old age. An exceedingly rich young man, the son of a wealthy lawyer and liberal politician who owned vast estates in Southern Russia, the Wolf-Man, traveling with his valet and private doctor, arrived in Freud's consulting room suffering from a severe neurosis. He was said to be "entirely incapacitated and completely dependent upon other people," and he had for some while unsuccessfully sought a cure in various nursing homes and sanatoria.

"I can remember, as though I saw them today, [Freud's] two adjoining studies, with the door open between them and with their windows opening on a little courtyard," the Wolf-Man later wrote.

> There was always a feeling of sacred peace and quiet here. The rooms themselves must have been a surprise to any patient, for they in no way reminded one of a doctor's office but rather of an archaeologist's study. Here were all kinds of statuettes and other unusual objects, which even the layman recognized as archaeological finds from ancient Egypt. Here and there on the walls were stone plaques representing various scenes of long-vanished epochs. A few potted plants added life to the rooms, and the warm carpet and curtains gave them a homelike note. Everything here contributed to one's feeling of leaving the haste of modern life behind, of being sheltered from one's daily cares.

But Freud's working hours were fully booked and at first it appeared that the Wolf-Man would have to continue his journey to Switzerland, where he planned to visit a doctor in Berne. However, Freud mentioned that he had to visit the Cottage Sanatorium every afternoon. He could see the Wolf-Man there. "This proposal disconcerted us, and we reconsidered continuing our journey to Switzerland," the Wolf-Man recalled. "But Freud had made such a favorable impression upon me that I persuaded Dr. D. that I should follow Freud's suggestion." There then began an analysis that was to continue for four years and, after a disappointing start, was to end with the patient apparently cured.

In 1910 he was suffering from a frustrated love affair and later admitted that the most important question for him was whether Freud would agree to his returning to his mistress, Thérèse. "Had Professor Freud, like the other doctors whom I had seen previously, said 'No,' I would certainly not have stayed with him." He constantly brought up the question and recalled how on one occasion Freud raised his hands above his head and cried out, "For twenty-four hours now I have not heard the sacred name Thérèse!" After some weeks the patient was allowed to visit the woman. He eventually brought her to Freud, who was much impressed. The Wolf-Man subsequently married her.

"During these first months in analysis with Professor Freud, a completely new world was opened to me, a world known to only a few people in those days," the Wolf-Man has written. "Much that had been ununderstandable in my life before that time began to make sense, as relationships which were formerly hidden in darkness now emerged into my consciousness."

While the analysis sought to remove the neurosis from which the Wolf-Man was suffering in 1910, little was actually said about it in the paper, "From the History of an Infantile Neurosis," which Freud wrote four years later. Instead, the paper described how an infantile neurosis can be recovered and explained during analysis for totally different mental troubles many years later.

Just before his fifth birthday the patient had experienced a nightmare in which he had seen six or seven white wolves sitting in a walnut tree outside his bedroom window. For six years he suffered from obsessional neurosis and a phobia of wolves, these symptoms then gradually disappearing until, at the age of seventeen, he began suffering from the mental disturbances for whose treatment he now, at the age of twenty-three, came to Freud. By an ingenious line of reasoning Freud traced his patient's earlier disorders back to an infant seduction by his sister and the sight, at the age of one and a half, of his parents having intercourse. The latter was the vital point, not only for the Wolf-Man analysis but for a serious divergence of opinion that had arisen between Freud on the one hand, and Adler and Jung on the other. Freud maintained that the recollections of seeing parental intercourse frequently reported by his patients were recollections of real events, whereas Adler and Jung contended that they were merely fantasies of adult life even though indistinguishable in a patient's mind from genuine recollections.

Freud devoted a good deal of his paper to subtle arguments tending to show that in the case of the Wolf-Man the recollection was of a real event; but he then went on to say that his patient may have watched animals copulating on his father's estate and transposed the memory on to his parents. "I should myself," he admits, "be glad to know whether the primal scene in my present patient's case was a phantasy or a real experience." Faced with an apparently insoluble problem, Freud nevertheless produced an answer that satisfied him: "I must admit that the answer to this question is not in fact a matter of very great importance." If this is the case, it has been suggested, "then Freud's polemics with Adler and Jung must have been a storm in a teacup and this paper should have been entitled 'Much Ado About Nothing.' " Against this item on the debit side of the ledger there should be noted Freud's honesty at admitting his own uncertainty. There seems little doubt that he had embarked on the paper hoping that it would provide a weapon with which to beat his enemies; but although it turned out to be nothing of the sort, he still kept the record straight.

He had been inhibited from describing the Wolf-Man's current neurosis in too great a detail for fear of the patient being identified. This was unfortunate since after four years with but few results to show, there came an unexpected success. In the spring of 1914 Freud warned his patient that he would be breaking off the treatment for good when he started his summer holiday as usual in July. The shock worked, and by early July the patient appeared to have been cured. Certainly he went back to Russia in apparent good health, not returning to Freud until November 1919 with a totally different kind of trouble.

Long before this—in fact, as analysis of the Wolf-Man was starting—Freud was engaged in creating the body which he hoped would direct the spread of psychoanalysis throughout the world and which would, in turn, be controlled by him. The idea had been discussed by Freud, Jung, Ferenczi and Jones at the Clark University celebrations, and it had been tentatively agreed that Jung, who had organized the Salzburg gathering the previous year, should arrange a Congress for 1910 at which there would be founded a permanent international psychoanalytical association. "If I had to say which of us took the lead in planning the constitution of the new Association," Jones later recalled, "I should name Ferenczi, and it was he who moved the necessary resolutions when the time came for the meeting."

Nevertheless, Jones himself was a major influence on the setting up of the organization, of which he was later to be president for many years. At Worcester, as Freud had shrewdly noted, a doubt had crossed Jones's mind about the part he was to play in the growing movement. That doubt had been completely resolved by the spring of 1910. Jones had then written to Freud, telling him "about six or eight months ago I determined not only to further the cause by all the means in my power, which I had always decided on, but also to further it by whatever means you personally decided on, and to follow your recommendations as exactly as possible."

A few weeks later he explained the reservations Freud had sensed at Worcester, and at the same time renewed his allegiance. "Shortly put," he wrote,

> my resistances have sprung not from any objections to your theories, but partly from an absurd jealous egotism and partly from the influences of a strong "Father-complex." You are right in surmising that I had at one time hoped to play a more important part in the movement in England and America than I now see is possible; it must, and should, be directed by you, and I am content to be of any service in my power along the lines you advise.

All was now set for Freud's next step forward, the creation of an organization which he would command from behind the scenes if necessary. Many motives have been attributed to him. As the creator of a new therapy he naturally wanted to maintain his position as leader, the reward for two decades of uphill struggle. As the founder of a movement, or a cause, he had a quasi-religious belief in his duty to remain in undisputed control. There is also the reason which has been put forward, in detail and with a good deal of plausibility, by Thomas S. Szasz. "What happened," he has said, "was that Freud abandoned the kind of leadership we associate with the progress of science and adopted in its stead the kind of leadership typical of big business or of imperialistic nationalism." A complex of motives no doubt guided him, and he would presumably have been the last to deny that some of them were unconscious.

Freud put down his version in *On the History of the Psycho-Analytic Movement,* a polemic admittedly written to help drive Jung from the movement. "I considered it necessary to form an official association," he said, "because I feared the abuses to which psychoanalysis would be subjected as soon as it became popular. There should be some headquarters whose business it would be to declare: 'All this nonsense is nothing to do with analysis; this is not psychoanalysis.' " And in a private letter to Eugen Bleuler he went slightly further, saying, "It appeared to me necessary to create an organization with a central office which would conduct its external policies and give authentic information about what should be permitted to be called psychoanalysis." The significance of the ominous "permitted" was revealed in a subsequent letter when Freud gave two specific reasons for the foundation of the International Psycho-Analytical Association: "First, the need to present to the public genuine psychoanalysis and protect it from imitations which soon would arise, and second . . . that we must be ready now to answer our opponents and that it is not proper to leave these answers up to the whim of individuals. It is in the interest of our cause to bring a personal sacrifice and relegate polemics to a central office." The words have a similarity to those used a quarter of a century later by Hitler's scientific fuehrer, Johannes Stark, while the concept of protection being needed for a new and deeper science of the mind was curious. Darwin, as it has been pointed out, never claimed to have founded a science different from biology; James Clerk Maxwell laid no claim to a new physics; and Max Planck never claimed to have founded a new science of the quantum. Only psychoanalysis, it appeared, needed special protection.

The best case for the closed-shop atmosphere of the Association, and for Freud's insistence that ground rules should be laid down for defining what was psychoanalysis and what was not, rests on the need for the toughest discipline in the early stages of what was bound to be a tough battle. Opponents of the new therapy were numerous, strong and constantly on the lookout for the unguarded remark or the unjustified paper that could be used to discredit it. Dangers from within were hardly less than those from without. Psychoanalysts were, as Freud was never tired of stressing, human beings like the rest and just as susceptible to the wildness of overenthusiasm. Moreover, once the value of their methods became firmly established they would inevitably attract the charlatans and the hangers-on. In spite of all this, the closed society with its dogma of beliefs, which could be amended only after approval by the leader, suggested religion rather than science; the International Psycho-Analytical Association, itself born of historical necessity, gave Freud's critics a handy weapon.

There was another entry on the debit side. During the first decade of the twentieth century psychoanalysis had gained only a tiny bridgehead in Europe's academic world: that within Bleuler's Burghölzli at Zurich. If it were to fulfill its mission as Freud hoped, that bridgehead would have to be enlarged; over the years, psychoanalysis would have to become embodied in established teaching so that it was no longer a separate island of beliefs and practices. Yet the formation of a closed body of specialists, allowed to think only along lines laid down from above, was a development more likely than any other to make such a transition almost impossible. Bleuler was to resign a few months after the foundation of the Association, mainly due to what he regarded as its antiscientific attitude. The resignation was an event more ominous than Freud realized, and it has been speculated that without it "the future isolation of psychoanalysis from the universities and academic institutions never would have occurred, and psychoanalysis would have developed as an integral part of medicine to be taught in medical schools."

Ernest Jones was to maintain that the action of Bleuler and a few of his supporters was due to one thing alone: "It was against their principles to belong to an international body—a forerunner of Switzerland's attitude toward the League of Nations and the United Nations Organization. Evidently that was only a rationalization on Bleuler's part." Bleuler's own letters to Freud suggest that Jones, with his excuse of Swiss feeling, may have been the rationalizer.

"There is a difference between us," Bleuler wrote to Freud on being pressed to rejoin the organization, "which I decided I shall point out to you, although I am afraid that it will make it emotionally more difficult for you to come to an agreement. For you evidently it became the aim and interest of your whole life to establish firmly your theory and to secure its acceptance. . . . For me, the theory is only one new truth among other truths . . . for me it is not a major issue, whether the validity of these views will be recognized a few years sooner or later. I am therefore less tempted than you to sacrifice my whole personality for the advancement of the cause." Within a few months he was to add that while "the principle 'all or nothing' is necessary for religious sects and for political parties. . . . for science I consider it harmful. . . ." Two years later he was to be even more specific. "Scientifically," he wrote, "I still do not understand why for you it is so important that the whole edifice [of psychoanalysis] should be accepted. But I remember I told you once that no matter how great your scientific accomplishments are, psychologically you impress me as an artist. From this point of view it is understandable that you do not want your art product to be destroyed. In art we have a unit which cannot be torn apart. In science you made a great discovery which has to stay. How much of what is loosely connected with it will survive is not important."

This was the type of compliment that Freud could do without—and, in the circumstances, with good enough reason. Despite the understandable difficulty in producing the hard, incontrovertible data that the physical sciences demanded, Freud had from the first maintained that psychoanalysis was a science, a claim whose validity rests very largely on the definition of science. Justifiable or not, this claim was no doubt a necessary defense against opponents who had little scruple in glossing over the undeniable contributions that psychoanalysis had already made to an understanding of the mind and dismissing the subject as a mixture of old wives' tale and confidence trick. Yet it was a defense quickly undermined if too much emphasis were placed on the intuitive insights which Freud believed he and his followers could contribute to nonmedical subjects. Bleuler was using the word "art" in the loosest possible way, but he no doubt recalled to Freud an attitude widely held by his medical colleagues.

Peter F. Drucker, who as a boy was introduced by his parents to Freud—"the most important man in Austria, and perhaps in Europe"—has described the feeling in the Austrian capital:

The most bothersome question for the Viennese physicians was whether Freud (and his disciples) were talking about healing the sick or about art criticism. One minute they were trying to cure a specific ailment, such as fear of crossing the street, or impotence. The next they applied the same method, the same vocabulary, the same analysis, to Grimms's *Fairy Tales* or to *King Lear*. The physicians were perfectly willing to concede that, as Thomas Mann put it in his speech on Freud's 80th birthday, "psychoanalysis is the greatest contribution to the art of the novel." Freud as the powerful, imaginative, stimulating critic of culture and literature, of religion and art was one thing; it was readily conceded by a good many that he had opened a window on the soul that had long been nailed shut. This is what made him "the most important man in Austria." But was psychoanalysis then likely to be therapy any more than were Newton's physics or Kant's metaphysics or Goethe's aesthetics? This was precisely what Freud and his followers claimed, and it was a claim Viennese physicians, by and large, could not accept.

Freud knew that the struggle for acceptance would be long and difficult, but could report encouraging signs when the Congress, at which the international organization was founded, was held in March in Nuremberg. His hopes for the future were outlined in his address on "The Future Prospects of Psycho-Analytic Therapy." He recalled the time, not so very long before, when his patients had "looked round my modest abode, reflected on my lack of fame and title, and regarded me like the possessor of an infallible system at a gaming resort, of whom people say that if he could do what he professes, he would look very different himself." Those days were ending. Now, he went on, they could look forward to a substantial improvement in therapeutic prospects, to be brought about by progress in their own work and by their greater prestige. Prestige, and the faith which it transmitted to patients, was important. Talking of earlier times, Freud recalled that nobody had then believed in him, "just as, even today, people do not much believe any of us. Under such conditions not a few attempts were bound to fail." The admission that faith played an important part in cure certainly added something to the picture of psychoanalysis as a religion but is unlikely to have impressed the medical profession. More important was the prognostication made by Freud when he speculated on the growth of psychoanalytical knowledge and future improvements in technique. "I hope you will have formed an impression," he went on, "that . . . our medical procedure will reach a degree of precision and certainty of success which is not to be found in every specialized field of medicine."

However, at Nuremberg the future of psychoanalysis as a therapy was almost overshadowed in Freud's mind by the need to create an international organization which he could control. By 1910 he had become convinced of two things. He believed that the danger of psychoanalysis being considered a Jewish idea was as great as its being considered pornographic. And he also believed that it now required a figurehead unhandicapped by the weight of criticism that he had attracted during the first decade of the century. His defense of the leadership cult as outlined in retrospect by Ernest Jones is revealing:

> Freud was too mistrustful of the average mind to adopt the democratic attitude customary in scientific societies, so he wished there to be a prominent "leader" who should guide the doings of branch societies and their members; moreover he wanted the leader to be in a permanent position, like a monarch. In this, especially in the first half of it, I feel sure he was right, for one cannot understand anything about the development of psychoanalysis if one puts it on a level with old-established and relatively unemotional branches of science, with astronomy, geology, and so on. A strong steadying influence, with a balanced judgment and a sense of responsibility, was in the circumstances highly desirable.

As far as Freud was concerned there was only one possible candidate for the monarchy. This was Jung, "the Siegfried of the Burghölzli" as Wittels called him, a counterweight in the eyes of the world to the Viennese Jews and, Freud still believed, a man over whom he could exercise the necessary influence and control. The choice, Jones acknowledged, although with hindsight, "was the first indication I had that Freud, despite his extraordinary genius in penetrating the deepest layers of the mind, was not a connoisseur of men."

Freud arrived in Nuremberg, where between fifty and sixty analysts had gathered, with the elevation of Jung a major aim. The signs were not propitious. In spite of a growing rift between Bleuler and Jung, the Swiss as a bloc did usefully counterbalance the Viennese; but Freud's worry was shown in a letter to Pfister two weeks before the conference: "I still have not got over your not coming to Nuremberg," he wrote. "Bleuler is not coming either, and Jung is in America, so that I am trembling about his return. What will happen if my Zürichers desert me?" The answer, of course, was that he would have to make do with his Viennese, but he had little wish for that. "I no longer get any pleasure from [them]," he had written to Abraham a few weeks earlier. "I have a heavy cross to bear with the older generation, Stekel, Adler, Sadger. They will soon be feeling that I am an obstacle and will treat me as such, but I can't believe that they have anyone better to substitute for me."

There was little chance by this time of the Viennese aiding Jung's elevation in the hierarchy. However, a willing instrument was present in Ferenczi, a neutral Hungarian in any Austro-Swiss unpleasantness, and it was Ferenczi who proposed at Nuremberg that the International Psycho-Analytical Association should be founded with Jung as permanent president. He was to have extraordinary powers, including the appointment and deposition of analysts, and the prepublication vetting of whatever members should write on psychoanalysis. If this were not enough to rouse anger, Ferenczi, more through lack of tact than intention, suggested that this was the natural course for events since the Viennese—with the exception of Freud himself—were in some ways inferior to the Swiss. Whatever the merits or demerits of the case as a whole, prepublication vetting was obviously an absurdity if psychoanalysis were to be taken seriously, the main point made in a half-hour protest by Wilhelm Stekel.

No verbatim account of the ensuing discussion has apparently survived, but the fact that after it had taken place during a morning session the chairman suspended sittings until the following day is an indication of the heat engendered. Before the resumption, however, the Viennese had been called by Stekel to a meeting in his bedroom in the Grand Hotel. Freud was not invited.

Suddenly, Stekel later wrote in describing the event,

> the door opened; we looked around and saw it was Freud. He was greatly excited and tried to persuade us to accept Ferenczi's motion; he predicted hard times and a strong opposition by official science. He grasped his coat and cried: "They begrudge me the coat I am wearing; I don't know whether in the future I will earn my daily bread." Tears were streaming down his cheeks. "An official psychiatrist and a Gentile must be the leader of the movement."

Stekel's version must not be taken too literally, and the picture of Freud with tear-stained cheeks is hard to credit. Yet even Ernest Jones, rarely one to show the founder of psychoanalysis in less than the best of lights, later reported him as dramatically throwing back his coat and declaring, "My enemies would be willing to see me starve; they would tear my very coat off my back." The most credible account is given by Fritz Wittels, who has Freud saying to the Viennese:

> Most of you are Jews, and therefore you are incompetent to win friends for the new teaching. Jews must be content with the modest role of preparing the ground. It is absolutely essential that I should

form ties in the world of general science. I am getting on in years, and am weary of being perpetually attacked. We are all in danger. . . . They won't even leave me a coat to my back. The Swiss will save us—will save me, and all of you as well.

A compromise eventually sufficed. The following motion, finally carried, omitted the power of censorship, and it was agreed that while the presidency should go to Jung, it was to be not for life but for only two years. Since Freud was himself to play the leading part in eventually driving Jung from the movement, the compromise forced on him in Nuremberg was an example, albeit unwitting, of a man's friends saving him from himself. But for them, Jung might have ruled supreme for more than half a century until his death in 1961.

The Viennese gained one other small concession. It was agreed that another journal, the *Zentralblatt für Psychoanalyse,* should be founded. Adler and Stekel would be joint editors, but Freud would also read the articles submitted and each of the three men would have the power of veto. Within a few months Stekel produced for its pages "The Obligation of the Name." Freud vetoed it.

If the Nuremberg Congress had not quite gone Freud's way, a good deal had been accomplished, notably the foundation of the Association, whose purpose was: "The cultivation and promotion of the psychoanalytic science as inaugurated by Freud, both in its form as pure psychology and in its application to medicine and the humanities; mutual assistance among members in their endeavors to acquire and foster psychoanalytic knowledge." A few days later he wrote to Ferenczi, "With the Nuremberg *Reichstag* closes the childhood of our movement; that is my impression. I hope now for a rich and fair time of youth."

But Freud had been forced to show his hand. "[He] does not think much of us, his Viennese pupils," Fritz Wittels wrote. "If he knew the Swiss as well as he knows us, he would like them still less!" Yet he had been able to staple Jung into position as his chief of staff, a success whose importance was shown in two remarks to Ludwig Binswanger. "I wish I lived closer to Jung in order to support him in his youthful authority, on which much of the future seems to depend," he wrote later in 1910; and, early the following year: "When the empire I have founded is orphaned, no one but Jung must inherit the whole thing. As you see, my politics incessantly pursues this aim, and my behavior toward Stekel and Adler fits into the same scheme."

In spite of such hopes, the bitter feelings between the Viennese and the Swiss came to the surface again when the Vienna

Psychoanalytical Society met on April 6, 1910, and the members heard Freud outline the consequences of the Congress. The Society, he pointed out, would have to fall into line with the requirements of the International Association. Until now, Freud went on, the members had been his guests, but in future this would no longer be feasible, and they would have to form a constitution, meet formally elsewhere and choose a president, a post to which Adler was elected.

Freud was followed by other speakers, including Dr. Hitschmann and Fritz Wittels. Hitschmann gave his own impression of the Congress, "which is that the Zürichers, as a breed, are totally different people from us in Vienna. But for all that we do not underestimate our inner qualities." Wittels was even more revealing, as much of his own group as of the opposition. "The Zürichers are trained clinically to become Freudians," he is reported as saying; "they would probably champion any other doctrine with the same righteousness and the same tearful tone. The Vienna society, on the other hand, has grown historically; each one of us has a neurosis, which is necessary for entry into Freud's teachings; whether the Swiss have, is questionable." As an illustration of St. Luke's injunction to physicians, Wittels' admission is possibly unique.

In spite of the contretemps between the Viennese and the Swiss, the Nuremberg Congress had got the international psychoanalytic movement safely off the ground. The progress foreshadowed in the United States was continuing, and Freud had every reason to be satisfied with the outlook. "About myself," he had written to the Roumanian friend of his youth, Edouard Silberstein,

I can only say that I encountered many unforeseen labors, that I found unexpectedly a great deal of work; however, on the whole, I am not dissatisfied with the outcome. My scientific expectations are slowly materializing. I am earning as much as we need; in fact, I could have been a well-to-do man had I not preferred to have a large family. I am in the midst of a great movement concerning the concept and therapy of nervous diseases, which is probably not unknown in Roumania.

It was not only knowledge of psychoanalysis which was spreading by this time. The area in which its principles could be applied was also extending, and before the end of 1911 Freud was using them to throw fresh light on the psychoses, those illnesses whose severity can render their victims *non compos mentis*. Freud's sortie into this field where, as he himself admitted, psychoanalysis could rarely be of great help, was notable for the unusual details of the case itself; for the fact that analysis was made without personal contact with the "patient," being based solely on the latter's written memoirs, and for the fact that Freud's paper on the subject contained the seeds of disagreement with Carl Jung and with Freud's intimate friend Sandor Ferenczi.

In 1903 there had appeared in Leipzig the *Memoirs of my Nervous Illness* of Daniel Paul Schreber. The story they revealed was an extraordinary one. Schreber came from a distinguished family and in the autumn of 1884 had been presiding judge at the Landsgericht in Chemnitz. He was also standing as a candidate for the Reichstag but in October became afflicted with what was described as a nervous illness. He was admitted to the Psychiatric Clinic of the University of Leipzig, was discharged after six months, and before the end of 1885 had resumed his judicial duties. Eight years later he was appointed president of the Judges Panel at the Supreme Court of the Kingdom of Saxony. But only six weeks after taking office Schreber again fell ill. This time a brief stay in the Leipzig Clinic was followed by committal to Sonnenstein Asylum, where he was kept until obtaining his discharge in 1902.

During his years of incarceration Schreber showed the symptoms of acute paranoia. He had to be placed in a padded cell at night, attended by three men during the day, and forcibly fed. He was, according to the judge who considered his appeal for discharge, "dominated by delusions . . . considered himself chosen to redeem the world and to restore to it the lost state of Blessedness. This however he could only do by first being transformed from a man into a woman. In this sexual transformation the patient imagined himself the object of continuous divine miracles, and believed he could hear the birds and the winds talking to him, which fortified him in his belief in miracles." He believed he was being persecuted, particularly by his former doctor; that he was changing sex; and that "there sometimes appeared when I was in bed—not sleeping but awake—all sorts of large, queer, almost dragonlike shapes, immediately next to my bed, and almost as big as my bed." Such however, were only the highlights of the case. "So manifold were the symptoms [Schreber] displayed at one time or another," it has been said, "that almost the whole symptomatology of the entire field of psychiatric abnormality is described."

Freud's interest in paranoia went back to the 1890s when he had sent Fliess a long draft on the subject in which he noted: "People become paranoiac about things that they cannot tolerate—provided always that they have a particular psychical disposition." By the early 1900s he was beginning to suspect that this special disposition might be a state of repressed homosexuality. However, as he pointed out, it was difficult for a doctor in private practice to make detailed studies of paranoiacs, since such patients were usually institutionalized. Schreber's *Memoirs* offered a second-best alternative, for his hallucinations had not prevented him from giving a detailed and coherent account of them and of his experiences in the asylum.

Eugen Bleuler quoted extensively from the *Memoirs* in his classic *Dementia Praecox, or the Group of Schizophrenias*, written in 1908 although not published until 1911, and it was most probably Bleuler who drew Freud's attention to the *Memoirs* after the Salzburg Congress of 1908. Freud is known to have discussed the subject with Ferenczi while they were on holiday in Sardinia during the summer of 1910, and during the last weeks of the year he wrote "Psychoanalytic Notes on an Autobiographical Account of a Case of Paranoia (Dementia Paranoides)." The paper attributed Schreber's illness to an upsurge of unconscious homosexuality which he was unable to accept, the subsequent internal conflict leading to his withdrawal from reality. It was a verdict which remained largely unchallenged for more than forty years, although Bleuler himself, while agreeing that unconscious homosexuality was a factor, doubted whether it was the only one. Then, in 1955 two psychiatrists, Ida Macalpine and R. A. Hunter published what Jones has called "a tartly written criticism" of Freud's findings. They added major qualifications to his conclusions, seeing Schreber's failure to produce a son as the precipitating factor in his illness. Nearly two decades later there came Morton Schatzman's *Soul Murder*, which convincingly linked Schreber's delusions to his upbringing by a tyrannical father. "What," it has recently been asked, "would Freud have made of the case if he had known the true story, and why, since he was particularly interested in childhood experience, did he not take the trouble to to find out more about Schreber's background?"

Freud's Schreber paper, with its attempt to show how psychoanalysis could stretch back to explain the actions of the dead, was typical of the new vigor which followed the founding of the International Psycho-Analytical Association. The cause was growing, and it was in a spirit of expanding optimism that he now began preparations for a Congress to which he hoped he could attract the Americans. It was therefore agreed that the meeting should be held in the autumn of 1911, a more suitable season for the hoped-for visitors than the spring. At first it looked as though the extra time would be useful for another reason, since it seemed likely that Freud might now be losing his invaluable contact in North America, Ernest Jones.

Once again Jones had suffered a misfortune. This time he was being accused by a woman patient of having had sexual intercourse with her. She had denounced Jones to the president of the University of Toronto and had also threatened legal proceedings. The state of her mind is indicated by the fact that she had threatened to murder Jones who was, he wrote to Putnam, being guarded by an armed detective. He had, as he admitted, foolishly paid the woman $500 "to prevent a scandal which would be almost equally harmful either way."

It looked as if Jones's job might be in danger and that promotion to a chair, which he had been expecting, was extremely unlikely. He had therefore, he told Freud, decided to leave Canada for Europe the following September. If he did get the chair, then he would return to Toronto to lecture for one session and would then resign. In the meantime, he went on, he would try to get a post in the United States. In any case, he would continue to work for the cause.

Freud responded immediately, offering help, advice and encouragement. Eventually inquiries showed that the woman was a psychopath, a morphine addict and a failed suicide. The president refused to accept her story. Jones was appointed associate professor of psychiatry, and held the appointment until he returned to London in November 1913. Remaining in Toronto, he was thus able to smooth the way for attendance of Americans at the autumn Congress of 1911. Locarno was first suggested as the site, but later dropped in favor of Weimar, and here the third Congress was held in September. The American party included Brill, T. H. Ames, Beatrice Hinkle and, most important of all, James Putnam, whose presence gave the occasion an accolade it would otherwise have lacked.

Throughout August and early September, Freud was on holiday with his family at Bolzano in the Dolomites. He then traveled to Weimar by way of Zurich, where he was met by Jung and taken to the latter's home at Küsnacht, a few miles out of town on the Lake of Zurich. James Putnam was already a guest. Judging by a letter from Emma Jung to Freud a few weeks later, Freud was in a depressed mood. She recalled "the conversation on the first morning after your arrival, when you told me about your family. You said then that your marriage had long been 'amortized,' now there was nothing more to do except—die . . . you said you didn't have time to analyze your children's dreams because you had to earn money so that they could go on dreaming. Do you think this attitude is right?"

At Küsnacht, Freud took the opportunity of giving Putnam a six-hour analysis, an operation whose somehat surprising outcome the elderly American took with understanding. "I remember," he recalled, "that Dr. Freud pointed out to me, in the very first of our few conferences in Zurich, that I was a murderer! Think of that. But did he mean, or did I suppose he meant, that I was to go and jump overboard, or give myself up to the hangman? Not a bit of it. I was to be healthier-minded from then on, and happier, and better able to stop being a murderer."

The Weimar Congress was held in the city's best hotel, and attended by representatives from Holland, Sweden and Germany, as well as by the Austrian, Swiss and American contingents. Freud was at the top of his form, reading an elegant postscript to the Schreber paper in which he referred to Schreber's illusion of being able to look at the sun without being dazzled, and the myth that the eagle always forced its young to look at the sun without blinking, throwing out of the eyrie those which failed. "And when Schreber boasts that he can look into the sun unscathed and undazzled," he went on, "he has rediscovered the mythological method of expressing his filial relation to the sun, and has confirmed us once again in our view that the sun is a symbol of the father."

The remark allowed the Congress to show its adulation when Stekel rose after Freud's paper. Alfred Adler had by this time seceded from the Vienna group and was preparing to take a number of followers with him. The point was not lost on the Weimar audience when Stekel reminded them that Freud had left in Vienna an eagle who had dared to look at the sun. They dutifully applauded.

The only shadow at Weimar was that cast by the first signs of a difference between Freud and Putnam. The two men were to remain firm friends until Putnam's death in 1918, and Putnam was never to fall away from his faith in psychoanalysis as, to Freud's dismay, did Stanley Hall. Freud never doubted the value of the American's support and after reading Putnam's paper "On the Aetiology and Treatment of the Psychoneuroses," declared that he had never been as proud or as satisfied with himself. "You convince me," he added, "that I have not lived and worked in vain, for men such as you will see to it that the ideas I have arrived at in so much pain and anguish will not be lost to humanity. What more can one desire?" And to Abraham he had confirmed his view of Putnam's value: "That old gentleman," he wrote, "is a magnificent acquisition." The "old" was a reminder of the exchange which had started when Freud, writing to Putnam after his return from America, had commented, "Although you are a decade older than I am. . . ." It is not clear whether Putnam received the letter before passing the proofs of his account of the Clark University visit for the *Journal of Abnormal Psychology*, but here he wrote, "Though little known among us, Freud is no longer a young man." This rankled with Freud who in a note to his translation of Putnam's "On the Aetiology and Treatment of the Psychoneuroses" added—simply as "an act of vengeance," as he described it to Jung—that Putnam had "left his youth far behind him."

Nevertheless, Putnam was certainly an acquisition; and Freud knew that acquisitions usually have to be paid for. In this case the price was the effort needed to counter Putnam's desire to harness psychoanalysis to the chariot wheels of his own brand of Hegelian philosophy, an aim which became clear with his Weimar paper on "The Importance of Philosophy for the Further Development of Psychoanalysis." Raised on strict religious principles, which had enabled him to absorb the revelations of late nineteenth-century science without undue discomfort, Putnam believed "that philosophy provided insights as valid as those of science," and that a place for the revelations of psychoanalysis should be found within his own framework of Christian ethics. To Freud, such a framework was at the best superfluous, at the worst a hindrance. As he explained to Putnam,

> I feel no need for a higher moral synthesis in the same way that I have no ear for music. But I do not consider myself a better man because of that. I console myself with this reflection: the idealistic truths which you are not willing to give up cannot be so certain if the basic principles of the science on which we do agree are so difficult to determine. But I respect you and your views. Although I am resigned to the fact that I am a God forsaken "incredulous Jew" [two quoted words in English], I am not proud of it and I do not look down on others. I can only say with Faust, "There have to be odd fellows like that too."

At Weimar, Freud began to realize for the first time that the differences between Putnam and himself were more than personal differences of approach. He had become quite experienced in fighting off the accusations that psychoanalysis had little scientific foundation, and the protests that even if it had, it dealt with matters that were best left undiscussed. Now he sensed a more formidable danger: the idea that psychoanalysis should be part of an idealistic philosophy, teaching that basic psychic tension arose from the contrast between man's recognition of his own transitory existence and the reality of the infinite: that although one manifestation was, indeed, the psychic sexual conflict, it was only a partial manifestation of a greater whole.

Putnam's address at Weimar was treated with respect, but its reception can be gauged from the reaction of Pfarrer Pfister, a listener certainly sympathetic to the spiritual approach. "I can still vividly remember the impression that was made by Putnam's paper," he wrote more than a decade later. "The audience, under the spell of a profound spiritual achievement, was glowing with the noblest sentiments, but the copious rush of thoughts left behind a certain bewilderment. . . . This obscure metaphysics which advances with victorious mien and haughtily demands that empirical science shall follow in its triumphant train. Putnam left out of consideration the unhappy experiences of psychology during the time when it was struggling in the net of metaphysics." Freud summed up his reaction more succinctly. "Putnam's philosophy," he said, "is like a beautiful table centre; everyone admires it but nobody touches it."

Although Freud's differences with Putnam were directly relevant to the future of psychoanalysis, they aroused no bitterness, a circumstance not entirely accounted for by the fact that for most of their lives the two men were separated by the breadth of the Atlantic. But with Putnam there could be no personal rivalry for position or power, a factor quite as important in maintaining equable terms as Freud's need of an ambassador within the American medical establishment.

The case of Alfred Adler, whose final break with Freud came a few weeks after the Weimar Congress, was very different. The motives in the controversy were numerous and interlinked; the position at times took on the air of a struggle not of right against wrong but of right against right, while Freud himself occasionally showed an enthusiasm for political intrigue not untouched by bitterness. "Personal differences—jealousy or revenge or some other kind of animosity always came first," he himself later admitted when discussing the upheavals of the movement's early days; "scientific discoveries came later. If people were really friendly, differences of scientific opinion would not make enemies of them." Nevertheless, he could proclaim that Adler's views had little relation to psychoanalysis as he had created it and as he intended to keep it, whatever personal motivations or jealousies were involved.

As a child Adler had been crippled by rickets and unable to walk until the age of four. He had then suffered badly from pneumonia and, apparently due to his disabilities, had been involved in several street accidents. Thus it was perhaps more natural for Adler than for the basically vigorous Freud to see the search for power, rather than sex, as the mainspring of life and the "inferiority complex," a term which he popularized, as the basis of human struggle. There were other differences. Freud had remained a Jew, while Adler became a Christian "as a protest against the isolation that he felt was a spiritual danger in the Orthodox Jewish faith." And while Freud made it not only his practice but a cardinal point of his teaching that patients should be kept at emotional arm's length— that if their problems were to be relieved, this could only come about with the help of an analyst who was dispassionate, objective, aloof—Adler operated in another way. He became friends with his patients.

In addition, Adler was a Social Democrat and, as one competent observer remarked, seemed "to have attempted to reconcile the Marxist doctrine of class struggle with his own ideas about the psychic conflict." Significantly, the members of the Vienna Psychoanalytical Society who eventually seceded with him—a quarter of the membership—were all Social Democrats. Whatever the professional differences between Freud and Adler, however strong the human disagreements, their break had a whiff of political revolt. There was nothing disreputable about this, and it is revealing of the varied issues involved that Jones, Freud's faithful paladin, should write almost contemptuously of Adler's socialism that it was "of the type whose views were based rather on a sense of social inferiority, with consequent envy and resentment, than on more objective grounds. He came to psychoanalysis attracted by the stress it laid on suppression of personal wishes, and hoping to get from it some scientific support for his Socialistic strivings."

In 1907 Adler, a doctor at first specializing in ophthalmology, had published his *Study of Organ Inferiority and Its Psychical Compensation.* Although the seeds of his later apostasy were contained in the book, its thesis at first seemed acceptable enough to Freud and his colleagues. Adler, like most doctors, knew that damage to one organ in the human body was sometimes followed by a compensatory reaction, among the most common being the increased functioning of one kidney or lung if the other were damaged. Surely, he argued, there could be the psychic equivalent of such reactions.

The first hint of trouble ahead appeared the following year when, on June 3, Adler read to the Society a paper on "Sadism in Life and in Neurosis." Freud agreed with most of Adler's points but mainly, it appears from the secretary's minute, because "what Adler calls aggressive drive is our libido." Freud went on to make a number of comparatively mild criticisms, and the minutes note that a long debate followed "on the identity of or difference between Adler's aggressive drive and our libido." Almost exactly a year later, when Adler read a paper on "The Oneness of the Neuroses," criticism came not only from Freud but from other members of the Society.

The basic differences between the theories that Freud had been developing for more than two decades and those which had occupied Adler for about half the time were simple enough to understand. Whereas Freud believed that neuroses arose from maladjustments to sexual development, to Adler they represented a compensation for inferior psychic or physical attributes. Within this concept of power as the mainspring of the human machine, the Oedipus complex could be accommodated, if at all, only when downgraded in significance and transformed into something far less dramatically shocking than Freud's lust for mother or father.

Adler's theories were thus in direct opposition to those of Freud. It might not have mattered had the Vienna Psychoanalytical Society and the international body been groups whose main aim was the search for truth. But the purpose of the International Association was to promote "the psychoanalytic science as inaugurated by Freud," and its Viennese branch had aims not much less rigid or narrow. Adler's resignation therefore became essential. Ensuring this was a task to which Freud devoted much skill.

What could have been a perfectly respectable agreement to differ was, moreover, being compounded by the struggle for power between the Viennese group, headed by Adler, and the Zurichers, headed by Freud's chosen Crown Prince. Freud's adroit handling of the situation at Nuremberg in the spring of 1910, and his gift of the *Zentralblatt* to Adler and Stekel, had prevented what would then have been a disastrous explosion of anger. But Kipling's "If you once have paid him the Dane-geld, You never get rid of the Dane" was applicable to the Viennese. Before the end of 1910 it was clear to Freud that Adler was consolidating the position from which he continued to propagate ideas that were seriously worrying to those of the true faith. "Adler," he was writing to Jung in November,

> is a very decent and highly intelligent man, but he is paranoid; in the *Zentralblatt* he puts so much stress on his almost unintelligible theories that the readers must be utterly confused. He is always claiming priority, putting new names on everything, complaining that he is disappearing under my shadow, and forcing me into the unwelcome role of the aging despot who prevents young men from getting ahead. They are also rude to me personally and [referring to Adler and Stekel] I'd gladly get rid of them both. But it won't be possible.

The defeatist attitude changed early in 1911. Adler was invited to give the Viennese Society an explanation of his ideas, and a number of evenings were allocated for this. He seized the opportunity, hoping that he might be able to convince his teacher. Freud could not have hoped for more. In a confrontation the scales would be heavily weighted in his favor.

Accounts of Adler's exposition, and of the debate that followed, come mainly from Adler's supporters, but Freud put his own point of view to Pfister at the height of the argument. Adler's theories, he said, were

> departing too far from the right path, and it [is] time to make a stand against them. He forgets the saying of the apostle Paul, the exact words of which you know better than I: "And I know that ye have not love in you." He has created for himself a world system without love, and I am in the process of carrying out on him the revenge of the offended goddess Libido. I have always made it my principle to be tolerant and not to exercise authority, but in practice it does not always work. It is like cars and pedestrians. When I began going about by car I got just as angry at the carelessness of pedestrians as I used to be at the recklessness of drivers.

His principle of exercising tolerance was finally abandoned in the debate that followed the conclusion of Adler's statements. According to Wittels, who admittedly got his account from the Adlerian supporter Wilhelm Stekel, "Freud had a sheaf of notes before him, and with gloomy mien seemed prepared to annihilate his adversary." Freud's supporters, he states, "made a mass attack on Adler, an attack almost unexampled for its ferocity even in the fiercely contested field of psychoanalytical controversy." Freud's reply, as sifted through the ameliorating secretarial work of those who kept the minutes, was critical, although it gave a firm impression of trying to be fair in the face of provocation.

The older members of the Society tended to support him, although, as he admitted to Jung, the younger and newer men showed considerable sympathy with Adler. Among the latter was Stekel, after whose intervention Freud retorted: "while Stekel asserts that he does not see any contradiction between Adler's views and Freud's doctrines, one has to point out that two of the persons involved do find this a contradiction: Adler and Freud." For Stekel himself, Freud had a mixture of bitterness and contempt. To Herman Nunberg, an early member of the Society, he said after Stekel's departure from the Vienna group, "Henceforth we can work peacefully and undisturbed," and to Jones he said, "I am afraid he will find life very hard and suffer the fate of the inflated frog." Years later, sending a new patient to a colleague, he wrote: "The last experience she has had to go through was a six-month treatment by Stekel. The fact that she remained impervious to his imbecile suggestions cannot be counted to her discredit."

Adler had been outmaneuvered, and the Society's minutes for March 1, 1911, report that he resigned from the presidency "on the grounds of the incompatability between his scientific position and his position in the Society. . . . and that Stekel has joined him." There was a glimmer of the coming fission when Dr. Fürtmüller, who had earlier been so unhappy about Wittels' attack on Kraus, denied that there was any incompatibility, a point of view which Freud regarded as "a criticism we could spare Adler and an overture we could spare ourselves."

Freud's observations on the schism are almost conversational. "Pretty interesting things have come to pass in the Vienna group," he reported to Jones. "We had a series of Adler debates and as the incompatibility of his views with our psychoanalysis came clearly out, he resigned his leadership. . . . Stekel followed his example, and so I have to accept the honor he dropped on Wednesday next and will [sic] the matter into my own hands again."

This was reasonable enough. But from now on there is no doubt that an accommodation with Adler was the last thing for which Freud was hoping. However, Adler and Stekel were still in charge of the Zentralblatt. "Naturally I am only waiting for an occasion to throw them both out," he confided to Jung, "but they know it and are being very cautious and conciliatory, so there is nothing I can do for the present. Of course I am watching them more closely, but they put up with it. In my heart I am through with them." Adler's ego, he went on, "behaves as the ego always behaves, like the clown in the circus who keeps grimacing to assure the audience that he has planned everything that is going on. The poor fool!"

The letter to Jones was no doubt the basis of Jones's statement that Freud now "somewhat reluctantly agreed" to resume the presidency. Reporting to Jung, Freud himself put a different gloss on the situation. "I have decided," he wrote, ". . . to take the reins back into my own hands, and I mean to keep a tight hold on them."

Stekel, whose Die Sprache des Traumes (The Language of Dreams) had just appeared, got no better treatment. The book, Freud admitted, was rich in content: "the pig finds truffles," he went on, "but otherwise it's a mess, no attempt at coherence, full of hollow commonplaces and new lopsided generalizations, all incredibly sloppy." However, to Stekel himself Freud wrote in other terms later the same summer. When he sent the sloppy generalizer an agate bowl from Karlsbad, where he was taking the waters, he enclosed a note saying: "I cannot conceive that anything could ever come between us."

But the poor fool and the sloppy generalizer were still in charge of the *Zentralblatt*. In April, 1911, Freud told Jung that he would like "to throw [Adler] out on the next occasion; but Stekel wants to keep him and promises to make him see the light. . . ." However, in May he succeeded. Opinions differ as to exactly what happened. Freud has said that he "pressed" Bergman, the publisher, to dismiss Adler, and the Adlerians maintain that while Adler was on holiday Freud informed the publisher that he would withdraw his name unless Adler's was removed from the title page. According to the Freud version, Adler "twisted and turned, and finally came up with a strangely worded statement which can only be taken as his resignation," while in his subsequent *On the History of the Psycho-Analytic Movement* Freud openly admitted: ". . . I was obliged to bring about Adler's resignation from the editorship of the *Zentralblatt*. . . ." His statement was confirmed in the August number of the journal in which Adler gave notice as follows: "I wish to bring to the attention of the readers of this periodical that I am resigning from the editorial staff. The publisher, Professor Freud, was of the opinion that such diverging views exist between him and me that a common publication of this periodical does not appear feasible. I have therefore decided to resign voluntarily."

Two things are certain: that Freud himself was in control of events and that he forced Adler's resignation. As he admitted in a long letter to Jones from Klobenstein am Ritten, the village in the Tyrolese Dolomites where he was spending the summer holiday, he had ripened the crisis. He expected that Adler's resignation would be followed by the departure of others, and he was not particularly unhappy at the prospect. To Jung he wrote in similar terms. "The damage is not very great," he said. "Paranoid intelligences are not rare and are more dangerous than useful. As a paranoiac, of course he is right about many things, though wrong about everything. A few rather useless members will probably follow his example."

The members did so at the first meeting of the Society after the summer recess when, with Adler, they withdrew completely. "Most of these men did not share Adler's views," reported Hanns Sachs; "their decision was influenced by their belief that the whole proceeding violated the 'freedom of science.' It may well be that Freud's incisive and harsh criticism had hurt soft feelings and made them willing to think that Adler's complaint of intolerance was justified."

Neither then, nor in the aftermath of the upheaval, did Freud admit that the freedom of science was involved. "Rather tired after battle and victory," he wrote to Jung the following day, October

12, 1911. "I hereby inform you that yesterday I forced the whole Adler gang (six of them) to resign from the Society. I was harsh but I don't think unfair."

Neither was he forgiving. As one commentator put it, although Freud disposed conclusively of Adler's case against him, he disposed of it week after week, for years. In 1914 he wrote of the "specific venomousness" of Adler, the "loathsome individual," and in *On the History of the Psycho-Analytic Movement* he drew attention to "the profusion of petty outbursts of malice which disfigure [Adler's] writings and . . . the indications they contain of an uncontrolled craving for priority." The bitterness went on. So much so that, as Ernest Jones reported, Freud made a distinctly unusual comment to Arnold Zweig after Adler had dropped dead of a cerebral hemorrhage while attending a meeting of the British Association for the Advancement of Science in Aberdeen. "For a Jew boy out of a Viennese suburb," he is quoted as writing, "death in Aberdeen is an unheard-of career in itself and a proof of how far he had got on. The world really rewarded him richly for his service in having contradicted psychoanalysis." When the Freud–Zweig correspondence was later edited by Freud's son Ernst the bitter reference was cut out—presumably because Ernst realized better than Jones how the word "Jew-boy" would be viewed as pejorative by Gentile readers.

Shortly after Adler's secession in the autumn of 1911 he and his followers set up the Society for Free Psychoanalytic Research. It had been started, said their official explanation, since it was felt that "attempts were being made to commit the members of the old society to the whole of Freud's scientific doctrines and theories. Such a proceeding seemed to them not only difficult to reconcile with the basic tenets of scientific research, but especially dangerous in a science as young as psychoanalysis. In their opinion it also called in question the value of previous achievements if people were expected to commit themselves hastily to certain formulas and give up the possibility of attempting new solutions. Their conviction of the decisive importance of the psychoanalytical method of work and approach caused them to see that their scientific duty was to ensure a place for completely independent psychoanalytical research."

Adler's "individual psychology," as his "free psychoanalysis" soon became, not only survived but flourished, and its popularity was no doubt one factor in keeping Freud's bitterness alive. "But a theory such as this is bound to be very welcome to the great mass of the people," he was to admit, "a theory which recognizes no complications, which introduces no new concepts that are hard to grasp, which knows nothing of the unconscious, which gets rid at a single blow of the universally oppressive problem of sexuality and which restricts itself to the discovery of the artifices by which people seek to make life easy." And here he quoted Schiller: "Were the idea not so confounded clever, I'd be inclined to call it really stupid." In fact, Adler's psychology, he would conclude, had "very little to do with psychoanalysis but, as a result of certain historical circumstances, leads a kind of parasitic existence at its expense."

There is no doubt that Freud believed Adler's activities faced psychoanalysis with very real danger, and he considered it a triumph that he had been able to cast his opponent into what he believed was outer darkness. What he failed to realize was that to some, and possibly to many, his treatment of Adler, and later of other dissidents, was very similar to the unthinking opposition which he himself had met a decade and more earlier. Though a great admirer of Cromwell, he omitted to follow the advice offered by the Protector to the Kirk of Scotland: "I beseech you, in the bowels of Christ, think it possible you may be mistaken."

Criticism did not come only from the Adlerians. "Freud . . . insisted . . . that if one followed Adler and dropped the sexual basis of psychic life, one was no more a Freudian," wrote Max Graf. "In short, Freud, as head of the church, banished Adler; he ejected him from the official church. Within the space of a few years I lived through the whole development of church history; from the first sermons to a small group of apostles, to the strife between Arius and Athanasius." The comparison with a faith, however high-pitched the protests it brings from Freudians, was clear enough to those who knew Freud well. His concentration on psychoanalysis, noted Hanns Sachs, "burned with a steady and all-consuming flame. Like every other faith, it imposed on the life of the believer severe restrictions and regulations. Everything from the small details of everyday routine to the most momentous decisions was shaped by its dictation."

The role of defender of the faith rather than seeker after truth, played out in many later quarrels with followers who became renegades, deviants or deserters must be understood, even if it cannot be excused. Ernest Jones has written in his own memoirs, published long after Freud's death, that while a scientist has to place truth before all things, "there is one situation in which it is quite peculiarly hard to uphold this grand ideal." This is, he continues, "when it has cost much to come to the conclusion in question, or, put in modern language, when one has overcome an emotional resistance that had stood in the way of perceiving the truth of the conclusions. Truths so painfully won are apt to be defended with great tenacity, and this may often interfere with the desirable readiness to modify them in the light of still more evidence. What began as a piece of insight hardens into a conviction and may at the end petrify into a prejudice; it did so with the great Lord Lister and his antiseptic spray."

Much the same can be said of Freud. In the case of Adler he paid a penalty, for Adler did not wither in the outer darkness. Instead, the weekly meetings which he soon inaugurated showed signs of turning into the nucleus of a genuine psychotherapeutic movement, a development which quickly became something of an embarrassment to Freud, forced as he was to take defensive action.

The strength of Adler's position was underlined when in the autumn of 1912 there arrived in Vienna Lou Andreas-Salomé, one of the more remarkable of Freud's followers. The daughter of a Russian general, Lou was a woman with a past that included as lovers Nietzsche and Rilke, and was later to operate a respected psychoanalytic practice in the German university town of Göttingen. She had attended the Weimar Congress with Poul Bjerre, a doctor who earlier in the year had launched his career by reading a paper on psychoanalysis to the Association of Swedish Physicians, had read most of Freud's writings and had very soon become the most devoted of converts.

On the face of it, Lou Andreas-Salomé might have been planted in the psychoanalytic movement by those intent on destroying it. Her private life, particularly after her marriage to Friedrich Carl Andreas in 1887, though conducted with transparent sincerity, was enough, had its details been known, to confirm Freud's most virulent critics in their belief that excessive sexuality was the rock on which the cause had been founded. And although her intellectual ability could not be faulted, her looks, her personality and her facility for attracting men more than offset any position she might occupy as a bluestocking. If this were not enough to make her a potential danger to psychoanalysis, there was the influence which she soon began to exercise over Freud himself. In retrospect, his relations with Lou Andreas-Salomé add to his stature. After his death it was to be maintained that "nowhere in his writings is it possible to divine he was aware of the passion, tenderness, poetry, and beauty of love, nor all the shades of regard, affection, and friendship which are not sexually motivated." It was, in fact, just such feelings that Freud evinced for Lou during the quarter century of their friendship. "There are some people," he once told a colleague, "who have an intrinsic superiority. They have an inborn nobility. She is just one of those people."

Lou arrived in Vienna on October 25, 1912, having previously obtained Freud's permission to attend his university lectures. But she arrived with an open mind and had arranged that after listening to Freud on Wednesday evenings she would attend the meetings held in Adler's rooms on Thursdays. Freud soon had to explain that this would not do. "Since you have informed me of your intention to attend Adler's Discussion Evenings, I shall take the liberty of saying a few words to you unasked, so that you may be enlightened as to this disagreeable state of affairs," he told her. "The relationship between the two groups is not such as ought to result from analogous, even if divergent, endeavors. They frequently carry on something else besides psychoanalysis. We found ourselves obliged to break off all contact between Adler's splinter group and our own, and even our medical guests are asked to choose between one or the other. That is not pleasant, but the personal behavior of those who have left our ranks left us no choice." However, he would not make this stipulation with Lou, a wise decision since to a newcomer such a ban might have looked like weakness.

The situation, moreover, now gave him an observer in the enemy camp, as is clear from a cryptic entry in Lou's diary. "Freud's official account of Stekel's withdrawal," she wrote after attending the meeting of the Vienna Psychoanalytical Society on November 6; "(as if it concerned the local Vienna society only—whereas I know from Adler what Stekel's intentions are, and Freud also now recognizes them. But on this I had to be silent)." However complete the silence, it would be remarkable if Freud did not gather from her at least something of what was going on, particularly as the disagreement with Stekel centered on his refusal to allow Victor Tausk, the ambitious new recruit to psychoanalysis, to supervise the reviews in the *Zentralblatt*.

This was not without significance since within a few weeks of arriving in Vienna, Lou had become Tausk's mistress, thus creating, with her idolatry for Freud, an eternal triangle with a difference. From Lou, Freud received detailed news of Tausk's professional work. From Freud, Tausk received an encouragement that might otherwise have been withheld—"I would have dropped him long ago if *you* hadn't raised him so in my estimation," Freud was to tell Lou a few years later. From Tausk, Lou gained the satisfaction of adding yet another scalp to her trophies.

The disagreement with Stekel had broken out earlier in the year and had simmered throughout the summer and autumn, Stekel comparing himself to Freud with the statement that a dwarf on the shoulders of a giant could see farther than the giant. Current relationships are revealed by Freud's retort: "That may be true, but a louse on the head of an astronomer does not." Eventually, early in November, Stekel resigned from the Vienna Psychoanalytical Society. But, as Freud was probably warned by Lou, he had no intention of relinquishing editorship of the journal. Freud was technically director, and Jones later asked him why he had not exercised his right to appoint another editor. "The excuse he gave me," Jones wrote, "was that Stekel had too much influence with the publisher, but it may well be that he preferred withdrawing to having an open fight." Jung, whom Freud kept closely informed of events, put it more bluntly. "Unfortunately," he told the American psychologist, Trigant Burrow, "the publisher remained on the side of Stekel, hence Stekel kept the *Zentralblatt* and Freud was dismissed." Freud himself told Putnam, "Stekel's treason forced me to give up the *Zentralblatt* to him." But he put the best face possible on the matter, telling Abraham that it was a blessing to have got rid of such a doubtful character as Stekel. He now circularized contributors, asking them not to write for the *Zentralblatt* but to support a new publication he would start. No time was lost. Before the end of the month Freud and his supporters met in Munich, and from their discussions came the *Internationale Zeitschrift für Psychoanalyse*, edited by Ferenczi, Rank and Jones, all dedicated to following the strict Freudian line. Stekel's *Zentralblatt* carried on, rather lamely, until publication ceased with the outbreak of the First World War.

Lou was not only a useful informant inside the Adlerian camp. Within less than a month of arriving in Vienna she had become a focus of Freud's attentions. "I missed you yesterday at the lecture," he wrote on November 10, "and I am happy to hear that your absence was not occasioned by a visit to the camp of the masculine protest. I have acquired the bad habit of directing my lecture to a particular person in the audience, and yesterday I stared spellbound at the vacant chair reserved for you." For her part, she was intrigued by the simplicity of Freud's expositions, remembering almost two decades later how he had, as she expressed it, exposed a neurosis to its bottom-most layer, then "suddenly with a flip of the hand, the way one tilts a cake out of its tin baking mold, lifted it to our view in its unimpaired entirety."

Freud's wisdom in condoning Lou's attendances in both the Freudian and the Adlerian camps paid dividends. She returned to Göttingen the following April a convinced disciple and spoke of the months in Vienna as her turning point. "The turning," says her biographer, Rudolph Binion, "was one against Adler."

14

The Break with Jung

So we are at last rid of them, the brutal, sanctimonious Jung and his disciples.

FREUD, in a letter to Karl Abraham

By the autumn of 1912 Freud had successfully defeated the first attempt to question his authority. He was now in charge, and he was determined to remain so. His star was rising, and the fact was known to both his followers and his family. Yet not even Freud can have been entirely happy at the outcome of the Adler controversy. Adler had certainly been forced overboard, but he had not sunk without trace. "Individual psychology" could not draw upon either the notoriety of Freud's name or the extensive background of practice Freud could use either for therapy or to convince unbelievers. Nevertheless, Adler survived. He showed, in fact, every indication that he would continue to survive. Moreover, it was by now becoming only too clear that Freud might soon have to deal with a far more important defection: that of his Crown Prince and chief of staff, Carl Jung.

The faint hint of possible differences which had marked their early correspondence and meetings had soon evaporated. It did not materialize again for some while, and Freud's attitude was well expressed by his letter to Pfister soon after the 2nd International Congress. "I hope you agree with the Nuremberg decisions and will stand loyally by our Jung," it said. "I want him to acquire an authority that will later qualify him for leadership of the whole movement." In the autumn of 1911 he still regarded Jung as both the organizer of victory and the Crown Prince destined to take over control when he himself was removed by age or death.

For his part, Jung showed no reluctance to play the role laid down for him by Freud. Indeed, at times he gave the impression that it was no more than his due. Yet despite the bonds that linked these two decent men, each devoted to what was basically the same cause, forces were already moving them apart and preparing to turn them toward each other on a collision course. The ostensible reason was to be Jung's reinterpretation of Freud's beliefs and, in particular, his devaluation of the importance which Freud had always given to sexuality. The latter was more than a mere difference of emphasis or a variation on a theme that could be passed off with a shrug of the shoulders; it made a conflict between the two men inevitable, and it almost as certainly meant that the psychoanalytic movement would split yet again. Nevertheless the break would have generated less bitterness had it not been for Freud's role as commander in chief and his belief that if any changes in the governing body of opinion were to be ordered, they must be ordered by him. This was not all. Freud needed his Zürichers as troops to fight the battle for psychoanalysis; but he frequently regarded them as levies, and the point did not escape them. In addition there was the question of race. He had soon noted a touch of prejudice in Jung's make-up, and almost as soon had begun to see in him the Gentile superiority that had riled him since his school days.

Thus the confrontation between the two men arose from a complex of reasons—professional and personal—complicated by the conviction of each that his motives were above reproach and eventually heightened by Freud's anger that his position as leader should even be questioned. Accounts of the rupture have been given by adherents of Freud and of Jung, but only now is it possible to follow the month-by-month development of the crisis and to understand the strength of the feelings aroused. It was Winston Churchill who once said that chronology is the key to history; certainly it provides an understanding of the bitterness that marked the Freud–Jung clash. At times Freud was no doubt badly treated, but he does not need much pity on that account. When it came to intellectual rough-and-tumble he was well able to look after himself and the cause, and to defend both without paying too much attention to Queensberry Rules.

It was Emma Jung, the perceptive wife, who first noted signs of the coming storm. On October 30, 1911, she wrote Freud a letter of which, she emphasized, her husband knew nothing at all. "Since your visit," she began, "I have been tormented by the idea that your relation with my husband is not altogether as it should be, and since it definitely ought not to be like this I want to try to do whatever is in my power." When Freud had visited them at Küsnacht before the Weimar Congress, she went on, he had avoided all mention of Jung's *Wandlungen und Symbole der Libido (Transformations and Symbols of the Libido)*, the first part of which had been published in the *Jahrbuch für psychoanalytische und psychopathologische Forschungen.* Was this perhaps the trouble? "Or is it something else?" she persisted. "If so, please tell me what, dear Herr Professor; for I cannot bear to see you so resigned. . . . Please do not take my action as officiousness and do not count me among the women who, you once told me, always spoil your friendships."

The warning made little impression on Freud. It still appeared inconceivable to him that the trouble with Adler would be repeated. "The indestructible foundation of our personal relationship," he wrote to Jung early in 1912, "is our involvement in PA but on this foundation it seemed tempting to build something finer though more labile, a reciprocal intimate friendship. Shouldn't we go on building?"

They might possibly have done so but for one incident. In March 1912 Ludwig Binswanger, the young Swiss psychiatrist with whom Freud had forged a close friendship since Binswanger's visit to Vienna in 1907, had to undergo a serious operation for removal of a tumor. There was a danger that death might follow within a few years, and Freud responded to the news with a letter to Binswanger on April 14, 1912. "As an old man who has no right to complain if his life ends in a few years (and who has made up his mind not to complain)," he said, "I experience a particular pain learning from one of the thriving young ones that his life span has become uncertain; from one of those who should continue my own life." He would like to visit his friend at his home in Kreuzlingen, at the northern end of Lake Constance. "How about Whitsun?" he asked. "Let me know whether this would be all right for you."

The date was convenient, and Freud arrived in Kreuzlingen on Saturday May 25 for a forty-eight-hour visit that was to cost him almost as many hours on the train from, and back to, Vienna.

Now, Kreuzlingen was an easy forty-mile journey from Jung's home in Küsnacht. It would therefore seem the most natural thing in the world for Jung to seize the opportunity of visiting Freud in Kreuzlingen. However, it is equally possible that one of them, or both, wanted to avoid such a meeting, a possibility which makes it unwise to be too certain about the reasons for what actually happened.

According to Freud's account to Ernest Jones, he had written to both Binswanger and Jung on the same day, May 23, saying he would be in Kreuzlingen for the coming weekend and apparently assuming that Jung would visit him. Jung did not do so, later maintaining that Freud's letter had only arrived on Monday, the day Freud was leaving Kreuzlingen, but later adding, according to the Freud–Jones version, that he himself had been away from home that weekend. Binswanger, however, was later to record that Freud's letter had been written on May 16, in which case it would seem unlikely that posting would have been delayed until the twenty-third. This inevitably points toward a deliberate slighting of Freud by Jung. While Jones was insistent that Freud had expected Jung to come to Kreuzlingen, Binswanger's story is that Jung reproached Freud for not having met him in Zurich. Whatever the truth about the contretemps, it seems that it could readily have been removed by either man picking up the telephone.

Whether the result of a simple misunderstanding or of an unconscious wish to avoid the meeting, the Kreuzlingen incident further exacerbated relations between the two men. Jung reproached Freud for the insult of sending the letter too late. Freud explained to Pfister that if only he had met Jung he could have told him that "he is at perfect liberty to develop views divergent from mine, and that I ask him to do so without a bad conscience." Later in the month Freud received a querulous letter from Jung and revealed in a letter to Jones the way his attitude was developing. Jung's letter could not, he told Jones, "but be construed into formal disavowal of our hitherto friendly relations. I am sorry, not more on personal motives but for the future of the Verein and the cause of P/A, but I am resolved to let things go and not to try to influence him any more. P/A is no more my own affair but it concerns you and so many others besides as well."

By this time the second part of Jung's *Transformations and Symbols of the Libido* was about to appear. Jones had apparently secured a proof and without delay told Freud of its contents. Freud acquired a copy of his own and immediately saw that even without the clash of personal relationships, Jung's new concept of the libido had brought them to the parting of the ways. At the turn of the century the word had been variously used to mean "sexual desire" or "sexual instinct" in the narrowest meanings of the words. Freud had used the word more widely but was, at this date, still retaining its purely sexual connotations. But now Jung introduced the idea of the libido as being composed of psychic energy as a whole, an idea which if accepted would have struck away one of the main props supporting the Freudian structure. Furthermore, and equally important in a situation of potential personal confrontation, Jung used the paper as a vehicle for quoting passages from Freud's Schreber paper and for then elucidating them in terms which contrasted strongly with Freud's sexual explanations.

It was at this point, in the summer of 1912, as genuine technical disagreement ominously enlarged the personal rift between Freud and Jung, that the romantic Celt in Jones came to the surface with the proposal of a Praetorian Guard whose members would in an emergency rally round their leader. There did indeed seem to be some need of this. Adler had walked out with an unhappily large section of the Vienna Society. Stekel had followed, and it needed less than outstanding perception to see that Jung, a more formidable figure than any of the other defectors, might soon be raising his own standard. Hence, Jones argued, the need for an inner circle with whom Freud would regularly discuss the affairs of the international organization, and whose members would agree not to announce any radical innovation to psychoanalytic theory or practice until it had been discussed by them all.

The exact part played by Jones in the genesis of the "Committee," as it came to be called, is not entirely clear. "The idea of a united small body designed, like the Paladins of Charlemagne, to guard the kingdom and policy of their master, was a product of my own romanticism," he was to write to Freud shortly after the idea had been launched, "and I did not venture to speak about it to the others until I had broached it to you." However, writing forty years later, he explained that he had in fact discussed the plan with Ferenczi and Rank.

On July 30, 1912, he wrote to Freud. He could not, he said, "help wishing that things at the top, gathered around you, were more satisfactory." In Vienna, he continued, some one, probably Ferenczi, had "expressed the wish that a small group of men could be thoroughly analyzed by you, so that they could represent the pure theory unadulterated by personal complexes and thus build an unofficial inner circle in the Verein and serve as centers where others (beginners) could come and learn the work. If that were only possible it would be an ideal solution."

Freud replied by return. He welcomed the idea—not unnaturally, since it gave him back at least some of the control he had lost at Nuremberg. "What took hold of my imagination immediately is your idea of a secret council composed of the best and most trustworthy among our men to take care of the future development of psychoanalysis and defend the cause against personalities and accidents when I am no more," he said. But the idea did not appear to be new, or even Ferenczi's. In two sentences which Jones omitted when publishing Freud's response, Freud suggested that he himself might have originated the idea when he had hoped that Jung would collect such a circle.

He was, however, shrewdly aware of the dangers. "I know there is a boyish and perhaps romantic element too in this conception," he went on, "but perhaps it could be adapted to meet the necessities of reality. I will give my fancy free play and leave you to the part of censor." Freud's one injunction was that the Committee should be strictly secret both in its existence and in its actions. There was considerable wisdom in this. Had it become known that the founding fathers of psychoanalysis were banding themselves together with some of the trappings of a schoolboys' secret society, the cause would no doubt have suffered. Even Jones himself later thought it best to play down that aspect of the Committee after Freud had given each member an antique Greek intaglio which the recipient wore in a gold ring. "Don't be misled by the boyish business of the rings," he warned. "They didn't amount to anything, and at least two members of the Committee were embarrassed to wear them. . . ."

Original members were Ferenczi, Rank, Sachs, Abraham and Jones. "When I introduced Rank to [Freud] as the latest recruit to our little group," Jones later wrote, "Ferenczi eyed him keenly and put the question to him: 'I suppose you will always be loyal to psychoanalysis?'. . . Rank answered, 'Assuredly.' " It was, says Jones, "an odd coincidence that those two were in years to come the only ones who did not stay faithful to our undertaking of mutual consultation."

Other trusted friends were eventually brought into the charmed circle, Eitingon apparently being among the first. Rings were given to Lou Andreas-Salomé; Freud's daughter Anna; Princess Marie Bonaparte, Freud's later friend and supporter; Anna's friend Dorothy Burlingham; and Ernest Jones's wife Katherine. Other names, including those of Stefan Zweig, Ferenczi's wife Gisela, Ruth Mack-Brunswick, Edith Jackson, Henny Freud and Eva Rosenfeld, have been included on lists of those said to have received rings. Whatever the accuracy of the details, the idea of an exclusive secret body of policymakers was certainly diluted by time.

When proposing the Committee, Jones had in mind the widening rift he saw opening between Jung and Freud. Yet he himself was not above suspicion. Shortly after he had suggested the scheme to Freud, Freud received a letter from Ferenczi: "It has seldom been so clear to me as now what a psychological advantage it signifies to be born a Jew. . . . ," it said; "you must keep Jones constantly under your eye and cut off his line of retreat."

It was against this background of gathering distrust that Jung left Zurich in the early autumn for his second visit to the United States. He had been invited to the Jesuit Fordham University in the Bronx, and here he gave nine lectures on "The Theory of Psychoanalysis" to nearly a hundred psychiatrists and neurologists. In the first he discussed Breuer's Anna O. case; stated that observant doctors would confirm that distressing events often lay at the root of neurotic illness; and then, revealing the cloven hoof, added: "This truth was already known to the older physicians." He admitted in a foreword to the lectures that Freud's experience and insight were far greater than his own but nevertheless went on to say, " . . . it seems to me that certain of my formulations do express the observed facts more suitably than Freud's version of them . . . ," the formulations including a dilution of the importance given to the sexual factor in mental ill health. However, it was when he came specifically to the Oedipus complex, a term which "seems the most unsuitable one possible," that Jung began to undermine an essential foundation of Freud's theory. While the tragic conflict of Oedipus was that he had unknowingly married his mother and then killed his father,

> the term "Oedipus complex" naturally does not mean conceiving this conflict in its adult form, but rather on a reduced scale suitable to childhood. All it means, in effect, is that the childish demands for love are directed to mother and father, and to the extent that these demands have already attained a certain degree of intensity, so that the chosen object is jealously defended, we can speak of an "Oedipus complex."

If there remained any doubt that Jung was transforming Freud's unconscious desire for incest into a cosy nursery normality, it was removed a few minutes later. "If I now say," he told his audience, "that the Oedipux complex is in the first place only a formula for childish desires in regard to the parents and for the conflict which these desires evoke—as every selfish desire must—the matter may seem more acceptable."

Of this last point there could certainly be no doubt. Neither, on reflection, could there be doubt about the effect of Jung's lectures on Freud's whole theory. "He . . . takes the tendency towards incest to be an absolutely concrete sexual wish, for he calls this complex the root complex, or nucleus, of the neuroses," Jung stressed, "and is inclined, viewing this as the original one, to reduce practically the whole psychology of the neuroses, as well as many other phenomena in the realm of the mind, to this one complex." But this complex, it now appeared, was something very different from what Freud had been claiming it to be. Commander in chief and chief of staff had almost totally different ideas of what they were fighting for.

The Fordham lectures left some vintage Freud intact, but not very much. In the opinion of Putnam, who had met Jung in New York, the latter was rejecting the most valuable elements of psychoanalysis. "What Dr. Jung said, in effect," he wrote to Jones,

> was that while he still held to the importance of the psychoanalytic technique, he had come to rate the infantile fixations as of far less importance than formerly as an etiological factor, and, indeed, as I understood him, as an almost negligible factor in most cases— though I hardly think he could really maintain this if he were pushed for a positive opinion. At any rate, the point on which he seems now inclined to lay emphasis is the difficulty of meeting new problems and environmental conditions which arise at the time of the actual onset of the neurosis. It seems to me that we all recognize the importance of these influences, and I cannot as yet feel that anything is won through minimizing the significance of the other factor.

Freud had reason to feel aggrieved, since Jung had not discussed with him in advance the major revisions to Freudian theory he was expounding. But the omission revealed a lack of courtesy more than anything else, and there was a good deal in Jung's protest that the lectures, whose publication was to give considerable publicity to his views throughout the United States, could hardly be regarded as schismatic unless psychoanalysis was a faith.

For some while Freud knew only the barest details of these activities. Had he known more, he would have been more perturbed. For in his lectures Jung not only had soft-pedaled what Freud regarded as the central tenet of psychoanalysis, but had gained personal publicity, which enabled him to put forward his own ideas with some success. For example, the outcome of a lengthy interview with a reporter from the *New York Times* was a 5,000-word article, occupying four fifths of a page and headed "'AMERICA FACING ITS MOST TRAGIC MOMENT'—DR. CARL JUNG." As recorded by the interviewing reporter, Jung used the word "sex" on a solitary occasion—and in reference to Athens in 500 B.C. The bulk of the article, which stated, "It was [Jung] who brought Dr. Sigmund Freud to the recognition of the older school of psychology," was deeply critical of the United States. One reason for its inhabitants' unhappy situation, Jung submitted, was their "prudery." However, this little failing appeared to be less important than the repercussions of the American need to subjugate first the indigenous inhabitants and then their environment. While the American Indians had "fallen back," contemporary white Americans were in Jung's opinion, "influenced by the negro race, which not so long ago had to call you master." As for the environment: "There is no question but that you have sacrificed many beautiful things to achieve your great cities and domination of your wildernesses. To build so great a mechanism you must have smothered many growing things, but there must be somewhere a cause, and when you have discovered that, your mechanism will not have its danger for you that it has today." Jung has been accused of covering his ideas in an immense "lather of verbosity," and some of his more mystical statements justify the criticism. Yet here he was making a penetrating comment on the situation in the early years of the century to which at least some Americans were not averse to listening. Jung, sternly staring from the page in a photograph across three columns, gained considerable attention.

When it came to attacking Freud, he was assured of listeners. It is true that following the support of men such as Putnam it was becoming increasingly difficult to convince a medical audience that consideration of psychoanalysis was entirely a waste of time. However, what military men were to call the "strategy of indirect approach" could always be used. Thus Moses Allen Starr, addressing the New York Academy of Medicine's Section on Neurology, after Putnam had read a paper dealing with "Comments on Sex Issues from the Freudian Standpoint," chose to make a slighting attack on Freud himself. He had, he declared, known Freud well in Vienna, "Vienna is not a particularly moral city," he continued, "and working side by side with Freud in the laboratory all through one winter, I learned that he enjoyed Viennese life thoroughly. Freud was not a man who lived on a particularly high plane. He was not self-repressed. He was not an ascetic. I think his scientific theory is largely the result of his environment and of the peculiar life he led."

As a mixture of non sequitur and smear by association this part of Starr's statement was of a high order, but Freud, after hearing from Putnam of Starr's statement, remained cool. He had, he asserted, never known Starr. "Nor did the issue, no matter what its precise origin could have been, seem important enough," he went on. "His information about my early years amused me mightily. Would that it had been true!" Whether Putnam ever faced Starr with Freud's reply is not known. If so, Starr might have described the days when he and Freud had worked together at a bench in Meynert's laboratory while medical students and the occasions on which he had sent abstracts of Freud's first papers to American journals. A student named M. Allen Starr had certainly worked there.

While Putnam naturally made the most of his opponent's de-

Sigmund Freud, about eight years old, photographed with his father, Jacob Freud, in Vienna.

Martha Bernays, Freud's future wife, aged twenty-one, in 1882.

Bertha Pappenheim (1859-1936), the 'Anna O' of Breuer's famous case history.

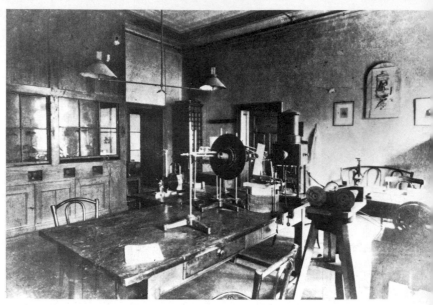

Dr Ernst Brücke's laboratory in the Physiological Institute, Vienna, 1900.

Schloss Bellevue, outside Vienna, where, in July 1895, Freud interpreted 'the dream of Irma's injection.'

Freud with Wilhelm Fliess (1858-1928), *right,* his confidant during the early years of psychoanalysis.

A family celebration at No 19 Berggasse, about 1898. Standing *left to right:* Martin, Sigmund. *Seated, left to right:* Oliver, Martha, Minna Bernays, *Front:* Sophie, Anna, Ernst.

Freud's children playing in the woods near Berchtesgaden, 1899, *Left to right:* Anna, Mathilde, Sophie, Oliver, Martin and Ernst.

James Putnam's camp in Keene Valley, New York, showing the chalets where Freud, Jung and Ferenczi stayed in 1909. (Adirondack Museum, Blue Mountain Lake)

The 3rd International Psychoanalytical Congress, held in Weimar, September 21-22, 1911: 1 Sigmund Freud, 2 Otto Rank, 3 Ludwig Binswanger, 4 O. Rothenhäusler, 5 Jan Nelken, 6 R. Forster, 7 Ludwig Jekels, 8 A. A. Brill, 9 Edward Hirtschmann, 10 J. E. G. von Emden, 11 Alphonse Maeder, 12 Paul Federn, 13 Adolf Keller, 14 Alfred von Winterstein, 15 J. Marcinowski, 16 Isidor Sadger, 17 Oskar Pfister, 18 Max Eitingon, 19 Karl Abraham, 20 James J. Putnam, 21 Ernest Jones, 22 Wilhelm Stekel, 23 Paul Bjerre, 24 Eugen Bleuler, 25 Maria Moltzer, 26 Mira Gineburg, 27 Lou Andreas-Salomé, 28 Beatrice Hinkle, 29 Emma Jung, 30 M. von Stack, 31 Antonia Wolff, 32 Martha Böddinghaus, 33 Franz Riklin, 34 Sandor Ferenczi, 35 C. G. Jung, 36 Leonhard Seif, 37 K. Landauer, 38 A. Stegmann, 39 W. Wittenberg, 40 Guido Brecher.

Freud on the verandah of No 19 Berggasse, photographed by one of his sons, about 1912.

Freud and Ernest Jones in 1919, at one of their first meetings after the First World War.

Princess Marie Bonaparte photographs Freud at Bergasse 19.

The commander-in-chief at home.

Freud and friend in his study, near the end of his career.

Flanked by Princess Marie Bonaparte and William Bullitt, the American ambassador to France, Freud arrives in Paris.

London, 1938: In the garden of his Hampstead home, where the Royal Society's Charter Book had been brought for him to sign.

Oskar Pfister (1873-1

Lou Andreas-Salomé (1861-1937).

Alfred Adler (1870-1937).

Karl Abraham (1887 1925).

Hanns Sachs (1881-1947).

scent to the personal, out of place in a scientific body, Starr did on this occasion speak up for what he called psychoanalysis, even though it appeared to be the Adlerian version: "As a matter of fact," he said,

> I believe that Freud, in the theory which all you gentlemen have praised so highly, has turned into a frivolous vein the really serious new science of psychoanalysis, by which we neurologists are enabled to study the mental processes of our patients as exactly, and as mathematically, as we have previously been able to study the human body by the use of the microscope and the scalpel. There are many other causes which give rise to complex psychoses in human life, besides the sex instinct. An equally strong instinct, for example, is the self-preservative instinct. In America this self-preservative instinct is represented by the struggle for wealth. It is my opinion that if we American physicians recognize the equal value of the self-preservative instinct in shaping our patients' lives and mental states, we will have much greater success.

Dr. Starr concluded his speech by asking Dr. Putnam and his colleagues to state categorically whether, even if Freud's theory were true, it would be of any practical benefit to physicians in diagnosing a case. In the confused argument which followed, Putnam was unable to reply.

With a sizable body of opinion happy to build on the pronouncements of such men as Starr, Jung was encouraged by his reception in New York. Certainly he was far from abashed at having in effect walked out of the Freudian camp, and on his return to Europe was quite ready to explain his position. "Naturally," he wrote to Freud in a conspicuously bumptious letter, "I also made room for those of my views which deviate in places from the hitherto existing conceptions, particularly in regard to the libido theory. I found that my version of PA won over many people who until now had been put off by the problem of sexuality in neurosis. . . ." He then turned the knife in the wound. "As soon as I have an offprint, I shall take pleasure in sending you a copy of my lectures in the hope that you will gradually come to accept certain innovations already hinted at in my libido paper. I feel no need to let you down provided you can take an objective view of our common endeavors. . . ." As a final irritant, he added: "Your Kreuzlingen gesture had dealt me a lasting wound."

Freud's reply started ominously enough with "Dear Doctor Jung" rather than the usual "My friend." He acknowledged Jung's success, but he warned against putting lack of resistance to his views in the credit column; the farther he departed from what was new in psychoanalysis "the more certain you will be of applause and the less resistance you will meet." It was a friendly letter until he came to the end. "I must own," he said, "that I find your harping on the 'Kreuzlingen gesture' both incomprehensible and insulting, but there are things that cannot be straightened out in writing."

It was possibly of this stage that he was thinking a decade later when he referred to the break in a letter to Abraham. "When Jung used his first independent experiences to shake himself free of analysis, we both knew that he had strong neurotic and selfish motives that took advantage of this discovery. I was then able to say with justification that his twisted character did not compensate me for his lopsided theories."

However, even at this stage a complete break had not come about, and in November 1912, when a meeting was called in Munich to discuss both Stekel's refusal to give up the *Zentralblatt* and the founding of a new journal, it seemed that a final break might be fended off indefinitely. Jung proposed the adoption of Freud's plan for the future of the publications; no one raised objections, and the meeting ended without signs of rancor.

Freud and Jung then went for a stroll together. Their failure to meet at Kreuzlingen now appeared, on the surface, to be satisfactorily explained. According to Jones's story of what happened during the stroll, Jung admitted that he had been away for the Whitsun weekend, had not received Freud's letter in time, and had not subsequently looked at the postmark before complaining. The explanation would of course be irrelevant if Freud had in fact posted his letter on the sixteenth rather than on the twenty-third as Jones infers.

In his account of the Munich meeting, Jones makes a second point against Jung. Although he, Jones, had been staying in Florence, "Jung sent the notification of the meeting to my father's home in Wales and also gave the date as November 25 instead of November 24. In the meantime I heard the correct date from Vienna, and so arrived in time. The look of surprise on Jung's face told me the mistake belonged to the class called parapraxes, but when I told Freud of Jung's unconscious slip he replied: 'A gentleman should not do such things even unconsciously.'"

At the luncheon in Munich, Freud had another temporary blackout, possibly due to his bottled-up emotions at having, as he thought, buried the hatchet with Jung, rather than in Jung. According to Jones, Freud "fell on the floor in a dead faint." According to Jung, who no doubt remembered the occasion when, a few years earlier, Freud had fainted in Bremen, everyone clustered helplessly round him. I picked him up, carried him into the next room, and laid him on a sofa. As I was carrying him, he half came to, and I shall never forget the look he cast at me. In his weakness he looked at me as if I were his father. Whatever other causes may have contributed to this faint—the atmosphere was very tense—the fantasy of father-murder was common to both cases.

On recovering consciousness, Jones has stated, Freud exclaimed, "How sweet it must be to die." Freud insisted that he merely fainted for a moment and then got up by himself.

Within the next few weeks, the fainting episode was mulled over in considerable and contradictory detail, Freud giving various accounts to Ferenczi, to Jones and to Binswanger. To the last he wrote, in December: "I am resigned to being declared a candidate for eternity on the basis of my attack in Munich. Recently Stekel wrote that my behavior was already showing the 'hypocritical feature.' All of them can hardly wait for it, but I can answer them as Mark Twain did under similar circumstances: 'Reports of my death grossly exaggerated'."

Two weeks later he felt less worried about his candidacy for eternity. "My fainting attack in Munich," he told Binswanger,

was surely provoked by psychogenic elements, which received strong somatic reinforcements (a week of troubles, a sleepless night, the equivalent of a migraine, the day's tasks). I had had several such attacks; in each case there were similar contributory causes, often a bit of alcohol for which I have no tolerance. Among the psychic elements there is the fact that I had had a quite similar seizure in the same place, in Munich, on two previous occasions, four and six years ago. In the light of a most careful diagnosis, it seems scarcely possible to attribute my attacks to a more serious cause, for instance, a weak heart. Repressed feelings, this time directed against Jung, as previously against a predecessor of his, naturally play the main part.

Freud appears to have fainted in the same room of the same hotel when in Munich with Fliess on one of their "Congresses"—although more than six years previously—and his use of the word "predecessor" shows the strong similarity between his relationship with Fliess and that with Jung.

Years later Jung supported the repression theory. According to a note in Jones's papers, Jung said to a friend, who passed the information on to Jones, that after the name Amenhotep IV had been brought up in conversation as the founder of a religion, Freud commented that he was the ruler who had scratched out his father's name on monuments. "Yes, he did," replied Jung, "but you cannot dismiss him with that. He was the first monotheist among the Egyptians. He was a great genius, very human, very individual. That is his main merit. That he scratched out his father's name is not the main thing at all." At that point Freud, apparently identifying with the scratched-out father, fainted. Jung interpreted this, as well as the earlier fainting fit in Bremen, as sensitivity to criticism or to any challenge to his authority, later commenting: "He could not stand a critical word. Just like a woman. Confront her with a disagreeable truth: she faints."

However strongly Freud felt that he was being pushed into the role of Amenhotep IV's scratched-out father, it did look as though the principal trouble with Jung might now be over, and a few days after the Munich incident Freud wrote happily to Putnam:

> A talk between us swept away a number of unnecessary personal irritations. I hope for further successful cooperation. Theoretical differences need not interfere. However, I shall hardly be able to accept his modification of the libido theory since all my experience contradicts his position.

They had agreed to disagree, and if their differences had been only those of psychoanalytic interpretation, it is just possible that the personal bitterness would still have been avoided. But their underlying antogonisms were by this time so great that an incident of even less than "Kreuzlingen" importance was to end their friendship. Earlier in the year Freud had pointed out to Jung that the latter's idea of the incest complex had some similarity with that of Adler, a view which rankled with Jung, who had no wish to be linked with Adler on any grounds at all. He now wrote to Freud, protesting that "even Adler's cronies do not regard me as one of theirs." At least, that was what he had intended to write. But a small slip of the pen—the writing of "*ihrigen*" with a capital letter instead of a small one, in these circumstances a classic Freudian slip—caused him to write "one of yours." Freud pointedly referred to the error, and on December 18 Jung replied with a scathing letter that for all practical purposes brought contact between the two men to a finish. He admitted the ambivalence of his feelings toward Freud before continuing:

> I would, however, point out that your technique of treating your pupils like patients is a *blunder.* In that way you produce either slavish sons or impudent puppies (Adler-Stekel and the whole insolent gang now throwing their weight about in Vienna). I am objective enough to see through your little trick. You go around sniffing out all the

symptomatic actions in your vicinity, thus reducing everyone to the
level of sons and daughters who blushingly admit the existence of
their faults. Meanwhile, you remain on top as the father, sitting
pretty. For sheer obsequiousness nobody dares to pluck the prophet
by the beard and inquire for once what you would say to a patient
with a tendency to analyze the analyst instead of himself. You would
certainly ask him: *"Who's got the neurosis?"*

After more in the same vein, Jung concluded:

> I shall continue to stand by you publicly while maintaining my own
> views, but privately shall start telling you in my letters what I really
> think of you. I consider this procedure only decent.
>   No doubt you will be outraged by this peculiar token of friendship,
> but it may do you good all the same.
>   With best regards.

Freud's answer showed no sign of outrage. On the contrary, it
is difficult to read his reply, written with a calm assurance from
what he saw as the higher ground, without feeling that Jung, losing
his temper at last, had done just what Freud hoped he would do.
"It is a convention among us analysts," Jung was told,

> that none of us need feel ashamed of his own bit of neurosis. But one
> who while behaving abnormally keeps shouting that he is normal
> gives ground for the suspicion that he lacks insight into his illness.
> Accordingly, I propose that we abandon our personal relations en-
> tirely. I shall lose nothing by it, for my only emotional tie with you
> has long been a thin thread—the lingering effect of past disappoint-
> ments—and you have everything to gain, in view of the remark you
> recently made in Munich, to the effect that an intimate relationship
> with a man inhibited your scientific freedom.

One more letter from Freud to Jung has survived, and it seems
likely that it was the last he wrote to the man he had believed could
protect the cause from the accusation of being a Jewish invention.
In it he reported that a secret contract appeared to have been
signed some eighteen months before between Stekel and the publishers of the *Zentralblatt,* providing for Freud's dismissal if he came
into conflict with Stekel. "A pretty piece of treachery," he concluded in a judgment which indicates the feelings among what had
once been a band of brothers.
     The breach with Jung quickly widened, and on the first day of
1913 Freud wrote to Pfister: "Do not have too much confidence in
a lasting personal agreement between me and Jung. He demands

too much of me, and I am retreating from my overestimation of him. It will be sufficient if the unity of the association is maintained." Only a few weeks later he reported to Abraham that Jung was "following in Adler's wake, without being as consistent as that pernicious creature."

However confident Freud may still have been about the situation, Jones was not quite so happy and now sent a warning note to Freud which included the accusation of mental derangement that was to become almost endemic when certain analysts were describing those who disagreed with them. "I am deeply impressed," he said,

> by the success of Jung's campaign, for he appeals to formidable prejudices. It is, in my opinion, the most critical period that psychoanalysis will ever have to go through and we formed the Committee not at all too early; there is much to discuss about devising proper measures to meet his propagandism, and I am eagerly looking forward to coming to Vienna, if for this reason alone. I have written a strong protest to Jung at his treatment of me, but in such a form that it need not lead to an open rupture, which I am not eager to provoke. If I had written earlier, it would have been much angrier. Still, I do not expect he will answer me, for his recent conduct in America makes me think more than [ever] that he does not react like a normal man, and that he is mentally deranged to a serious extent; he produced quite a paranoiac impression on some of the psychoanalytic psychiatrists on Ward's Island [where the Psychiatric Institute of the New York State hospitals was situated].

The prospect of trouble ahead held no terrors for a man as committed as Jones, and after outlining plans for further expansion of the international movement he finished up: "It is a grand time to be alive in, better than any other period in history because it is fuller of fighting on which so much depends. . . . Yours enthusiastically, Jones."

Freud himself was now coming round to the view that the Crown Prince had finally to be disposed of; but he was well aware of the dangers. "Jung is crazy," he wrote to Abraham, "but I have no desire for a separation and should like to let him wreck himself first. Perhaps my *Totem* paper will hasten the breach against my will. . . ."

In August Jung attended the seventeenth International Congress of Medicine in London and here, in a series of lectures, outlined his position, giving to his body of views the name "analytical psychology" in contrast to Freud's "psychoanalysis." Psychoanalytic theory, he said, should "be freed from the purely sexual standpoint. In place of it I should like to introduce an *energetic viewpoint* into the psychology of neurosis." And on some aspects of dreams he found himself "in entire agreement with the views of Adler"; in other words, in entire disagreement with the views of Freud.

Furthermore, Jung was also giving extraordinary weight to what he described as the "collective unconscious." His first interest had been archaeology; medicine had been its successor, and he now discerned the directives of mental activity in the farthest human past. All humans, he insisted, were born with minds on which were imprinted vestigial traces of the collective beliefs and myths of the race to which they belonged: an inheritance that, as he was eventually to maintain, contained all the wisdom and experience of uncounted centuries. Freud, it is true, was in his later speculations on the beginnings of human society to make a somewhat similar assumption but he long regarded as only tentative what Jung defined from the first as a fact of human existence. Both men, indeed, ignored what was virtually established even by the start of the twentieth century: that acquired characteristics could not be inherited, a fact which reduced the collective unconscious to what Krafft-Ebing might well have described as another "scientific fairy tale." As one modern commentator has aptly put it: "In short, for the Freudian theory, which is hard enough to test but has some degree of support, Jung [had] substituted an untestable system which flies in the face of current genetics."

These pronouncements should ostensibly have ruled Jung out of court at the 4th International Psycho-Analytical Congress held in Munich in September 1913. That they did not do so is further evidence that Jung was not a man to bow off the stage at the first sign of opposition. The reigning president, he sat with his supporters at a separate table, facing Freud's, and the mood of the group was well described by Lou Andreas-Salomé. "Their behavior toward Freud can be characterized in a word," she later wrote:

> it is not so much that Jung diverges from Freud, as that he does it in such a way as if he had taken it on himself to rescue Freud and his cause *by* these divergences. . . . Two years ago Jung's booming laughter gave voice to a kind of robust gaiety and exuberant vitality, but now his earnestness is composed of pure aggression, ambition and intellectual brutality. . .

Jung's almost heretical "The Psychology of the Unconscious," its views in line with those of the Fordham Lectures, had by this time been published. Now, at the Congress, his colleague Al-

phonse Maeder read a paper on dreams that led listeners directly
away from Freud's theory of wish fulfillment. Freud described the
proceedings as "fatiguing and unedifying" and added that they
were "conducted by Jung in a disagreeable and incorrect manner;
the speakers were restricted in time and the discussions overwhelmed the papers." His tone, more that of the annoyed schoolmaster than of a commander in chief, no doubt reflected his feeling
that control of the movement might be beginning to slip from his
hands.

The situation, as was obvious early in the Congress, would be
intensified when it came to the vital question of re-electing Jung
for a further two years as president. Freud's supporters rightly
claim that of those entitled to vote, no less than twenty-two out of
fifty-two abstained. But Jung could equally well point out that he
was nevertheless re-elected. Moreover, according to Ferenczi, the
abstentions were due primarily to the way in which Jung conducted
the proceedings. "It was only the absolutely improper way in which
you as Chairman of the Congress dealt with the suggestions we put
forward, the quite one-sided and partial comments you made on
all the papers read, and also the personal behavior on the part of
your group, that caused us to protest by voting with blank cards,"
Ferenczi wrote. Jung apparently took some of the abstentions to
heart. He might have been resigned to the Viennese Jews failing
to support him, but he had expected something different from
Ernest Jones to whom he said, according to Jones's biography of
Freud: "I thought you were a Christian"; or, according to Jones's
autobiography written a few years later, "I thought you had ethical
principles."

Nevertheless, Jung was left securely in the saddle. "We dispersed," says Freud of his Crown Prince, "without any desire to
meet again."

Freud's first reaction to the Munich decision was to propose to
Abraham that the International Association be dissolved. If Jung
objected, then surely the Vienna, Berlin and Budapest groups
could each resign and start the organization afresh. But the plan
would have left Jung in command and, after protests from
Abraham and Jones, Freud agreed to leave things as they were, at
least for the time being. "You know," he wrote to Abraham, "that
in these matters I gladly let myself be advised by my friends, as
since being taken in by Jung my confidence in my political judgment has greatly declined."

There was to be wisdom in waiting for the following month,
since Jung then resigned from his editorship of the *Jahrbuch*, ostensibly because he had heard that Freud doubted his *bona fides*. "I

have by no means walked into Freud's trap," he told Alphonse Maeder, "for I consider it of no advantage to Freud to have sickened me off. A committee of enquiry is out of the question because the *Jahrbuch* is not, after all, run by a club and I *won't* collaborate with Freud any longer. It will make a very bad impression all round. But inner successes count more with me than the howling of the mob."

However, Jung was still president of the International Association and it was clear to Freud that something must be done before the Congress planned for 1914. The situation, he realized, was not too promising. "We are mostly dependent on [Jung] for helping us by his foolish ways," he confided to Jones on November 17. "If he were clever there would be no chance." Five days later he repeated his view. "We know J's position is a very strong one," he said, "our hope is still he will ruin himself. You will have to fight him for the influence in England and America and it may be a long and hard struggle."

It was in this frame of mind that he decided to take firm and uncompromising action, driven on as he was by two spurs, one personal, one professional. His personal dislike of Jung was unequivocally expressed to Putnam: "I found [him] sympathetic so long as he lived blindly, as I did," he wrote. "Then came his religious-ethical crisis with higher morality, 'rebirth,' Bergson, and at the very same time, lies, brutality and anti-semitic condescension towards me. It has not been the first or the last experience to reinforce my disgust with saintly converts."

But it was not only personal feeling that moved him. Psychoanalysis he regarded as his own exclusive contribution to man's self-knowledge, and he regarded as an almost sacred duty the task of keeping it free of both pollution and dilution. "In the execution of this duty," Sachs has recorded, "he was untiring and unbending, hard and sharp like steel, a 'good hater' close to the limit of vindictiveness." When it came to dealing with Jung, personal and professional feelings were inextricably mixed. "Differences in theory are unavoidable in the development of a science," Freud wrote to Putnam; "even errors may contain elements of progress, as my own experience has taught me. But that such departures and theoretical innovations must be accompanied by so much injury to legitimate personal feelings surely does little credit to human nature." To Stanley Hall, also, he made his feelings uncompromisingly plain. "Jung, who was with me [in Worcester in 1911] is my friend no longer, and our work together is approaching a rupture," he said, adding, "Such changes are very disagreeable, but they cannot be helped."

In the last weeks of 1913 he began to write for the next issue of the *Yearbook* what he called a "polemic," *On the History of the Psycho-Analytic Movement.* "The aim," says James Strachey, in an editor's note to the Standard Edition, ". . . was to state clearly the fundamental postulates and hypotheses of psychoanalysis, to show that the theories of Adler and Jung were totally incompatible with them, and to draw the inference that it would lead to nothing but general confusion if these contradictory sets of views were all given the same name. . . ."

The aim was respectable enough, and there is no doubt that Freud felt strongly about theories and therapies being expounded and practiced under the name of psychoanalysis when they differed so fundamentally from his own ideas. Nevertheless his publicly proclaimed intention was not his only one, as he made clear privately. On December 8 he wrote to Jones, noting that there was "a delicious silence about Zurich now," and added: "May it last until July 14, when my paper on the 'P/A movement' in the new *Jahrbuch* will cut definitely all connection between us."

To Lou Andreas-Salomé he was even more outspoken. "I am," he wrote, "busy writing contributions to the history of the psychoanalytical movement for our *Jahrbuch* and expect that this statement of mine will put an end to all compromises and bring about the desired rupture." To Putnam he regretted what he found it necessary to do. "As usual," he complained,

the hardest task falls to me; in this instance, I must protect myself against people who have called themselves my pupils for many years and who owe everything to my stimulus. Now I must accuse them and reject them. I am not a quarrelsome person, nor do I share the widespread opinion that a scientific quarrel brings about clarity and progress. However, I am not in favor of sloppy compromises, nor would I sacrifice anything for the sake of an unproductive reconciliation.

By March 1914 he had completed a draft of the *History*. "I was," he subsequently wrote to Lou,

only able to carry out this inescapable task by writing as if I myself were the sole arbiter involved and by concerning myself as little as possible with a jury to whose favor I might have been appealing. Hence I intentionally gave everyone a good clobbering and to my closest friends who needed no winning over I paid as many compliments as I chose. . . .

Of course I know that the adversaries, diluters and misinterpreters also perform an important mission in that they garnish the otherwise unpalatable fodder for the digestive organs of the masses. But one must not acknowledge this openly, and I can only support them in the proper execution of this mission, if I am allowed to abuse them for the pollution which the cause suffers at their hands.

He sent a draft of the *History* to Jones and also to Abraham, on whose advice he toned down some of the more critical passages. Abraham was in no doubt of Freud's intentions. "I have read it over and over again and have increasingly come to see how important a weapon it is," he declared. Jones objected to one phrase—unfortunately unknown—adding to Freud in May: "This is of course absolutely true, and in principle I am in favor of no mercy being shown in such an important war, but none the less I find this rather strong personally and fear it would weaken, by its personal note, the general effect of the essay rather than strengthen it. One does not want to put weapons in the hands of the enemy. . . ."

On April 20 Jung resigned from the presidency. His reasons are obscure, although Jones believed the resignation acknowledged "the untenability of his position." It is possible that he had already got wind of what Freud was writing in the *History*. Freud himself was exultant. "You were certainly just as surprised as I was at how meticulously Jung carried out our own intentions," he wrote revealingly to Abraham. "But our reserve has now indeed borne fruit; somehow we shall get rid of him, and perhaps of the Swiss altogether."

But Jung was still a member of the Association. He was about to visit England, and Freud, who had by this time told Jones that he was tired of leniency and kindness, anxiously awaited the explosion of his bombshell. "I expect no immediate success but incessant struggling," he told Jones. "Anyone who promises mankind liberation from the hardship of sex will be hailed as a hero, let him talk whatever nonsense he chooses."

"I am not in the least afraid of whatever he does but I affirm that no one can foretell what he will do," he added a few days later. "Perhaps not even God or the Devil knows it at this moment. I do not consider it necessary for you to follow his steps in England and contradict him on the spot, except perhaps on a single occasion which you may choose to your pleasure. Let him talk, and defy him afterward in print drily and mercilessly." Jung, he went on, was now showing "unveiled adherence to Bergson. So you see he had found another Jew for his father complex. I am no longer jealous. . . ."

At the end of the month Freud was still wondering what would happen, although his letter to Abraham on the twenty-fifth assumed that advance copies of the *Jahrbuch* were available. "So the bombshell has now burst," he wrote, "we shall soon discover with what effect. I think we shall have to allow the victims two or three weeks' time to collect themselves and react; also I am not sure they will respond to the blandishments bestowed upon them by resigning."

Within three weeks the bombshell had indeed had its effect. Jung resigned, adding for good measure that no analyst from Zurich would attend the meeting in Dresden planned for September 1914. "I cannot suppress a cheer," Freud wrote to Abraham on July 18. Four days later the Zurich group voted, by fifteen votes to one, to withdraw from the International Association, one reason given being "the endangering of indepent research." Freud wrote in delight to Abraham:

> So we are at last rid of them, the brutal, sanctimonious Jung and his disciples. I must now thank you for the vast amount of trouble, the exceptional clear-sightedness, with which you supported me and our common cause. All my life I have been looking for friends who would not exploit and then betray me, and now, not far from its natural end, I hope I have found them.

The *History* was not, however, Freud's only weapon for attacking Jung and, to a lesser extent, Alfred Adler. There was also Freud's important essay "On Narcissism: An Introduction," which appeared in the same issue of the *Jahrbuch* and which, in the campaign against the defectors, was complementary to it. Since the turn-of-the-century, narcissism—a word introduced independently but almost simultaneously by Paul Näcke and Havelock Ellis —had been used to describe self-love as it expressed itself in sexual perversion. There were, however, various expressions of this tendency so much less acute that they could in no way be considered as perversions. In such cases psychoanalysis had always considered that the amount of love devoted to the self was reciprocal to that devoted to other objects or persons.

This simple and apparently satisfactory explanation had been contradicted in Jung's *Wandlungen und Symbole der Libido*. There he had, moreover, maintained that Freud had abandoned his idea of the libido in his Schreber paper. Ferenczi had loyally denied the charge in a lengthy review of Jung's book but Freud, working up toward the final break with Jung, had then taken the opportunity of further correcting Jung and of putting forward a new, more complex but essentially more plausible explanation of narcissism. He wrote it in Rome, whence he had retired after the ructions of the Munich Congress, toward the end of September 1913. Then, back in Vienna early in 1914, preparing the polemical *History,* he rewrote the technical article in a month.

Before the end of the year he was also at work on his account of the Wolf-Man. It was an interesting story; it was also a useful one, and Freud admitted that it had been written as a response to the reinterpretations which Jung and Adler were giving to psychoanalysis.

Even before he had achieved his main objective in the summer of 1914 Freud had decided on his next move. On Jung's resignation he had written to the presidents of the six European branch societies, suggested that arrangements for a fifth Congress should be temporarily suspended and that meanwhile a provisional president should be elected, his own choice being Abraham. On the face of it, Freud had won game, set and match. The "desired rupture" had been achieved. Control of the international organization was now finally back in Freud's hands, and the members of the Committee were available to see that matters stayed that way. The future seemed assured.

The break with Jung, now complete, was the most important of those that Freud felt it necessary to bring about. Jung was, like Freud himself, in a different league from all the other early psychoanalysts, he stood the best chance of taking over the leadership, and discussion of the rupture has, like discussion of other dissensions in the movement, often been phrased in terms of pure white or deepest black. Michael Balint, Ferenczi's executor, is one of the comparatively few who has balanced one view against another in discussing the underlying causes of the successive rifts. "It is true," he wrote to Ernest Jones,

> that whenever a crisis broke out Freud invariably showed himself what he really was, a truly great man, who was always accessible and tolerant to new ideas, who was always willing to stop, think anew, even if it meant re-examining even his most basic concepts, in order to find a new possibility for understanding what might be valuable in any new idea. It has never been asked whether something in Freud has or has not contributed to a critical increase of tension during the period preceding a crisis. Still less has any analyst bothered to find out what happened in the minds of those who came into conflict with Freud and what in their relationship to him and to psychoanalysis led to the exacerbation. We have been content to describe them as the villains of the piece.

Freud himself had a briefer explanation. He was asked by Paul Häberlin, who visited him in April 1913 with Ludwig Binswanger, why it was the older of his followers who had broken away.

"Precisely because they too wanted to be Popes," he replied.

It might have seemed by the summer of 1914 that the potential Pope Jung had been adequately disposed of. However, the International Congresses provided only one forum for ideas. Jung had by this time begun to establish himself. Now, while being excoriated by Freud, he addressed the annual meeting of the British Medical Association in Aberdeen on "The Importance of the Unconscious in Psychopathology." He thanked Freud for having called attention to the importance of dreams, but he did not mention the word psychoanalysis, and after his paper a lengthy discussion ended with a qualified welcome for his ideas. He also lectured in London where, Jones told Freud in a long letter, he unfortunately had a great success. By the summer of 1914 there were thus three competing schools in operation: Freud's, Adler's and Jung's.

Whatever plans each had for the future, they were soon to be overwhelmed by events. On June 28 a Bosnian revolutionary assassinated Archduke Francis Ferdinand of Austria and his wife in Sarajevo. Freud, like most other Europeans, had no premonition of what was to come, and on July 7 he wrote to his nephew Samuel Freud in Manchester: "Today my youngest daughter, Anna, now a girl of 18 1/2 years, has set [out] for a journey to Berlin, Hamburg, and England, where she will arrive the 15th. or 16th. with the 'Amerika.'" Money was being sent from Vienna to Manchester, and Samuel was asked "to play the role of her banker until the end of Sept., when we are to meet in Holland." Freud himself meanwhile completed preparations for his journey to Karlsbad where he was to take the cure.

A week later came Austria's ultimatum to Serbia, the Empire's declaration of war and the Austrian bombardment of Belgrade. Freud was still as unaware as anyone else that what looked like a local war would soon engulf most of Europe. Yet in his case events might have caused particular distress by separating him for the duration from Anna, who was already developing into her father's professional secretary and assistant.

Luckily, Anna's friends in England acted quickly, and in time. Before the end of August she was safely back in Vienna, having traveled home by way of Gibraltar and Genoa in the care of the Austrian ambassador. By this time what had begun as a Balkan confrontation had, with Germany's invasion of Belgium, developed into the First World War, and Anna had been saved from four years' internment in Britain as an enemy alien.

15

New Fields for Conquest

Psychoanalysis must "conquer the whole field of mythology. . . . We must also take hold of biography . . ."

FREUD, in a letter to C. G. Jung

The fission of the psychoanalytic movement on the eve of the First World War into two parties, one following Freud, the other Jung, with a less important group of Adlerians waiting in the wings, had been caused by differing views on mental illness and its amelioration or cure. Freud's unquenchable determination to lead the movement and to ensure that it kept strictly within approved lines had, with Jung's equal confidence in Jung, brought matters to a head. But although the argument had centered on the medical aspects of psychoanalysis, there were by this time other aspects of growing importance; indisputable evidence that human actions could be, and often were, the result of unknown impulses hidden deep in the unconscious was already leading to the application of psychoanalysis in nonmedical fields.

Once it had been recognized that men could be driven on by motives of which they were unaware, it was inevitable that the fact should be used to help elucidate the riddles of history and biography. If the great captains were in this respect no different from other men—and there was no reason to suppose they were—then the fate of nations might have been decided on grounds which could only now be brought to light. So, too, with statesmen and even scientists. What was it that had really driven Bismarck to bestride Europe, or Newton to derive from the falling apple a system that was to last for two and a half centuries until Einstein glimpsed an oddity in Newton's picture of the universe? Now, as psychoanalysis got into its stride, it might be possible to find out. But surely, also, the work of writers and artists might be the result not, as their creators mistakenly supposed, of a multiplicity of known pressures but of unconscious urges of which they were totally unaware? Once this possibility was accepted it could be claimed that the actions of history's great dramatic characters could be better explained with the help of psychoanalysis.

There was, indeed, something to be said for all this, although not as much as many psychoanalysts contended. Freud was at times aware of the limitations and was to see at least some sorties into nonmedical psychoanalytic interpretation in a far less certain light than did many of his followers. Their enthusiasm was understandable, but in the long term considerably damaging. Their weakness was not so much that of using speculations derived from the clinical experience of psychoanalysis; it was, rather, the belief of many of them that the new tool for investigating the past could replace, instead of supplement, the essential specialist knowledge required, be it military, political or artistic. Fritz Wittels, who had meandered on before the Vienna Psychoanalytical Society about the big organ and the little organ of the Kraus family, would be an example too trite to mention were he not an omen of things to come.

The failure of many psychoanalytic writers to do their homework before turning to history or biography naturally attracted criticism. An historian, reviewing a book on the life of Woodrow Wilson that Freud was to write with William Bullitt in the 1930s, and considering what the Freudian method could do for history, wrote: "The answer must be that as an instrument of illumination it can do much—on one condition: let it for God's sake be applied by a responsible historian." The lesson had to be learned slowly and patchily, and the reviewer of a volume on symbolism in fairy tales, another subject to which psychoanalysts began to devote their expertise, noted the "growing tendency on the part of the Freudians to enter other fields, outside their own, with the same airy disregard of the fact that these departments of knowledge have developed methods of investigation at least as rigid as the technique of psychoanalysis itself."

Nevertheless, the method had its valid uses when properly applied to history or biography. The validity decreased as it was brought to bear on the workings of the creative mind and then on to the mental processes of the artists' creations, the men and women who had never lived. I. A. Richards discusses the danger of the first in his *Principles of Literary Criticism*, where he points out:

Whatever psychoanalysis may aver, the mental processes of the poet are not a very profitable field for uncontrollable conjecture ... even if we knew far more than we do about how the mind works, the attempt to display the inner working of the artist's mind by the evidence of his work alone must be subject to the gravest dangers. And to judge by the published work of Freud upon Leonardo da Vinci or of Jung upon Goethe ... psychoanalysts tend to be peculiarly inept as critics.

Speculation on the motives which drove on the great characters of fiction and drama does make an interesting intellectual party game; but it should be remembered that Sterne created and directed his characters for purposes of plot, and that Shakespeare directed his to keep an audience on edge until curtain-fall.

Despite these considerable limitations it was to be expected that Freud would apply psychoanalysis to the creative mind and its products. Toward the end of the nineteenth century his confidence that he had "touched upon one of the great secrets of nature" had grown, and as early as 1897 he was considering what light psychoanalysis might throw on folklore. "Stories about the devil, the vocabulary of popular swear words, the rhymes and habits of the nursery, are all gaining significance for me," he wrote to Fliess. He wanted to know why "were the confessions extracted under torture [from witches] so very like what my patients tell me under psychological treatment," while later in the year he struck what was to be a rich vein with his submission that "the mechanism of creative writing is the same as that of hysterical phantasies."

Almost at the same time, discussing his discovery of the Oedipus complex with Fliess, he let loose the hare which he was to pursue for the rest of his life: the proposal that the complex might lie at the root of *Hamlet*. "I am not thinking of Shakespeare's conscious intentions, but supposing rather that he was impelled to write it by a real event because his own unconscious understood that of his hero," he wrote. The idea was given additional plausibility when he read that *Hamlet* had been written soon after the death of Shakespeare's father in 1601, "that is, under the immediate impact of his bereavement and, as we may well assume, while his childhood feelings about his father had been freshly revived." Although there was no evidence that the death of Shakespeare's father, even if it had, indeed, taken place before *Hamlet* was written, had awakened the memory of the poet lusting after his mother, as the death of Jacob Freud had awakened his son's, it was an idea to which Freud was to cling almost as tenaciously as to the Oedipus complex itself.

It was to Fliess that, in 1898, he sent his first application of psychoanalysis to a work of literature, a five hundred-word commentary on C. F. Meyer's short story "Die Richterin." One of the first examples of applied psychoanalysis claiming to uncover the latent psychological meanings hidden within the manifest content of a work of art, it began with a glib assurance that many might take to be a prototype of Freudian judgment: "There is no doubt that this is a defense against the writer's memory of an affair with his sister," a verdict possibly connected with the regretfully abandoned seduction theory.

Before his sighting-shot at the psychoanalytic interpretation of literature was followed up, Freud had proposed another nonclinical application. Psychoanalysis, he felt sure, could help determine the innocence or guilt of the accused in a court of law. Attempts had been made to do this with the help of Jung's association experiments during mock trials held by law students in a University of Vienna seminar, and in 1906 Freud was asked to lecture by its president, Professor Alex Löffler. What he suggested in a paper on "Psychoanalysis and the Establishment of Facts in Legal Proceedings" was a variation of the association test. The result would not be the only factor governing the verdict, and he foresaw a long period during which the value of the method would have to be tested. It might be arranged for you, he told students,

> even to the extent of becoming a duty, to undertake such examinations for a series of years in all actual cases of accusation, *without your conclusions being allowed to influence the decision of the judge.* It would, indeed, be best if the latter never knew the conclusions which you drew from your experiments with regard to the guilt of the accused. After years of collecting and comparing the results thus obtained, all doubt with regard to the value of this psychological method of examination should be solved.

The following year, 1907, Freud returned to his speculations on the unconscious sources of literature with a lecture on "Creative Writers and Day-Dreaming," given to a specialist audience in a hall at Heller's publishing house. "It passed off without mishap, which is good enough for me," he told Jung; "it must have been heavy fare for all the writers and their wives. . . . If nothing else, it was an incursion into territory that we have barely touched upon so far, but where I might easily settle down."

It was in the same year, 1907, that Freud followed up his "Die Richterin" analysis. The successor was "Delusions and Dreams in Jensen's *Gradiva,* " in which Freud dealt with a novella by Wilhelm

Jensen, first mentioned to him by Jung and with an archaeological setting in Pompeii, which Freud had visited with his brother Alexander in 1902. The book told the story of the fictitious Norbert Hanold, a German archaeologist who became obsessed by the plaster cast in the Vatican of a relief showing a young girl. In a dream he saw her at the time of Pompeii's destruction in A.D. 79, traveled to the ruins, met what he at first believed was her ghost, and then found that the "ghost" was a childhood acquaintance. The attraction of the story for Freud went beyond its setting, and for one very good reason: although Jensen knew nothing of either Freud or psychoanalysis when he wrote *Gradiva,* he made his hero's dream run very closely along the lines that Freud had laid down in his *The Interpretation of Dreams.*

Jensen's reaction to Freud's work, which drew more attention to his short book than it would otherwise have received, appears to have been equivocal. On receiving a copy, he replied that the analysis followed his own aims. But on receiving another letter from Freud he replied cautiously. Jung later sent Freud copies of three more stories by Jensen, and Freud then took part in a discussion at the Vienna Psychoanalytical Society after Max Graf had read a paper on "The Methods Used in the Study of the Psychology of Creative Writers." Jensen, Freud concluded, had been deeply attached in his youth to a young girl, possibly his sister, and had suffered great unhappiness, perhaps through her death. The girl, he suggested, might have suffered from some disability such as a club foot, which Jensen had turned into the beautiful gait of Gradiva. Asked for comments, Jensen said that he had never had a sister but that his first love had been a childhood friend who had died of consumption at the age of eighteen. Later he had fallen in love with another girl who reminded him of the first, but she too had died. According to Herbert Marcuse, Jensen refused to meet Freud, and there the matter rested, leaving usable ammunition with Freud's supporters and with his opponents.

Whatever the relevance of Freud's *Gradiva* essay to the future of psychoanalysis, it was beautifully written and aroused considerable interest. Freud himself appears to have become almost as obsessed with the cast as was Jensen and, after visiting the Vatican in 1907, wrote to Martha of the joy he had felt on seeing the cast there— "a dear familiar face!," as he called it. Copies were made soon after publication of Freud's essay and quickly became a familiar sight in psychoanalysts' consulting rooms. Twenty years later the girl became a cult image among the surrealists, Salvador Dali making numerous drawings of her after translation of the essay into French.

During the year following publication of Freud's essay on *Gradiva,* he was occupied with his practice, with the aftermath of the Salzburg Congress and then with preparations for his visit to the United States. Not until the spring of 1910 did he complete the short excursion into literature and art that was to arouse more controversy than any of his nonmedical writings until publication of *Moses and Monotheism* nearly thirty years later. Entitled "Leonardo da Vinci and a Memory of his Childhood," it took one sentence from Leonardo's notebooks as starting point for an elaborate explanation of Leonardo's psychosexual life.

Freud first became interested in Leonardo in 1898 during a discussion with Wilhelm Fliess on the possible connections between bilaterality and bisexuality. "Leonardo, of whom no love affair is recorded, was perhaps the most famous case of left-handedness," he wrote on October 9. "Can you use him?" Nine years later, replying to a newspaper questionnaire asking for the titles of his favorite books, Freud included Merezhkovsky's novel, *The Romance of Leonardo da Vinci.* Not until 1909, however, did the full potentialities of applying psychoanalysis to such figures of the past really become apparent. In a letter to Jung, Freud declared that psychoanalysis must "conquer the whole field of mythology." He continued:

> We must also take hold of biography. I have had an inspiration since my return. The riddle of Leonardo da Vinci's character has suddenly become clear to me. That would be a first step in the realm of biography. But the material concerning L. is so sparse that I despair of demonstrating my conviction intelligibly to others. . . . Do you remember my remarks in the "Sexual Theories of Children" to the effect that children's first primitive researches in this sphere were bound to fail and that this first failure could have a paralyzing effect on them? . . . Well, the great Leonardo was such a man; at an early age he converted his sexuality into an urge for knowledge and from then on the inability to finish anything he undertook became a pattern to which he had to conform in all his ventures: he was sexually inactive or homosexual.

One of his own patients, Freud went on, seemed to have the same constitution as Leonardo, without his genius. It was Freud's interest in the man which triggered off plans that had been growing for some time, and a few weeks later he spoke to the Vienna Psycho-Analytical Society on the subject.

Freud finished his Leonardo study the following May. Previously, however, Ernest Jones had sent him Walter Pater's famous description of the Mona Lisa, and Freud wrote in acknowledging the excerpt:

> You must not expect too much of Leonardo who will come out in the next month, neither the secret of the Vierge aux Rochers nor the solution of the Monna [sic] Lisa puzzle; keep your hopes on a lower level, so it is likely to please you more. Many thanks for the page from Pater; I knew it and had quoted some lines out of the fine passage. I think L. was "bimanual," but that is about the same thing as left-handed. I have not inquired further into his handwriting, because I avoided by purpose all biological views, restraining myself to the discussion of the psychological ones.

In view of the controversy aroused by the Leonardo work, Freud's correspondence with his friends at the time of publication is significant. To Ferenczi he wrote: "Don't be concerned about the Leonardo. I have long written only for the small circle which every day widens, and if the other people don't rail about the Leonardo, I should have gone astray in my opinion of them." To Pfarrer Pfister he noted that the essay would "cause plenty of offense, but I write really only for a small circle of friends and followers." Most of them were happy. "[The study] has a very dainty analysis, with all sorts of suggestive remarks in it," Jones noted to Putnam. "What a lot there is to learn!"

Freud himself appears at the time to have taken the subject rather less seriously, noting to Binswanger of another project that it was a "stupid idea . . . a private amusement, something like Leonardo." It is probable that his own verdict, as distinct from that propagated by his admirers, would have been that of Havelock Ellis who said of Freud's *Gradiva* and "Leonardo": "It would be fantastic to find any trace of science in either of these delightful essays, and yet they are typically Freudian."

The rock on which the Leonardo hypothesis was built consisted of one sentence in a German translation of Leonardo's notebooks, whose English version ran: "To write thus clearly of the kite would seem to be my destiny, because in the earliest recollections of my infancy it seemed to me when I was in the cradle that a kite came and opened my mouth with its tail, and struck me within upon the lips with its tail many times." In the German work used, the Italian word for kite was incorrectly translated as *"Geier"* or "vulture." The difference was important, since Leonardo's statement, Freud suggested, referred not to a genuine recollection but to a fantasy which Leonardo had conceived in adult life. When the psychoanalytic searchlight was trained on the sentence, a great deal appeared to be revealed. For the vulture, as Leonardo would have known, was the ancient Egyptian hieroglyph not only for the vulture-headed goddess Mut but also for "mother." In the fantasy the vulture's phallic tail in the child's mouth represented the mother's breast, and in Freud's reasoning there was justification for the hypothesis in the little that was known of Leonardo's first years. He was an illegitimate child and had, it was possible to speculate, been brought up during his first years by his mother alone, being taken into his father's house only after the father, Piero da Vinci, had married a woman of his own class. The real mother, lonely and unsatisfied, had lavished all her care and attention on the son, cultivated his early eroticism and helped set him on the road to homosexuality.

Once Leonardo had been taken into his father's house, he could be considered as having two mothers; the first Caterina, the peasant girl who had borne him, the second his father's wife. This, according to Freud, was the explanation behind Leonardo's painting of the Virgin and Child with Saint Anne in the Louvre, a picture in which the Virgin looked the same age as Saint Anne, her traditional mother, and in which both women wore the enigmatic Mona Lisa smile. Leonardo, according to Freud, had earlier met Mona Lisa, who had aroused his latent sexuality, reawakened his unconscious memory of Caterina, and thus paved the way for the picture in which his two mothers were represented. It was these circumstances, no doubt, which induced Freud to describe the paper as trying "to prove an especially crass example of the impact of accidental family constellations."

"Leonardo and a Memory of his Childhood" outlined what Freud admitted was only a possibility. Indeed, to the German artist Hermann Struck he wrote: "As a matter of fact it is also partly fiction. I wouldn't like you to judge the trustworthiness of our other discoveries by this example." The work was, however, a *tour de force*. Freud himself described it to Lou Andreas-Salomé as "the only truly beautiful thing I have ever written," and its persuasiveness slowly transformed its content from a tentative theory into an article of faith to be defended by all good Freudians. Jung discerned the outline of a vulture in the picture of the Virgin and Child that Freud had reproduced. Pfarrer Pfister, visiting the Louvre, discovered a better one in the blue robes of Leonardo's Virgin, a classic example of the searcher finding what he was looking for and a development which induced Freud to make the pronouncement: "The key to all his achievements and misfortunes lay hidden in the childhood phantasy of the vulture." In 1931, moreover, he wrote that the Louvre picture could not really be understood "without some knowledge of Leonardo's peculiar child-hood."

By the early 1920s, however, some points which could be talked away only with difficulty by even the most dedicated Freudians had come to light. The first revelation was that Leonardo had not, in fact, made any mention of a vulture in the crucial sentence on which Freud had based his essay. The word *"nibbio"* means "kite" and is correctly translated as *"Hühnergeier"* in many German editions of Leonardo. Freud was unlucky enough to use the Herzfeld translation, which incorrectly turned *"nibbio"* into "vulture," and on the mistake erected the structure of the Egyptian hieroglyph, the goddess Mut and the word "mother," all of which collapsed as the bird's species was correctly identified. However, the editors of the Vienna Psychoanalytical Society's minutes, illustrating the lengths to which Freudian loyalty can run, later protested that, after all, "a 'keith' like a vulture, is a bird," a "pathetic justification of Freud's error," as it has been called.

The elimination of the vulture, by Eric Maclagan as early as 1923 in the January issue of the British art journal the *Burlington Magazine,* was followed by the suggestion that the Caterina of whose significance Freud had made so much was not, in fact, Caterina the mother but a woman of the same name whom Leonardo had employed as a housekeeper in adult life. There was also the question of how long Leonardo had spent with his mother before being taken into his father's household. There could be genuine doubt about this in 1910, when Freud was writing, even though in his library he had marked a passage in one biography which said: "Leonardo missed that maternal influence to which every great man who respects himself must submit." The statement of a single author need not be accepted unquestioningly, yet later evidence did suggest that Leonardo had been taken into his father's house soon after his birth, a circumstance which, as one writer had said, "would have contradicted Freud's hypothesis of a long period after [the] marriage when the young genius was alone with his doting and love-starved mother."

More important was the incontestable background to the picture of the Virgin, Saint Anne and the infant Christ. According to Freud, the painting had been executed following the meeting with Mona Lisa, and the portrayal of mother and daughter was a direct outcome of Leonardo's unconscious memory of his childhood with two mothers. But a few years earlier the cult of Saint Anne had received a considerable stimulus when the Pope issued an indulgence for those who recited a prayer to her. The prayer was printed on the indulgence ticket, and a woodcut showing Saint

Anne, the Virgin and the Child was often included. The woodcuts were produced in great numbers and had, by the time Leonardo set to work on the picture, acquired a great vogue throughout Catholic Europe.

Other writers with more knowledge than Freud of Renaissance Italy have drawn attention to other unjustifiable assumptions in the Leonardo essay. Freud assumed, for instance, that Leonardo's releasing of captive birds—a habit described in his essay as significant—revealed traces of a converted sadistic impulse; but it has been pointed out that Renaissance men often did release birds as a means of attracting good luck, and that it would, in any case, have been a perfectly natural act for Leonardo, who had an insatiable interest in the mechanisms of flight.

Far from being "struck throughout the book by Freud's vast literary knowledge, a burden he wore lightly and of which he never made any display," as Ernest Jones remarks, it is difficult not to see "Leonardo" as an illustration of the psychoanalyst stepping into a specialist field and erecting there a major construction on the most rickety of foundations. Remarkably enough, this was admitted by Freud himself a decade later after investigations by the psychoanalyst Rudolf Reitler had forced him to modify the second edition of the book.

Nevertheless, the essay was to become a new Ark of the Covenant for the faithful, and as the persuasiveness of its argument grew weaker, increasingly tortuous propositions were put forward to salvage something from the wreckage.

The "Leonardo" did psychoanalysis as little good as Wittels' contortions over Karl Kraus and *Die Fackel*, and its essential weakness has been pointed out by the psychoanalyst Charles Rycroft:

> The fallacy in using the clinical notion of childhood reconstruction as a technique of aesthetic and historical research is, I believe, two-fold. First, in the absence of a patient able to give or withhold his assent, the number of alternative interpretations available is so great that the subject can easily become a screen onto which the analyst projects his own personal and theoretical predilections; and secondly it ignores the fact that a shift of meaning occurs when the notion of "interpretation," which applies in the first instance to communications made to patients in a therapeutic setting, is transferred to the public arena.

Yet something remained, apart from the quality of the writing, the imagination and the ingenuity of Freud's argument. "His conclusions," Kenneth Clark has written, have been rejected with horror by the majority of Leonardo scholars, and no doubt the workings of a powerful and complex mind cannot be deduced from a single sentence nor explained by a rather one-sided system of psychology. Freud's study, though it contains some passages of fine intuition, is perhaps as oversimplified as that of Vasari. Yet it helps our conception of Leonardo's character by insisting that he was abnormal.

The "Leonardo" was indicative of the way in which psychoanalysis was from now on to permeate wider areas. The expansion aroused opposition, even before the specific dangers were revealed, and Freud was well aware that this would be so. He was aware, also, that the prospect of psychoanalytic investigation into nonmedical fields might attract not only the fully qualified but the second-rate. His fears were to be amply justified, and two decades later he could write:

> The result has been that analysts, as amateurs with an equipment of greater or less adequacy, often hastily scraped together, have made excursions into such fields of knowledge as mythology, the history of civilization, ethnology, the science of religion and so on. They were no better treated by the experts resident in those fields than are trespassers in general: their methods and their findings, in so far as they attracted attention, were in the first instance rejected.

One reason for rejection was the high percentage of practitioners with "less adequacy." Another was the suspicion with which a great deal of the professional world continued to regard psychoanalysis itself. The second factor led Freud to progress cautiously in encouraging nonmedical applications, and it was not until 1912, when the International Association was apparently over the hump, that the journal *Imago* came into existence. Founded by Hanns Sachs, it was to be edited jointly by Freud and Rank. The title was taken from the novel by Carl Spitteler in which the unconscious is shown both as affecting conscious action and stimulating the creative powers; but, significantly, the word also stands for the final form of an insect after metamorphosis, and the journal was to deal not with the medical aspects of psychoanalysis but with the nonmedical possibilities that had emerged from them.

In the first issue Freud stressed the need to extend the scope of psychoanalytic research to fields such as language, customs, religion and the law. Subjects as varied as mythology and aesthetics, literature and the history of art, philology, folklore, criminology and moral theory were all to be included. They were ambitious plans and they were to grow more ambitious with time. Two decades later Freud was writing that psychoanalysis could "become indispensable to all the sciences which are concerned with the evolution of human civilization and its major institutions such as art, religion and the social order."

Imago also published the first of four essays which, later appearing together as *Totem and Taboo,* represented Freud's application of psychoanalysis to social and anthropological problems. The short book, which outlined nothing less than his view of how human society originated, had been conceived more than a decade earlier. The parallel between the analyst delving into successive layers of the mind and the archaeologist stripping successive layers of physical deposits had then combined with the mystery of ancient civilizations—"only a good-for-nothing is not interested in his past," Freud once said—to arouse his interest in archaeology. Schliemann at Troy had been followed by Sir Arthur Evans on Crete, and their spectacular discoveries had led Freud to speculate on the beliefs of man's earliest ancestors. "Zeus seems originally to have been a bull," he wrote to Fliess after reading of Evans' excavations at Knossos. "The God of our own fathers, before the sublimation instigated by the Persians took place, was worshiped as a bull. That provides food for all sorts of thoughts which it is not yet time to set down on paper. . . ."

From then on, the possibility of psychoanalysis being able to throw light on the beginnings of religion and its relationship to human society was a constant preoccupation. In "Obsessive Actions and Religious Practices," written in 1907, Freud compared the compulsive acts of neurotics with the rituals of religion and came to an unpopular conclusion: that religion itself was a universal obsessional neurosis, and obsession an individualized religion. The following year, in "Civilised Sexual Morality and Modern Nervous Illness," he discussed the persistent suppression of the instincts as human society had taken shape.

However, Freud was well aware of his own limitations, as he acknowledged to Professor Ernst Oppenheim, a specialist in classical mythology and folklore who had attended his university lectures in 1906. Considering one of his papers which discussed psychoanalytic observations in relation to folklore, Freud told him that it

makes me regret once again—as I have so often done before—that so little has been added to my knowledge of antiquity since my schooldays . . . I have long been haunted by the idea that our studies on the content of the neuroses might be destined to solve the riddle of the formation of myths, and that the nucleus of mythology is nothing other than what we speak of as "the nuclear complex of the neuroses."

Two of his pupils, Karl Abraham in Berlin and Otto Rank in Vienna, he went on, had tried to invade mythology and make conquests in it with the help of psychoanalysis. "But we are," he admitted, "amateurs, and have every reason to be afraid of mistakes. We are lacking in academic training and familiarity with the material."

His modesty evaporated within the next few years, possibly under the influence of Jung's confident assertions that prehistory had as great an effect on man as his own individual past. Jung's first interest had been archaeology; compared with Freud he was a professional, and he quickly showed a competence to which Freud reacted with a combination of encouragement and dismay. With his concern for priorities he soon confessed to Jung that it was "a torment to me to think, when I conceive an idea now and then, that I may be taking something away from you or appropriating something that might just as well have been acquired by you. . . . Why in God's name did I allow myself to follow you into this field?" Jung himself was not too happy about what the commander in chief was doing, admitting that "the outlook for me is very gloomy if you too get into the psychology of religion." Despite the dangers, they both worked on, Freud later being encouraged by Putnam's address at Weimar; for if the American was really trying to hitch the star of psychoanalysis to religion, then Freud was ready to demonstrate the futility of the exercise.

He began his *Totem and Taboo* in the spring of 1911, telling Jung that he hoped to be finished by the summer; "for that," he added, "I need a room where I can be alone and a forest nearby." In early August he took a different view, reporting that the psychology of religious faiths on which he was at work was likely to occupy him for years. He knew that it would be as unpopular as his views on sex and wrote to Binswanger from the Alps: "The frequency of images of god here in the Tyrol, where until recently they have been more common that the pilgrims, has induced me to undertake religious-psychological studies, something of which may perhaps see the light of day later on. After I've published them I won't probably be readmitted to the Tyrol." To Ferenczi he admitted in November: "The Totem work is a beastly business. I am reading thick books without being really interested in them since I already know the results; my instinct tells me that. But they have to slither their way through all the material on the subject. In that process one's insight gets clouded, there are many things that don't fit and

yet mustn't be forced. I haven't time every evening, and so on."
And to Putnam he confided about the work that "On the whole,
doing this makes me feel like an elderly gentleman who contracts
a second marriage late in life. *L'Amour coûte cher aux vieillards* [Love
is expensive for old men]."

By the second day of 1912 he appears to have been unusually
depressed, telling Abraham, "My work on the psychology of religion is proceeding very slowly, and I would prefer to drop it
altogether." However, he survived the depression and finished the
first of the four chapters, "The Horror of Incest," published in
Imago under the title "Some Points of Agreement between the
Mental Lives of Savages and Neurotics." Of the final three essays,
Freud completed two later in the year and the last in the spring of
1913—"the most daring enterprise I have ever ventured," as he
described it to Jones. "'On Religion, Ethics and quibusdem aliis'
God help me!" All three were read to the Vienna Psychoanalytical
Society, the first in a three-hour lecture, and the four parts were
published later in 1913 as *Totem and Taboo*.

To some friends Freud was disarmingly honest about his motives for pressing on with *Totem and Taboo;* it would, he told Binswanger, "'smuggle' psychoanalysis into ethnopsychology." There
was, moreover, another reason, which he revealed as he discussed the enterprise with Abraham, Jones and Ferenczi. All
three were strong critics of the Zurich group, and reading Freud's
remarks to them it is clear that he regarded *Totem and Taboo* as a
useful, if fortuitous, weapon against Jung and his supporters.
Abraham was told that the final important essay would appear
before the Munich Congress and would "serve to cut us off cleanly
from all Aryan religiousness. Because that 'will certainly be the
consequence." If there were any doubt about Freud's attitude, it
would be settled by his prediction to Ferenczi. After saying of
Totem and Taboo that he had not worked on anything with such
certainty and elation since *The Interpretation of Dreams*, he added:
"The reception will be the same: a storm of indignation except
among those near to me. In the dispute with Zurich it comes at the
right time to divide us as an acid does a salt." As Wittels has
maintained with some exaggeration: "In *Totem and Tabu*, Freud
wreaked a scientific vengeance on Jung, following the latter into
the domain of folk psychology, and there annihilating Jung on his
own vantage ground."

"Annihilating" was certainly an extravagant word, and it would
have been more accurate to say that while both men assumed that
human action was influenced by the customs of the earliest societies, they had contrasting ideas of the ways in which the influence

was transmitted. Jung had already attributed it to a collective unconscious, inherited over countless generations; Freud accounted
for it by the evolution of a changing but ever-present network of
social customs and taboos.

As published in 1913, *Totem and Taboo* consisted of "The Horror
of Incest," "Taboo and Emotional Ambivalence," "Animism,
Magic and the Omnipotence of Thought" and "The Return of
Totemism in Childhood." Freud, like Jung, delved back into the
deepest ancestral past; but while Jung's raw material had consisted
very largely of primitive myths and almost incomprehensible
sagas, Freud drew upon the reports of contemporary savages still
living in the South Seas and Australia, and it was their customs and
taboos that he saw as the end product of a social evolution, which
with the help of psychoanalysis he traced back to the start of
human history.

His observations were taken from Sir James Frazer whose *The
Golden Bough* had appeared twenty years earlier; from Darwin, from
whom Freud had borrowed the hypothesis that human beings
originally lived in small hordes, each of which was under the despotic rule of an older male who appropriated all the females and
castrated or disposed of the younger males, including his sons;
from Atkinson who had conceived the idea of a revolution in which
the older male was killed and eaten; and from Robertson Smith
from whose totem theory he assumed the evolution of the totemic
brother-clan.

In length, as well as in the extent of speculative interpretation,
the four essays were very different. All, however, were persuasively
written, and if they contained many dogmatic phrases—"will be
bound to show," "these . . . must be the oldest and most powerful
of human desires"—they also contained a plethora of honest ad-
missions that the ideas put forward were speculative and must, at
the best, be only tentatively held. It was as well since, as Freud had
expected, *Totem and Taboo* was to arouse criticism just as deep and
sustained as that aroused by the theory of infantile sexuality.

The first, a 18,000-word essay, surveyed the taboos on incest,
which Frazer and others had found among contemporary primitive
peoples—a mass of material from a culturally distant past seen by
Freud as evidence of the Oedipus complex, which much of the
twentieth century still rejected as a psychoanalyst's nightmare.
"We are," he concluded,

> driven to believe that this rejection is principally a product of the
> distaste which human beings feel for their early incestuous wishes,
> now overtaken by repression. It is therefore of no small importance

that we are able to show that these same incestuous wishes, which are later destined to become unconscious, are still regarded by savage peoples as immediate perils against which the most severe measures of defense must be enforced.

The claim that evidence from the cultural past supported one part of psychoanalytic theory was developed in the second and longer essay. The taboos of primitive people were very similar to the obsessional prohibitions of neurotics, as Freud had already suggested in his case of the "Rat Man"; now he went on to propose "that the moral and conventional prohibitions by which we ourselves are governed may have some essential relationship with these primitive taboos, and that an explanation of taboo might throw a light upon the obscure origin of our own 'categorical imperative.' " The idea was developed with the aid of comparisons drawn between many primitive taboos and the obsessions of his patients whose causes he had been able to uncover; and, in the third essay, by comparison with his psychoanalytic assessment of man's evolving view of the universe as revealed by the anthropologists.

But it was in the fourth essay that, having carefully prepared the ground, he came to the nub of the matter. He had already shown to his own satisfaction that the totem animal, normally revered but killed and eaten on certain festive or religious occasions, was a substitute for the father. "If, now," he went on, "we bring together the psychoanalytic translation of the totem with the fact of the totem meal and with Darwin's theories of the earliest state of human society, the possibility of a deeper understanding emerges —a glimpse of a hypothesis which may seem fantastic but which offers the advantage of establishing an unsuspected correlation between groups of phenomena that have hitherto been disconnected."

The hypothesis began with Darwin's "primal horde," a fine phrase by which Darwin meant no more than a small self-supporting group under the control of "the father," who exercised absolute rule over other men in the group and kept all the women for his own use. Freud believed that eventually the young men revolted, killed and ate the father, and in atonement forbade the killing of the totem animal which represented the father. But in order to prevent a repetition of the original crime during competition for the liberated women, marriage within the group was forbidden, as was killing within it. Thus, explains Freud, they "created out of their filial sense of guilt the two fundamental taboos of totemism, which for that very reason inevitably corresponded to the two repressed wishes of the Oedipus complex. Whoever contravened those taboos became guilty of the only two crimes with which primitive society concerned itself"—murder and incest.

The idea, which Freud was later to describe as a "hypothesis, or, I would rather say, vision," had, he admitted, "a monstrous air"; it also had one irresistible attraction: if true, it showed that his Oedipus complex, the core of psychoanalysis as he saw it, was as important to the development of society as to the development of the individual. As he himself put it, it showed "that the beginnings of religion, morals, society and art converge in the Oedipus complex. This is in complete agreement with the psychoanalytic finding that the same complex constitutes the nucleus of all neuroses, so far as our present knowledge goes."

Yet in spite of Freud's natural inclination toward such a hypothesis, he was emphatic that it was only speculative. A few years later he underlined the point even more strongly:

> To be sure, [it] is only a hypothesis, like so many others with which archaeologists endeavor to lighten the darkness of prehistoric times —a "Just-So-Story," as it was amusingly called by a not unkind English critic; but I think it is creditable to such a hypothesis if it proves able to bring coherence and understanding into more and more new regions.

The critic was Robert Ranulph Marett, reviewing *Totem and Taboo* in the *Athenaeum*. The comment was remarked upon nineteen years later by the American anthropologist Alfred L. Kroeber, writing *"Totem and Taboo* in Retrospect" in the *American Journal of Sociology.* "It is a felicitous phrase coming from himself," Kroeber noted. "Many a tale by Kipling or Andersen contains a profound psychological truth. One does not need therefore to cite and try it in the stern court of evidential confrontation." Freud's acceptance of the comment, which he quoted in his paper on "Group Psychology and the Analysis of the Ego," makes more understandable his remark in 1921 to Abram Kardiner, a student who was to set up the first psychoanalytic training school in the United States. Referring to his theory of primal parricide, Freud said, "Oh, don't take that seriously—I made that up on a rainy Sunday afternoon."

Freud's belief that his hypothesis might "lighten the darkness" of prehistoric times was perhaps hardly the phrase to describe *Totem and Taboo*'s impact on the obscurities of the past, and even in 1913 two criticisms could fairly be made of it. One was that its acceptance required a belief in the inheritance of acquired characteristics, which Lysenko revived in Stalin's Russia, where it was encouraged largely for political reasons. The aberration was not particularly surprising. Even Ernest Jones has admitted that "Freud remained from the beginning to the end of his life what one must call an obstinate adherent of this discredited Lamarckism." More surprising was Freud's acceptance of the collective unconscious as an essential part of his hypothesis, an assumption which, admittedly with wider implications, was a central point in Jung's beliefs. This demanded not merely Lamarckian belief in the transmission of acquired characteristics but the transmission of memory traces over hundreds of generations, a concept based on as little evidence as was Fliess's semimystical numerology.

Almost as important, and possibly more so in the United States, was the fact that Freud had leaned so heavily on the work of anthropologists belonging to the English evolutionary school. Much of his material came from Sir James Frazer's *Totemism and Exogomy* published a few years before, which he augmented with anecdotes from earlier field anthropologists. But doubt was soon being cast on such material as a reliable basis for anthropological theory, while the unilineal cultural evolutionism which Freud assumed was already quite out-of-date. "The conventional American anthropologist," as a result, "dismissed Freud's anthropology as bad and his conclusions as worthless. With regrettable but familiar illogic, psychoanalytic method and theory were therewith rejected."

Support for Freud's assumptions steadily weakened as belief in the material he had used to justify them was eroded by anthropologists in the field. In particular, work with primitive people showed that the concept of the primal horde was not viable, while the varied ways in which society does in fact evolve came slowly to light. Malinowski found that in the Trobriand Islands it was not the father but the maternal brother who was a child's guardian, a state of affairs which suggested that the Oedipus complex should not be given the simple universality which Freud gave it. Nevertheless, it was the idea of the complex which led to Malinowski's kinship theory, and despite the use made of his discoveries by the opponents of psychoanalysis, Malinowski himself tended to regard his findings as supplementary to Freud's rather than as contradicting them. A decade later, Margaret Mead and Ruth Benedict were to be among those demonstrating that the great variety of human development against different cultural backgrounds was making Freud's views increasingly untenable. But, as with Malinowski, both would probably have acknowledged a considerable debt to Freud's insight even while disagreeing with the theories of *Totem and Taboo*.

His delving into prehistory and mythology was not the first occasion on which psychoanalysis had been used to cast light on the distant past. Otto Rank, in particular, had earlier made more than one foray, while the growing interest in anthropology and archaeology would, quite apart from Freud's personal enthusiasm, have made inevitable the growth of such excursions. However, his work on *Totem and Taboo,* discussed freely among his supporters for some time before publication, encouraged a spate of work in the field, and the curious pathways down which the explorations could sometimes lead were described by Ernest Jones in March 1914. "I have completely re-written my Madonna essay for the *Jahrbuch,*" he told Freud,

adding both some valuable material and what I think is an important deepening of the theory (relation of flatus to castration); the last part of it was sent to Sachs a fortnight ago. Toward the end an amusing episode occurred. The crocodile part all depended on the fact that these animals, like frogs, have no external penis. On reading Wallis Budge's book on Osiris, which by the way is very good, I was horrified to read that the Egyptians performed certain rites with the *penis* of the crocodile. I telephoned in a panic to various professors of zoology, none of whom could tell me what I wanted, and the next day went to the Zoological Gardens to investigate the point. None of the keepers knew, so the only thing to do was to turn over an undoubted male crocodile on to his back by means of poles, etc. This proved to be an appallingly difficult task, and created an exciting scene. I found, also later from textbooks, that the animal's *penis* is *entirely* concealed within the cloaca, so that the psychological assumption that it must be invisible from outside proved correct. What a dull life an ordinary doctor leads in comparison with that of a psychoanalyst!

If psychoanalytic explanation of ancient rites was to be investigated with greater energy after Freud had shown the way, so too was the light which the theories could throw on art and artists. Freud himself was to demonstrate how far the process could be taken, for following fast on *Totem and Taboo* there came a paper, "The Moses of Michelangelo," above which *Imago* published the following note: "Although this paper does not, strictly speaking, conform to the conditions under which contributions are accepted for publication in this Journal, the editors have decided to print it, since the author, who is personally known to them, moves in psychoanalytic circles, and since his mode of thought has in point of fact a certain resemblance to the methodology of psychoanalysis." This was indeed true. The author was Freud himself, as he acknowledged ten years later; the paper, "The Moses of Michelangelo," an unexpected work explicable to some extent by Freud's self-identification with Michelangelo's subject.

On the fourth day of his first visit to Rome, he had entered the church of San Pietro in Vincoli and stood before Michelangelo's huge statue, part of the uncompleted work designed for the tomb of Julius II and intended for the Vatican. A copy of the statue stood in the Vienna Academy of Art, and it is probable that Freud's long identification with Moses had already prompted him to study it. Certainly that is suggested by his words on a post card to Martha: "I have come to understand the meaning of the statue by contemplating Michelangelo's intention." More than a decade later he noted to Martha: ". . . every day I pay a visit to Moses in S. Pietro in Vincoli, on whom I may perhaps write a few words."

He returned to the statue on many of his visits to Rome, but it was only in September 1913 that he became seized of it. He later wrote:

> My relationship to this work is something like that to a love child. Every day for three lonely weeks in September of 1913 I stood in the church in front of the statue, studying it, measuring and drawing it until there dawned on me that understanding which in the essay I only dared to express anonymously. Not until much later did I legitimize this nonanalytic child.

On returning to Vienna, he began to read up the subject. He also asked Ernest Jones, then in Florence, to send him photographs of certain statues in the Duomo, one of which, by Donatello, was said to have inspired Michelangelo into his work on the Moses. "This shook Freud badly," says Jones, "since it opened the possibility of the reason for the pose being a purely artistic one without any special ideational significance. I then sent him two photographs from Rome, and at his request had some also specially taken of the lower edge of the Tables, which Moses is shown holding."

Jones did more than send material. "Do you," he asked, "find anything curious about the *left* [*sic*] hand, the first two fingers are in the beard, and the other tightly clasping the clothing in a rather unnecessary way."

Now, the fingers in the beard and the unnecessary clasping of the clothing were significant factors leading to Freud's conclusion. The Michelangelo shows a fierce Moses clasping the Tables he had just received on Mount Sinai. Most commentators concluded—and in spite of Freud still do—that he was depicted when first catching sight of the Israelites dancing around the Golden Calf and as he was about to fling down the sacred Tables. Freud's version was entirely different. "What we see before us," he wrote, is not the inception of a violent action but the remains of a movement that has already taken place. In his first transport of fury, Moses desired to act, to spring up and take vengeance and forget the Tables; but he has overcome the temptation, and he will now remain seated and still, in his frozen wrath and in his pain mingled with contempt.

By an ingenious process of what might be called sculptural analysis he evolved the theory that Michelangelo had

modified the theme of the broken Tables; he does not let Moses break them in his wrath, but makes him be influenced by the danger that they will be broken and makes him calm that wrath, or at any rate prevent it from becoming an act. In this way he had added something new and more than human to the figure of Moses; so that the giant frame with its tremendous physical power becomes only a concrete expression of the highest mental achievement that is possible in a man, that of struggling successfully against an inward passion for the sake of a cause to which he has devoted himself.

This was the conclusion he had arrived at as he completed his paper in the first days of 1914. But he was not at all anxious to sign it, asking Jones why he should disgrace Moses by putting his name to it and adding, "It is a fun and perhaps no bad one." To Abraham he added what he called "shame at the obvious amateurishness" of the essay and his doubts about the conclusion he had arrived at. He approached more than one artist but without much success. "The last . . . I consulted showed me what the way of artists in such matters is and made me afraid of too sharp an interpretation. Meaning is but little with these men, all they care about is line, shape, agreement of contours. They are given up to the Lustprinzip. I prefer to be cautious."

Eventually, and largely under pressure from Rank and Sachs, the editors of *Imago*, the essay was published anonymously. Its conclusion was speculative, even if the speculation was ingenious. It reveals nothing about Michelangelo, and the only revelation about Moses is that the Biblical account of his actions could be wrong. However, "The Moses of Michelangelo" implies quite a lot about Freud. The paper was written during the final stages of his break with Jung, and to a Freud already identifying with Moses it was easy to believe that Michelangelo had seen in Moses a model that he must follow; he must restrain his anger against the deserters, the Adlers and Stekels and Jungs who, like the Israelites, had been impudent enough to betray their leader. A year earlier, when the battle with Jung was in progress, he had written to Ferenczi: "At the moment the situation in Vienna makes me feel more like the historical Moses than the Michelangelo one." But whatever he felt, he had to restrain his emotions. By 1914 it was comparatively easy; for he was by then, as he had written to Abraham, "rid of them, the brutal, sanctimonious Jung and his disciples."

Freud's enthusiastic excursions into nonmedical subjects during the decade before the First World War would have done the long-term interests of the cause little good even had his tentative suppositions not been hardened into articles of faith by his supporters. Yet in this field Freud himself was particularly reluctant to abandon ideas which served the cause, although at times he had doubts about their validity. This is illustrated by his tenacious clinging on to the Oedipal theory of *Hamlet.* He had developed the idea outlined to Fliess in the last years of the nineteenth century in *The Interpretation of Dreams.* Here he had maintained that the play was "built up on Hamlet's hesitations over fulfilling the task of revenge that is assigned to him; but its text offers no reasons or motives for these hesitations and an immense variety of attempts at interpreting them have failed to produce a result." To Freud there was a simple explanation:

> Hamlet is able to do anything—except take vengeance on the man who did away with his father and took that father's place with his mother, the man who shows him the repressed wishes of his own childhood realized. Thus the loathing which should drive him on to revenge is replaced in him by self-reproaches, by scruples of conscience, which remind him that he himself is literally no better than the sinner whom he is to punish.

The speculation that Shakespeare was plagued by Oedipal guilt feelings after the death of his father—as Freud himself had been—and that he had fashioned *Hamlet* as a result, is weakened by the fact that Hamlet's alleged hesitation in taking vengeance is entirely a matter of opinion. It has often been pointed out that until the play is half over, Hamlet has only the word of the Ghost that King Claudius is a murderer—and Shakespeare, like most Elizabethans, believed not only in ghosts but that they might be lying demons in disguise. Moreover, it must be remembered that even when the doubt is removed, Hamlet does not plan to kill Claudius during the duel. The occasion presents itself accidentally and is not an act of foresight on his part. As the Shakespearean scholar John Ashworth has pointed out, "Freud's description of Hamlet's character was based on a wrong premise. Because he couldn't perceive Hamlet's motives, he swallowed the nonsense that a workmanlike dramatist like Shakespeare had written a play without showing the motives of the central character." In addition, he overlooked the fact that had Shakespeare killed off Claudius any earlier, he would have robbed himself of a full-length play.

Freud's theory was further elaborated by Ernest Jones in "The Oedipus Complex as an Explanation of Hamlet's Mystery," and it was with some concern that early in 1921 Freud informed Jones of a new edition of Brandes' *William Shakespeare*, in which the author quoted a recently discovered note. "This note," Brandes wrote, "seems to have been written before January 1599, for Spenser, who died about this date, is mentioned as if he was living then. Essex, who too is spoken of as a person alive, was executed in February 1601. The consequence seems to be that *Hamlet* was enacted before the death of Spenser, in any case before the death of Essex, that is to say much earlier than was believed hitherto." Edmund Spenser had in fact died in 1599, and it now appeared from Brandes that *Hamlet* had probably been performed before 1601. "Now remember," wrote Freud at the end of his letter to Jones, "Shakespeare's father died in the year 1601! Will you think of defending our theory?"

Jones replied that he would do what he could; but he did not think that Brandes' passages proved the date, since they might have been written in the historical present.

However, in replying to Jones, Freud made a remarkable avowal of his own doubts and of the very basis on which his psycholiterary work had been carried out. "I am glad to hear you will keep your eyes on [the Hamlet question]," he replied.

Yet it is evident that there is much slippery ground in many applications of P/A to biography and literature. I got a similar impression referring to the findings of Reitler on Leonardo [Rudolf Reitler, who in 1917 had published a short paper on the subject. Although noting it, Freud did not, apparently, feel inclined to accept it without reserve] (which I inserted into the 2nd. edition) and if I must not be prepared to retract as well in my own conclusions about this great man, my predilection may be simply and solely the extreme dearth of the material. It is the danger inherent in our method of concluding from faint traces, exploiting trifling signs. The same as in criminal cases, where the murderer has forgotten to relinquish his *carte de visite* and full address on the *Tatort*.

Freud's honest admission that psychobiography was in fact being built on faint traces and the exploitation of trifling signs was a warning that when psychoanalysts stepped into the highly technical fields of art criticism or biography, it was especially easy for them to make fools of themselves. He himself was far more aware of this danger than some of his followers, and emphasized it a few years later after reading *Elizabeth and Essex* by Lytton Strachey, the brother of his colleague, friend and translator, James Strachey. "You are aware," he wrote in a long letter to Lytton,

> of what other historians so easily overlook—that it is impossible to understand the past with certainty, because we cannot divine men's motives and the essence of their minds and so cannot interpret their actions. Our psychological analysis does not suffice even with those who are near us in space and time, unless we can make them the object of years of the closest investigation, and even then it breaks down before the incompleteness of our knowledge and the clumsiness of our synthesis. So that with regard to the people of past times we are in the same position as with dreams to which we have been given no associations—and only a layman could expect us to interpret such dreams as those.

However, Freud remained reluctant to abandon his Hamlet thesis, and in his short autobiographical study written in 1924, repeated his view of the play's Oedipal conception, noting that "Shakespeare wrote *Hamlet* very soon after his father's death." Five years afterward, in a new edition of *The Interpretation of Dreams*, he added to his discussion of the subject: "Incidentally, I have in the meantime ceased to believe that the author of Shakespeare's works was the man from Stratford." Almost unbelievably, he added no rider to this sentence, which appeared to strike away the props from beneath the alleged Oedipal motivation of the play.

When his autobiographical study appeared in another edition five years later, Freud added a footnote saying that he would like to withdraw the construction that *Hamlet* had been written shortly after the death of Shakespeare's father. The reason, he went on, was that having read *Shakespeare Identified,* a book by the English schoolmaster J. Thomas Looney, he was convinced that "Shakespeare" was Edward de Vere, Earl of Oxford. No reference was made to the collapse of the original Oedipal interpretation. However, all was not lost, as Freud indicated in *An Outline of Psychoanalysis,* which he wrote in 1938. The Earl of Oxford's father had died when the son was a boy, and his mother had remarried shortly afterward: as good a peg for an Oedipus complex as any believer could hope for.

It is, of course, possible that if Shakespeare was Shakespeare, then he was conditioned by his father's death to transform a *Hamlet* of uncertain background, although uncertainty about dates was quite sufficient to justify Freud's alarm in 1921. It is equally possible that if Shakespeare was Oxford, then the noble earl's history could be summoned up to save the Oedipus connection. Freud was certainly anxious that this should be done. His theory of the genesis of *Hamlet* was the touchstone of his other psychoanalytical speculations about Shakespeare just as these were the touchstone of his belief that psychoanalysis could lead to a better understanding of the creations of other authors. Apart from his more obvious gaffes—such as naming childlessness as the tragedy of Lady Macbeth, a mistake followed by Jones, who subsequently admitted that his own similar error illustrated his subservience to Freud's *dicta*—Freud's position was essentially insecure. As the Shakespearean scholar Dr. Gareth Lloyd Evans has pointed out, "you cannot psychoanalyse Macbeth for the simple reason that, *because* it is a fiction, the author has *selected* the 'evidence' in order to make a calculated design upon the audience's imagination. A psychoanalyst requires infinitely more evidence than the dramatist, by definition, can or ought to provide."

However, the argument about Freud's Oedipal theory of *Hamlet* has continued with unabated vigor, and Norman N. Holland's *Psychoanalysis and Shakespeare* contains a closely packed six-page bibliography of more than a hundred items which covers this one point alone, in papers running from highest praise to deepest ridicule. This huge exegesis, still growing year by year, was but one result of the increase in the psychoanalytic interpretation of drama and fiction which took place after the prospects for the cause had been revolutionized by the First World War and the demand for change which followed it.

16

Wartime Acceptance

This is the first time that a German physician, basing himself firmly and without patronizing condescension on psychoanalysis . . . backs this with examples, and is also completely honest on the question of sexual aetiology.

FREUD, in a letter to Karl Abraham

The First World War, the outbreak of which so nearly coincided with the final secession of Jung and his followers from the cause, was to have significant effects on the acceptance of psychoanalysis throughout the world. In the summer of 1914 Freud was as outspokenly patriotic and as unthinkingly optimistic as most other citizens of the Central Powers and of the Allies. If anything, he was rather more so, writing to Abraham on July 26, as the Austrians mobilized on the Russian frontier, "for the first time for thirty years I feel myself to be an Austrian and feel like giving this not very hopeful Empire another chance." Shortly afterward, while Einstein and George Nicolai, professor of physiology at the University of Berlin and later the famous conscript-turned-pacifist, were drawing up the "Manifesto to Europeans" which deplored the German aggression and the consequent rupture of intellectual and cultural cooperation, Freud was living "from one German victory to the next" and eagerly awaiting news of the fall of Paris. Although doubts began to creep in during the first weeks of 1915, he was, as late as September 1916, urging his daughter Sophie to "keep cheerful and not take things too much to heart. Hindenburg has just said that our prospects are good." Only slowly, with the outlook for the war extending through the next year, then the next and the next, did he begin to question the certainty of victory. At the same time, even the patriotic Freud was beginning to wonder whether it had been justifiable to start the war at all.

As pessimism grew, a despair with humanity, never very far below the surface, rose to the surface of his consciousness where it was to remain for the rest of his life. Generalizing from his own particular case and feelings, he began to see human motivations in an even less happy light; he revised his views accordingly, and if justification were needed it came in 1918 and 1919 with the abandonment of Wilson's Fourteen Points and the blockade-imposed starvation in Austria and Germany, which Freud saw as unfortunately typical of the human race. He wrote to Pfister during the last weeks of the war:

> I do not break my head very much about good and evil, but I have found little that is "good" about human beings on the whole. In my experience most of them are trash, no matter whether they publicly subscribe to this or that ethical doctrine or to none at all. That is something that you cannot say aloud, or perhaps even think, though your experiences of life can hardly have been different from mine. If we are to talk of ethics, I subscribe to a high ideal from which most of the human beings I have come across depart most lamentably.

If the war influenced the background to the theoretical structure which Freud had built to explain the workings of the human mind, the fortunes of psychoanalysis itself were just as critically affected. At first the passions roused by the lengthening casualty lists provided a new reason in Allied countries for attacking an idea and a therapy that was considered essentially Germanic. In an age when the British mob banned Wagner and kicked dachshunds because of their origin, psychoanalysis became an even easier target for attack. Yet by the closing years of the war, the debit entry in the account was fast being counterbalanced, not only in Europe but in Britain and the United States, by one awkward fact that even the most virulent opponent of Freudian ideas found it difficult to ignore: of the war casualties limping in by the thousand from the battlefields, large numbers were suffering from mental breakdowns lumped together under the phrase "shell shock." Not only was this a condition which could sometimes be eased by psychoanalytic treatment but it was one whose investigation tended to confirm the underlying assumptions of psychoanalysis. By 1918 both the Central Powers and the Allies were running military hospitals at which psychoanalysis was being used as a method of cure.

In the summer of 1914, as preparations continued for the International Congress to be held in Dresden in September, Freud could not foresee these developments. On Monday June 29 he was visited by the Wolf-Man, now completely cured. Some weeks earlier he had taken the risky step of telling the patient that, whatever the current success of the therapy, treatment would have to cease when he started his summer holiday in July. The shock had worked. So much so that the Wolf-Man had brought his mistress, Thérèse, to visit Freud, who said that she "looked like a czarina"; he had resolved to marry her, and was now finally taking leave of his analyst.

The killings at Sarajevo had happened the previous day. "How little one then suspected that the assassination . . . would lead to World War I," the Wolf-Man has said, "is clear from the remark of Professor Freud (who, to be sure, was a stranger to political life) that if Franz Ferdinand had come to power, there would probably have been a war between Austria and Russia." The Emperor himself took a casual view of his heir's assassination. He had never condoned the Archduke's morganatic marriage and now that death had ensured dynastic purity merely remarked: "A higher power has reasserted the rules that I was unable to maintain." Unawareness continued throughout the next few weeks even as the armies of Europe prepared for mobilization. Not until July 27 did Ferenczi, who had planned to visit Jones in England, discover that he would not be allowed to leave Hungary since he was on the active list. Two days later Freud, observing to Eitingon that "one cannot predict what things will be like in another two months," still felt that he could add, "Perhaps by then most of them will be in order again." Even on July 31 Abraham, in Berlin, was convinced that no great power would declare war on another. The next day Germany declared war on Russia.

If the confidence of Freud and his colleagues looks strange, it should be remembered that in Britain J. J. Thomson, soon to be president of the Royal Society, was as late as the end of July to sign a plea that "War upon [Germany] in the interests of Serbia and Russia will be a sin against civilization." And on July 31 Lord Edmond Fitzmaurice, the man who would have been Foreign Secretary had Grey refused the appointment in 1906, wrote, "I can see no mortal reason why we should be dragged into this affair unless Grey has given pledges of which the House of Commons knows nothing."

At the beginning of August Freud was forced to admit to himself that a world war was in the making, though he saw it as a war forced on a reluctant Austria and Germany, and one which the two powers would bring to a successful conclusion without much disruption of normal life. On the 2nd he wrote to Mathilde in Vienna, telling her that he and Martha, who had been in Karlsbad since mid-July, intended to remain for the time being at the spa; but mobilization was already making it impossible to travel, and Ernst and Martin in Salzburg were apparently facing difficulties in getting home. Within the next few days Freud saw that he would have to abandon his plans for a leisurely journey to the Dolomites and a return to Vienna by way of Dresden, where the International Congress was to be held. On August 5, Austria-Hungary declared war on Russia, and the next day he and his wife started for home.

The Vienna to which he returned and in which he had not spent an August for almost thirty years, resounded with the movement of troops, and his thoughts turned naturally enough to his children. His eldest son, Martin, was about to join up, remarking that he would now, without changing his religion, be able to see Russia, a country then forbidden to Jewish visitors. He was soon followed by Ernst. Oliver, by this time a qualified engineer, was quickly employed on construction work. His eldest daughter, Mathilde, had been married for five years and was living in Vienna with her husband, Robert Hollitscher. Sophie, who had been married a year and a half when war broke out, was living in Hamburg with her husband, Max Halberstadt. Worry was thus concentrated on Anna in England, but by mid-August she had arrived safely back in Vienna.

For some weeks Freud hardly knew what to do. He was reluctant to reopen his practice before the normal date, and spent most of the time listing his collection of antiquities and, with the still-faithful Rank, cataloguing his library. In September he visited his daughter Sophie in Hamburg, called on Abraham in Berlin and then returned to Vienna to start work as usual. In October he had only two patients, in the following month only one. He was still uncertain of himself, at last beginning to wonder seriously what the war would mean. With little else at hand, he began to write the case history of the Wolf-Man, and not only because of its intrinsic importance. It was, James Strachey has pointed out, "largely designed as an empirical refutation of Adler and Jung, and contains many attacks on their theories."

By the end of the year depression had set in, although he still felt sure of German victory. In November he wrote to Lou Andreas-Salomé:

I do not doubt that mankind will survive even this war, but I know for certain that for me and my contemporaries the world will never again be a happy place. It is too hideous. And the saddest thing about it is that it is exactly the way we should have expected people to behave from our knowledge of psychoanalysis. Because of this attitude to mankind I have never been able to agree with your blithe optimism. My secret conclusion has always been: since we can only regard the highest present civilization as burdened with an enormous hypocrisy, it follows that we are organically unfitted for it. We have to abdicate, and the Great Unknown, He or It, lurking behind Fate will someday repeat this experiment with another race.

But he still held out for Germany and victory. "I know," he continued, "that science is only apparently dead, but humanity seems to be really dead. It is a consolation that our German people have behaved best in all this; perhaps because it is certain of victory. The tradesman faced with bankruptcy is always a swindler." After 1918 he forgot the attitude he had taken. Indeed, as early as 1925 he was writing that "during the World War, when a chorus of enemies were bringing against the German nation the charge of barbarism . . . it none the less hurt deeply to feel that my own experience would not allow me to contradict it." He had, in fact, contradicted it quite forcefully.

While Freud superficially appeared to be at a loose end during the first months of war, he was in fact husbanding his energies for an extraordinary spurt of work which was to produce five important essays during six weeks early in 1915 and another five in six more weeks. Meanwhile, opinion about his theories was being polarized in both America and Britain by the effects of the war.

In the United States psychoanalysis had already begun to develop along the lines that he had feared. By 1915 the number of self-styled psychoanalysts practicing in New York ran into three figures, while other American cities had seen a comparable increase. Many practitioners would have found it difficult to pass even the most elementary tests of efficiency and they tended to justify the current opinion among psychologists that while Freud might have to be noticed, his views need not be taken seriously. The damage done would have been greater had it not been for the efforts of the professional American societies and associations. The American Psychoanalytic Association, founded in 1911, did not admit laymen to full membership and required its members, despite their medical qualifications, to undergo a rigorous training before practicing as analysts. Other organizations did much the same. Nevertheless, they were unable to do more than inhibit the spread of garbled versions of what psychoanalysis was and did.

The opportunity for quackery, which Freud himself had intuitively foreseen, opened him to attack even from psychologists who might otherwise have veered round to his views. "As his popularity grew," it has been said, "they gave grudging notice by dumping him in the ragbag category of faith-healing along with Yoga, Christian Science, divine healing, animal magnetism and osteopathy. One text published in 1912 included psychotherapy in the section on 'Spiritualism and Mediumship,' remarking that it might have pragmatic value through suggestion, but had no scientific standing whatsoever. Another psychologist stressed that therapeutic success was no test of the correctness of the theory offered to explain it."

The classifying of psychoanalysis as a fringe medicine did little to deter its popularization. Max Eastman wrote a series of articles in the American *Everybody's Magazine,* prophesying that the therapy, born of the wizard Freud, would produce a wonder-cure for every ailment under the sun. *Good Housekeeping* gave the subject treatment almost as sensational, while Mabel Dodge described her psychoanalytic experiences in measured terms for the mass readership of the Hearst press. At a different level, both *The New Republic* and *The Nation* did their best to explain the subject to the educated layman, the former using the powerful advocacy of Walter Lippmann, about to launch out on his distinguished career, the latter being strongly critical.

Lippmann had been a pupil of William James at Harvard and a few years before the war had been preparing his first book, *A Preface to Politics.* A close friend was Alfred Booth Kuttner, a former patient of Brill who was now at work on a new translation of Freud's *The Interpretation of Dreams.* Kuttner had a cabin in the Maine woods, and he and Lippmann worked there together. "I read the translation as he worked on it and discussed it with him and began to see how much Freud had to contribute to the psychology which I had learned at College," Lippmann later wrote. "If you care to examine *A Preface to Politics* you will see the effects."

Lippmann was a useful convert. In "Freud and the Layman," published in *The New Republic,* he pointed out that ordinary men and women could not fail to be interested in Freud for one very good reason: "We ourselves are the subject matter of his science, and in the most intimate and drastic way." The article was a formidable defense of Freud, written with a sharp cutting edge. Lippmann said:

> When I compare his work with the psychology that I studied in
> college, or with most of the material that is used to controvert him,
> I cannot help feeling that for his illumination, for his steadiness and
> brilliancy of mind, he may rank among the greatest who have con-
> tributed to thought. I know how easy it is to be deceived, but I take

it that this is a small risk in comparison with the necessity for recognizing in his own lifetime a man of outstanding importance. . . . He has set up a reverberation in Human thought and conduct of which few as yet dare to predict the consequences.

The New Republic was almost alone in its advocacy, and the general attitude was reflected by *The Nation,* under Paul Elmer More, which expressed a view compounded of conservative moral outrage and a feeling that Freud had betrayed science with what had been called reactionary occultism. To this there were added the protests of the group headed by Amy Lowell who suggested that Freud's theories were applicable at best only to certain undesirable types of Austrians.

Weir Mitchell, who earlier had dismissed Freud's work as "filth," had in 1913 managed to strike a blow even when lecturing on "The Medical Department in the Civil War." "Today," he said, "aided by German perplexities we would ask the victims a hundred and twenty-one questions, consult their dreams as to why they wanted to go home, and do no better than to let them go as hopeless." And in the year that war broke out Boris Sidis could seriously claim: "Psychoanalysis is a conscious and more often a subconscious or unconscious debauching of the patient. Nothing is so diabolically calculated to suggest sexual perversion as psychoanalysis. Psychoanalysis . . . is a menace to the community. . . . Better Christian Science than psychoanalysis!"

At a time when such views could be sincerely held, the repercussions of the German invasion of Belgium and France should have caused little surprise. Yet it was in France that Freud was most unexpectedly defended against the chauvinism of the times. "In Paris itself," he had written during the first months of 1914, "a conviction still seems to reign (to which Janet himself gave eloquent expression at the Congress in London in 1913) that everything good in psychoanalysis is a repetition of Janet's views with insignificant modifications, and that everything else in it is bad." Yet when Freud was attacked in June 1914, at a meeting of the Société de Psychothérapie, it was Janet who rose to defend him. Against the errors and exaggerations of psychoanalysis, he said, there should be balanced the contribution it had made to an understanding of the human mind. "Let us acknowledge these merits," he went on; "our unavoidable criticisms should not prevent us from acknowledging the fine work and important observations of our Viennese colleagues." The defense was, moreover, published the following year, after the artillery of the Central Powers had been pushed to within earshot of Paris.

Elsewhere, reaction was very different. Although America still held aloof from the war, the sinking by a German submarine of the *Lusitania* in May 1915, with the loss of eleven hundred lives, one hundred of them American, turned the mood of public sympathy toward the Allies. By contrast, all things "German"—and in North American eyes this included all things Austrian—began to assume a new unpleasantness. Freud's Olympian "Thoughts for the Times on War and Death," written in 1915, soon became "a subtle apology for the Central Powers" and "an admirable essay in propaganda Teutonica"—a forerunner of the later indictment that it was "little less than a justification of the Prussian theory of the supremacy of the state over morals and ethics."

As for psychoanalysis, the war now offered the explanation for which so many were looking. "The German mind," it was claimed, "is (as has often been pointed out) to a certain extent undeveloped when contrasted with the logical and moral sanity of the non-German civilized nations," and the "right-minded reader of Freudian literature" was exhorted to agree with the views approvingly put forward by the same Gustav Aschaffenburg who had been in dispute with Jung in 1906: that "the doctrines of so-called psychoanalysis are well-founded neither theoretically nor empirically, that its therapeutic effect is unproved, that its permanent gain for clinical psychiatry is nil, that it conveys the impression of unscientific method, that its pursuit is dangerous for the patient and compromising for the physician, and finally that its only permanent interest is in the field of the history of Kultur." The last point was important for the writer in *The Nation;* he supported these opinions on the grounds that "psychoanalysis is most intimately bound up with German Kultur." Poor Freud! It was not Jewishness which was now being hung round the neck of his infant but the very "Germanism" which both Vienna and Berlin had claimed it was lacking.

Only a few of the comparatively popular journals—from which the majority of politically middle-of-the-road, educated laymen tended to get their information on subjects like psychoanalysis—successfully held the balance between uncritical praise and horrified condemnation. One was the *New York Times,* which devoted half a page to a favorable review when the translation of *The Psychopathology of Everyday Life* appeared in the United States in the autumn of 1914. Early in 1916 there had been what the paper called "a display of mingled ignorance and impudence" in a local court when suit had been brought to have a child removed from the household where his mother was living with her lover. In defense it was stated that the man had studied under Jung and believed in the doctrines of psychoanalysis: that, it was inferred, was enough to justify any sort of immoral behavior. The case was emotionally presented, and its impact could easily have been considerable but for the moderating effect of the *New York Times* common-sense observations. It pointed out:

> "Belief" in [psychoanalysis] has not more to do with regularity or irregularity of life than has the "belief" that quinine is a remedy for malaria, or that early operation for cancer is to be commended. The fervent psychoanalyst, like the fervent scorner of Freud, can have good morals or bad, as he or she pleases, can follow any religion or none, can pick any philosophy of life that seems sound, but in no case will these decisions be affected, one way or the other, by his or her judgment of Freud and Freud's contentions as to the origin and cure of hysteria.

Brill followed up a few days later with the response that the principal aim of psychoanalysis "is to adjust the individual to his environment. It is no more a philosophy of morals than any other branch of medicine."

The *New York Times,* judicially holding the ring, was in a minority, and throughout the United States the more general reaction was what Freud had feared since his visit in 1909: scorn and disbelief, encouraged by the activities of quacks and charlatans, and only partly offset by the support of a few specialists like Putnam and Brill, and an even smaller number of laymen like Lippmann. As war fever offered a fresh stick with which to beat psychoanalysis, the *bouleversement* of opinion, which in the 1920s was to transform the new method into a panacea for all mental troubles, would have seemed not just dangerous but impossible.

Across the Atlantic in Britain, where by the first months of 1915 the prospect of a long bloodletting war had begun to open out alarmingly, there was perhaps more excuse, if as little reason, for the condemnation of Freud as merely an addition to the "monstrous regiment of German professors that has so long sustained us." Such attacks would have been more effective had it not been for the influence of a small number of men who had been gathering support for psychoanalysis during the immediate prewar years. Prominent among them was of course Ernest Jones who had returned from Canada in 1913 and begun private practice in London, after having visited Budapest and being psychoanalyzed by Ferenczi. The analysis confirmed his dedication to the cause but appears to have made him slightly allergic to his analyst.

By the outbreak of war Jones had some foundation on which to build, although not very much. As early as 1910 Dr. T. W. Mitchell had published, in the *Proceedings* of the Society for Psychical Research, the first paper in England devoted mainly to psychoanalysis. The following year David Eder, among the earliest men to practice psychoanalysis in Britain, faced head-on the opposition of the medical establishment at the summer meeting of the British Medical Association. Here he read a paper before the Association's Neurological Section which described, in simple language, the treatment by Freudian methods of a case of hysteria and obsession. When he finished, the chairman of the section, and the audience of about nine, walked out without saying a word.

Some eighteen months later Eder arrived in Vienna, hoping to be taken into analysis by Freud. But Freud, too busy, handed him over to Tausk, and Eder, while still in Vienna, showed signs of swinging toward Jung's analytical psychology. So much so that following his return to Britain, he prepared to read a paper on Jung's and Adler's modifications of Freud's theories to the British Medical Association. Jones quickly warned Freud. "Without denying these gentlemen the right to have whatever modifications that may please them," he wrote, "I certainly think this is a very malaprop time to discuss them in England, before the audience knows about the theory that is to be modified."

Jung himself was in London the following month but made little headway, with or without Eder. He "played a quiet part, made a few courteous generalities, and was in the background," according to Jones. "Very few Germans were there, if any; mostly English so he had a disadvantage in speaking German."

A further sign that things might be moving Freud's way came with a debate at the Psycho-Medical Society in which Jones took part. "After the meeting," he told Freud, "Sir James Crichton-Browne, the President of the Section and Senior Lunacy Commissioner, came up, shook hands, and warmly congratulated me, thanking me in the name of the Committee for having made 'a much needed protest against these misrepresentations,' and spoke very highly of psychoanalysis. A number of other notable men did the same, and the whole attitude was very cordial and full of English 'fair play.'" The approbation of Crichton-Browne was a significant indication of the way things were going. He was one of the most distinguished physicians and psychologists of his time, and where Crichton-Browne led, others frequently followed. Freud was impressed. "'Fair play' is what we want and it is likely that it may be got better in England than anywhere else," he wrote to Jones.

Publication of Jones's *Papers on Psychoanalysis* and Bernard Hart's *The Psychology of Insanity*, both in 1912, had begun to present many of Freud's views to British readers for the first time, and support could now be at least faintly discerned. It was thus in a comparatively encouraging climate that Jones founded the London Psycho-Analytical Society in October 1913, shortly after papers on Freud's theories of dreams and of the unconscious had been read at the annual British Medical Association meeting. Secretary of the London Society, which had nine original members of whom four were practicing psychoanalysts, was David Eder, temporarily recovered from Jungian leanings. Its early days were hampered first by Pierre Janet's attack on Freud at the International Congress of Medicine in London, rebutted by Jones in the *Journal of Abnormal Psychology* where he bluntly accused Janet of dishonesty; then by schisms within the Society. Eder began to introduce recruits with Jungian tendencies, and in the words of Edward Glover, a later member, "the society became a hotbed of dissension, and after the first two years meetings were suspended—most of the members being on war service anyway." Havelock Ellis was among those who had refused to join, Jones told Freud, "on the ground that he belongs to *no* society on principle."

Foundation of the London Psycho-Analytical Society was only the most important item in Jones's campaign to establish psychoanalysis in Britain. A little later he was warmly applauded when he spoke to the psychiatric section of the Royal Society of Medicine. The following year a symposium on Freud's theory of forgetting was held at a joint meeting of psychologists and philosophers in Durham, while the occasional paper on psychoanalysis in medical journals no longer caused shocked surprise. Before the outbreak of war, Jones was able to tell Freud that in the examination for M.D. London (Psychiatry branch), only four out of six questions had to be answered, and four of those were on psychoanalysis. "My man swept the board and I hope may get the Gold Medal," he added.

Thus by the outbreak of war there was a small but determined body of Freudian supporters who had created a bridgehead in Britain. They were to be needed. Brill's translation of *The Psychopathology of Everyday Life* appeared in Britain during the first winter of the war, and an attacking review in the *British Medical Journal* by Charles Mercier, one of Freud's most persistent critics, was supported by a demand for immediate action. "Surely," wrote one correspondent,

the time has at last come when all psychologists, psychiatrists, and medical societies should join with Dr. Mercier in ceasing to regard this modern and alien jargon about the "unconscious" as matter for serious consideration, and follow the better course of killing the abounding nonsense of the Freudian "Philosophy" by ridicule, or by letting it perish, at least in this country, from neglect of cultivation. At present it plays the part of a virulent pathogenic microbe in the wells whence the psychiatrists drink.

Although the writer was himself strongly criticized for attacking the existence of the unconscious rather than Freud's theories about it, his attitude reflected the strong undertow of opinion typified by one critic in the *British Medical Journal:* "In order to understand how the Germanic obsession has held a majority of our profession in thrall for so many years," he said, "a rough contrast of the British and German temperaments is useful." The Germans' *"Deutschland Über Alles"* was compared with the British soldiers' "Tipperary," and through a process of guilt by association the "Germanic" theories of Freud were compared with the simpler and cleaner theories of the untainted British.

Even among those willing to give Freud a hearing, the alleged difference between British and German habits was a point not to be forgotten in wartime. St. John Bullen, noting in the *Journal of Medical Science* that Freud's emphasis on sex had impeded acceptance of his views, excused the reaction by admitting: "It is, however, too often lost sight of that Freud is dealing with a people whose general materialism and attitude towards sexual life is largely different from our own." This was, it appeared, an indication of "the extraordinary protrusion of sex matters into the life of the Teuton." And when Charles Mercier protested against the use of psychoanalysis in wartime Britain, he was rebuffed by the president of the Medico-Psychological Association on the ground that the subject would not be taken seriously. "Surely," the president protested, "it is notorious that the dirty doctrines of Freud, Jung and Co. have met with scant support among British psychiatrists either in their teachings or writings." Even scant support was, nevertheless, too much for some, and a few days later "Decency" asked in the columns of the *British Medical Journal* whether it was "known that psychoanalysts (some have been given commissions) are at their pernicious work in the lunacy wards of our great war hospitals."

It was, moreover, not only the more conservative medical men who still refused to take Freud seriously. Harold Laski, the political theorist of distinctly forward-looking ideas, protested to Justice [Oliver Wendell] Holmes: "I believe that the tendency to Bergsonise or Freudianise everything is just so much nonsense and I want to be back in the good old straight-backed chair where Hume

and Descartes give you the creeps about your own existence and
only the sudden discovery that you have pins and needles in your
feet makes you admit the reality of matter."

In Vienna, Freud knew little of the growing emotional forces
which, beyond the frontiers of the Central Powers, were beginning
to influence opinion about his work. For a time Jones maintained
contact through various neutral countries; and until America was
drawn into the war Putnam could write to Vienna. However, Jones
seems to have been mainly concerned with warning Freud that the
prospects of a German victory looked very different from across
the Channel, while Putnam's letters suggest that by now he had
little contact with the broader movement of public opinion. Freud
thus remained unaware of the new, anti-German bias now being
given to attacks on psychoanalysis until, in the later stages of the
war, they began to be counterbalanced by the views of Army doctors on both sides of the battlefront.

Meanwhile, he had enough to worry him and to make him grieve,
since among the last news to reach him from Britain was the account of how his half-brother Emanuel had been killed by falling
from a train between Southport and Manchester. In Vienna the
meetings of the Psychoanalytical Society had been suspended at
the outbreak of war and were later resumed on a basis of only one
meeting every three weeks. His practice failed to pick up, and like
many middle-class Viennese he was faced with the combined problems of reduced income and rising prices. Ernst had followed
Martin into the Army while Oliver, turned down for military service on medical grounds, was employed on a succession of engi-
neering tasks. Freud moved into the New Year of 1915 in a mood
of depression that matched the doldrums of his work. "At present," he wrote to Abraham, "I am as in a polar night and am
waiting for the sun to rise."

It rose during the next few weeks as he started work on a series
of essays and articles which were completed with unprecedented
speed, among them "Thoughts for the Times on War and Death."
Written to fill space in *Imago*, Freud described it to Putnam as "a
topical essay on the disappointment this war has brought, which
gives me no pleasure whatsoever and probably will not please
others either." To Abraham he described it as "a piece of topical
chit-chat about war and death to keep the self-sacrificing publisher
happy." The deprecatory note was unnecessary, if only because
the essay showed, at least by inference, that the conflict had
confirmed at least two of the theories expounded in psychoanalysis. Freud stressed the fact in a letter written to an old Dutch
friend, Dr. Frederick van Eeden, during the last days of 1914.

Psychoanalysis had, he said, inferred that the evil impulses of mankind had not vanished but merely lay waiting in the unconscious; and, furthermore, that the intellect which apparently kept them in check was a feeble thing which easily became the tool of the emotions. "If you will now observe what is happening in this war—the cruelties and injustices for which the most civilized nations are responsible, the different way in which they judge their own lies and wrong-doings and those of their enemies, and the general lack of insight which prevails—you will have to admit that psychoanalysis has been right in both its theses."

It was the uncivilized method of conducting the war, rather than the war itself, which prompted the disillusionment of Freud's paper. He had, apparently, expected that the war would be "a chivalrous passage of arms, which would limit itself to establishing the superiority of one side in the struggle, while as far as possible avoiding acute suffering that could contribute nothing to the decision, and granting complete immunity for the wounded who had to withdraw from the contest, as well as for the doctors and nurses who devoted themselves to their recovery." In his strictures on the combatants' failure to adhere to such high ideals, Freud did his best to remain impartial in the face of propaganda. Yet in one paragraph at least he did warrant the criticism that the essay was a subtle apology for the Central Powers. This came after he had deplored the fact that civilized nations could turn on each other with such hate and loathing.

> Indeed, one of the great civilized nations is so universally unpopular that the attempt can actually be made to exclude it from the civilized community as "barbaric," although it has long proved its fitness by the magnificent contributions to that community which it has made. We live in hopes that the pages of an impartial history will prove that that nation, in whose language we write and for whose victory our dear ones are fighting, has been precisely the one which has least transgressed the laws of civilization. But at such a time who dares to set himself up as a judge in his own cause?

Putnam, whose countrymen were to fund the rebuilding of the unique Louvain university library in Belgium, burned by the Germans a few months earlier, may indeed have been displeased.

A second essay, "Our Attitude Towards Death," first delivered to the B'nai B'rith in April 1915, dealt with the implications of the great change which the war had made in man's view of his inevitable fate. Civilized man had become accustomed to holding the thought of death at arm's length, but this was no longer possible,

Freud concluded; it would be in keeping with the times to alter the old saying "If you want to preserve peace, arm for war" into "If you want to endure life, prepare yourself for death."

Once the two pieces for *Imago* were out of the way he embarked on an ambitious enterprise: a dozen essays which would make up a book to be called *Introduction to Metapsychology*. This was a word he had first used in describing to Fliess the "psychology which leads behind consciousness" and whose meaning has been broadened over the years into the description of what in the sciences would be called "general theory." Freud, however, used the word specifically to describe mental phenomena in their relationship to the psychic apparatus, to the instincts involved and to the distribution within the apparatus of the energy generated.

The aim of the series, he stated, was "to clarify and carry deeper the theoretical assumptions on which a psychoanalytic system could be founded." It is perhaps surprising that only at this point, some twenty years after *Studies on Hysteria* had launched psychoanalysis on the world, did he find it necessary to create a new and more complicated structure into which it would be possible to fit his observations of the previous two decades. Yet in itself this supports Freud's constant assertion that his prognostications on the workings of the mind were the result not of theorizing but of careful clinical observation. Most of his first attempt to build an encompassing theoretical structure, the long-unpublished "Project," had soon been abandoned, and what remained had been reshaped to become the final chapter of *The Interpretation of Dreams;* a number of his subsequent works had included short discussions on theory, but not until 1915—with a dearth of patients and more time on his hands—did he turn to the task once more.

The first two papers, "Instincts and Their Vicissitudes" and "Repression," were completed within three weeks. The third, "The Unconscious," took no longer and contained an elaboration of the central idea on which Freud had built the whole of psychoanalysis. It was followed by "A Metapsychological Supplement to the Theory of Dreams" and by "Mourning and Melancholia."

Whether Freud ever did write the rest of the essays is unclear, and conflicting evidence is provided by his letters to Lou Andreas-Salomé. On July 30, 1915, he wrote to her of a "book consisting of twelve essays" and reported that it was "finished except for the necessary revision caused by the arranging and fitting in of the individual essays." Yet some four years later, on April 2, 1919, he told her that his *Metapsychology* had "not yet been written" but went on to add that a further contribution to it would "be found in an essay of mine entitled 'Beyond the Pleasure Principle.' "

With the first five metapsychological essays finished, Freud began to prepare for his usual lectures at the university. They were to be given from October to March, during the winter terms of 1915–16 and 1916–17, to doctors and laymen drawn from all faculties. Unlike his other university lectures, they were to be published, thus revealing for the first time to a wider public the masterly way in which he encouraged his listeners to follow his arguments; but with the air of assumed modesty he often displayed, Freud himself disparaged his work in private correspondence, describing the lectures to Lou as "crude stuff meant for the masses."

They were delivered every Saturday, from seven to nine, in a room at the Vienna Psychiatric Clinic, and it is a measure of Freud's ability as a lecturer that he not only managed to hold his audience for two unbroken hours—usually without notes—but that the audience grew from about seventy to more than a hundred. In his preface to the lectures, published as *Introductory Lectures on Psycho-Analysis,* he cautioned that in the circumstances it "was not possible . . . to preserve the unruffled calm of a scientific treatise." Neither was it possible to avoid starting with a warning. Thus he began by saying that among his listeners there might be one who was not satisfied with a casual knowledge of psychoanalysis but might decide to enter into a more permanent relationship with it. "As things stand at present, such a choice of profession would ruin any chance he might have of success at a University," he pointed out, "and if he started in life as a practicing physician, he would find himself in a society which did not understand his efforts, which regarded him with distrust and hostility, and unleashed upon him all the evil spirits lurking within it."

Four lectures dealt with parapraxes, and at the end of the fourth Freud asked how it was that men and women continued to attribute them to chance and opposed their psychoanalytic elucidation with such vigor. He himself would not give the answer. "Instead," he said, "I will introduce you by degrees to fields of knowledge from which the explanation will force itself upon you without any contribution of mine."

His fields of knowledge were those of dreams, and for the rest of the session the audience listened to eleven lectures on the subject. Freud admitted the difficulties of interpretation, explained how they could be overcome and steadily led his listeners into an understanding of the manner in which dreams contained the key to the unconscious. "There is nothing else," he pointed out in the last lecture of the season, "from which one can so quickly arrive at a conviction of the correctness of the theses by which psychoanalysis stands or falls."

When the first series of lectures was finished, Freud made one of his rare spring excursions from Vienna. There was a special reason for this, since his son Oliver was helping to build a new and strategic railway tunnel under the Carpathians to improve the Berlin–Constantinople route. Freud visited him and was taken for a long walk up through the forest to the crest of the Jablunka Pass. After that they came down to the tunnel entrance, and Oliver gave his father a guided tour of the project that involved scrambling up, down and around a series of ladders, leading them deep into the heart of the mountain. Then they visited the nearby town of Teschen, where Freud had begun the "Project" some twenty years previously and where many of his books had since been printed in the big Prohaska works.

Freud returned from the Carpathians to a Vienna where the privations of the war were already beginning to be felt. He left in July for what was to be a shorter holiday than usual; first at Bad Gastein, then on to Salzburg, staying at the Hotel Bristol, where the first Congress had been held; then back to Bad Gastein before returning to Vienna and settling down to write the lectures he was to give in October.

At the start of the series he warned his listeners that he would not now be dealing with parapraxes and dreams—matters of which they had personal knowledge—but with the neuroses, phenomena which would be strange to all except the doctors in his audience. Even here, he disarmingly explained, he would use the same technique as during the previous year. "I do not wish to arouse conviction," he said; "I wish to stimulate thought and to upset prejudices. If as a result of lack of knowledge of the material you are not in a position to form a judgment, you should neither believe nor reject. You should listen and allow what I tell you to work on you." After which the audience was led with considerable persuasiveness through the general theory of the neuroses.

The *Introductory Lectures* were published in three separate parts, in 1916 and 1917, and became, with the possible exception of *The Psychopathology of Everyday Life*, the most read of all Freud's works, being translated into fourteen languages before his death and into another three after it.

Freud well knew that the lectures were, for the layman, one of the clearest expositions of psychoanalysis. They were also a considerable financial success. Nevertheless, the months that followed their conclusion in March 1917 found him even more then usually depressed. One reason, no doubt, was that in May he would be sixty-one years old, the age at which he had once convinced himself he was due to die. There was also growing pessimism about the outcome of the war, and it was clear that there would be increasing shortages of food and fuel during the autumn and winter. In addition to these material problems there was the unresolved fate of anything whose success rested on international acceptance.

Freud had continued to keep the word "International" on the title page of the *Zeitschrift,* but it was becoming more and more obvious that Von Schlieffen's unsuccessful attempt to capture Paris by invading neutral Belgium in 1914 had shocked world opinion and made it certain that international cooperation would be rebuilt but slowly when peace eventually came.

> Life bears too heavily on me [Freud wrote to Abraham in the summer]. I talk very little about this, because I know that others would take such statements as complaints and signs of depression, and not as objective descriptions, which would be unfair to me. I believe I have had my time, and I am not more depressed than usual, that is to say, I am very little depressed, and console myself with the assurance that my work lies in the good hands of men such as you and Ferenczi, and perhaps some others, who will carry it on. . . .

Meanwhile he began searching around for ideas that would give additional support to psychoanalysis. In 1917 he even turned to Lamarck. Early in the nineteenth century the French naturalist had put forward a theory of evolution which relied heavily on the idea that characteristics acquired by one generation could be passed on to the next. Even before the advent of Darwin the idea had begun to wither from lack of evidence, and by the start of the twentieth century it had become almost totally discredited. This did not deter Freud, who began to discuss the potential implications with Ferenczi. "The idea," he confided to Abraham,

> is to put Lamarck entirely on our ground and to show that the "necessity" that, according to him, creates and transforms organs is nothing but the power of unconscious ideas over one's own body, of which we see remnants in hysteria, in short the "omnipotence of thoughts." This would actually supply a psychoanalytic explanation of adaptation; it would put the coping stone on psychoanalysis.

Superficially it might appear that Freud, anxious about the unremitting attacks on psychoanalysis, was desperately grasping at any idea which might help the defense. It was not entirely so, since a belief in Lamarckism runs through the whole of his life. Indeed, in the 1930s the belief acquired an arrogance typified by the way in which he finished an argument with one visitor. Told that he was accepting the inheritance of acquired characteristics, Freud replied, "Of course, if one didn't believe in inheritance, there would be a great deal we could not explain." Then, told that most biologists did not agree, he settled the question with the words: "Psychoanalysis cannot accommodate itself to the beliefs of biologists —we must go our own way." Little wonder that Freud's Lamarckian tendencies were, as one of his strongest adherents admitted, "much regretted by many of us."

In 1917 Freud had at least a few things for which to be thankful. His two sons on active service had survived unscathed, as they were to survive until the end of the war, although Martin had been almost continuously at the front in either Galicia or Russia, and Ernst had had more than one narrow escape on the frontier with Italy. Only one of Freud's relatives, Herman Graf, the son of his sister Rosa, was to be killed. His married daughter Mathilde was living in Vienna, as was Anna, and apart from the constant thought of Martin and Ernst at the battlefront, his family problems at first consisted mainly of the difficulty of keeping in touch with his daughter Sophie in Hamburg.

But by the autumn the prospects of the Central Powers obstinately refused to brighten, living conditions became harder, and the only thing certain about the future was the coming shortage of food and fuel. However, a few events tended to lighten Freud's gloom. One was receipt of a letter from Georg Groddeck, a doctor working in a Baden-Baden military hospital. A man of unorthodox methods, Groddeck had for long defended them with a vigor which, of itself, would have earned Freud's encouragement. However, the gist of his letter was that he had successfully treated a patient in 1909 with methods which he now believed were those of psychoanalysis; but, he went on, he did not want to label himself a psychoanalyst if he was to be rejected by the leader of the movement.

"I arrived at my, or should I say your, views" he went on,

> not by studying neuroses but by observing complaints which are commonly called organic I owe my reputation as a doctor originally to my activities as a physiotherapist, more specifically as a masseur. For this reason my circle of patients is probably different from that of a psychoanalyst. Long before I met the above-mentioned patient in 1909 I had become convinced that the distinction between body and mind is only verbal and not essential, that body and mind are one unit, that they contain an It, a force which lives us while we believe we are living. Naturally I cannot claim this idea for myself, either, yet it was and is the basis of my activity. In other words, from

the first I rejected a separation of bodily and mental illnesses, tried to treat the individual patient, the It in him, and attempted to find a way into the unexplored and inaccessible regions. I am aware of the fact that I am at least close to the mystical approach, if not actually engaged in it. And yet simple facts force me to continue on this way.

Freud, greatly impressed by the fact that Groddeck was treating organic disease by psychological means, replied cordially. He had reservations, and there was always to remain a difference between Groddeck's and Freud's conception of the It. But here was one more recruit to the cause, and a potentially useful one.

Another event which gave Freud encouragement was the news that he had been proposed for a Nobel Prize. There had, in fact, been an earlier occasion when in 1914 the American psychiatrist W. A. White had been lobbying for Freud's name to be proposed; but nothing came of this and Freud himself does not seem to have known of the plan. Now his name was put forward by Robert Bárány, who had been awarded the Prize for Physiology and Medicine in 1914. But Freud had mixed feelings, since some years earlier he had refused to take Bárány as a pupil, and on hearing of his Nobel award had written sourly that it had "aroused sad thoughts about how helpless an individual is about gaining the respect of the crowd. You know it is only the money that would matter to me, and perhaps the spice of annoying some of my compatriots. But it would be ridiculous to expect a sign of recognition when one has seven-eighths of the world against one." To Lou Andreas-Salomé he wrote of a possible award: "I don't think I shall live to see the day, even if they no longer continue to postpone awarding it." He was right. There was no Nobel Prize after Bárány's proposal, nor after the similar effort later made by Romain Rolland, Arnold Zweig and others. "I got over the Nobel Prize passing me by for the second time excellently, and have also realized that any such official recognition would fit not at all into my style of life," he told Abraham. Eventually, an emigrant in England and within a year of his death, he decided that if by any strange chance that award was ever offered, he would refuse it. He was never allowed the pleasure.

Amid the gathering gloom of autumn 1917 there was one other small spark of encouragement: the British had captured Jerusalem and had issued the Balfour Declaration, which promised support for the establishment of a Jewish national home in Palestine—"the only thing that gives me any pleasure," as Freud described it to Abraham.

Yet although he was by now so deep in depression, the prospects for psychoanalysis were already slowly improving. In the United States Putnam could ask, at the Eighth Annual Meeting of the American Psychopathological Association, "Who would have dreamed, a decade or more ago, that today college professors would be teaching Freud's doctrines to students of both sexes, scientific men turning to them for light on the nature of the instincts and educators for hints on the training of the young?" In England the influential Wilfred Trotter, who had not thought it worthwhile to listen to Freud at the Salzburg Conference in 1908, was qualifying his views. While he noted "a certain harshness in [Freud's] grasp of facts and even a trace of narrowness in his outlook which tend to repel the least resistant mind and make one feel that his guidance in many matters—perhaps chiefly of detail —is open to suspicion," he added, ". . . Nevertheless with regard to the main propositions of his system there can be little doubt that their *general validity* will be increasingly accepted. . . ." And readers of *The Lancet,* which printed W. H. R. Rivers' paper on "Freud's Psychology of the Unconscious," read to the Edinburgh Pathological Club in March 1917, were asked if the medical profession was "to reject a helping hand with contumely because it sometimes leads us to discover unpleasant aspects of human nature and because it comes from Vienna?"

The reason for this change of emphasis within the medical profession was that its members were by now having to deal with a growing number of war casualties suffering from shell shock. In earlier wars, it is true, there had been cases of men breaking down mentally under the stress of battle, but their numbers had been small in comparison with those suffering from physical wounds or from disease. Static trench warfare on the Western Front, combined with heavy artillery bombardments, swiftly changed the situation, and interest in the nervous affections of battle steadily increased. Neurologists were attached to military hospitals, and nerve cases were studied in as much detail as were surgical and medical cases. As Freud was to write in 1920: "The terrible war which has just ended gave rise to a great number of illnesses of this kind [traumatic neuroses] but it at least put an end to the temptation to attribute the cause of the disorder to organic lesions of the nervous system brought about by mechanical force."

In the British Army more than one psychiatrist paid tribute to the value of the methods which were being virulently decried only a few years previously. Thus David Eder, having been commissioned into the Royal Army Medical Corps and put in charge of the psychoneurological department in Malta, described in *War-Shock: The Psycho-Neuroses in War Psychology and Treatment* the first one hundred consecutive cases of psychoneurosis that came under his care there. In only six of them could psychoanalysis, "the only method with which I am acquainted that lays bare the innermost secrets," be used for therapy; furthermore, military needs required that the patients be whisked away before treatment could be completed. Nevertheless here was Freud's method being used in an Army hospital. It was described, moreover, by an author who added that ". . . in some cases sex, in the form of the typical Oedipus myth, is very clearly brought out, while in other cases it was highly probable that adequate psychoanalysis would have laid bare a sexual complex which again would have shown to be itself symbolic of the individual's maladaptation."

Another indication of a changing attitude was given by C. Stanford Read, an R.A.M.C. major who had been in charge of a psychiatric block in another military hospital. In *Military Psychiatry in Peace and War* he quoted the passage in Freud's Clark University lectures describing the aggressive way in which doctors treated hysteria and continued: "This is unfortunately true enough, and Freud's remarks largely hold good for most mental disorders. Such an outlook can only be gradually eradicated by education, and this applies to civil as well as military psychiatry."

More important than either Eder or Read in breaking down the resistance against psychoanalysis by using it in the treatment of war casualties was W. H. R. Rivers, who in the spring of 1915 had joined the staff of the Maghull Military Hospital in Lancashire. This was a hospital extraordinarily enlightened for its times where, it has been said, the newcomer was "introduced to a society in which the interpretation of dreams and the discussion of mental conflicts formed the staple subjects of conversation." Rivers was later posted to the even more famous Craiglockhart Hospital, on the outskirts of Edinburgh, where he was responsible for about a hundred shell-shock patients, and it was while there that he gave the paper to the Edinburgh Pathological Club which stressed the significance of the war for psychoanalysis. "It is a wonderful turn of fate," he said in it,

> that just as Freud's theory of the unconscious and the method of psychoanalysis founded upon it should be so hotly discussed, there should have occurred events which have produced on an enormous scale just those conditions of paralysis and contracture, phobia and obsession, which the theory was especially designed to explain. Fate would seem to have presented us at the present time with an unexampled opportunity to test the truth of Freud's theory of the unconscious, in so far as it is concerned with the production of mental and functional nervous disorder.

He concluded by saying that it was agreed that mental disorders were due to the

> individual experience of the patient as well as of that ancestral experience which we call heredity. Of this ancestral experience and to a large extent of the individual experience, everyone will acknowledge that it is not accessible to the manifest consciousness of the patient and cannot be learnt from him by the ordinary methods of obtaining the history of the patient and his illness. The great merit of Freud is that he has provided us with a theory of the mechanism by which this experience, not readily and directly accessible to consciousness, produces its effects, while he and his followers have devised clinical methods by which these hidden factors in the causation of disease may be brought to light. For the physician who is not content to walk in the old ruts when in the presence of the greatest afflictions which can befall mankind, Freud has provided a working scheme of diagnosis and therapeutics to aid him in his attempts to discover the causes of mental disorder and to find means by which it may be remedied.

Rivers found, as Freud had found two decades earlier, that specific symptoms could be linked with specific traumatic events, and that when the memories were recovered the symptoms disappeared. Typical, he later reported, was that of an Army doctor who found himself unable to enter dugouts or other underground shelters. In childhood the officer had been attacked by a dog in a dark passage. When the incident was revealed, the phobia disappeared. Various mental abnormalities brought to the surface in battle had, Rivers went on, the common feature that they unfitted their subject for further participation in warfare, and thus solved the conflict between duty and the dangers that attended it.

Freud knew nothing of the developments in Britain and appears to have had little contact with the treatment of shell-shock cases in Austria. However, he may have been alerted to the possibilities by Victor Tausk. Called up as an Army psychiatrist in 1915, Tausk published a paper the following year on "Diagnostic Considerations Concerning the Symptomatology of the So-called War-psychoses." He was not alone in Europe in considering how psychoanalysis might be used in the treatment of war psychotics, and in February 1918 Freud received an eighty-four-page paper on "War Neuroses and Psychic Trauma" written by Ernst Simmel, a German doctor who on the outbreak of war had been posted to a field hospital as a medical staff officer. Simmel soon adopted what was considered a revolutionary policy: that of treating men who had broken down mentally under the strain of action as patients rather than as malingerers. He used hypnosis—as Freud had done some thirty years earlier—and he had constructed a human dummy on which his patients could discharge their repressed aggression.

"Few communications from beginners in psychoanalysis who are personally unknown to me have provided me with so much satisfaction as your article . . . ," Freud wrote in acknowledging the paper. He went on to criticize Simmel's use of hypnosis, but added, "I can understand very well and can approve of the reasons you give for it: the vast number of patients, the short time available, and the necessity for therapeutic success. I myself would reach back for the hypnotic method if faced with similar case material and for certain psychoses." Freud was in no doubt about the significance of the paper. "This is the first time that a German physician, basing himself firmly and without patronizing condescension on psychoanalysis, speaks of its outstanding usefulness in the treatment of war neuroses, backs this with examples, and is also completely honest on the question of sexual aetiology," he wrote to Abraham. ". . . I think a year's training would make a good analyst of him. His attitude is correct."

A few months earlier Simmel had submitted to the German Secretary of State for War a plan for the formation of a psychoanalytic institute for research on the neuroses, together with a clinic where advice would be given free and a sanatorium where patients could be treated. No decision appears to have been taken on this proposal. Nevertheless, the Germans were induced to send an official representative to the International Congress organized by Freud and his followers in 1918, and Austria and Hungary did likewise.

At first Breslau was chosen as the location, but this was later changed to Budapest, and here the Congress was held in September. Significantly, there were no Swiss, and of the forty-two men attending, three were Dutch, three German; the rest came from the tottering Austro-Hungarian Empire, and Freud must have had mixed feelings as he realized the reasons behind the first flicker of official interest from the Central Powers. Psychoanalysis, devised to unravel the mysteries of the mind and to alleviate human suffering, was now being considered as a means of sending men back to the battlefront as quickly as possible.

However, by the time the delegates assembled in the Hungarian Academy of Sciences on September 28, it seemed unlikely that the battlefront would exist in any form for very much longer. Two weeks earlier the Austro-Hungarian authorities had sent a peace offer to the Allies, and although this had been brusquely rejected, it was obvious that the great Empire, to whose capital Freud had come nearly sixty years before, was in the final stages of collapse.

On the second, and final, day of the Congress, neighboring Bulgaria signed an armistice with the advancing Allies, and even Paul von Hindenburg, chief of the German general staff, demanded that his government should sue for peace. Despite these ominous events, which were soon to bring Austria-Hungary to an end, the Budapest authorities gave psychoanalysis a luxurious welcome, putting a steamer on the Danube at the disposal of the delegates and organizing a splendid series of banquets and receptions.

The Congress, at which Ferenczi was elected the new president, was notable not only for Simmel's paper, which proposed the setting up of psychoanalytic clinics and which, in the words of one commentator, created a sensation; in addition, it was announced that the recurrent problem of funding the Association's publications, aggravated by wartime shortages and by the inflation which was already beginning to grip the Central Powers, had now been solved. Anton von Freund, an exceedingly wealthy Budapest brewer, friend of both Ferenczi and Freud, had agreed to finance the Association's own publishing house, a generous decision whose results were to be limited by the financial chaos of the peace, now only two months away.

Freud's paper, "Turnings in the Ways of Psycho-Analytic Therapy," was on its own account as much of an innovation as Simmel's. For once he read, instead of speaking from rough notes or none at all. He had said to Hanns Sachs that "a man who reads a paper word for word is like a host who invites a friend for an automobile trip and then gets into the car and lets the guest run along behind"; he probably made this an exception for one reason alone: he wanted to keep strictly to the letter of the proposals he had thought about with such care. Freud envisaged a future in which psychoanalysis would slowly but inevitably become available to all who needed it:

> Then clinics and consultation departments will be built to which analytically trained physicians will be appointed, so that the men who would otherwise give way to drink, the women who have nearly succumbed under their burden of privations, the children for whom there is no choice but running wild or neurosis, may be made by analysis able to resist and able to do something in the world. This treatment will be free. It may be a long time before the State regards this as an urgent duty. Present conditions may delay its arrival even longer; probably these institutions will first be started by private beneficence; some time or other, however, it must come.

Freud's belief in "psychoanalysis for all" had previously been rather ambivalent. Not too much should be made of his statement to the Vienna Psychoanalytical Society that there are two classes of human beings who are comparatively free from neurosis: "proletarians and princes." Neither class, it has been pointed out, sought psychoanalytic advice in the years before the First World War. Yet Freud qualified his regret that analytic therapy was almost unattainable for the poor. "Little can be done to remedy this," he had then admitted. "Perhaps there is some truth in the widespread belief that those who are forced by necessity to a life of heavy labor succumb less easily to neurosis. But at all events experience shows without a doubt that, in this class, a neurosis once acquired is only with very great difficulty eradicated. . . . The pity which the world has refused to his material distress the sufferer now claims by right of his neurosis and absolves himself from the obligation of combating his poverty by work. . . ."

He still retained the view when concluding his paper at Budapest. "We shall," he prophesied, "probably discover that the poor are even less ready to part with their neuroses than the rich, because the hard life that awaits them when they recover has no attraction, and illness in them gives them more claim to the help of others."

Some time was to elapse before even the faintest evidence was to be available to suggest whether he was right or wrong. Freud spoke toward the end of September 1918. On the last day of the month, with the German forces on the Western Front in full retreat, the German Chancellor resigned, and four days later a German-Austrian note to the United States asked for an armistice. Austria-Hungary signed on November 5, Germany on the eleventh, and within weeks both empires were disintegrating. In the northwest of Austria the people declared a Czechoslovak Republic. In the south an independent Yugoslavia came into being. In Vienna a republic was declared on November 11; in Budapest, four days later.

THE
FREUDIAN
AGE

17

Reaping the Whirlwind

I always thought that my theory would be seized upon at first by scoundrels and speculators.

FREUD, in a letter to Paul Häberlin and Ludwig Binswanger

The First World War had swept away more than the stern authoritarianism of the Kaiser's Germany and the Ruritanian contrasts of the Austro-Hungarian Empire. It had also destroyed the security of the middle classes who in Vienna, perhaps more than elsewhere in Europe, had provided the ballast which in the postwar world might have kept the ship of state on an even keel. In many ways they were typified by Freud, who had only reluctantly begun to suspect the Central Powers' plea of a just war, and had subsequently believed in the promises of President Wilson's Fourteen Points. His disillusion in the immediate postwar debacle was that much greater, and in 1921 he was still maintaining that a better understanding of psychoanalysis might have altered history, by implication for the better: "the hard treatment of the men by their superiors may be considered as foremost among the motive forces of [the war neuroses]. If the importance of the libido's claims on this score had been better appreciated, the fantastic promises of the American President's Fourteen Points would probably not have been believed so easily, and the splendid instrument [the German Army] would not have broken in the hands of the German leaders."

During the war he and his colleagues had often, as Hanns Sachs recalled, sat "in the unheated study in our overcoats and gloves, with our hats on our heads, suffering from the emptiness of our stomachs and frostbites on our hands." Now, as the country tried to struggle back to normalcy, there was little alleviation of the shortages of food and fuel. Marginal improvements were soon more than counterbalanced by the financial collapse which, with the value of the currency falling hour by hour, caused family savings to evaporate overnight. Austria and Germany were paying a grim price for the war, a circumstance which tended to keep alive Freud's underlying feeling that the Central Powers had not been unreservedly guilty. "It is too early to reach any conclusion which will have the slightest scientific value," he said of the war to a visiting American; "at least 10 years must elapse before we can approach this whole subject with the essential impartiality. Possibly a foreigner, who can look at the situation objectively, might arrive at the truth. But it would have to be one who not only knows the conditions, but who knew them before."

Direct and uncensored communication between Austria and Britain was reopened in April 1919, and within a few days Freud received a letter from Jones, "the first window opening in our cage," as he described it and the first of a series in which the future of the cause was to be discussed. Early in May came news from Samuel Freud of the relatives in England. Sigmund's nephew John had left his parents' home and was not to be heard of again. But Samuel was successfully carrying on his father's business; his sisters Pauline and Bertha—first "the girls" in Freud's regular letters to England that were now resumed, finally "the old ladies"—were both well.

Freud replied at once to Samuel with his own news, writing as he was always to write, in good if sometimes idiosyncratic English:

We are passing through bad times as you know by the papers, privations and uncertainty all around. Martin is still a prisoner near Genova, seems to be in good condition judging by his letters. Martha has just recovered from a severe attack of influenza-pneumonia, but she will be all right in a few weeks.

Ernest is staying at Munich, got his diploma as architect in these troublesome days [when a Soviet-style republic had been set up in Bavaria]. You know already I presume that Sophie has borne a second son—Heinz—now five months old. She is now at Hamburg with her husband.

Give my best love to your dear mother, Pauline and Bertha, and believe me,

Ever your affectionate
Sigm.

Within a few months it had become possible to send food from Britain to Austria, where conditions were still worsening, and Samuel wrote asking how badly off the family was, and what they would like sent.

Life is very hard with us [Freud replied], I do not know what the English papers tell you, maybe they don't exaggerate. The majority of provisions and the deterioration of money are pressing mostly on the middle classes and on those who earn their livelihood by intellectual work. You must keep in view that all of us have lost 19/20 of what we possessed in cash, that Austria never could produce as much as it wanted, that not only the former provinces of the Empire but also our own countries are boycotting Vienna in the most reckless way, that industry has come to a dead stop by want of coal and materials and that buying and importing from the foreign countries is impossible, when a crown is much less than a [British] penny (240=430 crowns). We are living on small diet (the first herring some days ago was a treat to me) no meat, not enough bread, no milk, potatoes and eggs extremely dear, at least in crowns.

But, he continued, they had been saved from the worst of suffering by the help sent by Eli, his brother-in-law in the United States, who was now a very rich man. His mother and two of his sisters had been sent for the winter to Ischl in the Salzkammergut of western Austria, where conditions were not as harsh as they were in Vienna, while Minna had gone to southern Germany until conditions improved. All his three sons had come safely through the war, and although he gave no further news of Martin he was able to report that both Ernst and Oliver the engineer had already found work—something of an achievement in the desperate conditions of postwar Austria. "As for me," he went on,

you know I have a big name and plenty of work but I cannot gain [earn] enough and am eating up my reserves.
In answer to your kind offer I give you a short list of the articles of food which we need most; fat, corned beef, cocoa, tea, english cake and what-not. But I warn you not to send anything unless you can send to the address of the English military mission at Vienna or it is *sure* to get lost on the railway. It would be a pity and I cannot imagine that you are eager to feed the customs officials or the railway workmen. If you cannot find the right way, I am sorry to say, your charming good-will may prove of no advantage for us.
I will send you a photograph in a few days executed by Max (Sophie's husband at Hamburg) which I hope you will still recognize, however changed the subject may be.
Give my love to your mother and sisters. We are so glad Ma has recovered,

Yours affectionately and thankfully,
Sigm.

Freud's letter was the signal for Samuel and his sisters to launch a succession of food parcels. The contents helped their Viennese relatives through the darkest months of the next two years, and their correspondence contains many cards and brief letters recording the despatch, and receipt, of coffee, tea, margarine and corned beef, eventually packed so that the margarine should not, in Freud's words, "become mixed with the tea and the cocoa in a mischevious [sic] way by the length of the journey." Martha preferred not only the expected tinned milk, oats and extract of meat but also spices such as white pepper and cinnamon, while Freud himself put in a word for cheese and marmalade.

There were other sources of help, from friends and pupils who brought food from Holland and Switzerland, while payment to Samuel presented no difficulty. Freud was soon accumulating funds in Amsterdam and was able to ask British or American patients or trainees to settle Samuel's bills in lieu of fees. James Strachey, for instance, paid part of his training fees with a £28 check to Manchester.

With food arrangements moving smoothly, other items could be asked for: a pair of boots and material for a new suit—"a soft Shetland cloth—pepper and salt or mouse-grey or Tête-de-nègre in colour" as Freud requested. Anna put in her own request for a dozen tennis balls, only to hear from Samuel that "tennis balls, not being articles of necessity, may not be included in parcels sent through the 'food' Agency to Vienna."

Such articles, as well as larger quantities of food, could apparently have been sent if Freud had filled in the necessary import forms but, as he protested, he had something better to do. "My time at least is still precious . . . ," he told Samuel and, after learning that he would be welcome in Britain, had reluctantly replied: "But business is very brisk now, so you will have to wait" —no doubt a reference to the Americans and British who were now coming to him for analysis or training.

In the summer of 1919 he had contrived to take his usual summer holiday in the Alps. But travel was difficult, and he reported to Ernst, who had survived the Communist revolution in Munich, and its suppression, on the "dreadful journey" to Bad Gastein. Here he joined Minna, who had been living in the town for a few weeks. Postal communications had virtually stopped, but he was able to keep contact with other members of the family by telegraph. Food was in better supply than in Vienna, and his only complaint concerned the shortage of cigars.

Returning home in the autumn, he found that his services were still much in demand, a fact which he did not want to be overlooked in Britain. Thus, after sending his love to "the girls," he added: "Are they aware that my name in the world at large and in England, too, is far more respectable than my riches?" Then, realizing that he might have been misunderstood, he explained in his next letter: "I am anxious that you could misconstrue my question about renown in England. I wanted to know how much of the noise had reached your quiet home. Popularity itself is utterly indifferent to me, must at the best be considered a danger for more serious achievements."

Moves to consolidate those achievements had begun soon after the first postwar letter from Jones, who optimistically believed that an International Congress could, and should, be held later in the year. "The Committee exists," he went on, "not only to direct the external side of the psychoanalytic movements, but also to coordinate the internal, scientific side, and so I hold it highly desirable that a couple of weeks before the Congress we have a private congress of our own for about a week, to discuss (1) plans and programs ready to be submitted to the congress etc. and (2) purely scientific problems of a more difficult and technical nature than those usually discussed in public." Freud should remember, he continued, that they had not been in touch with each other for some years and that it was essential that they presented a united front when international relations were resumed; "(Unity of command; the great cry of the Entente for the last two years)," he concluded.

Jones's letter was received with caution, some optimism and some pessimism. "I am still upright and hold myself not responsible for any part of the world's nonsense," wrote Freud in reply. "Psychoanalysis is flourishing I am glad to learn from everywhere. I trust that science will prove a consolation for you too."

He had barely begun to discuss plans for the future when, early in July 1919, there came a severe shock. The meetings of the Vienna branch of the International Association had been resumed, and on the morning of Wednesday, the second, Freud received a brief note from Victor Tausk, announcing that he would not be present that evening. "I am occupied in solving the decisive affairs of my life and I do not want by contact with you to be tempted to wish to resort to your help," this went. "I shall probably soon be free again to approach you. I intend to appear with a minimum of neurosis.

"In the meantime I remain with cordial respectful regards, gratefully yours, Tausk."

The note in itself was not particularly surprising. Since Tausk's return to Vienna from war service the previous November his relations with Freud had become steadily more difficult. He had resumed his psychoanalytic practice, but his considerable talent had been hobbled by two things: a growing feeling of rivalry with Freud, whom he almost obsessively thought of as plagiarizing his ideas, and a pathetically muddled personal life marked by a succession of broken love affairs. In December he had approached Freud, pleading to be taken into analysis. Freud had refused but had sent him to Helene Deutsch, a distinctly unusual procedure since Deutsch was then not only a young and relatively inexperienced analyst but was herself in analysis with Freud. She is reported to have described it as a "devilish arrangement." The situation became even more complicated when, in March 1919, she ended Tausk's analysis, apparently under pressure from Freud.

What Freud thought about the note of July 2 is not known. The shock came the following day, or possibly on the morning of the fourth, when he received a farewell letter from Tausk who had killed himself by blowing off part of his head after putting a noose round his neck, and thereby strangling himself at the same time. After asking Freud to help his fiancée, Tausk's note continued:

> I thank you for all the good which you have done me. It was much and has given meaning to the last ten years of my life. Your work is genuine and great, I shall take leave of this life knowing that I was one of those who witnessed the triumph of one of the greatest ideas of mankind.
>
> I have no melancholy, my suicide is the healthiest, most decent deed of my unsuccessful life. I have no accusations against anyone, my heart is without resentment, I am only dying somewhat earlier than I would have died naturally.
>
> I greet the Psychoanalytic Association, I wish it well with all my heart. I thank all those who helped me when I was in need. Those who have claim to this gratitude will know it for themselves.
>
> I hope you will have a long life, in health, strong and capable of working.
>
> I greet you warmly,
>
> Yours,
> Tausk
>
> Please look after my sons from time to time.

Freud's public reaction to the death of Victor Tausk was given in an obituary published in the *Internationale Zeitschrift für Psychoanalyse* where it was signed "Die Redaktion" (the Editorial Committee). He began rather oddly: "Among the sacrifices, fortunately few in number, claimed by the war from the ranks of psychoanalysis, we must count Dr. Victor Tausk. This rarely-gifted man, a

Vienna specialist in nervous diseases, took his own life before peace was signed." Freud's view that Tausk was "a victim of fate, a delayed victim of the war" was also put forward in a letter to Pfarrer Pfister. In the obituary there followed a eulogy which, after saying that Tausk believed psychoanalysis would be recognized in the near future, concluded: "There is no doubt that this man, of whom our science and his friends in Vienna have been prematurely robbed, has contributed to that aim. He is sure of an honorable memory in the history of psychoanalysis and its earliest struggles."

To Lou Andreas-Salomé, Freud reported that Tausk's farewell letters to his former wife, to the woman he was about to marry, and to Freud himself threw no light on the suicide.

> In his letter to me he swore undying loyalty to psychoanalysis, thanked me, etc. But what was behind it all we cannot guess. After all he spent his days wrestling with the father ghost. I confess that I do not really miss him; I had long realized that he could be of no further service, indeed that he constituted a threat to the future. I had an opportunity of taking a glance or two at the foundations on which his high-flown sublimations rested; and I would have dropped him long ago if *you* hadn't raised him so in my estimation. Of course I was still ready to do anything for his advancement, only latterly I have been quite powerless myself owing to the general deterioration of conditions in Vienna. I never failed to recognize his notable gifts; but they were denied expression in achievements of corresponding value. . . .

It would be remarkable if Tausk had not sensed Freud's feelings, and ingenuous to believe that they can have played no part in his suicide. But on the day of his death he was to have obtained a license to marry Hilde Loewi, a concert pianist sixteen years his junior who had for a brief while been his patient. With one failed marriage behind him and a string of equally failed liaisons, it seems possible that the future, with or without Freud's support, was more than he could face. His solution is not unknown even among men who have never taken psychoanalysis seriously.

In Freud's reaction to Tausk's death there is a contrast between public eulogy and private disavowal that cannot entirely be explained away by the difference between professional judgment and personal sentiment. It is also unfortunate that Freud's private emotions were concealed when the correspondence between himself and Lou Andreas-Salomé was first published in 1966; the vital sentences of criticism were removed on Anna Freud's instructions. She had, she subsequently explained, heard from one of Tausk's sons. "Evidently the memory of his father, whom he lost very early, is of the greatest concern to him," she wrote. ". . . If he read in print such a statement by my father this would have very bad consequences, which must be avoided under all circumstances."

Two years later, however, a young American professor, Paul Roazen, printed the unexpurgated text of Freud's letter in a book dealing with Freud and Tausk for which he was mercilessly savaged by Freud's disciples. The cut was restored when the English edition of the Freud–Lou letters was published in 1972.

In the summer of 1919 Freud was engrossed in the task of re-establishing psychoanalysis in the postwar world, a task that had absolute priority. In particular, certain things had to be done. First, the international links which had been broken for more than four years had to be restored. Then the wilder excesses of pseudo-psychoanalysis, which he had for long feared might discredit the cause, had to be brought under some sort of control. "I always thought that my theory would be seized upon at first by scoundrels and speculators," he had told Paul Häberlin and Ludwig Binswanger before the war; in its aftermath the iconoclasm which swept away so many standards and traditions of the nineteenth century had left the ground clear for just such extravagances as well as for genuine psychoanalysis. In addition, looming in the background, he felt the need to extend the metapsychology he had begun to create during the war and which was eventually to involve restructuring the foundations on which psychoanalysis was built.

Restoration of prewar links was hampered both by physical conditions on the Continent far worse than Jones, or most others in Britain, could easily appreciate, and by a bitterness toward the Central Powers that Freud, in his turn, was hardly able to understand.

Jones, with an encouraging forecast of more food and money in the fairly near future, was told in reply: "But it strikes me that you did not add in clear language where that plentiness should be, with ourselves or in England." And Jones's suggestion for an early International Congress was brusquely brushed aside with the blunt rebuke that he knew "nothing of the conditions we live in" and had learned nothing from the papers. Travel was still difficult, and after being asked where he was to spend the summer, Freud replied:

It all depends on the state of Europe in general and of this neglected unhappy corner in particular, on the signing of peace, on the improvement of our money, the opening of the borders, etc., and there is a great probability things will not be better two months hence than they are now. . . . I can't remember a time of my life when my horizon was so thickly veiled by dark clouds, or if so I was younger then and not vexed by the ailments of beginning old age. I know you had a bad time and bitter experiences yourself, and feel extremely sorry I have nothing better to report and no consolation to offer. When we meet, as I trust we shall in this year, you will find I am still unshaken and up to every emergency, but it is only in sentiment, my judgment is on the side of pessimism.

To his friend Ludwig Binswanger in Switzerland, he wrote: "Only the cause flourishes."

There were to be ample personal grounds for Freud's pessimism. Before the end of the year Anton von Freund, whose earlier generosity was to help launch the psychoanalytical publishing house in Vienna, was dying of cancer. "I go to have a look on him every day," Freud told Jones, "but it is not merry. . . ."

However, shortly after Freund's death, Freud had to face up to a far more bitter event: the sudden death in January 1920 of his daughter Sophie from the virulent influenza which was sweeping across an ill-nourished Europe. For Freud, whose three sons had come safely through the war, Sophie's death was a savage blow and one which confirmed his belief that if there were indeed a God, then He moved in a particularly mysterious way. Postal links between Austria and Northern Germany were uncertain, and a visit from relatives in Vienna to the distraught widower in Hamburg would have involved great complications. Freud responded with a letter to Max which was taken to Berlin by a friend who there posted it to Hamburg. "It seems to me," he said,

that I have never written anything more superfluous than this. You know how deeply we feel for you. We know how badly you yourself must feel. But I won't try to comfort you, just as you cannot comfort us. Perhaps you feel that I do not know what it means to lose a beloved wife and the mother of one's children, because I have not had to endure the experience. You are right, but I know how unbearable it must be to survive such an experience. I need not tell you that this misfortune does not change anything in my feelings towards you and that you remain our son as long as you wish to do so. It goes without saying that this follows from our earlier relationship. So why do I write to you? I think it is only because we are separated, and that in these miserable times we cannot meet, and thus I cannot say to you the things which I say to mother and to brothers and sisters. It is a senseless brutal act of fate which has taken our Sophie from us, something that one cannot wrack one's brain about, a blow under which we have to bow our heads, poor helpless human beings that we are. I think she was happy as long as she was with you, despite the difficult times of your short seven-year marriage, and her happiness was due to you.

Mama is completely broken. She wants to visit you as soon as possible but the nearest date would be the 29th. She wants to know what your plans are regarding the children and your household in the immediate future. I would prefer it if Math[ilde] and Robert [Freud's eldest daughter and her husband] came to you instead of her as I am not too confident of her strength. Math. is clever and warm-hearted. Robert is a good fellow and is very moved by the news. I am also glad that Oliver and Ernst can be close to you and most of all that we all met in the autumn.

Kiss both the boys for their grandfather. Take courage. With the most heartfelt greetings from Papa.

Recovering, Freud turned himself with renewed dedication to promoting the resumption of international relations. It was less easy to bring about than he had anticipated since the emotions aroused, not so complicated but more bitter than those of 1945, made it difficult for even scientists of the opposing sides to meet on the same platform. As late as the 1930s Lord Rutherford—of "science is international, and I trust will ever remain so"—was refusing to meet Fritz Haber, the German chemist who had developed poison gas. A decade earlier, in 1920, an international meeting of psychoanalysts could easily have been shipwrecked on such feelings, and Abraham's first proposal to Freud that an International Congress should be held in Berlin was wildly impractical.

Eventually the Hague was chosen and here, in September 1920, psychoanalysts from most of the belligerent nations, as well as from a number of neutral countries, met for the first International Congress of its kind to be held since the outbreak of war.

It is still pleasant to remember [Freud wrote fourteen years later] how kind our Dutch colleagues were to us starving, shabby Central Europeans. At the end of the Congress they gave us a dinner of really Dutch proportions, for which we were not allowed to pay, but we had also forgotten how to eat. When the *hors d'oeuvres* were handed round, we all enjoyed them but after that we were done; we could not take any more.

The Hague Congress was a considerable success. There was a British contingent of fifteen and a German contingent of eleven. There were sixteen Dutch psychoanalysts, as well as two from the United States, and the total of sixty-two members was made up of Austrians, Hungarians, a Pole and seven Swiss from the newly constituted and pro-Freudian Swiss Psychoanalytical Society. Freud addressed the Congress on "Supplements to the Theory of Dreams," qualifying the statement put forward two decades earlier that all dreams represented wish fulfillments. In addition, he now said, there were punishment dreams—which could be considered in some respects as wish fulfillments of the ego—and traumatic dreams.

The Congress was enlivened by Georg Groddeck, who blotted his copybook in a very distinctive way. He began by introducing himself with the words: "I am a wild analyst," either being ignorant of, or ignoring, the fact that "wild analyst" was the name given to those totally unqualified psychoanalysts frequently advocating free love, who were already getting the cause a bad name. In the words of his biographers: "then he proceeded to speak, in an informal, unorganized discursive demonstration of the process of free association. He made a few friends that day, and several enemies."

His thesis, that organic disease could be treated by psychoanalysis, was illustrated by his theory that visual difficulties were the result of emotional conflicts: not sometimes, but always. Myopia, presbyopia, retinal bleeding, and even organic changes in the eye were all, Groddeck claimed, efforts to defend against forbidden wishes and to express them. "This," it has been remarked, "was too much for most of those in the audience. Ernst Simmel, listening intently, adjusted his thick-lensed spectacles and smiled."

Freud was not particularly worried about the rambling, free-association method of Groddeck's delivery. But he did feel it necessary to ask whether the thesis was meant to be taken seriously or was merely a joke at the expense of the audience. It was, Groddeck replied, quite serious. There was, he maintained, a waking censor, and if "the repressed complexes become too intense, censorship is strengthened and the eye is rendered short-sighted. If this is still not enough, the unconscious destroys the retina with bleeding."

Freud, attracted by Groddeck "in spite of, or perhaps partly because of, his vagaries," as Ernest Jones puts it, accepted the explanation. His condemnation was on different grounds: the doctor had brought his mistress with him, thus deeply offending Freud's sense of propriety.

Only a few months later, Groddeck was to add to his reputation as the cuckoo in the psychoanalytic nest when his novel, *The Seeker of Souls,* was published. Its character can be gauged by the more-in-sorrow-than-in-anger tone of Ernest Jones's circular letter to the members of the Committee:

Ps-A has so many attractions for the popular entertainer that it seems to me better that we official representatives should lay stress on the dignified and scientific aspects, just those which our opponents deny in our work. On the other side it is not necessary for me to disocciate [*sic*] myself from the extreme critics of the book on puritanical lines. Pfister wrote this week to Barbara Low expressing the utmost indignation at its obscenity etc.; and saying that its publication was the severest blow that Ps-A had suffered for years! It appears that a special meeting of the Swiss Society was called to denounce the book, which they did unanimously and in unmeasured language.

The Hague Congress ended on September 11. It was to be followed by others held during the interwar years, at two-year intervals, in Berlin, Salzburg, Bad Homburg, Innsbruck, Oxford, Lucerne, Wiesbaden, Marienbad and Paris. Freud attended only the first but continued, from a watching position in the wings, to keep a control whose firmness declined only slowly with his fading health.

After the Hague Congress he had planned to visit England with Anna. He hoped to see his relatives in Manchester and had also arranged to visit Cambridge. The first setback, however, was that Anna's papers failed to arrive in time. Then, when he was contemplating going on his own, there came news of a family death in Berlin. His sister Marie had some years previously married Morris Freud, one of the cousins of Jacob Freud who in the mid-nineteenth century had emigrated from Galicia to Roumania. Now Morris had died suddenly of a heart attack. "I decided that I had to go back by Berlin in order to see [Marie] and the orphan and had only 4 days left for the trip to England, so I dropped it with a sore heart," he wrote to Samuel after his return to Vienna.

What he did manage to arrange while waiting for Anna's papers to come through was an unconventional tour of Holland—by steamer, canoe, and even on foot—organized by his Dutch hosts. Then he returned to Vienna, leaving Anna in Berlin en route. He barely had time to settle in before being brought into what inaccurately became known as the "Wagner-Jauregg Process," an event midway between inquiry and trial.

Julius von Wagner-Jauregg, professor of psychiatry at the university and director of the psychiatric division of the Vienna General Hospital, had been one of Freud's colleagues during the early 1880s, and their paths had continued to cross. While Freud had been establishing psychoanalysis, Wagner-Jauregg's work had led to the virtual extinction of cretinism in Europe by the countering of iodine deficiency, and to the malarial therapy of general paretics which was to bring him the Nobel Prize in 1927.

Wagner-Jauregg, like a handful of doctors in other hospitals, had been responsible for the psychiatric treatment of many casualties between 1914 and 1918. In the aftermath of defeat there were bitter complaints about the treatment of some troops, particularly by electric-shock methods, and in 1920 the Austrian government set up a commission of investigation. Freud and Emil Raimann, Wagner-Jauregg's assistant, were asked to submit memoranda, and were cross-examined on them when the commission opened on October 15. Due to the importance of Wagner-Jauregg's position, and to the fame of Freud, the hearings soon developed into a debate between their differing views on the treatment of war casualties. Wagner-Jauregg argued that many of the men were malingerers and that a taste of shock treatment soon revealed the fact. Freud argued that the malingerers would be small in numbers and would have been equally revealed by psychoanalysis. Both sides had a case, but Wagner-Jauregg strengthened his by pointing out that during the war he had dealt with many psychiatric casualties, Freud with none.

After Freud had declared, "I would have done it differently," Emil Raimann heightened the argument by asking, "Why in the subjunctive? Why did he not do it otherwise and show how one cures war neuroses psychoanalytically? He would have immediately been allotted a ward. . . . He has never seen war neuroses, and it requires some courage to give an expert report on these matters without knowing anything about them."

Two points should be made. Wagner-Jauregg had voluntarily treated thousands of officers and men throughout the war; Freud, only one year older, had been satisfied to devote himself to the cause. It was not unexpected that in the face of Wagner-Jauregg's defense the commission should decide that no case against him had been made. Secondly, the substance of that case should not obscure the new appreciation, in Germany and in Britain, of what psychoanalysis could do for the treatment of shell shock.

It was not merely the "Wagner-Jauregg Process" that occupied Freud in October. Waiting for him in Vienna on his return from the Hague Congress he had found an accumulation of letters, duties and patients. Every minute was taken up, he told Jones, and he felt pretty tired after the end of his first day's work. "I feel very proud of the Congress," he went on,

and, as I proclaimed in my improvisation, highly relieved by the conviction that men like you, Ferenczi, Abraham, Rank, etc. are apt and ready to carry on for me. The remainder of my time and powers I will have to devote to the duty of providing for my family, that is to say to making money, but if scientific interest, which just now is asleep with me, gets aroused in the course of time I may still be able to make some new contribution to our unfinished work.

Meanwhile, he was faced with the consequences, both good and bad, of the surging postwar interest in psychoanalysis. The reasons for this awakening were different among doctors and among laymen. The attitude among the first was typified by Sir Frederick Mott, the English neuropathologist, who pointed out that "the formation of a conscript army in which only physical difficulties were recognized as causes of unfitness, had shown that a large percentage of men were neuropathic and liable to neurosis, hysteria and neurasthenia, provided stress was sufficient." Not all such casualties were found responsive to psychoanalysis; but enough did benefit to make it difficult any longer to ignore its principles. One result, described by Brill in a slightly different context, was that Freud had

> wiped out the line of demarcation between mental medicine and the allied sciences. He [had] forced a sort of union between them. To understand the neuroses one must know something about biology, psychology, sociology, anthropology, and pedagogics; and vice versa, students in any of these disciplines must also have a knowledge of Freudian psychiatry.

So by the first years of the peace the status of psychoanalysis had been subtly changed; it might still be bludgeoned by its enemies but now as a new insider rather than as a derided outsider.

At the same time, the possibilities of dealing with mental illness were being enlarged by discoveries in other fields. Although Freud himself stressed that his theories merely added one more weapon in the armory against illness and that others would eventually be found, many psychoanalysts would have been reluctant to admit as much. Nevertheless the birth of genetics, which followed the rediscovery of Mendelism at the turn of the century, with its explanation of how inherited characteristics were passed on, now began to give evidence for what had previously been supposition. The discovery of the sex hormones, forecast in Freud's *Three Essays* of 1905, had much the same effect, while even schizophrenia was, before many years, to be at least partly explicable in terms of chemistry. Mental illness was thus becoming a subject linked as much with the possibilities of understanding as with the grim hopelessness of the asylum. This in itself meant that psychoanalysis, although only one potential method of treatment, became increasingly, if still usually skeptically, discussed by the medical profession.

During the immediate postwar years Freud was as a result able to note an encouraging growth of interest in many parts of the world. In 1920 Eitingon began to finance a Berlin clinic where, on lines already suggested by Simmel, the poor were treated and analysts were trained. In Budapest, Ferenczi tried, amid the chaos following Béla Kun's four-and-a-half-month Communist rule, to keep alive the Hungarian Psychoanalytical Society he had founded in 1913. In Switzerland the Swiss Psychoanalytical Society, on whose council there sat such staunch Freudians as Binswanger and Pfister, had come into existence early in 1919, and before long applications to join the International Association were being received from groups in Calcutta and Moscow.

In Vienna itself, what had started almost two decades previously as the Wednesday Society was flourishing once again as the Vienna branch of the International Association and attracting new members. Among them was Wilhelm Reich, a recently qualified Austrian doctor who after reading a paper to the Society on "The Libido Conflict and Delusion of Peer Gynt" became a member at the early age of twenty-three. Reich was another follower who was eventually to ride away from Freud's teachings on his own hobby-horse, although in his case his controversial orgasm theory, to be introduced in a paper read at the Salzburg International Congress of 1924, was not the only reason. Freud could accept this, or at least parts of it; what he could not accept was Reich's linking of Marxism and psychoanalysis, a view which saw the death instinct as a direct result of the capitalist system.

As Freud was reviving the Vienna branch of the International Psycho-Analytical Association, there began a reorganization of psychoanalysis in Britain. During the war a number of influential members of the London Psycho-Analytical Society had left the ranks of the Freudians and joined Jung's camp. Then, in February 1919, Jones, who had been congratulated by Freud on his plans to "purge" the British organization of "Jungish" members, dissolved the London society and formed the British Psycho-Analytical Society.

The growth in serious professional interest was also taking place in the United States, where, as in Britain, it was paralleled by a change in popular opinion among a lay public to whom the benefits of psychoanalysis could be, and often were, presented in the most extravagant terms. "Many of our former opponents are now strict adherents," Brill could claim in 1919. "Works on neurology and psychiatry, even of the most orthodox type, are forced to take note of us; we are constantly discussed at dinner parties; we are parodied in the theater and the press; and quacks, in the form of psychotic old ladies and disappointed litterateurs, are reaping a rich harvest through psychoanalytic treatment."

The two victorious Anglo-Saxon allies had indeed one thing in common: the belief that since it was the old ideas, in politics, in morals and in motivation, which had led to Armageddon, then any new ideas were worth considering; if they were dangerous, that was an item on the credit side, and if they were also heretical, so much the better. Newness was itself a virtue in the eyes of those described by one writer as

> The nephews and nieces of War
> As wise as our uncles were bold—
> Too wise to go out in the cold,
> Too witty and wise to complain and feel sore
> That all the best fruit has been handled before
> And all the good stories been told.

The shadowy figure of Freud, ready in the background, appeared to offer the chance of fresher fruit and better stories. "Repression" became one of the boss words of the early twenties. As Frederick J. Hoffman said:

> It was the peg upon which discontented Americans hung all of their resentment with the moral world about them. As a term of disapproval it relaxed disciplines and smoothed the way to seduction. It was the easiest form of rationalization of familiar impiety and extramarital indulgences. It made love "free" and helped to condemn fidelity as smug and conventional.

Following fast on the demand came those who could supply it. As it became the fashion to be "psyched," willing operators arose almost overnight, in practice unhampered by rule or regulation and attracted by the ability to extort high fees for uttering a few long words. Even the effort of coping with a patient on the couch was not always necessary since it was, according to advertisements, possible to be "psyched" by mail.

The change was particularly surprising in the United States. Here, in spite of the respectability given to the subject by Putnam's support, Ernest Jones's hard work and the number of occasions on which psychoanalysis was seriously discussed at medical meetings, it had, to most American psychiatrists, "remained a topic for cloakroom wisecracks or parlor discussions." Then, not overnight but after only a few years, the reverence for what has been called Emersonian Puritanism dissolved into an attitude which held nothing sacred. "It was a denial, by American authors, of the most American standard, almost the only American standard, we had," it has been said, "—a rejection of the austere morality of a New

England philosopher to make way for the biological theory of an Austrian physician to diseased minds."

Freud well knew the dangers involved in popularity of this kind. He "did not reciprocate this enthusiasm which intended to make him the gonfalonier [standard-bearer] of the march toward a new and better order," his friend Hanns Sachs has explained. "He refused to cooperate in making psychoanalysis the instrument for any other purpose than the study and the best possible understanding of the human mind. He knew too well that those who now sang 'Hosannah' with the loudest voice would be the first to cry 'crucify' as soon as the trends of the time changed."

The American public was certainly not allowed to forget the growing importance of psychoanalysis when in 1924 two rich young men, Leopold and Loeb, killed a boy in what they had hoped to be "the perfect murder." Desperate, and successful, efforts were made to save them from execution, and both Colonel McCormick of the *Chicago Tribune* and William Randolph Hearst asked Freud to name his own terms for coming to America to psychoanalyze the youths. Freud refused. But during the trial no less than ten psychiatrists were present, five for the defense and five for the prosecution, and, as it has been said, "the newspaper-reading public knew a great deal about fantasies, complexes, neuroses, psychoses, fixations, inhibitions, repressions and perversions. And it was determined to know still more." Leopold and Loeb were eventually convicted, although their lives were spared —not so much due to the psychiatric pleadings as to the inspired plea of Clarence Darrow, the world-famous defense lawyer, that nothing would be gained by their execution.

Any doubt that psychoanalysis had become the vogue was removed by the circulation of telling limericks, an indisputable sign of fame. One of the most popular was:

> A progressive young lady of Rheims
> Had confessed some astonishing dreams
> And was justly annoyed
> When the great Doctor Freud
> Said: "A surfeit of chocolate creams."

Another was repeated to Hanns Sachs by Freud himself. He said he had heard it in 1922 from an Englishman, then in analysis with him in Vienna, who said that it was current in New York and London. It went as follows:

> Young men who frequent picture palaces
> Have no use for psychoanalysis;
> If you mention Freud
> They are vastly annoyed
> And cling to their longstanding fallacies.

There is another version, given in Norman Douglas' *Some Limericks,*
which was more adventurous:

> The girls who frequent picture-palaces
> Set no store by psychoanalysis.
> And though Mr. Freud
> Is greatly annoyed,
> They cling to their old-fashioned phalluses.

Some psychoanalysts were themselves not averse to making light
of the subject and at a meeting of the New York Society of
Neurology and Psychiatry, after references were made to the importance of infantile sexuality, "Sachs declared he was under the
impression, which he could not give up, that the penis was attached
to the boy, whereas Freud and Brill were asking him to accept the
concept that the boy was attached to the penis."

H. L. Mencken in his "Rattling the Subconscious" was equally
light-hearted: "Hard upon the heels of the initiative and referen-
dum, the Gary system, paper-bag cookery, the Montessori method,
vers libre and the music of Igor Feodorovitch Stravinsky," he wrote,
"psychoanalysis now comes to intrigue and harass the sedentary
multipara who seeks refuge in the women's clubs from the horrible
joys of home life." Indeed, it has been said "that the reason the
denizens of Greenwich Village never recognized the fact of prohi-
bition was because at the time the Eighteenth Amendment was
proposed they were too busy discovering the variants of psychoanalysis to read about its passage."

Mencken was typical of those who turned their wit against the
excrescences of psychoanalysis. But he typified, also, the reaction
of those lucky persons who had never needed any form of psychotherapy and who therefore found it easy to look upon the subject
with profound skepticism. Those more introspective, more con-
templative or more troubled were likely to take a less critical view,
even if they had not personally benefited from analysis.

While Mencken's astringent comments may have done something to limit the extension of a therapy into a cult, the cause
continued to be embarrassed by practitioners over whom the professional American bodies were able to exercise less control than

they wished. As Henry F. May has said in *The End of American Innocence,* Freud was "represented in the popular press as a wizard, a surgeon of the soul who had a secret formula for ending mental disease and restoring social efficiency overnight, that is, for casting out devils."

It is easy to understand how it happened. Early in his work Freud had stressed what is now a commonplace but was in his day still strongly disputed: that mental normality is separated from abnormality not by a series of high steps but by almost imperceptible gradations, making the difference between mental health and ill health one of degree rather than of kind. Normality itself was thus relative, and so a wide variety of mental troubles could easily be presented, with no more than a minor sleight of hand, as susceptible to improvement by psychoanalysis.

Freud had always taken a strong stand against this, maintaining in his earlier days—even before the first bright confidence had worn off—that the new therapy was applicable only to particular categories of ill health and then only if patients fell into certain well-defined groups. To keep within these guidelines, however, would have been to limit the empire-building which inevitably attracts the adherents of any new movement, and in the turbulent iconoclasm of the postwar years, psychoanalysts, good, bad and indifferent, multiplied in numbers and often replaced the believers in the Puritan ethic whose authority had been undermined by the experiences of the war. The professional bodies did what they could; but hampered by their earlier reluctance to accept psychoanalysis at all, their influence was circumscribed. Within a few years a securely defended base of operations had been created for the new therapy and among successful psychoanalysts it became as dangerous to criticize any tenet of psychoanalysis as for Ralph Nader to criticize the entrenched positions of the automobile industry half a century later.

In addition to the growing number of nonqualified analysts and the growing popularity of a subject that was widely believed to encourage promiscuity, there was one side effect which at times caused Freud some worry: the way in which the adherents of Adler and Jung began to gain ground. Among the American population there were many seeking a better understanding of the mind but unwilling to consider Freud's application of Charcot's belief that "sex is always at the bottom of such cases, always, always, always." For them, either Adler or Jung offered acceptable alternatives. Freud was well aware of this, particularly after Jung's second visit to the United States in 1912. However, it is possible that his fears were exaggerated. The Clark University lectures had given him a head start, and with the help of such proselytes as Putnam, Brill and Jones, he managed to maintain the lead.

More dangerous was the new postwar popularity itself. From the time of his first visit to America Freud had feared that psychoanalysis might attract not only the charlatans but also the ignorant enthusiasts, the only partially qualified hacks whose ill-founded confidence would satisfy less critical patients and whose questionable operations might eventually destroy the cause. During the early 1920s this was beginning to happen. The Rev. C. F. Potter, speaking in the West Side Unitarian Church on "Psychoanalysis and Religion," praised Freud for the valuable work he and his colleagues were doing. But, he went on, while Freud was the Columbus who had discovered an unknown continent, there were "many sad derelicts in his wake floating on the sea of life who have found that leaky rowboats and poorly constructed rafts are not seaworthy craft." Then, using terms which Freud would have strongly applauded, Potter explained how he and other clergymen knew of "poor, pitiable, unnerved and nearly demented victims of quack psychoanalysts who are unscrupulously seizing upon the present craze as a means for exploiting their victims, financially and otherwise." It seemed incredible, he continued, that while a physician had to serve ten years' training before he could treat a man's body, "an analyst who presumes to treat that more delicate organism, the human mind, can hang out his shingle and charge twenty-five dollars a sitting, after no more preparation than ten days reading of Freud and Jung . . . and [then] 'drop a monkey wrench into the machinery' of the mind."

The famous Stephen Wise, rabbi of the Free Synagogue in New York, was equally condemnatory:

> It is deeply to be deplored that there is so serious a misuse of psychoanalysis by frauds and charlatans whom no one despises more than do the scientific medical practitioners. It is indeed to be regretted that an instrument of highest potential value to the race should be degraded by those who know of psychoanalysis only through hearsay, rather than study, into an excuse for verbal vulgarity and set obscenity.

The sudden blossoming into a fashionable cult brought about its own reactions. At an Atlantic City meeting of the American Psychoanalytic Association, members were exhorted by Dr. William A. White to "free American psychiatry from the domination of the Pope at Vienna." Dr. Frederick Peterson of New York, who in 1907 had set Brill on the path to the Burghölzli, was to describe Freudianism as a voodoo religion characterized by obscene rites and human sacrifices. And when Susan Glaspell's *Suppressed Desires*—a harmless enough attempt at comedy—was produced in 1923 it brought the protest that "it is the only blot on the record of the little theater movement that this most foul and insidious of German propaganda should have been innocently distributed by them."

It was not long before the booming popularity, equalled only by the reaction it engendered among opponents, produced one almost inevitable result. Early in December 1921 an audience, which included many members of Cornell University's faculty, packed the City Hall of Ithaca to hear a Dr. Vosberg, described as an intimate friend and pupil of Freud, lecture on the intricacies of psychoanalysis. It was in fractured English that Dr. Vosberg, tall and dark-bearded, told his audience: "A dreamer does know what he dreams, but he does not know what he knows and therefore believes what he does not know." This, with the rest of the lecture, was duly accepted, and the evening ended with a member of the university faculty thanking the speaker. A few days later postcards appeared showing "Dr. Vosberg" with beard and spectacles and the same man without them: Charles M. Stolz, a third-year student in Cornell's school of architecture.

Three months afterward something similar—"a good practical joke," as Ernest Jones described it to Freud—took place in Oxford where a lecture by Dr. Busch, of the University of Frankfurt, "the friend and colleague of Dr. Freud," was announced. The student, kitted out for the part by a local barber, "gave a quite nonsensical lecture, which was not detected and led to a discussion," Freud was informed. Several heads of colleges, invited by the "Home Counties Psychological Association," attended the lecture at which Dr. Busch, according to the *Oxford Chronicle,* said "he did not agree that man was the slave of circumstance. Man could, he believed, influence his career largely by autosuggestion. Asked whether the background was something additional to the sum total of the combined personalities, he thought not, as it was apparently more in the nature, so to speak, of a fluid."

"Dr. Busch" was in fact George Edinger, later a distinguished British journalist, who was not detected. "It shows," Jones reported, "the state of ignorance at Oxford, for several professors were also present and were also taken in."

Freud received little sympathy either in America or in Britain, where after the Cornell hoax *The Times* of London gave its views in a Delphic leading article:

The Freudian psychology is both exciting and difficult to under-stand; it is therefore misunderstood by many people who wish for excitement. And this misunderstanding is not prevented by Freud himself, who, though a man of genius, has also a turn for reducing his own theories to an absurdity and no great gift of lucid exposition. So, with the help of a few phrases and formulas, anyone can be a Freudian, can make of his own dreams and other people's what he will, and can discover that what we think we mean, in our conscious and waking life, is always the opposite of what we really do mean. . . . Hence the multitude of convinced, if rather vague, Freudians who provoke a natural prejudice against the new psychology. It is a pity that they should reduce certain very valuable, if still imperfect, dis-coveries to an absurdity, that they should be the drunken helots of a new science.

The exhortation then ended with the hope that "the very absurdi-ties of his followers may at least set Freud on guard against his own. He has a real, though intermittent, sense of humor and we may hope that some day, like Ibsen in *The Wild Duck,* he will turn to rend his own devotees."

In addition to the skeptics who refused to take psychoanalysis seriously there was also the deserter from the ranks. Notable among them was Dr. Samuel A. Tannenbaum who had been a practicing psychiatrist since 1912. Tannenbaum was well-known for his psychoanalysis of Floyd Dell after the author had come to a creative standstill in his work *Mooncalf.* Treatment enabled him to complete the work, and he dedicated his second book *The Briary Bush* to Tannenbaum in appreciation of his help.

As early as 1920 there had been a major disagreement between Tannenbaum and Freud, who was quick to impute the worst of motives to his opponent. "I am glad you agree with my letter to the knave T.," he wrote to Jones. "We will be able to stand his attacks. If America really is embracing Jungism, as he pretends, she will get what she deserves. Give me some millions (even of Kronen) more and I will never more be afraid of an adversary." The following year Tannenbaum began to study the results of his case histories and early in 1922 announced his revised views. "It is my experience," he said, "that patients can be cured without such [Freudian] interpretations, that their neuroses can be inter-preted in the light of other instincts that dominate human life. Sex is not responsible for all neuroses. Neuroses are due to the individ-ual's conflict with reality, with the world, irrespective of his love life."

After submitting that it had now "become fashionable for men and women who cannot earn their living in any other way to be-come psychoanalysts," Tannenbaum concluded: "Psychoanalysis is a pseudoscience like palmistry, graphology and phrenology. It has enough of a foundation, in fact, to deceive the uncritical and, as in Christian Science, there is a certain modicum of truth in it."

The blasts of serious critics, the insidious claims of quacks and the horrified declamations of adamantine opponents were all heard throughout the confused psychiatric scene in the United States in the early 1920s. It is difficult to assess how much damage was caused, but considering the speed with which the psychoanalytic community continued to grow, it was probably less than was feared at the time. One result, however, was to make it easy to capitalize on the failures of psychoanalysis. Among those seeking help for mental illness, failures were not unexpected, and the fact that patients do sometimes die under the anesthetic has rarely been cited as a reason for never operating. Nevertheless even the most tenuous links between psychoanalysis and suicide often provided useful ammunition for its opponents. When a young woman gassed herself in New York early in 1922 it was attributed to "taking up Freud." Physicians agreed, the *New York Times* reported, "that the practice of psychoanalysis by girls too ignorant to grasp its true meaning and not sufficiently learned to discriminate among its theories, had become so prevalent, an educational corrective was needed, since its devotees often derive only a dismal outlook on life from its teachings." But guilt by association could go too far and after a girl, also studying Freud, had jumped to her death from the *New York Times* building and earned the headline GIRL, WEARY FROM FREUD, A SUICIDE, there came a protest. The girl had probably bought a hat some time, one reader pointed out; so why not the headline: BUYS HAT—DIES; or, since she had probably eaten like most others, why not the headline: EATS POACHED EGG—DIES.

Some of the more responsible American newspapers tried to hold the scales fairly, even though not especially enthusiastic about psychoanalysis. The *New York Times*, admitting in an editorial that Freudians believed many mental ills to be the fault of repressions, pointed out that the Freudian answer was not "Do as you please," but sublimation to higher and proper uses. "Whoever does anything else," it went on, "who finds in psychoanalysis license instead of liberty—is not a follower of Freud . . . but a charlatan, certainly ignorant and probably vicious."

The United States, however, had no monopoly of charlatans, and the situation in Britain was in many respects comparable. Ernest Jones, reporting from London, gave Freud a startling picture. "Would you like to earn £1,000 a year as a psychoanalyst?" asked one advertisement in a London paper. "We can show you how to do it. Take eight postal lessons from us at four guineas a course." Some newspapers tried honestly to investigate the position, and Jones noted that the *Daily Graphic* had appointed a special commission of lawyers and doctors to report on the subject. "The animus," he wrote, "is chiefly directed again at the lay analyst, charlatans, quacks and spiritualists being the commonest epithets. Occasionally a distinction is drawn between quacks and 'genuine analysts,' but more often not." In January 1921 he added that an attempt was being made to get the London County Council to license and supervise lay analysis under the law relating to massage and other quasi-medical measures; but, as he forecast, the proposal came to nothing.

Just how strong a foothold the impostors and the unskilled were gaining in Britain is uncertain, but Jones warned Freud that they had to be taken seriously. "A well-known one in London boasted that the Queen had arranged with him to conduct a psychoanalysis on the Prince of Wales on his return from India, this to be kept secret from the King," he wrote. "Most likely the story is true, so Bryan and I wrote to the Queen's private secretary pointing out the dangers of the procedure: we received a grateful acknowledgment."

Attacks on the grounds of obscenity continued, these being brought to a new high pitch by publication in English of the *Tagebuch eines halbwüchsigen Mädchens (A Young Girl's Diary)*, ˙the detailed story of a young girl's sexual awakening which Freud had described as "a little gem." A reader's report to Allen & Unwin, to which the manuscript was submitted, recommended that it should be published, but warned that the best thing would be "to get some qualified and well-known writer to contribute a preface and to publish it as a scientific curiosity and sociological warning. To publish it as it is, with Dr. Freud's brief statement to the effect that it is 'a little gem' and ought to be made public—to offer it to the general public—would be to risk attracting the attention of the police." After the book had appeared, early in 1921, the *Evening Standard* called for prosecution, and, reported Jones, Stanley Unwin "came round to see me in a considerable panic. I wrote a letter congratulating him on the appearance of this valuable work, etc. which he can show to the police. . . . It has the advantage of making Unwin more dependent on us!"

The diary had been handed to Freud by Dr. Hermine von Hug-Hellmuth, a member of the Vienna Psychoanalytical Society. In acknowledging it he wrote to her: "I really believe it has never before been possible to obtain such a clear and truthful view of the mental impulses that characterize the development of a girl in our social and cultural stratum during the years before puberty." However, when James Strachey published the letter in the Standard Edition of Freud's works, he felt a footnote was necessary: "It should be added," this went, "that after its publication suggestions were made that the diary might have been touched up by the unidentified person who confided the manuscript to Frau von Hug-Hellmuth." In fact, the book was withdrawn in Germany where it was widely believed that a good deal of it was the product of Frau von Hug-Hellmuth's overstimulated imagination.

Attacks still continued, and were to do so for some time, on what might by now have been considered the least provocative works. In February 1921 a letter in the *Occult Review* found it possible to say of *The Interpretation of Dreams:* "Had we not the book before us one could never believe that a reputed scientist could endeavor to found a theory upon the filth and folly of semi-insane people and expect the theory to cover the facts of the normal mind and the dreams of healthy people." And as late as 1932 some three hundred citizens of North Carolina petitioned the governor against the inclusion in the state's university library of Freud's *General Introduction to Psychoanalysis.*

Even in more intellectual circles Freud sometimes got less approval than might have been expected. A typical attitude in Britain was that of a character in Rose Macaulay's *Dangerous Ages* who maintained that Freudianism could perform wonderful cures—for "shell shock, insomnia, nervous depression, lumbago, suicidal mania, family life—anything." Even his publishers had views that he would not have relished. In 1924 the Hogarth Press, founded by Leonard and Virginia Woolf, began to take over publication of psychoanalytical literature for the London Institute of Psycho-Analysis. Virginia Woolf was not enthusiastic, writing to Molly MacCarthy (wife of Desmond MacCarthy, author and critic): " . . . we are publishing all Dr. Freud, and I glance at the proof and read how Mr. A. B. threw a bottle of red ink on to the sheets of his marriage bed to excuse his impotence to the housemaid, but threw it in the wrong place, which unhinged his wife's mind—and to this day she pours claret on the dinner table. We could all go on like that for hours; and yet these Germans think it proves something—besides their own gull-like imbecility." J. M. Keynes, part of the same Bloomsbury establishment, writing in the *Manchester Guardian Commercial* on purely economic matters, noted that "With religion dead and philosophy dry, the public run to witchdoctors. In cut and material," he went on, "our fig leaves have fallen out of fashion, and we find them neither comfortable nor becoming. Freud tells us to strip them off; Coué to wear two pairs."

The reaction from Bloomsbury was the natural response to

Freud's picture of the writer and artist as a clever neurotic able to turn his own fantasies into fame and fortune. Roger Fry and Clive Bell were only two of those who objected, and the same view was held elsewhere, even by those who admitted their debt to psychoanalysis. Thus Thomas Mann was able to say:

> As far as I am concerned, at least one of my works, the short novel, *Death in Venice*, was created under the immediate influence of Freud. Without Freud I would never have thought of dealing with this erotic motive or would at least have treated it differently. If one can put it in military terms, I would say that Sigmund Freud's thesis represents a kind of general offensive against the Unconscious with the aim of its conquest. As an artist I have to confess, however, that I am not at all satisfied with Freudian ideas; rather, I feel disquieted and reduced by them. The artist is being X-rayed by Freud's ideas to the point where it violates the secret of his creative art.

In the face of this undertow of feeling, both in Britain and elsewhere—a feeling sometimes experienced, sometimes merely implied, sometimes only suspected—Jones pushed doggedly on, speaking to medical societies, preparing the ground for the Institute of Psycho-Analysis, which he set up in 1924, and devoting virtually all his considerable talents to furthering the cause. A small but typical indication of his problems is given by his report to Freud of a special dinner held by the Lyceum Club, a distinguished London club for ladies, at which psychoanalysis was to be described. A good deal of work had been necessary to prepare the way, and Jones had high hopes of the outcome:

> They had definitely promised me that no guests should be invited except with my approval, especially various outsider pseudo-analysts, and that there should be no debate. Actually they invited a number of objectionable people, who had the posts of honour to the detriment of many of our members. Barbara Low, Flugel, and I spoke—I believe all well, with a good impression—after dinner, and then the hostess, who throughout had behaved very discourteously, announced that this was a controversial subject, that we should all move from the dining-room to another room, where the debate would be opened by William Brown. There were nine members of our society there and we all left the Club at this point, with the exception of Flugel, who with his usual cowardice could not bring himself to behave "impolitely." I sent in a formal protest to the Club Committee afterwards, and the matter is still in discussion.

At the Lyceum Club, as well as elsewhere in both Britain and the United States, discussion of psychoanalysis centered on its validity for medical purposes and on whether its sexual emphasis was justified. Yet at the same time, in both countries, as well as to a lesser extent on the Continent, psychoanalytical methods were ever more frequently being extended into areas which had no connection with therapy and where Freudian theories could be applied, if at all, only with the greatest care and circumspection. "On a cruder level," as F. H. Matthews had pointed out in the *Journal of American Studies*, "[it] quickly became a universal polemic tool: 'puritanism' was exposed by the frustrations of Martin Luther, and the sordid roots of Theodore Roosevelt's progressivism were exposed by pseudo-Freudian analysis of his 'real' motives in splitting the Republican Party."

Yet it was in literature and biography that the ramifications already opened up by psychoanalysis were most far-reaching. This was to be expected. Once it had become established outside the purely medical world that men's actions could be governed by factors of which they themselves knew nothing, the scope for investigating established characters of fiction and famous characters of history—as Freud had done with his *Gradiva* and "Leonardo" essays—was almost limitless.

The prospect was distinctly attractive since it enabled readers to enjoy, beneath the overlay of clinical respectability, what they would have been ashamed to enjoy a few years earlier. At times the psychoanalytic background was assumed on rather dubious evidence, as with Sherwood Anderson. "As his work became known in the 1920s," says his biographer, Irving Howe,

> Anderson was quickly tagged a Freudian, usually by critics who assumed a causal connection between Freud's theories and the portraiture of neurotic character-types in *Winesburg*. He was often labeled the American writer most influenced by Freud and in "The Dial" Miss Alyse Gregory had a myopic vision of Anderson "like the anxious white rabbit in Alice in Wonderland clasping . . . the latest edition of Sigmund Freud." Regis Michaud, an extravagant Freudian critic, hailed [Anderson] as "the Freudian novelist *par excellence,*" and Camille McCole, a Catholic writer, denounced him in much the same terms.

Most critics concentrated on several references in the novel *Poor White* to what could be read as psychoanalytical concepts, and the remark in *Dark Laughter* that "if there is anything you do not understand in human life, consult the works of Doctor Freud." Yet to his friends Anderson continued to insist that he had not read Freud and in his *Memoirs* he was to add: "I never did read him."

Backing away from involvement with Freud was the reaction of many writers and artists whose work was influenced, to

lesser or greater extent, by growing public awareness of the unconscious. Thus D. H. Lawrence produced his "ecstatic anti-
Freudian tirades" and his essays on "Psychoanalysis and the
Unconscious" and "Fantasia of the Unconscious." Frieda Lawrence was, however, a great admirer of Freud and lengthily argued out her ideas with her husband. "Lawrence's conclusion,"
she has written, "was more or less that Freud looked on sex
too much from the doctor's point of view, that Freud's 'sex'
and 'libido' were too limited and mechanical and that the root
was deeper." Others among the intellectuals took a critical
view, notably Aldous Huxley with his contempt for Freudian
symbolism and his damaging lampoon of psychoanalysts at
work and play, "The Farcical History of Richard Greenow."
Nevertheless, Katherine Mansfield, Elizabeth Bowen and certainly Virginia Woolf—despite her judgment of "gull-like imbecility"—all wrote in a manner which would have been barely
comprehensible before the coming of Freud.

Yet the majority attitude in Britain was no doubt reflected accurately by two of its most important mirrors of contemporary taste
—*The Times Literary Supplement* and the humorous journal *Punch.* In
reviewing *Uncle Lionel,* a novel by the English writer S. P. B. Mais,
the *Supplement* noted that the author had been

> studying the theories of those two very estimable gentlemen, the
> sounds of whose names one is beginning to dislike, Messrs. Jung and
> Freud, and apparently this course of reading has induced in him the
> same spiritual shell-shock which it has lately been promulgating
> widely among novelists. Even if it is true that the unconscious mind
> influences thought and action to the extent which they suppose, why
> should the unconscious mind be given such a very bad reputation?
> Mr. Jung himself, one understands, has put in some good words for
> it; he has pointed out that its intentions are by no means always
> incestuous. Why, then, should the characters in the psychological
> novel be invariably horrid? When will it be possible for a novelist to
> write a decent and readable story and yet to be thought scientific?
> How long will the theory last that the science of psychology is a
> special device for giving novelists an insight which they do not pos-
> sess into the mental processes of the characters which they them-
> selves have created?

Punch, following up the review, devoted a ten-verse poem to
Freud and Jung, the writer claiming to have

> searched the last edition of the famous *Ency. Brit*
> And neither of this noble pair is even named in it.

He ended with the lines:

> But I, were I a despot, quite benevolent, of course,
> Armed with the last developments of high explosive force,
> I'd build a bigger "Bertha" [the Germans' long-range gun of the
>   First World War]
> And discharge it in the void
> Crammed with the novelists who brood on Messrs. Jung and Freud.

Samuel Freud, having sent a copy to Vienna, was told by Freud that he thought the poem rather silly. Moreover, *Punch* was wrong. Although Freud's name was not in the eleventh edition of the *Encyclopaedia Britannica*, Samuel was told, it was in the supplement issued in 1913.

Despite the implications of *The Times Literary Supplement*, many writers continued reluctant to acknowledge the unconscious as one of the mainsprings of their work, in strong contrast to André Breton, one of the early leaders of the surrealist movement and among the few artists to admit the influence of psychoanalysis. The reluctance was understandable. It had been an early premise of psychoanalysis that there is a close association between the life of the instincts and the life of the imagination, and that there is a similarity between the neurotic patient who gives up his neurosis under treatment and the artist who sublimates feelings in creative work. Professionals tended to take umbrage at this view of the creative act as "a subjective means of avoiding, rather than an objective plan for shaping, reality."

One notable exception to the novelist's habit of digging a ditch between himself and psychoanalysis was Theodore Dreiser, who once wrote:

> I shall never forget my first encounter with [Freud's] *Three Contributions to the Theory of Sex*, his *Totem and Taboo* and his *Interpretation of Dreams*. At that time, and even now, quite every paragraph came as a revelation to me—a strong, revealing light thrown on some of the darkest problems that haunted and troubled me and my work. And reading him has helped me in my studies of life and men. I said at that time and I repeat now, that he reminded me of a conqueror who has taken a city, entered its age-old hoary prisons and there generously proceeding to release from their gloomy and rusted cells the prisoners of formulae, faiths and illusions which have racked and worn man for hundreds and thousands of years. And I still think so.
>
> The light that he has thrown on the human mind! Its vagaries and destructive delusions and their cure! It is to me at once colossal and beautiful.

Perhaps more important than fiction, which either conscripted the reader's unconscious into an understanding of the text or set the plot against a psychoanalytic background, was psychobiography and psychohistory. Even if the more obvious *non sequiturs* of Freud's Leonardo essay tended to be counterbalanced by its felicity of style, the essay itself was not entirely blameless. "The striking novelty and the startling conclusions of [the essay]," said William L. Langer, president of the American Historical Association, speaking to the Association years later, "had much to do with precipitating the flood of psychoanalytic or, better, pseudo-biographical psychoanalytic writing during the 1920s, almost all of which was of such a low order—ill-informed, sensational, scandalizing—that it brought the entire Freudian approach into disrepute. I have no doubt that this, in turn, discouraged serious scholars— the historians among them—from really examining the possibilities of the new teachings."

Another discouragement may well have come from the early extravagances of the *International Journal of Psycho-Analysis,* started soon after the war, technically directed by Freud but for most practical purposes under the control of Ernest Jones. From the start, the *Journal* spread itself on nonclinical subjects. The first full-dress paper was "On the Character and Married Life of Henry VIII," and others which followed analyzed Lady Macbeth and Shylock. Some contributors pitched their claims rather high. "Not psychology alone but all contiguous disciplines, anthropology, folklore, religion, economics, sociology, history and even literary criticism, politics and biography are becoming indebted to psychoanalysis," stated James S. Van Teslaar in writing on "The Significance of Psycho-analysis in the History of Science." Nor was this all. "Already," the author continued,

> it is not premature to assert that psychoanalysis promises to accomplish for the whole group of the so-called *Geisteswissenschaften* (the cultural sciences, as contrasted to the exact disciplines) what the evolutionary theory—and specifically the work of Darwin—has done for the biological group of sciences. . . .
>
> Through psychoanalysis, at last, mental health, efficiency, education of mind and body, human welfare generally—racial as well as personal—become subject to purposive direction and control, exactly as the forces of nature are today in the engineer's hands.

With psychoanalysis being supported in such terms there was little need for its enemies to worry.

18

Reassessing the Unconscious

Thus in its relation to the id [the ego] is like a man on horseback,
who has to hold in check the superior strength of the horse; with this
difference, that the rider tries to do so with his own strength while
the ego uses borrowed forces.

FREUD, *The Ego and the Id*

In spite of the dangers of overpopularity, the extravagances of the
overenthusiastic and the operation of quacks and charlatans, psychoanalysis consolidated during the early 1920s the base it had
begun to gain during the later stages of the First World War. Its
practitioners and its patients increased annually, particularly in the
United States and Britain, where it continued to be granted a status
higher than in most Continental countries. Its use as an investigating tool that could help solve literary, biographical or historical
riddles of the past was exploited, sometimes with an amateurishness that attracted ridicule, but occasionally to good effect. The
growing acceptance of the unconscious as a factor in human affairs
increasingly influenced literature and art, and when the Surrealists
designed their own pack of playing cards, the Genius of the Dream
suit was Isidore Lucien Ducasse, the pseudonym of the French
poet the Comte de Lautréamont, the Siren was Carroll's Alice and
the Magus was Freud.

One potential threat to the cause came from the first stirrings of
the neo-Freudians, those analysts who, unlike Adler, Jung and the
other dissidents, accepted the basic Freudian principles but restated them with emphasis on factors that Freud had either ignored or had considered of only secondary importance. Thus
while the orthodox "Continental" school continued to maintain
that control of the psyche rested exclusively upon psychological
factors, other analysts—later to be typified by Fromm, Horney and

Sullivan—emphasized the importance of cultural or sociological pressures.

The Marxists stressed that psychoanalysis should take account of the economic motivations of human conduct, while Melanie Klein developed a technique for applying psychoanalysis to children only twenty-four months old. These and other extensions or modifications of Freud's work during the interwar years steadily changed what had for many Freudians been comparatively simple certainties into a network of varying theories, sometimes interlocking, sometimes competitive and often sustained with a dogmatic fervor that would have been a credit to Freud in his most fervid moments. More important was the influence of those critics who, while agreeing with Freud on the significance which he gave to the unconscious, could accept neither the development of his theories nor, indeed, even the validity of some of his basic beliefs. Professor William McDougall believed, as he stated in the preface to his *Outline of Abnormal Psychology,* "that Professor Freud has done more for the advancement of psychology than any student since Aristotle. . . . [but] I regard much of current psychoanalytic doctrine as ill-founded and somewhat fantastic." C. S. Myers, president of the International Congress of Psychology, took much the same view, and during an acrimonious argument with Jones, stated:

> My standpoint in regard to Freud is that there is hardly an explanation which, I should say, does not hold in *certain cases,* and that there is seldom a *generalization* which I should not be prepared to contest. My conviction is that we need far more unbiassed research and that committal to a "school" makes this impossible.

Nevertheless, it was clear that psychoanalysis had come to stay, which was at least some consolation to Freud as during the immediate postwar years he struggled with the financial problems that faced the self-employed Austrian professional classes even more menacingly than the rest of the population. In Vienna he was, in spite of his fame abroad, still comparatively unknown, even though more than one famous Viennese sought his help. Among them was Eisenbach, greatest of the capital's comedians; his trouble was severe depression.

Early in 1920 Freud was, it is true, at last made a full professor of the university, but it was not an appointment that gave him a seat on the board of the faculty. Recognition was still grudging, and when he was reminded that his fame had spread far beyond the frontier, he would brusquely assert that it did not begin until the frontier was reached. When his income tax was questioned on the grounds that his fame attracted patients who were able to pay high fees from foreign countries, he noted that it was the first official recognition his work had found in Vienna.

Even among his close neighbors, little was yet known of that work, let alone Freud's fame. One inhabitant of an apartment in No. 19, who always exchanged greetings with Martha, knew almost nothing of what her husband did. She would occasionally encounter Freud when entering or leaving the building, but her contacts were very different from the friendly exchanges with his wife. "There might be a brief greeting or a nod but these would have been unusual because the major recollection was one of no greeting at all," says an American who discussed Freud with her years later. "He might walk with his head bowed, or in any case, he would simply ignore her. She ascribed this to what she inferred was his intense preoccupation and absorption with his professional interests and intellectual concerns. The degree of detachment was impressive."

Within his home, the surroundings had not changed greatly since he had moved into the apartment more than thirty years previously. The waiting room still contained the rich red plush chairs of the 1880s. The framed diplomas still hung on the walls, and on the side tables there stood the statuettes, the archaeological curiosities and the fine pieces collected over the years. On the wall there hung a French print of a nude, unconscious woman. "She was stretched out and in the power of a demonic incubus, suggesting, as it were, the subject of psychoanalytic therapy," recalled one visitor. "To the left of the door on top of a cabinet there stood a big simple antique urn. Its concentrated stillness might have expressed something of Freud's yet unrevealed philosophy." When the door to the consulting room opened, the visitor was faced with an impressive figure. Freud looked his years, although his movements were still quick, his voice still crisp, his white beard still immaculately trimmed. Above all there were his eyes, deep set and brown, with a penetrating look that was difficult to forget. "His face in old age proclaimed him one in the midst of battle," an observer noted. "The deep wrinkle of the nose and cheek continued over the right eye like a streaming war standard, producing the effect both of beauty of the eyebrows and watchfulness of the hero who had devoted himself to works of peace, but has encountered deadly powers. Evidently he had learned to play with the extremes." This was the man, now in his mid-sixties, wondering whether the victory of "the cause" would be only transitory, who struggled to keep the Verlag in being, to guide the fortunes of psychoanalysis through his influence in the International Association and to make financial ends meet.

At the same time he managed to squeeze out time to play the

role of Freud the patriarch, the one member of the family to whom all others could turn for advice and from whom more than one was to receive the money needed for economic survival. It was a role he enjoyed. Beneath the dispassionate, slightly somber exterior, the façade of the man totally immersed in the clinical curiosities of his profession and the speculative theories to which they gave rise, there coursed a consanguineous response well shown in a letter to Samuel in England, written in December 1921 and apologizing for the break in his usual flow of letters. "I am very far from forgetting you, mother, and the girls," this went,

nor can many days pass by without bringing up the memory of my dear beloved elder brother. Do you think he would have enjoyed my actual popularity? It is a burden to me.

Not many events have happened since July. I passed part of the summer at Seefeld, Tirol. I cannot banish the illusion of having sent you several illustrated cards from this place, middle of Sept. I went to Berlin with Ernesti who had shared our summer as a companion. I saw Ernest, his wife Lucy (or Lux), his remarkable son, found Oliver back from Rumania, visited Aunt Marie, the widow, then I went over to Hamburg to spend some days in Sophie's orphaned house—you know, I am very fond of poor Max—indulged in the joys of a grandfather, fondled little Heinz, a charming naughty devil of a boy. The last week of September I was in the company of my nearest friends and adherents (Jones from London, Abraham from Berlin, Ferenczi fm B'pest, Rank from Vienna), travelling through the Harz: Hildesheim, Halberstadt, Goslar, etc. On the last of the month I was home a few days. I was deeply in work with 6 Americans, 3 Englishmen, 1 Swiss, listening and talking 9 hours a day and so I have gone on for these two months.

As I am earning foreign money, I am excepted from the miseries of our town. I have even succeeded in regaining a part of the amount of money lost by the war and as long as I can continue working, I am sure to be free of financial cares. I am glad to say none of the family is still dependent on the scarce and irreplaceable subsidies from Eli.

No big misfortune has occurred. Aunt Minna fell down in the street three weeks ago, fractured her right arm and is not very brilliant since but it is not serious. Anna is in splendid health and would be a faultless blessing, were it not that she had lived through her 26th birthday (yesterday) while still at home. Martha and I do feel the whims of old age growing upon us. Martin has got a respectable position, his boy is thriving well.

You will have gathered from the newspapers how desperate our public conditions are. Or perhaps there is no interest for Austria in your papers.

Old mother is remarkably sprightly, it seems to be a matter of habit

and exercise. Glad you tell the same about your mother.
My best love to all of you. Let me soon hear more.

Yours affectionately,

Sigm.

The Americans were important for Freud's economic survival. "I am dependent on foreign patients and scholars, as it would be impossible to get from Austrians fees sufficient to live thereon," he admitted to Samuel. "At the end of this month four of my patients (two Americans and two Englishmen) leave me, so I expect an easier yet a poorer time."

His position was underlined to one American to whom he remarked: "My fees are 10 dollars an hour or about 250 dollars monthly, to be paid in effective notes, not in checks which I could only change for crowns." Some of his visitors were patients; many more came for training—"the instruction of disciples" as he revealingly called it—and he had constant trouble in keeping the balance right. On one occasion he had one patient and seven trainees. On another, having agreed to take six Americans for training, he discovered he could squeeze in time for only five. "We all gathered the next day at 3 P.M. and were ushered into his office," Abraham Kardiner has written. Freud then announced that his daughter, his wife and he himself had reached a conclusion that he hoped would suit them all. "My daughter Anna made the best suggestion," he went on. "Being something of a mathematician, she figured out that $6 \times 5 = 30$, and $5 \times 6 = 30$. So if each of you will sacrifice one hour per week, I can accommodate all of you." One problem was language, since Freud's good understanding of English did not stretch to the variety of American accents displayed by his visitors. "Nine analytic sessions daily have become a greater strain because of the shift to English in five of the sessions," he wrote to Abraham. "I note with surprise how greatly the effort of listening and inwardly translating uses up one's free energy."

But financially it was no time to be unduly selective. He noted to Jones of one young man that he was not very clever—in fact, rather an ass. But, as he went on, five dollars were then worth 750 crowns. And as he told a colleague, Eduardo Weiss, "In the most unfavorable cases, one ships such people . . . across the ocean, with some money, let's say to South America, and lets them there seek and find their destiny."

It was not only the Americans who caused him trouble. Ernest Jones had asked whether there was any hope of his taking on for analysis a Mr. James Strachey. "He is a man of 30, well educated and of a well-known literary family. (I hope he may assist with translation of your works)," Jones went on. "I think a good fellow but weak and perhaps lacking in tenacity"—the latter a judgment hardly borne out by Strachey's subsequent translation and editing of the twenty-four-volume Standard Edition of Freud's works. Strachey offered to pay a guinea an hour. Freud replied that while financial considerations prevented him from taking a patient for such an amount, that of a pupil was different. As long as the English pound continued to be worth about 600 crowns, he would be willing to take him. Later he said that he did not regret the decision—even though Strachey's speech was so indistinct and strange that it was a torture to listen to.

The English patients helped, and it was a few English pounds, nearly as desirable in Austria as American dollars, that Freud sometimes passed on to the Wolf-Man, financially ruined by the Russian revolution, who now visited him again. "I was so thoroughly satisfied with my mental and emotional condition that I never thought of the possibility of needing more psychoanalytic treatment," the patient later wrote. "But when I told Professor Freud everything I could about my state of mind during the years since I had left Vienna, he thought that there was still a small residue of unanalyzed material and advised a short reanalysis with him." Freud not only carried out the analysis without fee but collected money for his poverty-stricken patient, continued to do so for a number of years and, when further treatment became necessary in 1926, ensured that the Wolf-Man was dealt with by one of his able colleagues, Ruth Mack-Brunswick.

To Americans seriously interested in psychoanalysis and its future he was willing to devote time even during his normally inviolate holidays, and he spent a long afternoon at Bad Gastein discussing a variety of psychoanalytic problems with Jeliffe, who reported:

> The precise discussion of many points was not reached, but he had a fine stroke, and cut into things very sharply and clearly. Bergson, he says, he does not understand. . . . As for Adler he has little use. Jung's recent material—particularly the prospective function of the dream—he called "trash" and he was content with the activities of his many pupils.

There were other less welcome visitors, and the man who found it difficult to suffer fools gladly found it almost impossible if they were Americans. One who knocked on his door unannounced stated that he was a doctor from Ohio. "I have heard so much about you, so I wanted to see you, shake hands, and have a few words with you before returning to my country," he added. Freud grasped him by the hand and, before closing the door, said: "Pleasant journey."

His deep-rooted anti-Americanism, grounded in the visit of 1909 to which he even now attributed chronic digestive troubles, and nourished by what he regarded as Wilson's reneging on the Fourteen Points, was never far below the surface and always ready to come up for air. It was hardly assuaged when both Jung and Adler were given honorary degrees by Harvard. But when one American, impressed by the number of his countrymen who were taking up psychoanalysis, remarked, "How odd, the Americans are supposed to be such practical people," Freud tartly replied that there were also among them a few who were idealists.

His feelings revealed themselves very openly when he was visited by Max Eastman, whose book on Marx had recently been published. It included a chapter on Freud and Marx, and Freud had written to the author complimenting him. Asked whether his tribute could be used publicly, he had replied, " 'No.' I will thank you for *not* mentioning any of the remarks in my letter in public. I seem thus far to have failed to accustom myself to the American life forms."

When Eastman called on him in Vienna he was met with: "But why should I support you? Can't you stand up on your own legs?" In spite of this discouraging beginning the two men were soon on comparatively good terms, although Eastman was surprised by Freud's attitude to all things American. When a difference over psychology arose, the visitor was told, "Perhaps you're a behaviorist. According to your John B. Watson, even consciousness doesn't exist. But that's just silly. That's nonsense. Consciousness exists quite obviously and everywhere—except perhaps in America." Then, before Eastman left, he was advised to write a book on "The Miscarriage of American Civilization." "You will find out the causes and tell the truth about the whole awful catastrophe," he was exhorted. "That book will make you immortal. You may not be able to live in America any more, but you could go and live very happily somewhere else."

During these immediate postwar years, while Freud was setting psychoanalysis on an international footing once more and striving to discourage the wilder excesses of its practice, he turned again to the metapsychology on which he had begun work during the war. He had used the term more than once in his letters to Fliess at the end of the nineteenth century. "I hope you will lend me your ear for a few metapsychological questions . . .," he had then written.

"When I was young, the only thing I longed for was philosophical knowledge, and now that I am going over from medicine to psychology I am in the process of attaining it." He had tightened the link in *The Psychopathology of Everyday Life*, noting there: "The obscure recognition (the endopsychic perception, as it were) of psychical factors and relations in the unconscious is mirrored . . . in the construction of a *supernatural reality*, which is destined to be changed back once more by science into the *psychology of the unconscious*. One could venture . . . to transform *metaphysics* into *metapsychology*."

Thus the position remained until, during the war, he planned his book of twelve essays which were to form an "Introduction to Metapsychology." It was in the third of these, "The Unconscious," that he had defined the word in the terms he was to use from now on. "I propose," he wrote, "that when we have succeeded in describing a psychical process in its dynamic, topographical and economic aspects, we should speak of it as a *metapsychological* presentation." Here the dynamic referred to the various instincts in conflict with each other: the topographical, an idea borrowed from Gustav Fechner, the founder of psychophysics, to the distinction within the psychic apparatus of the unconscious, the preconscious and the conscious; and the economic to that which "endeavors to follow out the vicissitudes of amounts of excitation and to arrive at least at some *relative* estimate of their magnitude."

The metapsychology that Freud had constructed during the war was self-contained, satisfactory and acceptable, and it was something of a shock to his friends and followers that as he struggled for survival among the financial disasters of the new Austrian Republic he should expound two ideas which called for considerable restructuring of the basis on which psychoanalysis rested. He had begun this in the spring of 1919, writing to Ferenczi: "Much of what I am saying in it is pretty obscure, and the reader must make what he can of it. Sometimes one cannot do otherwise. Still I hope you will find much in it that is interesting." He finished the essay, was dissatisfied with it, rewrote it, read an abstract to the Vienna Society in the summer of 1920 and saw it published in December.

Beyond the Pleasure Principle, as the paper was called, advanced a tentative theory that Freud described as "speculation, often far-fetched speculation, which the reader will consider or dismiss according to his individual predilection." In the closing pages he admitted that he did not know how much he himself believed in it. But, as was the case on other occasions, his more loyal followers accepted as unquestionable fact what he had tentatively put forward, a conviction that slowly became Freud's own. The ideas propounded in *Beyond the Pleasure Principle* did indeed meet opposition, but by the time it could make itself felt Freud was already seeing them as firmly established.

The paper began by reiterating his previous belief that the course of mental events was "automatically regulated by the pleasure principle. We believe, that is to say, that the course of those events is invariably set in motion by an unpleasurable tension, and that it takes a direction such that its final outcome coincides with a lowering of that tension—that is, with an avoidance of unpleasure or a production of pleasure." Yet there were notable exceptions to this principle. It had been found during treatment of war neurotics that many would constantly recall and relive in dreams the traumatic events which had caused their mental breakdown. In psychoanalysis some patients would insist on repeatedly acting out unpleasant experiences in their youth. Even children would recall and act out unpleasant as well as pleasant events. Freud saw the repetition-compulsion, as he called it, as an instinct as fundamental as the pleasure principle.

> At this point we cannot escape a suspicion that we may have come upon the track of a universal attribute of instincts and perhaps of organic life in general which has not hitherto been clearly recognized or at least not explicitly stressed. *It seems, then, that an instinct is an urge inherent in organic life to restore an earlier state of things* which the living entity has been obliged to abandon under the pressure of external disturbing forces; that is, it is a kind of organic elasticity or, to put it another way, the expression of the inertia inherent in organic life.

But once it was accepted that an instinct might automatically encourage regression to an earlier state, then the next step was hard to resist. "The attributes of life," Freud went on,

> were at some time evoked in inanimate matter by the action of a force of whose nature we can form no conception. It may perhaps have been a process similar in type to that which later caused the development of consciousness in a particular stratum of living matter. The tension which then arose in what had hitherto been an inanimate substance endeavored to cancel itself out. In this way the first instinct came into being: the instinct to return to the inanimate state.

Thus, by what appeared to be a logical argument it was possible to picture—in contrast to the pleasure principle—the death instinct, which encompassed the impulses aiming at destruction, death or escape from stimulation on the part of the individual.

The idea was by no means new. Novalis, Von Schubert, Fechner and Sabina Spielrein were only some of those who had presupposed a death instinct either similar to or identical with Freud's supposition, while in more recent times Stekel has acrimoniously stated in his autobiography: "Freud later adopted some of my discoveries without mentioning my name. Even the fact that in my first edition [of *Causes of Nervousness*] I had defined anxiety as the reaction of the *life instinct* against the upsurge of the *death instinct* was not mentioned in his later books, and many people believe that the death instinct is Freud's discovery." Discovery is of course the wrong word; what Freud had done was to incorporate the purely hypothetical idea into what he hoped was an acceptable framework.

Freud's "death instinct" was to raise almost as much controversy as the Oedipus complex, and inevitably there was speculation that both the phrase, and the kernel of the theory itself, were due not only to emotions aroused by the war but to Freud's loss of his daughter Sophie and of Anton von Freund, whose postwar financial support had been so important. Freud himself, always anxious to refute any suggestion that his theories originated from personal experience rather than from widespread observation of others, wrote to Eitingon on July 18, 1920, saying: "The 'Beyond' is finally finished. You will be able to certify that it was half finished when Sophie was alive and flourishing." However, that was not the entire story. Sophie had died on January 25, and Freud appears to have used the phrase "death instinct" for the first time in a letter to Eitingon less than three weeks later.

Beyond was only a first statement of the developing ideas which Freud was to firm up into a harder outline during the next few years, but it attracted the interest that was now being shown in everything he wrote. "For [it]," he wrote to Eitingon some months later, "I have been sufficiently punished. It is very popular, is bringing me lots of letters and expressions of praise. I must have done something very stupid there." On this last point he may have been right. Ernest Jones has admitted that in the decade following publication of *Beyond the Pleasure Principle,* only half of the papers discussing the subject agreed with Freud, that in the next decade only a third did so, "and in the last decade none at all."

Freud's belief in two contrasting drives forever in conflict with each other echoed his theory of the neuroses, which had assumed only two groups of essentially opposing instincts, those of sex and of self-preservation; now, in speculating on wider problems, he introduced the Life Instinct and the Death Instinct, Eros and Thanatos, the first including both the sexual and the self-preservation instincts and the latter an instinctive drive to return to the inanimate state. Jones has speculated that the dualism of Freud's ideas "must have sprung from some depths in [his] mentality, from some offshoot of his Oedipus complex, perhaps the opposition between the masculine and the feminine sides of his nature." A rather more plausible explanation has been put forward by Dr. Charles Rycroft who attributes it to a Continental weakness, illustrated by Hegel and Marx, for espousing dialectical theories.

While at work on *Beyond the Pleasure Principle* Freud had started on the draft of what he described to Ferenczi as a "simple idea that will serve as a psychoanalytic foundation for group psychology." For a man who appreciated how much he, and many others among his countrymen, had been misled by wartime propaganda, and who knew how the mob had taken over in many places as the Austro-Hungarian Empire collapsed, it was a logical development. The contemporary relevance of the subject, and its grim foreshadowing of the rise of Hitler little more than a decade ahead, has led to Freud's "simple idea" sometimes being regarded more as a treatise in social psychology than as an addition to the new picture of the mind he was creating. It did, in fact, as he explained to the French writer and Nobel Prize-winner Romain Rolland, show "a way from the analysis of the individual to an understanding of society," but in the process it threw new light on the way that the individual's mind worked.

"Group Psychology and the Analysis of the Ego," as Freud called his essay, quoted extensively from *The Crowd* by Gustave Le Bon—that "notorious, racist, political anti-Semite and intellectual servitor of the French military class" as he has been called. It drew on Trotter's *The Instincts of the Herd in Peace and War*, and it described the lowering of intellectual activity when an individual becomes merged in the mass. It is not surprising that a considerable contempt for the masses shows through, and it is no more surprising that this fact is made little of by most Freudians.

Freud's explanation for the deterioration in standards that comes with an individual's adherence to the group—whether the group comprises football fans, troops or members of the same nation—was that it represented an extension of more primitive loyalties: those to the family and, earlier, to the primal horde of *Totem and Taboo*. "The leader of the group is still the dreaded primal father; the group still wishes to be governed by unrestricted force; it has an extreme passion for authority; in Le Bon's phrase, it has a thirst for obedience. The primal father is the group ideal, which governs the ego in the place of the ego ideal."

However, Freud was about to change the significance of the ego itself, and to put it firmly within a new conceptual framework in which the interactions of three psychic agencies, the ego, the id and the super-ego, governed the course of all mental life. The history of his paper containing these new ideas—*The Ego and the Id* —is complicated by the fact that Georg Groddeck, who had begun to work a passage back into psychoanalytic respectability after his appearance at the Hague Congress, was not only simultaneously elaborating a somewhat similar idea but was sending it to Freud for his opinion.

It would be wrong to suggest that Freud took his concept of the ego and the id from Groddeck without acknowledgment; indeed, the ideas of the two men were very different in certain ways, although Freud stated in his paper that he was "following Groddeck in calling the other part of the mind, into which [the ego] extends and which behaves as though it were *Ucs* [unconscious], the 'id.'" Nevertheless, the cross-fertilization of ideas between them has only been fully revealed during the last few years.

In the early spring of 1921 Groddeck sent Freud five chapters of the book he was writing. Each chapter was in the form of a letter to an intelligent young woman who wished to know what psychoanalysis was about, and after the first chapter, each successive letter answered questions that might have been raised by the preceding one. In these letters Groddeck used the word *Es*—the German for "It"—to describe that portion of the unconscious which came into existence at birth. Translated as the "It"—and subsequently by Freud's translators into the "Id"—it reflected, as it has been said, "to an extreme degree, the old Romantic concept of an irrational unconscious. [Groddeck] conceived of the id as impersonal and full of aggressive and murderous impulses, and believed each drive had its obverse."

Freud had his reservations, as he explained when he replied to Groddeck on April 17. "I understand very well," he said,

> why the unconscious is not enough to make you consider the It dispensable. I feel the same. Yet I have a special talent for being satisfied with the fragmentary. For the unconscious is merely something phenomenal, a sign in place of a better acquaintanceship, as if I said: the gentleman in the havelock [the white cloth covering on a soldier's cap which protects the neck from the sun] whose face I cannot see distinctly. What do I do if he appears without this piece of clothing?

But Freud was enthusiastic nevertheless—"Your style is enchanting, your speech like music"—and remained so when further chapters were sent him: "As fascinating as the earlier ones, perhaps less whimsical." Groddeck's completed manuscript arrived on Freud's desk at the end of the year, together with three possible titles, from which he was asked to choose the most suitable.

Six months later Freud told Ferenczi that he was "occupied with something speculative, a continuation of *Beyond the Pleasure Principle;* it will result in either a small book or else nothing at all. I will not yet reveal to you the title, only that it has to do with Groddeck." The first indication of its contents came at the Berlin Congress in September 1922, when he addressed the audience on "Some Remarks on the Unconscious," but he continued to work on it until Christmas. Then he wrote to Groddeck, saying that both Groddeck's book, now called *The Book of the It,* and his own, to be called *The Ego and the Id,* were due for publication in the spring. "Do you remember, by the way," he later asked, in writing of his own book, "how early I accepted the It from you? It was a long time before I made your personal acquaintance, in one of my first letters to you. I made a drawing there, which will soon be published in almost the same form."

The Book of the It appeared in March 1923, and Freud told its author:

> I like the little book very much. I consider it a matter of merit to put people's noses up against the fundamentals of analysis from which they constantly try to withdraw. The work, moreover, argues the theoretically important point of view which I have dealt with in my own forthcoming book *The Ego and the Id.*
>
> The public will of course react to it with even more aversion and indignation than it did to *The Seeker of Souls,* which could be taken as an artistic treatment of the undesirable. Your self-esteem will hardly be affected by this.

To Pfister, Freud conceded that "Groddeck is quite certainly four-fifths right in his belief that organic illness can be traced to the It and perhaps in the remaining fifth he is also right."

Groddeck continued to hold Freud in high esteem, although a letter to the woman he had married since the Hague Congress, written after receiving a copy of Freud's *The Ego and the Id,* gives a rather different impression:

> [It] is pretty, but quite uninteresting to me. In reality it was written to appropriate secretly loans made by Stekel and me. And yet his Id is of only limited use for the understanding of neuroses. He ventures into the realm of organic illness only in a very sneaky way, with the help of a death instinct or destruction drive taken from Stekel and

Spielrein. He disregards the constructive aspect of my It, presumably to smuggle it in next time. Some of it is quite amusing.

His long letter to Freud expresses his feelings in more detail:

Many thanks for sending me *The Ego and the Id*. As the godfather of this term I am now expected to say something about it. Yet the only thing I can think of is a comparison which throws light on our interrelationship and our attitude to the world, but does not say anything about the book. In this comparison I appear to myself as a plough, and you as the peasant who uses the plough—or perhaps another one—for his purpose.

In *The Ego and the Id,* about which Groddeck obviously had ambivalent feelings, Freud had sharpened and refined his meaning of the ego, a concept he had used since the early days of his psychological writings. He had employed it in a variety of ways, and some psychoanalysts were to maintain that it was only given its real meaning in his description of the new psychical apparatus in 1923. Others have seen the outline of its ultimate meaning in his earlier writings and claim that throughout the years it was evolving into the later form. Whichever view is taken, there was no doubt that the ego of 1923 was a different conception from that of Freud's earlier years.

It was now a modified portion of the "Id," which was in some ways a successor to the unconscious—a word which Freud was now beginning to use as an adjective rather than as a noun. The id contained all that was present at birth and "we call it a chaos, a cauldron full of seething excitations . . . filled with energy reaching it from the instincts, but it has no organization, produces no collective will, but only a striving to bring about the satisfaction of the instinctual needs subject to the observance of the pleasure principle." But a layer of the id, adapted for the reception and exclusion of stimuli, and in direct contact with the external world, was molded by the pressures of that world into the ego, a force representing reason and common sense and ceaselessly trying to hold in check the unruly unconscious. "Thus in its relation to the id," Freud now wrote of the ego,

it is like a man on horseback, who has to hold in check the superior strength of the horse; with this difference, that the rider tries to do so with his own strength while the ego uses borrowed forces. The analogy may be carried a little further. Often a rider, if he is not to be parted from his horse, is obliged to guide it where it wants to go; so in the same way the ego is in the habit of transforming the id's will into action as if it were its own.

In addition to these two forces forever struggling for domination there was a third, the super-ego, coming into existence as a child begins to learn what its parents believe to be right or wrong, growing with the acceptance of moral ideas and reaching its full strength only in the first years of adult life. It "observes the ego, gives it orders, judges it and threatens it with punishments, exactly like the parents whose place it has taken," Freud was to maintain. At least, that was his conception. To Jung, it was merely "a furtive attempt to smuggle the time-honored image of Jehovah in the dress of psychological theory."

The Ego and the Id, while one of Freud's more speculative disquisitions, marked a watershed in his beliefs and teachings: after it, no one would be able to think of the mind's structure as they had previously thought of it. Yet his weakness for Lamarck's discredited theory—that acquired characteristics could be inherited—induced him to add a touch of the incongruous on which his enemies could seize. He maintained that although the experiences of the ego seemed at first to be lost for inheritance,

> when they have been repeated often enough and with sufficient strength in many individuals in successive generations, they transform themselves, so to say, into experiences of the id, the impressions of which are preserved by heredity. Thus in the id, which is capable of being inherited, are harbored residues of the existence of countless egos; and when the ego forms its super-ego out of the id, it may perhaps only be reviving shapes of former egos and be bringing them to resurrection.

There was also a bringing in of the Eros-Thanatos dichotomy, after the observation that some animals [i.e., insects] die in the act of copulation. "These creatures," Freud wrote, "die in the act of reproduction because, after Eros had been eliminated through the process of satisfaction, the death instinct has a free hand for accomplishing its purposes," a remark which succeeded in bringing the insect world within the orbit of psychoanalysis.

This structural theory of the mind which Freud had evolved between the mid-war years and 1923 was in the nature of things even more difficult to verify than his earlier theories, since traditional scientific methods can be used to study only those matters which can be accurately observed. The deviation of light when passing close to the sun—measured by Eddington in 1919 and supporting Einstein's General Theory of Relativity—has no satisfactory parallel in considerations of the id, the ego and the super-ego: neurophysiological studies may one day provide such evidence, but the day is not yet. Nevertheless, if the existence of three physiological structures functioning like the id, the ego and the super-ego is still largely speculative, the existence of three different types of mental processes has received support, and there is at least some evidence for three motivational factors in much behavior.

In 1923 Freud put forward his new theory on a purely tentative basis. To this extent he had abandoned the earlier arrogance of "We possess the truth" and had more nearly approached Einstein's conclusion: that the scientist can never hope to reach the truth but merely to get a little closer to it. But he had successfully launched his new ideas of the mind and could observe their fate without anxiety. The International Psycho-Analytical Association was flourishing, and if there were worries about the wilder ramifications of psychoanalysis, that was no more than he had feared and expected. Austria's fortunes appeared to have passed their lowest ebb, and with the Chancellor's negotiation of a large loan, made with the aid of the League of Nations in 1922, it was possible to see light at the end of the dark international tunnel. For Freud, too, the future began to look less gloomy.

19

Cancer

It has been decided that I must undergo a second operation, a partial resection of the maxiella, because my dear neoplasm has reappeared there.

FREUD, in a letter to Max Eitingon

Late one evening in April 1923, Freud surprised his doctor, Felix Deutsch, by asking him to look at something "unpleasant" in his mouth. "Be prepared," he added, "to see something you will not like." One glance was enough. "No sooner had I seen it, an obvious advanced cancer," Deutsch later said, "than Freud added, 'For what I intend to do I need a doctor. If you take it for cancer, I must find a way to disappear from this world with decency. There is only one difficulty. You may not know that my mother is still alive—she is eighty-seven years old. It would not be easy to do that to the old lady.'"

Deutsch later said that he did not believe that Freud, then approaching his sixty-seventh birthday, thought of committing suicide. Instead, he "wished only that I should spare him the suffering of a 'hopeless sickness' which cancer meant to him at that time. He apparently wanted to have the right of an euthanasia. I at least understood it that way."

Nevertheless, Deutsch had been caught by surprise. To gain time he took a second look and decided to diagnose the trouble as a bad case of leukoplakia, which required a biopsy and the removal of the diseased membrane by operation. "Freud agreed to follow this advice," Deutsch has said, "and he asked me for a handshake to seal the deal in case the biopsy should show cancer. I shook hands with him and he called my agreement an act of friendship."

It is not at all certain how far Freud was deceived, if at all. A third of a century earlier he had been able to dissemble with Fliess, to maintain either that smoking did him no harm or, if that argument failed, that the pleasure of the cigar, its arousal of his intellect and its stimulation to work, more than made up for the danger. In an age that knew little of the carcinogens in tobacco and even less of the statistical links between smoking and cancer, it was at least a respectable argument. But now he reluctantly had to admit that his life might be measured by something more inescapable than Wilhelm Fliess's numerological fantasies.

Arrangements were quickly made. "We drove to the hospital together with the understanding that he would be at his home immediately after the operation," Deutsch has written. "But he lost more blood than it was foreseen, and as an emergency he had to rest on a cot in a tiny room in a ward of the hospital, since no other room was available, with another patient who, by tragicomic coincidence, I might say, was an imbecile dwarf." Yet it was this very man who, when Freud suddenly suffered a profuse hemorrhage, alarmed a nurse and stayed with him until the doctor was summoned. He may have saved Freud's life. To attribute the casual treatment of such an eminent patient to the controversies which his work had aroused may seem extravagant. Nevertheless, a man as well-informed as Max Schur, Freud's doctor from 1928 on, has stated: "In view of the powerful hold that resistance to psychoanalysis and its findings has on the behavior of many people, we can assume that the very fact that the patient was Freud, the discoverer of psychoanalysis, actually contributed to the course of events during and after that first surgery."

Soon afterward, a course of radium was begun, the first in a long succession of treatments and operations that, it was optimistically hoped, might prevent an extension of the disease. By May 10 Freud, replying to Abraham's birthday congratulations, was able to write: "I can again chew, work and smoke, and I shall try your optimistic slogan: *many happy returns of the day and none of the new growth* [italicized words in English]." The letter was typical of the way in which Freud rose to the occasion and continued to do so, responding with a fortitude which gives a genuinely heroic quality to the last years of his life.

He was still recovering when he received another blow. Since the death of his daughter Sophie he had developed a great fondness for her younger son, Heinz Rudolf. The boy had the previous year, at the age of three and a half, contracted tuberculosis and on his recovery had come to stay in Vienna for some months with Freud's daughter Mathilde. At the end of May he fell ill. At first his illness could not be diagnosed. Then, Freud wrote to two friends, there came

> the slow but sure realization that he has a miliary tuberculosis, in fact that the child is lost. He is now lying in a coma with paresis, occasionally wakes up, and then he is so completely his own self that it is hard to believe. . . . After each waking and going to sleep one loses him all over again; the doctors say it can last a week, perhaps longer, and recovery is not desirable, fortunately not likely . . . I find this loss very hard to bear. I don't think I have ever experienced such grief; perhaps my own sickness contributes to the shock. I work out of sheer necessity; fundamentally everything has lost its meaning for me.

On June 19 the boy died. Freud, more affected than he had been even by the death of his daughter, later said that he found the blow heavier than that of his own cancer, and to Ludwig Binswanger he wrote: "It is the secret of my indifference—people call it courage —toward the danger to my own life."

Freud's exceptionally strong feelings for the boy were revealed in a letter which he wrote to the bereaved father early in July from Bad Gastein, where he was staying with Minna:

> I have spent some of the blackest days of my life in sorrowing about the child. At last I have taken hold of myself and can think of him quietly and talk of him without tears. But the comforts of reason have done nothing to help; the only consolation for me is that at my age I would not have seen much of him. I doubt if you realize how much we all loved him. We cared for him as we would have cared for one of our own children and cannot express our feelings for him. I think you never knew him properly. He was too small in Hamburg and the constant rivalry with his elder brother distorted things. Here [in Vienna] he developed beautifully and the way in which he learned to understand and conquer the world and the people around him one could only call wonderful. The pity of it is that one will never know how these feelings would have developed, since he never grew up. Even the three-quarters of a year during which he was constantly ill was a very happy time for him; even at the end he suffered less than us, so all of us who knew him still have vivid memories. I think you are right to take a holiday and hope that it will be effective. Ernestl [Heinz's elder brother who was staying with the rest of the Freud family elsewhere in the Tyrol] I saw two days ago. His outfit—coat, cap, case, has been admired. He himself was very happy, has enjoyed everything and has tried not to mention Heinele.

To the letter Aunt Minna added her own postscript, saying how strongly she felt about the boy's death, that she herself had been very "physically down" for some time, and that Papa [Freud] had arrived in a miserable state but was starting to recuperate.

The recuperation appeared to be continuing, a view supported by a doctor in Bad Gastein who inspected the operation scar. But Freud, who held a low opinion of the local man, was suspicious of the continuing discomfort. By early August he had left Bad Gastein for Lavarone where he was joined by his daughter Anna. Anna persuaded him to write at once to Felix Deutsch in Vienna.

Deutsch reacted promptly. Since April he had "wavered between the satisfaction of having prevented [Freud] from an irreversible act and the fear that he might discover the deception and the breach of confidence." Now he decided to travel from Vienna to see Freud for himself. He arrived quickly; and, as quickly, saw that the growth had spread and that another, more serious, operation would have to be carried out.

More than 2,000 feet below Lavarone, at San Cristoforo on Lake Caldanozzo, the Committee was to meet within the next few days. And since Freud had planned earlier in the year to leave Lavarone at the end of August for a visit to Rome, two questions now arose. Could the members of the Committee, who had so far been given no inkling of how serious Freud's condition was, persuade him to undergo the operation if, as seemed likely, he did not wish to have it? And should he make the projected trip to Rome or return to Vienna immediately?

The problem was made no easier by the fact that Freud himself had decided not to attend the meeting of the Committee. According to Ernest Jones, he had "proposed that we should try the experiment of meeting together to learn to achieve harmony without him; if we succeeded he would be pleased to meet us afterward." But it is difficult not to feel that Freud wished to avoid the various arguments, not connected with his illness, which he rightly expected would break out.

After the members of the Committee had arrived, Deutsch and Anna Freud walked down to San Cristoforo where Deutsch, anxious to hear their views when they were told the truth, described the position. When the question arose of how best to induce Freud to have the operation, and of deciding if an attempt should be made to stop the trip to Rome, Sachs suggested that Anna's help should be invoked. Rank had the more subtle suggestion of using Freud's mother to influence him. But the feeling was that Freud would not delegate the decision to someone else. Jones reports that he himself "protested that we had no right to take such a decision out of Freud's hands, and the other medical men present, Abraham, Eitingon and Ferenczi, supported me."

Apart from debating the question of the operation, the San Cristoforo meeting justified Freud's forebodings. Trouble had been simmering for some while between Rank and Jones, and now Rank—unnerved, it has been claimed, by the condition of Freud who was not only friend and colleague but also employer—called for Jones's expulsion from the Committee. His colleagues refused. Later Jones was to write publicly that "there was a very painful scene with Rank in uncontrollable anger and myself in a puzzled silence." During the next few months Rank's confrontation with Jones was augmented by a more serious argument with Abraham, and before the spring of 1924 the Committee had been formally dissolved. Only as moves for its reconstitution took place in the autumn of 1924 did Jones give another version of the San Cristoforo meeting. "Finding myself, largely because of Rank's skilful manoeuvring, faced with unanimous opposition and condemnation," he wrote in a circular letter to members of the Committee, "I saw how hopeless it would be for me to take a firm stand that would be tantamount to denunciation of Rank; this was the chief, though of course not the only, reason for my state of inhibition then. . . ."

Freud went to Rome and was also persuaded, apparently without difficulty, that the second operation should be carried out. But only after he had arrived back in Vienna was he personally told of the true seriousness of his condition; and only years later was he told how the Committee had decided not to let him know the real situation and, "with blazing eyes . . . asked, 'With what right?' "

Knowing the truth at last, he lost no time in passing it on to Eitingon. "Today," he said,

I can satisfy your need to have news from me. It has been decided that I must undergo a second operation, a partial resection of the maxilla, because my dear neoplasm has reappeared there. The operation will be performed by Professor Pichler, the greatest expert in these matters, who is also preparing the prosthesis that will be needed afterward. He promises that within 4–5 weeks I shall be able to eat and talk satisfactorily, so that for the time being I have postponed the beginning of my practice until November 1.

As he awaited the operation, there arrived a letter that gave him a good deal of satisfaction. Before leaving Lavarone in August he had been visited by a prospective analyst, an American who brought a letter of recommendation from Stanley Hall. The visitor was told that Hall had "very definitely taken sides with Adler and it cannot have escaped you that his doctrines involve a complete refutation of psychoanalysis." In these circumstances, Freud continued, he found it difficult to understand Hall's statement that his view of Freud's contribution to psychopathology remained unchanged. The visitor had reported back to Hall in the United States and the long letter that Freud now received as a result did much to set his mind at rest. Hall admitted that he had found some things useful in Adler's approach and also in Jung's, "mystical and unintelligible as much of his writing is to me." But he then put these statements in perspective:

> I think the world knows that both these men owe their entire impulsion to you and I also think that both illustrate the revolt against the father which you have so well explained. I do not know that psychoanalysis tells us what is the instinctive, or what ought to be, the attitude of the father toward his revolting sons. Wundt had the same feelings toward his own pupils who developed the methods of introspection. In my own very small sphere I, too, have had painful experiences with those whose model seemed to be *periunt illi qui nostra ante nos dixerunt.* I think the impulse to wish the death of those who said our things before we did is pretty strong, and it is most exasperating to those who suffer from it.
>
> But your own achievements are far and away beyond those of any psychologist of modern times; in fact history will show that you have done for us a service which you are not at all extravagant in comparing with that of Darwin for biology. It seems to me you can well afford to be magnanimous toward these revolting children. . . .
>
> For me, your work has been the chief inspiration of most that I have done for the last fifteen years. It has given me a totally new view of psychic life, and I owe to you more than to anyone else, living or dead.

There was much more on the same lines and Hall ended by apologizing for the length of his letter and expressing his "heart-felt wish that you may continue for many, many years the great work you have already established in the world."

By the time Freud read these words he was preparing for what he knew would be extensive and complicated surgery. Indeed, the problems involved were so considerable that Pichler found it necessary to experiment on a corpse before he could decide whether the operation would be feasible. Two operations were in fact needed. The first and minor one was carried out on October 4; a week later came the major operation. First the lip and cheek had to be slit wide open; then the whole upper jaw and palate on the affected right side removed, a surgery which turned the mouth and the nasal cavity into a single organ. This demanded the subsequent fitting of a metal prosthesis, in effect an artificial roof to the mouth which for the rest of Freud's life had to be regularly taken in and out, usually with considerable pain and often with the help of the surgeon.

The second operation lasted seven hours, was carried out under a local anesthetic plus some sedation—and in the days before antibiotics and intravenous feeding. Yet before the end of October he was back at No. 19 Berggasse. Awaiting him was the news that Maria Freud, Emanuel's wife whom he had known as a child in Freiberg, had just died. "As I returned home from the sanatorium yesterday, very much broken and enfeebled," he wrote to Samuel, "I found your letter with the distressing news which does away with another part of the cherished past."

Now, recuperating, he hoped that the worst was over. Within two weeks he was to be disillusioned. On November 12 the surgeon, who had earlier removed a specimen of tissue for investigation, reported continued malignancy. Pichler suggested further surgery; Freud agreed, and the operation was performed the same afternoon.

This time all appeared to be well, and before the end of December Freud was home and apparently recovering quickly. While he had been in hospital his brother-in-law Eli Bernays had died in New York of appendicitis, an event of which he informed Samuel in a cryptically revealing note. "He died a rich man and may have left almost a million dollars, all in favor of Anna [Bernays] who now promises to do something for her 88-year-old mother and four indigent sisters," he wrote, before adding, "Chi viorra verra [those who live will see]."

By the first days of the new year he was able to give Samuel encouraging news of his progress. "I am glad to let you know that I am rapidly recovering and was able to take up my work with this New Year," he said. "My speech may be impaired but both my family and my patients say it is quite intelligible. I am glad to have got so far. Now let us see how long this condition will endure. . . ."

Yet even though thirteen years were to pass before malignant cells were once again found, the ordeal was to continue. More than thirty more operations were to be required for the removal of the chronically inflamed areas, or of precancerous tissue. There also went on a lengthy process of trial and experiment in the construction of a new prosthesis to enable the normal functions of eating, drinking and speaking—and of smoking, which Freud still refused to give up—to be carried on with as little difficulty as possible.

What the future held could at best be painful and incapacitating, and there was ample justification for the occasion when, after one operation, a relative ceremoniously presented Freud with a gold piece inscribed as were the medals given to soldiers for bravery in battle. In this case the words were: "For Courageous Deportment in the Face of Enemy Forces."

20

Last Desertions

Now, after I have forgiven everything, I am through with him.
FREUD, in a letter to Hanns Sachs, of Otto Rank

By the late autumn of 1923 the cancer was being held at bay, and Freud stoically began to learn to live with "the Monster," as the prosthesis came to be called. His spirits rose, and he replied almost jauntily to his correspondents, congratulating Georg Groddeck on the news that he had at last married his mistress and adding: "at bottom I'm all for doing things the proper way." Even two years later it appeared that the enemy had been defeated, and he could write to Havelock Ellis: "I believe that I have got over my serious illness, although I feel distinctly the ineluctable influence of old age."

Freud had sixteen more years to live, and for a man of his years, with his disability, they were to be remarkably full. It would be artificial to categorize this decade and a half too distinctly into periods. Nevertheless, three strands of Freud's life during these years—the further defection of colleagues, his efforts to develop psychoanalysis, and the effect on him of world events—were important as the 1920s turned into the 1930s and the shadow of Hitler began to stretch longer across Europe. These fluctuating features had at least one constant background: the progress or otherwise of the cause whose fortunes were rarely far below the surface of his mind.

During the 1920s, as he was forced to cope with the most hurtful of all defections, Freud could see that psychoanalysis was consolidating the stronger position it had achieved toward the end of the war. The deep roots it had put down in the United States typified the situation in which, while suspicion remained, psychoanalysis was accepted as a therapy the medical fraternity had to acknowledge.

Analysts were by this time operating not only in most European countries but in Japan, Russia, Australia and South Africa; and in Britain the London Clinic of Psycho-Analysis opened to "bring a method of treatment that is lengthy, and therefore expensive, within the reach of those who cannot afford the usual, or indeed, any fees." Even in France, whose citizens were still allergic to anything connected with the detested Germans, a Société Psychanalytique was soon to be founded in Paris.

The French group was largely the creation of Princess Marie Bonaparte, a devoted supporter of the cause and an important figure in the fortunes of its next few years. Marie Bonaparte—"the Princess" to all within the magic circle—was a direct descendant of Lucien Bonaparte, Napoleon's brother who had devoted much of his life to science and art. Her own inclinations were along similar lines and as a girl she had wanted to become a doctor. Her ambition was frustrated, and instead she had married Prince George of Greece. The couple tended to go their own ways, and when, after the First World War, she developed an interest in psychoanalysis, her husband regarded it as no more than a harmless hobby.

In 1925 Marie Bonaparte arrived in Vienna for analysis with Freud. After a short interval she became first his student and then a family friend. For her, contact with Freud and with psychoanalysis was an intellectual adventure that helped develop her considerable literary talents that were to be revealed in, among other books, a study of Edgar Allan Poe and a lesser-known but remarkable book on the rumors and unsubstantiated beliefs which proliferated during the Second World War. For Freud, the Princess became not only a generous helper and colleague but also a confidante, and Ernest Jones was later to be staggered when he learned what intimate things about himself Freud had divulged to her. She was also a benefactor to the cause who saved the Verlag in 1929 when its finances were in desperate straits, and who helped found the *Revue Française de Psychanalyse* in 1927 and the Institut de Psychanalyse in Paris seven years later. Her support was useful in another way. Whatever deference Freud paid to rank in his seventies is immaterial, but he was a practical man and knew the benefit to the cause of having a Princess on its books.

By the mid-1920s it must have become apparent to him, even in his most depressed moods, that a good deal of the fight had been won. Revisionism would no doubt change the outline of the ideas he had propounded a third of a century earlier, and heresies as yet unthought-of might be accepted into its creed. But it was becoming, difficult to drop psychoanalysis into the rag bag with animal magnetism and other discarded eccentricities.

This appeared to be the verdict of a special committee of the British Medical Association. Its report, issued in May 1929, concluded of psychoanalysis that the committee members were "not in a position to express any collective opinion either in favor of the practice or in opposition to it." Nevertheless, the twenty-one-man Committee, which included Ernest Jones for the Freudians and H. Godwin Baynes for the Jungian school of analytical psychology as well as a number of skeptics, did present a serious and unbiased survey of the origins of psychoanalysis, of what it claimed to do and of how it tried to achieve its aims. The committee had met regularly for two years and in its report made a transparently objective attempt to assess the Freudian theories which, it admitted, were "of an extremely astonishing nature." Considerable space was given to current criticism of psychoanalysis, and beside this there was printed the psychoanalysts' reply, which helped to dissolve certain misconceptions still held by many medical men. Yet the final result was much in the nature of a "not proven" verdict, and after opting out of expressing any collective opinion, the Committee's final conclusion noted of psychoanalysis: "The claims of its advocates and the criticisms of those who oppose it must, as in other disputed issues, be tested by time, by experience, and by discussion." It is expressive of the opinion, then widely held, that Jones regarded such a verdict as "the accomplishment of my most difficult achievement on behalf of psychoanalysis."

It was in this distinctly less condemnatory atmosphere of the 1920s that the story of the prewar years began to repeat itself. First one, then another of the faithful deserted their leader, an apostasy that was to be followed, like the defections of Adler and Jung, by international events which again put psychoanalysis in jeopardy for a time; first, the war of 1914–1918 and then, in the 1930s, the rise of Hitler.

The first trouble came with Otto Rank, the follower who since the early days had always sat next to Freud, recording the minutes, anxious to serve. Despite his own pioneer work before the First World War, Rank had never aspired to independence or leadership. Instead, he radiated an aura of indispensability, as Freud acknowledged after it had seemed likely that Rank might be incapacitated by illness. "I had to tremble at the idea of his getting disabled for a longer time as he is—in every department of the work—the indispensable helpmate and a most intelligent companion," Freud told Jones. "If anyone of us is getting rich it will be his duty to provide for him in a satisfying way."

In 1919 Rank had returned to Vienna from his service with the Austrian Army in Poland a tougher, more confident person. At the time Jones appears to have been delighted at the change and told Freud how much he admired the quick brain and good judgment that Rank was now showing. Only later did his attitude radically change; and then his description of Rank's "failing mental integration" and of his entering the "manic phase of his cyclothymia" suggested partiality. Publication of Rank's biography by Mrs. Jessie Taft in 1958 showed that this was so.

As director of the International Psychoanalytic Publishing House in Vienna and joint editor with Jones of the *International Journal of Psycho-Analysis,* Rank had certainly begun to establish a special niche for himself. In view of what was to happen, the description by the psychoanalyst Lilla Veszy-Wagner, who had a close-up view of the situation, is instructive. "Otto Rank constantly poured into Freud's ears stories of how impossible Jones was as a colleague, particularly when Rank and Jones were jointly engaged in editing the *International Journal,"* she has written. "He accused Jones of . . . personal interference in every step of the editing process."

But with one editor in London and another in Vienna, it was inevitable that problems would arise. When the first language of one was German and the first language of the other was English, the opportunity for misunderstanding was complicated even further. It can hardly have been diminished as Jones, in London, reflected that Rank, in Vienna, had the ear of the master to a degree that he obviously lacked. This was no doubt the influence which drove Jones to complain of "Rank's custom of treating his colleagues as puppets," and of his issuing "reproofs couched in a hectoring tone that I would not accept from anyone else." Dislike of Rank even induced him to criticize Freud, and to Abraham he wrote:

I have renounced the hope of leading the Professor to any sort of objectivity where Rank is concerned. One must recognize with regret that even Freud has his human frailties and that age is bringing with it one-sidedness of vision and diminution of critical power. I hope, however, that Rank will recover from the severe trauma of being for once the criticized one and will in time learn to play his part among us as equal.

At one point Freud took sides against Jones, writing in 1922:

> I had to find out that you had less control of your moods and pas-
> sions, were less consistent, sincere and reliable than I had a right to
> expect of you and than was required of our conspicuous position.
> And although you yourself had proposed the Committee you did not
> refrain from endangering its intimacy by unjust susceptibilities. You
> know it is not my habit to suppress my true judgment in relations of
> friendship and I am always prepared to run the risk attaching to that
> behavior.
>
> You are quite right in asking that friends should not treat each
> other as unrelentingly as fate does, but just imagine how much more
> satisfactory it is to a friend to acknowledge, to praise or to admire
> the other man than to forgive him.

It was to Rank alone, moreover, that Freud had confided a premonition of his developing, but at this point still undiagnosed,
cancer: "It will not have escaped you that for some time now I have
not felt sure of my health," he had written. "I speak of it to no one
else because one gets to hear nothing but the usual insincerities.
You are still the youngest and freshest among us while one knows
that age so near seventy is quite a serious matter."

It was in this situation that in the spring of 1923 Rank, now the
most trusted of the trusted few, finished the manuscript of *The
Trauma of Birth*. The central argument of the book was that the
factor determining an individual's mental development was the
separation-anxiety experienced at birth. This, it was argued, took
pride of place over the Oedipus complex, the importance of which
was thereby drastically diminished. It was not, perhaps, the unqualified heresy which it appeared to be at first glance. As far back
as 1909 Freud himself had added a footnote to the second edition
of *The Interpretation of Dreams* asserting that "the act of birth is the
first experience of anxiety, and thus the source and prototype of
the affect of anxiety"; and at the end of *The Ego and the Id* he had
described birth as "the first great anxiety state." It was therefore
hardly surprising that Freud's first reactions to *The Trauma of Birth*
should have been mixed and that some months after publication
of the book, in December 1923, he should have told Ferenczi: "I
don't know whether 66 or 33 percent of it is true, but in any case
it is the most important progress since the discovery of psychoanalysis."

At this date Rank's only crime was that he had failed to discuss
the work in advance with the other members of the Committee.
"Neither Freud nor Ferenczi had read [the book] beforehand,
though they knew Rank was writing it, and it came as a great

surprise to the rest of us," Jones has stated. Sachs, too, has gone indignantly on record with: "He did not say a word about his new ideas to me until he presented me with a printed copy, although we had stayed at the same summer resort and had seen each other daily while he was writing the book." However, there was no need for Freud to read the published work, since in May 1923 he had accepted a copy of the manuscript from Rank as a birthday gift and later in the year, after his third operation, had written: "And now everything falls into place around this point that you [Rank] are the dreaded David who with his *Trauma of Birth* succeeds in depreciating my work. . . . Thus I can continue your interpretation. I hope to see you soon." Five days later, apparently after receiving a copy of the published book, he wrote:

Dear Dr. Rank:
   I gladly accept your dedication with the assurance of my most cordial thanks. If you could put it more modestly it would be all right with me. Handicapped as I am, I enjoy enormously your admirable productivity. That means for me, too, "Non omnis moriar." ("I shall not wholly die"—Horace—in other words, my works will survive me.)

Some five weeks later Freud reaffirmed his attitude, saying in a letter to members of the Committee that his acceptance of the dedication showed he was not completely out of sympathy with the content of Rank's book:

Complete agreement, in all detailed questions of science and its newly opened problems is not possible among half a dozen men of different personality, and is not even desirable. Only one condition is necessary for our fruitful cooperation, that nobody should desert the common ground of psychoanalytical presuppositions and we may be sure of that with every member of the Committee. . . . There is, furthermore, a circumstance not unknown to you, which makes me especially unfit to function as a despotic, ever-wakeful censor. It is not easy for me to feel my way into another person's thinking; as a rule I have to wait until I have found a connection with it in my own devious ways. So if you want to hold back a new idea every time until I can agree with it, it runs the risk of aging considerably in the meantime.

This is Freud at his best and most reasonable. But while he was for the moment willing to overlook the first signs of apostasy, some of his followers reacted differently. Abraham in particular felt that Rank was a potential danger. "Results of whatever kind obtained in a legitimate analytic manner would never give me cause for such grave doubts," he wrote. "This is something different. I see signs of an ominous development concerning vital issues of psychoanalysis. They force me, to my deepest sorrow, and not for the first time in the twenty years of my psychoanalytic life, to sound a warning." Jones, who was later to claim for Rank a psychotic illness of which no one else was aware, as yet saw nothing wrong with Rank's thesis, and in reading a paper on "Psycho-Analysis and Anthropology" to the Royal Anthropological Institute, declared that the importance of birth on primitive man's belief is one that would meet with extensive support from psychoanalysis and "is quite on the lines of a recent important study by Otto Rank."

But Rank had taken the unprecedented step of airing a major amendment to accepted theory without discussing it with his colleagues. "It would," his biographer Mrs. Taft has admitted, "be hard to imagine any greater assertion of omniscience or any greater insult to the Committee, who had not been informed in advance, much less consulted." Freud, who stood on higher ground than the Committee, now feared that the birth trauma would be the subject of acrimonious debate at the Congress to be held in Salzburg in April 1924. With what at first looks like a step toward abdication but was in fact a judicious move, he decided not to attend. Poor health was a good excuse ready at hand. While the rest of them argued, Freud, intellectually alone, would await whatever verdict the Congress decided to hand down.

But there was also the question of the Committee. After the dissension at San Cristoforo in August 1923 it had been virtually dead; the appearance of Rank's *The Trauma of Birth* had reduced the chances of its revival, and its resuscitation was made even more unlikely by the publication of *The Development of Psychoanalysis*, a book on which Ferenczi had collaborated with Rank. Abraham was now among those pleading for a strong line to be taken, while Freud, still torn between loyalty to his old friends Rank and Ferenczi and loyalty to the cause, unhappily did his best to wash his hands of the argument. "However justified your reaction to Ferenczi and Rank may be," he wrote to Abraham, "your behavior was certainly not friendly. And that is what has made it quite clear that the Committee no longer exists; because the sentiments are not there that would make a Committee out of this handful of people." But he did not like it. "I have survived the Committee that was to be my successor," he wrote to Ferenczi, "perhaps I shall yet survive the International Association. I only hope that psychoanalysis will survive me. But taken altogether it makes a sad ending to life." The position was formalized shortly afterward. A circular letter from Rank announced that the Committee had been dissolved.

At Salzburg a head-on collision between the Rank–Ferenczi axis and the rest was narrowly avoided, and Freud's blunt action in disposing of the magic circle may well have been one of the reasons, acting like a shot across the bows of the opposing factions. But although Abraham made his peace with Ferenczi, Rank was another matter, and the dispute with his colleagues was unresolved when, on the second day of the Congress, he left for the United States.

Rank's visit to America had been arranged some while before. He was to spend about six months in New York, and it should have been obvious that as one of Freud's most trusted lieutenants he would be treated with respect. What had not been appreciated was that the ideas he had tentatively outlined in *The Trauma of Birth* would begin to harden into what looked dangerously like a new basis for psychoanalysis.

Yet Freud still continued to be conciliatory, hoping that Rank would do well in the United States and playfully ending one letter with the request: "Give my regards to all the squirrels and also feed them with peanuts in my name. The real zoo to be visited is in the Bronx."

Slowly, however, Freud became disenchanted with *The Trauma of Birth.* In July he wrote:

In the months since our separation I am even further from agreeing with your innovations. I have seen nothing in two of my cases that have been completed that confirms your views and generally nothing that I did not know before. The final birth phantasy seems to me still to be the child that one gives, analytically, to the father. I am often much concerned about you. The exclusion of the father in your theory seems to reveal too much the result of personal influences in your life which I think I recognize, and my suspicion grows that you could not have written this book had you gone through an analysis yourself. Therefore I beg of you not to become fixed but to leave open a way back.

There were, indeed, a number of reasons why Freud was anxious to welcome Rank back into the fold, as he made clear to Lou Andreas-Salomé in a letter from the Semmering on August 11. "For fifteen years he was an irreproachable assistant and faithful son to me," he said. "Now, since he thinks he has made a great discovery, he is behaving so refractorily that I can only look forward to his return from America with great apprehension. . . . He would be difficult to replace in his various functions."

From Rank, he concealed his apprehension, writing to him on August 25 a letter obviously intended to heal the wound:

> Although I now look at most events *sub specie aeternitatis* and cannot expend violent emotions on them as I did in earlier years, I am not indifferent to the changes in my relation to you. My condition seems to indicate that I have still some life span left, and it is my strong wish that during this period you should not become lost to me. You left Europe, I hear, in a state of excitement and distrust. The knowledge that I have turned away to some extent from approval of your last work may have increased your mood. Probably, you overrate the affective importance of this theoretical difference and you believe that, during your absence, I have been accessible to influences inimical to you. The purpose of this letter is to assure you that this is not the case. I am not so easily accessible to others, and the others—I had for some days the visit of Eitingon and Abraham—are equally sincere in recognizing your great merits and regret deeply the rudeness with which you isolate yourself. There is no animosity toward you either with us or with my New York family. There is just time to exchange a letter before your return. I would like you to inform me and reassure me about your present state of mind.
>
> The difference of opinion concerning *The Trauma of Birth* carries no weight with me. Either, in the run of time—if there is enough time left—you will convince and correct me or you will correct yourself and separate the lasting new gains from what the bias of the discoverer has added. I know that you are not lacking acclaim for your innovation, but consider how few are able to judge and how strong the desire is in most of them to get away from the Oedipus wherever a path seems to open. Even if much is erroneous, in no case do you have to be ashamed of your product, rich in spirit and content, which brings new and valuable ideas even to the critics. But surely you should not assume that this work of yours must disrupt our relation founded on the intimacy of so many years.
>
> Adding to my cordial regards the expectation of seeing you soon,
>
> Freud

But Rank had already written to Freud. There are four different versions of his letter, only one of which was sent, and all indicate that even though Jones was later unnecessarily scathing about Rank's mental condition, New York had certainly produced an inflated confidence. After berating Freud for listening overmuch to Abraham, Rank continued: "Do not let us forget that the psychoanalytic movement as such is a fiction, and for the people who are now eager to work at a psychoanalytic movement, I confess, I have no sympathy."

Whatever Freud might have been able to accept in the way of recriminations against his colleagues, the description of his beloved cause as a fiction touched him on the rawest of raw nerves. He appears to have received Rank's letter the day after sending his long conciliatory appeal. He replied at once in terms of very different character. "To impute to Abraham 'profound ignorance,' to call him 'a noisy ranter,' that presupposes a disturbance of judgment only to be explained by a boundless affectivity, and fits ill with the overcoming of complexes," he said before making the final accusation of treason. "An evil demon makes you say that this psychoanalytic movement is a fiction, and puts in your mouth the very words of the enemy."

The following month Freud confided to Ferenczi that it now looked as if "from the very beginning [Rank] had the intention of establishing himself on the basis of his patent procedure which he kept secret, and wanted you to join him." He was surprised that Ferenczi had collaborated with Rank on *The Development of Psychoanalysis* and, to give emphasis to his feelings, passed on to Ferenczi one of Rank's letters. The move worked. Ferenczi decided to break with Rank, and passing him later in Pennsylvania Station, cut him dead. "He was my best friend, and he refused to speak to me," Rank bitterly remembered.

When Rank arrived back in Vienna in October, Freud still hoped for a reconciliation, and it was arranged that the two men should meet. But on the day that the visitor called at No. 19 Berggasse, Freud received a letter from Brill in New York, describing the effect of Rank's visit. Freud circulated the letter, which appears to have enlarged on the enormity of Rank's renegade views. Once again, circulation of a damaging letter did the trick as far as the psychoanalytic community in Vienna was concerned.

Even so, further interviews between Rank and Freud took place, and Freud appears to have retained a genuine hope that the differences between them could even now be smoothed over. However, there was a point beyond which he could not go, and when Rank set off for America again in December, it looked as if the break was final.

Then, in Paris, there occurred what Jones has described as "a miracle." Instead of continuing to the United States, Rank returned to Vienna, once again met Freud, and on December 26, 1924, sent a circular letter to the members of the Committee which said:

From a state which I now recognize as neurotic, I have suddenly returned to myself. Not only have I recognized the actual cause of the crisis in the trauma occasioned by the dangerous illness of the Professor, but I was able also to understand the type of reaction and its mechanism from my childhood and family history—the Oedipus and brother complexes. . . . From analytic interviews with the Professor, in which I could explain in detail the reactions based on affective attitudes, I gain the hope that I was successful in clarifying, first of all, the personal relationship, since the Professor found my explanations satisfactory and has forgiven me personally.

Rank had for the moment seen the error of his ways. But his circular letter is an astonishing one, similar in an uncanny way to the statements by prisoners of the Communists who have been brainwashed into confession. Nevertheless, the retraction is not unique in the annals of psychoanalysis. Almost a decade after Fritz Wittels had published his life of Freud, he wrote for the *Psychoanalytic Review* a lengthy paper entitled "Revision of a Biography." This went a great deal further than the amendments and qualifications that could readily be accounted for by fresh information or fresh judgments. In withdrawing the greater part of his accusations against Freud, Wittels adopted a tone typified by his opening statement: he could "no longer stand sponsor for the errors and misrepresentations which I have come to recognize as such."

In Rank's case the change was not to last. Back in the United States, susceptible to the attentions and high fees of those who still looked on him as Freud's disciple, he returned to the stance he had maintained before "the miracle." His last meeting with Freud took place on April 12, 1926, during a brief visit to Europe. Freud made two comments. "I was honest and hard," he wrote to Ferenczi, "but we have certainly lost him for good." And to Sachs: "Now, after I have forgiven everything, I am through with him."

As with the earlier desertions—an appropriate word since at one point Freud wrote to Jones, hoping that Rank would "again fight bravely in our ranks"—the situation was one of genuine disagreement about psychoanalytic theory and about personal relationships. The difference was that while with Adler, Stekel and Jung, Freud's professional disagreements were encouraged by his personal feelings, the reverse was the case with Otto Rank. But once his tolerance had evaporated, Freud was quick to give more substance to his criticism of *The Trauma of Birth.* In 1926 he dealt with it in "Inhibitions, Symptoms and Anxiety" and, a decade later, in "Analysis, Terminable and Interminable" delivered his final verdict. "Rank's argument was bold and ingenious," he decided, "but it did not stand the test of critical examination. Moreover, it was a child of its time, conceived under the stress of the contrast between the postwar misery of Europe and the 'prosperity' of America, and designed to adapt the tempo of analytic therapy to the haste of American life."

As to the contemporary view of Rank's trauma of birth, this depends very largely on whose view is sought, the differences tending to highlight the sometimes diametrically opposed opinions held on either side of the Atlantic. In Britain it is sometimes stated that the idea is now of little more than historical interest, thus vindicating Freud's dismissal. This view is often contested. In the United States there is Arthur Janov's primal scream therapy, largely based on the birth trauma and one which Freud might consider as "designed to adapt . . . to the haste of American life."

The correctness of his more general judgment on Rank became apparent years later when Anaïs Nin, the young French writer whose analyst Rank had become in the United States, published her *Journals*. They give a revealing picture of Rank when, following a succession of returns to Europe, he had finally settled in New York; and his description of psychoanalysis as he then considered it leaves no doubt about his basic differences with Freud. "I do not believe in long drawn-out psycho-analysis," Rank said, according to Nin.

> I do not believe in spending too much time exploring the past, delving into it. I believe neurosis is like a virulent abscess, or infection. It has to be attacked powerfully in the present. Of course, the origin of the illness may be in the past, but the virulent crisis must be dynamically tackled. I believe in attacking the core of the illness, through its present symptoms, quickly, directly. The past is a labyrinth. One does not have to step into it and move step by step through every turn and twist. The past reveals itself instantly, in today's fever or abscess of the soul.
>
> I believe analysis has become the worst enemy of the soul. It killed what it analyzed. I saw too much psychoanalysis with Freud and his disciples which became pontifical, dogmatic. That was why I was ostracized from the original group.

Freud's break with Ferenczi, which was never complete, had its genesis in the 1920s but did not reach its climax until 1932. The disagreements were genuine disagreements about two aspects of psychoanalysis, the less important concerning the relative weight that each gave to clinical and to nonclinical work. From the earliest days Freud had regarded the development of psychoanalysis as an investigation of the way in which the human mind works. Patients provided his raw laboratory material, but while he had as much desire as the next man to relieve suffering and cure illness, curiosity was always a spur. As his old friend Hanns Sachs admitted, "he had nothing of the *furor therapeuticus.*" Ferenczi, by contrast, had gradually become monopolized by a single interest, "the need to cure and to help," as Freud was to describe it. Whatever his interest in the theory and organization of psychoanalysis, and at times it was considerable, results from the couch came first.

But the difference between Freud and Ferenczi was here one of degree and was hardly important enough to produce serious argument between the two men, let alone a breach. More fundamental was the question of technique. Freud had always maintained for severely practical reasons that the role of the analyst was that of the objective outsider, listening to his patient's recollections, sifting, sorting, interpreting but never becoming personally involved. There were of course the problems of transference and countertransference, but they were known problems and could be dealt with by care, common sense and discipline.

Throughout the 1920s Ferenczi had come to adopt a more controversial approach. Lack of parental love, he believed, lay at the root of much mental trouble which could be removed if the analyst adopted a personal attitude toward his patient—what Freud was to call "[playing] mother and child with his female patients." Freud found the idea repugnant; it offended his own personal standards, and in an age when psychoanalysis was being attacked for its encouragement of sexual looseness it offered enemies a handy weapon. "I see that the differences between us come to a head in a technical detail which is well worth discussing," he wrote to Ferenczi at the end of 1931. "You have not made a secret of the fact that you kiss your patients and let them kiss you; I had also heard that from a patient of my own." Ferenczi, Freud said, would have the choice of publishing or concealing this when he gave a full-scale description of how he worked. To conceal the facts would be dishonorable, to publish might have unfortunate results. "There is," Freud continued,

no revolutionary who is not driven out of the field by a still more radical one. A number of independent thinkers in matters of technique will say to themselves: why stop at a kiss? Certainly one gets further when one adopts "pawing" as well, which after all doesn't make a baby. And then bolder ones will come along who will go further to peeping and showing—and soon we shall have accepted in the technique of analysis the whole repertoire of demi-viergerie and petting parties, resulting in an enormous increase of interest in psychoanalysis among both analysts and patients. The new adherent, however, will easily claim too much of this interest for himself, the younger of our colleagues will find it hard to stop at the point they originally intended, and God the Father Ferenczi gazing at the lively scene he has created, will perhaps say to himself: maybe after all I should have halted in my technique of motherly affection *before* the kiss.

Ferenczi took little notice, and the following year a delicate situation arose shortly before the Congress to be held in Wiesbaden. Eitingon was to resign as president, and Ferenczi was expected to succeed him. But the paper Ferenczi was to read was considered by some to be so controversial that Freud begged him not to read it. Ferenczi went ahead, the paper was passed as comparatively harmless and, after Ferenczi's decision that he was too busy to become president, Jones was elected in Eitingon's place.

Ferenczi's health was already deteriorating, and soon after the Congress Freud noted to Marie Bonaparte: "Ferenczi is a bitter drop in the cup. His wife has told me I should think of him as a sick child! You are right: psychical and intellectual decay is far worse than the unavoidable bodily one." Early the following year Freud acknowledged Ferenczi's New Year's greeting in a note that ended by saying he was "glad to hear of the restoration of your health, a precious piece of the more beautiful past."

However, within a few months Ferenczi was dead. According to Jones, he had mentally deteriorated, was subject to latent psychotic trends, had dropped into a "final delusional state," and at the end showed "violent paranoiac and even homicidal outbursts." According to Michael Balint, a psychoanalyst close to the heart of the movement, this was not true, and he subsequently wrote:

> I saw Ferenczi during the last months of his life on many occasions, once or twice a week, and I never found him deluded, paranoid or homicidal. On the contrary, though he was physically incapacitated by his ataxia, mentally most of the time he was quite fresh and often discussed with me the various details of his controversy with Freud and his plan to review some of his ideas published in his last papers —if he ever would again be able to write. I saw him on the Sunday before his death and though he was very weak his mind even then was completely clear.

The contradiction in the evidence can be explained at various levels. It has been suggested that Jones never "forgave" Ferenczi for the insight into his character derived from Ferenczi's Budapest analysis of him in 1913. More plausible is the idea behind Erich

Fromm's observation: "Apparently Jones assumes that only a diseased mind can accuse Freud of authoritarianism and hostility."

Of the authoritarianism there can be little doubt, despite the protestations of Freud's supporters who credit him with what would have been an almost inhuman, and certainly disabling, perfection. Fritz Wittels, for instance, could write as an admirer in 1924: "He has become a despot who will not tolerate the slightest deviation from his doctrine; holds councils behind closed doors; and tries to ensure, by a sort of pragmatic sanction, that the body of psychoanalytical teaching shall remain an indivisible whole."

Wittels overstates the case, yet it does seem to be true that some psychoanalysts left the International Association in circumstances which have not been adequately explained. Notable was the case of Wilhelm Reich. It is no doubt true that Reich's political views were as responsible as was his orgasm theory for his estrangement from the body of orthodox psychoanalytic opinion. Nevertheless, while the official version is that Reich resigned from the Association at the Lucerne Congress of 1934, Reich always maintained that he was expelled.

By this time Freud must have become only too well aware that he lived in constant danger of a stab in the back that was as likely to come from friend as from foe. The situation tended to make him more than usually careful in political negotiation for the cause, and more cautious than he might otherwise have been in qualifying the views of his earlier years.

21

Riding the Tiger?

Freud replied that there was implicit in this argument a false assumption that the validity of psychoanalytic findings and theories were definitely established, while actually they were still in their beginning, and needed a great deal of development and repeated verification and confirmation.

MARTIN W. PECK, "A Brief Visit with Freud,"
Psychoanalytic Quarterly

However fierce the internecine quarrels between members of the Committee, which Jones reestablished at the end of 1924, and however painful individual desertions might be to Freud personally, it was still impossible to challenge his position as originator and leader of a cause that was steadily though slowly gaining ground. As a consequence he inevitably became involved in the organizational and institutional controversies besetting an expanding movement.

Thus to Freud there came the first proposal that psychoanalysis should be presented to the public on the cinema screen. He reacted with horror and contempt, and not only because the approach had been made by the irrepressible Sam Goldwyn.

In December 1924, Goldwyn crossed the Atlantic to Europe, telling the *New York Times* on board ship that there was nothing so really entertaining on the screen as a great love story.

So I thought I would go and see Freud and at least have a talk with the greatest love specialist in the world. . . . The finished pictures produced with Professor Freud as collaborator will have audience appeal far greater than any productions made today, because these love revelations and psychological truths will strike fire with the deepest thoughts and feelings of the people who unquestionably react more strongly to the genuine in pictures.

So they might indeed. But Freud, who had remained generally antagonistic to the cinema since his first experience of it in New York, in 1909, had other ideas. "I do not intend to see Mr. Goldwyn," he announced.

The rejection was partly the result of Goldwyn's reputation for transforming history into fiction. Nevertheless, Freud's feelings went deeper than mere fear that the subject to which he had devoted his life would be vulgarized and trivialized for popular consumption: he did not believe that it would be possible to explain the theories of psychoanalysis on the silver screen. This became clear less than six months later when he learned that both Abraham and Sachs had been approached in Berlin by UFA— Universum Film Aktiengesellschaft, the largest film company in Germany—which wanted their advice on the making of a documentary on psychoanalysis. It was planned that the director would be G. W. Pabst, the Austrian whose film of the desperate poverty in Vienna, *Freudlose Gasse (Joyless Street)*, had recently exerted a profound influence, and it was clear that the company would go ahead with the project with or without the help of Freud or his colleagues.

For this reason, as much as for any other, Abraham did his best to enlist Freud's support, while agreeing that "this kind of thing is not really up my street." Freud was unconcerned about the money that might be made from the film and pointed out that if any did come his way, he would be glad to hand it over to the Verlag. But he was still adamant in his objection. "The film will be as unpreventable, it seems, as bobbed hair," he protested to Ferenczi, "but I'm not having mine cut, and neither will I have any personal connection with any film."

Nevertheless the making of the film was started, and it progressed in a desultory way throughout the summer, accompanied by a steady breakdown of Abraham's health, which threw more of the work on to Sachs, and by continuing doubts as to how much support should be given by psychoanalysts. Siegfried Bernfeld, another Viennese analyst, wrote his own script for a film and tried to bring Abraham into his project. The move brought an indignant complaint from Abraham to Freud, who appears to have taken a more lenient view of his Viennese. Abraham pointed out that in previous disagreements Freud had not always been right, and received the somewhat testy reply: "You are not necessarily always right. But should you turn out to be right this time too, nothing would prevent me from once again admitting it." Abraham's health continued to deteriorate and his death—from what now appears to have been undiagnosed lung cancer—came on Christmas Day 1925, virtually as the film was being completed.

Geheimnisse einer Seele (Secrets of a Soul) was released early in 1926, together with a monograph written by Hanns Sachs for those who saw the film. This traced the case of a genuine patient —details being changed to prevent identification—who had been suffering from a knife phobia and compulsions, and showed both the origins of the symptoms and the precipitating factors that brought them to the surface. It was followed by a visual record of the analysis which, in the days of silent films, had to be presented with the help of the words written in the analyst's notebook. Despite Freud's anxieties, *Secrets of a Soul* was an honest and at least partially successful explanation of psychoanalysis. What weighed most heavily on the debit side was probably the opportunity the film offered Freud's opponents to accuse him of promoting his wares in the cinema.

As *Secrets of a Soul* was being shown throughout Germany, Freud became more directly involved with a question that had been slumbering within psychoanalysis since its earliest years: the problem of lay analysis. Should the new therapy be practiced only by qualified doctors or should laymen also be allowed to practice?

During the early years of the century the problem had hardly arisen in practical terms. A few men who were not qualified doctors had joined Freud's group in Vienna, but only a handful had practiced, and they had not done so on any great scale. There was an Austrian law which forbade the administration of medical treatment by the unqualified, but this had been passed to hamper the operation of quacks and charlatans, and although the feeling against psychoanalysis was strong in the country, the law had never been invoked against it.

While the informed opinion prevalent in the United States was that only medical men should practice, in Austria analysis by laymen as well as by doctors was accepted. This view was no doubt influenced by the strong opinion held by Freud, who in a letter written in 1926 to Paul Federn, acting chairman of the Vienna Psychoanalytical Society, had said: "The battle for lay analysis must, at one time or the other, be fought to the finish. Better now than later. As long as I live I shall resist that psychoanalysis be swallowed up by medicine." Subsequently he explained his feelings in more detail when writing to Pfarrer Pfister about two of his own publications:

I do not know if you have detected the secret link between the "Lay Analysis" and the "Illusion." In the former I wish to protect analysis from the doctors and in the latter from the priests. I should like to hand it over to a profession which does not yet exist, a profession of *lay* curers of souls who need not be doctors and should not be priests.

In other countries positions between those of Vienna and America were taken up, by Jones in London, by Eitingon in Berlin and by numerous others who believed in the principle of lay analysis but felt that its practice should be safeguarded by certain restrictions —notably that it should be preceded by the recommendation of a doctor.

Events began moving toward a clash of views between Europeans and Americans after five European societies and the New York Psychoanalytic Society were admitted to the International Training Committee at the Bad Homburg Congress in 1925. The following year lay analysis was made illegal in New York State, formal recognition of a situation already causing dismay to some of Freud's associates. Arriving in the States as laymen, and expecting their services to be encouraged, they found exactly the reverse.

Such was the situation when, in 1926, Theodor Reik, a member of the Vienna Psychoanalytical Society, was accused under the rarely invoked Austrian law of treating a patient while having no medical degree. Freud immediately intervened, and not only because it was he himself who had passed the patient on to Reik.

Freud came to his colleague's aid by intervening with a favorably inclined government official to whom he cogently outlined the position as he saw it. He was unsuccessful, and the fact that the case against Reik was eventually withdrawn was due mainly to the weakness of the prosecution's evidence. However, Freud's long discussion with the authorities was not unproductive since it was the stimulus for "The Question of Lay Analysis," a 25,000-word exposition in which he put the case to an imaginary objector.

Freud was persuasive, but the argument continued to rumble on, complicated as it was by the fact that the issue was not as clear-cut as it appeared on the surface. After the *International Journal* and the *Zeitschrift* had published twenty-eight papers, airing a diversity of views on the subject, it was debated at length, but without much success for either side, at the Innsbruck Congress in 1927. Thereafter the fortunes of battle fluctuated. At the Oxford Congress in 1929—where Anna reported the College accommodation as "more tradition than comfort" and drew from Freud the reflection: "You know that the English, having created the notion of comfort, then refused to have anything more to do with it"— one advance was made. Diagnosis was separated from treatment, and it was agreed that no lay analyst could accept a consultation from a patient, or see any patient, except one referred to him by a medical analyst. Further discussions continued at Wiesbaden in 1932, at Lucerne in 1934 and at Paris in 1938. At none of the Congresses was the problem solved, even though both sides made concessions. By the end of the Second World War, death and emigration had so decimated the European psychoanalytic community that command of the field was effectively left to the Americans.

The first publication of "The Question of Lay Analysis" was in a volume which also contained a short essay called "An Autobiographical Study." It was in fact Freud's contribution to a four-volume work published in Leipzig under the title of *Die Medizin der Gegenwart in Selbstdarstellungen (Contemporary Medicine in Self-Portraits)*, and it traced the course of psychoanalysis rather than the life of its founder. Nevertheless it made clear in an extraordinary way how, as Freud was to write in a postscript to the essay ten years later, "psychoanalysis came to be the whole content of [his] life."

In the postscript Freud reminded readers that although he had carried out some important revisions of his psychoanalytic views in the 1920s, he had "made no further decisive contributions to psychoanalysis" since *Beyond the Pleasure Principle* and *The Ego and the Id;* "what I have written on the subject since then has been either unessential or would soon have been supplied by someone else." While this is technically correct, it should not be allowed to hide the fact that the important revisions, as Freud called them, were exceptionally so, and that during the next few years his output was to be remarkable for a sick man in his seventies: two considerable essays, one on religion, one on civilization, both treating their subjects psychoanalytically; a psychobiography of Woodrow Wilson; a series of essays written as an extension of his 1915–1917 lectures; and a book, *Moses and Monotheism,* which merged his life's interests in Jewish beliefs with his own views of unconscious motives and was almost defiantly flung in the face of his critics, both Jewish and Gentile. He had, as he often said, wanted to die in harness.

The revisions, which Ernest Jones considered the "most valuable clinical contribution Freud made in the period after the war years," were contained in "Inhibitions, Symptoms and Anxiety." In the 1890s, when he had first begun to investigate the neuroses, he had regarded anxiety neurosis as the result of undischarged sexual tension, an explanation soon extended to cover the anxiety of various psychoneuroses. It was developed in some of his early letters and drafts to Fliess, as well as in *The Interpretation of Dreams*, while as late as 1920 he added a footnote to *Three Essays,* saying that anxiety was a transformation of the libido, the two being related "in the same kind of way as vinegar is to wine." In spite of this belief, persisted in for more than a quarter of a century, there were times when Freud appeared to contradict the very theory he was expounding. To Fliess he wrote in November 1897 that he had decided to regard the cause of libido as different from the cause of anxiety. There followed, in the summer of 1909, the footnote in *The Interpretation of Dreams*—"the act of birth is the first experience of anxiety, and thus the source and prototype of the affect of anxiety"—and its repetition more than a decade later in *The Ego and the Id*.

After publication of Rank's *The Trauma of Birth* Freud began to examine his own views afresh. He now abandoned the theory that anxiety was a transformation of libido but found it impossible to give to the birth trauma the importance that both he and Rank had given it on various occasions. Instead, he provided a simpler explanation, one with which most people would have agreed even before the birth of psychoanalysis:

> Anxiety is a reaction to a situation of danger. It is obviated by the ego's doing something to avoid that situation or to withdraw from it. It might be said that symptoms are created so as to avoid the generating of anxiety. But this does not go deep enough. It would be truer to say that symptoms are created so as to avoid a *danger situation* whose presence has been signaled by the generation of anxiety.

Freud's new explanation was the last major revision to his beliefs about the workings of the mind. Yet from now onward it is possible to see a trace of qualification in more than one of his pronouncements about psychoanalysis: a qualification about its efficacy on which he placed considerably more emphasis than before. He still believed in the cause. Increasingly handicapped as he was by disease, with death and desertion claiming the founding fathers, and with new recruits emphasizing social and political factors to which he had given little attention, he still retained his faith in his life work. But he continued to remind his readers that it was wrong to believe that psychoanalysis could cure every kind of neurotic phenomena.

It was a warning he had given as early as 1922 in a long article written for the *Encyclopaedia Britannica*. Now he was to state that "so long as the organic factors remain inaccessible, analysis leaves much to be desired." Moreover, a few years later his "Analysis Terminable and Interminable" gave what his editor James Strachey admitted to be "an impression of pessimism in regard to the therapeutic efficacy of psychoanalysis." This was no more than the truth, since Freud had written:

> One has an impression that one ought not to be surprised if it should turn out in the end that the difference between a person who has not been analyzed and the behavior of a person after he has been analyzed is not so thoroughgoing as we aim at making it and as we expect and maintain it to be. . . . I really cannot commit myself to a decision on this point, nor do I know whether a decision is possible at the present time.

In spite of the constant insistence that every treatment by psychoanalysis had to surmount a number of hurdles, such views would have sounded dangerously like heresy a few decades earlier. Yet even they were more qualified than Freud's statement in 1937 to the American psychoanalyst Martin W. Peck. During a talk Peck said he felt that the time had come for closer cooperation between psychoanalysis and medicine. "Freud replied," he later wrote, "that there was implicit in this argument a false assumption that the validity of psychoanalytic findings and theories were definitely established, while actually they were still in their beginning, and needed a great deal of development and repeated verification and confirmation." Whatever gloss is put on the words, they are very different from the dogmatism of "We possess the truth."

Before the change of emphasis became so clearly visible, Freud had been affected by what he called an "alteration" in himself. "My interest, after making a lifelong *détour* through the natural sciences, medicine and psychotherapy, returned to the cultural problems which had fascinated me long before, when I was a youth scarcely old enough for thinking," he wrote. He had, he went on, begun to carry a stage further the work he had started in *Totem and Taboo*. "I perceived ever more clearly," he said, "that the events of human history, the interactions between human nature, cultural development and the precipitates of primaeval experiences (the most prominent example of which is religion) are no more than a reflection of the dynamic conflicts between the ego, the id and super-ego, which psycho-analysis studies in the individual—are the very same processes repeated upon a wider stage."

Freud turned to the work with an enthusiasm which had been accumulating during the previous decade, years during which he had devoted himself to building his new conceptual framework, struggled through the disasters of postwar Vienna, and dealt with the physical and mental trauma of cancer, and Otto Rank's defection. Now at last he could let himself go on the things he had felt so strongly about for years.

The first of his new essays was *The Future of an Illusion*, begun early in 1927, finished by the autumn and published in November. Religion itself was the illusion, and Freud knew that by submitting it to criticism in a set-piece essay he would once again be inviting attack. "The one person this publication may injure is myself," he admitted. "I shall have to listen to the most disagreeable reproaches for my shallowness, narrow-mindedness and lack of idealism or of understanding for the highest interests of mankind." But for Freud this would be no new experience, and "if a man has already learnt in his youth to rise superior to the disapproval of his contemporaries, what can it matter to him in his old age when he is certain soon to be beyond the reach of all favor or disfavor?" He wondered whether his attack would harm the cause. Yet, he reassured himself, psychoanalysis was a method of research, and if religion retreated under its scrutiny, then surely it would be religion rather than psychoanalysis that would be found wanting.

The cool appraisal was not the first he had given to the subject. Twenty years earlier, in "Obsessive Actions and Religious Practices," he had charted numerous similiarities between the actions of neurotics and those of the devout, and in *Totem and Taboo* he had claimed for religion a genesis which none considered flattering and few considered acceptable. *The Future of an Illusion* had been simmering for a long time, and one reason for Freud's delay in writing it had been his regard for his clerical friend, Pfarrer Pfister. Finally, as he put it, "the impulse became too strong. . . . I feared, and still fear, that such a public profession of my attitude will be painful to you." He was right. But Pfister was quite capable of defending himself; in reply to *The Future of an Illusion* he promptly responded with "The Illusion of a Future."

Freud threw a penetrating sidelight on his own essay during a visit by Binswanger to the Semmering in September 1927. The two men were discussing the problem of ensuring genuine collaboration between analyst and patient, a problem attributed by Binswanger to lack of "spirit." Binswanger later recalled:

> I could scarcely believe my ears when I heard [Freud] say, "Yes, the spirit is everything," even though I was inclined to surmise that by "spirit" he meant in this case something like intelligence.
> But then Freud continued: "Mankind has always known that it possesses spirit; I had to show it that there are also instincts. But men are always discontented, they cannot wait, they always want something whole and ready-made; however, one must begin somewhere

and one progresses only slowly." Encouraged by this admission I went one step further, saying that I had been forced to recognize something like a fundamental religious category in man; that at all events I found it impossible to admit that "the religious" was a phenomenon that could somehow be derived from something else. (Needless to say, what I had in mind was neither the "genesis" of a specific religion nor that of "religion" in general, but what I have since learned to describe as the religious I–Thou relationship). But now I had overreached the limits of our agreement, and aroused his opposition: "Religions originate in the child's and young mankind's fears and need for help," Freud said tersely, "it cannot be otherwise." As he said this, he pulled out his desk drawer: "Now is the moment for me to show you something," and he took out a completed manuscript that bore the title *The Future of an Illusion*, and looked at me with an inquiring smile. From the trend of our conversation I easily guessed the meaning of this title. It was time for me to go. Freud walked with me to the door. His last words, accompanied by a shrewd, slightly ironic smile, were: "I am sorry I cannot satisfy your religious needs."

In the essay Freud correctly maintained that he was adding little to the argument against religion, and that his exposition merely added "some psychological foundation to the criticisms of my great predecessors." Throughout he made no reference to any of the world's revealed religions—although in a predominantly Catholic Austria it was clear where his arrows were aimed. Instead, as he later wrote, he concentrated on what the common man understood by his religion—"the system of doctrines and promises which on the one hand explains to him the riddles of this world with enviable completeness and, on the other, assures him that a careful Providence will watch over his life and will compensate him in a future existence for any frustrations he suffers here." Such beliefs, Freud maintained, were generated by wishful thinking, and acted as a defense against the cosmic forces which man would never be able to understand.

The idea was by no means new, but in Freud's hands it was subtly supported by the findings which psychoanalysis had brought to the surface during the previous three decades. The reaction to *The Future of an Illusion* was as expected. In Britain, T. S. Eliot, among others, was critical. In New York, Rabbi Nathan Krass, speaking at Temple Emanu-El on Fifth Avenue, voiced a popular feeling in popular words. "In this country," he said,

we have grown accustomed to listening to men and women talk on all topics because they have done something notable in one field.

Because Edison knows about electricity we ask for and listen to his opinions of theology. Because a man has made a name for himself in aviation he is asked to make speeches on everything under the sun. All admire Freud, the psychoanalyst, but that is no reason why we should respect his theology.

But it was perhaps not only Freud's theology that worried some of his readers. If the late 1920s was not yet the age of Henry Wallace's "Common Man," it was already the age in which leadership, discipline, obedience were becoming suspect words and in which criticism of the common man was among the vilest of heresies. What, therefore, was one to make of Freud's discussion of this ticklish matter? "It is just as impossible to do without control of the mass by a minority as it is to dispense with coercion in the work of civilization," he argued. "For masses are lazy and unintelligent; they have no love for instinctual renunciation, and they are not to be convinced by argument of its inevitability; and the individuals composing them support one another in giving free rein to their indiscipline. It is only through the influence of individuals who can set an example and whom masses recognize as their leaders that they can be induced to perform the work and undergo the renunciations on which the existence of civilization depends." This was no more than an overdose of Gustave Le Bon, whose *The Psychology of Crowds* had influenced Freud's *Group Psychology*, but it was hardly likely to make Freud popular.

The Future of an Illusion was very largely concerned with spelling out in detail the convictions which he had previously put forward in more general terms. But the essay did disclose an appreciation of the scientific spirit which had not been overprominent in his earlier writings. Thus in upholding science against "the burden of religious doctrines" he could write: "The transformations of scientific opinion are developments, advances, not revolutions. A law which was held at first to be universally valid proves to be a special case of a more comprehensive uniformity or is limited by another law, not discovered till later; a rough approximation to the truth is replaced by a more carefully adapted one, which in turn awaits further perfectioning." It might be no more than a lesson learned from Einstein's achievement in subsuming Newtonian gravity into general relativity, although Freud appears to have had alarmingly optimistic ideas of the position in this field, judging by a remark reported by Ernest Jones: "I always envy the physicists and mathematicians who can stand on firm ground," he is quoted as saying. "I hover, so to speak, in the air. Mental events seem to be immeasurable and probably always will be so." This was a fair assessment of the difference between the problems facing psychoanalysts and those of the "hard" sciences; but it assumes a certainty which would hardly have been claimed by Rutherford, Einstein or Heisenberg, by Whitehead, Russell or Gödel.

Freud should have had every reason to be pleased at the reception given to *The Future of an Illusion,* since it confirmed his views about those who supported revealed religions. Nevertheless, he expressed a surprising lack of appreciation to at least one visitor. René Laforgue, one of his former analysands, had read the essay with enthusiasm. He wrote to Freud and was invited to call upon him at Schneewinkel, the hamlet above Berchtesgaden where he had finished *The Interpretation of Dreams* some thirty years previously. "[He] at once broached the subject," Laforgue wrote.

> He confessed that it was always a pleasure for an author to be complimented about one of his works, but he then poured cold water on my enthusiasm. "This is my worst book!" he said. "It isn't a book of Freud." Can you imagine my utter surprise? How I protested! He continued talking. "It's the book of an old man." Well, I nearly fainted. He added, laying stress on each word, "Besides, Freud is dead now, and believe me, the genuine Freud was really a great man. I am particularly sorry for you that you didn't know him better."
>
> I stammered something like, "But, Herr Professor, what makes you say that?" So he answered, *"Die Durchschlagskraft ist verloren gegangen* [The punch is lost]."

Freud's reaction was probably due to the battle with the prosthesis as much as to anything else. There was persistent trouble and struggle with it, and in the autumn of 1928 he was persuaded to visit Professor Schroeder, an oral surgeon in Berlin, so that a better one could be made. During the visit, accompanied by Anna, he stayed with Ernst Simmel, by this time running a psychoanalytic sanitarium in Schloss Tegel, on the outskirts of the city; and to Simmel he sent, following his return to Vienna a ring similar to those once "distinguishing a group of men who were united in their devotion to psychoanalysis, who had promised to watch its development as a 'secret committee,' and to practice among themselves a kind of analytical brotherhood."

Princess Marie Bonaparte and Ferenczi visited him during the two-month stay in Berlin. So did Lou Andreas-Salomé. They were now on such terms as could survive the worst buffets. They had even survived the occasion when Freud told her one day that he had just read Nietzsche's "Prayer to Life," written when she had been Nietzsche's mistress. He thought it atrocious. "Millennia to be, to think, to live," he quoted. "Hold me in both your arms with might and main! / If you have no more happiness to give: / Give me your pain." Freud protested. "No, no. I could not go along with that. A good head cold would cure me of all such wishes!" Lou was too fond of him to be hurt; too fond, even though it was she, and not Nietzsche, who had written the lines.

In Berlin she and Freud walked together in the parks stretching along the Tegelsee, where he picked her a bunch of the red, blue and purple pansies flowering in profusion. His cancer made talking difficult but they reminisced for hours about their experiences since they had first met nearly two decades earlier. "Suddenly," says her biographer, "Lou asked Freud whether he still remembered her 'Prayer to Life,' the poem which he thought Nietzsche had written." Freud did remember. "And then," Lou has written, "something happened that I did not understand myself, but no power in the world could have stopped me; my trembling lips in revolt against his fate and martyrdom, burst out: 'You have done what I, in my youthful enthusiasm, only raved about.' " Startled by her own words, Lou burst into tears. Freud did not answer. "I only felt his arms around me," she wrote.

Despite the handicap of his condition in Berlin, Freud made the most of his time in the German capital, visiting relatives and enjoying his first aircraft flight, which he described in a letter to Samuel Freud on his return to Vienna. "I found the sensation startling and rather pleasant," he noted.

It was not to be his last visit to the city in search of relief. The new prosthesis was a great improvement, but it was to be only one of a succession with whose help Freud tried to live a normal existence. But he was under no illusion about the future. "I will consider everything that life still has to offer me as a gift," he had written to Simmel after his first visit to Schloss Tegel, "and you know that one should not examine gifts too closely."

The underlying pessimism can be detected in his writings and was exemplified in the work to which he turned in the summer of 1929 when he was again staying at Schneewinkel. He still loved the mountains. He still enjoyed the flowers and the views. And Dr. Schur who visited him noticed "that all the suffering did not substantially impair his capacity for such enjoyment." Yet the long strenuous walks were no longer possible. He found it difficult to settle down to reading and, as he lamented to Lou, one could not smoke or play cards all day. He knew what the answer was. He turned to work "and in doing so the time passed quite pleasantly."

The result was a 30,000-word essay, virtually finished during the last days of July. Its title, *Unhappiness in Civilization,* before being changed to *Civilization and its Discontents,* reflected the pessimism of his cool and sometimes despairing look at man's problem of living with his fellow men. As with so much of Freud's writings, the effect of his own immediate and personal circumstances influenced the way in which he tackled the problem in hand. More than thirty years before, he had contended that one could hold civilization "responsible for the spread of neurasthenia." Now he was beginning to see the antagonism between instinct and civilization in wider terms.

He was not, initially at least, very satisfied with the thesis which he had developed. "It deals with civilization, guilt feelings, happiness and similar lofty matters," he told Lou, "and it strikes me, no doubt rightly, as quite superfluous in contrast to earlier works, which after all always derived from some inner urge. But what else should I do?"

A good part of the essay covered well-trodden ground. A group of men willing to restrict their instincts and work together for the common good would be stronger than any single individual; but such an embryonic civilization would inevitably produce in each member conflict between his own instincts and the demands of society. With the growth of civilization, Freud speculated, the conflict might have become unresolvable, civilization thus creating its own neurosis. It was hardly an original proposition, but in his spotlighting of man's innate aggression and his proposal that conflict between aggression and the ego produced a sense of guilt, Freud struck out along new lines. In fact it was, he said, his "intention to represent the sense of guilt as the most important problem in the development of civilization, and to show that the price we pay for our advance in civilization is a loss of happiness through the heightening of the sense of guilt."

Freud had written *Civilization and its Discontents* during the first weeks of what he had hoped would be his usual long summer break. But by mid-September he was forced to visit Berlin for further modification of the prosthesis. With Anna to look after him, he greatly enjoyed the time spent with his sons Ernst and Oliver, their wives and their four children. The only shadow was cast by the suicide of Jankef Seidman, the husband of his niece Martha. "He was an honest, nice and clever fellow," he told Samuel, "liked by all of us, but he had undertaken what seems impossible in our days, to build up a Verlag [publishing house] without money, and finally he could not stand the burden of debts and the shame of bankruptcy." Seidman had left a charming seven-year-old daughter, and Freud, always prepared to assume responsibility, noted that "in some way we will have to provide for the child."

Affection for even the more distant members of the family—in whose births, marriages and deaths Freud saw "growth and decay . . . as in plants, a comparison you may find in the old Homer"—became more marked as he grew older. "This night," he wrote to Samuel on one birthday anniversary,

> I found myself in the company of all of you—more than you are now —and to be sure I understand the meaning of the dream. It corresponded to my intention—to write to you on my 72nd. birthday and try a consolation for the grief that I am not to see you again, the living ones no more than the dear deceased and remembered.
>
> I do not enjoy life—I am not better than a wreck in several respects —but let us quickly turn to the other side. I am in possession of my mental powers, I continue doing work and earning money for our people. Mother is remarkably fresh at ninety-three. She insisted in calling on me at my house this afternoon. Martha is as healthy and active as ever, Anna splendid. The big children are honestly struggling for life, the little ones here and at Berlin are thriving well.
>
> This is a view of our present condition, not too bad, not altogether brilliant. Now let me hear good news about you, Pauline and Bertha, who in my dream had not changed from when I last saw them. With tender regards, Your Sigm.

The "not better than a wreck" was perhaps a minor exaggeration, and after the last visit to Berlin the prosthesis was considerably improved. But after thanking Samuel for news of "the girls" in England, Freud commented, "I wish they were better, but we have become a lot of old people and must be modest in our claims." During the summer of 1930 he was back in Berlin once more for yet further work on the prosthesis, a visit which was to lead to one of his most curious and least satisfactory ventures.

Also in Berlin during the same summer was William C. Bullitt, a United States diplomat who had taken part in the Paris Peace Conference of 1919, and whose second wife had once been a patient of Freud's. Bullitt, studying German archives before writing a book on the Conference, had met Freud a couple of times and now decided to call upon him.

He found him greatly depressed. "Somberly he said that he had not long to live and that his death would be unimportant to him or to anyone else, because he had written everything he had wished to write and his mind was emptied," Bullitt later recorded. In an attempt to divert the gloom, the visitor then mentioned his own current work, a book which would include studies of the leading figures at the Peace Conference. "Freud's eyes brightened and he became very much alive," Bullitt has written. "Rapidly he asked a number of questions, which I answered. Then he astonished me by saying he would like to collaborate with me in writing the Wilson chapter of my book."

Bullitt's astonishment would have been less had he followed the progress of psychoanalysis into history and biography. Freud's injunction to Jung almost a quarter century before that they should "take hold of biography" had been pursued, but sometimes with more enthusiasm than circumspection. There had been some bad examples where analysis had provided plausible explanations which had later been, if not destroyed, at least undermined by further investigation by the experts. This did not suggest that psychobiography should be abandoned; it did suggest caution.

Freud himself had sometimes skimped the necessary homework, producing as illustrations of psychoanalytic interpretation what would more reasonably have been put forward as tentative ideas. Thus he was to expound with some certainty to Emil Ludwig that the biographer was wrong in basing his interpretation of Kaiser Wilhelm's personality on the Kaiser's withered arm. "I told him it was not this which caused the inferiority but Wilhelm's mother's attitude toward the withered arm."

So, too, with Napoleon. To Arnold Zweig, Freud gave an analytic interpretation of Napoleon's Egyptian campaign. "Napoleon had a tremendous Joseph-complex," he explained. "That was the name of his elder brother and he had to marry a woman called Josephine." What is more, it was the dissolution of his marriage which led to his military downfall since, according to Freud writing to Thomas Mann, the "rash, poorly-prepared campaign against Russia . . . was like a self-punishment for his disloyalty to Josephine, for the regression from his love to his original hostility towards Joseph." Unconscious motives no doubt affected Napoleon as they affect the rest of men; but it might have been wiser if Freud had admitted that military and political motives were not insignificant.

With such a background of historical reinterpretation, Freud was naturally attracted to Bullitt's project. At first Bullitt protested. "Freud persisted," he wrote later,

saying that I might consider his proposal comic but it was intended to be serious. To collaborate with me would compel him to start writing again. That would give him new life. Moreover he was dissatisfied by his studies of Leonardo da Vinci and of the Moses statue by Michelangelo because he had been obliged to draw large conclusions from few facts, and he had long wished to make a psychological study of a contemporary with regard to whom thousands of facts could be ascertained.

But there was more to it than that. It was due to Wilson, Freud believed, that the Austrian Alto Adige had been ceded to Italy, thus disemboweling the Tyrol. The figure of the American President, "as it rose above the horizon of Europeans, was from the beginning unsympathetic to me," he wrote, "and . . . this aversion increased in the course of years the more I learned about him and the more severely we suffered from the consequences of his intrusion into our destiny." He had, in particular, been bitterly disillusioned by Wilson's failure to obtain agreement to his famous Fourteen Points, proposed by him in 1918 and the basis of the Central Powers' request for an armistice in November 1918. When Ernest Jones defended Wilson on the grounds that the peace settlement could not be dictated by one man, Freud had a simple reply: "Then he should not have made all those promises." And elsewhere he had said to an American, "You should not have gone into the war at all. Your Woodrow Wilson was the silliest fool of the century, if not of all centuries. . . . And he was also probably one of the biggest criminals—unconsciously, I am quite sure."

This hardly augured well for an impartial assessment of Wilson by Freud but might have been adequately countered had Bullitt been an American admirer who could offset opinions which seemed to blame Wilson for the downfall of the Austro-Hungarian Empire. However, Bullitt had an equally critical view of Wilson, although for different reasons. While attending the Peace Conference he had been sent by Wilson on a secret mission to the Communist leaders in Moscow, but the proposals with which he returned were brushed aside, a reaction which Bullitt regarded as mainly mistaken and largely the personal fault of Wilson.

Bullitt and Freud eventually agreed to collaborate, and Bullitt soon had 1,500 pages of notes which were first read by Freud and afterward discussed by them both. "Freud [then] wrote the first draft of portions of the manuscript and I wrote the first draft of other portions," Bullitt said in a foreword to the book. "Each then criticized, amended or rewrote the other's draft until the whole became an amalgam for which we were both responsible."

It was hardly a happy collaboration, and the resulting work was, Bullitt admitted, "the result of much combat. Both Freud and I were extremely pig-headed: somewhat convinced that each one of us was God. In consequence, each chapter: indeed each sentence: was the subject of an intense debate."

One reason was the dissimilarity in their beliefs on most things other than Wilson. "[Freud] was a Jew who had become an agnostic," Bullitt has written. "I have always been a believing Christian. We often disagreed but we never quarreled. On the contrary, the more we worked together, the closer friends we became." Nevertheless, there were perpetual disagreements and for some while it looked as if the book would never appear. In December 1933 Freud wrote despairingly to Marie Bonaparte: "From Bullitt no direct news. Our book will never see the light of day." It had, indeed, soon become clear that time alone would remove the considerable differences between the two authors, while as long as Mrs. Wilson was alive there remained the possibility of libel. Not until 1938 was Bullitt able to obtain Freud's approval to a final manuscript. Freud died little more than a year later and, once again, publication seemed unlikely, particularly as views among the Freud family were mixed. They can be gauged from the comment of one reviewer that *Thomas Woodrow Wilson, Twenty-eighth President of the United States: A Psychological Study*, eventually published in 1966, was received by the psychoanalytic fraternity "as if it were something between a forged First Folio and the Protocols of Zion."

The thesis put forward was that Wilson, ruled by a father complex, had faltered at most of the critical points in his career; this had culminated in his failure to dominate the Paris Peace Conference and to force the Fourteen Points down the throat of an unwilling Europe. As a psychological study the book was persuasive and entertaining, but it raised a question that was answered only damagingly at the end of a long—and typical—review in the *Atlantic Monthly*. "What," asked Barbara Tuchman, "can the Freudian method do for history? The answer must be that as an instrument of illumination it can do much—on one condition: let it for God's sake be applied by a responsible historian."

In the early 1930s Freud had hoped that publication of the Wilson book by the Verlag would give the publishing house a badly needed financial boost. When, early in 1932, the chances of publication still looked slim, he turned to something else which he hoped would help. This was the *New Introductory Lectures*, a series of seven—numbered as a continuation of the twenty-eight lectures given fifteen years earlier—that were never meant to be delivered as lectures.

Published as a book, they brought the theory and practice of psychoanalysis up-to-date. By tailoring new material together with old, and concluding with two lectures which concentrated on subjects whose links with psychoanalysis were slight, they skillfully disguised their conception as a pot-boiling act of good will. The first lecture, on revision of the dream theory, was largely a recapitulation of earlier material; the second, on dreams and occultism, suggested that psychoanalysis might throw light on at least some events usually regarded as occult. There followed three lectures on metapsychology, more complex than any in the former wartime series and introducing many fresh ideas as well as material from *The Ego and the Id* and "The Unconscious."

The final two incorporated Freud's views on a large number of peripheral subjects such as telepathy, education, religion and Communism. Some of it was very much against the "progressive" outlook of the times, and many readers were probably disappointed to learn from Freud that it was impossible to let children follow their impulses. "Accordingly," he went on, "education must inhibit, forbid and suppress, and this it has abundantly seen to in all periods of history." It did, he admitted, involve the dangers of neurotic illness, and thus education had to find its way "between the Scylla of noninterference and the Charybdis of frustration." His basically conservative outlook was further stressed when he warned that children should not be educated to be against "the established order of society." Psychoanalytic education, he continued,

> will be taking an uninvited responsibility on itself if it proposes to mold its pupils into rebels. It will have played its part if it sends them away as healthy and efficient as possible. It itself contains enough revolutionary factors to ensure that no one educated by it will in later life take the side of reaction and suppression. It is even my opinion that revolutionary children are not desirable from any point of view.

22

The Darkening Scene

We are moving towards dark times: the apathy of old age ought to enable me to rise above it all, but I cannot help the fact that I am sorry for my seven grandchildren.

FREUD, to Arnold Zweig

New Introductory Lectures was written as Europe was approaching the psychological watershed which divided into two the years between the end of the First World War and the start of the Second. Behind, there lay a period of slow-growing but genuine hope that peace could be maintained; in front, there lay the prospect of a decline into chaos and barbarism. Fear that the disasters of 1914–1918 were to be repeated on a greater scale encouraged a pessimism that shows through in much of Freud's writings; and it was a poor consolation that the future, dark as it appeared to be, seemed likely to confirm the gloomy prognostications which Freud saw in psychoanalysis.

It was from this period on that he and his work began to be recognized seriously outside the ranks of psychiatry. *New Introductory Lectures* was published in English within a year of its appearance in German, in itself a pointer to the recognition that was slowly being granted to psychoanalysis. In Austria the first official admission that Freud existed had been made by the Austrian Broadcasting System when it transmitted a commemorative address on his life and work at the time of his seventieth birthday in 1926. He had mixed feelings about the celebrations, as he confessed in a letter to his son-in-law Max Halberstadt who had proposed coming to Vienna for the occasion. "You won't be surprised to hear that I have got older and not exactly healthier," Freud wrote to him. "At the moment I am at the sanatorium having heart therapy. They say it is nothing serious but the need for such treatment is hardly a sign of perfect health. They promise to release me this month but I am aware that with all my smaller and my bigger ailments I won't find it easy to continue hard work." There were both pros and cons for making the birthday a big occasion, he continued; if they did so they would have to cope with strangers and uninvited guests; but if they did not, it would mean "keeping away all the dear ones we would like to see." His compromise was to leave free the period from his birthday on Thursday May 6 until the following Sunday. "But don't feel that you have to be tied down to this," he went on. "Come whenever you like; any time, early or late. I am not working all the time and shall always have time for you and your family."

Despite the doubts about his health, Freud was in fairly good spirits as he approached his birthday. "I have," he wrote to Samuel,

> continued to do some work. I give 5–6 hours treatment daily and my pupils or patients feign not to note my defects. I write a paper from time to time, the complete edition of my works is finished up to one volume, I am considered a celebrity; writers and philosophers who pass through Vienna call on me to have a talk, the Jews all over the world boast of my name, pairing me with Einstein. After all, I have no reason to complain and to look with fright at the near end of my life. After a long period of poverty I am earning money without hardship, and I dare say I have provided for my wife.

There followed the customary detailed account of how the members of the family were faring, ending with an account of Anna, "of whom we may well be proud. She has become a pedagogic [teaching] analyst," Freud went on,

> is treating naughty American children, earning a lot of money of which she disposes in a very generous way, helping various poor people. She is a member of the International P/A Association, has won a good name by literary work, and demands the respect of her co-workers. Yet she has just passed her 30th birthday, does not seem inclined to get married, and who can say if her momentary interests will render her happy in years to come when she has to face life without her father?
>
> Now I think I have largely made up for my silence; give me something in return, ample information about yourself and the dear girls.

The demand for information about "the dear girls" in England increased as the chances of Freud ever seeing them again slowly evaporated, and as the failing health of other relatives, notably his mother, could no longer be ignored.

Amalie Freud had for long kept her physical vitality and her mental alertness, although Freud, reporting to Samuel, had made a significant admission in describing her ninetieth birthday party in 1925. "We made a secret of all the losses in the family," he explained. "My daughter Sophie, her second son Heinele, Teddy in Berlin, Eli Bernays and your parents. . . . We had to use many precautions not to be discovered and so I did not give notice of the event before the term."

The following year Amalie Freud insisted on attending her son's seventieth birthday party, and on having a new dress for the occasion. "She had to be carried down the stairs from her own home and up the stairs to the Freud's," her niece has written, "but she did not mind that so long as she could be present to be honored and feted as the mother of her 'golden son' as she called her Sigmund."

Three years later her determination was as strong as ever, and although she was "beginning to lose her fine spirits," she insisted on leaving Vienna for her customary visit to Bad Ischl. The following summer she once again could not be dissuaded from making her annual journey to the Alps, even though she had to be carried on a stretcher to the train, looked after in the sleeping car by her doctor and taken to her apartment in the village by ambulance. "But once there," her niece has said, "she rallied for a while and sat on her balcony, enjoying both the view of the mountains and the consciousness that she was Ischl's oldest summer guest."

Freud was meanwhile staying with Martha at Grundlsee, an hour's drive away, and it was at Grundlsee that he learned of his award of the Goethe Prize for Literature. It was an honor about which he had mixed feelings, as he disclosed to Alfons Paquet, the poet who had put up a hard fight before finally persuading the Goethe Foundation, which administered the Prize awarded annually by the city of Frankfurt, to approve the nomination. "I have not been spoilt by public honors and have therefore accustomed myself to getting along without them," Freud told him. To Arnold Zweig he admitted: "The idea of a closer connection with Goethe is too tempting; the Prize itself is more of a bow made to the recipient than an assessment of his achievement. On the other hand, at my time of life such recognition has neither much practical value nor great emotional significance. For a reconciliation with my contemporaries it is pretty late; and that psychoanalysis will win through long after my time I have never doubted."

Not only was he frail; by this time the prosthesis prevented him from reading the speech of acceptance, so Anna traveled to Frankfurt to perform this duty while Paquet traveled to Grundlsee, where Freud was actually handed the award, the "great honor although not a big sum" as he described it to Samuel. Of the 10,000-mark award he sent 1,000 marks to Lou whose husband had recently died.

In mid-August he drove to Bad Ischl to congratulate his mother on her ninety-fifth birthday. "She is very weak," he told Samuel, "at times apathetic, but not out of her senses. She recognizes people and is accessible to all kinds of emotions." But the rally did not last. Early in September she returned to Vienna and on the twelfth, Freud, who had remained at Grundlsee, sent the expected news to Samuel. "Mother died peacefully this morning in her bedroom in Vienna. The funeral may be on Saturday. At 95 she well deserved to be relieved."

Meanwhile, many continental papers had been printing reports of Freud's own failing health. "They seem," he commented, "to be a reaction against the honors in francfort [sic] which are sure to have aroused great dislike among my contemporaries." The truth, he went on a week later, "is I am neither very young nor very solid but there is nothing new in it."

Dislike among his contemporaries was no doubt increased the following year when the Czechs decided to mount a commemorative plaque on the house in which he had been born. "Think what a treat it would have been for your grandfather and for your father to witness the ceremony," he proudly wrote to Samuel to whom he sent photographs of the occasion, attended as it was by his children Anna and Martin and his brother Alexander. "But of course grandfather had to be 116 years old at the time!"

To those outside the family he appeared skeptical of what the Czech gesture really meant; and the world's somewhat grudging acknowledgment tended to be overshadowed by something more than his own personal affliction. Any satisfaction which he might personally have felt was gradually qualified by despair at political events in Europe. There was, he forecast, "no likelihood of our being able to suppress humanity's aggressive tendencies," and for a Jew, considering a Europe in which Hitler's National Socialist German Workers' Party was, by September 1930, the second largest party in Germany, the forecast looked ominously correct. "We have been deprived by [the Soviet experiment] of a hope—and an illusion—and we have received nothing in exchange," he remarked to Arnold Zweig. "We are moving towards dark times: the apathy of old age ought to enable me to rise above it all, but I cannot help the fact that I am sorry for my seven grandchildren."

Even over his relations with Martha there had developed a small cloud whose existence he did his best to conceal from the world. Dr. Schur, who had become his doctor in 1928, noted what appeared to be Freud's understanding forgiveness of the pedantic attitude sometimes shown by his wife. During the 1930s there was even slight irritation—well controlled as Freud's reactions always were—and it seemed that there was little left of the earlier great love.

While Martha and Minna continued to run No. 19 Berggasse and to organize the social life of the family, Anna's position was becoming increasingly more important. Not only nurse, secretary and unfailing support in time of trouble, she was also, in view of her preeminence as an analyst, an almost natural successor to leadership of the cause. She had also, quite fortuitously, brought a new interest into the last years of her father's life. In the 1920s she had bought Wolf, an Alsatian, to accompany her on walks through Vienna. The dog had quickly become one of the family and on Freud's seventieth birthday he was presented with a photograph of the animal; attached to it was a poem in which Wolf offered his congratulations. Freud was always concerned when the dog was left on his own. If he found him in a dark room he would put on the light, and it became a family joke that Freud expected the dog to read a book if he was lonely. He used to feed him at table, or put down his own plate for the dog in defiance of Martha's objections and treated him with all the courtesy that he normally accorded human beings.

It was, moreover, not only for personal pets that Freud in his later years developed a new interest and understanding. Ernst Simmel has said that he would never forget an incident when he and Freud were walking in the grounds of Schloss Tegel and saw a chained-up police dog. Simmel warned Freud not to touch the animal because he was vicious. Freud disregarded him, unchained the dog, accepted friendly licks in response to friendly pats, and remarked, "If you had been chained up all your life, you'd be vicious too." Simmel declares that for him the action "revealed Freud's complete and unified personality: a man for whom theory and practice, percept and life, were one."

Yet there was something missing in his feelings for animals. He was presented by Marie Bonaparte with a fine white chow of which he became very fond. When the dog was killed in an accident the Princess sent Freud another dog. "A few weeks ago," he wrote to Lou, ". . . Jofi, a sister of my lost Lün, arrived. I miss her now almost as much as my cigar. She is a charming creature, so interesting, in her feminine characteristics too, wild, impulsive, gentle, intelligent and yet not so dependent as dogs often are. One cannot help feeling respect for animals like this." And to a patient who had described his own dog, Freud was to say: "The feeling for dogs is the same as we have for children; it is of the same quality. But do you know in what way it differs? . . . There is no ambivalence, no element of hostility"—and apparently no affection that was equal to that for a cigar.

However, the family dog from now on was part of Freud's life. She "sat in" on many sessions with patients, and Martin Freud maintained that his father never had to consult his watch to know when the analytical hour was finished. "When Jofi got up and yawned, the time was up; she was never late in announcing the end of a session, although father did admit that she was capable of an error of perhaps a minute, at the expense of the patient."

The patients continued to arrive, and it is a tribute to Freud's stamina that he found time to carry on as an analyst, to maintain a flow of psychoanalytical papers and at the same time keep up an enormous private correspondence. In 1932, moreover, his views on the ineradicable instincts of man caused him to enter what in the Europe of the early 1930s could easily be construed as political argument.

Although numerous theories have been formulated about Freud's political beliefs and influence, he himself tended to be apolitical, "an old-fashioned liberal," but one whose vestigial faith in the ability of liberalism to accomplish very much had evaporated during the First World War. He had little time for the concessions and maneuvering which are the small change of political life, and his personal experience of its exponents was minimal. On only one political subject were his feelings aroused, at once, and strongly: at the first hint of anti-Semitism he reached for his armor and his armaments, ready to do battle against all comers. Yet it was on the question of war rather than of anti-Semitism that he was now impelled to write a specific polemic.

Soon after the International Institute of Intellectual Cooperation had been founded by the League of Nations in 1926, it had been asked by the League "to encourage an exchange of letters between leaders of thought, on the lines of those which have always taken place at the great epochs of European history; to select subjects best calculated to serve the common interest of the League of Nations and of the intellectual life of mankind; and to publish this correspondence from time to time." One volume, *A League of Minds,* containing letters from Salavador de Madariaga, Gilbert Murray and Paul Valéry among others, was published in 1931. Later in the year Einstein was asked to suggest another.

"You have made an excellent proposal," he was told by Henri Bonnet, the Institute's director, in answer to his proposals; "an exchange of ideas in letters between you and Freud about the ways in which schools may be able, with the help of the new psychoanalytical knowledge, to direct children's ideas toward peace may be described, without doubt, as a most worthy contribution to the world of intellectual cooperation."

A few years earlier, when spending Christmas at Ernst Freud's Berlin home, Freud had been visited by Einstein. What they talked about is unknown, although it is possible that they recalled the occasion in 1912 when Einstein had supported the foundation of a new scientific association "quite indifferent to metaphysical speculation and so-called critical transcendental doctrine"; Freud, as well as his Viennese contemporary Ernst Mach, had been among those who signed a manifesto outlining the association's aims. Yet all that has been recorded of the first meeting between the world's two most famous living Jews, is Freud's verdict: "He is cheerful, sure of himself, and agreeable. He understands as much about psychology as I do about physics and we had a very pleasant talk."

On June 6, 1932, Freud replied to the Institute official who had proposed to him the exchange of letters suggested by Einstein. "I hasten to answer your letter," he said,

because you tell me you intend to use my comments when you meet Professor Einstein at the end of this month. While reading your letter I have indulged in as much enthusiasm as I am able to muster at my age (seventy-six) and in my state of disillusionment. The words in which you express your hopes and those of Einstein for a future role of psychoanalysis in the life of individuals and nations ring true and of course give me very great pleasure. It has been no little disappointment to me that at a time when we can continue our work only under the greatest social and material difficulties, I haven't seen the slightest sign of interest for our efforts on the part of the League of Nations. Thus practical and idealistic considerations combine to induce me to put myself with all that remains of my energies at the disposal of the Institute of Intellectual Cooperation.

I cannot quite imagine as yet what form my participation is going to take. It will devolve upon Einstein to make suggestions. I would prefer not to hold forth on my own and hope that the character of a discussion can be maintained in such a way, perhaps, that instead of answering one question put to me by Einstein, I respond from the point of view of psychoanalysis to statements in which he expresses his opinions. I would also prefer not to pick out a single topic from among those enumerated in your letter. It is rather a question of a number of problems of which the most important for practical purposes is the influence of psychoanalysis on education. But, as I say, in all these practical details, I am ready to follow Einstein's suggestions. When you see him you won't be able to tell him anything more about my personal relationship to him than he knows already, although I only once had the long-desired opportunity of talking to him.

As for yourself, please accept my cordial thanks for your interest in psychoanalysis.

Leon Steinig, the League official involved, subsequently met Freud in Vienna and explained the idea in more detail. But the more Freud heard of the proposal the less optimistic he became. "All my life," he told Steinig, "I have had to tell people truths that were difficult to swallow. Now that I am old I do not want to fool them."

His doubts were spelled out when he replied to Einstein's letter on July 30, 1932. Einstein had in effect asked one simple question —"Is there any way of delivering mankind from the menace of war?"—and had answered it optimistically. An international authority, strong enough to enforce peace, would make war impossible. There was, he admitted, the awkward fact that "man has within him a lust for hatred and destruction" but that, surely, was where psychoanalysis could help find an answer.

In his long discursive reply Freud agreed with most of the points that Einstein had made. He begged to differ only over the feasibility of the proffered solutions. "The upshot of [my] observations," he noted,

as bearing on the subject in hand, is that there is no likelihood of our being able to suppress humanity's aggressive tendencies. In some happy corners of the earth, they say, where nature brings forth abundantly whatever man desires, there flourish races whose lives go gently by, unknowing of aggression or constraint. This I can hardly credit; I would like further details about these happy folk. The Bolshevists, too, aspire to do away with human aggressiveness by ensuring the satisfaction of material needs and enforcing equality between man and man. To me this hope seems vain. Meanwhile they busily perfect their armaments, and their hatred of outsiders is not the least of the factors of cohesion amongst themselves.

War might one day conceivably be ended if man's cultural disposition was sufficiently affected by what Freud called "a well-founded dread of the form that future wars will take." But he was obviously pessimistic, even of the ultimate deterrent, a pessimism which later caused Havelock Ellis to remonstrate: "It is unfortu-

nate that Freud, and some other psychoanalysts—who seem sometimes to show a malicious pleasure in trying to give an evil aspect
to human impulses—should have regarded hate as a primary motive and love as a secondary derivative. From an evolutionary
standpoint it is not easy to make this work out; the reverse order
would be far more plausible. . . ." Ellis was to die two months
before Freud, a few weeks before the German invasion of Poland,
which for many of their contemporaries must have seemed to settle
the argument.

The Freud–Einstein correspondence was eventually published
under the title *Why War?* and, as Freud had insisted, it appeared
not only in French and English but also in German. But by this
time Adolf Hitler had become Chancellor of Germany and *Warum
Krieg?* was banned throughout the Third Reich.

The rise of Hitler at first merely reinforced the resigned pessimism with which Freud had met the rebuffs of his early years. To
the protest that a sculptor had made him look too cross, he replied:
"But I am cross. I am cross with mankind." Men, he complained,
were "a wolf pack, simply a wolf pack. They hunt down those who
would do good for them." Yet if the future seemed to hold out few
prospects, either for himself as an individual or for the human race
in general, one must still soldier on, hoping for the best, preparing
for the worst. However the rest of the world saw him, Freud still
saw himself in the role he had chosen at the end of the nineteenth
century—that of the leader, struggling on against adversity, if necessary alone. But if the leader demanded high standards of himself,
no less should be demanded of those who followed. "I saw him,"
Hanns Sachs has said, "when the news came that someone with
whom he had been on friendly terms for years had committed
suicide. I found him strangely unmoved by such a tragic event.
Suicide meant to him—except in certain extreme cases—the shirk-
ing of a task, an attempt to escape in the midst of action; he felt
it so strongly that his humanity was balanced by contempt. He was
willing to give his affection unsparingly where he thought it well
bestowed, but not to offer the alms of sentimentality."

In spite of the uncomfortable belief that the worst was yet to be,
Freud's response to the rise of the Nazi Party was at first strangely
muted. Shortly after it had become the second largest party in
Germany he had added a final sentence to *Civilization and its Discontents* in which he had speculated on the battle between the cultural
development of the human species and its self-destructive instincts. Initially he had written that it was "to be expected that the
other of the two 'Heavenly Powers,' eternal Eros, will make an
effort to assert himself in the struggle with his equally immortal

adversary." But as the menace of Hitler changed from nightmare to reality, he added a final few words—"But who can foresee with what success and with what result?"

When bad turned to worse, his response was half philosophical, half unbelieving, even though a letter to Samuel as early as July 1933, less than six months after Hitler's accession to power, gave a hint of things to come. "Life in Germany has become impossible for Oliver and Ernest," he told his nephew. "The latter is now in London . . . preparing his coming over for good, his family still at Berlin. Oliver has made up his mind to settle in France, he lives now at St. Brieuc, somewhere on the seashore with wife and little daughter Eva. His first task will be to learn the language. Neither of both is yet sure of finding a living. You know from the papers (I am now a regular reader of the Manch. Guardian) how unassured our situation in Austria is. The only thing I can say is that we are determined to stick it out here to the last. Perhaps it may not come out too badly."

And then, with words that were echoed in so many of his letters to England, he concluded: "And how are you and the girls? As I am now convinced I will never see any one of you again, I am the more eager to hear about you. Affectionately your, Sigm."

He continued to hope, assuring Marie Bonaparte that if the Nazi movement should spread to Austria there would be nothing comparable to the excesses of the German movement since the Austrians were not as brutal as the Germans—forgetting that the Austrian-born Hitler had settled in Linz and had lived in Freud's own Vienna before the First World War. In any case, he consoled himself, the Versailles Treaty forbade any *Anschluss* between Germany and Austria.

A decade earlier he had given an indication of his currently held attitude, certain that German nationalism was resurgent but unwilling to believe that its results could not be avoided. A young Jew had asked him to account for the fact that Hans Bluher, a propagandist for the rising German nationalist movement, was an apparent admirer of Freud.

Mass psychoses are invulnerable to reasoning [Freud replied]. The Germans in particular would have had all reason to learn this in this [sic] World War. But they do not seem capable of it. Let us leave them alone.

Bluher is one of the prophets of a time out of joint. Certainly not the most respectable among them. He has nothing to do with analytic science. As soon as analysis approaches his *typus universus,* he repudiates it, resorting to the sovereign intuition of his German soul. However often he quotes me, agrees with me, or subdues me—I shall never have a word for him.

Turn instead to matters that can lift the Jew out of all these frenzies and—do not take amiss this advice which is the result of lifelong experience—do not impose yourself upon the Germans.

Thirteen years later, writing to the same correspondent, he said: "You surely do not believe that I am proud of having been right? I was right as the pessimist against the enthusiast, as the old man against the youngster. It would have been better to have been wrong."

Freud had in fact every logical reason to fear for the future. He had experienced the anti-Semitism of Vienna at least since the great financial crash of 1873. His eyes had been opened, although late, to the facts of German aggression in 1914. In *Group Psychology* he had shown a despairing understanding of how the mob could be led to behave, and his attitude was summed up a few years later in a letter to Richard Dyer-Bennet, author of *Gospel of Living*. "What also seems overoptimistic to me," he said, "is your opinion that humanity has progressed far enough to react to an appeal such as yours. A very thin layer may come up to your expectations, otherwise all the old cultural levels—those of the Middle Ages, of the Stone Age, even of animistic prehistory—are still alive in the great masses."

Yet even the ominous warning of the Burning of the Books did not appear to alarm him too greatly. On May 10, 1933, 40,000 Berliners cheered the sight of 5,000 swastika-bearing students burning 2,000 books before the Berlin Opera House. Included were the works of Einstein, Thomas Mann, Erich Maria Remarque and Stefan Zweig, as well as of Freud, the last being thrown on the pyre with the words: "Against the soul-destroying overestimation of the sex life—and on behalf of the nobility of the human soul— I offer to the flames the writings of one, Sigmund Freud!"

"At least," Freud observed to a friend, "I burn in the best of company"; and to another, "What progress we are making! In the Middle Ages they would have burnt me; nowadays they are content with burning my books." In retrospect, the remark has a special horror: four of his five sisters were to die in concentration camps.

Freud's reluctance to take the personal threat seriously was slow to evaporate. From the spring of 1933, friends who believed that Hitler would incorporate Austria into the Reich at the first opportunity offered him refuge. It was proposed that he move to Switzerland, to France, to England, to America or even to the Argentine, to which he was invited by the Spanish poet Xavier Boveda and a group of sympathetic writers. To all he returned the same answer. To take flight, he felt, was quite unnecessary. "I don't believe there is any danger here," he wrote from Vienna on one occasion. "If they kill me—good. It is one kind of death like another. But probably that is only cheap boasting." As late as December 1933 he was writing: "The fact is that I do not underestimate at all the threatening menace for me (as well as for others) in case Hitlerism might establish itself by force in Austria. But I look calmly forward, prepared to endure what one will have to endure, and determined to stay here as long as it will be possible, generally speaking. However, it seems now that we in Austria will be spared from this German disgrace." Only to Arnold Zweig did he admit, in 1934, that the worst might happen. He would stick it out indefinitely in Vienna, but "if there really were a satrap of Hitler's ruling in Vienna, I would no doubt have to go, no matter where."

His attitude was compounded of the natural disinclination of an old man to uproot himself; of the feeling that he would be deserting his post; of the deep affection which beneath the surface he still felt for Vienna; and, in the face of his public protestations in *Why War?*, a reluctance to believe that even under Hitler the German government could behave as evilly as it appeared to behave.

To all this there was added his instinctive political neutrality. In contrast to the posthumous exegesis with which enthusiasts have linked his writings to almost every political creed, his true feelings were shown during one heated discussion reported by Joan Riviere, who translated many of his works between the wars. Freud, accused of being neither black nor red, neither Fascist nor Socialist, replied, "No, one should be flesh-colour"—the color of ordinary men.

Only gradually did he begin to see that "the world is turning into an enormous prison," and that "Germany [was] its worst cell." Of the Nazis he proclaimed: "They began with Bolshevism as their deadly enemy and they will end with something indistinguishable from it—except perhaps that Bolshevism after all adopted revolutionary ideals, whereas those of Hitlerism are purely medieval and reactionary." His sardonic sense of humor soon came into play. "Look how poverty stricken the poet's imagination really is," he remarked to a friend. "Shakespeare in *A Midsummer Night's Dream* has a woman fall in love with a donkey. The audience wonders at that. And now, think of it, that a nation of sixty-five million have . . ." And he ended the sentence with a wave of the hand.

Yet there was another side to the coin as he suggested to Arthur Koestler in the autumn of 1938, after he had emigrated to England. Koestler had passed some comment about the Nazis. "Freud looked with an absent, wondering look at the trees across the window," he later wrote, "and in a hesitating manner said: 'Well, you know, they are *abreacting* the aggression pent up in our civilization. Something like this was inevitable, sooner or later. I am not sure that from my standpoint I can blame them.' He probably put it into quite different words, but there could be no misunderstanding of the meaning."

Freud's first serious doubts about his own future in Austria came after Chancellor Dollfuss quelled a Socialist uprising in February 1934, and the balance of power within Austria shifted to the right. But leaving would mean abdication, a retreat from the battle, a step to be taken only in the direst circumstances. Quite apart from the upheaval for a sick man approaching eighty, he believed that outside Austria he would be unable to exercise his influence where it could have the greatest effect. The influence did not apply only to psychoanalysis, as he pointed out to one visitor as late as 1937. "The Nazis?" he said to René Laforgue who was urging that he leave Vienna without delay. "I am not afraid of them. Help me rather to combat my true enemy." Asked how or what that was, he replied, "Religion, the Roman Catholic Church."

It was not only personal issues that were involved. Soon after Hitler was granted unlimited power, psychoanalysts in Germany faced the traumatic problem that was to confront so many Europeans as Germany swallowed up Austria, then occupied France and the Low Countries. Was it better to move beyond control of those who ran the Third Reich, or was it better to remain and, with a show of collaboration, ease the lot of those with no choice but to live under Nazi rule? At one end of the spectrum there would be resolute resisters; at the other the self-seeking collaborators; in between there would be an almost infinite variety of positions, taken up by men and women under varying pressures and later justified by arguments that ranged from the honest to the specious.

For psychoanalysis, the first hint of trouble came when, a few weeks after Hitler's appointment as Chancellor, the government banned foreigners from sitting on the central executive of any medical society. Max Eitingon, the head of the Berlin Psychoanalytical Society, was a Russian Jew who in the postwar settlement of 1919 had chosen Polish nationality. Next in line to succeed him was Felix Boehm, a German Gentile who on hearing of the new decree asked whether it applied to psychoanalytical organizations. The answer, which needed little perspicacity to forecast, was "Yes," and on hearing this, Boehm visited Freud in Vienna to discuss the next move. His action in asking whether the decree affected psychoanalysts has been criticized, and after the war he felt it necessary to send to Anna Freud a long report on the fortunes of the Deutsche Psychoanalytische Gesellschaft from 1933 on. Certainly Freud appears to have believed that firmer action by Boehm could have ameliorated the conditions which now closed in round the society. Eitingon emigrated—eventually to Palestine —and Boehm took his place. Professor M. H. Göring, cousin of the newly appointed German Air Minister, was soon put in effective control and informed members that Hitler's *Mein Kampf* would in future serve as a basis for their beliefs.

With conditions still worsening, Boehm visited Vienna again, early in 1937, and gave Freud and a number of colleagues an account of the deepening difficulties in Berlin. After listening for three hours, Boehm later wrote, Freud intervened. "Enough!" he said. "The Jews have suffered during centuries for their convictions. Now the time has come that our Christian colleagues have to suffer in their turn for their convictions. I attach no importance to my name being mentioned in Germany as long as my work is represented correctly." He then left the meeting.

By this time Freud had a special reason for bitterness and for bringing up the antithesis between Jew and Gentile. Soon after Hitler had come to power in 1933, the German Society for Psychotherapy had been reorganized into the International General Medical Society for Psychotherapy. The existing president, Ernst Kretschmer, resigned in protest since under the new regime the practice of psychoanalysis would come under Nazi control. Into his place there stepped Carl Jung, who also became editor of the new Nazi-controlled *Zentralblatt für Psychotherapie*.

Jung's work for the new Society, which continued until his resignation in 1940, was to be vigorously condemned, and as vigorously defended. "What with the hue and cry against me it has been completely forgotten that by far the greatest number of psychotherapists in Germany are Jews," he protested, in March 1934 to Max Guggenheim. "People do not know, nor is it said in public, that I have intervened personally with the regime on behalf of certain Jewish psychotherapists."

Jung's claim, often repeated, that his intervention had aided many Jewish psychotherapists in Germany, may well be justified. Comparable claims were to be made after the war by many of those dubbed collaborators, men and women who had, indeed, worked with the occupying German forces but had done so in the hope that they could ameliorate conditions. But the case against Jung is not solely that he worked with the Nazi authorities. It is that the circumstances of the time brought into the open the anti-Semitism of which Freud had long accused him and which Jung was always vehemently to deny.

Freud himself was at the center of many statements now to be made by Jung. Thus in the *Zentralblatt für Psychotherapie* of January 1934, almost a year after Hitler had come to power, he boldly announced:

> The Aryan unconsciousness has a higher potential than the Jewish; that is the advantage and the disadvantage of a youthfulness not yet fully escaped from barbarism. In my opinion it has been a great mistake of all previous medical psychology to apply Jewish categories which are not even binding for all Jews, indiscriminately to Christians, Germans or Slavs. In so doing, medical psychology has declared that most precious secret of the Germanic people—the creatively prophetic depth of the soul—to be a childishly banal morass, while for decades my warning voice has been suspected of anti-Semitism. The source of this suspicion is Freud. He did not know the Germanic soul any more than did all his Germanic imitators. . . . Has the mighty apparition of National Socialism which the whole world watches with astonished eyes taught them something better?

These were, at the least, unusual words for a man of Jung's stature in an era which had already witnessed the burning of the books and in which the concentration camps were being prepared. Indeed, Wilhelm Stekel wrote to Chaim Weizmann in Jerusalem, bitterly asserting that Jung had "murdered judenrein." "The University in Jerusalem," he went on, "must now become the 'guardian place' of the Jewish science (Psychoanalysis). You have in Tel Aviv one of the most highly gifted of psychotherapists, Dr. Velikofsky, with whom it would be worthy for all scholars to unite, and in Jerusalem to create a center for Germany's prohibited branch of psychoanalysis."

It was not yet entirely prohibited. But the possibility was indicated when in February 1934 Jung wrote to Wolfgang Kranefeldt, one of the founders of the Berlin Institution:

> . . . As is known, one cannot do anything against stupidity, but in this instance the Aryan people can point out that, with Freud and Adler, specific Jewish points of view are publicly preached and, as can be proved likewise, points of view that have an essentially corrosive character. If the proclamation of this Jewish gospel is agreeable to the government, then so be it. Otherwise, there is also the possibility that this would not be agreeable to the government. . . .

Many correspondents wrote demanding an explanation of Jung's actions and of his criticisms of Freud. Typical was his reply to James Kirsch in May: ". . . As you know, Freud previously accused me of anti-Semitism because I could not abide his soulless materialism. The Jew directly solicits anti-Semitism with his readiness to scent out anti-Semitism everywhere." And to Gerhard Adler he wrote the following month: "It is typically Jewish that Freud can forget his roots to such an extent." To Abraham Roback, author of *The Jewish Influence in Modern Thought,* he wrote: "To [Freud] as to many other Jews, as I have seen with my own eyes, the re-establishment of the communication with the instincts means a true and vital find and source of satisfaction and joy."

Time and again he came back to the break with Freud in 1912–1914, to his book *Wandlungen und Symbole der Libido,* and to the fact that Freud had then accused him of anti-Semitism. "From this I must conclude that I had somehow trespassed against the Jews," he wrote in June 1934. "This prejudice has stuck to me ever since and has been repeated by all Freudians, thereby confirming every time that psychoanalysis is in fact a Jewish psychology which nobody else can criticize without making himself guilty of anti-Semitism."

Now, a quarter of a century after Freud had so eagerly recruited Jung as a defense against the charge that psychoanalysis was a Jewish development, the final solution to the question was emerging. Jung was now "proving" that psychoanalysis was Jewish.

Meanwhile the exodus from Germany had been growing, and both Freud and Anna, as well as the resolute Ernest Jones in London, became increasingly involved in the task of finding new posts for psychoanalysts no longer able to practice within the Third Reich. With two other refugees, Max Eitingon eventually founded the Psychoanalytic Society of Palestine. Some of his colleagues crossed the Atlantic, harbingers of an army which was within a decade to remove the mainsprings of psychoanalysis from Europe to North America. Many wished to settle in Britain, and Jones had the difficult job of explaining that even some British psychoanalysts were only partially employed. Even if newcomers spoke fluent English, which was rare, their chances of professional survival were poor.

As the shadows lengthened, Freud's concern with the future of psychoanalysis in Europe was paralleled by the course of the disease from which he had in 1923 been granted only a temporary respite. It was assiduously fought by his doctors with the aid of scalpel, radium and any other weapon which could be used to slow the enemy's advance. Some idea of his suffering is conveyed by his doctor's report after manipulation of the prosthesis had enabled Freud to speak with slightly less discomfort. "Some more chiselling," it runs. "Now rather difficult to insert prosthesis so that it clicks into channel. Patient will have to exercise it by biting on piece of wood with upper and lower right molars."

To the problem of the prosthesis there was added that of coping with the endless cycle of leukoplakia and precancerous lesions, each of which had to be treated either surgically, by electrocoagulation or by a combination of both. It was before this period that Dr. Max Schur came into Freud's life as his personal physician, mainly on the insistence of Marie Bonaparte, who had herself become acutely ill in Vienna. She had been in the care of Schur, one of the few Viennese doctors with a leaning toward psychoanalysis, was impressed by his ability and finally persuaded Freud to put himself in Schur's hands for a trial period. It lasted until Freud's death eleven years later.

"Before telling me his history or his present complaints," Schur has written,

> he wanted a basic understanding on the conditions for such a relationship. Mentioning only in a general way "some unfortunate experiences with your predecessors," he expressed the expectation that he would always be told the truth and nothing but the truth. My response must have reassured him that I meant to keep such a promise. He then added, looking searchingly at me: "Promise me one more thing: that when the time comes, you won't let me suffer unnecessarily." All this was said with the utmost simplicity without a trace of pathos, but also with complete determination. We shook hands at this point.

Freud's insistence that he should be told the truth indicates that he had some inkling of the testing times ahead. They were to be made more difficult by his refusal permanently to give up his beloved cigars, a refusal which Schur quickly saw was a main cause not only of the recurring heart trouble but of the difficulty in holding the cancer at bay. Freud of course knew this. But while he could sometimes be persuaded to stop smoking for a short spell, he always returned, usually excusing himself as he did in a letter to Eitingon. "Your question about the cigars induces me to confess that I am smoking again. Considering my age and the amount of discomfort which I have to bear day after day, abstinence and the prospect [of preventing new lesions] which it involves do not seem justified to me."

To Marie Bonaparte he wrote after another major operation carried out to remove a growth that might be malignant: "I am still quite below par and this time I have certainly taken a huge step out of the circle of life."

More operations followed. Dr. Schur was forced to leave his

patient in no doubt that the precancerous nature of the growth and the inflammation was caused by nicotine. "I therefore confronted Freud with Erdheim's report [a report by Jacob Erdheim, made after an earlier operation and implicating nicotine] and urged him even more emphatically than before to stop smoking. Freud shrugged his shoulders, making a typical gesture with his hand, and dismissed the suggestion . . . he would again and again submit to restrictions on his smoking when he was having trouble with his heart, but never on account of the danger of a lesion in the mouth developing into a new malignancy."

On one occasion he was unable to climb the stairs of No. 19 and considered himself under house arrest. A few months later he was getting radium treatment and reacting with the most frightful pain; but shortly afterward he told Arnold Zweig that he retained his capacity for enjoyment and was dissatisfied with the resignation forced on him. "It is a bitter winter here in Vienna," he went on, "and I have not been out for months. I also find it hard to adapt myself to the role of the hero suffering for mankind, which you kindly assign me."

As to the finality of death, Freud had no doubts; yet on the wider but allied riddles of the paranormal, the skepticism of his earlier years became steadily more qualified. To Romain Rolland he wrote: "I am not an out-and-out skeptic. Of one thing I am absolutely positive; there are certain things we cannot know now." When Victor von Weizsäcker, the founder of medical anthropology, admitted that he was "perhaps something of a mystic on the side," Freud reacted with a horrified "That is terrible"; but when Weizsäcker began to yield with "I meant to say there is also something which we don't know," Freud responded with "Oh, in that I more than match you."

Denying to an interviewer in 1935 that he had become credulous in his old age, he added, "I don't think so. Merely all my life I have learned to accept new facts, humbly, readily. I believe that telepathy is a psychical event in one man causing a similar psychical event in another man. It can be presumed that the connection between these two psychological phenomena is physical—perhaps similar to the receiver and the speaking tube of a telephone." He still did not entirely rule out the occult as is shown by a letter to Eduardo Weiss, an analyst who had translated some of his works into Italian. "The medium business, however, is a disagreeable chapter," he admitted. "The unquestionable deceptions on the part of mediums, the simple-minded and tricky nature of their performances, the difficulties of testing them in the peculiar conditions chosen by them, the obvious impossibilities of many of their claims—all that calls for the utmost caution. There must surely be better ways of

showing what is real in the occult." Apart from all this, the old
reason for being cautious still remained, as he told Weiss in another letter. "Naturally it would be unfavorable for the part you
play as the pioneer of psychoanalysis in Italy were you to proclaim
yourself at the same time a partisan of occultism."

Throughout the 1930s he continued to speculate on those subjects that he was still anxious to keep judiciously separate from the
cause of psychoanalysis. Meanwhile, his own private battle with
ever-present disease strengthened his jaundiced view of the world
and particularly of the prospects of psychoanalysis. "Let us make
no mistake," he maintained to Zweig, "this day and age has rejected me and all I had to give, and acclamations will not cause it
to revise its judgment. Probably my time will come but, I might
add, for the moment it is past." When Georg Fuchs, the author of
Wir Zuchthäusler, a book on prison reform, in asking for an introduction described him as the standard-bearer of cultural Germany,
Freud replied, "But it seems to me that I am *persona ingrata,* if not
ingratissima to the German nation—not only to the educated, but
also to the uneducated classes." And reporting that he had received several offers from British and American publishers to write
a Psychoanalysis of the Bible, he remarked, "I recognize the fact
that I am not famous, but I am 'notorious.'"

His attitude was exemplified in 1936 amid the celebrations of his
eightieth birthday, after Ludwig Binswanger had read a paper on
"Freud's Conception of Man in the Light of Anthropology." "I
rejoiced over your beautiful prose, your erudition, the scope of
your horizon, your tact in disagreement," was Freud's reaction.
"Truly, one can put up with infinite amounts of praise."

Then, referring to the dream analogy in which the lower level
is the unconscious id, while the upper floors are the conscious ego
and super-ego, he went on:

> *But, of course, I don't believe a word of what you say.* I've always lived only
> in the *parterre* and basement of the building. You claim that with a
> change of viewpoint one is able to see an upper storey which houses
> such distinguished guests as religion, art, etc. You're not the only
> one who thinks that; most cultured specimens of *homo natura* believe
> it. In that you are conservative, I revolutionary. If I had another
> lifetime of work before me, I have no doubt that I could find room
> for these noble guests in my little subterranean house.

Binswanger's celebratory address was only one event among
many as Freud reached the age of eighty. Thomas Mann spoke to
the Akademischer Verein für Medizinische Psychologie on "Freud
and the Future," a paper read before a number of other audiences

and finally to Freud in his home. In New York, Smith Ely Jelliffe delivered an anniversary paper on "Sigmund Freud as a Neurologist" to the American Neurological Association, an occasion which produced a classic Freudian slip. Jelliffe had recounted that between 1882 and 1884 four men, all of whom became famous, had worked together in Meynert's laboratory. One was Bernard Sachs, who in the ensuing discussions recalled: "How well I remember those student days with Meynert. There at the same table we four men were working together—there was my dear friend, M. Allen Starr, lately professor of neurology at Columbia University, Anton, later at Halle, myself and a fourth man. Somehow I forget his name, who was the fourth man." At this point the audience rose almost as one to shout the word: "Freud."

In Paris, Marie Bonaparte celebrated the birthday with an address on his work to the Sorbonne, while in London he was elected a Foreign Member of the Royal Society. His name had been proposed by the distinguished astronomer Sir Harold Jeffreys, and both Lord Adrian, the neurologist, and Wilfred Trotter, who had attended the Salzburg Congress of 1908, supported the application. "I do not know how to thank you," Freud wrote to Jeffreys on hearing the news of his election, "or how I have deserved it from you."

In Vienna the teachers' seminar of the Psychological Institute was in doubt about how best to deal with the occasion. Finally it was suggested that Freud would appreciate a bunch of flowers collected in the mountains, and a member of the staff was deputed to collect them. He arrived back in Vienna with a large bunch of primula auricula. A seventeen-year-old girl was sent out to deliver them and, to her surprise, Freud called her in, thanked her personally and emphasized how much he appreciated the gesture.

Yet he knew that despite all the honors he was still swimming against the tide. "Even my Viennese colleagues honored me, and betrayed by all manner of signs how much against the grain it went," he wrote to Arnold Zweig of the eightieth birthday celebrations. The Minister of Education, he pointed out, had certainly formally congratulated him, but the Austrian newspapers were then threatened with confiscation if they reported the fact.

He noted the same attitude elsewhere, writing to Ludwig Binswanger that

the people of Acad. Soc. and the speakers they have invited, except for you and the good Thomas Mann . . . are neither my friends nor friends of psychoanalysis. They are hostile neutrals, some more hostile, and some more neutral than others. What motives they have fo.

arranging such a celebration, is not easy to say. Certainly it is not any pure desire to express friendship and recognition. Perhaps it is, following the American model, the honoring of old age with the not too respectable intention of getting some publicity. I cannot rejoice over the whole thing, nor do I believe it is motivated by a sudden change of heart and of judgment at a time fixed beforehand.

In this case the chip on the shoulder was fully justified. Freud had no doubt noted that although the Imperial Austro-Hungarian Medal for Art and Science, instituted by the Emperor toward the end of the nineteenth century, was now being given once again by the Republic, he was not one of the recipients.

However, there was one birthday honor which did give him considerable pleasure. In May the Viennese student group, Kadimah, possibly the oldest Zionist society, sent Freud a congratulatory message. Acknowledging it, he signed himself: "Freud, who would have liked to belong to your *Alte Herren* [Old Boys]." On receiving this, the Kadimah decided to elect him an Honorary Member and asked his son Martin, who had joined the Kadimah years earlier, how his father would react to the proposal. Freud was delighted, and on September 6 a special delegation visited his holiday villa on the outskirts of Vienna, to present him with the red, purple and gold sash. "May I put it on?" he asked. "We did not dare to ask you to do so," replied one member of the delegation. Freud was then formally inaugurated—the sixth Honorary Member since the founding of the Kadimah in 1882.

One result of the eightieth birthday publicity which he did not enjoy was the flood of requests for interviews and for portrait sittings. He was perpetually suspicious of interviews, but was in two minds about sittings, as he made clear in a letter to the painter Professor Wilhelm Victor Krausz:

> It is a hard task, indeed, to deny anything to an artist. I want to explain my objections, as I have very little desire to be painted.
> What remains of my vanity of former decades is opposed to the representation of my actual decay and ugliness.
> But let us assume that I can overcome this infantile resistance and offer an acceptable model to the painter. I think that my face is not good for reproduction but you will say: "I am the better judge of that." Furthermore, even my limited experience has taught me that while an artist both intends and promises to take up only a few hours of his model's time, it generally turns out that the model has to sit for more than the "few hours." This is, however, exhausting for the poor victim who swears to himself, "Never again."
> Furthermore, I am not very agile as I am not allowed to mount

steps. The sittings would, therefore, have to take place in my house in Grinzing, or in its garden.

Also I am still in the middle of work, which for me means 9 one-hour sessions each day. I could not combine my work and yours. One would, therefore, have to wait for June or July when the holidays start.

And now, if you still want to paint me, please let me hear from you.

Yours devotedly,
Freud

If Freud was surprised by the aftermath of the birthday celebrations he was, as he admitted, "staggered" by an event which took place not so very many months later. Wilhelm Fliess, who had played such an important role in Freud's life in the 1890s, had died in Berlin in 1928. Frau Fliess had then asked Freud for the letters her husband had written to him. "As far as my memory goes," he replied, "I think that I destroyed the greater part of our correspondence some time after 1904." But some letters might have survived, and if he could find them they would "be held unconditionally at [her] disposal." No letters did go to Frau Fliess, but a subsequent remark by Freud to Marie Bonaparte casts a doubt on their fate. Frau Fliess still held Freud's letters, and in his reply to her he had added: "I would like to know that my letters to your husband, an intimate friend of longstanding, have found a fate that will protect them from future use." There is no record of Frau Fliess's answer to that question, and Freud apparently assumed that his letters had been destroyed. Now he was to be disillusioned.

A bookseller in Berlin, he was told by Marie Bonaparte, had visited her recently. "He has," she went on, "obtained from Fliess's widow your letters and manuscripts belonging to the Fliess estate." The widow had considered depositing them with the National Library of Prussia, had had second thoughts, then sold them to the bookseller from whom Marie Bonaparte had bought them.

"My dear Marie," Freud replied,

The matter of the correspondence with Fliess has stirred me deeply. After his death the widow requested the return of his letters to me and I agreed without question, but was unable to find them. I don't know till this very day whether I destroyed them or only hid them ingeniously. . . . Our correspondence was of the most intimate nature, as you can surmise. It would have been most painful to have it fall into the hands of strangers. It is therefore an extraordinary labor of love that you have gotten hold of them and removed them from danger. I only regret the expense you've incurred. May I offer to share half of it with you? I would have had to acquire the letters myself if the man had approached me directly. I don't want any of them to become known to so-called posterity.

The Princess managed to keep the letters physically out of Freud's hands, explaining that a condition of sale was that they would not be sold to the Freud family. Even had this not been the case she would probably have acted in the same way, since she later told Ernest Jones, "I did not hand them over to him as I was afraid he would destroy them." But Freud was obviously anxious to check what he had actually written so many years ago, and the delicate situation was at least partially resolved. "I . . . read a few of the most important ones to him during my analytic hours," Marie Bonaparte told Jones, "but without letting him have them."

Even this, however, was not entirely satisfactory. " Naturally it's all right with me if you don't read the letters either, but you should not assume that they contain no more than a good deal of indiscretion," Freud admitted. "In view of the intimate nature of our relationship, these letters cover all kinds of things, factual as well as personal topics; and the factual ones, which indicate all the presentiments and blind alleys of the budding psychoanalyst, are also quite personal in this case . . . For these reasons, it would be so desirable for me to know that this material was in your hands."

In Marie Bonaparte's hands it remained until, after the end of the Second World War, it was given to Anna Freud. A carefully edited selection of the letters was published in 1951, and the originals eventually found a home in the Library of Congress where it was planned that they would be kept unread until the end of the century.

In 1937 Freud thus won at least a partial victory. But he had more than enough to worry about as he tried, with the help of Ernest Jones among others, to keep some semblance of psychoanalytic training alive in Germany, where its prospects sank as Hitler's star rose.

Toward the end of the year he had to undergo yet another of what he was now calling his "normal" operations, and this time it was followed by unusually violent pain. "I had to cancel my work for 12 days," he told Zweig, "and I lay with pain and hot-water bottles on the couch which is meant for others." But early in the New Year he was back at work again, and by February 1938 there was even a note of optimism about the political situation in his letter to Eitingon: "Our brave, and in its way honest, government is at present more energetic in defending us against the Nazis than ever," he said, "although in view of the newest events in Germany no one can be sure what the outcome will be."

23

An Order for Release

"Finis Austriae"

Note in Freud's diary for March 11, 1938

The events that followed Freud's optimistic letter to Eitingon were noted on the white paper sheets which he kept on his desk as an unbound diary. These had for some while recorded both world events and personal history: the death of Masaryk, the Czech President, was sandwiched between the news that Emanuel Loewy was eighty and that another old friend had paid the Freuds a visit; the birthdays of members of the family and Minna's departure for hospital were intermingled with news of the now deteriorating political situation.

In February, besides noting Loewy's death, he recorded another operation in his mouth—this time for the removal of a suspicious wart on the site of his cancer—and, on the twenty-seventh, the single word "Schuschnigg." On the twenty-eighth he wrote: "Schlechte Tage"; dark days. Even darker days lay in the immediate future as any hope that Austria would be able to resist German demands steadily faded.

On March 9 the Austrian Chancellor, Kurt Schuschnigg, announced that a plebiscite to test whether the Austrian people wished to remain independent would be held on the twelfth. Whatever faith he may have had in the gesture it was obvious to others that events were closing in, and on the tenth, Freud recorded in his diary: "Wiley von Amerik Jesuitschaft." The reference was to John Cooper Wiley, appointed some months previously as consul general in Vienna on the recommendation of William Bullitt, now

United States ambassador in Paris, and charged with special instructions to keep a protecting eye on Freud and his family. Anna's friend Dorothy Burlingham lived in the same apartment block. The two homes were connected by internal telephone, and following Wiley's visit it was arranged that if there were trouble, then Dorothy Burlingham would telephone the American legation and an official would be dispatched from there on a purely "accidental" visit to the Freuds.

The precautions were soon to prove useful. On the eleventh, Schuschnigg obeyed Hitler's instructions to call off the plebiscite. But this was no longer enough, and in the afternoon he was forced to resign. On hearing the news Freud sent out the maid to buy a copy of *Abend,* the pro-Schuschnigg paper. "After gently taking the paper from Paula's hands, he read through the headlines," says Martin, "and then, crumpling it in his fist, he threw it into a corner of the room." And in his diary he wrote the words "Finis Austriae."

Max Schur was making the rounds at his hospital when the news of Schuschnigg's resignation was announced. He drove to the Berggasse without delay. "The streets were packed with marching [Austrian] storm-troopers," he later wrote. "A number of friends were gathered at Freud's home, and we all tried to convince [him] to leave. The following day he gave in but by then it was too late, and we had to wait for 'legal permission.' "

In Schuschnigg's place there was appointed the Austrian Nazi Seyss-Inquart. His first act was to invite the German Army into the country. The Germans had in fact already started to move, and by dawn their first tanks were rumbling through the streets of Vienna. In many places they were welcomed by cheering crowds, and it needed only a little imagination to see the ghost of Karl Lueger, Vienna's anti-Semitic mayor of many years earlier, saluting in the background.

On the morning of the twelfth, Hitler himself entered Austria and decided, apparently on the spur of the moment, that instead of setting up a puppet government, he would incorporate the country into the German Reich. "On the wireless," Freud told Zweig, "I was able to listen first to our challenge and then to our surrender, to the rejoicing and the counterrejoicing." In the course of this "eventful week"—a phrase which he wrote in English—"the last of my few patients have left me. I am not yet quite free from pain, so I cannot work and therefore I do absolutely nothing."

Freud's entries for three days of the eventful week were all equally ominous. On Sunday the thirteenth, "Anschluss an

Deutschland"; on Monday, "Hitler in Wien"; and on Tuesday, "Kontrolle in Verlag & Haus."

Luckily, by this time not only the resolute Mr. Wiley but also the equally resolute Ernest Jones had started the operations which eventually, almost three months later, were to open the route to Britain. This was as well. Freud's international fame was more than offset by his reputation as the founder of "Jewish psychoanalysis," a description which in Germany demarcated the technique from other forms of psychiatry as surely as "Jewish physics" made Einstein's relativity a theory which German scientists could accept only at their peril. Britain, France and the United States had for the previous five years done their, sometimes grudging, best to accommodate the flow of Jews from Germany, as well as some from Italy, and the prospects for those from Austria in 1938 were by no means good.

At first Freud seems to have aroused little interest among the British authorities. Since the early 1930s his name had been on the list of prominent Austrians prepared by the British embassy in Vienna each year for the Foreign Office in London, but the official attitude was typified by the remark of Sir Walford Selby made on Sir John Simon's list in 1936: "His numerous books on psychoanalysis and kindred subjects have made Professor Freud better-known [outside Austria] than in his own country, where no great fuss appears to be made of him." The Foreign Office was later told that while the Austrian government had congratulated Freud on his eightieth birthday, it had ensured "that no mention of this should appear in the Press." Thus the British government had become somewhat off-handed, and when the Prime Minister, Neville Chamberlain, received, on March 29, 1938, a telegram from an unidentified sender saying: "Demand instant news of Professor Freud," it was almost jocularly minuted: "A past—or future?—patient."

Freud's chances of survival would have been slim but for the help that now came from two complementary sources. In the United States the intervention of President Roosevelt, combined with the interest of Cordell Hull, Secretary of State, and William Bullitt, in Paris, gave him a measure of personal protection and eventually induced the Germans to let him leave Austria. In Britain, Ernest Jones's friendship with the Earl De La Warr, Lord Privy Seal, and with Sir Samuel Hoare, the Home Secretary, smoothed the way for granting permits to the Freuds which enabled them to live in Britain.

Jones flew to Austria on March 15 after effectively pulling a number of personal strings, and before he reached Vienna the

British ambassador in the city had already been informed by the Foreign Office: "Dr. Jones is anxious about the fate of Dr. Freud and if he applies to you for advice Lord Privy Seal would be grateful for anything you can do."

Arrived in the city, Jones went first to the offices of the Verlag. There, Martin Freud was under arrest, the offices were being thoroughly searched by the Germans and it was clear that there was no hope of the publishing house being spared because of its international character. Later that day Jones went to No. 19 Berggasse. Here he learned that the Americans had not only been alerted to Freud's danger but had already begun to exercise what was termed "friendly interest."

Interest had begun earlier in the day when Wiley had cabled Cordell Hull a message he wanted passed on to Bullitt: "Fear Freud, despite age and illness, in danger." In Washington, Hull had not only sent on the message to Bullitt but had raised the matter with Roosevelt. The President, apparently using his own private channels of communication, had learned that Freud would be welcomed in Paris by Marie Bonaparte if the French would grant him a visa, and had within a few hours instructed Hull to send the following message to Hugh Robert Wilson, the American ambassador in Berlin:

> Wiley reported in a telegram from Vienna yesterday that he fears that Dr. Freud despite age and illness is in danger. The President has instructed me to ask you to take the matter up personally and informally with the appropriate officials of the German Government and desires you to express the hope that arrangements may be made by the appropriate authorities so that Dr. Freud and his family may be permitted to leave Vienna and travel to Paris, where the President understands friends are willing and able to receive them. I think it would be preferable for you not to mention the President's name in this connection but to state that in view of Dr. Freud's outstanding position in the scientific world, such action on the part of the existing authorities in Austria could not help but create a very favorable impression in this country and on the part of this Government. Please telegraph the result of your conversation.

Before Wilson could reply, Wiley had reported to Hull that Freud had already received attention from the new masters of Vienna. "His house was searched, money and passport confiscated. Two officers of the Legation appeared during the search to show 'friendly interest.' He has not been molested since. Vienna Police President promises personal interest in case. French Legation states that visa will be granted if exit permit accorded."

Freud's home had, indeed, been one of the first marked out for attention by the S.A., who entered the apartment and put a sentry on the door. According to Jones, Martha had responded by inviting the sentry to sit down as she disliked seeing people standing in her home. She then added to the embarrassment of the visitors by putting all her housekeeping money on the table and asking them to help themselves. Anna Freud had meanwhile led the officers to another room where she produced about 6,000 Austrian schillings from the safe. At this point the door swung open and revealed Freud. He said nothing. He merely glared. The visitors, apparently discomfited, quickly left but warned that they would be back another day.

On the seventeenth the U.S. ambassador in Berlin was able to report on what he had done following Roosevelt's instructions:

> For reasons which I need not elaborate, I thought it best and most expeditious in the first instance to approach Weizsäcker in this matter. I told him that I had received a telegram from Washington informing me that Doctor Freud, now an old man and ill, was desirous of leaving Vienna with his family for Paris where he has friends who would take care of him. I added that he was widely and well known in the United States and that a permission accorded to him and his family to leave could not but create a favorable impression upon American opinion. I said that as Doctor Freud was presumably an Austrian subject my remarks were not an official representation but that I thought the German Government itself would be glad to know of the importance attached by my people to the favorable treatment of Doctor Freud. I then asked Weizsäcker for his friendly advice since I was so new at this post as to what procedure I had best follow in order to present this most efficaciously.
>
> Weizsäcker asked whether Doctor Freud had tried for permission to leave and been refused. I replied that I did not know. He then said that after reflection he thought the best procedure was to leave this in his hands. He would get into telephonic communication with von Stein, formerly Chargé d'Affaires of the German Legation in Vienna and now in charge of administration of the Ball Platz, and see what could be done about the matter. He added that he himself would inform Ribbentrop of my démarche and that he hoped there would be no difficulty. He will communicate by telephone as soon as he has any information.
>
> The foregoing was being coded when Weizsäcker telephoned to say that he had just spoken to von Stein in Vienna and that the latter had told him there was not a word of truth in the reports that Doctor Freud had been arrested, that he expected Doctor Freud to apply for a visa and that he "hoped there would be no difficulty." Weizsäcker added that of course the initiative of asking for a visa must come from Doctor Freud.

But Doctor Freud still showed no particular wish to leave Vienna. Imperturbable, self-assured, exhibiting a new confidence as if he were back in battle again, he made Ernest Jones's task of persuasion an extremely difficult one. He had no wish to settle in France and when Jones, persisting, said that he was prepared to return to Britain to see if he would be accepted there, Freud produced his final argument: to leave his native land would be like a soldier deserting his post. Jones was ready for this, and countered with a story which he must have known would tickle Freud's fancy. He recalled how Lightoller, the second officer of the *Titanic,* had been blown to the surface by the explosion of the boilers as the great liner had gone down. Later, being sternly questioned as to why he had left the ship, he had replied: "I never left the ship: she left me." Austria, as Freud had already acknowledged with his "Finis Austriae," had already left him. He saw the logic of the argument. He agreed to go.

Only later did he reveal why he had finally been persuaded. "The advantage the emigration promises Anna," he wrote to Jones, "justifies all our little sacrifices. For us old people (73–77–82) emigrating wouldn't have been worthwhile."

However, Freud's decision to leave Vienna enlarged in one way the Americans' problem of inducing the Germans to let him go and Jones's problem of obtaining British residence permits. This was disclosed when, on March 19, Wiley cabled Bullitt in some alarm. "Professor Freud," he said, "wishes to take with him his family of ten, including three in-laws, also maid, physician, latter's family of three, sixteen in all." Bullitt replied by return. "To support sixteen persons is, of course, entirely beyond any resources at my disposal. . . . At this distance it is impossible for me to give intelligent advice. I should perhaps limit myself to saying that I can make available immediately $10,000: but can not (repeat not) be responsible for more, although I might be able to obtain further contributions. Please make this perfectly clear." He was no doubt somewhat reassured when, the following day, he was told that Freud wanted to go to England and that the only problem involved was the exit visas, a matter which, Bullitt was informed on the twenty-second, Von Stein was "taking up . . . with Himmler."

Some idea of the close attention that Roosevelt's instructions had brought about was also given on the twenty-second, when Bullitt was advised: "Anna Freud just arrested. Have informed Berlin and Von Stein." The message was followed five hours later with the news: "Anna Freud released." She had, in fact, been taken away for a day's interrogation—giving Freud some of the worst hours of his life.

By the end of March the problems of persuading the Germans

to grant the exit permits and the British to grant the residence permits were still unsolved. A rather bizarre solution to the second problem was already being mooted in Britain by Commander Locker-Lampson, the splendid and eccentric British Member of Parliament who five years earlier had unsuccessfully tried to obtain British nationality for Einstein, unable to return safely to Germany after Hitler's rise to power.

On April 12 Locker-Lampson sought leave to bring in a bill extending Palestine nationality. Although the bill was specifically aimed at helping the large numbers of Jews trying to escape death in Germany, Locker-Lampson appeared to have had Freud particularly in mind, pleading in the debate that "in spite of Freud being old and dying, the Nazi monsters have deprived him of his liberty." Whether Freud would have made use of such a bill is very debatable indeed. In any case, the point was to be academic. The Commander was allowed to bring in his bill—although only by the grace of the Speaker's casting vote—but there was virtually no chance of its being approved. It was not only that Palestine nationality was regulated by the military commander in chief in that country and not by Parliament; as a minute from a Foreign Office official noted of the bill: "Only by the most remote chance of good luck in the ballot for private members bills next autumn—a 600 to 1 chance—would it [come before the House]. Even then it would have no chance of becoming law without Government support and unless it were very different from its description it would be opposed by the Government."

By this time there had been at least one tentative suggestion that Freud should be induced to settle in the United States. Toward the end of March, Geoffrey Parsons, editor of the *New York Herald Tribune,* had written to Felix Frankfurter, pointing out that it should be emphasized to Roosevelt that refugees from Austria would be of high intellect and very unlikely to become a charge upon the United States. "I am thinking," he said, "of people like the Stolpers from Berlin [Dr. Gustav Stolper was a former Reichstag deputy] for example. Such recruits to Americanism are precious, I feel. It would ·be an extraordinarily effective move, for example, if Freud could be persuaded to come to this country, assuming that he is strong enough to travel and can escape." Frankfurter passed on the gist of Parsons' letter to the President, but his reaction appears to have been noncommittal.

However, the problem of Freud's residence in Britain was eventually settled by Jones's efforts after he had returned to London. By this time Sir Samuel Hoare had been given a slight prod about the problem of Austrian refugees by Cosmo Lang, the Archbishop of Canterbury, who had informed him: "I have received information from Vienna of the miserable plight of the Jews in that city and in Austria and of their apprehension and even terror. I am told that those who may succeed in getting out of Austria would not be allowed to enter England." Hoare was genuinely doing what he could to deal humanely with a prickly situation, and now suggested to Jones that in the case of Freud he should enlist the help of Sir William Bragg, president of the Royal Society. Jones was later to express surprise at the naïveté of Bragg's question, "Do you really think the Germans are unkind to the Jews?" He might have been less surprised had he known that Bragg, when asked some years earlier to support Rutherford's Academic Assistance Council—created largely to help refugee scientists from Germany—had remarked, "It is possible, I suppose, to do more harm than good by angering the people in power in Germany."

In 1938, however, Bragg went so far as to petition Lord Halifax, the Foreign Secretary, on behalf of Austrian scientists who were being treated with great severity: "Can we possibly, through the Embassy, or in any other way, do something to help them?" In the background, moreover, there was the influence of the Lord Privy Seal, and it was soon evident that although the paper work involved in getting Freud and his family into Britain was considerable, the powers-that-be would help. Thus a familiar characteristic of British society became apparent; Jones's friendship with the Lord Privy Seal and membership of the same skating club as Sir Samuel turned the scales, and Freud was saved not by what his friends knew but by whom they knew.

The exit permits appeared to present a more intractable problem, even though the British had somewhat languidly put their shoulder to the wheel early in April when, on the eighth, the British ambassador in Berlin, Sir Neville Henderson, was told that the Lord Privy Seal was interesting himself in Freud's case and that President Roosevelt had apparently intervened. "If, as is understood to be possible, the U.S. Ambassador presses the German authorities for a reply, you might consider the desirability of supporting his action officially," Sir Neville was instructed.

By mid-April it looked as if only one more hurdle had to be cleared. "Freud's departure," Cordell Hull was informed by Wiley, "temporarily held up by liquidation of his publishing house on which exit permit depends. Princess of Greece here and actively interested. She will probably arrange matters by purchase of publishing rights. Freuds intend to settle in England."

The "liquidation" was apparently a means of extorting the maximum money from Freud before his exit permits were granted, since the German Psychoanalytic Society had already taken over the assets of the International Psycho-Analytical Association and of the Verlag. A Dr. Anton Sauerwald had been appointed administrator; although a convinced anti-Semite, Sauerwald proved more helpful than expected, largely due to the fact that he had studied chemistry at the University of Vienna under one of Freud's oldest friends. Nevertheless, the Nazis struck a hard bargain. Martin Freud had, before the *Anschluss,* sent for safety to Switzerland all the bound copies of Freud's *Collected Works* held by the Verlag. But the dispatch had been recorded in the office, and the Germans now demanded that the books should be brought back, at the Verlag's expense, before any exit permits were issued. They were then destroyed.

Even by the end of the first week in May, the matter of hard cash was still holding up the exit permits as Wilson in Berlin made clear to Cordell Hull. A member of the American embassy staff who had visited Vienna, Hull was told, "also enquired regarding the case of Freud and was informed by Gestapo official handling the case that the police had no further objection to the departure of Freud abroad and that all papers were in order. He said, however, that Freud's departure was delayed on account of an indebtedness of approximately 32,000 s[c]hillings due his publisher and that negotiations were going on between Freud and his creditors to satisfy this claim. He asserted further that Freud had sufficient funds to satisfy the creditors but that Freud had not yet agreed upon what he considered to be a just amount, that as soon as this transaction was settled Freud was free to depart." Eventually it was Marie Bonaparte who paid the financial blackmail money; whether, in the process, she bought the publishing rights of the Verlag was not immediately established.

Some weeks still had to pass before the Freuds were allowed to go, and there were times when hope faded. At one point the prospects looked particularly dark, and Anna asked her father, "Wouldn't it be better if we all killed ourselves?" "Why?" was Freud's reply. "Because they would like us to?"

During May, Marie Bonaparte, back in Vienna from Paris, joined Anna and her father in sorting his papers. Freud, following the habit of years, was all for destruction; Marie Bonaparte all for preservation. The result, Anna said later, was that she "rescued things from waste-baskets which my father had thrown there."

A major problem was presented by Freud's considerable library. There was a limit to what he could take out of the country, and when this had been reached there remained about 800 volumes, many of them annotated by him over the years. These he handed to

Heinrich Hinterberger, a Viennese bookseller, with instructions to sell them for the best price he could get. With the anti-Semitic and anti-psychoanalytic tide in full flood, Hinterberger had to be careful: in his next catalogue the collection was advertized merely as "brought together over nearly 50 years by a famous Viennese scientific explorer, very likely to constitute the nucleus of a library of neurology and psychiatry." The price asked was 1,850 German marks, or roughly $500 at the time—about 60 cents for each of Freud's 800 volumes. Dr. Jacob Schatzky, librarian of the New York State Psychiatric Institute, had a feeling that the "scientific explorer" might be Freud, and before the end of 1939 the collection had arrived in New York.

While Hinterberger was deciding how to dispose of his fortuitous windfall, the Freud family's exit papers had begun to come through. On May 5 Minna Bernays was allowed to leave Vienna for Britain. "Two prospects keep me going in these grim times," Freud wrote a week later to Ernst in England; "to rejoin you all and —to die in freedom. I sometimes compare myself with the old Jacob who, when a very old man, was taken by his children to Egypt, as Thomas Mann is to describe in his next novel. Let us hope that it won't also be followed by an exodus from Egypt. It is high time that Ahasuerus came to rest somewhere."

Martin's papers arrived in time for him to leave on the fourteenth. Ten days later Freud's eldest daughter Mathilde and her husband Robert were allowed to depart. "We packed and left our housekeeper behind to supervise the transport of the furniture and everything else," she later wrote. "Neighbors, friends, all our tradesmen, came to say goodbye; housekeeper, charwoman, caretaker of the house in Turkenstrasse, stood on the pavement weeping; a member of the firm for whom Robert had been working during the last years, and a schoolmaster of mine, came to the Westbahnhof—and so we left for the new life in England."

Alexander Freud, the transport expert, had been quick off the mark, moving into Switzerland as the *Anschluss* took place and eventually arriving in London on his way to a new life in Canada.

For Freud, there was another week of waiting. Then, at last, the necessary pieces of paper arrived. So, as a parting gesture, did the Gestapo. They brought a document to which they demanded Freud's signature. It stated that he had been properly treated. Freud signed. Then he added his own few words: "I can heartily recommend the Gestapo to anyone."

By the beginning of June everything was ready, and on the second, he received the final clearance from the authorities for himself, his wife and his youngest daughter. On the following day

Freud left the city that had been his home for nearly eighty years, traveling first on the Orient Express to Paris with Martha and Anna, two maids and a doctor, Josephine Stross, who at the last minute had replaced Dr. Schur, unexpectedly taken to hospital for an appendix operation. With them went the family chow.

In London Ernst Freud had already completed arrangements for his father's new home, and before leaving Vienna, Freud was able to scribble a brief note to Samuel, whom he had not seen since before the First World War. "Leaving Vienna for good today," he wrote. "Next address 39 Elsworthy Road, London, N.W.3. Any chance of our meeting after so many years."

24

Into the Promised Land

Over the Rhine bridge and we were free.

FREUD, in a letter to Max Eitingon

Freud and his family left Vienna accompanied by a member of the U.S. legation staff, ordered to ensure that no hitches occurred before the frontier with France was reached. His choice by the American officials in Vienna adds an ironic last note to Freud's departure from his own country. "When I saw [this U.S. official] just after World War Two," a friend wrote years later, "he told me about the trip and also vehemently described his personal feelings of repugnance for Freud, his friends and relatives, Jews, and psychoanalysis. I assure you he took that trip only because he was ordered to do so."

At three next morning the party reached Kehl, on the outskirts of Strasbourg, and the train clanked its way across the long iron girders into France. "Over the Rhine bridge and we were free," Freud wrote to Max Eitingon.

By ten they were in Paris. Here they were met by Marie Bonaparte, William Bullitt, Freud's nephew Harry and his son Ernst. They passed the day in Marie Bonaparte's house, where she presented Freud with a number of Greek terra-cotta figures she had bought for him as a surprise addition to his collection.

That night they left Paris for the night ferry to England, whose white cliffs Freud saw once again after an interval of thirty-one years. Jones had done his staff work well. Earl De La Warr had arranged that the whole party should be granted diplomatic privilege, and there was no examination of luggage or other formality, either at Dover or in London. Jones even succeeded in diverting much of the inevitable press attention, collecting Freud and Martha in his own car and making a quick getaway before the reporters caught up.

The first stop was 39 Elsworthy Road, rented by Ernst while searching for a permanent home for his parents. The house stood on the edge of Primrose Hill, north of Central London, and from its windows Freud could look out onto a small tree-surrounded garden beyond which lay green slopes. It was remarkably like the prospect from the summer home he had often occupied in Grinzing on the outskirts of Vienna, a pleasant change from the cooped-up quarters of the Berggasse to which he had been largely confined throughout the previous winter. The enchantment of the place, he told Max Eitingon, made him want to shout "Heil Hitler!"

Freud still had more than a year's life left to him, and for a man in his eighties, constantly accompanied by the pain and the inhibiting limitations of the prosthesis, it was to be remarkably full. During those months the physical distress was to be at least partly counterbalanced by the remarkable welcome he was given in Britain, not only by those official medical and Jewish bodies who had special reason to acknowledge him but also by the ordinary people. They had not, overnight, been converted to psychoanalysis; most of them still regarded Freud and his theories with a combination of skepticism and incredulity, when they considered them at all. There was still, within the national ethos, more than a trace of anti-Semitism which had not been shamed into extinction by the excesses of Hitlerite Germany. But enough of Freud's uncompromising courage had become known to arouse a feeling of respect as much as of sympathy. It was Chesterton who had maintained, on behalf of all Britons, that one man fighting against five was always a fine sight; a man in his eighties, disastrously stricken with cancer, persuaded to seek refuge only after the desperate efforts of his friends, presented much the same spectacle. Freud seems to have been surprised that, as he told his brother, "the newspapers have made us popular." Taxi drivers, the bank manager, shop assistants who served Martha—still maintaining her Viennese custom of doing her own shopping—exhibited a friendliness which had more to do with Freud's personality than with psychoanalysis.

For Freud himself there was a particular pleasure in his reception. From his first visit in 1875, the idea of settling in England had attracted him at fairly regular intervals. His position as an Anglophile was brought out when Sir Arthur Tansley, the botanist who had been his student after the First World War, once suggested to him that the continental condemnation of English "hypocrisy" might be justified. "But surely," said Freud, indignantly rejecting the idea, "you cannot doubt that England is rightly held to be morally pre-eminent." As Tansley was later to observe, Freud was the last man in the world to pretend what he did not believe, "and he used the word 'moral' in no narrow sense."

In 1938 Martha, writing to Freud's sisters still in Vienna, reflected Freud's own feelings:

> If one's thoughts were not always with the dear ones one has left behind, one would be completely happy. You cannot imagine how honored this town feels at having our modest beloved old man in their midst. Every day we receive letters welcoming him. Although we have only been here two weeks, letters arrive without any indication of the street: simply, "Freud, London"; and they arrive without delay despite the great size and magnificence of this city of ten million people.

Freud rallied quickly after the journey and was ready when, three days after his arrival in London, there appeared in Elsworthy Road one much-awaited visitor: Samuel Freud, the "sharp and deep chap" whom he had never expected to see again. It was a moving occasion.

Under the influence of his new surroundings, and with Anna's help, Freud was soon coping with the deluge of letters that poured into the new home. There were many from friends, almost as many from complete strangers who just wished him luck. There were also, inevitably, the autograph hunters and the "cranks, lunatics, and pious men who send tracts and texts from the Gospels which promise salvation, attempts to convert the unbeliever and shed light on the future of Israel."

Thomas Looney, whose *Shakespeare Identified* had made it easy for Freud to believe that Shakespeare was the Earl of Oxford, wrote, welcoming him to Britain. So did numerous Jewish organizations and Jewish scholars. Professor Malinowski, whose anthropological researches had qualified the findings of *Totem and Taboo*, called to pay his respects. So did Chaim Weizmann, president of the Jewish Agency. Nandor Fodor, the former research director of the Institute for Psychical Research, invoked Freud's help, alleging that he had been sacked because his report on a celebrated case of haunting had attributed it to sexual trauma. Freud read Fodor's account and was intrigued by it despite the fact that, as he wrote, he was a man "unwilling to believe in supernormal happenings."

Another visitor was Josef Breuer's granddaughter. Before leaving Vienna, Freud had been asked to help her mother to emigrate.

He had induced A. A. Brill to supply the necessary American affidavits, and the granddaughter now called on Freud with her husband. "Even though Freud could speak only with great difficulty," wrote the husband, Robert A. Kann, "he was very kind, showed us some of his Egyptian statues, and when my wife admired a beautiful white flower in a bowl he presented it to her." Freud went on to ask about many members of the family, in fact all except one. "While the motivation of his action was obviously focussed on Dr. Breuer," wrote Kann, "he did not refer to him with one syllable, even though he reviewed the fate of all other members of the family known to him."

Salvador Dali was introduced by Stefan Zweig, and in his autobiography gives a vivid picture of the man whom the surrealists had chosen as their patron saint: "While I was crossing the old professor's yard," he wrote,

> I saw a bicycle leaning against the wall, and on the saddle, attached by a string, was a red rubber hot-water bottle which looked full of water, and on the back of the hot-water bottle walked a snail! The presence of that assortment seemed strange and inexplicable in the yard of Freud's house.
>
> Contrary to my hopes we spoke little, but we devoured each other with our eyes. Freud knew nothing about me except my painting, which he admired, but suddenly I had the whim of trying to appear in his eyes as a kind of dandy of universal intellectualism. I learned later that the effect I produced was exactly the opposite.
>
> Before leaving I wanted to give him a magazine containing an article I had written on paranoia. I therefore opened the magazine at the page of my text, begging him to read it if he had time. Freud continued to stare at me without paying the slightest attention to my magazine. Trying to interest him, I explained that it was not a surrealist diversion, but was really an ambitious scientific article, and I repeated the title pointing to it at the same time with my finger. Before his imperturbable indifference, my voice became involuntarily sharper and more insistent. Then, continuing to stare at me with a fixity in which his whole being seemed to converge, Freud exclaimed, addressing Stefan Zweig, "I have never seen a more complete example of a Spaniard. What a fanatic!"

For his part, Freud admitted that until Dali's visit he had looked upon surrealists as cranks. "The young Spaniard, however, with his candid fanatical eyes and his undeniable technical mastery, has made me reconsider my opinion," he now conceded. "It would in fact be very interesting to investigate analytically how a picture like this [a surrealist picture] came to be painted. From the critical point of view it could still be maintained that the notion of art defies expansion as long as the quantitative proportion of unconscious material and preconscious treatment does not remain within definite limits. In any case these are serious psychological problems."

But there was one picture that Freud was prevented from investigating analytically. During the conversation Dali had been sketching his head. "I dared not show it to Freud," Zweig later wrote, "because clairvoyantly Dali had already incorporated death in the picture."

Freud was also visited by Charles Singer, the historian of medicine and science. Shortly afterward, Singer received a letter from H. G. Wells, who had met Freud a few years earlier in Vienna. "When I talked with [him then] . . .," Wells had written, "he did not seem to feel as I do about death. He is older than I and he was in bad health, but he seemed to be clinging to life and to his reputation and teaching much more youthfully than I do to mine." Now that Freud was a refugee in Britain, Wells was anxious to help; he believed that money was needed but did not like to raise the matter himself. Would Singer do so for him? Soon afterward Singer mentioned Wells's offer, only to be told that Freud was not really hard up, despite his losses on leaving Austria. But was there, Wells insisted, nothing else that Freud wanted? Singer said he would ask. "[Freud] gave the odd reply," he later wrote, "that the only thing he would really like was to die a British subject." Wells called on Freud and, in November 1938, wrote suggesting another meeting before he left England for the Continent. Freud replied that it would indeed be a good thing if they met before Wells again went abroad, since there was "so much uncertainty in our lives and in my life especially." But neither Wells nor the indefatigable Locker-Lampson, by now trying to gather support for a bill conferring immediate British citizenship on Freud, had any success.

On June 23 there came visitors who especially delighted him. They were the Secretaries of the Royal Society, bringing the Society's Charter Book for him to sign. He was unable to make the journey to the Society's headquarters, so the Book was brought to the signer, an honor previously accorded only to the King. "They left a facsimile of the book with me," Freud told Arnold Zweig, "and if you were here I could show you the signatures from I. Newton to Charles Darwin. Good company." For once he signed "Sigm. Freud," instead of the usual "Freud," explaining to Zweig in a footnote that he had been told "it is reserved for Lords to sign with the surname only. Altogether a strange country."

By the following month he was at work again. The task he now set himself was "to bring together the tenets of psychoanalysis and to state them, as it were, dogmatically—in the most concise form and in the most unequivocal terms. Its intention is naturally not to compel belief or to arouse conviction." If these few words in a two-paragraph preface suggested sweet reasonableness, the next tended to remind the reader of the earlier Freud for whom no exterior criticism of the cause was possible. "The teachings of psychoanalysis," he went on, "are based on an incalculable number of observations and experiences, and only someone who has repeated those observations on himself and on others is in a position to arrive at a judgment of his own upon it." Only psychoanalysts, in other words, could be judges of psychoanalysis. Nearing the end of the road, he was restaking his claims for the cause.

Within half a century Freud had seen many of these claims slowly accepted, even though grudgingly and with qualifications that have become further justified since his death. Even *The Lancet*, which had once given great space to his enemies, had said on his arrival in Britain: "His teachings have in their time aroused controversy more acute and antagonism more bitter than any since the days of Darwin. Now, in his old age, there are few psychologists of any school who do not admit their debt to him. Some of the conceptions he formulated clearly for the first time have crept into current philosophy against the stream of willful incredulity which he himself recognized as man's natural reaction to unbearable truth." In the United States acceptance had come more quickly and with fewer reservations but in a pattern which caused Freud much dismay. "A remark of yours saying that psychoanalysis has spread in the United States more widely than deeply struck me as particularly true," he wrote to Jelliffe. "I am by no means happy to see that analysis has become the handmaid of psychiatry in America and nothing else."

It was, moreover, about to experience both in America and in Britain an expansion which not even Freud himself could have foreseen as he reflected on his life work during the months he knew would be his last. One cause of this was the Second World War, now only a few months away. Psychoanalysts were to be used by most of the belligerents, both for advising on their own psychological warfare campaigns and for analyzing those of the enemy. Freud's follower Ernst Kris was to organize a special government department in Britain for the analysis of German broadcasts and was later to do the same in North America. The use of psychoanalysts in the treatment of battle casualties was from the start to be greater than in the First World War. As one example from

many, a psychoanalyst in the United States was to be put in charge
of an air force rehabilitation hospital, directing there a major psychiatric program carried out by psychiatrists, general practitioners,
social workers and chaplains. With this there went a growing
awareness that in war—and perhaps even in the peace to come—
psychoanalysis could play a part in fitting the right men, and
women, to the right job.

All this lay in the future—as did Russia's claim that "the legions
of Freud armed with the analyst's couch are the secret weapon of
capitalist imperialism," and that psychoanalysis itself was "one of
the most reactionary and pseudo-scientific manifestations of bourgeois ideology"—as Freud settled down to *An Outline of Psycho-
Analysis.* In it he restated the basic theories in the light of the id,
ego and super-ego construction, and hinted in more than one
place that he had new ideas to elaborate. He was never to do so.

Late in July 1938, Dr. Schur, now in Britain and given special
permission to act as Freud's physician in London before passing
the required British professional examinations, noticed a suspicious swelling in his patient's mouth. Freud was at first unwilling
to take the new development seriously and only reluctantly allowed Pichler to be called from Vienna early in September. "He
pointed out that even now he would have to make a large external
excision through the cheek and lips, and asked if I thought Freud's
heart would take the strain," Dr. Schur later wrote. "I voiced my
conviction that it was safe to go ahead, but we left the final decision
to Freud, who gave his consent."

The operation took place in the London Clinic on September 8
and appeared to have been successful. Nevertheless, that evening
Anna ended a letter to Marie Bonaparte with the sentence: "I am
very glad that it is already today, and no longer yesterday."

The Elsworthy Road house had been rented for only a short
period, and before the end of September, Freud was recuperating
in a more permanent home in Maresfield Gardens, little more than
a mile from Elsworthy Road, another big old house with a pleasant
patch of tree-hung garden at the rear. By now his furniture and
personal collections had arrived from Vienna, so Anna and the
maid were able to "reconstruct," in a room on the ground floor,
a replica of Freud's Viennese study, putting the furniture in the
same position and placing on the tables the same statuettes and
pictures he had known in the Berggasse for so many years.

This was to be the Freud family's final home. Freud himself was
to spend his last months here, and his wife and sister-in-law were
to live here until their deaths in 1951 and 1941. It was also to
remain the home of Anna, the daughter whose future prospects

had induced Freud to leave Vienna. She was, indeed, to justify what he had called "all our little sacrifices." Already a skilled child analyst, she was ideally equipped to start a center for homeless children when the intensive German bombing of London began in the autumn of 1940. She was soon to be helped by Americans and later was to write that "the Hampstead War Nursery was a colony of the Foster Parents' Plan for War Children, Inc., New York, and as such owed its whole existence to American generosity." Following the end of the war there came the Hampstead child-therapy center which she was to build up into today's internationally famous clinic.

In the Maresfield Gardens house Freud settled down for what he knew could not be many months. The majority of his close relatives were safe by this time. Mathilde and her husband, together with Martin and Ernst and their families, were in England; Oliver and his family were in France; and his son-in-law Max Halberstadt had emigrated to South Africa from Hamburg with his son a year or two previously. His brother Alexander was soon to be en route to Canada, where he was to spend the rest of his life, while Alexander's son Harry was to cross the Atlantic and spend the later years of the coming war in the U.S. Army.

But there was one shadow. Freud was with good reason worried about "the four old women between 75 and 80," as he described them to Marie Bonaparte—his four sisters still living in Austria. Before leaving Vienna he and his brother had given them 160,000 schillings [roughly $32,000 or £8,000 at the then rate of exchange], enough to keep them for some time unless the money was confiscated by the Germans. Nevertheless, efforts were made to get them to France. The efforts failed. But Freud was to die without knowing that his four elderly sisters were to be deported by the Nazis and killed in various concentration camps.

By the autumn of 1938 he had little energy left. What there was, he expended on his last explosive piece of writing. This was *Moses and Monotheism,* originally three essays and two prefaces written some years earlier and giving psychoanalytical support for the theory—already put forward a number of times—that Moses was an Egyptian. Coming from any quarter, a dissertation attempting to justify an idea so controversial was bound to provoke dissent; coming from one who, disregarding his rejection of the Jewish religion, sincerely believed that he had "probably the main thing" in common with his fellow Jews, the book could easily be classed as intellectual treason.

Freud's intense feeling of Jewishness had never been in doubt, a fact which made the impact of *Moses and Monotheism* on the Orthodox that much greater. Years earlier when Max Graf, the father of "Little Hans," had told Freud that to improve his son's chances he might follow the example of Adler and have him baptized, Freud had responded unequivocally: "If you do not let your son grow up as a Jew, you will deprive him of the sources of energy which cannot be replaced by anything else. He will have to struggle as a Jew, and you ought to develop in him all the energy he will need for that struggle. Do not deprive him of that advantage." As far back as 1909 he had told Jung that he was to be the Joshua destined to explore the promised land of psychiatry which Freud, like Moses, was only to see from afar. To Arthur Schnitzler he had written after being congratulated on his seventieth birthday, "Emotionally, Jewishness is still very important to me," and to the editor of the Swiss-Jewish weekly, *Jüdische Pressen-Zentrale,* "I have always felt a strong feeling of kinship with my race and have also fostered it in my children. . . ." When the local branch of YIVO, the Jewish Scientific Institute, welcomed his arrival in Britain, he had replied with a categorical: "You no doubt know that I gladly and proudly acknowledge my Jewishness, though my attitude toward any religion, including ours, is critically negative."

He could still be decidedly crisp on the subject, as he showed in his reply to Lady Rhondda, the editor of *Time and Tide,* who asked for a contribution to a special issue on anti-Semitism. "Don't you think," he asked, "you ought to reserve the columns of your special number for the utterances of non-Jewish people, less personally involved than myself?" He was, he went on, deeply affected by the acknowledgment in her letter of "a certain growth of anti-Semitism even in this country," and suggested that the current persecution ought rather to give rise to a wave of sympathy.

Yet it was only after Hitler rose to power, with his theory that the Jews were a distinct and evil species of mankind, that Freud began to speculate on what really constituted the essence of Jewishness, on how it had developed historically and on how it had traditionally led to persecution. His solution was a resurrection of the story that Moses was an Egyptian who disagreed with the religion of the royal house and gathered about himself a band of followers whom he led out of Egypt in the Exodus. *The Man Moses, a historical novel,* was to be the title, he had then told Arnold Zweig, before going on to say that the work would probably never be published. The reason, reached by a fairly extravagant argument, was that Austria was in the grip of Catholics, and the Catholics would be offended by the thesis. If it were put forward by the founder of psychoanalysis, they might be risking a ban on psychoanalysis and the suspension of their publications in the country.

Another, and more plausible, reason for Freud's initial hesitation about publication was given some weeks later in further letters to Arnold Zweig and Eitingon. He was, he admitted, on shaky historical ground. "Experts," he wrote, "would find it easy to discredit me as an outsider." Indeed, to Zweig he added: "let us leave it aside."

But it was not to be left for long since "it tormented [him] like an unlaid ghost." In 1937 he resolved the problem by working over the first two of the three essays and publishing them in *Imago*. The first put forward once again the simple thesis that Moses was an Egyptian. The second, "If Moses was an Egyptian . . . ," ingeniously restated the Biblical version of history on the assumption of the first essay. However, provocative as they were, they did avoid the argument of the final, much longer essay which, as Freud described it, "was really open to objection and dangerous—the application [of these findings] to the genesis of monotheism and the view of religion in general." This he held back, apparently intending that it should be held back forever.

When revising the first two essays for *Imago*, he had done the same with the third, and early in 1938 had once again worked over the long last essay. It had a particular fascination for him, reinforcing as it did the conclusion he had arrived at in *Totem and Taboo*—a conclusion "which reduces religion to a neurosis of humanity and explains its enormous power in the same way as a neurotic compulsion in our individual patients. . . ." But despite his disclaimer in a prefatory note, written before leaving Vienna, that he had anything new to say, "Moses, His People and Monotheist Religion" had a cutting edge sharper than that of *Totem and Taboo*. There he had prognosticated about the birth of religion in some prehistoric past; here he was dynamiting the Jewish faith and the Christian Church in a single argument. But Hitler—"the new enemy, to whom we want to avoid being of service, [and who] is more dangerous than the old one with whom we have already learned to come to terms"—had not yet subjugated Austria. The old enemy must still be placated and the conclusion was obvious. The last part of *Moses and Monotheism* might be "preserved in concealment till some day the time arrives when it may venture without danger into the light, or till someone who has reached the same conclusions and opinions can be told: 'there was someone in darker times who thought the same as you.' "

All that was changed by the *Anschluss* and Freud's emigration to London. "I had scarcely arrived in England before I found the temptation irresistible to make the knowledge I had held back accessible to the world, and I began to revise the third part of my study to fit it on to the two parts that had already been published," he wrote. The result, as he himself admitted in another further preface written in London, was artistically inept. Nevertheless, its impact on Jewry would be considerable, and when his plans became known he was visited by many Jewish scholars imploring him not to publish, notably Professor Abraham Yahuda, possibly the most distinguished Jewish Biblical expert of his day.

Freud was well aware of what he was doing. "Needless to say, I don't like offending my own people either," he wrote to Charles Singer. "But what can I do about it? I have spent my whole life standing up for what I have considered to be the scientific truth, even when it was uncomfortable and unpleasant for my fellow men. I cannot end up with an act of disavowal."

He pressed on. Indeed, although publication of the German edition had already been arranged in Amsterdam, he wrote persistently to Ernest Jones, whose wife was translating the book for the English publisher, asking for the work to be hurried up. Initially, it must be remembered, it was fear for the future of psychoanalysis in Austria, not fear of Jewish protest, which had deterred him from publishing, but he made his position clear when visited by the president of the London branch of YIVO, Jacob Meitlis. "His voice showed signs of pain, but he controlled his suffering, and as he spoke his tired face became animated, wrinkles seemed to disappear and his eyes shone with a friendly light," Meitlis later wrote. "His voice, too, grew warmer as he alternated from earnestness to wit, and from humor to wisdom."

Freud lost no time in coming to his theory of monotheism, no doubt stimulated by his visitor, as anxious as were most of the Jewish community to know what Freud was facing them with. "He had no preference for any religion," Meitlis reported. "All religions were matters created by human beings, and he could discern no trace of sanctity in any of them. It was the function of science to reveal this truth and to liberate spiritual movement from all later additions and extraneous elements. He realized that he would be hated for his efforts. . . . But despite this he was glad that his book would soon appear. 'It will anger Jews,' he added. . . ."

Moses and Monotheism was published in Amsterdam, in German, early in March 1939, and on the day that Freud received his first copies he wrote to Hanns Sachs: "The *Moses*, printed in German by Allert de Lange, made its appearance here today in two copies. Quite a worthy exit, I believe. . . ." To Zweig, if to few others, he appears to have revealed second thoughts, apparently regretting that he had published the book in Jewry's most terrible hour: "now that everything is being taken from them, I had to go and take their best man."

He was in no doubt that the Jewish reaction was the same as that of the public to *Three Essays* a third of a century earlier, and when Jacob Meitlis asked if his name could be used in a YIVO appeal Freud replied: "Because of the active opposition which my book *Moses and Monotheism* evoked in Jewish circles I doubt whether it would be in the interests of YIVO to bring my name before the public eye in such a capacity. I leave the decision to you."

Moses and Monotheism has generally been accepted—and not only by Orthodox Jewry—as one of Freud's less successful works. An obvious reason was the rickety structure resulting from the way in which it had been written, revised and rewritten. Age, too, had imposed its limitations, as Ernest Jones was privately to admit to one critical reviewer. "In his later years," he wrote,

> [Freud] had a way of being very selective in his quotations, using only those he wanted to support a particular point and not reviewing the general literature as in his earlier years. This habit was connected with the small store of energy he had left and his conciseness. You and others, for instance, reproach him with not having used various Hebrew sources of Moses legends, which he had no opportunity to investigate. There was little left of his strength when he was eighty-two.

Freud himself knew of other faults, as he acknowledged in a footnote:

> I am very well aware that in dealing so autocratically and arbitrarily with Biblical tradition—bringing it up to confirm my views when it suits me and unhesitatingly rejecting it when it contradicts me—I am exposing myself to serious methodological criticism and weakening the convincing force of my arguments. But this is the only way in which one can treat material of which one knows definitely that its trustworthiness has been severely impaired by the distorting influence of tendentious purposes.

Yet in its basic thesis *Moses and Monotheism* survives the attack of Biblical scholars better than those of the biologists. For here, as in *Totem and Taboo,* the inheritance of acquired characteristics, the essence of Lamarckianism, was not only an integral part of the argument but was held to account for the continuation of guilt in Jewish history, transmitted through generations of descendants.

The month which saw the publication of *Moses and Monotheism* was also for Freud a month of bitterly contrasting news. On March

10, 1939, when the twenty-fifth anniversary of the British Psycho-Analytical Society's foundation was celebrated with a dinner at the London Savoy, the guests and speakers were very different from those which might have been forecast a quarter of a century previously. Earl De La Warr, now president of the Board of Education, proposed the toast to the Society. Walter Elliot, Minister of Health, was among the speakers; others present included two of the most distinguished doctors in Britain: Lord Dawson of Penn, past president of the Royal Society of Medicine and of the British Medical Association, former physician-in-ordinary to King George V; and Lord Horder, whose patients had included King George VI and more than one British Prime Minister.

Whatever individuals might think of psychoanalysis, the meeting of March 10 acknowledged that it was, with whatever qualifications, a method of therapy. Recognition came, ironically enough, as Freud learned of what he realized was his death sentence. During the previous autumn there had been strong hopes that he was recovering from the September operation, and in October he had written to Jelliffe, reporting: "I have overcome another of my habitual operations, and am still fit to work." He was glad, he said, to have escaped the *furor teutonicus* and was "waiting for patients who so far have not arrived." Shortly afterward, he was once more conducting four analyses daily.

The New Year had brought a change. By mid-January another swelling had appeared far back in his mouth. "At first it looked like another bone necrosis, but soon the lesion took on an appearance which looked ominous to me," Dr. Schur has written. There was disagreement about the seriousness of the development, and even Wilfred Trotter, the surgeon who had last seen Freud more than thirty years previously at the Salzburg Congress, now drawn in to give an opinion, could not evaluate it with any certainty. Before the end of February, Dr. Lacassagne from the Institut Curie in Paris came to advise on the probable effects of radiotherapy. Meanwhile, further tests were made. The results were decisive. The cancer had returned, its position made an operation impossible, and by March it was clear that the best to be hoped for was palliative treatment.

Freud was to live six more months. He faced them stoically, refusing the drugs that could have alleviated the constant pain, carrying on with the psychoanalysis of his few patients to within a few weeks of his death. The treatment, he wrote to Eitingon, "gives a kind of life insurance for several weeks, and probably permits the continuation of my analytic work during that time. . . ." He was, he added in a postscript, "prepared for an onslaught by the Jews on [*Moses and Monotheism*]." And to Arnold Zweig he wrote that with publication of the book he no longer need "be interested in any book of mine again until my next reincarnation." There was, he added by way of explanation, no doubt that the latest trouble was "a recurrence of my dear old cancer, with which I have been sharing my existence for 16 years."

In April Dr. Schur had to leave, although only temporarily, for the United States. He had become eligible for a U.S. visa, and unless he now crossed the Atlantic and took out his first papers for American citizenship, the chance might not be given again—either to him or to his family. Reluctantly, he left England on April 21.

Freud was by this time becoming incapable of looking after himself. "Some kind of intervention that would cut short this cruel process would be very welcome," he wrote to Marie Bonaparte. But he still refused to give up, rationally describing his prospects two months later in a letter to H. G. Wells and proposing another teatime meeting.

But Schur, returning to England in July, found his patient physically weaker and, more ominously, mentally apathetic. He was now living permanently in a ground-floor room which looked out onto the garden. While Martha, as always, devoted herself to the efficient running of the house, the indispensable Anna attended to the day and night nursing that was now required. During August Freud began to sink quickly. There were last visits, from relatives and from friends.

On August 12 his nephew Harry, preparing to cross the Atlantic, said that he would come again when he returned for Christmas. Freud smiled sadly as he said, "You won't see me here when you return."

Shortly after the Second World War started in September 1939, the air-raid sirens sounded in London for the first time and Freud's bed was moved into the "safe" zone of the house, an operation which he followed with interest. Soon afterward he and Dr. Schur were listening to a broadcast which spoke of "the war to end all wars," and Schur asked if Freud thought this would indeed be the last. "My last war," he replied.

He was unable to follow details and almost certainly missed the irony of Hitler's speech in Danzig on September 19 when the Füehrer, on whose orders psychoanalysis had been hounded, claimed that the Poles showed all manner of barbaric treatment of others because of their inferiority complex. For once Freud might have smiled at the use of an Adlerian phrase.

Throughout the month he continued to slip downhill. Eating, drinking and sleeping all became more difficult. On the morning of the twenty-first, while Schur was sitting by his bed, Freud spoke to him: "My dear Schur, you certainly remember our first talk. You promised then not to forsake me when my time comes. Now it's nothing but torture and makes no sense any more."

Schur had not forgotten. Freud thanked him and added, without the slightest trace of emotion or self-pity, "Tell Anna about this."

"When he was again in agony," Schur has written, "I gave him a hypodermic of two centigrams of morphine. He soon felt relief and fell into a peaceful sleep. The expression of pain and suffering was gone. I repeated this dose after about twelve hours. Freud was obviously so close to the end of his reserves that he lapsed into a coma and did not wake up again. He died at 3.00 A.M. on September 23, 1939."

The eulogies that followed were to be expected, even in a world already being enveloped in the smoke of history's most disastrous war. In the United States the *American Journal of Sociology* devoted its entire November issue to papers assessing Freud's influence, and elsewhere the tributes and obituaries were lengthier than might have seemed likely even a few years previously.

Critical assessments have proliferated in number and complexity during the last forty years; but the argument has too frequently polarized between those who take as an article of faith the literal truth of everything that Freud wrote, and those who consider the greater part of the same material to be, at best, unproven speculation. Opposition between the two groups has often been conducted with the fanaticism, and sometimes the venom, of a religious war. Freud's followers must be held responsible for some of the dogmatism with which the arguments have been conducted, although he himself cannot be absolved from having encouraged, throughout much of his life, an attitude that leans more on blind faith than is usual among those claiming common cause with a scientific discipline.

His attitude was molded by many factors. In the early days of psychoanalysis, ambition demanded that no doubt, no hesitation, be visible to impede the progress of the cause. Like the religious leader, or the commander in chief, he knew that whatever qualifications might be discussed with the disciples or with the staff, the outer world must be presented with an image of men who were confident, inflexible, determined—and bound to succeed. Privately, pessimism might occasionally take over; publicly, questioning or dissent must be carefully controlled and, if necessary, ruthlessly extirpated. The justification for firm action was reinforced as Freud's personal ambition was subsumed into his conviction that the spread of psychoanalysis would reduce the total of human suffering.

These factors alone would have been sufficient to give his promotion of "the cause" a proselytizing fervor. They were reinforced by the condemnation of a medical establishment whose members often relied not on argument but on religious dogma or social convention, a method of attack which at times induced Freud himself to abandon argument for the appeal to faith.

Any honest assessment of how that faith appears today, forty years after his death, must necessarily be complex and qualified. It should also treat separately the foundations of the Freudian establishment and the huge and sometimes unsound structures which have been erected on it. The importance of the unconscious in motivating human conduct, which Freud was the first to utilize in trying to cure mental illness, is now part of accepted knowledge; so, too, is the existence of infantile sexuality, even though its role appears to be less ubiquitous than Freud believed. Had he done nothing more than make these two discoveries, which were to shed so much light on the workings of the mind, his fame would have been assured.

It is against such achievements that contemporary reservations about Freud's theories should be seriously balanced. Even a former president of the British Psycho-Analytical Society has admitted that "direct observation does not confirm the degree of importance given to the Oedipus Complex by the psychoanalyst." While psychosexual development through the oral and anal stages is generally accepted, Freud's belief that adult personality traits are dependent on the efficient control of these stages is often questioned. The death instinct and the trauma of birth have diminishing roll calls of supporters, and both the theory of dreams and the stratification of the mind into id, ego and super-ego are ringed with qualifications which in Freud's day would hardly have been raised by believing psychoanalysts.

Yet much of this psychoanalytical revisionism is the natural result of advances in biochemistry and in the knowledge of the linkages between mind and matter which have taken place during the last three quarters of a century. Freud would not have been surprised at these, or at comparable developments in medicine. He spoke more than once of the uses of endocrinology in influencing the mind. In 1930 he wrote to Marie Bonaparte that psychoanalysts "should study analytically every case of psychosis because the knowledge thus gained will one day direct the chemical therapy." And he had later noted: "Let the biologists go as far as they can and let us go as far as we can—one day the two will meet."

It is from this meeting that future methods of treating the mind appear most likely to emerge, although it seems inevitable that the result will be a further dilution of Freud's classical theory. Already the years-long treatment that was so often the inevitable but accepted handicap to the psychoanalysis of Freud's heyday has given way to analytic treatment on a totally different time scale; already the Freudian rule inhibiting social contact between patient and doctor has been worn paper-thin, while the "wild analysts" which he feared are thicker on the ground.

These changes, disturbing though they no doubt are to the more doctrinaire Freudian followers, may well be seen in the long perspective of history as little more than the changes which follow most successful revolutions. Throughout his life Freud, constrained by the need to fight a series of battles against implacable enemies, found it necessary to discourage any developments which might be schismatic; like all pioneers he had to gain limited objectives, one by one. Yet in his own line of country he was not unlike "The Explorer" of Rudyard Kipling, one of his favorite poets, the pioneer who "heard the mile-wide mutterings of unimagined rivers, / And beyond the nameless timber saw illimitable plains." It seems unlikely that he would be worried because the base he had secured after so much hard struggle was now a starting point for ventures into fresh territory.

Yet if it is now possible to see with some clearness, beneath the idolatry and the antagonisms, what Freud's achievements really were, it is at first rather more difficult to adjudicate between the contrasting accounts of what he was like as a human being. He himself, with his almost obsessional insistence on privacy and his weakness for destroying personal papers, is partly responsible. Martha Freud's determination to remain in the background gives to some aspects of his life a shadowy ambiguity, while his unusually close relationship with his sister-in-law, almost certainly sexually innocent, has handed a useful weapon to those of his opponents not too sensitive in dividing evidence from gossip. And the attempts of family and followers to limit criticism either of psychoanalysis or of its founder—signs of a rather unconsidered defense mechanism at work—tend to encourage a picture reminiscent of those erected by the devout in a holy shrine. The way has thus been left open for the portrait of loving father to be matched against that of autocratic paterfamilias; for the Puritan whose strict personal code alone allowed him to discuss the unspeakable details of sexuality to be matched with the man who must, it is averred, have been a dedicated, if unrevealed, libertine.

There is no reason to believe that Sigmund Freud was less complex than most men. But the known circumstances of his life, filled in by the multitudinous detail of a very considerable correspondence, suggest that those who see in his theories a covert personal sexuality, or who provide him with a lurid clandestine love life, are covering a sheep with wolf's clothing. Perhaps the best indication of what he was like has been given by his widow in a letter she never thought would be published. "How good, dear Dr.," she wrote to Ludwig Binswanger, "that you knew him when he was still in the prime of his life, for in the end he suffered terribly, so that even those who would most like to keep him forever had to wish for his release! And yet how terribly difficult it is to have to do without him. To continue to live without so much kindness and wisdom beside one! It is small comfort for me to know that in the fifty-three years of our married life not one angry word fell between us, and that I always sought as much as possible to remove from his path the misery of everyday life. Now my life has lost all content and meaning."

To those unable or unwilling to understand the world in which Freud lived, or who fail to realize that despite his qualities he was a human like the rest, the letter may come as a surprise. To some there will be, perversely, a hint of failure in the fact that the great Sigmund Freud and his devoted *Hausfrau* should, after the evaporation of the first careless rapture, have continued to live a happy life together.

Except to them, Martha's letter is not a bad epitaph.

Sources and Bibliography

Few pioneer writings have been published in more scholarly form than those of Sigmund Freud. The 24-volume *Standard Edition*, edited by James Strachey and replacing the earlier *Collected Edition*, is a model of its kind. All students of Freud must regard it as the starting point for their work, and all commentators on Freud must be deeply indebted to it. The volumes contain only his psychological and psychoanalytical writings; publications dealing with his earlier and other interests —notably his neurological papers, those on cocaine and his book *On Aphasia*— must be sought elsewhere. However, bibliographical details of these and similar nonpsychoanalytical writings are contained in the final Index volume compiled by Angela Richards, an incomparable guide to the growth of psychoanalysis which contains, among much other scholarly matter, an extensive bibliography of papers and books by writers other than Freud.

The documentary material for a life of Freud has been considerably increased since Ernest Jones wrote the official life a quarter of a century ago. Research in what is now Czechoslovakia has produced significant new information concerning the first years of Freud's life in Moravia, and the U.S. National Archives in Washington have now released details of America's part in his emigration from Vienna during his last years, following the German occupation of Austria in 1938.

A number of letters from Freud to Emil Flüss, a friend of his youth, have come to light, as have many scores of letters to Eduard Silberstein, an intimate friend with whom Freud corresponded regularly during his formative years at the University of Vienna. Much family material is now available in the Library of Congress—although much is embargoed until the year 2000—and an intriguing series of family letters between Freud and his nephew Samuel, born in Britain in 1865, has been discovered in Manchester, England. Many personal reminiscences of Freud, unrecorded during his lifetime, have been made public, while the extensive Freud-Jones correspondence, only parts of which were used by Jones in his biography of Freud or in his own later autobiography, throws fresh light on the early days of psychoanalysis in North America.

Max Schur, Freud's doctor for the last decade of his life, has included in a long and revealing paper many portions of the Freud-Fliess correspondence which were excised from the selection of Freud-Fliess letters published in *The Origins of Psycho-Analysis*, while his medical history of Freud has also drawn on hitherto unavailable material. The correspondence between Freud and Jung, Karl Abraham, Lou Andreas-Salomé, Oskar Pfister, Arnold Zweig, James Putnam, Ludwig Binswanger, Georg Groddeck and Eugen Bleuler has also been published, together with, in many cases, editorial material elucidating old riddles.

Many analyses have been made of the "Anna O." case—the starting point of psychoanalysis—notably those of Professor Henri F. Ellenberger, and they have put into perspective Freud's reaction to this seminal case. In addition, there has been an enormous exegesis on Freud's work, much of it discussing its relationship with his life. Its scope is illustrated by a bibliography in Norman Holland's *Psychoanalysis and Shakespeare* of more than a hundred items dealing solely with Freud's Oedipal theory of the conception of *Hamlet*.

In addition to the new manuscript material and the individual books and articles listed in the bibliography, the files of many specialist journals have been consulted. These include, among many others, those of the *American Imago, Brain: A Journal of Neurology*, the *Bulletin of the Menninger Clinic*, the *International Journal of Psycho-Analysis*, the *Journal of Abnormal Psychology*, the *Journal of the History of the Behavioral Sciences*, the *Journal of Nervous and Mental Disease*, the *Psychoanalytic Quarterly*, the *New York Medical Journal* and the *Psychoanalytic Review*.

Bibliography

Abraham, Hilda C., and Freud, Ernst L., eds., *A Psycho-Analytic Dialogue: The Letters of Sigmund Freud and Karl Abraham, 1907–1926*, trans. by Bernard Marsh and Hilda C. Abraham. London: Hogarth Press and the Institute of Psycho-Analysis, 1965.

Abraham, Karl, *Selected Papers on Psycho-Analysis*. London: Hogarth Press, 1949.

Adams, Grace, "The Rise and Fall of Psychology." *Atlantic Monthly*, Vol. CLIII, No. 1 (Jan. 1934), pp. 82–92.

Adler, Gerhard, ed., *C. G. Jung: Letters*. Selected and edited by Gerhard Adler in collaboration with Aniela Jaffé. Translations from the German by R. F. C. Hull. Vol. I: 1906–1950; Vol. II: 1951–1961. London: Routledge & Kegan Paul, 1973 and 1976.

Alexander, Franz, "Recollections of Berggasse 19." *Psychoanalytic Quarterly*, Vol. IX (1940), pp. 195–204.

Alexander, Franz; Eisenstein, Samuel; and Grotjahn, Martin, eds., *Psychoanalytic Pioneers*. New York and London: Basic Books, 1966.

Alexander, Franz, and Selesnick, Sheldon, "Freud–Bleuler Correspondence." *Archives of General Psychology*, Vol. XII (1965), pp. 1–9.

Amacher, Peter, "Freud's Neurological Education and Its Influence on Psychoanalytic Theory," published as *Psychological Issues*, Vol. IV, No. 4. Monograph 16. New York: International Universities Press, 1965.

American Psychiatric Association, *One Hundred Years of American Psychiatry*. New York: Columbia University Press, 1944.

Anderson, Sherwood, *Memoirs*. New York: Harcourt, Brace, 1942.

———, *Dark Laughter*. London: Jarrolds, n.d.

Andersson, Ola, *Studies in the Prehistory of Psychoanalysis*. Stockholm: Svenska Bokförlaget/Norstedts, 1962.

Andreas-Salomé, Lou, *The Freud Journal of Lou Andreas-Salomé*, trans. by Stanley A. Leavy. London: Hogarth Press and the Institute of Psycho-Analysis, 1965.

———, *Lebensrückblick. Grundriss einiger Lebenserinnerungen*. Frankfurt am Main: Insel Verlag, 1968. Aus dem Nachlass Herausgegeben von Ernst Pfeiffer.

———, *In der Schule bei Freud. Tagebuch eines Jahres 1912/1913*. Zurich: Max Niehans Verlag A.G., 1958. Aus dem Nachlass Herausgegeben von Ernst Pfeiffer.

Aron, Willy, "Notes on Sigmund Freud's Ancestry and Jewish Contacts." *YIVO Annual of Jewish Social Sciences*, Vol. XI (1956–1957), pp. 286–295.

Ashworth, John, "Olivier, Freud and Hamlet." *Atlantic Monthly*, Vol. CLXXXIII, No. 5 (May 1949), pp. 30–33.

Bakan, David, *Sigmund Freud and the Jewish Mystical Tradition.* New York: Van Nostrand, 1958.

Becker, Hortense Koller, "Carl Koller and Cocaine." *Psychoanalytic Quarterly,* Vol. XXXII (1963), pp. 309–373.

Bell, Sanford, "A Preliminary Study of the Emotion of Love between the Sexes." *American Journal of Psychology,* Vol. XIII, No. 3 (July 1902), pp. 325–354.

Beloff, John, *The Existence of Mind.* London: Macgibbon & Kee, 1962.

Beloff, Max, *Imperial Sunset,* Vol. I: *Britain's Liberal Empire, 1897–1921.* London: Methuen, 1969.

Bennet, E. A., *C.G. Jung.* London: Barrie and Rockliff, 1961.

Bernays, Anna Freud, "My Brother, Sigmund Freud." *American Mercury,* Vol. LI (Nov. 1940), pp. 335–342.

Bernfeld, Siegfried, "An Unknown Autobiographical Fragment by Freud." *American Imago,* Vol. IV, No. 1 (1946), pp. 3–19.

_____, "Freud's Scientific Beginnings." *American Imago,* Vol. VI, No. 3 (1949), pp. 163–196.

_____, "Sigmund Freud, M.D. 1882–1885." *International Journal of Psycho-Analysis,* Vol. XXXII (July 1951), pp. 204–217.

_____, "Freud's Studies on Cocaine, 1884–1887." *Journal of the American Psychoanalytic Association,* Vol. I, No. 4 (Oct. 1953), pp. 581–613.

_____, and Bernfeld, Suzanne Cassirer, "Freud's First Year in Practice, 1886–1887." *Bulletin of the Menninger Clinic,* Vol. XVI, No. 2 (March 1952), pp. 37–49.

Bernfeld, Suzanne C., "Freud and Archaeology." *American Imago,* Vol. VIII (1951), pp. 107–128.

Binion, Rudolph, *Frau Lou, Nietzsche's Wayward Disciple.* Princeton, N.J.: Princeton University Press, 1968.

Binswanger, Ludwig, *Sigmund Freud: Reminiscences of a Friendship.* New York and London: Grune & Stratton, 1957.

Blanton, Smiley, *Diary of My Analysis with Sigmund Freud.* New York: Hawthorn, 1971.

Bloch, Joseph S., *Erinnerungen aus meinem Leben.* Vienna and Leipzig: R. Löwit Verlag, 1922.

Boadella, David, *Wilhelm Reich: The Evolution of his Work.* London: Vision Press, 1973.

Bonaparte, Marie; Freud, Anna; and Kris, Ernst, eds., *The Origins of Psycho-Analysis: Letters to Wilhelm Fliess, Drafts and Notes: 1887–1902, by Sigmund Freud.* Authorized translation by Eric Mosbacher and James Strachey. Introduction by Ernst Kris. London: Imago, 1954.

Börne, Ludwig, "Die Kunst in drei Tagen ein Original-Schriftsteller zu werden (1823)," in *Gesammelte Schriften,* Vollständige Ausgabe. Erster Band. Vienna: Zendler (Julius Grosser), 1868.

Bottome, Phyllis, *Alfred Adler: Apostle of Freedom.* London: Faber & Faber, 1939.

Breton, André, *Les Pas Perdus.* Paris: Gallimard, 1924.

_____, *Les Vases Communicants.* Paris: Edition des Cahiers Libres, 1932.

Brill, A. A., *Psychanalysis: Its Theories and Practical Application,* Second Edition, thoroughly revised. Philadelphia and London: Saunders, 1914.

_____, *The Basic Writings of Sigmund Freud.* New York: The Modern Library, Random House, 1938.

_____, "Facts and Fancies in Psychanalytical Treatment." *New York Medical Journal,* Vol. CIX, No. 26 (June 28, 1919), pp. 1117–1120.

_____, "The Introduction and Development of Freud's Work in the United States." *American Journal of Sociology,* Vol. XLV (Nov. 1939), pp. 318–325.

Brill, A. A., "Reflections, Reminiscences of Sigmund Freud." *Medical Leaves* (Chicago), Vol. III (1940), pp. 18–29.

————, "A Psychoanalyst Scans His Past." *Journal of Nervous and Mental Disease*, Vol. XCV, Part 1 (May 1942), pp. 537–549.

Brome, Vincent, *Freud and His Early Circle: The Struggles of Psycho-Analysis.* London: Heinemann, 1967.

————, *Jung: Man and Myth.* London: Macmillan, 1978.

Brunswick, David, and Lachenbruch, Ruth, "Freud's Letters to Ernst Simmel," trans. by Frances Deri and David Brunswick. *Journal of the American Psychoanalytic Association*, Vol. XII, No. 1 (Jan. 1964), pp. 93–109.

Bry, Ilse, and Rifkin, Alfred H., "Freud and the History of Ideas: Primary Sources, 1886–1910," in Masserman, Jules H., ed. *Science and Psychoanalysis*, Vol. V, *Psychoanalytic Education*, pp. 6–36. New York, London: Grune & Stratton, 1962.

Bullen, St. John, "Remarks on the Interpretation of Dreams, according to Sigmund Freud and Others." *Journal of Mental Science*, Vol. LXI (1915), pp. 17–36.

Burnham, John Chynoweth, *Psychoanalysis and American Medicine: 1894–1918.* New York: International Universities Press, 1967.

Carus, Carl Gustav, *Psyche zur Entwicklungsgeschichte der Seele.* Pforzheim: Flammer und Hoffmann, 1846.

Chodorkoff, Bernard, and Baxter, Seymour, "*Secrets of a Soul:* An Early Psychoanalytic Film Venture." *American Imago*, Vol. XXXI, No. 4 (Winter 1974), pp. 319–334.

Choisy, Maryse, *Sigmund Freud: A New Appraisal.* London: Peter Owen, 1963; New York: Philosophical Library, 1963.

Cioffi, Frank, ed., *Freud: Modern Judgments.* London: Macmillan, 1973.

Clark, Kenneth, *Leonardo da Vinci. An Account of his Development as an Artist.* (The Ryerson Lectures delivered October and November 1936 at the School of the Fine Arts, Yale University, New Haven, Connecticut.) Cambridge at the University Press, 1939.

Clarke, J. Michell, "Hysteria and Neurasthenia." *Brain: A Journal of Neurology*, Vol. XVII (1894), pp. 119–78 and 263–321.

————, *Brain: A Journal of Neurology*, Vol. XIX (1896), pp. 401–414.

Clouston, T. S., quoted "The Progress and Promise of Psychiatry in America" in Notes and Comment (April 1898). *American Journal of Insanity*, Vol. LIV (1897–98), p. 638.

Cox, C. B., and Dyson, A. E., eds., *The Twentieth Century Mind: History, Ideas and Literature in Britain,* Vol. I, 1900–1918. London, Oxford, New York: Oxford University Press, 1972.

Cranefield, Paul F., "Josef Breuer's Evaluation of His Contribution to Psycho-Analysis." *International Journal of Psycho-Analysis*, Vol. XXXIX (1958), pp. 319–322.

Cromer, Ward, and Anderson, Paula, "Freud's Visit to America: Newspaper Coverage." *Journal of the History of the Behavioral Sciences*, Vol. VI (1970), pp. 349–353.

Dali, Salvador, *The Secret Life of Salvador Dali.* London: Vision, 1948.

Decker, Hannah S., "The Medical Reception of Psychoanalysis in Germany, 1894–1907: Three Brief Studies." *Bulletin of History of Medicine*, Vol. XLV (Baltimore, 1971), pp. 461–481.

De Forest, Izette, *The Leaven of Love.* New York: Harper, 1954.

Delisle, Françoise, *Friendship's Odyssey.* London: Heinemann, 1946.

Dempsey, Peter J. R., *Freud, Psychoanalysis, Catholicism.* Cork, Ireland: Mercier Press, 1956.

de Saussure, Raymond, "Sigmund Freud." *Schweizerische Zeitschrift für Psychologie und ihre Anwendungen,* 15 (1956), pp. 136–139, in Ruitenbeek, Hendrik M., ed., *Freud as We Knew Him.* Detroit: Wayne State University Press, 1973, pp. 357–359.

Deutsch, Helene, "Freud and His Pupils: A Footnote to the History of the Psychoanalytic Movement." *Psychoanalytic Quarterly,* Vol. IX, (1940), pp. 184–194.

Douglas, Norman. *Some Limericks. Collected for the use of Students, & ensplendour'd with Introduction, Geographical Index, and with Notes Explanatory and Critical.* Florence: G. Orioli (privately), 1928.

Dreiser, Theodore, Remarks (read by A. A. Brill at dinner on May 6, 1931), printed in *Psychoanalytic Review,* Vol. XVIII (1931), p. 250.

Drucker, Peter F., "What Freud Forgot." *Human Nature,* New York (March 1979), pp. 40–47.

Du Bois-Reymond, Estelle, ed., *Jugendbriefe von Emil Du Bois-Reymond an Eduard Hallmann* zu seinem Hundertsten Geburtstag dem 7 November 1918. Berlin: Dietrich Reimer (Ernst Vohsen), 1918.

Dujardin, Edouard, *Le Monologue Intérieur: son Apparition, ses Origines, sa Place dans l'Oeuvre de James Joyce.* Paris: Albert Messein, 1931.

Eastman, Max, *Heroes I Have Known: Twelve Who Lived Great Lives.* New York: Simon & Schuster, 1942.

Eder, M. D., *War-Shock: The Psycho-Neuroses in War Psychology and Treatment.* London: Heinemann, 1917.

Edes, Robert T., "The New England Invalid." *Boston Medical and Surgical Journal,* Vol. CXXXIII (1895), pp. 53–57, 77–81 and 101–107.

Efron, Arthur, "Freud's Self-Analysis and the Nature of Psychoanalytic Criticism." *International Review of Psycho-Analysis,* Vol. IV (1977), pp. 253–280.

Einstein, Albert, and Freud, Sigmund, *Why War?* An International Series of Open Letters, Vol. II. Trans. from the original German by Stuart Gilbert. Paris: International Institute of Intellectual Cooperation, 1933.

Eissler, K. R., *Leonardo da Vinci: Psychoanalytic Notes on the Enigma.* New York: International Universities Press, 1961.

———, *Medical Orthodoxy and the Future of Psychoanalysis.* New York: International Universities Press, 1965.

———, *Talent and Genius: The Fictitious Case of Tausk contra Freud.* New York: Quadrangle Books. 1971.

Eliot, George, *The Mill on the Floss.* Edinburgh and London: Blackwood, MDCCCLX.

Ellenberger, Henri F., "The Unconscious Before Freud." *Bulletin of the Menninger Clinic,* Vol. XXI (1957), pp. 3–15.

———, *The Discovery of the Unconscious: The History and Evolution of Dynamic Psychiatry.* New York: Basic Books, 1970.

———, "The Story of 'Anna O.': A Critical Review with New Data." *Journal of the History of the Behavioral Sciences,* Vol. VIII, No. 3 (July 1972), pp. 267–279.

———, "L'Histoire d' 'Emmy von N.' " *L'Evolution Psychiatrique* (Toulouse), Vol. XLII, No. 3 (1977) pp. 519–540.

Ellis, Havelock. *The World of Dreams.* London: Constable, 1911.

———, "Freud's Influence on the Changed Attitude Towards Sex." *American Journal of Sociology* (Nov. 1939), pp. 309–317.

Engelman, Edmund, *Berggasse 19: Sigmund Freud's Home and Offices, Vienna, 1938.* The Photographs of Edmund Engelman, With an Introduction by Peter Gay. New York: Basic Books, 1976.

Erikson, Erik H., "The First Psychoanalyst." *Yale Review,* N. S. 46 (Sept. 1956).

Escalona, Sybylle, "Problems in Psycho-Analytic Research." *International Journal of Psycho-Analysis*, Vol. XXXIII (1952), pp. 11–21.

Eve, A. S., *Rutherford, Being the Life and Letters of the Rt. Hon. Lord Rutherford, O.M.* Cambridge University Press, 1939.

Federn, Ernst, "How Freudian are the Freudians? Some Remarks to an Unpublished Letter." *Journal of the History of the Behavioral Sciences*, Vol. III, No. 3 (July 1967), pp. 269–281.

Ferenczi, Sandor, "Ten Letters to Freud." *International Journal of Psycho-Analysis*, Vol. XXX, Part 4 (1949), pp. 243–250.

Fine, Reuben, *The Development of Freud's Thought*. New York: Jason Aronson, 1973.

Fisher, Seymour, and Greenberg, Roger P., *The Scientific Credibility of Freud's Theories and Therapy*. Hassocks, Sussex: Harvester Press, 1977, and New York: Basic Books, 1977.

Fliess, Elenore, *Robert Fliess, 1895–1970*. Croydon: Roffey & Clark, 1974.

Fliess, Wilhelm, *In eigener Sache; gegen Otto Weininger und Hermann Swoboda*. Berlin: E. Goldschmidt 1906.

Fodor, Nandor, "Freud and the Poltergeist." *Psychoanalysis: Journal of Psychoanalytic Psychology*, Vol. IV, No. 2 (Winter 1955–56).

Forrest, D. W., *Francis Galton: The Life and Work of a Victorian Genius*. London: Paul Elek, 1974.

Fraenkel, Josef, "Professor Sigmund Freud and the Student Society 'Kadimah.' " *The Gates of Zion* (London, Apr. 1964).

Freud, Anna, in collaboration with Dorothy Burlingham, *Infants Without Families and Reports on the Hampstead Nurseries, 1939–1945*. London: Hogarth Press, 1974.

Freud, Ernst L., ed., *Letters of Sigmund Freud, 1873–1939*, trans. by Tania and James Stern. London: Hogarth Press, 1961, and New York: Basic Books, 1975.

———, *The Letters of Sigmund Freud and Arnold Zweig*, trans. by Professor and Mrs. W. D. Robson-Scott. London: Hogarth Press and the Institute of Psycho-Analysis, 1970.

———, "Some Early Unpublished Letters of Freud." *International Journal of Psycho-Analysis*, Vol. L (1969), pp. 419–427.

Freud, Ernst, and Freud, Lucie, *Sigmund Freud: Briefe 1873–1939*, Zweite, Erweiterte Auflage. Frankfurt am Main: S. Fischer Verlag, 1968.

Freud, Ernst; Freud, Lucie; and Grubrich-Simitis, Ilse, eds., *Sigmund Freud: His Life in Pictures and Words*, with a biographical sketch by K. R. Eissler; trans. by Christine Trollope. London: André Deutsch, 1978.

Freud, Harry, "My Uncle Sigmund," in Ruitenbeek, Hendrik M., ed., *Freud as We Knew Him*. Detroit: Wayne State University Press, 1973, pp. 312–313.

Freud, Martin, *Glory Reflected: Sigmund Freud—Man and Father*. London: Angus and Robertson, 1957.

Freud, Sigmund, *The Standard Edition of the Complete Psychological Works of Sigmund Freud*. Trans. from the German under the general editorship of James Strachey, in collaboration with Anna Freud, assisted by Alix Strachey and Alan Tyson, and Angela Richards.

Vol. I *Pre-Psycho-Analytic Publications and Unpublished Drafts* (1886–1899)

Vol. II *Studies on Hysteria* (1893–1895). By Josef Breuer and S. Freud

Vol. III *Early Psycho-Analytic Publications* (1893–1899)

Vol. IV *The Interpretation of Dreams* (I) (1900)

Vol. V *The Interpretation of Dreams* (II) and *On Dreams* (1900–1901)

Vol. VI *The Psychopathology of Everyday Life* (1901)

Vol. VII *A Case of Hysteria, Three Essays on Sexuality and Other Works* (1901–1905)

Vol. VIII *Jokes and their Relation to the Unconscious* (1905)

Vol. IX *Jensen's "Gradiva," and Other Works* (1906–1908)

Vol. X *The Cases of "Little Hans" and the "Rat Man"* (1909)

Vol. XI *Five Lectures on Psycho-Analysis, Leonardo and Other Works* (1910)

Vol. XII *Case History of Schreber, Papers on Technique, and Other Works* (1911–1913)

Vol. XIII *Totem and Taboo and Other Works* (1913–1914)

Vol. XIV *On the History of the Psycho-Analytic Movement, Papers on Metapsychology and Other Works* (1914–1916)

Vol. XV *Introductory Lectures on Psycho-Analysis* (Parts I and II) (1915–1916)

Vol. XVI *Introductory Lectures on Psycho-Analysis* (Part III) (1916–1917)

Vol. XVII *An Infantile Neurosis and Other Works* (1917–1919)

Vol. XVIII *Beyond the Pleasure Principle, Group Psychology and Other Works* (1920–1922)

Vol. XIX *The Ego and the Id and Other Works* (1923–1925)

Vol. XX *An Autobiographical Study, Inhibitions, Symptoms and Anxiety, Lay Analysis and Other Works* (1925–1926)

Vol. XXI *The Future of an Illusion, Civilization and its Discontents and Other Works* (1927–1931)

Vol. XXII *New Introductory Lectures on Psycho-Analysis and Other Works* (1932–1936)

Vol. XXIII *Moses and Monotheism, An Outline of Psycho-Analysis and Other Works* (1937–1939)

Vol. XXIV *Indexes and Bibliographies* (Compiled by Angela Richards, 1974)

(London: Hogarth Press and the Institute of Psycho-Analysis, 1953–1974.)

Freud, *Collected Papers.* Authorized translation under the supervision of Joan Riviere.

Vol. I *Early Papers and History of Psycho-Analytical Movement*

Vol. II *Clinical Papers; Papers on Technique*

Vol. III *Case Histories*

Vol. IV *Metapsychology: Papers on Instinct and the Unconscious; Papers on Applied Psycho-Analysis*

Vol. V *Miscellaneous Papers, 1888–1938* (edited by James Strachey)

(London: Hogarth Press and the Institute of Psycho-Analysis, 1924–1950.)

————, *The Origins of Psycho-Analysis. Letters to Wilhelm Fliess, Drafts and Notes: 1887–1902.* Edited by Marie Bonaparte, Anna Freud, Ernst Kris; authorized translation by Eric Mosbacher and James Strachey. Introduction by Ernst Kris. London: Imago, 1954.

————, "Über Coca." Neu durchgesehener und vermehrter Separat-Abdruck aus dem *Centralblatt für die gesamte Therapie*, II Vienna, July 1884, pp. 289–314, Vienna: Verlag von Moritz Perles, 1885.

————, "Über die Allgemeinwirkung des Cocains," *Medizinisch-chirurgisches Centralblatt*, XX, Nr. 32 (7 Aug. 1885), pp. 374–375.

————, *Wit and Its Relation to the Unconscious.* Authorized English edition; introduction by A. A. Brill. London: T. Fisher Unwin, 1916.

————, *Zur Geschichte der psychoanalytischen Bewegung*, Leipzig, Vienna, Zurich: Internationaler Psychoanalytischer Verlag, 1924.

————, [*Zur Auffassung der Aphasien*] *On Aphasia: A Critical Study.* Authorized translation by E. Stengel. London: Imago, 1953.

————, *The Cocaine Papers.* Vienna, Zurich: Dunquin Press, 1963.

————, and Bullitt, William C., *Thomas Woodrow Wilson, Twenty-eighth President of* the United States: A Psychological Study. London: Weidenfeld & Nicolson, 1967.

Freud, Sigmund, and Einstein, Albert, Why War? (See Einstein, Albert)

Freud, S[igmund], and Oppenheim, D. E., Dreams in Folklore. Trans. from the German and the Original German Text by A. M. O. Richards; edited with an Introduction by James Strachey. New York: International Universities Press, 1958.

Freud—Letters

Collections of correspondence are listed under their editors, i.e.:

Sigmund Freud, see Freud, Ernst L. (ed.)

with Karl Abraham, see Abraham, Hilda C., and Freud, Ernst L. (eds.)

with Lou Andreas-Salomé, see Pfeiffer, Ernst (ed.)

with Eugen Bleuler, see Alexander, Franz, and Selesnick, Sheldon

with Sandor Ferenczi, see Ferenczi, Sandor

with Wilhelm Fliess, see Bonaparte, Marie; Freud, Anna; Kris, Ernst (eds.)

with Georg Groddeck, see Groddeck, Georg

with C. G. Jung, see McGuire, William (ed.)

with Oskar Pfister, see Meng, Heinrich, and Freud, Ernst L. (eds.)

with J. J. Putnam, see Hale, Jr., Nathan G. (ed.)

with Ernst Simmel, see Brunswick, David, and Lachenbruch, Ruth

with Edoardo Weiss, see Weiss, Edoardo

with Arnold Zweig, see Freud, Ernst L. (ed.)

Fromm, Erich, Sigmund Freud's Mission: An Analysis of His Personality and Influence. New York: Harper, 1959.

———, The Dogma of Christ and Other Essays on Religion, Psychology and Culture. London: Routledge & Kegan Paul, 1963.

Galdston, Iago, "Freud and Romantic Medicine." Bulletin of the History of Medicine, Vol. XXX, No. 6 (Nov.–Dec. 1956), pp. 489–507.

Galton, Francis, "Psychometric Experiments." Brain: A Journal of Neurology, Vol. II (July 1879), pp. 149–162.

Gardiner, Muriel, ed., The Wolf-Man and Sigmund Freud. London: Hogarth Press and the Institute of Psycho-Analysis, 1972.

Garrison, Fielding H., An Introduction to the History of Medicine: With Medical Chronology, Suggestions for Study and Bibliographical Data. Philadelphia and London: Saunders, 1922.

Gartenberg, Egon, Mahler: The Man and His Music. London: Collins, and New York: Schirmer, 1978.

Gedo, John E., and Pollock, George H., eds., Freud: The Fusion of Science and Humanism: The Intellectual History of Psycho-Analysis. Psychological Issues, Vol. IX, Nos. 2/3, Monograph 34/35. New York: International Universities Press, 1976.

Gervais, Terence White, "Freud and the Culture-Psychologists." British Journal of Psychology, Vol. XLVI, Part 4 (Nov. 1955), pp. 293–305.

Gicklhorn, Renée, "The Freiberg Period of the Freud Family." Journal of the History of Medicine," Vol. XXIV (Jan. 1969), pp. 37–43.

———, Sigmund Freud und der Onkeltraum—Dichtung und Wahrheit. Horn, Austria: Ferdinand Berger, 1976.

Gifford, Jr., George E., "Freud and the Porcupine." Harvard Medical Alumni Bulletin, Vol. XLVI, No. 4 (Mar.–Apr. 1972), pp. 28–31.

Glover, Edward, Freud or Jung. London: Allen & Unwin, 1950.

Goldhammer, Leo, "Herzl and Freud." Herzl Year Book, Vol. I, New York, 1958, pp. 194–196.

Goldman, Emma, Living My Life. New York: Knopf, 1931.

Graf, Max, "Reminiscences of Professor Sigmund Freud." *Psychoanalytic Quarterly,*
Vol. XI (1942), pp. 465–476.

Grinker, Roy R., "Reminiscences of a Personal Contact with Freud." *American
Journal of Orthopsychiatry,* Vol. X (1940), pp. 850–854.

Groddeck, Georg, *The Meaning of Illness.* Selected Psychoanalytic Writings, including his correspondence with Sigmund Freud. Selected and with an Introduction by Lore Schacht, translated by Gertrud Mander. London: Hogarth Press
and the Institute of Psycho-Analysis, 1977.

Grossman, Carl M., and Grossman, Sylva, *The Wild Analyst: The Life and Work of
Georg Groddeck.* London: Barrie and Rockliff, 1965.

Grotjahn, Martin, "Sigmund Freud and the Art of Letter Writing." *Journal of the
American Medical Association,* Vol. CC, No. 1 (Apr. 3, 1967), pp. 13–18.

Grünwald, Max, *History of the Jews in Vienna.* Philadelphia: Jewish Publication
Society of America, 1936.

Guillain, Georges, *J.-M. Charcot: His Life—His Work.* London: Pitman, 1959.

Gutheil, Emil A., ed., *The Autobiography of Wilhelm Stekel: The Life Story of a Pioneer
Psychoanalyst.* Introduction by Mrs. Hilda Stekel. New York: Liveright, 1950.

Hale, Jr., Nathan G., *Freud and the Americans: The Beginnings of Psychoanalysis in the
United States, 1876–1917.* New York: Oxford University Press, 1971.

————, ed. with introductory essay, *James Jackson Putnam and Psycho-
analysis: Letters between Putnam and Sigmund Freud, Ernest Jones, William James, Sandor
Ferenczi and Morton Prince, 1877–1917,* translation of German texts by Judith
Bernays Heller. Cambridge, Mass.: Harvard University Press, 1971.

Hall, G. Stanley, *Life and Confessions of a Psychologist.* New York, London: Appleton,
1923.

Hart, Bernard, "The Psychology of Freud and his School" (read British Psychological Society, Oxford, May 7, 1910). *Journal of Mental Science,* Vol. LVI (July
1910), pp. 431–452.

Hawthorne, Nathaniel, *The Scarlet Letter: A Romance.* Boston: Ticknor, Reed and
Fields, MDCCCL.

Hearnshaw, L. S., *A Short History of British Psychology 1840–1940.* London: Methuen, 1964.

————, "Psychology," in Cox, C. B., and Dyson, A. E., eds., *The Twentieth-Century
Mind: History, Ideas and Literature in Britain,* Vol. I, 1900–1918. London, Oxford,
New York: Oxford University Press, 1972, pp. 225–247.

Heer, Friedrich, "Freud, the Viennese Jew," in Jonathan Miller, ed., *Freud the
Man, His World, His Influence.* London: Weidenfeld and Nicolson, 1972, pp.
1–20.

Heller, Judith Bernays, "Freud's Mother and Father: A Memoir." *Commentary,*
Vol. XXI, No. 5 (May 1956), pp. 418–421.

Henry, W. E.; Sims, J. H.; and Spray, S. L., *The Fifth Profession (Becoming a Psychotherapist).* San Francisco: Jossey-Bass, 1971.

Hobman, J. B., ed., *David Eder: Memoirs of a Modern Pioneer.* London: Gollancz,
1945.

Hoffman, Frederick J., *Freudianism and the Literary Mind.* Baton Rouge: Louisiana
State University Press, 1945.

Holland, Norman N., *Psychoanalysis and Shakespeare.* New York, Toronto, London:
McGraw-Hill, 1964, 1966.

Holmes, Oliver Wendell, *Mechanism in Thought and Morals: An Address with Notes and
Afterthoughts.* London: Sampson Low, Son, & Marston, 1871.

Holroyd, Michael, *Lytton Strachey,* Vol. II. London: Heinemann, and New York:
Holt, 1968.

Howe, Irving, *Sherwood Anderson*. London: Methuen, 1951.

Howe, Mark DeWolfe, ed., *Holmes-Laski Letters: The Correspondence of Mr. Justice Holmes and Harold J. Laski, 1916–1935*. London: Geoffrey Cumberlege, Oxford University Press, 1953.

Huxley, T. H., "Nature: Aphorisms by Goethe." *Nature*, Vol. I (Nov. 4, 1869), pp. 9–11.

Illing, Hans A., "Freud and Wagner-Jauregg." *American Imago*, Vol. XV, No. 3 (Fall 1958), pp. 267–273.

Jaffé, Aniela, ed., *C.G. Jung. Memories, Dreams, Reflections*. Translated from the German by Richard and Clara Winston. London: Collins and Routledge & Kegan Paul, 1963.

James, Henry, ed., *The Letters of William James*, 2 Vols. London: Longmans, Green, 1920.

James, William, *The Varieties of Religious Experience. A Study in Human Nature*, being the Gifford Lectures on Natural Religion delivered at Edinburgh in 1901–1902. London, New York and Bombay: Longmans, Green, 1902.

Janet, Pierre, *Principles of Psychotherapy*, trans. by H. M. and E. R. Guthrie. London: Allen & Unwin, 1925.

——, "Valeur de la psychanalyse et de Psychol de Freud" (read Société de Psychothérapie, June 1914). *Revue de Psychothérapie et de Psychologie Appliquées*, Vol. XXIX (1915), pp. 16–52.

——, "Contribution a l'étude des accidents mentaux chez les hystériques." Thèse méd. Paris, 1892–93, No. 432, pp. 252–257. Paris: Rueff, 1893.

Janik, Allan, and Toulmin, Stephen, *Wittgenstein's Vienna*. London: Weidenfeld & Nicolson, 1973.

Jelliffe, S. E., "Sigmund Freud as a Neurologist." *Journal of Nervous and Mental Disease*, Vol. LXXXV (June 1937), pp. 696–711.

Jones, Ernest, *Sigmund Freud: Life and Work*. Vol. I, *The Young Freud, 1856–1900;* Vol. II, *Years of Maturity, 1901–1919;* Vol. III, *The Last Phase, 1919–1939*. London: Hogarth Press, 1953, 1955, 1957, and New York: Basic Books, 1953, 1955, 1957.

——, *Sigmund Freud: Four Centenary Addresses* (The Nature of Genius; Our Attitude Towards Greatness; Psychiatry Before and After Freud; Sigmund Freud: The Man and His Achievements). New York: Basic Books, 1956.

——, *Free Associations: Memories of a Psycho-Analyst*. London: Hogarth Press, 1959.

——, "Psycho-Analysis and Anthropology." *Journal of the Royal Anthropological Institute*, Vol. LIV (1924), pp. 47–66.

——, "The Individual and Society." *Sociological Review*, Vol. XXVII, No. 3 (July 1935), pp. 245–263.

——, "Reminiscent Notes on the Early History of Psycho-Analysis in English-Speaking Countries." *International Journal of Psycho-Analysis*, Vol. XXVI (1945), pp. 8–10.

——, "Freud's Early Travels." *International Journal of Psycho-Analysis*, Vol. XXXV, Part 2 (1954), pp. 81–84.

Jung, C. G., *Collected Works of C. G. Jung*, eds. Sir Herbert Read, Michael Fordham and Gerhard Adler, trans. R. F. C. Hull. Vol. 4 *Freud and Psychoanalysis*, Vol. 7 *Two Essays on Analytical Psychology*. London: Routledge & Kegan Paul, 1961, 1953.

——, *Memories, Dreams, Reflections*. Recorded and edited by Aniela Jaffé. Translated from the German by Richard and Clara Winston. London: Collins and Routledge & Kegan Paul, 1963.

——, *C. G. Jung: Letters*. Selected and edited by Gerhard Adler in collaboration with Aniela Jaffé, translations from the German by R. F. C. Hull. Vol. I: 1906–1950, Vol. II: 1951–1961. London: Routledge & Kegan Paul, 1973, 1976.

Kanzler, Mark, ed., *The Unconscious Today: Essays in Honor of Max Schur.* New York: International Universities Press, 1971.

Kardiner, Abram, "Freud—The Man I Knew, The Scientist and His Influence," in Nelson, Benjamin, ed., *Freud and the 20th Century.* London: Allen & Unwin, 1958, pp 46–58.

———, *My Analysis with Freud: Reminiscences.* New York: Norton, 1977.

Kline, Paul, *Fact and Fantasy in Freudian Theory.* London: Methuen, 1972.

Kluckhohn, Clyde, "The Influence of Psychiatry on Anthropology in America during the past One Hundred Years," in the American Psychiatric Association, *One Hundred Years of American Psychiatry.* New York: Columbia University Press, 1944, pp. 589–617.

Koelsch, William A., "Freud Discovers America." *Virginia Quarterly Review,* Vol. XLVI, No. 1 (Winter 1970), pp. 115–132.

Koestler, Arthur, *The Invisible Writing,* Being the second volume of *Arrow in the Blue,* An Autobiography. London: Collins with Hamish Hamilton, 1954.

Koller, Carl, "Historical Notes on the Beginnings of Local Anesthesia." *Journal of the American Medical Association,* Vol. XC, No. 21 (1928), pp. 1742–1743.

———, "Über die Verwendung des Cocains zur Anaesthesierung am Auge." *Wien Med. Wochenschr.,* No. 43, pp. 1276–1278 and No. 44, pp. 1309–1311 (1884).

Kris, Ernst, *Psychoanalytic Explorations in Art.* London: Allen & Unwin, 1953.

———, "Freud in the History of Science." *The Listener* (May 17, 1956), pp. 631–633.

Kroeber, Alfred L., "*Totem and Taboo:* An Ethnologic Psychoanalysis." *American Anthropologist,* Vol. XXII (1920), pp. 48–55.

———, "*Totem and Taboo* in Retrospect." *American Journal of Sociology,* Vol. XLV, No. 3 (Nov. 1939), p. 446–451.

Krüll, Dr. Marianne, "Freuds Absage an die Verführungstheorie im Lichte seiner eigenen Familiendynamik." *Familiendynamik: Interdisziplinäre Zeitschrift für Praxis und Forschung.* Stuttgart: Klett-Cotta, 1978, pp. 102–129.

Laforgue, René, "Au delà du Scientisme, Ier Chapitre Freud et le Monothéisme." *Psyché,* Vol. IV (Paris, 1949), pp. 2–29.

———, "Personal Memories of Freud" (Geneva: Action Pensée, 1956), in Ruitenbeek, Hendrik M., ed., *Freud as We Knew Him.* Detroit: Wayne State University Press, 1973, pp. 341–349.

Langer, William L., "The Next Assignment." *American Imago,* Vol. XV (1958), pp. 235–266.

Leavy, Stanley A., *The Freud Journal of Lou Andreas-Salomé.* Translated and with an Introduction by Stanley A. Leavy. London: Hogarth Press and the Institute of Psycho-Analysis, 1965.

Linklater, Eric, *Poet's Pub.* London: Jonathan Cape, MCMXXIX.

Lippmann, Walter, "Freud and the Layman." *The New Republic* (Apr. 17, 1915).

Loewenstein, R. M.; Newman, L. M.; Schur, M.; and Solnit, A. J., eds., *Psychoanalysis—A General Psychology: Essays in Honor of Heinz Hartmann.* New York: International Universities Press, 1966.

Lothar, Ernst, *Das Wunder des Überlebens: Erinnerungen und Ergebnisse.* Hamburg, Vienna: Paul Zsolnay Verlag, MCMLX.

Macalpine, Ida, "Tribute to Freud." *Journal of the History of Medicine and Allied Sciences,* Vol. XI, No. 3 (July 1956), pp. 247–260.

———, and Hunter, Richard A., eds., of Schreber, Daniel Paul, *Memoirs of my*

Nervous Illness. Translated and edited by Ida Macalpine and Richard A. Hunter, with Notes and Discussion. London: Dawson, 1955.

Macaulay, Rose, *Dangerous Ages.* London: Collins, 1921.

McCarthy, Mary, *The Company She Keeps.* London: Nicolson & Watson, 1943.

MacCurdy, Edward, ed., *The Notebooks of Leonardo da Vinci.* Arranged, rendered into English and Introduced by Edward MacCurdy, Vols. I and II. London: Jonathan Cape, 1938.

McDougall, William, *Psycho-Analysis and Social Psychology.* London: Methuen, 1936.
_____, *An Outline of Abnormal Psychology.* London: Methuen, 1926. McGuire, William, ed., *The Freud/Jung Letters: The Correspondence between Sigmund Freud and C. G. Jung.* Translated by Ralph Manheim and R. F. C. Hull. London: Hogarth Press and Routledge & Kegan Paul, 1974, and Princeton, N.J.: Bollingen Series XCIV, Princeton University Press, 1974.

Marett, R. R., "Psycho-Analysis and the Savage." *Athenaeum,* No. 4685 (Feb. 13, 1920), pp. 205–206.

Masserman, Jules H., ed., "Science and Psychoanalysis." Vol. V, *Psychoanalytic Education.* New York, London: Grune & Stratton, 1962.

Matthews, F. H., "The Americanization of Sigmund Freud: Adaptations of Psychoanalysis Before 1917." *Journal of American Studies,* Vol. I, No. 1 (1967), pp. 39–62.

Matthiessen, F.O., *The James Family: Including Selections from the Writings of Henry James, Senior, William, Henry and Alice James.* New York: Knopf, 1948.

May, Henry F., *The End of American Innocence: A Study of the First Years of our Own Time, 1912–1917.* New York: Knopf, 1959.

Medawar, P. B., *The Hope of Progress.* London: Methuen, 1972.

Mencken, H. L., "Rattling the Subconscious." *The Smart Set* (Sept. 1918), reprinted as "The Advent of Psychoanalysis" in William H. Nolte, ed., *H. L. Mencken's "Smart Set" Criticism.* Ithaca, N.Y.: Cornell University Press, 1968, pp. 147–151.

Meng, Heinrich, and Freud, Ernst L., eds., *Psycho-Analysis and Faith: The Letters of Sigmund Freud and Oskar Pfister,* translated by Eric Mosbacher. London: Hogarth Press and the Institute of Psycho-Analysis, 1963.

Merlan, Philip, "Brentano and Freud." *Journal of the History of Ideas,* Vol. VI, No. 3 (June 1945), pp. 375–377.

Meyers, Jeffrey, "Freud, Hitler and Vienna." *London Magazine* (Aug.–Sept. 1974), pp. 67–79.

Miller, Jonathan, ed., *Freud: The Man, His World, His Influence.* London: Weidenfeld & Nicolson, 1972.

Moore, Merrill, "Note on a Limerick." *American Imago,* Vol. XIII (1956), pp. 147–148.

Munthe, Axel, *The Story of San Michele.* London: John Murray, 1929.

Myers, F. W. H., "The Subliminal Consciousness." *Proceedings of the Society for Psychical Research,* Vol. IX (1893–94), pp. 3–128. London: Kegan Paul, Trench, Trübner, 1894.

Natenberg, Maurice, *The Case History of Sigmund Freud: A Psycho-Biography.* Chicago: Regent House, 1955.

Needleman, Jacob, *Being-in-the-World: Selected Papers of Ludwig Binswanger.* Translated and with a Critical Introduction to His Existential Psychoanalysis. New York, London: Basic Books, 1963.

Nelson, Benjamin, ed., *Freud and the 20th Century.* London: Allen & Unwin, 1958.

Neumarkt, Paul, "The Freud-Tausk Controversy: A Symposium of Disharmonies." *International Review of Psycho-Analysis*, Vol. IV (1977), pp. 363–373.

Nicolson, Nigel, ed., *A Change of Perspective: The Letters of Virginia Woolf*, Vol. III, 1923–1928. London: Hogarth Press, 1977.

Nin, Anaïs, *The Journals of Anaïs Nin*, edited and with an Introduction by Gunther Stuhlman. London: Peter Owen, 1966, 1967.

Nolte, William H., ed., *H. L. Mencken's "Smart Set" Criticism*. Ithaca, N.Y.: Cornell University Press, 1968.

Nunberg, Herman, and Federn, Ernst, eds., *Minutes of the Vienna Psychoanalytic Society*, Vol. I, 1906–1908, Vol. II, 1908–1910, Vol. III, 1910–1911, Vol. IV, 1912–1918. New York: International Universities Press, 1962, 1967, 1974, 1975.

Oberndorf, C. P., *A History of Psychoanalysis in America*. New York: Grune & Stratton, 1953.

———, "Forty Years of Psycho-Analytic Psychiatry." *International Journal of Psycho-Analysis*, Vol. XXX (1949), pp. 153–161.

Orgler, Hertha, *Alfred Adler, The Man and His Work: Triumph over the Inferiority Complex*. London: C. W. Daniel, 1939.

Owen, Professor A. R. G., *Hysteria, Hypnosis and Healing: The Work of J.M. Charcot*. London: Dennis Dobson, 1971.

Peck, Martin W., "A Brief Visit with Freud." *Psychoanalytic Quarterly*, Vol. IX (1940), pp. 205–206.

Perry, Ralph Barton, *The Thought and Character of William James; As revealed in unpublished correspondence and notes, together with his published writings*. Vol. I, *Inheritance and Vocation;* Vol. II, *Philosophy and Psychology*. Boston: Little, Brown, 1935.

Peters, H. F., *My Sister, My Spouse: A Biography of Lou Andreas-Salomé*. London: Gollancz, 1963.

Pfeiffer, Ernst, ed., *Sigmund Freud and Lou Andreas-Salomé Letters*, trans. William and Elaine Robson-Scott. London: Hogarth Press and the Institute of Psycho-Analysis, 1972.

Pfennig, A. R., *Wilhelm Fliess und seine Nachentdecker: O. Weininger und H. Swoboda*. Berlin: E. Goldschmidt, 1906.

Pfister, Oskar, *Some Applications of Psycho-Analysis*. London: Allen & Unwin, 1923.

Popper, Karl R., *Conjectures and Refutations: The Growth of Scientific Knowledge*. London: Routledge & Kegan Paul, 1963.

Putnam, J. J., "Recent Experiences in the Study and Treatment of Hysteria at the Massachusetts General Hospital; with Remarks on Freud's Methods of Treatment by 'Psychoanalysis.' " *Journal of Abnormal Psychology*, Vol. I (Apr. 1906), pp. 26–41.

———, "Personal Impressions of Sigmund Freud and His Work, with Special Reference to his Recent Lectures at Clark University." *Journal of Abnormal Psychology*, Vol. IV (Dec. 1909–Jan. 1910), pp. 293–310, and (Feb.–Mar. 1910), pp. 372–379.

———, "The Work of Sigmund Freud," read 8th Annual Meeting of American Psychopathological Association, May 24, 1917. *Journal of Abnormal Psychology*, Vol. XII (Aug. 1917), pp. 145–160.

———, *Addresses on Psycho-Analysis*. London, Vienna, New York: International Psycho-Analytical Press, 1921.

Read, C. Stanford, *Military Psychiatry in Peace and War*. London: H. K. Lewis, 1920.

Reik, Theodor, *From Thirty Years with Freud*. London: Hogarth Press and the Institute of Psycho-Analysis, 1942.

———, *Listening with the Third Ear: The Inner Experience of a Psychoanalyst*. New York: Farrar, Straus, 1948; Pyramid, 1964.

Reik, Theodor, *Fragment of a Great Confession: A Psychoanalytic Autobiography.* New York: Citadel Press, 1965.

Richards, I. A., *Principles of Literary Criticism.* London: Kegan Paul, Trench, Trübner; and New York: Harcourt, Brace, 1925.

Rieff, Philip, *Freud: The Mind of the Moralist.* London: Gollancz, MCMLX.

———, "Origins of Freud's Political Psychology." *Journal of the History of Ideas,* Vol. XVII (1956), pp. 235–249.

Rivers, W. H. R., *Conflict and Dream.* London: Kegan Paul, Trench, Trübner, and New York: Harcourt Brace, 1923.

———, "Freud's Psychology of the Unconscious," read Edinburgh Pathological Club. *The Lancet* (June 16, 1917), pp. 912–914.

Riviere, Joan, "An Intimate Impression." *The Lancet* (Sept. 30, 1939), pp. 765–767.

Roazen, Paul, *Brother Animal: The Story of Freud and Tausk.* New York: Knopf, 1969.

———, *Freud and His Followers.* New York: Knopf, 1975.

———, "Reading, Writing and Memory: Dr. K. R. Eissler's Thinking." *Contemporary Psychoanalysis,* Vol. XIV, No. 2 (1978), pp 345–353.

Roback, A. A., *Freudiana.* Cambridge, Mass.: Sci-Art Publishers, 1957.

Rosner, Henry, "Psychoanalytic Papers of Max Schur," in Kanzler, Mark, ed., *The Unconscious Today: Essays in Honor of Max Schur.* New York: International Universities Press, 1971.

Ruitenbeek, Hendrik M., ed., *Freud as We Knew Him.* Detroit: Wayne State University Press, 1973.

Russell, Bertrand, *Human Knowledge: Its Scope and Limits.* London: Allen & Unwin, 1948.

Rycroft, Charles, ed., *Psychoanalysis Observed.* London: Constable, 1966.

———, *A Critical Dictionary of Psychoanalysis.* London: Penguin, 1972.

———, *The Innocence of Dreams.* London: Hogarth Press, 1979.

Sachs, Hanns, *Freud: Master and Friend.* London: Imago, 1945, and Cambridge: Harvard University Press, 1944.

Sajner, Josef, "Sigmund Freuds Beziehungen zu seinem Geburtsort Freiberg (Příbor) und zu Mähren." *Clio Medica,* Vol. III (1968), pp. 167–180 (Pergamon Press).

Schapiro, Meyer, "Leonardo and Freud: An Art-Historical Study." *Journal of the History of Ideas,* Vol. XVII (Apr. 1956), pp. 147–178.

Schmidl, Fritz, "Sigmund Freud and Ludwig Binswanger." *Psychoanalytic Quarterly,* Vol. XXVIII (1959), pp. 40–58.

Schneck, Jerome M., "A Note on Freud's Neighbor." *American Journal of Psychotherapy,* Vol. XIII (1959), pp. 139–141.

Schorske, C. E., "Politics and Patricide in Freud's Interpretation of Dreams." *American Historical Review,* Vol. LXXVIII, Part 1 (1973), pp. 328–347.

Schur, Max, *Drives, Affects, Behavior,* Vol. II, *Essays in Memory of Marie Bonaparte.* New York: International Universities Press, 1965.

———, "Some Additional 'Day Residues' of 'The Specimen Dream of Psychoanalysis,' " in Loewenstein, R. M.; Newman, L. M.; Schur, M.; and Solnit, A. J., eds., *Psychoanalysis—A General Psychology, Essays in Honor of Heinz Hartmann.* New York: International Universities Press, 1966.

———, *Freud: Living and Dying.* London: Hogarth Press and the Institute of Psycho-Analysis, 1972.

Schusdek, Alexander, "Freud on Cocaine." *Psychoanalytic Quarterly,* Vol. XXXIV (1965), pp. 406–412.

———, "Freud's 'Seduction Theory': A Reconstruction." *Journal of the History of the Behavioral Sciences*, Vol. II, No. 2 (Apr. 1966), pp. 159–166.

Shaw, Bernard, *Man and Superman. A Comedy and a Philosophy*. Westminster: Archibald Constable, 1903.

Shlien, J. M., ed., *Research in Psychotherapy*. Washington, D.C.: American Psychological Association, 1968.

Sidis, Boris, *Symptomatology, Psychognosis and Diagnosis of Psychopathic Diseases*. Boston: R. G. Badger, 1914, and Edinburgh: E. & S. Livingstone, 1921.

Simmel, Ernst, "Sigmund Freud: The Man and His Work." *Psychoanalytic Quarterly*, Vol. IX (1940), pp. 163–176.

Simon, Ernst, "Sigmund Freud, the Jew." Leo Baeck Institute *Yearbook*, II, London (1957), pp. 270–305.

Sours, John A., "Freud and the Philosophers." *Bulletin of the History of Medicine*, Vol. XXXV (1961), pp. 326–345.

Spector, Jack J., *The Aesthetics of Freud: A Study in Psychoanalysis and Art*. London: Allen Lane, 1972.

Stafford-Clark, David, *What Freud Really Said*. London: Macdonald, 1965.

Stanescu, H., "Young Freud's Letters to his Rumanian Friend, Silberstein." *The Israel Annals of Psychiatry and Related Disciplines*, Vol. IX, No. 3 (Dec. 1971), pp. 195–207.

Stewart, Walter S., *Psychoanalysis: The First Ten Years, 1888–1898*. London: Allen & Unwin, 1969.

Storr, Anthony, "The Concept of Cure," in Rycroft, Charles, ed., *Psychoanalysis Observed*. London: Constable, 1966.

Stuhlmann, Gunther, ed., *The Journals of Anaïs Nin: 1931–1934*, Vols. I & II. Edited and with an Introduction by Gunther Stuhlmann. London: Peter Owen, 1966, 1967.

Sullivan, Mark, *Our Times: The United States, 1900–1925*, Vol. IV, *The War Begins 1909–1914*. New York, London: Scribner's, 1932.

Szasz, Thomas S., *Karl Kraus and the Soul-Doctors: A Pioneer Critic and His Criticism of Psychiatry and Psychoanalysis*. London & Henley: Routledge & Kegan Paul, 1977.

———, "Freud as a Leader." *Antioch Review*, Vol. XXIII, No. 2 (Summer 1963), pp. 133–144.

Tabori, Cornelius, *My Occult Diary*. Translated and edited by Paul Tabori. London: Rider & Co., 1951.

Taft, Jessie, *Otto Rank: A Biographical Study Based on Notebooks, Letters, Collected Writings, Therapeutic Achievements and Personal Associations*. New York: Julian Press, 1958.

Taylor, A. J. P., *Europe: Grandeur and Decline*. Harmondsworth, Middlesex: Penguin, in association with Hamish Hamilton, 1967.

Thompson, Clara, *Psychoanalysis: Evolution and Development*. London: Allen & Unwin, 1952.

Timpanaro, Sebastiano, *The Freudian Slip: Psycho-Analysis and Textual Criticism*, translated by Kate Soper. London: N.L.B., 1976.

Tobler, George Christoph, "The Fragment," afterward known as *"Die Natur,"* first published anonymously in the *Tiefurter Journal* in 1782 (edited by The Duchess Anna Amalia and privately circulated for 2–3 years in Weimar Literary Circle), and sometimes attributed to Goethe.

Trotter, Wilfred, *The Instincts of the Herd in Peace and War, 1916–1919*. London: Oxford University Press, 1953.

Tuchman, Barbara W., "Can History Use Freud? The Case of Woodrow Wilson." *Atlantic*, Vol. CCXIX (Feb. 1967), pp. 39–44.

Van Teslaar, James S., "The Significance of Psycho-analysis in the History of Science." *International Journal of Psycho-Analysis*, Vol. II (Part 3/4) (Sept.–Dec. 1921), pp. 339–353.

Von Weizsäcker, Viktor, "Reminiscences of Freud and Jung," in Nelson, Benjamin, ed., *Freud and the 20th Century*. London: Allen & Unwin, 1958, pp. 59–74.

Walter, Bruno, *Theme and Variations: An Autobiography*, translated from the German by James A. Galston. London: Hamish Hamilton, 1947.

Weiss, Edoardo, *Sigmund Freud as a Consultant: Recollections of a Pioneer in Psychoanalysis*. New York: Intercontinental Medical Book Corp., 1970.

Wells, H. G., *Experiment in Autobiography*, Vol. I. London: Gollancz, Cresset Press, 1934.

Whitehorn, John C., "A Century of Psychiatric Research in America," in the American Psychiatric Association, *One Hundred Years of American Psychiatry*. New York: Columbia University Press, 1944, pp. 167–193.

Whyte, Lancelot Law, *The Unconscious Before Freud*. London: Tavistock, 1962.

Wilson, Edmund, *To the Finland Station: A Study in the Writing and Acting of History*. London: Secker & Warburg, 1941.

Winnicott, D. W., *The Child, the Family, and the Outside World*. Harmondsworth, Middlesex, England: Penguin, 1964.

Wittels, Fritz, *Sigmund Freud: His Personality, His Teaching, & His School*, translated from the German by Eden and Cedar Paul. London: Allen & Unwin, 1924.

———, "Revision of a Biography." *Psychoanalytic Review*, Vol. XX, No. 4 (Oct. 1933), pp. 361–374.

Wolf-Man, The, "My Recollections of Sigmund Freud," and "The Memoirs of the Wolf-Man," in Gardiner, Muriel, ed., *The Wolf-Man and Sigmund Freud*. London: Hogarth Press and the Institute of Psycho-Analysis, 1972.

Wolpe, Joseph, and Rachman, Stanley, "Psychoanalytic 'Evidence': A Critique Based on Freud's Case of Little Hans." *Journal of Nervous and Mental Disease*, Vol. CXXXI, No. 2 (Aug. 1960), pp. 135–148.

Wortis, Joseph, "Fragments of a Freudian Analysis." *American Journal of Orthopsychiatry*, Vol. X (1940), pp. 843–849.

Zweig, Stefan, *The World of Yesterday*. London: Cassell, 1953.

Notes and References

Full details of the sources quoted, manuscript and printed, are given with bibliographical information in "Sources and Bibliography," pages 531–47. The page numbers of the American editions of Ernest Jones's *Sigmund Freud: Life and Work* and of *The Letters of Sigmund Freud* are italicized.

1 *Jewish Boyhood*

page 4   "one of the saddest and strangest of all landmarks": P. B. Medawar, *The Hope of Progress*, p. 68.

4   "family's cramped living quarters . . .": Max Schur, *Freud: Living and Dying*, p. 119 (afterward referred to as "Schur").

5   The woman listed: Register of Jews living in Freiberg in 1852, dated Jan. 23, 1853, Director, Okresní Archiv v. Novém Jičíně.

5   The initial discovery: Details of the Freud family's years in Freiberg are contained in:

(1) Josef Sajner, "Sigmund Freuds Beziehungen zu seinem Geburtsort Freiberg (Příbor) und zu Mähren," *Clio Medica*, Vol. III, (1968), pp. 167–180.

(2) Renée Gicklhorn, "The Freiberg Period of the Freud Family," *Journal of the History of Medicine*, Vol. XXIV (Jan. 1969), pp. 37–43 (afterward referred to as "Gicklhorn").

(3) Dr. Marianne Krüll, "Freuds Absage an die Verführungstheorie im Lichte seiner eigenen Familiendynamik," *Familiendynamik: Interdisziplinäre Zeitschrift für Praxis und Forschung*, pp. 102–129.

6   "As is known I deal in cloth": Abraham Sisskind Hoffman—Magistrate, July 24, 1844, Státní Archiv v. Opavě.

7   an official search: Státní Archiv v. Opavě—author, June 27, 1978.

7   "Maybe Rebecca was repudiated": Gicklhorn, p. 41.

8   "that because Freud had a certain neurotic symptom": Kurt Eissler, quoted Leslie Adams—Ernest Jones, Oct. 11, 1953, the Institute of Psycho-Analysis, London (afterward referred to as "Institute").

8   "My son Shlomo Sigismund": quoted Willy Aron, "Notes on Sigmund Freud's Ancestry and Jewish Contacts," *YIVO Annual of Jewish Social Sciences*, Vol. XI (1956–57), p. 288 (afterward referred to as "Aron").

9   "Prophecies of this kind": Sigmund Freud, *The Interpretation of Dreams* (1900), James Strachey, ed., *The Standard Edition of the Complete Psychological Works of Sigmund Freud* (afterward referred to as "*S. E.*"), Vols.

page

IV (pp. 1–338) and V (pp. 339–627) (afterward referred to as "*Dreams*"), here p. 192. (The year of writing is given in brackets. The year of publication is given in parentheses.)

9   "Could this have been": *Dreams*, p. 192.

9   "taking the edge off some of my indiscretions": Preface to the First Edition, *Dreams*, p. xxiv.

10   "The actuarial data . . .": Schur, p. 22.

10   "But what should have made": Freud, "Screen Memories" (1899), *S. E.* Vol. III, p. 310 (afterward referred to as "Screen Memories").

10   ". . . welcomed [his] one-year-younger brother": Freud–Wilhelm Fliess, Oct. 3, 1897, Freud, *The Origins of Psycho-Analysis. Letters to Wilhelm Fliess, Drafts and Notes: 1887–1902*, p. 219 (afterward referred to as "*Origins*").

10   "I see a rectangular": "Screen Memories," p. 311.

11   "I never felt really comfortable": "Screen Memories," p. 312.

11   "You see, there is a survival of my old agoraphobia": quoted Theodor Reik, *Listening with the Third Ear: The Inner Experience of a Psychoanalyst*, p. 25 (afterward referred to as "Reik, *Third Ear*").

11   "The common symptom of agoraphobia . . .": Anthony Storr, "The Concept of Cure," in Charles Rycroft, ed., *Psychoanalysis Observed*, p. 56.

12   "My parents were Jews": Freud, *An Autobiographical Study* (1925 [1924]), *S. E.* Vol. XX, p. 7 (afterward referred to as "*Auto. Study*").

12   "A Christian came up to me": quoted *Dreams*, p. 197.

13   Freud wrote: Freud–Eduard Silberstein, Sept. 9, 1875. Freud's scores of letters to Silberstein are now held in the Library of Congress, Washington. Microfilm of the letters is held by the copyright holders, Sigmund Freud Copyrights Ltd., Colchester, England (afterward referred to as "Colchester"), as here. Typed transcripts of many of the letters exist elsewhere outside the United States. Many letters have been quoted by H. Stanescu in "Young Freud's Letters to his Rumanian Friend, Silberstein," *The Israel Annals of Psychiatry and Related Disciplines*, Vol. IX, No. 3 (Dec. 1971), pp. 195–207 (afterward referred to as "Stanescu").

14   ". . . deeply buried within me": Freud–Burgomaster of Příbor, Oct. 25, 1931, *S. E.* Vol. XXI, p. 259.

14   "the living ones no more than": Freud–Samuel Freud, May 6, 1928, The John Rylands University Library of Manchester, Manchester, England (afterward referred to as "Rylands").

15   "long and difficult years followed": "Screen Memories," p. 312.

15   "When he isn't exactly grouchy": Freud–Martha Bernays, Aug. 14, 1882, Ernst L. Freud, ed., *Letters of Sigmund Freud, 1873–1939*, p. 40 (afterward referred to as "*Letters*"), 22.

16   the handling of forged banknotes: Renée Gicklhorn, *Sigmund Freud und der Onkeltraum—Dichtung und Wahrheit*.

17   "Not easy to justify": *Dreams*, p. 172.

17   "first understandings of a civilization": Freud, "Zur Psychologie des Gymnasiasten" (1914), *Gesammelte Schriften*, Vol. XI, p. 288.

17   "called up our fiercest opposition": Freud, "Some Reflections on Schoolboy Psychology" (1914), *S. E.* Vol. XIII, p. 242 (afterward referred to as "Schoolboy Psychology").

page 18　"At the North Station in Vienna": Anna Freud Bernays, "My Brother, Sigmund Freud," *American Mercury,* Vol. LI (Nov. 1940), p. 338 (afterward referred to as "My Brother").

18　"While he did this": "My Brother," p. 338.

19　"that if a man has been": Freud, "A Childhood Recollection from *Dichtung und Wahrheit"* (1917), *S. E.* Vol. XVII, p. 156.

19　"He appealed to my mother to remove the piano": "My Brother," p. 337.

19　"If I had a book": "My Brother," p. 337.

19　"All through the years of his school": "My Brother," p. 336.

19　"I seem to remember that through the whole of this time": "Schoolboy Psychology," p. 242.

19　"will let his wife starve": Bernard Shaw, *Man and Superman. A Comedy and a Philosophy,* p. 22.

2 Ambitious Youth

21　"extremely strong motives for concealing": Ernest Jones, *Sigmund Freud: Life and Work,* Vol. I, *The Young Freud 1856–1900;* Vol. II, *Years of Maturity 1901–1919;* Vol. III, *The Last Phase 1919–1939* (afterward referred to as "Jones, I," "II" and "III"), here II, p. 456, *409.*

21　"We were friends": Freud–Martha Bernays, Feb. 7, 1884, Ernst and Lucie Freud, eds. *Sigmund Freud: Briefe 1873–1939,* second enlarged edition, Frankfurt am Main (1968), pp. 103–104.

22　"I really believe we shall never part": Freud–Silberstein, Sept. 5, 1875, quoted Stanescu, p. 205.

22　"I suggest that we decide": Freud–Silberstein, Sept. 7, 1877, Colchester.

22　"the man feeling his way": Stanescu, p. 196.

22　"feel sentimental": Freud–Martha Bernays, Oct. 28, 1883, quoted Ernst L. Freud, "Some Early Unpublished Letters of Freud." *International Journal of Psycho-Analysis,* Vol. L (1969), p. 419 (afterward referred to as "Early Unpublished Letters").

23　"another passion": Freud–Silberstein, Sept. 4, 1872, Colchester.

23　"translated esteem for the mother": Freud–Silberstein, Sept. 4, 1872, Colchester.

23　"I would venture to surmise": Jones, II, p. 456, *409.*

23　"It was my first calf-love": "Screen Memories," p. 313.

23　"Did I ever tell you that Gisela": Freud–Martha Bernays, Oct. 28, 1883, "Early Unpublished Letters," p. 419.

23　"the quite extraordinary precautions": Jones, II, p. 455, *409.*

23　"But if you want me to entertain you": Freud–Emil Flüss, Sept. 28, 1872, "Early Unpublished Letters," p. 421.

24　"which I keep only for you": Freud–Silberstein, Aug. 17, 1872, Colchester.

24　"Gisela's beauty is wild": Freud–Silberstein, Sept. 4, 1872, Colchester.

24　"I was very sad": Freud–Silberstein, Sept. 4, 1872, Colchester.

25　"I was raving the whole day": Freud–Silberstein, Sept. 4, 1872, Colchester.

25　"deviated from the subject dear to me": Freud–Silberstein, Sept. 4, 1872, Colchester.

26　"She obviously recognizes": Freud–Silberstein, Sept. 4, 1872, Colchester.

page 26   "My regards to your esteemed mother . . .": Freud–Emil Flüss, Sept. 28, 1872, "Early Unpublished Letters," p. 421.

26   "Evidently not without the Flüsses": Freud–Silberstein, Jan. 24, 1875, quoted Stanescu, p. 203.

27   "nothing but a derision, a scoffing": Stanescu, p. 203.

27   "considers as 'Antediluvian' ": Stanescu, p. 203.

27   "the theory of repression is the cornerstone": Freud, *On the History of the Psycho-Analytic Movement* (1914), *S.E.* Vol. XIV, p. 16 (afterward referred to as *"History"*).

28   "On Nature": George Christoph Tobler's Essay, "The Fragment," afterward known as "Die Natur," first published anonymously in the *Tiefurter Journal* in 1782 (edited by The Duchess Anna Amalia and privately circulated for 2–3 years in Weimar Literary Circle), and sometimes attributed to Goethe.

28   "it is written by a well-known hand": J. W. von Goethe–Chancellor F. T. A. H. von Müller, May 26, 1828, quoted T. H. Huxley, "Nature: Aphorisms by Goethe," *Nature*, Vol. I (Nov. 4, 1869), p. 9 (afterward referred to as "Huxley").

28   "Nature! We are surrounded and embraced by her": T. H. Huxley's translation of "Die Natur," Huxley, p. 9.

28   "As for me, I can report": Freud–Emil Flüss, Mar. 17, 1873, "Early Unpublished Letters," p. 423.

28   "I have decided to be a Natural Scientist": Freud–Emil Flüss, May 1, 1873, "Early Unpublished Letters," p. 424.

29   "Neither at that time, nor indeed in my later life": *Auto. Study*, p. 8.

30   "[It] does not suit me a bit": Freud–Emil Flüss, May 1, 1873, "Early Unpublished Letters," p. 424.

30   "Interesting, but it didn't bowl me over": Freud–Emil Flüss, June 16, 1873, *Letters*, p. 22.

30   "In Latin we were given a passage from Virgil": Freud–Emil Flüss, June 16, 1873, "Early Unpublished Letters," p. 425.

31   "As to the first year at the university": Freud–Silberstein, July 11, 1873, Colchester.

31   "I have no knowledge of having had any craving": Freud, Postscript (1927) to *The Question of Lay Analysis: Conversations with an Impartial Person* (1926), *S. E.* Vol. XX, p. 253 (afterward referred to as *"Lay Analysis"*).

32   "perhaps as a true Italian,": Freud–Silberstein, Apr. 15, 1876, quoted Stanescu, p. 204.

32   "I was made familiar with the fate": *Auto. Study*, p. 9.

32   "Should you, in 20 or 30 years from now": Freud–Emil Flüss, May 1, 1873, "Early Unpublished Letters," p. 423.

33   "The exalted chick": Freud–Silberstein, Aug. 22, 1874, Colchester.

33   "I am indeed a Republican": Freud–Silberstein, Mar. 7, 1875, Colchester.

33   "Those crazy rulers": Freud–Silberstein, Aug. 15, 1877, Colchester.

34   "It was a little essay, a Biblical study": Freud–Silberstein, July 24, 1873, Colchester.

34   "I should be very sorry": Freud–Silberstein, Nov. 8, 1874, Colchester.

34   "We sent him a letter": Freud–Silberstein, Mar. 7, 1875, Colchester.

35   "to that group of human beings": Freud–Silberstein, Aug. 13, 1874, Colchester.

35   "I do not say": Freud–Silberstein, Aug. 22, 1874, Colchester.

page 36 "I have decided": Freud–Silberstein, Jan. 24, 1875, quoted Stanescu, p. 198.

36 "Should I be [in Berlin]": Freud–Silberstein, Jan. 24, 1875, quoted Stanescu, p. 198.

36 "It was in England that Sigmund resolved": "My Brother," p. 340.

37 "The day before yesterday": Freud–Silberstein, Sept. 9, 1875, Colchester.

38 "You have given us great pleasure": Emanuel Freud–Freud family, n.d., quoted "My Brother," p. 340.

39 "with [his] own eyes the detestable tower of St. Stephen's": Freud–Martha Bernays, Mar. 10, 1886, *Letters*, p. 224, *212*.

39 "I hate Vienna with a positively personal hatred": Freud–Fliess, Mar. 11, 1900, *Origins*, p. 311.

39 "is Vienna": Freud–Fliess, Apr. 16, 1900, *Origins*, p. 317.

39 "in the Vienna you like so little": Lou Andreas–Freud, Oct. 29, 1913, Ernst Pfeiffer, ed., *Sigmund Freud and Lou Andreas-Salomé: Letters*, p. 14 (afterward referred to as "Lou Letters"). [Louise (Lolja) von Salomé married Friedrich Carl Andreas in 1887. She is addressed by Freud first as "Frau Andreas" and later as "Lou"]."

39 "And my own feeling": Martin Freud, *Glory Reflected: Sigmund Freud—Man and Father*, p. 48 (afterward referred to as "*Glory Reflected*").

39 "Like you I have an indomitable affection for Vienna": quoted Ernst Lothar, *Das Wunder des Überlebens: Erinnerungen und Ergebnisse*, p. 40 (afterward referred to as "Lothar").

39 "Austro-Hungary is no more": quoted Lothar, p. 41.

40 "You are right": quoted Lothar, p. 41.

40 "The feeling of triumph on being liberated": Freud–Max Eitingon, June 6, 1938, *Letters*, p. 441, *446*.

40 "No one ever [had] found a mature male eel": Freud, S.: "Beobachtungen über Gestaltung und feineren Bau der als Hoden beschriebenen Lappenorgane des Aals." Von Sigmund Freud, stud. med. (Mit 1 Tafel) Arbeiten aus dem zoologisch-vergleichend-anatomischen Institut der Universität Wien. "Sitzungsber. der Kais. Akademie der Wissenschaften Wien." Abt. 1, Bd. 75. April-Heft 1877, pp. 419–431 (Tafel: "Gez. v. Verf."), quoted Siegfried Bernfeld, "Freud's Scientific Beginnings," *American Imago*, Vol. VI, No. 3 (1949), p. 165 (afterward referred to as "Bernfeld, 'Scientific Beginnings' ").

40 "Physiologically I only know that they like walking": Freud–Silberstein, Apr. 15, 1876, quoted Stanescu, p. 203.

40 "it is unfortunately forbidden to dissect humans": Freud–Silberstein, Apr. 15, 1876, quoted Stanescu, p. 203.

41 "always self-assured—at places even cocky": Bernfeld, "Scientific Beginnings," p. 166.

41 "Brücke and I pledged a solemn oath": Émil Du Bois-Reymond–Eduard Hallmann, May 1842, Estelle Du Bois-Reymond, ed., *Jugendbriefe von Emil Du Bois-Reymond an Eduard Hallmann* zu seinem Hundertsten Geburtstag dem 7 November 1918, p. 108.

42 "One morning he turned up punctually": *Dreams*, p. 422.

42 "From Freud's self-analysis": Bernfeld, "Scientific Beginnings," p. 169.

43 "At length in Ernst Brücke's": *Auto. Study*, p. 9.

43 "brought psychoanalysis into being": Freud, First Lecture, "Five Lec-

page   tures on Psychoanalysis" (1910 [1909]), delivered at Clark University, Worcester, Massachusetts, Sept. 1909, *S. E.* Vol. XI, p. 9 (afterward referred to as "Clark Lectures").

43   "Let's see what old Goethe has to say about it": quoted Fritz Wittels, *Sigmund Freud: His Personality, His Teaching, & His School*, p. 16 (afterward referred to as "Wittels").

44   "on the nature of man": Bernfeld, "Scientific Beginnings," p. 176.

44   "My demon drove me to visit Stricker's laboratory": Freud–Silberstein, Aug. 14, 1878, quoted Stanescu, p. 199.

45   "Brentano . . . named my name": Freud–Heinrich Gomperz, June 9, 1932, quoted Philip Merlan, "Brentano and Freud," *Journal of the History of Ideas*, Vol. VI, No. 3 (June 1945), p. 375.

45   "A thinking man is his own legislator": Freud–Silberstein, Feb. 27, 1875, Colchester.

45   "I adhere to the old ways": Freud–Martha Bernays, Nov. 15, 1883, *Letters*, p. 91, 76.

45   "A few weeks ago, while we were at table": Freud, "On Dreams" (1901), *S. E.* Vol. V, p. 638 (afterward referred to as "*On Dreams*").

46   "Woman, whom culture has burdened with a heavier load": Freud at Scientific Meeting on May 15, 1907, quoted Herman Nunberg and Ernst Federn, eds. *Minutes of the Vienna Psychoanalytic Society*, Vol. I 1906–1908, Vol. II 1908–1910, Vol. III 1910–1911, Vol. IV 1912–1918 (afterward referred to as "*Minutes* I, II, III and IV"), here I, p. 199.

46   "women must be regarded": Freud, Lecture XXXIII, "Femininity,." *New Introductory Lectures on Psycho-Analysis* (1933 [1932]), *S. E.* Vol. XXII, p. 134 (afterward referred to as "*New Intro. Lectures*").

46   "That is a practical impossibility": quoted Joseph Wortis, "Fragments of a Freudian Analysis," *American Journal of Orthopsychiatry*, Vol. X (1940), p. 847 (afterward referred to as "Wortis").

46   "that envy and jealousy": Freud, Lecture XXXIII, "Femininity," *New Intro. Lectures*, p. 125.

46   "The doctor then examined him": Freud, Lecture XXXIV, "Explanations, Applications and Orientations," *New Intro. Lectures*, p. 141.

47   "decidedly negligent": *Auto. Study*, p. 10.

47   "I no longer believe": Freud–Carl Koller, July 23, 1880, quoted Hortense Koller Becker, "Carl Koller and Cocaine," *Psychoanalytic Quarterly*, Vol. XXXII (1963), p. 316 (afterward referred to as "Becker").

47   "After a short collapse": Freud–Koller, July 23, 1880, quoted Becker, p. 317.

48   "In pharmacology": Freud–Koller, July 24, 1880, quoted Becker, p. 318.

3 Determined Doctor

49   "The turning point came in 1882": *Auto. Study*, p. 10.

50   "One would have imagined": "My Brother," p. 340.

50   "When making a decision of minor importance": Reik, *Third Ear*, p. 7.

51   "Do you really think one can employ": quoted René Laforgue, "Personal Memories of Freud" (1956), (afterward referred to as "Laforgue"), in Hendrik M. Ruitenbeek, ed., *Freud as We Knew Him*, p. 342 (afterward referred to as "Ruitenbeek").

page 51   "any physical experiences": Jones, I, p. 110, *99*.

51   "I stand for a much freer sexual life": Freud–Putnam, July 8, 1915, Nathan G. Hale, Jr., ed. *James Jackson Putnam and Psychoanalysis: Letters between Putnam and Sigmund Freud, Ernest Jones, William James, Sandor Ferenczi, and Morton Prince, 1877–1917*, p. 189 (afterward referred to as "Putnam Letters").

51   "sexual excitation is of no more use": Freud–Fliess, Oct. 31, 1897, *Origins*, p. 227.

51   "Up to the present I have not yet found": Freud's letter (n.d.) in answer to questionnaire on the essence of love contained in "Au delà de l'amour" published by *Les Cahiers Contemporains*, Paris, 1926, quoted Theodor Reik, *From Thirty Years with Freud*, p. 157 (afterward referred to as "Reik, *Thirty Years*").

52   "I never saw her more disappointed": Maryse Choisy, *Sigmund Freud: A New Appraisal*, p. 47 (afterward referred to as "Choisy").

52   "I think there is a general enmity": quoted Jones, I, p. 123, *111*.

53   "Here I think we have a situation": Charles Biederman–Ernest Jones, Oct. 19, 1955, Institute.

53   "I can foresee more than one opportunity": quoted Jones, I, p. 128, *116*.

53   "the enemy of our love": quoted Jones, I, p. 136, *123*.

54   "whoever needs more than five hours of sleep": quoted Jones, I, p. 71, *63*.

54   "A germanic caveman": Freud–Martha Bernays, Oct. 5, 1882, *Letters*, p. 48, *31*.

55   "at the behest of some extraordinary whim": Freud–Minna Bernays, Feb. 21, 1883, *Letters*, p. 53, *38*.

55   "It is hard to find material": Freud–Martha Bernays, Jan. 16, 1884, *Letters*, p. 104, *89*.

55   "A man must get himself talked about": Freud–Martha Bernays, Feb. 7, 1884, *Letters*, p. 112, *96*.

55   "now comes the worry about holding one's own": Freud–Martha Bernays, Feb. 14, 1884, *Letters*, p. 114, *99*.

55   "Strange creatures are billeted in my brain": Freud–Martha Bernays, Oct. 9, 1883, *Letters*, p. 82, *68*.

56   "don't be disappointed if I write again": Freud–Martha Bernays, Aug. 23, 1883, *Letters*, p. 60, *45*.

56   "I see your methods alone will make you famous yet": quoted Freud–Martha Bernays, Oct. 25, 1883, *Letters*, p. 87, *73*.

56   "Now that you have the weapon": quoted Freud–Martha Bernays, Oct. 25, 1883, *Letters*, p. 88, *73*.

56   "the years of waiting for my darling": Freud–Martha Bernays, Oct. 25, 1883, *Letters*, p. 88, *74*.

56   "So, I have allotted the various parts of the body": Freud–Martha Bernays, Oct. 12, 1883, quoted Jones, I, p. 223, *203*.

56   "Had he started with the psychiatry of his time": A. A. Brill, "A Psychoanalyst Scans His Past," presidential address given at combined meeting of the New York Neurological Society and the section of Neurology of the New York Academy of Medicine, Oct. 7, 1941, printed *Journal of Nervous and Mental Disease*, Vol. XCV, Part I (1942), p. 540 (afterward referred to as "Brill, 'His Past'").

page 57   "Today I put my case histories in order": Freud–Martha Bernays, Jan. 7, 1884, *Letters,* p. 99, *84.*

57   "Just imagine your timid lover": Freud–Martha Bernays, Feb. 14, 1884, *Letters,* p. 114, *98.*

57   "in one field of science": Freud–Martha Bernays, Apr. 19, 1884, *Letters,* p. 120, *105.*

57   "eye to pecuniary considerations": *Auto. Study,* p. 11.

57   "few specialists in that branch of medicine": *Auto. Study,* p. 11.

58   "I am also toying now": Freud–Martha Bernays, Apr. 21, 1884, *Letters,* p. 122, *107.*

58   "walk, run or climb mountains": *Chambers Encyclopaedia,* Vol. III (1889), p. 222.

58   "Bavarian soldiers, weary as a result of hardships": T. Aschenbrandt, quoted Freud, "Über Coca," Neu durchgesehener und vermehrter Separat-Abdruck aus dem *Centralblatt für die gesamte Therapie,* II (Vienna, July 1884), p. 14 (afterward referred to as "Über Coca").

58   "I have now ordered some of it": Freud–Martha Bernays, Apr. 21, 1884, *Letters,* p. 123, *107.*

59   "I first took 0.05 gram": "Über Coca," p. 11.

59   "We would take the alkaloid": C. Koller, "Historical Notes on the Beginnings of Local Anesthesia," *Journal of the American Medical Association,* Vol. XC, No. 21 (1928), pp. 1742–1743, quoted Becker, p. 330.

59   "Woe to you, my Princess": Freud–Martha Bernays, June 2, 1884, quoted Jones, I, p. 93, *84.*

60   "I said to him: 'I think I can help you' ": quoted Hanns Sachs, *Freud: Master and Friend,* p. 69 (afterward referred to as "Sachs").

60   "Where the main aim": "Über Coca," p. 16.

60   "Time after time": "Über Coca," p. 17.

60   "the recollection that American publications": Alexander Schusdek, "Freud on Cocaine," *Psychoanalytic Quarterly,* Vol. XXXIV (1965), p. 411.

60   According to an account: Reported Albert Hirst–Ernest Jones, Oct. 19, 1953, Institute.

61   "He stepped into Professor Stricker's laboratory": J. Gärtner, "Die Entdeckung der Lokalanaesthesie," in *Der Neue Tag* (Vienna, 1919), quoted Becker, p. 331.

61   "Now it was necessary": J. Gärtner, "Die Entdeckung der Lokalanaesthesie," in *Der Neue Tag* (Vienna, 1919), quoted Becker, p. 332.

61   "Cocaine was brought into the foreground": C. Koller, "Über die Verwendung des Cocaïn zur Anaesthesierung am Auge," *Wiener medizinische Wochenschrift,* Vol. XXXIV, No. 43, pp. 1276–1278; No. 44, pp. 1309–1311, (1884), quoted Becker, p. 334.

62   "not been thorough enough": *Dreams,* p. 170.

62   "but I bore my fiancée no grudge": *Auto. Study,* p. 15.

62   "I should unhesitatingly advise": Freud, "Über die Allgemeinwirkung des Cocaïns," read before Psychiatrischen Verein, March 5, 1885, printed *Medizinisch-chirurgisches Centralblatt,* XX, No. 32 (Aug. 7, 1885), pp. 374–375, in Sigmund Freud, *The Cocaine Papers,* p. 49.

62   "the third scourge of humanity": A. Erlenmeyer, "Über die Wirkung des Cocaïn bei der Morphiumentziehung," *Centralblatt für die Nervenheilkunde,* VIII (July 1885), pp. 289–299.

63   "Dr. Freud is a man with a good general education": Brücke, Commit-

page

tee Report to Faculty Meeting, Feb. 28, 1885, quoted Siegfried Bernfeld, "Sigmund Freud, M.D. 1882–1885," *International Journal of Psycho-Analysis*, Vol. XXXII (July 1951), p. 215.

63   "as yet unborn and unfortunate people": Freud–Martha Bernays, Apr. 28, 1885, *Letters*, p. 152, *140*.

63   "I have destroyed all my notes": Freud–Martha Bernays, Apr. 28, 1885, *Letters*, pp. 152–153, *140–141*.

63   "Freud was a confessor . . .": Reik, *Third Ear*, p. 21.

64   "It seems to me that the public has no concern": Freud–Fritz Wittels, Dec. 18, 1923, quoted Wittels, p. 11.

64   "Anyone turning biographer": Freud–Arnold Zweig, May 31, 1936, *Letters*, p. 426, *430*.

65   "You cannot imagine how dilapidated these princes": Freud–Martha Bernays, June 8, 1885, *Letters*, p. 163, *151*.

65   "if it weren't for the lack": Freud–Martha Bernays, June 8, 1885, *Letters*, p. 164, *152*.

65   "Oh, how wonderful it will be!": Freud–Martha Bernays, June 20, 1885, *Letters*, p. 166, *154*.

4 Paris

66   "I walked through the whole town": Freud–Martha Bernays, October 1885, quoted Ernest Jones, "Freud's Early Travels," read 18th International Psycho-Analytical Congress, London, July 27, 1953, printed *International Journal of Psycho-Analysis*, Vol. XXXV, Part 2 (1954), p. 83 (afterward referred to as "Jones, 'Freud's Early Travels' ").

67   "had to last until I got to Paris": Freud–Martha Bernays, Oct. 1885, quoted Jones, "Freud's Early Travels," p. 83.

67   "Imagine, a genuine obelisk": Freud–Martha Bernays, Oct. 19, 1885, *Letters*, p. 184, *173*.

67   "a few wonderful things": Freud–Martha Bernays, Oct. 19, 1885, *Letters*, p. 185, *173*.

67   "Apart from some subjective and scientific profit": Freud–Martha Bernays, Oct. 19, 1885, *Letters*, p. 183, *172*.

68   "Short of stature": Axel Munthe, *The Story of San Michele*, p. 284.

69   "But my stay here is going to be well worth it": Freud–Martha Bernays, Oct. 21, 1885, *Letters*, p. 188, *176*.

70   "must stop abusing me": Freud–Martha Bernays, Oct. 21, 1885, Colchester.

70   "I will tell you in detail": Freud–Martha Bernays, Nov. 24, 1885, *Letters*, p. 196, *184*.

71   "was not at all adapted to the reception": Freud, "Report on my Studies in Paris and Berlin" (1956 [1886]), *S. E.* Vol. I, p. 8 (afterward referred to as "Paris Report").

71   "to understand something of the riddles of the world": Freud, Postscript (1927) to *Lay Analysis*, p. 253.

72   "He used to look again and again": Freud, "Charcot" (1893), *S. E.* Vol. III, p. 12 (afterward referred to as "Charcot").

72   "In a series of researches he . . .": Freud, "On the Psychical Mechanism of the Hysterical Phenomena: A Lecture" (1893), *S. E.* Vol. III, p. 27.

73   "assured him for all time . . .": Charcot, p. 22.

73   "that this would not be the moment": Freud–Martha Bernays, Dec. 12, 1885, *Letters*, p. 201, *189*.

page 73 "As you realize, my heart is German provincial": Freud–Minna Bernays, Dec. 3, 1885, *Letters*, p. 200, *188*.

74 "It is bound to make me known": Freud–Martha Bernays, Dec. 12, 1885, *Letters*, p. 201, *189*.

74 "What a magic city this Paris is!": Freud–Martha Bernays, Feb. 10, 1886, *Letters*, p. 218, *206*.

74 "I couldn't help thinking what an ass I am": Freud–Martha Bernays, Feb. 10, 1886, *Letters*, p. 221, *208*.

74 "You are right in thinking": Freud–Koller, Oct. 13, 1886, quoted Becker, p. 357.

75 "No, dear friend, we will publish that together": quoted Freud–Martha Bernays, Jan. 17, 1886, *Letters*, p. 203, *191*.

75 "My appearance was immaculate": Freud–Martha Bernays, Jan. 20, 1886, *Letters*, p. 207, *195*.

75 "smoked like a chimney": Freud–Martha Bernays, Jan. 20, 1886, *Letters*, p. 208, *196*.

75 "These were my achievements": Freud–Martha Bernays, Jan. 20, 1886, *Letters*, p. 208, *196*.

76 "given favorable conditions I could achieve more than Nothnagel": Freud–Martha Bernays, Feb. 2, 1886; *Letters*, p. 214, *202*.

76 "You may as well be prepared": Freud–Minna Bernays, Feb. 7, 1886, *Letters*, p. 218, *205*.

76 "As long as their brains are free of disease": Freud–Martha Bernays, Mar. 10, 1886, *Letters*, p. 224, *212*.

76 "Although I have already been here for a week": Freud–Rosa Freud, Mar. 8, 1886, Colchester.

77 "[He] had, as it were, started from the ranks": R. Brun, "Sigmund Freud's Leistungen auf dem Gebiete der organische Neurologie," *Schweizer Archiv für Neurologie und Psychiatrie,* 37 (1936), pp. 200–207, quoted S. E. Jelliffe, "Sigmund Freud as a Neurologist," *Journal of Nervous and Mental Disease,* Vol. LXXXV (June 1937), p. 711.

5 Early Days in Practice

82 "[The typical doctor] cannot understand hysteria": First Lecture, Clark Lectures, p. 12.

83 "The French school of neuropathology": Paris Report, p. 5.

83 "had been met in our countries": Paris Report, p. 6.

83 "gladly seized the opportunity": Paris Report, p. 6.

83 "my true enemy": Freud–René Laforgue, quoted Laforgue, p. 344.

84 "The Jews are no longer our fellow citizens": quoted Joseph S. Bloch, *Erinnerungen aus meinem Leben,* p. 59.

84 "In [Freud's] personality": Reik, *Thirty Years,* p. 18

84 "I am not basically interested in therapy": quoted Abram Kardiner, "Freud—The Man I Knew, The Scientist and His Influence" (afterward referred to as "Kardiner"), in Benjamin Nelson, ed., *Freud and the 20th Century,* p. 51 (afterward referred to as "Nelson").

84 "I have told you that psychoanalysis": Freud, Lecture XXXIV, "Explanations, Applications and Orientations." *New Intro. Lectures,* p. 156.

85 "We both of us had nothing": Freud–C. G. Jung, Mar. 9, 1909, William McGuire, ed. *The Freud/Jung Letters: The Correspondence between Sigmund Freud and C. G. Jung,* p. 210 (afterward referred to as *"Freud/Jung Letters"*).

page 85 "In a few weeks the money": Freud–Martha Bernays, May 6, 1886, *Letters*, p. 228, *216*.

85 "In spite of everything my position here": Freud–Martha Bernays, May 13, 1886, *Letters*, p. 230, *218*.

85 "So, the battle of Vienna is in full swing": Freud–Martha Bernays, May 13, 1886, *Letters*, p. 230, *218*.

86 "Because the attitude of all my friends demanded it": Freud–Fliess, Aug. 29, 1888, *Origins*, p. 58.

86 "It is difficult for most people": Freud, "Review of August Forel's *Hypnotism*" (1889), *S. E.* Vol. I, p. 92.

86 "If you want to give me something": Freud–Koller, Oct. 13, 1886, Becker, p. 358.

87 "His case is complicated by his relationship": Freud–Martha Bernays, May 13, 1886, *Letters*, p. 230, *217*.

87 "It seemed weird to me": Freud–Martha Bernays, May 13, 1886, *Letters*, p. 230, *217*.

87 "Here I am counting every Gulden": Freud–Martha Bernays, May 13, 1886, *Letters*, p. 230, *217*.

87 "However, it went better with me": Freud–Koller, Oct. 13, 1886, Becker, p. 357.

88 "great confidence among military and civilians": Freud's Military Report, quoted Henri F. Ellenberger, *The Discovery of the Unconscious: The History and Evolution of Dynamic Psychiatry*, p. 459 (afterward referred to as "Ellenberger").

88 "Honest, firm character, cheerful": Ellenberger, p. 459.

88 "Obedient and open, moreover modest": Ellenberger, p. 459.

88 "Friendly": Ellenberger, p. 459.

88 "Benevolent and exerting a good influence": Ellenberger, p. 459.

88 "Very decent and modest, pleasant manners": Ellenberger, p. 459.

88 "An officer is a miserable creature": Freud–Josef Breuer, Sept. 1, 1886, *Letters*, p. 232, *219*.

89 "It was hard to get tenants": "My Brother," p. 341.

89 "Freud aus Wien" and "Freud aus Asien": Martha Freud–Ernest Jones, August 1947, Institute.

89 "My little wife": Freud–Koller, Oct. 13, 1886, Becker, p. 358.

89 "I remember very well her telling me": Elliott Philipp–Ernest Jones, Oct. 28, 1953, Institute.

91 "Everyone in that room knew": Rudolf von Urban–Ernest Jones, n.d., Institute.

91 "Gentlemen, When on October 15 I had the honor": Freud, "Observation of a Severe Case of Hemi-Anaesthesia in a Hysterical Male" (1886), *S. E.* Vol. I, p. 25.

92 "This time I was applauded": *Auto. Study*, pp. 15–16.

92 "I couldn't bring myself to do it": Reik, *Thirty Years*, p. 17.

93 ". . . but I must start with the confession": Freud–Fliess, Nov. 24, 1887, *Origins*, p. 51.

94 "Our correspondence": Freud–Princess Marie Bonaparte, Jan. 3, 1937, quoted Schur, p. 487.

94 "nothing sensational": Editors' note, *Origins*, p. ix.

94 "The selection was made": Editors' note, *Origins*, p. ix.

95 "almost unbelievable lengths to rationalize his faith": Arthur Efron, "Freud's Self-Analysis and the Nature of Psychoanalytic Criticism,"

page   *International Review of Psycho-Analysis*, Vol. IV (1977), p. 254.

95   "an even greater visionary than I": Freud–Fliess, Oct. 31, 1895, *Origins*, p. 130.

96   "That wouldn't have bothered Fliess": quoted Jones, I, p. 320, *291*.

96   "universal specialist from Berlin": Freud–Fliess, Sept. 3, 1899, *Origins*, p. 285.

96   "If you have really solved the problem": Freud–Fliess, May 25, 1895, *Origins*, p. 120.

96   "doubts must be cast upon the rigidity": Freud, *Beyond the Pleasure Principle* (1920), *S. E.* Vol. XVIII, p. 45 (afterward referred to as *"Pleasure Principle"*).

96   "The relationship between the chain": Freud, *On Aphasia: A Critical Study*, p. 55 (afterward referred to as *"On Aphasia"*).

97   "Anxiety, chemical factors, etc.": Freud–Fliess, June 30, 1896, *Origins*, p. 169.

97   "I am not in the least in disagreement": Freud–Fliess, Sept. 22, 1898, *Origins*, p. 264.

97   "When I talked to you": Freud–Fliess, Aug. 1, 1890, *Origins*, p. 60.

97   "People like you should not die out": Freud–Fliess, Jan. 1, 1896, quoted Jones, I, p. 328, *298*.

97   "that I partake": Freud–Frau Fliess, Dec. 22, 1896, quoted Elenore Fliess, *Robert Fliess, 1895–1970*, p. 14.

98   "and he had always remembered": Siegfried Bernfeld and Suzanne Cassirer Bernfeld, "Freud's First Year in Practice, 1886–1887," *Bulletin of the Menninger Clinic*, Vol. XVI, No. 2 (Mar. 1952), pp. 37–49.

99   "you never know who is pulling": Julius von Wagner-Jauregg–Wittels, quoted Wittels, p. 31.

99   "This gives me the advantage": Josef Breuer and Sigmund Freud, *Studies on Hysteria* (1893–1895), *S. E.* Vol. II, p. 267 (afterward referred to as *"Studies"*).

99   "My therapeutic arsenal": *Auto. Study*, p. 16.

99   "If it is a merit": First Lecture, Clark Lectures, p. 9.

6 Prospecting the Unconscious

100   "the germ cell of the whole of psychoanalysis": Josef Breuer–August Forel, Nov. 21, 1907, quoted Paul F. Cranefield, "Josef Breuer's Evaluation of his Contribution to Psycho Analysis," *International Journal of Psycho-Analysis*, Vol. XXXIX (1958), p. 320 (afterward referred to as "Cranefield").

100   "the patient had not been cured": H. F. Ellenberger, "The Story of 'Anna O.': A Critical Review with New Data," *Journal of the History of the Behavioral Sciences*, Vol. VIII, No. 3 (July 1972), p. 279 (afterward referred to as "Ellenberger, 'Anna O.' ").

101   "a lengthy medical conversation": Freud–Martha Bernays, July 13, 1883, *Letters*, p. 56, *41*.

101   "There were extremely rapid changes of mood": *Studies*, p. 24.

101   "she completely ignored [him]": *Studies*, p. 27.

102   "against her will": Josef Breuer's original report of 1895, quoted Ellenberger, "Anna O.," p. 268.

102   "without deceit, but by force": Josef Breuer's Unknown Report of 1882, quoted Ellenberger, "Anna O.," p. 276.

102   "She would take up the glass of water": *Studies*, p. 34.

page 102   the "talking cure" or "chimney-sweeping": quoted *Studies*, p. 30.

102   "She took a great step forward": *Studies*, p. 35.

103   "My merit lay essentially": Breuer–Forel, Nov. 21, 1907, quoted Cranefield, p. 319.

103   "This would mean that the illness": Ellenberger, "Anna O.," p. 279.

104   "free from the innumerable disturbances": *Studies*, p. 40.

104   "On the evening of the day": Freud–Stefan Zweig, June 2, 1932, *Letters*, p. 408, *413*.

104   "Seized by conventional horror": Freud–Stefan Zweig, June 2, 1932, *Letters*, p. 409, *413*.

104   "It would seem that Breuer had developed": Jones, I, p. 246, *224*.

104   "Though profoundly shocked": Jones, I, p. 247, *225*.

104   "fraught with impossibilities": Ellenberger, p. 483.

104   "The poor patient did not fare so well": Freud–Martha Bernays, Aug. 5, 1883, quoted Jones, I, p. 247, *225*.

105   "hysterical features": Ellenberger, "Anna O.," p. 277.

105   "disparaging judgments": Ellenberger, "Anna O.," p. 277.

105   "lack of insight": Ellenberger, "Anna O.," p. 278.

105   "In spite of her recovery": Freud, Lecture XVIII, "Fixation to Traumas–The Unconscious," *Introductory Lectures on Psycho-Analysis* (1916–1917 [1915–1917]), *S. E.* Vols. XV (pp. 1–239) and XVI (pp. 241–463) (afterward referred to as *"Intro. Lectures"*), here XVI, p. 337.

106   "that a fairly severe case": Breuer–Forel, Nov. 21, 1907, quoted Cranefield, p. 320.

106   "It was impossible for a 'general practitioner' ": Breuer–Forel, Nov. 21, 1907, quoted Cranefield, p. 320.

106   "an educated and literate social class": Breuer and Freud, Preface to the First Edition, *Studies*, p. xxix.

106   "I began, with Breuer's constant co-operation": Freud, "On the Psychical Mechanism of Hysterical Phenomena: A Lecture" (1893), *S. E.* Vol. III, p. 30.

107   "The benefit of tears in emotional shock": F. W. H. Myers, "The Subliminal Consciousness," *Proceedings of the Society for Psychical Research*, Vol. IX (1893–4), p. 13 (afterward referred to as "Myers").

107   "He frankly admitted to me": *Auto. Study*, p. 18.

108   "If only we had the means of putting": quoted *Studies*, p. 108.

108   "The hypnotist . . . plays the role of the drill sergeant": Brill, "His Past," p. 542.

109   "Breuer's reception of [the book]": Freud–Minna Bernays, July 13, 1891, *Letters*, p. 239, *229*.

110   "the best brains of German and foreign neurology": *On Aphasia*, p. 1.

110   "I shall endeavor to demonstrate": *On Aphasia*, p. 1.

110   "I have been very cheeky in [*On Aphasia*]": Freud–Fliess, May 2, 1891, *Origins*, p. 61.

110   "My darling Son Shlomo": quoted Aron, p. 289.

111   "shares with me responsibility": Freud–Fliess, Aug. 16, 1895, *Origins*, p. 122.

111   "It was not a pious household": Judith Bernays Heller, "Freud's Mother and Father: A Memoir," *Commentary*, Vol. XXI, No. 5 (May 1956), p. 419 (afterward referred to as "Heller").

111   "My little Mathilde is thriving": Freud–Fliess, Feb. 4, 1888, *Origins*, p. 54.

page 112   "goes on tolerably well here": Freud–Fliess, May 28, 1888, *Origins*, p. 56.

112   "Though she never really assumed the full responsibility": Judith Bernays Heller–Ernest Jones, n.d., Institute.

7 *The Birth of Psychoanalysis*

115   "Just what he himself understood by it": quoted Reik, *Thirty Years*, p. 61.

115   "The key to the knowledge": Carl Gustav Carus, *Psyche zur Entwicklungsgeschichte der Seele*, p. 1.

115   "Around 1870 the 'unconscious' was not merely topical": Lancelot Law Whyte, *The Unconscious Before Freud*, p. 163.

116   "We maintain not merely the existence": quoted Ida Macalpine, "Tribute to Freud," *Journal of the History of Medicine and Allied Sciences*, Vol. XI, No. 3 (July 1956), p. 248.

116   "The body and the mind are as a jerkin and its lining": Laurence Sterne, *Tristram Shandy*.

116   "had come closer to the fundamental truths": Reik, *Thirty Years*, p. 61.

116   "are valuable allies": Freud, "Delusions and Dreams in Jensen's *Gradiva*" (1907 [1906]), *S. E.* Vol. IX, p. 8.

117   "the direct introduction of the reader": Edouard Dujardin, *Le Monologue Intérieur: son Apparition, ses Origines, sa Place dans l'Oeuvre de James Joyce*, p. 58.

117   "I am pretty well alone here": Freud–Fliess, May 21, 1894, *Origins*, p. 83.

118   "I myself would reach back": Freud–Ernst Simmel, Feb. 20, 1918, David Brunswick and Ruth Lachenbruch, "Freud's Letters to Ernst Simmel," *Journal of the American Psychoanalytic Association*, Vol. XII, No. 1 (Jan. 1964), p. 97 (afterward referred to as "Simmel Letters").

118   "At first, I must confess": Second Lecture, Clark Lectures, p. 22.

118   "But he did not accept this": *Studies*, p. 109.

118   "I decided to start from the assumption": *Studies*, p. 110.

119   "dissociate the patient's attention": *Studies*, p. 271.

119   "what one does not know": Freud–Putnam, Mar. 10, 1910, Putnam Letters, p. 97.

119   "I abandoned hypnotism": *Auto. Study*, p. 28.

119   "the mothers of the nomadic tribes": Choisy, p. 125.

119   "One female patient exploiting this situation": The Wolf-Man, "My Recollections of Sigmund Freud" (afterward referred to as "The Wolf-Man, 'Recollections'), in Muriel Gardiner, ed., *The Wolf-Man and Sigmund Freud*, p. 142 (afterward referred to as "Gardiner").

120   "Take a few sheets of paper": Ludwig Börne, "Die Kunst, in drei Tagen ein Original-Schriftsteller zu werden" (1823), *Gesammelte Schriften*, Vollständige Ausgabe, Erster Band, p. 138.

120   "When I read this one again": Freud–Sandor Ferenczi, Apr. 9, 1919, quoted Ernst Freud, Lucie Freud and Ilse Grubrich-Simitis, eds., *Sigmund Freud: His Life in Pictures and Words*, p. 73 (afterward referred to as *Life in Pictures*).

120   "apparently always engaged": Francis Galton, "Psychometric Experiments," *Brain: A Journal of Neurology*, Vol. II (July 1879), p. 155 (afterward referred to as "Galton").

page 120   "Perhaps the strongest of the impressions": Galton, p. 162.

120   "It is perhaps unimportant": D. W. Forrest, *Francis Galton: The Life and Work of a Victorian Genius*, p. 148.

121   "For example, my use . . .": R. S. Woodworth, Columbia University-editor of *The Nation*, Oct. 13, 1916, *The Nation*, Vol. CIII, No. 2678 (Oct. 26, 1916), p. 396.

121   "So far as analytic procedure is concerned": Wortis, p. 844.

122   "After such an analysis": quoted The Wolf-Man, "Recollections," in Gardiner, p. 148.

122   "One thing more, before you begin": Freud, "Further Recommendations in the Technique of Psycho-Analysis: On Beginning the Treatment. The Question of the First Communications. The Dynamics of the Cure" (1913), *Collected Papers*, Vol. II, p. 355 (afterward referred to as "On Beginning the Treatment").

123   "We have only one aim": Freud–Eva Rosenfeld, quoted Jones, III, p. 163, *153*.

123   "If we write the dream down": quoted Ernest Simon, "Sigmund Freud, the Jew," Leo Baeck Institute: *Yearbook*, II, London, 1957, p. 291 (afterward referred to as "Simon").

123   "brings to mind the characteristic form": Simon, p. 291.

124   "moved back from the scene": *History*, p. 10.

124   "It appeared that psychoanalysis could explain nothing": *History*, p. 10.

125   "At first the analyzing physician could do no more": *Pleasure Principle*, p. 18.

125   "This extension is justified genetically": Freud, "Observations on 'Wild' Psycho-Analysis" (1910), *Collected Papers*, Vol. II, p. 299.

126   "I happened to be standing": *History*, p. 13.

126   "These things are always *secrets d'alcôve!*": *History*, p. 13.

127   "Soldiers are standing by": *Neue Freie Presse*, May 1, 1890.

127   "Kraus saw that the actual root of [hysteria]": Allan Janik and Stephen Toulmin, *Wittgenstein's Vienna*, p. 76.

128   "The more I set about looking for such disturbances": Freud, "My Views on the Part Played by Sexuality in the Aetiology of the Neuroses" (1906 [1905]), *S. E.* Vol. VII, p. 271.

128   "made up of two parts": Freud, "The Future Prospects of Psychoanalytic Therapy" (1910), delivered as an address at the opening of the 2nd Psycho-Analytical Congress, Nuremberg, March 30 and 31, 1910, *S. E.* Vol. XI, p. 141.

129   "I unhesitatingly sacrificed my growing popularity": *History*, p. 21.

129   "The sexual business attracts people": Freud–Fliess, Oct. 6, 1893, *Origins*, p. 77.

129   "arose from no inclination towards the subject": Breuer–Forel, Nov. 21, 1907, quoted Cranefield, p. 320.

130   "a long battle with my collaborator": Freud–Fliess, Dec. 18, 1892, *Origins*, p. 64.

131   "It brings to an end the operative force": Breuer and Freud, "On the Psychical Mechanism of Hysterical Phenomena: Preliminary Communication" (1893), *Studies*, p. 17.

131   "happy to see that the results of my findings": Pierre Janet, "Contribution à l'étude des accidents mentaux chez les hystériques", Thèse méd. Paris, 1892-3, No. 432 (Paris: Rueff, 1893), pp. 252–57.

131   "Then the connection between the latter": J. Michell Clarke, "Hyste-

page   ria and Neurasthenia," *Brain: A Journal of Neurology*, Vol. XVII (1894), p. 125.

131   "That extraordinary potency of subliminal action": Myers, p. 15.

132   "The therapeutic success on the whole": *Studies*, p. 101.

133   "This of course applies especially": Preface to the First Edition, *Studies*, p. xxix.

133   "the sexual instinct is undoubtedly": *Studies*, p. 200.

134   "touched on one of the great secrets of nature": Freud–Fliess, May 21, 1894, *Origins*, p. 83.

134   "they are important": Freud–Fliess, Aug. 29, 1894, *Origins*, p. 101.

134   "with a beating heart": Freud–Fliess, Mar. 10, 1898, *Origins*, p. 247.

134   "changed first of all the terms I was using": Pierre Janet, *Principles of Psychotherapy*, p. 41.

135   "in taking up the uninterpreted experiments": *The Times* (May 25, 1931).

135   "requires a penetrating investigation": Adolf von Strümpell, review in *Deutsche Zeitschrift für Nervenheilkunde*, 8, (1896), p. 159, quoted footnote, *Origins*, p. 156.

135   "able to laugh at the lack": *Auto. Study*, p. 23.

135   "nothing but the kind of psychology": Alfred Freiherr von Berger, review in *Neue Freie Presse* (Feb. 2, 1896), quoted Frank Cioffi, ed., *Freud: Modern Judgments*, p. 5 (afterward referred to as "Cioffi").

135   "very sensitive article": Freud–Fliess, Feb. 6, 1896, *Origins*, p. 156.

136   "been long recognized in the Roman Church": J. Michell Clarke, review in *Brain: A Journal of Neurology*, Vol. XIX (1896), p. 407 (afterward referred to as "Michell Clarke").

136   "interesting to note a return": Michell Clarke, p. 414.

136   "only on severe, indeed on the severest cases": Freud, "On Psychotherapy" (1905 [1904]), *S. E.* Vol. VII, p. 263 (afterward referred to as "On Psychotherapy").

137   "simply non-testable, irrefutable": Karl R. Popper, *Conjectures and Refutations: The Growth of Scientific Knowledge*, p. 37.

137   "I actually spend the whole day": Freud–Fliess, June 22, 1894, *Origins*, p. 95.

137   "postulated not molecules and motion": Iago Galdston, "Freud and Romantic Medicine," *Bulletin of the History of Medicine*, Vol. XXX, No. 6 (Nov.–Dec. 1956), p. 494.

138   "I was walking home": Rudolf von Urban–Ernest Jones, Oct. 10, 1955, Institute.

139   "Instinctively, he opened his arms": Hanna Breuer–Ernest Jones, Apr. 21, 1954, Institute.

139   "Breuer, so it would appear": Jones, I, p. 281, 255.

139   "One owes respect to the living": Voltaire, *Lettres sur Oedipe*, i, note.

139   "need not be reproduced": Jones, I, p. 281, 255.

139   "His look of downright pity and superiority": Ludwig Binswanger, *Sigmund Freud: Reminiscences of a Friendship*, p. 4 (afterward referred to as "Binswanger").

8 Splendid Isolation: Disaster

140   "splendid isolation": *History*, p. 22.

141   "At that time I had reached the peak of loneliness": Freud–Ferenczi, July 9, 1913, *Letters*, p. 307, 301.

141   "What personal pleasure is to be derived": Freud–Oskar Pfister, Dec.

page

25, 1920, Heinrich Meng and Ernst L. Freud, eds., *Psycho-Analysis and Faith: The Letters of Sigmund Freud and Oskar Pfister*, p. 79 (afterward referred to as "Pfister Letters").

142   "such a great boon to live": Freud–Fliess, Nov. 17, 1893, quoted Schur, p. 42.

142   "the specific pharmacological effect of nicotine": Schur, p. 61.

142   "I am inclined to the opinion": Schur, p. 62.

144   "an enormous extension of our definite knowledge": T. S. Clouston, quoted "The Progress and Promise of Psychiatry in America," in Notes and Comment (Apr. 1898), *American Journal of Insanity*, Vol. LIV (1897–1898), p. 638.

144   "In this house on July 24th, 1895": Freud–Fliess, June 12, 1900, *Origins*, p. 322.

145   "first great error": Freud–Karl Abraham, July 5, 1907, Hilda C. Abraham and Ernst L. Freud, eds., *A Psycho-Analytic Dialogue: The Letters of Sigmund Freud and Karl Abraham, 1907–1926*, p. 2 (afterward referred to as "Abraham Letters").

145   "most beautiful things": Freud–Fliess, Nov. 29, 1895, *Origins*, p. 134.

145   "I have trouble in fitting everything in": Freud–Fliess, Dec. 8, 1895, *Origins*, p. 136.

145   "that this year for the first time": Freud–Fliess, May 4, 1896, *Origins*, p. 162.

145   "It had been a hot summer afternoon": *Dreams*, p. 469.

146   "attended by an audience of eleven": Freud–Fliess, Nov. 5, 1897, *Origins*, p. 228.

146   "A thing I remember from my boyhood": Freud–Fliess, Sept. 21, 1899, *Origins*, p. 298.

146   "It is my busy time now": Freud–Fliess, Mar. 11, 1900, *Origins*, p. 311.

147   "a sheet-anchor during those difficult times": Freud, Lecture XXIX, "Revision of the Theory of Dreams." *New Intro. Lectures*, p. 7.

148   "better, but not quite well": *Dreams*, p. 106.

148   "with the idea of giving it to Dr. M.": *Dreams*, p. 106.

148   "A large hall—numerous guests, whom we were receiving": *Dreams*, p. 107.

149   "The dream acquitted me of the responsibility": *Dreams*, p. 118.

149   "I would be grateful": Freud–Fliess, Mar. 4, 1895, quoted Max Schur, "Some Additional 'Day Residues' of 'The Specimen Dream of Psychoanalysis' " (afterward referred to as "Schur, 'Day Residues' "), in R. M. Loewenstein, L. M. Newman, M. Schur, and A. J. Solnit, eds., *Psychoanalysis—A General Psychology*, p. 55.

149   "probably upset you as much": Freud–Fliess, Mar. 8, 1895, quoted Schur, "Day Residues," p. 59.

150   "suddenly pulled out something": Freud–Fliess, Mar. 8, 1895, quoted Schur, "Day Residues," p. 59.

150   "This is the strong sex": Freud–Fliess, Mar. 8, 1895, quoted Schur, "Day Residues," p. 57.

150   "*we had misjudged her*": Freud–Fliess, Mar. 8, 1895, quoted Schur, "Day Residues," p. 60.

150   "one of the not too uncommon surgical 'parapraxes' ": Schur, p. 80.

150   "never glad confident morning again": Robert Browning, "The Lost Leader."

page 150   "Of course no one blames you": Freud–Fliess, Mar. 8, 1895, quoted
              Schur, "Day Residues," p. 60.

       150   "a very nice reasonable girl": Freud–Fliess, Mar. 28, 1895, quoted
              Schur, "Day Residues," p. 62.

       150   "you will always remain the healer": Freud–Fliess, Apr. 20, 1895,
              quoted Schur, "Day Residues," p. 67.

       151   "You were correct": Freud–Fliess, Apr. 26, 1896, quoted Schur, "Day
              Residues," p. 80.

       151   "Emma has a scene [in mind]": Freud–Fliess, Jan. 17, 1897, quoted
              Schur, "Day Residues," p. 83.

       151   "Meaning the hemorrhage": Schur, "Day Residues," p. 83.

       151   "I will not pretend": *Dreams*, p. 120.

       152   "never been so intensely preoccupied": Freud–Fliess, Apr. 27, 1895,
              Origins, p. 118.

       152   "to see how the theory of mental functioning": Freud–Fliess, May 25,
              1895, *Origins*, p. 119.

       152   "devoted every free minute to such work": Freud–Fliess, May 25,
              1895, *Origins*, p. 120.

       152   "Saying anything now": Freud–Fliess, June 12, 1895, *Origins*, p. 121.

       152   "This psychology is really an incubus": Freud–Fliess, Aug. 16, 1895,
              Origins, p. 123.

       153   "Shortly before Teschen": Freud–Fliess, Sept. 15, 1895, The Jewish
              National and University Library, Jerusalem (afterward referred to as
              "The Jewish Library").

       153   "is to furnish a psychology": Freud, "Project for a Scientific Psychol-
              ogy" (1950 [1895]), *S. E.* Vol. I, p. 295.

       154   "Everything fell into place": Freud–Fliess, Oct. 20, 1895, *Origins*, p.
              129.

       154   "concocted": Freud–Fliess, Nov. 29, 1895, *Origins*, p. 134.

       154   "I cannot conceive how I came": Freud–Fliess, Nov. 29, 1895, *Origins*,
              p. 134.

       154   "We are taken a step further": Freud, "The Unconscious" (1915), *S.
              E.* Vol. XIV, p. 174 (afterward referred to as "The Unconscious").

       155   "in the fact that the quantities of energy": Freud–Pfister, Jan. 18,
              1928, Pfister Letters, p. 120.

       155   "not among those who place psychoanalysis": Freud–Alexander Lip-
              schütz, Aug. 12, 1931, *Letters*, p. 406, 407.

       155   "One great enigma": John Beloff, *The Existence of Mind*, p. 236.

       156   "Note that among other things I suspect the following": Freud–Fliess,
              Oct. 8, 1895, *Origins*, p. 126.

       156   "Have I revealed the great clinical secret": Freud–Fliess, Oct. 15,
              1895, *Origins*, p. 127.

       156   "Foremost among those guilty of abuses like these": Freud, "Further
              Remarks on the Neuro-Psychoses of Defense" (1896), *S. E.* Vol. III,
              p. 164.

       156   "some objections to the aetiological theory": Freud, "Heredity and
              the Aetiology of the Neuroses" (1896), *S. E.* Vol. III, p. 143 (afterward
              referred to as "Heredity and the Neuroses").

       156   *"the subject's sexual life"*: Heredity and the Neuroses, p. 149.

       157   "What gives its distinctive character": Heredity and the Neuroses, p.
              149.

       157   "I am quite sure that this theory": Heredity and the Neuroses, p. 149.

page 157   "Gentlemen—When we set out": Freud, "The Aetiology of Hysteria" (1896), *S. E.* Vol. III, p. 191 (afterward referred to as "Aetiology of Hysteria").

157   "If his work is crowned with success": Aetiology of Hysteria, p. 192.

158   "It sounds like a scientific fairy tale": quoted Freud–Fliess, Apr. 26–28, 1896, Schur, p. 104.

158   "I no longer believe": Freud–Fliess, Sept. 21, 1897, *Origins*, p. 215.

158   "aetiology broke down": *History*, p. 17.

158   "an icy reception from the asses ...": Freud–Fliess, Apr. 26–28, 1896, quoted Schur, p. 104.

158   "only to condemn the absurdity": C. H. Hughes, ed., editorial, "Aetiology of Hysteria," *The Alienist and Neurologist*, Vol. XVII, No. 3 (St. Louis, Oct. 1896), p. 520.

158   "as a curiosity of the absurd lengths": C. H. Hughes, editorial, "Sigmund Freud's Foolish Conclusion," *The Alienist and Neurologist*, Vol. XX, No. 1 (St. Louis, Jan. 1899), p. 114.

159   "aggressive pursuit of evidence to substantiate it": Nathan Schlessinger, John E. Gedo, Julian A. Miller, George H. Pollock, Melvin Sabshin and Leo Sadow, "The Scientific Styles of Breuer and Freud and the Origins of Psychoanalysis," in John E. Gedo and George H. Pollock, eds., *Freud: The Fusion of Science and Humanism: The Intellectual History of Psycho-Analysis. Psychological Issues*, Vol. IX, Nos. 2/3, Monograph 34/35, p. 204 (afterward referred to as "Gedo and Pollock").

159   "once generalized": Leo Sadow, John E. Gedo, Julian A. Miller, George H. Pollock, Melvin Sabshin and Nathan Schlessinger, "The Process of Hypothesis Change in Three Early Psychoanalytic Concepts," in Gedo and Pollock, p. 273.

159   "in every case the father, not excluding my own": Freud–Fliess, Sept. 21, 1897, "Extracts from the Fliess Papers" (1950 [1892–1899]), *S. E* Vol. I, p. 259.

159   letter as published in *The Origins of Psycho-Analysis:* Freud–Fliess, Sept. 21, 1897, *Origins*, p. 215.

159   "error into which I fell for a while": *Auto. Study*, p. 33.

159   "Associations which were not deemed adequate": Alexander Schusdek, "Freud's 'Seduction Theory': A Reconstruction," *Journal of the History of the Behavioral Sciences*, Vol. II (1966), p. 163.

160   "The old man died on the night of the twenty-third": Freud–Fliess, Oct. 26, 1896, *Origins*, p. 170.

160   "It revolutionized my soul": Freud–Jones, Feb. 12, 1920, Colchester.

160   "By one of the obscure routes": Freud–Fliess, Nov. 2, 1896, *Origins*, p. 170.

160   "Not long ago I dreamt": Freud–Fliess, May 31, 1897, *Origins*, p. 206.

161   "Let me tell you straight away": Freud–Fliess, Sept. 21, 1897, *Origins*, p. 215.

161   "it was hardly credible": Freud–Fliess, Sept. 21, 1897, *Origins*, p. 215.

161   "happened by chance to include": Freud, "My Views on the Part played by Sexuality in the Aetiology of the Neuroses" (1906 [1905]), *S. E.* Vol. VII, p. 274.

161   "the vast majority of physicians": Ernest Jones, "The Nature of Genius," delivered to the New York Psychoanalytical Society and Institute, Apr. 23, 1956, printed Ernest Jones, *Sigmund Freud: Four Centenary Addresses,*   (afterward referred to as "Jones, *Centenary Addresses*").

page 161   "well-recognized difficulty in forming": "The Nature of Genius," Jones, *Centenary Addresses*, p. 23.

161   "I was at last obliged": *Auto. Study*, p. 34.

161   "I do not believe even now": *Auto. Study*, p. 34.

162   "We need not be afraid, therefore, of telling the patient": *Studies*, p. 295.

162   "liable to make statements": Michell Clarke, p. 414.

162   "boldly demand confirmation": Freud, "Sexuality in the Aetiology of the Neuroses" (1898), *S. E.* Vol. III, p. 269.

162   "Quite often we do not succeed": Freud, "Constructions in Analysis" (1937), *S. E.* Vol. XXIII, p. 265.

162   "We do not know how many patients": Seymour Fisher and Roger P. Greenberg, *The Scientific Credibility of Freud's Theories and Therapy*, p. 366 (afterward referred to as "Fisher and Greenberg").

162   "Analysis had led back to these": *History*, p. 17.

162   "made uncertain by that first great error": Freud–Abraham, July 5, 1907, Abraham Letters, p. 2.

162   "open every step of the way": Freud–Jung, May 23, 1912, *Freud/Jung Letters*, p. 507.

162   "The hope of eternal fame was so beautiful": Freud–Fliess, Sept. 21, 1897, *Origins*, p. 217.

163   "It is curious that I feel not in the least disgraced": Freud–Fliess, Sept. 21, 1897, *Origins*, p. 217.

163   "the aetiological factor of seduction": Freud, footnote added 1924, "Further Remarks on the Neuro-Psychoses of Defence" (1896), *S. E.* Vol. III, p. 168.

163   "to cover up the auto-erotic activity": *History*, p. 18.

163   "from behind the phantasies": *History*, p. 18.

9 Splendid Isolation: Recovery

164   "The chief patient I am busy with is myself": Freud–Fliess, Aug. 14, 1897, *Origins*, p. 213.

164   "We are all human": Captain J. P. Farrar, quoted Ronald W. Clark, *An Eccentric in the Alps*, p. 175.

165   "I soon saw the necessity of carrying out": *History*, p. 20.

165   "the danger of incompleteness is particularly great": Freud, "The Subtleties of a Faulty Action" (1935), *S. E.* Vol. XXII, p. 234.

165   "So it may seem tempting to take the easy course": Freud, "From the History of an Infantile Neurosis" (1918 [1914]), *S. E.* Vol. XVII, p. 14 (afterward referred to as "Freud, Wolf-Man Case").

166   "sound partly contradictory": Schur, p. 125.

166   "supreme achievement, a discovery fit to rank": Paul Kline, *Fact and Fantasy in Freudian Theory*, p. 348 (afterward referred to as "Kline").

166   ". . . that my 'primary originator' [of neurosis]": Freud–Fliess, Oct. 3, 1897, *Origins*, p. 219.

166   "my instructress in sexual matters": Freud–Fliess, Oct. 3-4, 1897, *Origins*, p. 220.

167   "I have found love of the mother": Freud–Fliess, Oct. 15, 1897, *Origins*, p. 223.

168   "The idea has passed through my head": Freud–Fliess, Oct. 15, 1897, *Origins*, p. 224.

page 168   "it is not so much that Freud brought": Norman N. Holland, *Psychoanalysis and Shakespeare*, p. 59.

168   "moves us only because it might have been ours": *Dreams*, p. 262.

168   "if psychoanalysis could boast of no other achievement": Freud, "An Outline of Psycho-Analysis" (1940 [1938]), *S.E.* Vol. XXIII, p. 192 (afterward referred to as "Outline of Psycho-Analysis").

168   "He wishes to possess her physically": "Outline of Psycho-Analysis," p. 189.

169   "You will of course object that after all": Freud, Lecture XXXII, "Anxiety and Instinctual Life," *New Intro. Lectures*, p. 86.

169   "It is our suspicion": Freud, Lecture XXXII, "Anxiety and Instinctual Life," *New Intro. Lectures*, p. 86.

169   "In this sense": Freud, Lecture XXI, "The Development of the Libido and the Sexual Organizations," *Intro. Lectures*, p. 337.

170   "by remarking that the point": Freud at Scientific Meeting on Feb. 25, 1914, quoted *Minutes*, IV, p. 231.

170   "obvious enough": Freud at Scientific Meeting on Apr. 8, 1914, quoted *Minutes*, IV, p. 254.

170   "It is our task to establish": Freud at Scientific Meeting on Apr. 8, 1914, quoted *Minutes*, IV, p. 254.

170   "inclined to regard this relationship": M. D. Eder, *War-Shock: The Psycho-Neuroses in War Psychology and Treatment*, p. 73 (afterward referred to as "Eder").

170   "In other words, the one set of thinkers": Jones, "The Individual and Society," read before the Sociology Society, London School of Economics, Mar. 8, 1935, printed *Sociological Review*, Vol. XXVII, No. 3 (July 1935), p. 261.

171   "Freud's persuasive sweep": Fisher and Greenberg, p. 223.

171   "in one case that boys and girls do have sexual feelings": Kline, p. 348.

172.   "Direct observation does not confirm": D. W. Winnicott, *The Child, the Family and the Outside World*, p. 149.

172   "responses to his own intellectual needs": Jones, "Prefatory Note," *British Journal for the Philosophy of Science*, Vol. VII, No. 25 (May 1956), p. 1.

172   "The real sin which [he] has committed": T. A. Ross, letter in *British Medical Journal* (Jan. 9, 1915), p. 94.

172   "I am only a literary man": Georg Brandes quoted Freud, Lecture XXXIV, "Explanations, Applications and Orientations," *New Intro. Lectures*, p. 139.

173   "his tone became urgent": C. G. Jung, *Memories, Dreams, Reflections*, p. 147 (afterward referred to as "Jung, *Memories*").

173   "I can still recall vividly": Jung, *Memories*, p. 147.

174   "I have such unruly dreams": Freud–Martha Bernays, June 30, 1882, quoted Jones, I, p. 385, *351*.

174   "heard from [Gomperz] the first remarks": Freud–Elise Gomperz, Nov. 12, 1913, quoted *Life in Pictures*, p. 85.

174   "For several weeks I found myself obliged": *Studies*, p. 69.

174   "My desire for knowledge had not at the start been directed": *History*, p. 19.

175   "Find out all about dreams": quoted Ernest Jones, footnote added 1914, *Dreams*, p. 569.

page 175   "When, after passing through a narrow defile": *Dreams*, p. 122.

175   "portion of my own self-analysis": Preface to the Second Edition, *Dreams*, p. xxvi.

176   "I am deep in the dream book": Freud–Fliess, Feb. 9, 1898, *Origins*, p. 244.

176   "The dream book is irremediably at a standstill": Freud–Fliess, Oct. 23, 1898, *Origins*, p. 269.

176   "I have decided . . .": Freud–Fliess, May 28, 1899, *Origins*, p. 281.

176   "I am reasonable enough to recognise": Freud–Fliess, June 9, 1898, quoted Schur, "Day Residues," p. 74.

176   "The gap made by the big dream": Freud–Fliess, Aug. 1, 1899, quoted Schur, "Day Residues," p. 76.

177   "I don't know till this very day": Freud–Princess Marie Bonaparte, Jan. 3, 1937, quoted Schur, p. 487.

177   "I work at finishing off the dreams": Freud–Fliess, Aug. 1, 1899, *Origins*, p. 288.

177   "It was unusual for him to discuss his work": *Glory Reflected*, p. 67.

177   "Next month I shall begin the last": Freud–Fliess, Aug. 20, 1899, *Origins*, p. 292.

177   "my own dung-heap": Freud–Fliess, May 28, 1899, *Origins*, p. 281.

178   "Insight such as this": Preface to the Third (Revised) English Edition, *Dreams*, p. xxxii.

178   "The only dreams open to my choice": Preface to the First Edition, *Dreams*, p. xxiii.

178   "I might pursue the intricate trains of thought": *Dreams*, p. 206.

178   "there were some [thoughts] among them": *On Dreams*, p. 671.

178   "sexual preoccupations apparently play no role": André Breton, *Les Vases Communicants*, p. 32.

178   "I believe that if I have not analyzed my own dreams": Freud–André Breton (n.d.), quoted Jack J. Spector, *The Aesthetics of Freud: A Study in Psychoanalysis and Art*, p. 154 (afterward referred to as "Spector").

179   "were subject to an undesirable complication": Preface to the First Edition, *Dreams*, p. xxiii.

181   "Somewhere inside me": Freud–Fliess, Sept. 21, 1899, *Origins*, p. 298.

181   "It is no exaggeration to say": James Strachey, Editor's Introduction, *Dreams*, p. xv.

181   "not a leaf has stirred": Freud–Fliess, Mar. 11, 1900, *Origins*, p. 311.

181   "Seldom has an important book": Jones, I, p. 396, *361*.

181   "many details of a highly stimulative value": William Stern, review in *Zeitschrift für Psychologie und Physiologie der Sinnesorgane*, Vol. XXVI (1901), p. 131.

181   "farther in effort": W. Weygandt, review in *Zentralblatt für Nervenheilkunde*, Vol. XXIV (1901), pp. 548–49.

182   "I have readers here too": Freud–Fliess, Dec. 9, 1899, *Origins*, p. 304.

182   "an ironic and malicious journalistic distortion": Max Burckhard, review in *Die Zeit*, Jan. 6 and 13, 1900, footnote, *Origins*, p. 307.

182   "[The review] is unflattering": Freud–Fliess, Jan. 8, 1900, *Origins*, p. 307.

182   "but unfortunately also no respect": Freud–Fliess, Jan. 26, 1900, *Origins*, p. 309.

182   "I do not believe I shall get a review here": Freud–Fliess, Dec. 21, 1899, *Origins*, p. 306.

page 182   "He lent me his new book": Emil A. Gutheil, ed., *The Autobiography of Wilhelm Stekel: The Life Story of a Pioneer Psychoanalyst*, p. 105 (afterward referred to as "Stekel").

182   "retain this book": quoted Leo Goldhammer, "Herzl and Freud," *Herzl Year Book*, Vol. I (New York, 1958), p. 196.

183   "An appearance filled with glory": Simon, p. 274.

183   "This man has something to say to us": Phyllis Bottome, *Alfred Adler: Apostle of Freedom*, p. 69 (afterward referred to as "Bottome").

183   "like meeting the 'femme fatale' ": Sachs, p. 1.

183   "My psychiatric colleagues seem to have taken": Freud, Preface to the Second Edition, *Dreams*, p. xxv.

183   "by one of the profoundest": Havelock Ellis, *The World of Dreams*, p. vi.

184   "If its earlier function was to offer": Freud, Preface to the Sixth Edition, *Dreams*, p. xxix.

184   "In the pages that follow": *Dreams*, p. 1.

184   "the building of a huge structure": review in *The Nation*, Vol. XCVI, No. 2498 (May 15, 1913), p. 504.

184   "as one whose scientific judgment": review in *The Nation*, Vol. XCVI, No. 2498 (May 15, 1913), p. 505.

184   "Such a method would reduce": W. H. R. Rivers, *Conflict and Dream*, p. 6 (afterward referred to as "Rivers").

184   "Not only does it prune": G. Elliot Smith, Preface, Rivers, p. vii.

185   "To attempt—as Freud did—": Bertrand Russell, *Human Knowledge: Its Scope and Limits*, p. 60.

185   "precisely before the genuine dream-thought": Freud, Lecture XXIX, "Revision of the Theory of Dreams," *New Intro. Lectures*, p. 12.

185   "just beneath his reassuring bravado": Note 42, Fisher and Greenberg, p. 78.

185   "it has, of course, received the least attention": Freud, supplement to later German edition of *Dreams*, quoted A. A. Brill, *Basic Writings*, p. 186.

185   "The new century": Freud–Fliess, Jan. 8, 1900, *Origins*, p. 307.

10 Founding the Cause

190   "educators, pediatricians, sociologists": Sybylle Escalona, "Problems in Psycho-Analytic Research," *International Journal of Psycho-Analysis*, Vol. XXXIII (1952), p. 11.

190   "Today I have made a discovery": quoted Max Born, "Max Karl Ernst Ludwig Planck," *Obituary Notices of Fellows of The Royal Society*, Vol. VI (No. 17) (Nov. 1948), p. 161.

191   "let me tell you what a dirty-minded": quoted Vincent Brome, *Freud and His Early Circle: The Struggles of Psycho-Analysis*, p. 31 (afterward referred to as "Brome").

191   "I know that my work is odious": Freud–Fliess, Apr. 4, 1900, *Origins*, p. 316.

191   "In those days when one mentioned": Max Graf, "Reminiscences of Professor Sigmund Freud," *Psychoanalytic Quarterly*, Vol. XI (1942), p. 469 (afterward referred to as "Graf").

191   "If the patient loved his mother": quoted Peter F. Drucker, "What Freud Forgot," *Human Nature* (New York, Mar. 1979), p. 43 (afterward referred to as "Drucker").

page 191   "She listened outside the door": Rudolf von Urban–Jones, Oct. 8, 1950, Institute.

192   "Psychoanalytic teaching shifted the balance": L. S. Hearnshaw, "Psychology," in C. B. Cox and A. E. Dyson, eds., *The Twentieth Century Mind: History, Ideas and Literature in Britain*, Vol. I, 1900–1918, p. 236.

192   "there is nothing which man": Freud–Ludwig Binswanger, May 28, 1911, quoted Fritz Schmidl, "Sigmund Freud and Ludwig Binswanger," *Psychoanalytic Quarterly*, Vol. XXVIII (1959), p. 46.

193   "They may abuse my doctrines": quoted Jones, "Our Attitude Towards Greatness," read before American Psychoanalytic Association, Chicago, April, 28, 1956, printed Jones, *Centenary Addresses*, p. 46.

193   "I went from one prominent doctor": Bruno Walter, *Theme and Variations: An Autobiography*, p. 181 (afterward referred to as "Walter").

193   "professionally interested in a possible connection": Walter, p. 181.

193   "In short": Walter, p. 181.

193   "But I can't move my arm": Walter, p. 184.

193   "by dint of much effort": Walter, p. 184.

194   "not firmly established": Egon Gartenberg, *Mahler: The Man and His Music*, p. 173 (afterward referred to as "Gartenberg").

194   "I analyzed Mahler": quoted Theodor Reik, "The Haunting Melody," quoted Gartenberg, p. 174.

195   "The attitude of friends and acquaintances": Sachs, p. 71.

195   "The truth is that my father's respectable address": *Glory Reflected*, p. 24.

195   "the happiest women": George Eliot, Book Sixth, "The Great Temptation," *The Mill on the Floss*, Vol. III, p. 43.

195   "great kindliness and deep humanity": Sachs, p. 74.

196   "I felt as though I were despised": Freud, "Address to the Society of B'nai B'rith," on May 6, 1926 (1941 [1926]), *S. E.* Vol. XX, p. 273.

196   "After the exaltation and feverish activity": Freud–Fliess, Mar. 11, 1900, *Origins*, pp. 311–312.

197   "for the sake of any patient": Freud–Fliess, Aug. 7, 1901, *Origins*, p. 333.

197   "When father came down from his room": *Glory Reflected*, p. 62.

197   "At about this time of year": Freud–Pfister, June 13, 1909, Pfister Letters, p. 25.

197   "enthusiastic appreciation of nature": Schur, p. 415.

197   "I am sitting in my room in Grinzing": Freud–Arnold Zweig, May 2, 1935, Ernst L. Freud, ed., *The Letters of Sigmund Freud and Arnold Zweig*, p. 106 (afterward referred to as "Zweig Letters").

198   "I should love to go to our lovely Italy": Freud–Fliess, Apr. 3, 1898, *Origins*, p. 251.

198   "the evenings and mornings are delightful": Freud–Fliess, June 12, 1900, *Origins*, p. 321.

198   "The first climb of the season": Freud–the Family, Apr. 20, 1905, *Letters*, p. 257, *247*.

198   "I have given up [mountain] climbing": Freud–Fliess, June 22, 1894, quoted Schur, p. 51.

198   "Monday morning I climbed the Rax": Freud–Fliess, May 25, 1899, quoted Schur, p. 194.

198   "delightful solitude—mountain, forest, flowers": Freud–the Family, Apr. 20, 1905, *Letters*, p. 257, *248*.

page 198   "Yesterday after dragging my weary bones": Freud–Jung, July 19, 1909, *Freud/Jung Letters*, p. 242.

199   "Although father loved climbing": *Glory Reflected*, p. 85.

199   "a wonderful wood full of ferns": Freud–Fliess, June 12, 1897, *Origins*, p. 210.

199   "Alpine roses coming right down to the roadway": Freud–Fliess, July 4, 1901, *Origins*, p. 331.

199   "he would run to it": *Glory Reflected*, p. 59.

200   "Literary work there is nothing but a pleasure": Freud–Abraham, June 7, 1908, Abraham Letters, p. 40.

200   "Father and Uncle Alexander": *Glory Reflected*, p. 59.

200   "the wish to go to Rome": *Dreams*, p. 196.

201   "Learning the eternal laws of life": Freud–Fliess, Aug. 27, 1899, *Origins*, p. 294.

201   "at the season of the year": *Dreams*, p. 194.

201   "if we take [Freud] on his own principles": Peter J. R. Dempsey, *Freud, Psychoanalysis, Catholicism*, p. 50.

201   "as synonymous with intolerance": Choisy, p. 91.

202   "to break with my strict scruples": Freud–Fliess, Mar. 11, 1902, *Origins*, p. 342.

203   "By parapraxes, then, I understand": Freud, "The Claims of Psycho-Analysis to Scientific Interest" (1913), *S. E.* Vol. XIII, p. 166.

204   "able to prove . . .": Freud–Fliess, Aug. 26, 1898, *Origins*, p. 261.

204   "How can I make this seem credible": Freud–Fliess, Sept. 22, 1898, *Origins*, p. 265.

204   "when someone makes a slip of the tongue": Freud, "Psycho-Analysis and the Ascertaining of Truth in Courts of Law" (1906). Lecture delivered to Prof. Löffler's Seminar in June 1906, *Collected Papers*, Vol. II, p. 15 (afterward referred to as "Psycho-Analysis in Courts of Law").

205   "contributed towards circumscribing the field": Psycho-Analysis in Courts of Law, p. 15.

205   "We made no scruples, for instance": A. A. Brill, interpolation in his English translation of *The Psychopathology of Everyday Life*, in *The Basic Writings of Sigmund Freud*, p. 57.

205   "I go to a locked drawer": Havelock Ellis, review in *Journal of Mental Science*, Vol. LIII (Oct. 1907), p. 832.

206   "We shall, I think, have stated the facts": Freud, *The Psychopathology of Everyday Life: Forgetting, Slips of the Tongue, Bungled Actions, Superstitions and Errors* (1901), *S. E.* Vol. VI, p. 7 (afterward referred to as "*Everyday Life*").

206   "The view of 'slips of the tongue' ": *Everyday Life*, p. 100.

206   "*Exoriar(e) Aliquis nostris ex ossibus ultor*" ("Let someone [*aliquis*] arise from my bones as an avenger!"): Virgil, *Aeneid*, IV, 625, quoted *Everyday Life*, p. 9.

207   "He would have had no difficulty": Sebastiano Timpanaro, *The Freudian Slip: Psycho-Analysis and Textual Criticism*, p. 44.

208   "The question can indeed now pose itself": Frederic Raphael, review of *The Freudian Slip* by Sebastiano Timpanaro, in *The New Statesman*, July 9, 1976, p. 51.

209   "if a certain Böcklin": Freud–Fliess, Mar. 11, 1902, *Origins*, p. 343.

page 209   "Congratulations and bouquets keep pouring in": Freud–Fliess, Mar. 11, 1902, *Origins*, p. 344.

209   "His friend Professor Herzig": Ernst Freud–Jones, Nov. 8, 1952, Institute.

211   "His method of exposition": Wittels, p. 129.

211   "Swear": William Shakespeare, *The Tragedy of Hamlet: Prince of Denmark*, I, v (afterward referred to as *"Hamlet"*).

211   "O day and night, but this is wondrous strange": *Hamlet*, I, v.

211   "And therefore as a stranger give it welcome": *Hamlet*, I, v.

211   "So I, too, shall ask you first": quoted, Reik, *Thirty Years*, p. 21.

211   "If you attack the symptom directly": quoted Sachs, p. 45.

211   "For instance the experimenter says 'Horse' ": quoted Sachs, p. 43.

211   "If I am not mistaken": quoted Sachs, p. 44.

211   "Then you have unintentionally": quoted Sachs, p. 44.

212   "His simplicity and earnestness": Emma Goldman, *Living My Life*, Vol. I, p. 173.

212   "We cannot help thinking": quoted Wittels, p. 130.

212   "To many physicians, even today": "On Psychotherapy," p. 257.

212   "I am actually not at all a man of science": Freud–Fliess, Feb. 1, 1900, quoted Schur, p. 201.

213   "I was the apostle of Freud": Stekel, p. 106.

213   "On the first night": Stekel, p. 116.

213   "Once a year we had a business meeting": Sachs, p. 59.

214   "had driven an adit deep into the mental life": Wittels, p. 131.

214   "to marry his [youngest] daughter": quoted Gunther Stuhlmann, ed., *The Journals of Anaïs Nin: 1931–1934*, p. 279.

214   "Now I am more than ever in need": Sandor Ferenczi–Freud, Jan. 18, 1908, Sandor Ferenczi, "Ten Letters to Freud," *International Journal of Psycho-Analysis*, Vol. XXX, Part 4 (1949), p. 243.

215   "were held together by their common discontent": Hermann Nunberg, Introduction, *Minutes*, I, p. xx.

215   "They knew that man is a social being": Nunberg, Introduction, *Minutes*, I, p. xxvii.

215   "I was not highly impressed": Ernest Jones, *Free Associations: Memories of a Psycho-Analyst*, p. 169 (afterward referred to as "Jones, *Free Associations*").

216   *Un parterre des rois*: quoted Jones, I, p. 376, 342.

216   "We foregathered in Freud's waiting room": Wittels, p. 133.

216   "This is the kind of paper": reported Kardiner, p. 50.

216   "This may all very well be so": Jerome S. Bruner–Jones, Oct. 12, 1955, Institute.

217   "Does reading menus fill your stomach?": Freud–Theodor Reik, quoted Reik, *Thirty Years*, p. 22.

217   "We won't be divided into an Upper House": quoted Sachs, p. 50.

217   "When a speaker's remarks": Nunberg, Introduction, *Minutes*, I, p. xxvi.

217   "There was an atmosphere of the foundation": Graf, p. 471.

218   "enlist many partisans": Freud–Putnam, June 25, 1912, Putnam Letters, p. 143.

218   "We can say with pride": Stekel, announcement of 3rd Psycho-Analytical Congress, *Zentralblatt für Psychoanalyse*, Vol. I (1911), p. 53.

page

quoted C. P. Oberndorf, *A History of Psychoanalysis in America*, p. 110 (afterward referred to as "Oberndorf").

218   "We possess the truth": Freud–Ferenczi, May 13, 1913, quoted Brome, p. 132.

219   "convictions of the truth of his theories": Ellenberger, p. 463.

219   "Everyone here is staggered": Jung–Freud, Jan. 18, 1911, *Freud/Jung Letters*, p. 385.

219   "really . . . an arrogant ass": Freud–Jung, Mar. 3, 1911, *Freud/Jung Letters*, p. 399.

219   "No great loss . . .": Freud–Jung, Nov. 2, 1911, *Freud/Jung Letters*, p. 453.

219   "highly intelligent . . .": Freud–Jung, Nov. 25, 1910, *Freud/Jung Letters*, p. 373.

219   "the Adlerian buffoons": Freud–Ferenczi, Sept. 16, 1930, *Letters*, p. 400, *401*.

220   "can no more be created": Wilhelm Fliess, quoted Ernst Kris, Introduction, *Origins*, p. 7.

220   "These rhythms": Fliess, quoted Kris, Introduction, *Origins*, p. 7.

220   "a sample of that type of insolence": Freud–Fliess, Apr. 14, 1898, quoted Schur, p. 144.

220   "You will see in this another confirmation": Freud–Jung, Apr. 16, 1909, *Freud/Jung Letters*, p. 220.

220   "Thus it was plausible to suppose": Freud–Jung, Apr. 16, 1909, *Freud/Jung Letters*, p. 219.

220   "Freud cannot be characterized": Schur, p. 233.

220   "really uncanny how often": Freud–Jung, Apr. 16, 1909, *Freud/Jung Letters*, p. 219.

221   "with fatalistic licence": Freud–Jung, Apr. 16, 1909, *Freud/Jung Letters*, p. 219.

221   "According to the large conception": *Pleasure Principle*, p. 45.

221   "that 'the thought-reader merely reads . . .' ": Freud–Fliess, Aug. 7, 1901, *Origins*, p. 334.

221   "On that occasion Freud showed": Fliess, *In eigener Sache; gegen Otto Weininger und Hermann Swoboda*, quoted footnote, *Origins*, p. 324.

222   "perhaps the only occasion in Freud's life": Jones, I, p. 346, *315*.

222   "The facts of the matter seem to me": Freud–Fliess, Jan. 4, 1898, *Origins*, p. 242.

222   "drawn somewhat apart from each other": Freud–Fliess, Aug. 7, 1901, *Origins*, p. 334.

222   "And now for the most important thing of all": Freud–Fliess, Aug. 7, 1901, *Origins*, p. 334–335.

223   "I certainly had no intention": Freud–Fliess, Sept. 19, 1901, *Origins*, p. 337.

223   "a sick genius": quoted Kardiner, p. 47.

223   "glimpse into his unconscious": Wittels, p. 67.

223   "That's all I know about the matter": quoted Jones, I, p. 346, *315*.

224   "It is not our task to criticize": A. R. Pfennig, *Wilhelm Fliess und seine Nachentdecker: O. Weininger und H. Swoboda*, quoted Brome, p. 12.

224   "A reader, who is rarely your follower": Sigmund Freud, Eight Lines on Sigmund Freud's Calling Card, Oct. 2, 1904, in "The Fackel Archives," mimeographed (Vienna: Heinrich Hinterberger, 1973), quoted Thomas Szasz, *Karl Kraus and the Soul-Doctors: A Pioneer Critic*

page   *and His Criticism of Psychiatry and Psychoanalysis*, p. 20 (afterward referred to as "Szasz").

225   "That I find my name": Freud–Karl Kraus, Jan. 12, 1906, *Letters*, p. 259, *249*.

225   "accused of the most flagrant plagiarism": Freud–Kraus, Jan. 12, 1906, *Letters*, p. 259, *250*.

225   "absurd slander": Freud–Kraus, Jan. 12, 1906, *Letters*, p. 260, *250*.

11 Early Skirmishes

227   "It is certainly true that the dreamer": Freud–Fliess, Sept. 11, 1899, *Origins*, p. 297.

227   "I . . . found that their essence": *Auto. Study*, p. 66.

228   "Such a far-reaching agreement": Freud, *Wit and Its Relation to the Unconscious*, p. 126 (afterward referred to as *"Wit"*).

228   "as if I were his equal": Hirsch-Hyacinth in Heine's "Reisebilder," quoted *Wit*, p. 15.

228   "Hood once remarked": A. A. Brill, *Psychanalysis: Its Theories and Practical Application*, p. 334.

228   "Why, he is going to draw houses": quoted *Wit*, p. 44.

228   "It is a fragment of an analysis": Freud–Fliess, Jan. 25, 1901, *Origins*, p. 326.

229   "meet the gaze of an astonished public": Freud–Fliess, June 9, 1901 (unpublished), quoted Editor's Note, Freud, "Fragment of an Analysis of a Case of Hysteria" (1905 [1901]), *S. E.* Vol. VII, p. 4 (afterward referred to as "Dora").

229   "In the first place I wished to supplement": Dora, p. 114.

229   "be accused of giving information": Freud, Prefatory Remarks, Dora, p. 7.

229   "that case histories that are not": Freud at Scientific Meeting on Apr. 21, 1909, *Minutes*, II, p. 213.

230   "the case has opened smoothly": Freud–Fliess, Oct. 14, 1900, *Origins*, p. 325.

230   "a warm, but platonic, homosexual relationship": Jones, II, p. 287, *256*.

230   "sexual questions will be discussed": Freud, Prefatory Remarks, Dora, p. 9.

230   "were by no means disappointed": Dora, p. 59.

231   "The conclusion now presents itself": Freud, *Three Essays on the Theory of Sexuality* (1905), *S. E.* Vol. VII, p. 171 (afterward referred to as *"Three Essays"*).

232   "only be demonstrable in *children*": Three Essays, p. 172.

232   "a difficulty in the way of regarding children": Wittels, p. 106.

232   "The emotion of sex-love": Sanford Bell, "A Preliminary Study of the Emotion of Love between the Sexes," *American Journal of Psychology*, Vol. XIII, No. 3 (July 1902), p. 328.

233   "In brief, therefore, it must be concluded": Kline, p. 92.

233   "In the foreground we find the effects of seduction": Three Essays, p. 190.

234   "Among these [infantile] tendencies": *Three Essays*, p. 227.

234   "Forel stands as far below the level": Otto Soyka, review-essay in *Die Fackel*, 191 (Dec. 21, 1905), pp. 6–11, quoted Szasz, p. 28.

234   "Certainly no one can read these essays": "Three Contributions to

page   Sexual Theory," review in *British Medical Journal* (June 3, 1911), p. 1337.

235   "even a psychoanalyst may confess": Freud, "Analysis of a Phobia in a Five-Year-Old Boy" (1909), *S. E.* Vol. X, p. 6, (afterward referred to as "Little Hans").

235   "be told many things": Little Hans, p. 104.

235   "robbed of his innocence": Freud, Postscript (1922), Little Hans, p. 148.

235   "He declared that he was perfectly well": Postscript, Little Hans, p. 148.

236   "indeed the first true insight": Jung–Jones, quoted Jones–Putnam, June 1, 1909, Putnam Letters, p. 208.

236   "that it does not provide anything": Joseph Wolpe (of the department of neurology and psychiatry, University of Virginia School of Medicine, Charlottesville, Virginia) and Stanley Rachman (of the Institute of Psychiatry, Maudsley Hospital, London), "Psychoanalytic 'Evidence': A Critique Based on Freud's Case of Little Hans," *Journal of Nervous and Mental Disease*, Vol. CXXX, No. 8, p. 146.

236   "I well remember the first patient": Jones, "Reminiscent Notes on the Early History of Psycho-Analysis in English-Speaking Countries," *International Journal of Psycho-Analysis*, Vol. XXVI, Parts I and II (1945), p. 9.

237   "was based on the illogical expectation": Hannah S. Decker, "The Medical Reception of Psychoanalysis in Germany, 1894–1907: Three Brief Studies," *Bulletin of History of Medicine*, Vol. XLV (Baltimore, 1971), p. 480.

237   "When I first read Freud's writings": C. G. Jung, "Freud's Theory of Hysteria: A Reply to Aschaffenburg" (afterward referred to as "Jung, 'Reply' "), in *Freud and Psychoanalysis, Collected Works*, Vol. IV, p. 7 (afterward referred to as "Jung, *Freud and Psychoanalysis* ").

238   "How in the world were you able to bear": quoted Jung, *Memories*, p. 128.

238   "In a way I regarded the woman": Jung, *Memories*, p. 128.

238   "My scientific conscience did not allow me": Jung–Christian Jensen, May 29, 1933, Gerhard Adler, ed., *C. G. Jung: Letters*, p. 122 (afterward referred to as "Jung Letters").

239   "that everything I have said": Freud–Jung, Apr. 11, 1906, *Freud/Jung Letters*, p. 3.

239   "on the whole [a] very moderate and cautious criticism": Jung, "Reply," p. 3.

239   "Freud has not examined all the hysterias": Jung, "Reply," p. 4.

239   "may not be entirely in agreement": Jung–Freud, Oct. 5, 1906, *Freud/Jung Letters*, p. 4.

240   "building explanations of complex phenomena": Meyer Schapiro, "Leonardo and Freud: An Art-Historical Study," *Journal of the History of Ideas*, Vol. XVII, No. 2 (Apr. 1956), p. 177.

240   "the first emissary to reach the lonely man": Freud–Eitingon, Jan. 7, 1913, quoted Martin Grotjahn, "Sigmund Freud and the Art of Letter Writing," *Journal of the American Medical Association*, Vol. CC, No. 1 (Apr. 3, 1967), p. 18.

240   "The day after our arrival": Binswanger, p. 2.

240   "holding himself more like a soldier": *Glory Reflected*, p. 109.

page 240   "We met at one o'clock in the afternoon": Jung, *Memories*, p. 146.

240   "We talked about everything": Jung, quoted *Time*, Feb. 14, 1955.

240   "Above all, Freud's attitude towards the spirit": Jung, *Memories*, p. 147.

241   "Yes, so it is": Jung, *Memories*, p. 147.

241   "Apparently a duel was planned": Freud–Jung, Apr. 14, 1907, *Freud/Jung Letters*, p. 33.

241   "Whether you have been or will be lucky": Freud–Jung, Sept. 2, 1907, *Freud/Jung Letters*, p. 82.

241   "That voice was yours": Freud–Jung, Sept. 2, 1907, *Freud/Jung Letters*, p. 82.

241   "Unfortunately, he made the mistake": Jones, II, p. 126, *112*.

241   "uncommonly far-reaching and significant analogies": Jung, "The Freudian Theory of Hysteria" (1908), translated from "Die Freud'sche Hysterietheorie," *Monatsschrift für Psychiatrie und Neurologie* (Berlin), XXIII (1908), in Jung, *Freud and Psychoanalysis*, p. 23.

242   "I now realize that I am as replaceable": Freud–Jung, Apr. 7, 1907, *Freud/Jung Letters*, p. 27.

242   "I don't know whether you're right": Freud–Enrico Morselli, 1926, quoted Friedrich Heer, "Freud, the Viennese Jew," in Jonathan Miller, ed. *Freud: The Man, His World, His Influence*, p. 15 (afterward referred to as "Miller").

242   "The great Jewish minds": Edmund Wilson, *To the Finland Station*, p. 306 (afterward referred to as "Wilson").

243   "Our Aryan comrades": Freud–Abraham, Dec. 26, 1908, Abraham Letters, p. 64.

243   "anti-semitic condescension towards me": Freud–Putnam, July 8, 1915, Putnam Letters, p. 189.

243   "In brief, analysts were predominantly upwardly mobile": W. E. Henry, J. H. Sims, and S. L. Spray, *The Fifth Profession (Becoming a Psychotherapist)*, reported Fisher and Greenberg, p. 298.

243   "once the English have become acquainted": Freud–Jung, Dec. 8, 1907, *Freud/Jung Letters*, p. 102.

243   "I don't believe that Germany": Freud–Jung, Aug. 18, 1907, *Freud/Jung Letters*, p. 77.

244   "The interest [there] is very great at present": Jung–Freud, Feb. 15, 1908, *Freud/Jung Letters*, p. 118.

244   "Why don't you come to Vienna": A. A. Brill, "Reflections, Reminiscences of Sigmund Freud," *Medical Leaves*, Vol. III (Chicago, 1940), p. 19 (afterward referred to as "Brill, 'Reflections' ").

244   "They are doing the Freud work there": A. A. Brill, "The Introduction and Development of Freud's Work in the United States," *American Journal of Sociology*, Vol. XLV, No. 3 (Nov. 1939), p. 318 (afterward referred to as "Brill, 'Development of Freud's Work' ").

244   "Under the wise guidance of Bleuler": Brill, "Development of Freud's Work," p. 318.

244   "The magnitude of this task": Brill, "His Past," p. 539.

245   "atrocious 'English' ": Putnam–Jones, Sept. 14, 1910, Putnam Letters, p. 229.

245   "conscientious rather than beautiful": Freud–Putnam, Dec. 5, 1909, Putnam Letters, p. 90.

246   "I wish to inform you": quoted Brome, p. 29.

page 246   "the obligation to speak": Memorandum to Scientific Meeting on Feb. 12, 1908, *Minutes*, I, p. 314.

246   "Personal invectives and attacks": Isidor Sadger's motion at Scientific Meeting on Feb. 5, 1908, *Minutes*, I, p. 300.

246   "If the situation is such": Freud at Scientific Meeting on Feb. 5, 1908, *Minutes*, I, p. 301.

247   "intellectual communism": Paul Federn's motion at Scientific Meeting on Feb. 5, 1908, *Minutes*, I, p. 299.

247   "considered it his duty": Wilhelm Stekel at Scientific Meeting on Feb. 5, 1908, *Minutes*, I, p. 302.

247   "Every intellectual property set forth": Alfred Adler's motion as amended by Maximilian Steiner at Scientific Meeting on Feb. 5, 1908, *Minutes*, I, p. 303.

247   "From many quarters the followers of Freud's teachings": Jung, printed circular, posted ca. June 18–20, 1908, *Freud/Jung Letters*, p. 110.

248   "I remember vainly protesting": Jones, *Free Associations*, p. 165.

248   "make a better impression abroad": Freud–Jung, Feb. 18, 1908, *Freud/Jung Letters*, p. 122.

248   "It astonished me": Jones, II, p. 47, *43*.

248   "The chief features of his disorder": Freud, "Notes upon a Case of Obsessional Neurosis" (1909), *S. E.* Vol. X, p. 158 (afterward referred to as "Rat Man").

249   "It would not surprise me to hear": Rat Man, p. 169.

249   "Delivered without any notes": Jones, *Free Associations*, p. 166.

249   "Freud had no followers of any weight in Vienna": Jones, *Free Associations*, p. 166.

250   "I console myself with the thought": quoted Jones, *Free Associations*, p. 168.

250   "So you too are pleased with our meeting": Freud–Jung, May 3, 1908, *Freud/Jung Letters*, p. 144.

251   "No less than twenty doctors appeared": Abraham–Freud, Oct. 13, 1907, Abraham Letters, p. 11.

251   "In the course of the battle . . . I defended": Abraham–Freud, Apr. 4, 1908, Abraham Letters, p. 33.

251   "it acts like a red rag to a bull": Abraham–Freud, Nov. 10, 1908, Abraham Letters, p. 55.

251   "might advance in the second half of the winter": Abraham–Freud, Nov. 10, 1908, Abraham Letters, p. 56.

251   "becoming more and more convinced": Abraham–Freud, June 11, 1908, Abraham Letters, p. 41.

251   "Unless the most improbable changes take place": Freud–Abraham, Nov. 12, 1908, Abraham Letters, p. 58.

252   "There are still so few of us": Freud–Abraham, May 3, 1908, Abraham Letters, p. 34.

252   "as a Christian and a pastor's son": Freud–Abraham, May 3, 1908, Abraham Letters, p. 34.

252   "I deceived myself momentarily": Abraham–Freud, May 11, 1908, Abraham Letters, p. 36.

252   "I nurse a suspicion": Freud–Abraham, July 23, 1908, Abraham Letters, p. 46.

page 253 "much younger than when he came here": Freud–Mathilde Freud, postcard, Sept. 5, 1908, Library of Congress.

253 "overcome his vacillation": Freud–Abraham, Sept. 29, 1908, Abraham Letters, p. 51.

253 "My selfish purpose": Freud–Jung, Aug. 13, 1908, *Freud/Jung Letters*, p. 168.

253 "No, the dawn is not yet": Freud–Jung, Nov. 29, 1908, *Freud/Jung Letters*, p. 181.

253 "It's really too nice of him": Freud–Jung, Jan. 17, 1909, *Freud/Jung Letters*, p. 196.

254 "that our psychiatric work has been taken up": Freud–Oskar Pfister, Jan. 18, 1909, Pfister Letters, p. 15.

254 "the totally nonreligious Freud household": Anna Freud, Pfister Letters, p. 11.

254 "I am very much struck by the fact": Freud–Pfister, Feb. 9, 1909, Pfister Letters, p. 17.

254 "I apologised for my appearance": *Glory Reflected*, p. 166.

254 "If only one could get the better people": Freud–Pfister, July 12, 1909, Pfister Letters, p. 27.

255 "what can be stated as the direct outcome": Freud–Pfister, Mar. 30, 1909, Pfister Letters, p. 22.

255 "Public debate of psychoanalysis is hardly possible": Freud–Pfister, May 28, 1911, Pfister Letters, p. 50.

12 A Sortie to America

257 "From the cradle to the grave": Samuel White, president of the New York State Medical Society. Address on Insanity delivered before the New York State Medical Society, Feb. 7, 1844, quoted Oberndorf, p. 22.

257 "hysteria is frequently caused": quoted the American Psychiatric Association, *One Hundred Years of American Psychiatry*, p. 215.

257 "strove to go deep into his patient's bosom": Nathaniel Hawthorne, *The Scarlet Letter: A Romance*, p. 147 (afterward referred to as "Hawthorne").

257 "at some inevitable moment": Hawthorne, p. 148.

257 "The more we examine the mechanism of thought": Oliver Wendell Holmes, *Mechanism in Thought and Morals: An Address with Notes and Afterthoughts*, p. 57.

258 "an independent corroboration of Janet's views": William James, review in *Psychological Review*, Vol. I, No. 2 (March 1894), p. 199 (afterward referred to as "James").

258 "thorns in the spirit": James, p. 199.

258 for a patient to scream: Robert T. Edes, "The New England Invalid," Shattuck Lecture read before the Massachusetts Medical Society, June 11, 1895, printed *Boston Medical and Surgical Journal*, Vol. CXXXIII (1895), pp. 53–57, 77–81 and 101–107.

258 "In the wonderful explorations by Binet": William James, *The Varieties of Religious Experience: A Study in Human Nature*, being the Gifford Lectures on Natural Religion delivered at Edinburgh in 1901–1902, p. 234.

259 "In the relief of certain hysterias": William James in Lowell Lecture on psychopathology in 1896, quoted F. O. Matthiessen, *The James*

page

Family: including Selections from the writings of Henry James, Senior, William, Henry and Alice James, footnote p. 226.

259   "a man of science": *Dictionary of American Biography,* 1928–36, Vol. XV, p. 283.

259   "reacted with tragic bitterness": Marian C. Putnam, Foreword, Putnam Letters, p. xii.

259   "not that the 'psychoanalytic' method is useless": Putnam, "Recent Experiences in the Study and Treatment of Hysteria at the Massachusetts General Hospital; with Remarks on Freud's Methods of Treatment by 'Psychoanalysis,'" *Journal of Abnormal Psychology,* Vol. I (Apr. 1906), p. 35.

260   "To me it is clear": Jones–Freud, May 7, 1920, Institute.

260   "I heartily agree with you": Freud–Jones, Nov. 20, 1908, Colchester.

260   ". . . I am not very hopeful of the present wave of interest": Jones–Freud, Dec. 10, 1908, Colchester.

261   "I well remember the shiver": Jones, *Free Associations,* p. 189.

261   "William James couldn't come": Jones–Freud, Feb. 7, 1909, Colchester.

262   "a delightful old man": Jones–Freud, Feb. 7, 1909, Colchester.

262   "are peculiar to the Anglo-Saxon race": Jones–Freud, Feb. 7, 1909, Colchester.

262   "a series of fads or crazes": G. Stanley Hall, quoted William A. Koelsch, "Freud Discovers America," reprinted from *Virginia Quarterly Review,* Vol. XLVI, No. 1 (Winter 1970), p. 117 (afterward referred to as "Koelsch").

262   "a publicist for research": Koelsch, p. 117.

262   "too many outsiders got in": quoted Koelsch, p. 119.

263   "Although I have not the honor": Hall–Freud, Dec. 15, 1908, quoted Koelsch, p. 121.

263   "Janet, who has visited this country": Hall–Freud, Apr. 13, 1909, Clark University, Worcester, Mass.

263   "not wealthy enough": Freud–Jung, Dec. 30, 1908, *Freud/Jung Letters,* p. 193.

263   "I must admit that this has thrilled me": Freud–Jung, Mar. 9, 1909, *Freud/Jung Letters,* p. 210.

263   "Perhaps it will annoy some people in Berlin": Freud–Abraham, Mar. 9, 1909, Abraham Letters, p. 75.

263   "I have some misgivings": Freud–Hall, May 2, 1909, quoted Koelsch, p. 122.

263   "a wide and deep interest in your coming": Freud–Hall, Aug. 9, 1909, quoted Koelsch, p. 122.

264   "changes my whole feeling about the trip": Freud–Pfister, June 13, 1909, Pfister Letters, p. 25.

264   "Such a beginning will take you far": Freud–Jung, June 18, 1909, *Freud/Jung Letters,* p. 234.

264   "the invitation is the main thing": Freud–Jung, June 18, 1909, *Freud/Jung Letters,* p. 234.

264   "I am finding it very difficult": Freud–Jung, June 30, 1909, *Freud/Jung Letters,* p. 238.

264   "But I have asked for so much money": Freud–Jung, July 7, 1909, *Freud/Jung Letters,* p. 239.

265   "Afterward he said to me that he was convinced": Jung, *Memories,* p. 153.

265   "[It] was surely provoked": Freud–Binswanger, Jan. 1, 1913, Binswanger, p. 49.

page 265 "seemed to be mostly concerned with cares": Jones, II, p. 62, 55.

265 "Freud had a dream": Jung, *Memories*, p. 154.

265 "Won't they get a surprise": quoted E. A. Bennet, *C. G. Jung*, p. 40 (afterward referred to as "Bennet").

265 "How ambitious you are": quoted Bennet, p. 41.

265 "Me? I'm the most humble of men": quoted Bennet, p. 41.

266 "That's a big thing": quoted Bennet, p. 41.

266 "a magnified Prater": Jones, II, p. 62, 56.

266 "transfer the difficulty to the side of the hearers": Freud–Hall, Sept. 1, 1909, quoted Koelsch, p. 123.

266 "plump, jolly, good-natured and extremely ugly": Jung–Emma Jung, Sept. 6, 1909, Jung, *Memories*, p. 336.

266 "The house is furnished in an incredibly amusing fashion": Jung–Emma Jung, Sept. 6, 1909, Jung, *Memories*, p. 336.

267 "In the morning, before the time had come": Freud, "Sandor Ferenczi" (1933), *S. E.* Vol. XXII, p. 227.

267 "In Europe I felt as though I were despised": *Auto. Study*, p. 52.

267 "If it is a merit to have brought": First Lecture, Clark Lectures, p. 9.

267 *"our hysterical patients suffer from reminiscences"*: First Lecture, Clark Lectures, p. 16.

268 "Yet every single hysteric": First Lecture, Clark Lectures, p. 17.

268 "not possible to make them much clearer": First Lecture, Clark Lectures, p. 20.

268 "complete theories do not fall": First Lecture, Clark Lectures, p. 20.

268 "I was held back": Third Lecture, Clark Lectures, p. 33.

268 "would not reject the results": Third Lecture, Clark Lectures, p. 39.

268 "arrogance of consciousness": Third Lecture, Clark Lectures, p. 39.

269 "exactly what I have just told you": Fourth Lecture, Clark Lectures, p. 42.

269 "You can, if you like": Fourth Lecture, Clark Lectures, p. 48.

269 "The neuroses have no psychical content": Fifth Lecture, Clark Lectures, p. 50.

269 "a certain portion of the repressed libidinal impulses": Fifth Lecture, Clark Lectures, p. 54.

269 "I must thank you for your invitation": Fifth Lecture, Clark Lectures, p. 55.

269 "a tremendous amount of ceremony": Jung–Emma Jung, Sept. 14, 1909, Jung, *Memories*, p. 338.

270 "Sigmund Freud of the University of Vienna": quoted Koelsch, p. 127.

270 "This is the first official recognition": quoted Koelsch, p. 127.

270 "We are gaining ground here": Jung–Emma Jung, Sept. 8, 1909, Jung, *Memories*, p. 337.

270 "an ordinary reader would gather": quoted Jones, II, p. 63, 57.

270 "by no means atypical": Jones, II, p.63, 57.

270 "I cannot pretend to have verified": Putnam, "Personal Impressions of Sigmund Freud and His Work, with Special Reference to his Recent Lectures at Clark University," *Journal of Abnormal Psychology*, Vol. IV (Dec. 1909–Jan. 1910), pp. 293–310 and (Feb.–Mar. 1910), pp. 372–379, here p. 379 (afterward referred to as "Putnam, 'Personal Impressions'")

270 "for one day in order to see": William James–Theodore Flournoy, Sept. 28, 1909, Henry James, ed., *The Letters of William James*, Vol. II, p. 327 (afterward referred to as "James Letters").

page 270   "I shall never forget one little scene . . .": *Auto. Study*, p. 52.

271   "And he put his hand to his breast pocket": Jung–Virginia Payne, July 23, 1949, Jung Letters, I, p. 531.

271   "with his arm around my shoulder": Jones, II, p. 64, 57.

271   "The future of psychology belongs to your work": quoted Jones, II, p. 64, 57.

271   "I strongly suspect Freud": James–Professor Mary W. Calkins, Sept. 19, 1909, Ralph Barton Perry, *The Thought and Character of William James; As revealed in unpublished correspondence and notes, together with his published writings*, Vol. II, p. 123.

271   "I hope that Freud and his pupils": James–Flournoy, Sept. 28, 1909, James Letters, p. 327.

271   "William James was impressed": quoted Koelsch, p. 126.

271   "that James's well-known affinity": Koelsch, p. 126.

272   "spoke of his works": Worcester *Gazette*, Sept. 6–11, 1909, quoted Ward Cromer and Paula Anderson, "Freud's Visit to America: Newspaper Coverage," *Journal of the History of the Behavioral Sciences*, Vol. VI (1970), p. 349 (afterward referred to as "Cromer and Anderson").

272   "developed his method of psychic analysis": Worcester *Telegram* (Sept. 8, 1909), quoted Cromer and Anderson, p. 350.

272   "Conference Brings Savants together": Worcester *Telegram* (Sept. 12, 1909).

272   "enthusiastic over the sacrifice": Boston *Transcript* (Sept. 8, 1909), quoted Cromer and Anderson, p. 351.

272   "One sees at a glance": Boston *Transcript* (Sept. 11, 1909), quoted Cromer and Anderson, p. 352.

273   "certainly gave his hearers much food for thought": Editorial, "Twentieth Anniversary of Clark University," *Boston Medical and Surgical Journal*, Vol. CLXI, No. 12 (Sept. 16, 1909), p. 412.

273   "Because the newpaper coverage was limited": Cromer and Anderson, p. 353.

273   "I remember the first time": Freud–Jones, Feb. 24, 1912, Colchester.

273   "Let the old fellow go first": quoted Brome, p. 108.

273   sending a tourist postcard: Freud–Sophie Freud, Sept. 13, 1909, Library of Congress.

273   "Abe, Freud, Ferenczi and Jung": "Kindest Regards": postcard from Brill, Freud, Ferenczi and Jung–Mrs. Brill, Sept. 13, 1909, Library of Congress.

274   "Dr. James Putnam arrived from Boston": Putnam Camp Log Book, Sept. 16, 1909, quoted George E. Gifford, Jr., "Freud and the Porcupine," *Harvard Medical Alumni Bulletin*, Vol. XLVI, No. 4 (Mar.–Apr. 1972), p. 29 (afterward referred to as "Gifford").

274   "It is four weeks today": Freud–Freud family, Sept. 16, 1909, Adirondack Museum, Blue Mountain Lake, N.Y.

275   "it was helpful to provide a lightning conductor": Jones, II, p. 66, 59.

275   "They started the climb up a rather gentle hill": Joseph T. Wearn, quoted Gifford, p. 30.

275   "very meaningful for our work": Freud–Mathilde Hollitscher, Sept. 23, 1909, Library of Congress.

276   "East, West; Home Best": Freud–Mathilde Hollitscher, Sept. 23, 1909, Library of Congress.

page 276   "I confront the despiritualized furniture": Freud–Jung, Apr. 16, 1909, *Freud/Jung Letters*, p. 218.

276   "I can see that you two are not to be held back": Freud–Ferenczi, May 11, 1911, quoted editorial note, *Freud/Jung Letters*, p. 421.

276   "In matters of occultism": Freud–Jung, June 15, 1911, *Freud/Jung Letters*, p. 429.

276   "I am not one of those who dismiss": Freud–Hereward Carrington, July 24, 1921, *Letters*, p. 339, *334*.

277   "By it you would be throwing a bomb": Freud–Ferenczi, Mar. 20, 1925, quoted Jones, III, p. 421, *394*.

278   "[He] produced the following argument": Jones–Putnam, Aug. 14, 1910, Putnam Letters, p. 225.

278   "some such formal move": Jones–Putnam, Sept. 9, 1910, Putnam Letters, p. 227.

278   "America is the most grandiose experiment": quoted Sachs, p. 84.

278   "Yes, America is gigantic": quoted, Jones, *Free Associations*, p. 191.

278   "an honest boy when I knew him": Freud–Jones, Mar. 8, 1920, Colchester.

278   "the mad and wicked side . . .": Freud–Stefan Zweig, Feb. 7, 1931, *Letters*, p. 401, *402*.

278   "He foresaw the coming storm": Wittels, p. 137.

279   "You should talk more clearly": quoted Wortis, p. 844.

279   "Quite particularly often we find in American physicians": Freud, "Introduction to the Special Psychopathology Number of *The Medical Review of Reviews*" (1930), *S. E.* Vol XXI, p. 254.

13 First Defections

280   "One of the most agreeable phantasies": Freud–Pfister, Oct. 4, 1909, Pfister Letters, p. 29.

280   "that precisely for this reason": *History*, p. 32.

281   "I often fear that when the triumph will come": Freud–Brill, May 2, 1909, quoted Brill, "Reflections," p. 20.

281   "Indeed we must conclude": Fisher and Greenberg, p. 285.

281   "I have many limitations as an analyst": quoted Kardiner, p. 51.

281   "Since [Freud] had not been analyzed himself": Raymond de Saussure, "Sigmund Freud" (1956), *Schweizerische Zeitschrift für Psychologie und ihre Anwendungen*, 15 (1956), pp. 136–39, in Ruitenbeek, p. 359.

281   "This impatience": Max Schur–Ernest Jones, n.d., Institute.

281   "dates, the text of dreams": Freud, "Recommendations for Physicians on the Psycho-Analytic Method of Treatment," first published in *Zentralblatt*, Bd. II (1912), *Collected Papers*, Vol. II, p. 326.

281   "the name (1) of a procedure": Freud, "Two Encyclopaedia Articles" (1923 [1922]), *S. E.* Vol. XVIII, p. 235.

283   "Nothing appealed less": Sachs, p. 34.

283   "the household gave an impression": Sachs, p. 19.

283   "Father, aware of this power": *Glory Reflected*, p. 39.

283   "rather a stern, serious face": *Glory Reflected*, p. 192.

284   "Nervous? I couldn't afford to be nervous": Martha Freud–Ella and Theodor Reik, quoted Reik, *Fragment of a Great Confession: A Psychoanalytic Autobiography*, p. 373.

284   "A spirit of congeniality": Brill, "Reflections," p. 21.

page 284   "well advised to withdraw to his tent": Field Marshal Montgomery, "The Conduct of War," privately circulated.

285   "With sixty seconds' worth of distance run": Rudyard Kipling, "If."

285   "Oh, he's crazy!": Kardiner, p. 46.

285   "You have probably heard": quoted Franz Alexander, Samuel Eisenstein and Martin Grotjahn, eds., *Psychoanalytic Pioneers*, p. 336 (afterward referred to as *"Psychoanalytic Pioneers"*).

285   "This is not a topic for discussion": quoted David Stafford-Clark, *What Freud Really Said*, p. 21.

285   "The discussion mainly consisted of a number": Abraham–Freud, Oct. 18, 1910, Abraham Letters, p. 93.

285   "The situation recalled what was actually put in practice": Freud, Lecture XXXIV, "Explanations, Application and Orientations," *New Intro. Lectures*, p. 137.

285   "Only Raimann from Vienna stood out": Abraham–Freud, Oct. 18, 1910, Abraham Letters, p. 93.

285   "Genuine criticism of Freud's work": Bernard Hart, "The Psychology of Freud and his School," read before British Psychological Society, Oxford, May 7, 1910, printed *Journal of Mental Science*, Vol. LVI (July 1910), pp. 450 and 452.

287   "By all means we should concede more": Karl Kraus, *Die Fackel*, No. 239 (Dec. 31, 1907), p. 34, quoted Szasz, p. 29.

287   "The speaker takes off from the question": Dr. Wittels, at Scientific Meeting, Jan. 12, 1910, *Minutes*, II, p. 382.

287   "the *Presse* is the father's organ": Dr. Wittels, at Scientific Meeting, Jan. 12, 1910, *Minutes*, II, p. 384.

288   "Furtmüller would like to put forward": C. Furtmüller, at Scientific Meeting, Jan. 12, 1910, *Minutes*, II, p. 393.

288   "the further admonition": Freud, at Scientific Meeting, Apr. 14, 1910, *Minutes*, II, p. 476.

288   "entirely incapacitated and completely dependent": Freud, Wolf-Man Case, p. 7.

289   "I can remember, as though I saw them today": The Wolf-Man, "Recollections," Gardiner, p. 139.

289   "This proposal disconcerted us": The Wolf-Man, "Recollections," Gardiner, p. 137.

289   "Had Professor Freud": The Wolf-Man to Muriel Gardiner, Oct. 23, 1970, quoted editorial footnote, Gardiner, p. 89.

289   "For twenty-four hours now": quoted The Wolf-Man, "The Memoirs of the Wolf-Man" (afterward referred to as "The Wolf-Man, 'Memoirs'"), Gardiner, p. 85.

289   "During these first months in analysis": The Wolf-Man, "Memoirs," Gardiner, p. 83.

290   "I should myself be glad to know": Freud, Wolf-Man Case, p. 97.

290   "I must admit that the answer": Freud, Wolf-Man Case, p. 97.

290   "then Freud's polemics with Adler and Jung": Charles Rycroft, review "Not So Much a Treatment, More a Way of Life," *New York Review of Books*, Vol. XVII, No. 6 (Oct. 21, 1971).

291   "If I had to say which of us took the lead": Jones, *Free Associations*, p. 214.

291   "about six or eight months ago": Jones–Freud, Oct. 17, 1909, Colchester.

page 291   "Shortly put, my resistances have sprung": Jones–Freud, Dec. 18, 1909, Colchester.

292   "What happened was that Freud abandoned": Thomas S. Szasz, "Freud as a Leader," *Antioch Review*, Vol. XXIII, No. 2 (Summer 1963), p. 134.

292   "I considered it necessary to form": *History*, p. 43.

292   "It appeared to me necessary to create": Freud–Eugen Bleuler, Sept. 28, 1910, Franz Alexander and Sheldon T. Selesnick, "Freud–Bleuler Correspondence," *Archives of General Psychiatry*, Vol. XII, 1965, p. 2 (afterward referred to as "Bleuler Letters").

292   "First, the need to present to the public": Freud–Bleuler, Oct. 16, 1910, Bleuler Letters, p. 4.

293   "the future isolation of psychoanalysis": Bleuler Letters, p. 1.

293   "it was against their principles": Jones, II, p. 79, *72*.

293   "There is a difference between us": Bleuler–Freud, Oct. 19, 1910, Bleuler Letters, p. 5.

294   "the principle 'all or nothing' ": Bleuler–Freud, Mar. 11, 1911, Bleuler Letters, p. 5.

294   "Scientifically I still do not understand": Bleuler–Freud, Nov. 5, 1913, Bleuler Letters, p. 6.

294   "the most important man": Drucker, p. 40.

295   "looked round my modest abode": Freud, "The Future Prospects of Psycho-Analytic Therapy" (1910), *S. E.* Vol. XI, p. 146 (afterward referred to as "Future Prospects").

295   "I hope you will have formed an impression": "Future Prospects," p. 146.

296   "Freud was too mistrustful": Jones, *Free Associations*, p. 214.

296   "the Siegfried of the Burghölzli": Wittels, p. 187.

296   "was the first indication I had": Jones, *Free Associations*, p. 215.

296   "I still have not got over": Freud–Pfister, Mar. 17, 1910, Pfister Letters, p. 35.

296   "I no longer get any pleasure from [them]": Freud–Abraham, Feb. 24, 1910, quoted Jones, II, p. 78, *71*.

297   "the door opened": Stekel, p. 128.

297   "My enemies would be willing": quoted Jones, II, p. 77, *69*.

297   "Most of you are Jews": Wittels, p. 140.

298   "The cultivation and promotion": Statutes of the International Psycho-Analytic Association, quoted *Freud/Jung Letters*, p. 568.

298   "With the Nuremberg *Reichstag*": Freud–Ferenczi, April 3, 1910, quoted Jones, II, p. 79, *71*.

298   "[He] does not think much of us": Wittels, p. 177.

298   "I wish I lived closer to Jung": Freud–Binswanger, Nov. 6, 1910, Binswanger, p. 26.

298   "When the empire I have founded is orphaned": Freud–Binswanger, Mar. 14, 1911, quoted Binswanger, p. 31.

299   "which is that the Zürichers": Eduard Hitschmann at Scientific Meeting on Apr. 6, 1910, *Minutes*, II, p. 467.

299   "The Zürichers are trained clinically": Wittels at Scientific Meeting on Apr. 6, 1910, *Minutes*, II, p. 468.

299   "About myself, I can only say": Freud–Silberstein, Apr. 1910, quoted Stanescu, p. 205.

300   "dominated by delusions": Judgment of the Royal Superior Country Court, Dresden, July 14, 1902, quoted Ida Macalpine and Richard A. Hunter, trans. and eds., Daniel Paul Schreber, *Memoirs of my Nervous*

page

Illness, p. 330 (afterward referred to as "Macalpine and Hunter").

300 "there sometimes appeared when I was in bed": Daniel Paul Schreber, *Memoirs of my Nervous Illness,* in Macalpine and Hunter, p. 190.

300 "So manifold were the symptoms": Introduction, Macalpine and Hunter, p. 8.

300 "People become paranoiac about things": Draft H. "Paranoia," enclosed with Freud–Fliess, Jan. 23, 1895, *Origins,* p. 109.

301 "a tartly written criticism": Jones, II, p. 306, *273.*

301 "What would Freud have made": Anthony Storr, "A Disciple's Chronicle," *The New York Times Book Review* (Aug. 5, 1979), p. 29.

302 "to prevent a scandal": Jones–Putnam, Jan. 13, 1911, Putnam Letters, p. 253.

302 "the conversation on the first morning": Emma Jung–Freud, Nov. 6, 1911, Jung Letters, p. 456.

303 "I remember that Dr. Freud pointed out to me": Putnam–Fanny Bowditch, Dec. 10, 1913, Putnam Letters, p. 40.

303 "And when Schreber boasts": Freud, Postscript (1912 [1911]), "Psychoanalytic Notes on an Autobiographical Account of a Case of Paranoia (Dementia Paranoides)" (1911), *S. E.* Vol. XII, p. 81.

303 "You convince me that I have not lived": Freud–Putnam, Sept. 29, 1910, Putnam Letters, p. 107.

303 "That old gentleman": Freud–Abraham, Dec. 18, 1910, Abraham Letters, p. 98.

303 "Although you are a decade older": Freud–Putnam, Dec. 5, 1909, Putnam Letters, p. 89.

304 "Though little known among us": Putnam, "Personal Impressions," p. 294.

304 "an act of vengeance": Freud–Jung, Apr. 27, 1911, *Freud/Jung Letters,* p. 419.

304 "left his youth far behind him": Freud, footnote to "James J. Putnam" (1919), *S. E.* Vol. XVII, p. 272.

304 "that philosophy provided insights": Putnam Letters, p. 43.

304 "I feel no need for a higher moral synthesis": Freud–Putnam, Aug. 18, 1910, Putnam Letters, p. 105.

305 "I can still vividly remember": Pfister, *Some Applications of Psycho-Analysis,* pp. 178–9.

305 "Putnam's philosophy is like a beautiful table centre": quoted Jones, *Free Associations,* p. 189.

305 "Personal differences—jealousy or revenge": quoted Wortis, p. 848.

306 "as a protest against the isolation": Bottome, p. 24.

306 "to have attempted to reconcile": Nunberg in Introduction, May 1959, *Minutes,* I, p. xxv.

306 "of the type whose views were based": Jones, *Free Associations,* p. 217.

306 "what Adler calls aggressive drive": Minute of Scientific Meeting, June 3, 1908, *Minutes,* I, p. 408.

306 "on the identity of or difference between": Minute of Scientific Meeting, June 3, 1908, *Minutes,* I, p. 410.

307 "If you once have paid him the Dane-geld": Rudyard Kipling, "What Dane-Geld Means."

307 "Adler is a very decent and highly intelligent man": Freud–Jung, Nov. 25, 1910, *Freud/Jung Letters,* p. 373.

page 308 "departing too far from the right path": Freud–Pfister, Feb. 26, 1911, Pfister Letters, p. 48.

308 "Freud had a sheaf of notes before him": Wittels, p. 151.

308 "made a mass attack on Adler": Wittels, p. 151.

308 "while Stekel asserts": Freud at Scientific Meeting on Feb. 22, 1911, Minutes, III, p. 173.

308 "Henceforth we can work peacefully": quoted editorial footnote, Minutes, I, p. 300.

308 "I am afraid he will find life": Freud–Jones, Nov. 8, 1912, Colchester.

308 "The last experience she has had": Freud–Lou, Jan. 20, 1925, Lou Letters, p. 147.

309 "on the grounds of the incompatibility": Dr. Hitschmann at Scientific Meeting on Mar. 1, 1911, Minutes, III, p. 178.

309 "a criticism we could spare Adler": Freud at Scientific Meeting on Mar. 1, 1911, Minutes, III, p. 179.

309 "Pretty interesting things have come to pass": Freud–Jones, Feb. 2, 1911, Colchester.

309 "Naturally I am only waiting for an occasion": Freud–Jung, Mar. 14, 1911, Freud/Jung Letters, p. 403.

309 "somewhat reluctantly agreed": Jones, II, p. 149, 132.

309 "I have decided . . . to take the reins back": Freud–Jung, Mar. 3, 1911, Freud/Jung Letters, p. 400.

309 "the pig finds truffles": Freud–Jung, Mar. 14, 1911, Freud/Jung Letters, p. 404.

309 "I cannot conceive": quoted Wittels, p. 226.

310 "to throw [Adler] out": Freud–Jung, Apr. 27, 1911, Freud/Jung Letters, p. 418.

310 "pressed": Freud–Jung, June 15, 1911, Freud/Jung Letters, p. 428.

310 "twisted and turned": Freud–Jung, June 15, 1911, Freud/Jung Letters, p. 428.

310 ". . . I was obliged to bring about Adler's resignation": History, p. 51.

310 "I wish to bring to the attention": Alfred Adler, notice in Zentralblatt für Psychoanalyse, Herausgegeben von Prof. S. Freud, Verlag J. F. Bergmann, Wiesbaden, 1 Jarhgang, Heft 10–11, August 1911, quoted Hertha Orgler, Alfred Adler: The Man and His Work: Triumph over the Inferiority Complex, p. 25.

310 "The damage is not very great": Freud–Jung, June 15, 1911, Freud/Jung Letters, p. 428.

310 "Most of these men did not share": Sachs, p. 51.

310 "Rather tired after battle and victory": Freud–Jung, Oct. 12, 1911, Freud/Jung Letters, p. 447.

311 "specific venomousness" and "loathsome individual": Freud–Frau Andreas, July 7, 1914, Lou Letters, p. 19.

311 "the profusion of petty outbursts of malice": History, p. 51.

311 "For a Jew boy out of a Viennese suburb": Freud–Arnold Zweig, June 22, 1936, quoted Jones, III, p. 223, 208.

311 "attempts were being made to commit members": Declaration of Alfred Adler and his followers, quoted Life in Pictures (Note 214), p. 332.

311 "But a theory such as this": Freud, Lecture XXXIV, "Explanations, Applications and Orientations," New Intro. Lectures, p. 142.

page 312   "Were the idea not so confounded clever": Schiller, "Die Pic-colomini," II, 7, quoted Lecture XXXIV, "Explanations, Applications and Orientations," *New Intro. Lectures,* p. 142.

312   "very little to do with psychoanalysis": Freud, Lecture XXXIV, "Explanations, Applications and Orientations," *New Intro. Lectures,* p. 140.

312   "I beseech you": Oliver Cromwell–The General Assembly of the Kirk of Scotland, Aug. 3, 1650, in Robert Woodrow's Collection of Pamphlets Vol. 203, National Library of Scotland, Edinburgh.

312   "Freud . . . insisted . . . that if one followed Adler": Graf, p. 473.

312   "burned with a steady and all-consuming flame": Sachs, p. 70.

312   "there is one situation": Jones, *Free Associations,* p. 202.

313   "nowhere in his writings": Maurice Natenberg, *The Case History of Sigmund Freud: A Psycho-Biography,* p. 43.

313   "There are some people": A. Kardiner, *My Analysis with Freud: Reminiscences,* p. 77 (afterward referred to as "Kardiner, *Analysis*").

314   "Since you have informed me of your intention": Freud–Frau Andreas, Nov. 4, 1912, Lou Andreas-Salomé, *In der Schule bei Freud,* p. 23.

314   "Freud's official account of Stekel's withdrawal": Lou Andreas Salomé; Nov. 6, 1912, *In der Schule bei Freud,* pp. 23–24.

314   "I would have dropped him": Freud–Frau Andreas, Aug. 1, 1919, Lou Letters, p. 98.

314   "That may be true": Freud, quoted Jones II, 154, *136.*

315   "The excuse he gave me": Jones, II, p. 154, *137.*

315   "Unfortunately the publisher remained on the side of Stekel": Jung–Trigant Burrow, Dec. 26, 1912, Jung Letters, p. 27.

315   "Stekel's treason": Freud–Putnam, Nov. 28, 1912, Putnam Letters, p. 150.

315   "I missed you yesterday at the lecture": Freud–Frau Andreas, Nov. 10, 1912, Lou Letters, p. 11.

315   "suddenly with a flip of the hand": editorial note, Rudolph Binion, *Frau Lou, Nietzsche's Wayward Disciple,* p. 363 (afterward referred to as "Binion").

315   "The turning was one against Adler": Binion, p. 337.

14 *The Break with Jung*

316   "I hope you agree with the Nuremberg decisions": Freud–Pfister, May 2, 1910, Pfister Letters, p. 37.

317   "Since your visit": Emma Jung–Freud, Oct. 30, 1911, *Freud/Jung Letters,* p. 452.

318   "The indestructible foundation": Freud–Jung, Mar. 5, 1912, *Freud/Jung Letters,* p. 492.

318   "As an old man who has no right": Freud–Binswanger, Apr. 14, 1912, Binswanger, p. 39.

319   "he is at perfect liberty": Freud–Pfister, July 4, 1912, Pfister Letters, p. 57.

319   "but be construed into formal disavowal": Freud–Jones, July 22, 1912, Colchester.

320   "The idea of a united small body": Jones–Freud, Aug. 7, 1912, Colchester.

320   "help wishing that things at the top": Jones–Freud, July 30, 1912, Colchester.

320   "expressed the wish": Jones–Freud, July 30, 1912, Colchester.

page 320　"What took hold of my imagination": Freud–Jones, Aug. 1, 1912, quoted Jones, II, p. 173, *153*.

320　"I know there is a boyish": Freud–Jones, Aug. 1, 1912, quoted Jones, II, p. 173, *153*.

321　"Don't be misled by the boyish business": Jones–Brome, quoted Brome, p. 160.

321　"When I introduced Rank to [Freud]": Jones, *Free Associations*, p. 227.

321　"an odd coincidence": Jones, II, p. 173, *153*.

321　"It has seldom been so clear to me": Ferenczi–Freud, Aug. 16, 1912, quoted Brome, p. 154.

322　"This truth was already known": C. G. Jung, "A Review of the Early Hypotheses" in "The Theory of Psychoanalysis," being a series of lectures delivered at Fordham University in Sept. 1912 (afterward referred to as "Jung, Fordham Lectures"), printed Jung, *Freud and Psychoanalysis*, p. 89.

322　". . . it seems to me": Jung, Foreword to the First Edition, "The Theory of Psychoanalysis," Jung, Fordham Lectures, p. 86.

322　"seems the most unsuitable one possible": Jung, "The Oedipus Complex," Jung, Fordham Lectures, p. 152.

322　"the term 'Oedipus complex' ": Jung, "The Oedipus Complex," Jung, Fordham Lectures, p. 152.

322　"If I now say": Jung, "The Oedipus Complex," Jung, Fordham Lectures, p. 153.

322　"He . . . takes the tendency towards incest": Jung, "The Oedipus Complex," Jung, Fordham Lectures, p. 156.

323　"What Dr. Jung said, in effect": Putnam–Jones, Oct. 24, 1912, Putnam Letters, p. 276.

323　" 'America Facing Its Most Tragic Moment' ": *New York Times* (Sept. 29, 1912).

323　"It was [Jung] who brought Dr. Sigmund Freud": *New York Times* (Sept. 29, 1912).

324　"lather of verbosity": Edward Glover, *Freud or Jung*, p. 31.

324　"Vienna is not a particularly moral city": *New York Times* (Apr. 5, 1912).

324　"Nor did the issue": Freud–Putnam, June 25, 1912, Putnam Letters, p. 143.

325　"As a matter of fact": quoted *New York Times* (Apr. 5, 1912).

325　"Naturally I also made room for those of my views": Jung–Freud, Nov. 11, 1912, *Freud/Jung Letters*, p. 515.

325　"Dear Doctor Jung": Freud–Jung, Nov. 14, 1912, *Freud/Jung Letters*, p. 517.

326　"When Jung used his first independent experiences": Freud–Abraham, Mar. 4, 1924, Abraham Letters, p. 352.

326　"Jung sent the notification": Jones, II, p. 164, *145*.

326　"fell on the floor in a dead faint": Jones, I, p. 348, *317*.

327　"everyone clustered helplessly": Jung, *Memories*, p. 153.

327　"How sweet it must be to die": quoted Jones, I, p. 348, *317*.

327　"I am resigned to being declared": Freud–Binswanger, Dec. 16, 1912, quoted Binswanger, p. 48.

327　"My fainting attack in Munich": Freud–Binswanger, Jan. 1, 1913, quoted Binswanger, p. 49.

327　"Yes, he did": Jung, quoted Jones note, 1954, Institute.

page 328   "A talk between us swept away": Freud–Putnam, Nov. 28, 1912, Putnam Letters, p. 150.

328   "even Adler's cronies": Jung–Freud, Dec. [11–14, 1912,] *Freud/Jung Letters*, p. 533.

328   "I would, however, point out": Jung–Freud, Dec. 18, 1912, *Freud/Jung Letters*, p. 534.

329   "It is a convention among us analysts": Freud–Jung, Jan. 3, 1913, *Freud/Jung Letters*, p. 539.

329   "A pretty piece of treachery": Freud–Jung, Jan. 27, 1913, *Freud/Jung Letters*, p. 541.

329   "Do not have too much confidence": Freud–Pfister, Jan. 1, 1913, Pfister Letters, p. 59.

330   "following in Adler's wake": Freud–Abraham, Mar. 27, 1913, Abraham Letters, p. 137.

330   "I am deeply impressed by the success": Jones–Freud, Apr. 25, 1913, Colchester.

330   "It is a grand time to be alive in": Jones–Freud, Apr. 25, 1913, Colchester.

330   "Jung is crazy": Freud–Abraham, June 1, 1913, Abraham Letters, p. 141.

330   "be freed from the purely sexual standpoint": Jung, "On Psychoanalysis," read before 17th International Medical Congress, London, 1913, printed as "Psychoanalysis and Neurosis," in Jung, *Freud and Psychoanalysis*, p. 247.

331   "in entire agreement with the views of Adler": Jung, "Psychoanalysis," read before Psycho-Medical Society, London, Aug. 5, 1913, printed as "General Aspects of Psychoanalysis," in Jung, *Freud and Psychoanalysis*, p. 240.

331   "In short, for the Freudian theory": Kline, p. 324.

331   "Their behavior toward Freud": Lou Andreas-Salomé, Sept. 7/8, 1913, Stanley A. Leavy, *The Freud Journal of Lou Andreas-Salomé*, p. 168.

332   "fatiguing and unedifying": *History*, p. 45.

332   "It was only the absolutely improper way": Ferenczi–Jung, Nov. 13, 1913, quoted Brome, p. 136.

332   "I thought you were a Christian": quoted Jones, II, p. 115, *102*.

332   "I thought you had ethical principles": quoted Jones, *Free Associations*, p. 224.

332   "We dispersed without any desire to meet again": *History*, p. 45.

332   "You know that in these matters": Freud–Abraham, Nov. 9, 1913, Abraham Letters, p. 157.

332   "I have by no means walked into Freud's trap": Jung–Alphonse Maeder, Oct. 29, 1913, Jung Letters, p. 28.

333   "We are mostly dependent": Freud–Jones, Nov. 17, 1913, Colchester.

333   "We know J's position": Freud–Jones, Nov. 22, 1913, Colchester.

333   "I found [him] sympathetic": Freud–Putnam, July 8, 1915, Putnam Letters, p. 189.

333   "In the execution of this duty": Sachs, p. 115.

333   "Differences in theory are unavoidable": Freud–Putnam, Jan. 1, 1913, Putnam Letters, p. 153.

333   "Jung, who was with me": Freud–Stanley Hall, Nov. 23, 1913, Clark University.

334   "The aim . . . was to state clearly": Editor's note, *History*, p. 4.

page 334   "a delicious silence": Freud–Jones, Dec. 8, 1913, Colchester.

334   "I am busy writing contributions": Freud–Frau Andreas, Jan. 12, 1914, Lou Letters, p. 16.

334   "As usual the hardest task falls to me": Freud–Putnam, June 19, 1914, Putnam Letters, p. 176.

334   "I was only able to carry out": Freud–Frau Andreas, June 29, 1914, Lou Letters, p. 17.

335   "I have read it over and over again": Abraham–Freud, Apr. 2, 1914, Abraham Letters, p. 169.

335   "This is of course absolutely true": Jones–Freud, May 18, 1914, Colchester.

335   "the untenability of his position": Jones–Freud, Apr. 22, 1914, Colchester.

335   "You were certainly just as surprised": Freud–Abraham, Apr. 24, 1914, Abraham Letters, p. 173.

335   "I expect no immediate success": Freud–Jones, May 17, 1914, Colchester.

335   "I am not": Freud–Jones, June 2, 1914, Colchester.

336   "So the bombshell has now burst": Freud–Abraham, June 25, 1914, Abraham Letters, p. 181.

336   "I cannot suppress a cheer": Freud–Abraham, July 18, 1914, Abraham Letters, p. 184.

336   "So we are at last rid of them": Freud–Abraham, July 26, 1914, Abraham Letters, p. 186.

337   "It is true that whenever a crisis broke out": Michael Balint–Jones, May 31, 1957, Institute.

338   "Precisely because they too wanted to be Popes": quoted Binswanger, p. 9.

338   "Today my youngest daughter": Freud–Samuel Freud, July 7, 1914, Rylands.

15 *New Fields for Conquest*

340   "The answer must be": Barbara Tuchman, "Can History Use Freud? The Case of Woodrow Wilson," *Atlantic Monthly,* Vol. CCXIX, No. 2. (Feb. 1967), p. 44 (afterward referred to as "Tuchman").

340   "growing tendency on the part of the Freudians": Review of Dr. Franz Ricklin's *Wishfulfillment and Symbolism in Fairy Tales, The Nation,* Vol CIII, No. 2662 (July 6, 1916), p. 13.

341   "Whatever psychoanalysis may aver": I. A. Richards, *Principles of Literary Criticism,* p. 20.

341   "Stories about the devil": Freud–Fliess, Jan. 24, 1897, *Origins,* p. 189.

341   "were the confessions extracted under torture": Freud–Fliess, Jan. 17, 1897, *Origins,* p. 188.

341   "the mechanism of creative writing": Draft N, Notes (III), dated May 31, 1897, enclosed with Freud–Fliess, May 31, 1897, *Origins,* p. 208.

341   "I am not thinking of Shakespeare's conscious intentions": Freud–Fliess, Oct. 15, 1897, *Origins,* p. 224.

341   "that is, under the immediate impact": *Dreams,* p. 265.

342   "There is no doubt": Freud–Fliess, June 20, 1898, *Origins,* p. 256.

342   "even to the extent": Psycho-Analysis in Courts of Law, p. 24.

342   "It passed off without mishap": Freud–Jung, Dec. 8, 1907, *Freud/Jung Letters,* p. 103.

page 343   "a dear familiar face!": Freud–Martha Freud, Sept. 24, 1907, *Letters*, p. 276, *267*.

344   "Leonardo, of whom no love affair": Freud–Fliess, Oct. 9, 1898, *Origins*, p. 268.

344   "conquer the whole field of mythology": Freud–Jung, Oct. 17, 1909, *Freud/Jung Letters*, p. 255.

345   "You must not expect too much of Leonardo": Freud–Jones, Apr. 15, 1910, quoted Jones, II, p. 388, *347*.

345   "Don't be concerned about the Leonardo": Freud–Ferenczi, June 6, 1910, quoted Jones, II, p. 389, *347*.

345   "cause plenty of offense": Freud–Pfister, Mar. 6, 1910, Pfister Letters, p. 34.

345   "[The study] has a very dainty analysis": Jones–Putnam, June 19, 1910, Putnam Letters, p. 219.

345   "stupid idea . . . a private amusement": Freud–Binswanger, apparently June 29, 1912, Binswanger, p. 45.

345   "It would be fantastic": Havelock Ellis, "Freud's Influence on the Changed Attitude Towards Sex," *American Journal of Sociology* (Nov. 1939), p. 316.

345   "To write thus clearly of the kite": Leonardo da Vinci Notebook C.A. 66 v.b., quoted Edward MacCurdy, ed., *The Notebooks of Leonardo da Vinci*, Vol. II, p. 521.

346   "to prove an especially crass example": Freud–Else Voigtländer, Oct. 1, 1911, *Letters*, p. 294, *285*.

346   "As a matter of fact it is also partly fiction": Freud–Hermann Struck, Nov. 7, 1914, *Letters*, p. 312, *306*.

346   "the only truly beautiful thing I have ever written": Freud–Frau Andreas, Feb. 9, 1919, Lou Letters, p. 90.

347   "The key to all his achievements": Freud, "Leonardo da Vinci and a Memory of his Childhood" (1910), *S.E.* Vol. XI, p. 136 (afterward referred to as "Leonardo").

347   "without some knowledge of Leonardo's peculiar childhood": Freud–Dr. Max Schiller, Mar. 26, 1931, *Letters*, p. 404, *405*.

347   "a 'keith' like a vulture, is a bird": *Minutes*, II, p. 341.

347   "pathetic justification of Freud's error": Spector, p. 57.

347   "Leonardo missed that maternal influence": quoted Spector, p. 57.

347   "would have contradicted Freud's hypothesis": Spector, p. 57.

348   "struck throughout the book": Jones, II, p. 387, *346*.

348   "The fallacy in using the clinical notion": Charles Rycroft, "Leonardo Psychoanalysed," *Observer Weekend Review* (Apr. 8, 1962).

348   "His conclusions have been rejected": Kenneth Clark, *Leonardo da Vinci: An Account of his Development as an Artist*, p. 4.

349   "The result has been that analysts": Freud, Lecture XXXIV, "Explanations, Applications and Orientations," *New Intro. Lectures*, p. 145.

350   "become indispensable to all the sciences": *Lay Analysis*, p. 248.

350   "only a good-for-nothing is not interested in his past": quoted Suzanne C. Bernfeld, "Freud and Archaeology," *American Imago*, Vol. VIII (1951), p. 111.

350   "Zeus seems originally to have been a bull": Freud–Fliess, July 4, 1901, *Origins*, p. 333.

350   "The God of our own fathers": Freud–Fliess, July 4, 1901, *Origins*, p. 333.

page 350 "makes me regret once again": Freud–D. E. Oppenheim, Oct. 28, 1909, Sigmund Freud and D. E. Oppenheim, *Dreams in Folklore*, p. 13.

351 "a torment to me to think": Freud–Jung, Nov. 12, 1911, *Freud/Jung Letters*, p. 459.

351 "the outlook for me is very gloomy": Jung–Freud, Nov. 14, 1911, *Freud/Jung Letters*, p. 460.

351 "for that I need a room where": Freud–Jung, Feb. 12, 1911, *Freud/Jung Letters*, p. 391.

351 "The frequency of images of god here in the Tyrol": Freud–Binswanger, Sept. 10, 1911, quoted Binswanger, p. 36.

351 "The Totem work is a beastly business": Freud–Ferenczi, Nov. 30, 1911, quoted Jones, II, p. 394, *352*.

352 "On the whole": Freud–Putnam, Dec. 25, 1911, Putnam Letters, p. 135.

352 "My work on the psychology of religion": Freud–Abraham, Jan. 2, 1912, *Letters*, p. 294, *286*.

352 "the most daring enterprise I have ever ventured": Freud–Jones, Apr. 9, 1913, quoted, Jones, II, p. 396, *353*.

352 " 'smuggle' psychoanalysis into ethnopsychology": Freud–Binswanger, Mar. 15, 1912, quoted Binswanger, p. 39.

352 "serve to cut us off cleanly": Freud–Abraham, May 13, 1913, Abraham Letters, p. 139.

352 "The reception will be the same": Freud–Ferenczi, May 13, 1913, quoted Jones, II, p. 396, *354*.

352 "In *Totem and Tabu* Freud wreaked": Wittels, p. 191.

353 "will be bound to show": Freud, *Totem and Taboo: Some Points of Agreement between the Mental Lives of Savages and Neurotics* (1913 [1912–13]), *S. E.* Vol. XIII, p. 1 (afterward referred to as *"Totem and Taboo"*).

353 "these . . . must be the oldest": *Totem and Taboo*, p. 32.

353 "We are driven to believe": *Totem and Taboo*, p. 17.

354 "that the moral and conventional prohibitions": *Totem and Taboo*, p. 22.

354 "If, now, we bring together": *Totem and Taboo*, p. 141.

354 "created out of their filial sense of guilt": *Totem and Taboo*, p. 143.

355 "hypothesis, or, I would rather say, vision": *Auto. Study*, p. 68.

355 "a monstrous air": footnote, *Totem and Taboo*, p. 142.

355 "that the beginnings of religion": *Totem and Taboo*, p. 156.

355 "To be sure, [it] is only a hypothesis": Freud, *Group Psychology and the Analysis of the Ego* (1921), *S. E.* Vol. XVIII, p. 122 (afterward referred to as *"Group Psychology"*).

355 "It is a felicitous phrase": Alfred L. Kroeber, *"Totem and Taboo* in Retrospect," *American Journal of Sociology*, Vol. XLV, No. 3 (Nov. 1939), p. 446.

355 "Oh, don't take that seriously": Freud–Kardiner, quoted Anna Quindlen, *New York Times* (May 7, 1977).

356 "Freud remained from the beginning": Jones, III, p. 333, *311*.

356 "The conventional American anthropologist": Clyde Kluckhohn, "The Influence of Psychiatry on Anthropology in America during the past One Hundred Years," in The American Psychiatric Association, *One Hundred Years of American Psychiatry*, p. 594.

357 "I have completely rewritten my Madonna essay": Jones–Freud, Mar. 13, 1914, Colchester.

page 357   "Although this paper does not": Freud, "The Moses of Michelangelo" (1914), *S. E.* Vol. XIII, p. 211 (afterward referred to as "Moses of Michelangelo").

358   "I have come to understand the meaning": Freud–Martha Freud, postcard, Sept. 6, 1901, quoted Jones, II, p. 409, *365.*

358   ". . . every day I pay a visit to Moses": Freud–Martha Freud, Sept. 25, 1912, *Letters,* p. 302, *293.*

358   "My relationship to this work": Freud–Edoardo Weiss, Apr. 12, 1933, quoted Edoardo Weiss, *Sigmund Freud as a Consultant: Recollections of a Pioneer in Psychoanalysis,* p. 74 (afterward referred to as "Weiss").

358   "This shook Freud badly": Jones, II, p. 409, *365.*

358   "Do you find anything curious about the *left* [*sic*] hand": Jones–Freud, Oct. 30, 1912, Colchester.

358   "What we see before us": "Moses of Michelangelo," p. 229.

359   "modified the theme of the broken Tables": "Moses of Michelangelo," p. 233.

359   "It is a fun and perhaps no bad one": Freud–Jones, Jan. 16, 1914, Colchester.

359   "shame at the obvious amateurishness": Freud–Abraham, Apr. 6, 1914, Abraham Letters, p. 171.

359   "The last . . . I consulted": Freud–Jones, Feb. 8, 1914, Colchester.

359   "At the moment the situation in Vienna": Freud–Ferenczi, Oct. 17, 1912, quoted Jones, II, p. 411, *367.*

360   "built up on Hamlet's hesitations": *Dreams,* p. 264.

360   "Hamlet is able to do anything": *Dreams,* p. 265.

360   "Freud's description of Hamlet's character": John Ashworth, "Olivier, Freud and Hamlet," *Atlantic Monthly,* Vol. CLXXXIII, No. 5 (May 1949), p. 30.

361   "This note seems to have been written": Georg Brandes, quoted Freud–Jones, Jan. 24, 1921, Colchester.

361   "Now remember, Shakespeare's father died": Freud–Jones, Jan. 24, 1921, Colchester.

361   "I am glad to hear you will keep your eyes": Freud–Jones, Feb. 7, 1921, Colchester.

361   "Feel inclined": "Leonardo," p. 115.

362   "You are aware": Freud–Lytton Strachey, Christmas Day 1928, quoted Michael Holroyd, *Lytton Strachey,* Vol. II, p. 615.

362   "Shakespeare wrote *Hamlet*": *Auto. Study,* p. 63.

362   "Incidentally, I have in the meantime": footnote, added 1930, *Dreams,* p. 266.

363   "You cannot psychoanalyse Macbeth": Dr. Gareth Lloyd Evans–author, Feb. 11, 1978.

16 *Wartime Acceptance*

364   "for the first time for thirty years": Freud–Abraham, July 26, 1914, Abraham Letters, p. 186.

364   "from one German victory to the next": Freud–Abraham, Aug. 25, 1914, Abraham Letters, p. 193.

364   "keep cheerful": Freud–Sophie Halberstadt, Sept. 1916, Library of Congress.

365   "I do not break my head": Freud–Pfister, Oct. 9, 1918, Pfister Letters, p. 61.

page 366   "looked like a czarina": The Wolf-Man, "Recollections," in Gardiner, p. 90.

366   "How little one then suspected": The Wolf-Man, "Recollections," in Gardiner, p. 90.

366   "A higher power has reasserted the rules": quoted A. J. P. Taylor, *Europe: Grandeur and Decline*, p. 79.

366   "one cannot predict": Freud–Eitingon, July 29, 1914, quoted Jones, II, p. 192, *170*.

366   "War upon [Germany]": *Cambridge Daily News* (Aug. 1, 1914).

366   "I can see no mortal reason": Lord Edmond Fitzmaurice–J. A. Spender, July 31, 1914, Spender Papers (British Library), Add. 46392, quoted Max Beloff, *Imperial Sunset*, p. 177.

366   On the 2nd he wrote: Freud–Mathilde Hollitscher, Aug. 2, 1914, Library of Congress.

367   "largely designed as an empirical refutation": Editor's note, *History*, p. 4.

367   "I do not doubt that mankind will survive": Freud–Frau Andreas, Nov. 25, 1914, Lou Letters, p. 21.

368   "during the World War": *Auto. Study*, p. 49.

368   "As his popularity grew": F. H. Matthews, "The Americanization of Sigmund Freud: Adaptations of Psychoanalysis Before 1917," *Journal of American Studies*, Vol. I No. 1 (1967), p. 42 (afterward referred to as "Matthews").

369   "I read the translation": Walter Lippmann–Frederick J. Hoffman, Nov. 18, 1942, quoted Frederick J. Hoffman, *Freudianism and the Literary Mind*, p. 54 (afterward referred to as "Hoffman").

369   "We ourselves are the subject matter": Walter Lippmann, "Freud and the Layman," *The New Republic* (Apr. 17, 1915).

370   "filth": S. Weir Mitchell, quoted Oberndorf, p. 52.

370   "Today aided by German perplexities": S. Weir Mitchell, "The Medical Department in the Civil War," address at Chicago, Feb. 1913, quoted Oberndorf, p. 52.

370   "Psychoanalysis is a conscious": Boris Sidis, *Symptomatology, Psychognosis and Diagnosis of Psychopathic Diseases*, p. vii.

370   "In Paris itself, a conviction still seems to reign": *History*, p. 32.

370   "Let us acknowledge these merits": Pierre Janet, "Valeur de la psychanalyse et de Psychol de Freud," read before Société de Psychothérapie, June 1914, printed *Revue de Psychothérapie et de Psychologie Appliquées*, Vol. XXIX (1915), pp. 16–52.

371   "a subtle apology for the Central Powers": E. E. Southard, quoted in Introduction, Cioffi, p. 8.

371   "an admirable essay in propaganda Teutonica": E. E. Southard, quoted in Introduction, Cioffi, p. 8.

371   "little less than a justification": "More German than Germans," *The New York Times Magazine* (Aug. 24, 1919), p. 11.

371   "The German mind": C. Ladd Franklin letter, *The Nation*, Vol. CIII, No. 2677 (Oct. 19, 1916), (afterward referred to as "Franklin").

371   "right-minded reader of Freudian literature": Franklin.

371   "the doctrines of so-called psychoanalysis": Franklin.

371   "psychoanalysis is most intimately bound up": Franklin.

371   "a display of mingled ignorance and impudence": Editorial, *New York Times* (Feb. 14, 1916).

page 372   " 'Belief ' in [psychoanalysis] has not": Editorial, *New York Times* (Feb. 14, 1916).

372   "is to adjust the individual": A. A. Brill, *New York Times* (Feb. 17, 1915).

372   "monstrous regiment of German professors": Charles Mercier, quoted in Introduction, Cioffi, p. 7.

373   "Without denying these gentlemen": Jones–Freud, July 22, 1913, Colchester.

373   "played a quiet part": Jones–Freud, Aug. 8, 1913, Colchester.

373   "After the meeting Sir James Crichton-Browne": Jones–Freud, Aug. 8, 1913, Colchester.

373   " 'Fair play' is what we want": Freud–Jones, Aug. 10, 1913, Colchester.

374   "the society became a hotbed of dissension": Edward Glover, quoted *Psychoanalytic Pioneers*, p. 536.

374   "on the ground that he belongs": Jones–Freud, Oct. 4, 1913, Colchester.

374   "My man swept the board": Jones–Freud, Dec. 11, 1913, Colchester.

374   "Surely the time has at last come": "H. B. D.," letter, *British Medical Journal* (Dec. 12, 1914), p. 1048.

375   "In order to understand how the Germanic obsession": B. H. Shaw, letter, *British Medical Journal* (Jan. 9, 1915), p. 94.

375   "It is, however, too often lost sight of": St. John Bullen, "Remarks on the Interpretation of Dreams, according to Sigmund Freud and Others," *Journal of Mental Science*, Vol. LXI (1915), p. 36 (afterward referred to as "Bullen").

375   "the extraordinary protrusion of sex matters": Bullen, p. 36.

375   "Surely it is notorious": D. G. Thomson, letter, *British Medical Journal* (Jan. 6, 1917), p. 32.

375   "known that psychoanalysts": "Decency," letter, *British Medical Journal* (Jan. 13, 1917), p. 64.

375   "I believe that the tendency": Harold Laski–Mr. Justice [Oliver Wendell] Holmes, Dec. 18, 1917, Mark DeWolfe Howe, ed., *Holmes–Laski Letters: The Correspondence of Mr. Justice Holmes and Harold J. Laski, 1916–1935*, p. 120.

376   "At present I am as in a polar night": Freud–Abraham, Jan. 25, 1915, quoted Jones, II, p. 207, *184*.

376   "a topical essay on the disappointment": Freud–Putnam, Mar. 9, 1915, Putnam Letters, p. 181.

376   "A piece of topical chit-chat": Freud–Abraham, Mar. 4, 1915, Abraham Letters, p. 213.

377   "If you will now observe": Freud–Frederick van Eeden, Dec. 28, 1914, Appendix to Freud, "Thoughts for the Times on War and Death" (1915), *S. E.* Vol. XIV, p. 301 (afterward referred to as "Thoughts on War and Death").

377   "a chivalrous passage of arms": Thoughts on War and Death, p. 278.

377   "Indeed, one of the great civilized nations": Thoughts on War and Death, p. 279.

378   "If you want to preserve peace, arm for war" and "If you want to endure life, prepare yourself for death": Thoughts on War and Death, p. 300.

page 378 "psychology which leads behind consciousness": Freud–Fliess, Mar. 10, 1898, *Origins*, p. 246.

378 "to clarify and carry deeper": editorial footnote, Freud, "A Metapsychological Supplement to the Theory of Dreams" (1917 [1915]), *S. E.* XIV, p. 222.

378 "book consisting of twelve essays": Freud–Frau Andreas, July 30, 1915, Lou Letters, p. 32.

378 "not yet been written": Freud–Frau Andreas, Apr. 2, 1919, Lou Letters, p. 95.

379 "crude stuff meant for the masses": Freud–Frau Andreas, July 14, 1916, Lou Letters, p. 48.

379 "was not possible . . . to preserve": Freud, Preface (1917), *Intro. Lectures*, p. 9.

379 "As things stand at present": Freud, Lecture I, Introduction, *Intro. Lectures*, p. 16.

379 "Instead I will introduce you by degrees": Freud, Lecture IV, "Parapraxes" (concluded), *Intro. Lectures*, p. 79.

379 "There is nothing else": Freud, Lecture XV, "Uncertainties and Criticisms," *Intro Lectures*, p. 239.

380 gave his father a guided tour: Oliver Freud–Jones, Nov. 1955, Institute.

380 "I do not wish to arouse conviction": Freud, Lecture XVI, "Psychoanalysis and Psychiatry," *Intro. Lectures*, p. 243.

381 "Life bears too heavily on me": Freud–Abraham, May 20, 1917, Abraham Letters, p. 251.

381 "The idea is to put Lamarck": Freud–Abraham, Nov. 11, 1917, Abraham Letters, p. 261.

382 "Of course if one didn't believe in inheritance": quoted Wortis, p. 847.

382 "Psycho-analysis cannot accommodate itself": quoted Wortis, p. 847.

382 "much regretted by many of us": Ernst Kris, "Freud in the History of Science," *The Listener* (May 17, 1956), p. 632.

382 "I arrived at my, or should I say your": Georg Groddeck–Freud, May 27, 1917, quoted Georg Groddeck, *The Meaning of Illness*, p. 32 (afterward referred to as "Groddeck").

383 "aroused sad thoughts": Freud–Ferenczi, Oct. 31, 1915, quoted Jones, II, p. 213, *189*.

383 "I don't think I shall live to see the day": Freud–Frau Andreas, July 13, 1917, Lou Letters, p. 61.

383 "I got over the Nobel Prize": Freud–Abraham, Oct. 31, 1920, Abraham Letters, p. 317.

383 "the only thing that gives me any pleasure": Freud–Abraham, Dec. 10, 1917, Abraham Letters, p. 264.

384 "Who would have dreamed": Putnam, "The Work of Sigmund Freud," read before 8th Annual Meeting of American Psychopathological Association, May 24, 1917, printed *Journal of Abnormal Psychology*, Vol. XII (Aug. 1917), p. 146.

384 "a certain harshness in [Freud's] grasp of facts": Wilfred Trotter, *The Instincts of the Herd in Peace and War, 1916–1919*, p. 54.

384 "to reject a helping hand": W. H. R. Rivers, "Freud's Psychology of the Unconscious," read before Edinburgh Pathological Club, Mar. 7,

page   1917, printed *The Lancet* (June 16, 1917), p. 914 (afterward referred
            to as "Rivers, *Lancet*").

384   "The terrible war which has just ended": *Pleasure Principle*, p. 12.

385   "the only method with which I am acquainted": Eder, p. 11.

385   ". . . in some cases sex": Eder, p. 12.

385   "This is unfortunately true enough": C. Stanford Read, *Military Psychiatry in Peace and War*, p. 161.

385   "introduced to a society in which": G. Elliot Smith, Preface, W. H. R.
            Rivers, *Conflict and Dream*, p. viii.

385   "It is a wonderful turn of fate": Rivers, *Lancet*, p. 913.

386   "individual experience of the patient": Rivers, *Lancet*, p. 914.

387   "Few communications from beginners in psychoanalysis": Freud–
            Simmel, Feb. 20, 1918, Simmel Letters, p. 97.

387   "This is the first time that a German physician": Freud–Abraham,
            Feb. 17, 1918, Abraham Letters, p. 271.

388   "a man who reads a paper": Sachs, p. 161.

388   "Then clinics and consultation departments": Freud, "Turnings in
            the Ways of Psycho-Analytic Therapy," *Collected Papers*, Vol. II, p. 401
            (afterward referred to as "Psycho-Analytic Therapy").

389   "proletarians and princes": Freud at Scientific Meeting on Dec. 5,
            1906, *Minutes*, I, p. 73.

389   "Little can be done to remedy this": "On Beginning the Treatment,"
            p. 353.

389   "We shall probably discover": "Psycho-Analytic Therapy," p. 402.

17 *Reaping the Whirlwind*

393   "the hard treatment of the men": *Group Psychology*, p. 95.

393   "in the unheated study in our overcoats": Sachs, p. 154.

394   "It is too early to reach any conclusion": Freud interviewed in Vienna
            by Charles J. Rosebault, *New York Times* (Aug. 24, 1919).

394   "the first window opening in our cage": Freud–Jones, Apr. 18, 1919,
            Colchester.

394   "We are passing through bad times": Freud–Samuel Freud, May 22,
            1919, Rylands.

395   "Life is very hard with us": Freud–Samuel Freud, Oct. 27, 1919,
            Rylands.

396   "become mixed with the tea and the cocoa": Freud–Samuel Freud,
            Oct. 2, 1920, Rylands.

396   "a soft Shetland cloth": Freud–Samuel Freud, Feb. 22, 1920, Rylands.

396   "tennis balls": Samuel Freud–Anna Freud, Mar. 20, 1920, Rylands.

396   "My time at least is still precious": Freud–Samuel Freud, Dec. 17,
            1919, Rylands.

396   "But business is very brisk now": Freud–Samuel Freud, Feb. 15, 1920,
            Rylands.

396   "dreadful journey": Freud–Ernst Freud, July 19, 1919, Library of
            Congress.

397   "Are they aware that my name": Freud–Samuel Freud, Oct. 15, 1920,
            Rylands.

397   "I am anxious that you could misconstrue": Freud–Samuel Freud,
            Nov. 5, 1920, Rylands.

397   "The Committee exists": Jones–Freud, Apr. 2, 1919, Institute.

397   "I am still upright": Freud–Jones, Apr. 18, 1919, Colchester.

397   "I am occupied in solving the decisive affairs": Victor Tausk–Freud,

page   July 2, 1919, quoted Paul Roazen, *Brother Animal: The Story of Freud and Tausk*, p. 122 (afterward referred to as "Roazen").

398   "devilish arrangement": quoted Paul Roazen, "Reading, Writing and Memory: Dr. K. R. Eissler's Thinking," *Contemporary Psychoanalysis*, Vol. XIV, No. 2 (1978), p. 347.

398   "I thank you for all the good": Tausk–Freud, July 3, 1919, quoted Roazen, p. 127.

398   "Among the sacrifices": Freud, "Victor Tausk," *Internationale Zeitschrift für Psychoanalyse*, Vol. 5 (1919), p. 225, where it was signed by "Die Redaktion" [The Editorial Committee], *S. E.* Vol. XVII, p. 273 (afterward referred to as "Tausk").

399   "a victim of fate": Freud–Pfister, July 13, 1919, Pfister Letters, p. 71.

399   "There is no doubt that this man": Tausk, p. 275.

399   "In his letter to me he swore": Freud–Frau Andreas, Aug. 1, 1919, Lou Letters, p. 98.

399   "Evidently the memory of his father": Anna Freud–S. Fisher Verlag, n.d., quoted K. R. Eissler, *Talent and Genius: The Fictitious Case of Tausk contra Freud*, p. 17.

400   "I always thought that my theory": quoted Binswanger, p. 9.

400   "But it strikes me": Freud–Jones, Feb. 18, 1919, Colchester.

400   "nothing of the conditions we live in": Freud–Jones, May 28, 1919, Colchester.

400   "It all depends on the state": Freud–Jones, May 28, 1919, Colchester.

401   "Only the cause flourishes": Freud–Binswanger, Feb. 16, 1919, quoted Binswanger, p. 66.

401   "I go to have a look on him every day": Freud–Jones, Dec. 11, 1919, Colchester.

401   "It seems to me that I have never written": Freud–Max Halberstadt, Jan. 25, 1920, Library of Congress.

402   "science is international": Lord Rutherford, Radio address from Broadcasting House, London to Fifth Pacific International Science Congress, Vancouver, on May 11, 1933, quoted A. S. Eve, *Rutherford, Being the Life and Letters of the Rt. Hon. Lord Rutherford, O. M.*, p. 373.

402   "It is still pleasant": Freud–Arnold Zweig, July 15, 1934, Zweig Letters, p. 86.

403   "I am a wild analyst": quoted Carl M. Grossman and Sylva Grossman, *The Wild Analyst: The Life and Work of Georg Groddeck*, p. 13 (afterward referred to as "Grossman").

403   "then he proceeded to speak": Grossman, p. 13.

403   "This was too much for most of those": Grossman, p. 97.

403   "the repressed complexes become too intense": Groddeck–Freud, Sept. 11, 1920, Groddeck, p. 52.

403   "in spite of, or perhaps partly because of": Jones, III, p. 202, *189*.

403   "Ps-A has so many attractions": Jones–Members of Committee, Feb. 11, 1921, Institute.

404   "I decided that I had to go back": Freud–Samuel Freud, Oct. 2, 1920, Rylands.

404   an unconventional tour: Anna Freud–Jones, Jan. 21, 1955, Institute.

405   "I would have done it differently": quoted Ellenberger, p. 838.

405   "I feel very proud of the Congress": Freud–Jones, Oct. 4, 1920, Colchester.

406   "the formation of a conscript army": Sir Frederick Mott presenting prizes at Charing Cross Hospital, *New York Times* (Jan. 15, 1922).

page 406   "wiped out the line of demarcation": Brill, "Development of Freud's Work," p. 325.

407   "purge": Freud–Jones, Feb. 18, 1919, Colchester.

407   "Many of our former opponents": A. A. Brill, "Facts and Fancies in Psychoanalytical Treatment," *New York Medical Journal,* Vol. CIX, No. 26 (June 28, 1919), p. 1117.

408   "The nephews and nieces of War": Eric Linklater, *Poet's Pub,* p. 80.

408   "It was the peg": Hoffman, pp. 30–31.

408   "remained a topic for cloakroom wisecracks": John C. Whitehorn, "A Century of Psychiatric Research in America," in *One Hundred Years of American Psychiatry,* p. 174.

408   "It was a denial": Mark Sullivan, *Our Times: The United States 1900–1925,* Vol. IV, *The War Begins 1909–1914,* p. 172 (afterward referred to as "Sullivan").

409   "did not reciprocate this enthusiasm": Sachs, p. 153.

409   "the newspaper-reading public": Grace Adams, "The Rise and Fall of Psychology," *Atlantic Monthly,* Vol. CLIII, No. 1 (Jan. 1934), p. 86 (afterward referred to as "Adams").

409   "A progressive young lady of Rheims": quoted Reik, *Thirty Years,* p. 174.

410   "Young men who frequent picture palaces": Freud–Sachs, quoted Merrill Moore, "Note on a Limerick," *American Imago,* Vol. XIII (1956), p. 147.

410   "The girls who frequent picture-palaces": Norman Douglas, *"Some Limericks. Collected for the use of Students, & ensplendour'd with Introduction, Geographical Index, and with Notes Explanatory and Critical,* p. 80.

410   "Sachs declared he was under the impression": *Psychoanalytic Pioneers,* p. 218.

410   "hard upon the heels of": H. L. Mencken, "Rattling the Sub-conscious," *The Smart Set* (Sept. 1918), reprinted as "The Advent of Psychoanalysis" in William H. Nolte, ed., *H. L. Mencken's "Smart Set" Criticism,* p. 147.

410   "that the reason the denizens": Adams, p. 85.

411   "represented in the popular press": Henry F. May, *The End of American Innocence: A Study of the First Years of our Own Time, 1912–1917,* p. 234.

412   "many sad derelicts": Rev. C. F. Potter, "Psychoanalysis and Religion," in West Side Unitarian Church on Mar. 29, 1925, reported *New York Times* (Mar. 30, 1925).

412   "It is deeply to be deplored": Rev. Stephen Wise, Rabbi of the Free Synagogue, New York, quoted *New York Times* (Nov. 21, 1921).

412   "free American psychiatry": quoted Oberndorf, p. 136.

413   "it is the only blot on the record": Bobby Edwards, editorial in *Quill,* Vol. XIII (1923), p. 14, quoted Hoffman, p. 76.

413   "A dreamer does know what he dreams": Dr. Vosberg, *New York Times* (Dec. 1921).

413   "a good practical joke": Jones–Freud, Apr. 1, 1922, Institute.

413   "he did not agree that man was the slave of circumstance": Dr. Busch, reported *Oxford Chronicle* (Mar. 17, 1922).

413   "It shows the state of ignorance at Oxford": Jones–Freud, Apr. 1, 1922, Institute.

414   "The Freudian psychology is both exciting": Editorial, "A Useful Hoax," *The Times* of London (Dec. 17, 1921).

page 414 "I am glad you agree with my letter": Freud–Jones, May 24, 1920, Colchester.

414 "It is my experience": Samuel A. Tannenbaum, reported *New York Times* (Mar. 19, 1922).

415 "taking up Freud": *New York Times* (Jan. 4, 1922).

415 "that the practices of psychoanalysis by girls": *New York Times* (Jan. 4, 1922).

415 "Girl, Weary From Freud, A Suicide": *New York Times* (Mar. 24, 1922).

415 "Buys Hat—Dies" and "Eats Poached Egg—Dies": *New York Times* (Mar. 27, 1922).

415 "Do as you please": Editorial, *New York Times* (Mar. 29, 1921).

415 "Would you like to earn £1,000 a year": Jones–Freud, Feb. 11, 1921, Colchester.

416 "The animus is chiefly directed": Jones–Freud, Jan. 11, 1921, Institute.

416 "A well-known one in London": Jones–Freud, Jan. 11, 1922, Institute.

416 "a little gem": Freud–Dr. Hermine von Hug-Hellmuth, Apr. 27, 1915, *S. E.* Vol. XIV, p. 341.

416 "to get some qualified and well-known writer": Reader's report–Allen and Unwin, n.d.

416 "came round to see me in a considerable panic": Jones–Freud, Feb. 1, 1921, Institute.

416 "I really believe it has never before been possible": Freud–Dr. Hermine von Hug-Hellmuth, Apr. 27, 1915, *S. E.* Vol. XIV, p. 341.

417 "It should be added": editorial footnote, "Letter to Dr. Hermine von Hug-Hellmuth" (1919 [1915]), *S. E.* XIV, p. 341.

417 "Had we not the book before us": P. H. Palmer to ed., n.d., *Occult Review*, Vol. XXXIII, No. 2 (Feb. 1921), p. 116.

417 three hundred citizens of North Carolina petitioned: Sullivan, p. 169.

417 "shell shock, insomnia, nervous depression": Rose Macaulay, *Dangerous Ages*, p. 63.

417 ". . . we are publishing all Dr. Freud": Virginia Woolf–Molly MacCarthy, Oct. 2, 1924, Nigel Nicolson, ed., *A Change of Perspective: The Letters of Virginia Woolf*, Vol. III (1923–1928), p. 134.

417 "With religion dead and philosophy dry": J. M. Keynes, "The Underlying Principles," *Manchester Guardian Commercial* (Jan. 4, 1923).

418 "As far as I am concerned": Thomas Mann in "Stampa," June 1925, quoted *Internationale Zeitschrift für Psychoanalyse*, XI Band, Heft 2 (1925), p. 247.

418 "They had definitely promised me that no guests": Jones–Freud, n.d., Institute.

419 "On a cruder level": Matthews, p. 59.

419 "As his work became known in the 1920s": Irving Howe, *Sherwood Anderson*, p. 180.

419 "if there is anything you do not understand": Sherwood Anderson, *Dark Laughter*, p. 207.

419 "I never did read him": Sherwood Anderson, *Memoirs*, p. 243.

420 "ecstatic anti-Freudian tirades": Spector, p. 203.

420 "Lawrence's conclusion was more or less": Frieda Lawrence–Frederick J. Hoffman, Nov. 12, 1942, quoted Hoffman, p. 154.

420 "studying the theories": *The Times Literary Supplement* (Feb. 26, 1920), p. 139.

page 420   "searched the last edition": C. L. Graves, "Freud and Jung," *Punch, or The London Charivari* (Mar. 10, 1920), p. 196.

421   Samuel was told: Freud–Samuel Freud, Nov. 28, 1920, Rylands.

421   "a subjective means of avoiding": Hoffman, p. 97.

421   "I shall never forget my first encounter": Theodore Dreiser, remarks read by A. A. Brill, at dinner on May 6, 1931, printed *Psychoanalytic Review*, Vol. XVIII (1931), p. 250.

422   "The striking novelty and the startling conclusions": William L. Langer, presidential address at annual dinner of the American Historical Association, Dec. 29, 1957, printed "The Next Assignment," *American Imago*, Vol. XV (1958), p. 239.

422   "Not psychology alone": James S. Van Teslaar, "The Significance of Psycho-analysis in the History of Science," *International Journal of Psycho-Analysis*, Vol. II, p. 340.

18 *Reassessing the Unconscious*

424   "that Professor Freud has done more": Professor William McDougall, Preface, *An Outline of Abnormal Psychology*, p. viii.

424   "My standpoint in regard to Freud": C.S. Myers–Jones, July 16, 1926, Institute.

425   "There might be a brief greeting or a nod": Jerome M. Schneck, "A Note on Freud's Neighbor," *American Journal of Psychotherapy*, Vol. XIII (1959), pp. 139–141.

425   "She was stretched out": Viktor von Weizsäcker, "Reminiscences of Freud and Jung," in Nelson, p. 60 (afterward referred to as "Weizsäcker").

425   "His face in old age": Weizsäcker, p. 60.

426   "I am very far from forgetting": Freud–Samuel Freud, Dec. 4, 1921, Library of Congress.

427   "I am dependent": Freud–Samuel Freud, Jan. 21, 1921, Rylands.

427   "My fees are 10 dollars an hour": Freud–A. Kardiner, Apr. 1921, quoted Kardiner, *Analysis*, p. 15.

427   "the instruction of disciples": Freud–Wilfred Lay, Dec. 13, 1920, Four Unpublished Letters, *Psychoanalytic Quarterly*, Vol. XXV (1956), p. 152.

427   "We all gathered": Kardiner, *Analysis* p. 18.

427   "Nine analytic sessions daily": Freud–Abraham, Oct. 31, 1920, Abraham Letters, p. 317.

427   "In the most unfavorable cases": Freud–Edoardo Weiss, Oct. 3, 1920, quoted Weiss, p. 28.

427   "He is a man of 30": Jones–Freud, May 7, 1920, Institute.

428   Freud replied: Freud–James Strachey, June 4, 1920, Strachey Papers, British Library.

428   "I was so thoroughly satisfied": The Wolf-Man, "Memoirs," in Gardiner, p. 111.

428   "The precise discussion of many points": Smith Ely Jelliffe–William A. White, Aug. 1921, quoted *Psychoanalytic Pioneers*, p. 226.

428   "I have heard so much about you": Dr. Smith of Plainville, Ohio–Freud, reported Oberndorf, p. 147.

429   "How odd, the Americans are supposed to be": Vienna University Professor–Freud, reported Oberndorf, p. 139.

429   " 'No.' I will thank you": quoted Max Eastman, *Heroes I Have Known:*

page   *Twelve Who Lived Great Lives*, p. 263 (afterward referred to as "Eastman").

429   "But why should I support you?": quoted Eastman, p. 265.

429   "Perhaps you're a behaviorist": quoted Eastman, p. 266.

429   "You will find out the causes": quoted Eastman, p. 272.

429   "I hope you will lend me your ear": Freud–Fliess, Apr. 2, 1896, *Origins*, p. 161.

430   "The obscure recognition": *Everyday Life*, p. 258–259.

430   "I propose that when we have succeeded": The Unconscious, p. 181.

430   "endeavors to follow out": The Unconscious, p. 181.

430   "Much of what I am saying": Freud–Ferenczi, Mar. 31, 1919, quoted Jones, III, p. 42, *40*.

430   "speculation, often far-fetched speculation": *Pleasure Principle*, p. 24.

431   "automatically regulated by the pleasure principle": *Pleasure Principle*, p. 7.

431   "At this point we cannot escape": *Pleasure Principle*, p. 36.

431   "The attributes of life were at some time": *Pleasure Principle*, p. 38.

432   "Freud later adopted some of my discoveries": Stekel, p. 138.

432   "The 'Beyond' is finally finished": Freud–Max Eitingon, July 18, 1920, quoted Schur, p. 329.

432   "For [it] I have been sufficiently punished": Freud–Eitingon, Mar. 27, 1921, quoted Schur, p. 343.

432   "and in the last decade none at all": Jones, III, p. 287, *266*.

433   "must have sprung from some depths": Jones, III, p. 287, *267*.

433   "simple idea that will serve": Freud–Ferenczi, May 12, 1919, quoted Jones, III, p. 45, *42*.

433   "a way from the analysis of the individual": Freud–Romain Rolland, Mar. 4, 1923, quoted Schur, p. 350.

433   "notorious, racist, political anti-Semite": Philip Rieff, "Origins of Freud's Political Psychology," *Journal of the History of Ideas*, Vol. XVII (1956), p. 238.

433   "The leader of the group": *Group Psychology*, p. 127.

434   "following Groddeck in calling the other part of the mind": Freud, *The Ego and the Id* (1923), S. E. Vol. XIX, p. 23 (afterward referred to as *"The Ego and the Id"*).

434   "to an extreme degree": Ellenberger, p. 844.

434   "I understand very well why the unconscious": Freud–Groddeck, Apr. 17, 1921, Groddeck, p. 58.

434   "Your style is enchanting": Freud–Groddeck, Apr. 17, 1921, Groddeck, p. 58.

435   "As fascinating as the earlier ones": Freud–Groddeck, Aug. 27, 1921, Groddeck, p. 65.

435   "occupied with something speculative": Freud–Ferenczi, July 21, 1922, quoted Jones, III, 104, *99*.

435   "Do you remember, by the way": Freud–Groddeck, Christmas 1922, Groddeck, p. 76.

435   "I like the little book very much": Freud–Groddeck, Mar. 25, 1923, Groddeck, p. 77.

435   "Groddeck is quite certainly four-fifths right": Groddeck, p. 106.

435   "[It] is pretty": Groddeck–Mrs. Groddeck, May 15, 1923, Groddeck, p. 13.

page 436   "Many thanks for sending me": Groddeck–Freud, May 27, 1923, Groddeck, p. 79.

436   "We call it a chaos": Freud, Lecture XXXI, "The Dissection of the Psychical Personality," *New Intro. Lectures*, p. 73.

436   "Thus in its relation to the id": *The Ego and the Id*, p. 25.

437   "observes the ego": Outline of Psycho-Analysis, p. 205.

437   "a furtive attempt to smuggle": "Der Gegensatz Freud und Jung," *Kölnische Zeitung* (Cologne) (May 7, 1929), p. 4, quoted Jung, *Freud and Psychoanalysis*, p. 339.

437   "when they have been repeated often enough": *The Ego and the Id*, p. 38.

437   "These creatures die": *The Ego and the Id*, p. 47.

437   "We possess the truth": Freud–Ferenczi, May 13, 1913, quoted Brome, p. 132.

19 *Cancer*

439   "Be prepared to see something you will not like": quoted Schur, p. 350.

439   "No sooner had I seen it": Felix Deutsch, "Reflections on the 10th Anniversary of Freud's Death," Institute (afterward referred to as "Deutsch, 'Reflections' "). First written as "10th Anniversary," then amended and given, as "Reflections on Freud's One Hundredth Birthday" to meeting of American Psychosomatic Society in Boston, Mar. 24, 1956; printed, *Psychosomatic Medicine*, Vol. XVIII (1956), pp. 279–83.

439   "wished only that I should spare him": Deutsch, "Reflections."

439   "Freud agreed to follow this advice": Deutsch, "Reflections."

440   "We drove to the hospital together": Deutsch, "Reflections."

440   "In view of the powerful hold": Schur, p. 354.

440   "I can again chew": Freud–Abraham, May 10, 1923, Abraham Letters, p. 338.

441   "the slow but sure realization": Freud–Kata and Lajos Levy, June 11, 1923, *Letters*, p. 349, *344*.

441   "It is the secret of my indifference": Freud–Binswanger, Oct. 15, 1926, quoted Jones, III, p. 97, *92*.

441   "I have spent some of the blackest days": Freud–Max Halberstadt, July 7, 1923, Library of Congress.

441   "physically down": Minna Freud–Max Halberstadt, postscript to Freud's letter of July 7, 1923, Library of Congress.

442   "wavered between the satisfaction": Deutsch, "Reflections."

442   "proposed that we should try the experiment": Jones, III, p. 58, *56*.

442   "protested that we had no right": Jones, III, p. 98, *93*.

443   "there was a very painful scene": Jones, III, p. 58, *56*.

443   "Finding myself, largely because of Rank's skilful manoeuvring": Jones–Members of Committee, Nov. 1924, Institute.

443   "with blazing eyes . . . asked": Jones, III. p. 98, *93*.

443   "Today I can satisfy your need": Freud–Eitingon, Sept. 26, 1923, quoted Schur, p. 361.

443   "very definitely taken sides with Adler": Freud–Hall, Aug. 28, 1923, Clark University.

444   "mystical and unintelligible": Hall–Freud, Sept. 24, 1923, Clark University.

page 444   "I think the world knows": Hall–Freud, Sept. 24, 1923, Clark University.

445   "As I returned home": Freud–Samuel Freud, Oct. 25, 1923, Rylands.

445   "He died a rich man": Freud–Samuel Freud, Dec. 19, 1923, Rylands.

445   "I am glad to let you know": Freud–Samuel Freud, Jan. 9, 1924, Rylands.

445   "For Courageous Deportment": Anna Freud letter quoted Mark Kanzler, ed., *The Unconscious Today: Essays in Honor of Max Schur*, p. 7 (afterward referred to as "Kanzler").

20 *Last Desertions*

446   "at bottom I am all": Freud–Groddeck, Nov. 25, 1923, Groddeck, p. 84.

446   "I believe that I have got over": Freud–Havelock Ellis, Nov. 8, 1925, The Yale University Library.

447   "bring a method of treatment": Public announcement, Institute.

448   "not in a position to express": Supplementary Report of Council, British Medical Association, *British Medical Journal* (June 29, 1929), p. 270. Report of Psychoanalysis Committee (afterward referred to as "Committee Report").

448   "of an extremely astonishing nature": Committee Report, p. 265.

448   "The claims of its advocates": Committee Report, p. 270.

448   "the accomplishment of my most difficult achievement": Jones, III, p. 155, *145*.

448   "I had to tremble at the idea": Freud–Jones, June 8, 1913, Colchester.

449   "failing mental integration": Jones, III, p. 47, *46*.

449   "manic phase of his cyclothymia": Jones, III, p. 49, *47*.

449   "Otto Rank constantly poured into Freud's ears": quoted *Psychoanalytic Pioneers*, p. 43.

449   "Rank's custom of treating his colleagues as puppets": Jones–Freud, Nov. 16, 1922, Institute.

449   "I have renounced the hope": Jones–Abraham, Jan. 1, 1923, Institute.

450   "I had to find out": Freud–Jones, Jan. 7, 1922, Colchester.

450   "It will not have escaped you": Freud–Otto Rank, Aug. 4, 1922, quoted Jessie Taft, *Otto Rank: A Biographical Study Based on Notebooks, Letters, Collected Writings, Therapeutic Achievements and Personal Associations*, p. 77 (afterward referred to as "Taft").

450   "the act of birth is the first experience": footnote added 1909, *Dreams*, p. 400.

450   "the first great anxiety state": *The Ego and the Id*, p. 58.

450   "I don't know whether 66 or 33 percent": Freud–Ferenczi, Mar. 24, 1924, quoted Jones, III, p. 61, *59*.

450   "Neither Freud nor Ferenczi had read": Jones, III, p. 60, *58*.

451   "He did not say a word about his new ideas": Sachs, p. 58.

451   "And now everything falls into place": Freud–Rank, Nov. 26, 1923, quoted Taft, p. 79.

451   "Dear Dr. Rank, I gladly accept": Freud–Rank, Dec. 1, 1923, quoted Taft, p. 85.

451   "Complete agreement in all detailed questions of science": Freud–Committee Members, Jan. 9, 1924, quoted Taft, pp. 86 and 87.

451   "Results of whatever kind": Abraham–Freud, Feb. 21, 1924, Abraham Letters, p. 349.

page 452　"is quite on the lines": Jones, "Psycho-Analysis and Anthropology," read before the Royal Anthropological Institute, Feb. 19, 1924, printed *Journal of the Royal Anthropological Institute*, Vol. LIV (1924), p. 57.

452　"It would be hard to imagine": Taft, p. 84.

452　"However justified your reaction to Ferenczi and Rank may be": Freud–Abraham, Mar. 31, 1924, quoted Jones, III, p. 69, *66.*

452　"I have survived the Committee": Freud–Ferenczi, Mar. 20, 1924, quoted Taft, p. 91.

453　"Give my regards to all the squirrels": Freud–Rank, May 23, 1924, quoted Taft, p. 96.

453　"In the months since our separation": Freud–Rank, July 23, 1924, quoted Taft, p. 99.

453　"For fifteen years": Freud–Lou, Aug. 11, 1924, Lou Letters, p. 138.

454　"Although I now look at most events": Freud–Rank, Aug. 25, 1924, quoted Taft, p. 104.

454　"Do not let us forget": Rank–Freud, Aug. 9, 1924, quoted Taft, p. 103.

455　"To impute to Abraham": Freud–Rank, Aug. 27, 1924, quoted Taft, p. 108.

455　"An evil demon": Freud–Rank, Aug. 27, 1924, quoted Taft, p. 108.

455　"from the very beginning [Rank]": Freud–Ferenczi, Sept. 9, 1924, quoted Jones, III, p. 73, *70.*

455　"He was my best friend": quoted Taft, p. xvi.

455　"a miracle": Jones, III, p. 75, *72.*

455　"From a state which I now recognize as neurotic": Rank–Committee Members, Dec. 26, 1924, quoted Taft, p. 110.

456　"no longer stand sponsor": Fritz Wittels, "Revision of a Biography," *Psychoanalytic Review*, Vol. XX, No. 4 (Oct. 1933), p. 361.

456　"I was honest and hard": Freud–Ferenczi, Apr. 23, 1926, quoted Brome, p. 194.

456　"Now, after I have forgiven everything": quoted Sachs, p. 148.

456　"again fight bravely in our ranks": Freud–Jones, Jan. 6, 1925, quoted Jones, III, p. 78, *74.*

456　"Rank's argument was bold and ingenious": Freud, "Analysis Terminable and Interminable" (1937), *S. E.* Vol. XXIII, p. 216 (afterward referred to as "Analysis Terminable and Interminable").

457　"I do not believe in long-drawn-out psycho-analysis": Rank, quoted Gunther Stuhlman, ed., *The Journals of Anaïs Nin, 1931–1934,* p. 277.

458　"he had nothing of the *furor therapeuticus*": Reik, *Thirty Years*, p. 18.

458　"the need to cure and to help": Freud, "Sandor Ferenczi" (1933), Obituary, *S. E.* Vol. XXII, p. 229.

458　"[playing] mother and child with his female patients": Freud–Eitingon, Apr. 18, 1932, quoted Jones, III, p. 183, *171.*

458　"I see that the differences between us": Freud–Ferenczi, Dec. 13, 1931, quoted Jones, III, p. 174, *163.*

458　"There is no revolutionary": Freud–Ferenczi, Dec. 13, 1931, quoted Jones, III, p. 175, *164.*

459　"Ferenczi is a bitter drop in the cup": Freud–Marie Bonaparte, Sept. 11, 1932, quoted Jones, III, p. 185, *174.*

459　"glad to hear of the restoration of your health": Freud–Ferenczi, Jan. 11, 1933, quoted Jones, III, p. 189, *177.*

page 459 "final delusional state": Jones, III, p. 188, *176.*

459 "violent paranoiac and even homicidal outbursts": Jones, III, p. 190, *178.*

459 "I saw Ferenczi during the last months of his life": Michael Balint–Jones, Nov. 28, 1957, Institute.

460 "Apparently Jones assumes": Erich Fromm, *The Dogma of Christ and Other Essays on Religion, Psychology and Culture,* p. 98.

460 "He has become a despot": Wittels, p. 18.

21 *Riding the Tiger?*

461 "So I thought I would go and see Freud": Sam Goldwyn interviewed by Maurice Arnold, *New York Times* (Dec. 21, 1924).

462 "I do not intend to see Mr. Goldwyn": quoted according "Stunde," *New York Times* (Jan. 24, 1925).

462 "this kind of thing": Abraham–Freud, June 7, 1925, Abraham Letters, p. 382.

462 "The film will be as unpreventable, it seems": Freud–Ferenczi, Aug. 14, 1925, quoted *Life in Pictures,* p. 224.

462 "You are not necessarily always right": Freud–Abraham, Nov. 5, 1925, Abraham Letters, p. 399.

463 "The battle for lay analysis must": Freud–Paul Federn, Mar. 27, 1926, quoted Ernst Federn, "How Freudian are the Freudians? Some Remarks to an Unpublished Letter," *Journal of the History of the Behavioral Sciences,* Vol. III, No. 3 (July 1967), p. 269.

463 "I do not know if you have detected": Freud–Pfister, Nov. 25, 1928, Pfister Letters. p. 126.

464 "more tradition than comfort": quoted Freud–Lou, July 28, 1929, Lou Letters, p. 182.

464 "you know that the English": Freud–Lou, July 28, 1929, Lou Letters, p. 182.

465 "psychoanalysis came to be the whole content": Freud, Postscript, *Auto Study,* p. 71.

465 "made no further decisive contributions": Postscript, *Auto. Study,* p. 72.

465 "what I have written on the subject": Postscript, *Auto. Study,* p. 72.

465 "most valuable clinical contribution": Jones, III, p. 274, *253.*

465 "in the same kind of way as vinegar is to wine": Freud, footnote, *Three Essays,* p. 224.

466 "the act of birth is the first experience of anxiety": footnote added 1909, *Dreams,* p. 400.

466 "Anxiety is a reaction to a situation of danger": Freud, "Inhibitions, Symptoms and Anxiety" (1926 [1925]), *S.E.* XX, p. 128.

466 "so long as the organic factors remain inaccessible": Wortis, p. 849.

467 "an impression of pessimism": Editor's note, "Analysis Terminable and Interminable," p. 211.

467 "One has an impression": "Analysis Terminable and Interminable," p. 228.

467 "Freud replied that there was implicit in this argument": Martin W. Peck, "A Brief Visit with Freud," *Psychoanalytic Quarterly,* Vol. IX (1940), p. 206.

467 "We possess the truth": Freud–Ferenczi, May 13, 1913, quoted Brome, p. 132.

page 467   "alteration": Postscript, *Auto. Study*, p. 72.

467   "My interest, after making a life-long *détour*": Postscript, *Auto. Study*, p. 72.

467   "I perceived ever more clearly": Postscript, *Auto. Study*, p. 72.

468   "The one person this publication may injure": Freud, *The Future of an Illusion* (1927), *S. E.* Vol. XXI, p. 35 (afterward referred to as *"The Future of an Illusion"*).

468   "if a man has already learnt in his youth": *The Future of an Illusion*, p. 36.

468   "the impulse became too strong . . .": Freud–Pfister, Oct. 16, 1927, Pfister Letters, p. 109.

468   "I could scarcely believe my ears": Binswanger, p. 81.

469   "some psychological foundation to the criticisms": *The Future of an Illusion*, p. 35.

469   "the system of doctrines and promises": Freud, *Civilization and its Discontents* (1930 [1929]), *S. E.* Vol. XXI, p. 74 (afterward referred to as *"Civilization and its Discontents"*).

469   "In this country we have grown accustomed": Rabbi Nathan Krass at Temple Emanu-El, New York, Jan. 22, 1928, "Psychoanalyzing a Psychoanalyst," *New York Times* (Jan. 23, 1928).

470   "It is just as impossible to do without control": *The Future of an Illusion*, p. 7.

470   "the burden of religious doctrines": *The Future of an Illusion*, p. 54.

470   "The transformations of scientific opinion": *The Future of an Illusion*, p. 55.

470   "I always envy the physicists": Freud–Marie Bonaparte, reported Jones, II, p. 466, *419*.

471   "[He] at once broached the subject": René Laforgue, "Au delà du Scientisme, Chapitre Ier, Freud et le Monothéisme," *Psyché* (Paris) Vol. IV (1949), p. 4.

471   "distinguishing a group of men": Freud–Simmel, Nov. 11, 1928, Simmel Letters, p. 104.

471   "Millennia to be, to think, to live": H. F. Peters, *My Sister, My Spouse: A Biography of Lou Andreas-Salomé*, p. 277 (afterward referred to as "Peters").

472   "No, no.": Peters, p. 277.

472   "Suddenly Lou asked Freud whether he still remembered": Peters, p. 288.

472   "And then something happened": Lou Andreas-Salomé, *Lebensrückblick*, p. 213.

472   "I only felt his arms around me": Lou Andreas-Salomé, *Lebensrückblick*, p. 213.

472   "I found the sensation": Freud–Samuel Freud, Dec. 6, 1928, Rylands.

472   "I will consider everything that life still has to offer": Freud–Simmel, Dec. 25, 1928, Simmel Letters, p. 105.

472   "that all the suffering did not substantially impair": Schur, p. 415.

472   "and in doing so the time passed": Freud–Lou, July 28, 1929, *Letters*, p. 389, *390*.

473   "responsible for the spread of neurasthenia": Freud, "Sexuality in the Aetiology of the Neuroses" (1898), *S. E.* Vol. III, p. 278.

473   "It deals with civilization": Freud–Lou, July 28, 1929, quoted Schur, p. 416.

page 473 "intention to represent the sense of guilt": *Civilization and its Discontents*, p. 134.

473 "He was an honest, nice and clever fellow": Freud–Samuel Freud, Dec. 6, 1929, Rylands.

473 "in some way we will have to provide for the child": Freud–Samuel Freud, Dec. 6, 1929, Rylands.

474 "growth and decay...": Freud–Samuel Freud, May 4, 1924, Rylands.

474 "This night I found myself": Freud–Samuel Freud, May 6, 1928, Rylands.

474 "I wish they were better": Freud–Samuel Freud, Dec. 6, 1929, Rylands.

474 "Somberly he said that he had not long to live": William C. Bullitt, Foreword, Sigmund Freud and William C. Bullitt, *Thomas Woodrow Wilson, Twenty-eighth President of the United States: A Psychological Study*, p. vii (afterward referred to as *"Woodrow Wilson"*).

474 "Freud's eyes brightened": Bullitt, Foreword, *Woodrow Wilson*, p. vii.

475 "I told him it was not this": Smiley Blanton, *Diary of My Analysis with Sigmund Freud*, p. 39 (afterward referred to as "Blanton").

475 "Napoleon had a tremendous Joseph-complex": Freud–Arnold Zweig, Nov. 6, 1934, Zweig Letters, p. 97.

475 "rash, poorly-prepared campaign": Freud–Thomas Mann, Nov. 29, 1936, *Letters*, p. 430, *433*.

475 "Freud persisted": Bullitt, Foreword, *Woodrow Wilson*, p. viii.

476 "as it rose above the horizon of Europeans": Freud, Introduction, *Woodrow Wilson*, p. xi.

476 "Then he should not have made all those promises": quoted Jones, III, p. 17, *17*.

476 "You should not have gone into the war at all": Eastman, p. 268.

476 "Freud [then] wrote the first draft": Bullitt, Foreword, *Woodrow Wilson*, p. ix.

476 "the result of much combat": W. C. Bullitt–Jones, July 22, 1955, Institute.

476 "[Freud] was a Jew": Bullitt, Foreword, *Woodrow Wilson*, p. ix.

477 "From Bullitt no direct news": Freud–Marie Bonaparte, Dec. 7, 1933, quoted Schur, p. 449.

477 "as if it were something": Tuchman, p. 40.

477 "What can the Freudian method do for history": Tuchman, p. 44.

478 "Accordingly education must inhibit": Freud, Lecture XXXIV, "Explanations, Applications and Orientations," *New. Intro. Lectures*, p. 149.

478 "between the Scylla of noninterference": Freud, Lecture XXXIV, "Explanations, Applications and Orientations," *New. Intro. Lectures*, p. 149.

478 "the established order of society": Freud, Lecture XXXIV, "Explanations, Applications and Orientations," *New Intro. Lectures*, p. 150.

478 "will be taking an uninvited responsibility": Freud, Lecture XXXIV, "Explanations, Applications and Orientations," *New Intro. Lectures*, p. 151.

22 The Darkening Scene

479 "You won't be surprised": Freud–Max Halberstadt, Apr. 17, 1926, Library of Congress.

page 480   "keeping away all the dear ones": Freud–Halberstadt, Apr. 17, 1926, Library of Congress.

480   "But don't feel that you have to be tied": Freud–Halberstadt, Apr. 17, 1926, Library of Congress.

480   "I have continued to do some work": Freud–Samuel Freud, n.d., Rylands.

480   "of whom we may well be proud": Freud–Samuel Freud, n.d., Rylands.

481   "We made a secret of all the losses": Freud–Samuel Freud, Aug. 21, 1925, Rylands.

481   "She had to be carried down the stairs from her own home": Heller, p. 420.

481   "beginning to lose her fine spirits": Freud–Samuel Freud, June 2, 1929, Rylands.

481   "But once there she rallied for a while": Heller, p. 421.

481   "I have not been spoilt by public honors": Freud–Alfons Paquet, July 26, 1930, *Letters*, p. 397, 397.

481   "The idea of a closer connection with Goethe": Freud–Arnold Zweig, Aug. 21, 1930, *Letters*, p. 399, 399.

482   "great honor although not a big sum": Freud–Samuel Freud, Aug. 18, 1930, Rylands.

482   "She is very weak": Freud–Samuel Freud, Aug. 18, 1930, Rylands.

482   "Mother died peacefully this morning": Freud–Samuel Freud, Sept. 12, 1930, Rylands.

482   "They seem to be a reaction": Freud–Samuel Freud, Sept. 12, 1930, Rylands.

482   "is I am neither very young nor very solid": Freud–Samuel Freud, Sept. 21, 1930, Rylands.

482   "Think what a treat it would have been": Freud–Samuel Freud, Dec. 1, 1931, Rylands.

482   "no likelihood of our being able": Freud–Albert Einstein, Sept. 1932, Albert Einstein and Sigmund Freud, *Why War?*, p. 47 (afterward referred to as *"Why War?"*)

482   "We have been deprived by [the Soviet experiment]": Freud–Arnold Zweig, Dec. 7, 1930, Zweig Letters, p. 25.

483   Dr. Schur noted: Schur–Jones, Sept. 30, 1955, Institute.

483   "If you had been chained up all your life": quoted, Ernst Simmel, "Sigmund Freud: The Man and His Work," *Psychoanalytic Quarterly*, Vol. IX (1940), p. 163–176 (afterward referred to as "Simmel").

483   "revealed Freud's complete and unified personality": Simmel, p. 174.

483   "A few weeks ago . . . Jofi": Freud–Lou, May 8, 1930, Lou Letters, p. 188.

484   "The feeling for dogs": Freud–Smiley Blanton on Sept. 2, 1929, quoted Blanton, p. 24.

484   "When Jofi got up and yawned": *Glory Reflected*, p. 191.

484   "to encourage an exchange of letters": League of Nations, Archives, Geneva (afterward referred to as "League Archives").

485   "You have made an excellent proposal": Henri Bonnet–Albert Einstein, Nov. 10, 1931, League Archives.

485   "quite indifferent to metaphysical speculation": Ronald W. Clark, *Einstein: The Life and Times*, p. 154.

page 485 "He is cheerful, sure of himself, and agreeable": Freud–Ferenczi, Jan. 2, 1927, quoted Jones, III, p. 139, *131.*

485 "I hasten to answer your letter": Freud–Leon Steinig, June 6, 1932, League Archives.

486 "All my life I have had to tell people": Freud–Steinig, n.d., League Archives.

486 "Is there any way of delivering mankind": Einstein–Freud, July 30, 1932, *Why War?*, p. 11.

486 "man has within him a lust": Einstein–Freud, July 30, 1932, *Why War?*, p. 18.

486 "The upshot of [my] observations": Freud–Einstein, Sept. 1932, *Why War?*, p. 47.

486 "a well-founded dread of the form": Freud–Einstein, Sept. 1932, *Why War?*, p. 56.

486 "It is unfortunate that Freud": quoted Françoise Delisle, *Friendship's Odyssey*, p. 289.

487 "But I am cross": Freud–Oskar Nemon, quoted Oberndorf, p. 151.

487 "a wolf pack, simply a wolf pack": quoted Reik, *Thirty Years*, p. 16.

487 "I saw him when the news came": Sachs, p. 147.

487 "to be expected that the other of the two": *Civilization and its Discontents*, p. 145.

488 "But who can foresee": *Civilization and its Discontents*, p. 145.

488 "Life in Germany has become impossible": Freud–Samuel Freud, July 31, 1933, Rylands.

488 "And how are you and the girls?": Freud–Samuel Freud, July 31, 1933, Rylands.

488 "Mass psychoses are invulnerable to reasoning": Freud–Erich Leyens, July 4, 1923, "Four Unpublished Letters," *Psychoanalytic Quarterly,* Vol. XXV (1956), p. 149.

489 "You surely do not believe": Freud–Erich Leyens, July 25, 1936, "Four Unpublished Letters," *Psychoanalytic Quarterly,* Vol. XXV (1956), p. 150.

489 "What also seems overoptimistic to me": Freud–Richard S. Dyer-Bennet, Dec. 9, 1928, *Letters*, p. 384, *384.*

489 "Against the soul-destroying overestimation": quoted Schur, p. 446.

489 "At least I burn in the best of company": quoted Reik, *Thirty Years*, p. 36.

489 "What progress we are making!": quoted Jones, III, p. 194, *182.*

490 "I don't believe there is any danger here": Freud–Marie Bonaparte, Mar. 16, 1933, quoted Jones, III, p. 187, *175.*

490 "The fact is that I do not underestimate": Freud–Xavier Bóveda, Dec. 6, 1933, "Four Unpublished Letters," *Psychoanalytic Quarterly,* Vol. XXV (1956), p. 154.

490 "if there really were a satrap": Freud–Arnold Zweig, Feb. 25, 1934, Zweig Letters, p. 65.

490 "No, one should be flesh-colour": quoted Joan Riviere, "An Intimate Impression" (1939), *The Lancet* (Sept. 30, 1939), p. 766.

490 "the world is turning into an enormous prison": Freud–Marie Bonaparte, June 10, 1933, quoted Jones, III, p. 194, *181.*

490 "They began with Bolshevism": Freud–Marie Bonaparte, June 10, 1933, quoted Jones, III, p. 194, *182.*

page 490   "Look how poverty stricken the poet's imagination": Reik, *Thirty Years*, p. 35.

491   "Freud looked": Arthur Koestler, *The Invisible Writing*, p. 409.

491   "The Nazis? I am not afraid of them": quoted Laforgue, p. 344.

491   "Religion, the Roman Catholic Church": quoted Laforgue, p. 344.

492   "Enough! The Jews have suffered": Felix Boehm, "Deutsche Psychoanalytische Gesellschaft Report on Events from 1933 to the Amsterdam Congress in August 1951," Institute.

492   "What with the hue and cry against me": Jung–Max Guggenheim, Mar. 28, 1934, Jung Letters, I, p. 156.

493   "The Aryan unconsciousness has a higher potential": Jung, *Zentralblatt für Psychotherapie* (Jan. 1934).

493   "murdered judenrein": Wilhelm Stekel–Chaim Weizmann, n.d., The Jewish Library.

493   ". . . As is known, one cannot do anything": Jung–Wolfgang Kranefeldt, Feb. 9, 1934, quoted, *International Review of Psychoanalysis*, Vol. IV (1977), p. 377.

494   ". . . As you know, Freud previously accused me": Jung–James Kirsch, May 26, 1934, Jung Letters, I, p. 162.

494   "It is typically Jewish": Jung–Gerhard Adler, June 9, 1934, Jung Letters, I, p. 164.

494   "To [Freud] as to many other Jews": Jung–Abraham Aaron Roback, Dec. 19, 1936, Jung Letters, I, p. 224.

494   "From this I must conclude": Jung–C. E. Benda, June 19, 1934, Jung Letters, I, p. 167.

494   "Some more chiselling": Case History of Professor Sigmund Freud, Mar. 14, 1924, quoted Appendix B., Jones, III, p. 503, *475*.

495   "Before telling me his history": Schur, p. 408.

495   "Your question about the cigars": Freud–Eitingon, June 1, 1931, quoted Schur, p. 412.

495   "I am still quite below par": Freud–Marie Bonaparte, May 10, 1931, quoted Schur, p. 429.

496   "I therefore confronted Freud": Schur, p. 433.

496   "It is a bitter winter here in Vienna": Freud–Arnold Zweig, Feb. 13, 1935, Zweig Letters, p. 101.

496   "I am not an out-and-out skeptic": Freud–Romain Rolland, Jan. 19, 1930, *Letters*, p. 393, *393*.

496   "perhaps something of a mystic on the side": Weizsäcker, p. 66.

496   "That is terrible": quoted Weizsäcker, p. 66.

496   "I meant to say that there is something": Weizsäcker, p. 66.

496   "Oh, in that I more than match you": quoted Weizsäcker, p. 67.

496   "I don't think so": quoted Cornelius Tabori, *My Occult Diary*, p. 219.

496   "The medium business, however": Freud–Edoardo Weiss, Oct. 8, 1932, quoted Weiss, p. 71.

497   "Naturally it would be unfavorable": Freud–Edoardo Weiss, Apr. 24, 1932, quoted Jones, III, p. 484, *454*.

497   "Let us make no mistake": Freud–Arnold Zweig, Jan. 28, 1934, Zweig Letters, p. 59.

497   "But it seems to me that I am *persona ingrata*": Freud–Georg Fuchs, n.d., quoted Brill, "Reflections," p. 20.

497   "I recognize the fact that I am not famous": Freud–Arnold Zweig, Dec. 20, 1937, Zweig Letters, p. 154.

page 497 "I rejoiced over your beautiful prose": Freud–Binswanger, 1936, quoted Jacob Needleman, *Being-in-the-World; Selected Papers of Ludwig Binswanger,* Translated and with a Critical Introduction to His Existential Psychoanalysis, p. 4.

498 "How well I remember these student days": Bernard Sachs, quoted C. P. Oberndorf, "Forty Years of Psycho-Analytic Psychiatry," *International Journal of Psycho-Analysis,* Vol. XXX (1949) p. 158.

498 "I do not know how to thank you": Freud–Sir Harold Jeffreys, Royal Society, July 1, 1936, St. Johns College, Cambridge.

498 "Even my Viennese colleagues honored me": Freud–Arnold Zweig, May 31, 1936, Zweig Letters, p. 127.

498 "the people of Acad. Soc.": Freud–Binswanger, Apr. 4, 1936, quoted Binswanger, p. 91.

499 "Freud, who would have liked": Freud–the Kadimah, n.d., quoted Josef Fraenkel, "Professor Sigmund Freud and the Student Society 'Kadimah,' " *The Gates of Zion* (London, Apr. 1964), p. 17 (afterward referred to as "Fraenkel").

499 "May I put it on?": quoted Fraenkel, p. 17.

499 "It is a hard task, indeed,": Freud–Wilhelm Victor Krausz, May 22, 1936, Library of Congress.

500 "staggered": Freud–Marie Bonaparte, Jan. 3, 1937, quoted Jones, III, p. 227, 212.

500 "As far as my memory goes": Freud–Frau Fliess, Dec. 17, 1928, The Jewish Library.

500 "be held unconditionally at [her] disposal": Freud–Frau Fliess, Dec. 17, 1928, The Jewish Library.

500 "I would like to know that my letters": Freud–Frau Fliess, Dec. 17, 1928, The Jewish Library.

500 "He has obtained from Fliess's widow": Marie Bonaparte–Freud, Dec. 30, 1936, quoted Max Schur, ed. *Drives, Affects, Behavior,* Vol. II, *Essays in Memory of Marie Bonaparte,* p. 12 (afterward referred to as "Schur, *Drives*").

500 "My dear Marie, The matter of the correspondence": Freud–Marie Bonaparte, Jan. 3, 1937, quoted Schur, *Drives,* Vol. II, p. 13.

501 "I did not hand them over to him": Marie Bonaparte–Jones, Nov. 8, 1951, Institute.

501 "I . . . read a few of the most important ones": Marie Bonaparte–Jones, Nov. 8, 1951, Institute.

501 ". . . Naturally it's all right with me": Freud–Marie Bonaparte, Jan. 10, 1937, quoted Schur, *Drives,* Vol. II, p. 16.

501 "I had to cancel my work for 12 days": Freud–Arnold Zweig, Mar. 21, 1938, Zweig Letters, p. 158.

501 "Our brave, and in its way honest, government": Freud–Eitingon, Feb. 6, 1938, quoted Jones, III, p. 232. 217.

23 An Order for Release

502 "Schuschnigg," "Schlechte Tage" and "Wiley": Freud's diary entries, Colchester.

503 "After gently taking the paper": *Glory Reflected,* p. 205.

503 "Finis Austriae": diary entry, Colchester.

503 "The streets were packed": Schur, p. 495.

page 503 "On the wireless": Freud–Arnold Zweig, Mar. 21, 1938, Zweig Letters, p. 158.

504 "His numerous books on psycho-analysis": Sir Walford Selby–Sir John Simon, Feb. 13, 1935, Foreign Office File No. 371: 19484, Public Record Office, Kew, London (afterward referred to as "P. R. O.")

504 "that no mention of this": Report on Freud, F. O. File No. 371: 21115, P. R. O.

504 "Demand instant news": F. O. File No. 371: 22321, P. R. O.

505 "Dr. Jones is anxious": F. O.–Mack, Mar. 15, 1938, F. O. File No. 371: 22321, P. R. O.

505 "Fear Freud": Wiley–Cordell Hull, Mar. 15, 1938, National Archives, Washington (afterward referred to as "Nat. Arch.")

505 "Wiley reported": Hull–Wilson, Mar. 16, 1938, Nat. Arch.

505 "His house was searched": Wiley–Hull, Mar. 17, 1938, Nat. Arch.

506 "For reasons": Wilson–Hull, Mar. 17, 1938, Nat. Arch.

507 "I never left the ship": quoted Jones, III, p. 235, *220*.

507 "The advantage the emigration promises": Freud–Jones, May 13, 1938, *Letters*, p. 440, *444*.

507 "Professor Freud": Wiley–Bullitt, Mar. 19, 1938, Nat. Arch.

507 "To support sixteen persons": Bullitt–Wiley, Mar. 19, 1938, Nat. Arch.

507 "taking up . . . with Himmler": Wiley–Bullitt, Mar. 22, 1938, Nat. Arch.

507 "Anna Freud just arrested": Wiley–Secretary of State, Washington, for Bullitt, Mar. 22, 1938, Nat. Arch.

507 "Anna Freud released": Wiley–Secretary of State, Washington, for Bullitt, Mar. 22, 1938, Nat. Arch.

508 "in spite of Freud": Commander Locker-Lampson, Apr. 12, 1938, Hansard, Column 943.

508 "Only by the most remote chance": F. O. Minute–Sir Maurice Peterson, June 9, 1938, F. O. File No. 371: 21876, P. R. O.

508 "I am thinking": Geoffrey Parsons–Felix Frankfurter, quoted Frankfurter–President Roosevelt, Mar. 31, 1938, Franklin D. Roosevelt Library, Hyde Park, New York.

509 "I have received information": Archbishop Cosmo Lang–Sir Samuel Hoare, Mar. 22, 1938, Templewood Papers, Cambridge University Library.

509 "Do you really think the Germans": quoted Jones, III, p. 237, *222*.

509 "It is possible": Sir William Henry Bragg–Lord Rutherford, May 4, 1933, Rutherford Papers, Cambridge University Library.

509 "Can we possibly": Bragg–Lord Halifax, Apr. 25, 1938, F. O. File No. 371: 21876, P. R. O.

509 "If, as is understood": F. O.–Sir Neville Henderson, Apr. 8, 1938, F. O. File No. 371: 21876, P. R. O.

509 "Freud's departure": Wiley–Hull, Apr. 13, 1938, Nat. Arch.

510 "also enquired": Wilson–Hull, May 6, 1938, Nat. Arch.

510 "Wouldn't it be better": quoted Max Schur in Henry Rosner, "Psychoanalytic Papers of Max Schur," in Kanzler, p. 69.

510 "rescued things from waste-baskets": Anna Freud, quoted *Freud/Jung Letters*, p. xx.

511 "brought together over nearly 50 years": Heinrich Hinterberger catalogue, quoted *New York Times* (May 18, 1978).

page 511   "Two prospects": Freud–Ernst Freud, May 12, 1938, *Letters*, p. 438, *442*.

511   "We packed and left": Mathilde Hollitscher–Jones, n.d., Institute.

511   "I can heartily recommend": quoted Jones, III, p. 241, *226*.

512   "Leaving Vienna for good today": Freud–Samuel Freud, June 4, 1938, Rylands.

24 *Into the Promised Land*

513   "When I saw": Bruce R. Merrill, M.D.–Jones, Jan. 23, 1938, Institute.

513   "Over the Rhine bridge": Freud–Eitingon, June 6, 1938, *Letters*, p. 441, *445*.

514   "the newspapers": Freud–Alexander Freud, June 22, 1938, *Letters*, p. 443, *448*.

515   "But surely you cannot doubt" and "and he used the word 'moral'": Sir Arthur Tansley, Obituary Notices of Fellows of the Royal Society, 1940, p. 274.

515   "If one's thoughts": Martha Freud–Freud's sisters, June 22, 1938, Library of Congress.

515   "sharp and deep chap": Freud–Silberstein, Sept. 9, 1875, Colchester.

515   "cranks, lunatics": Freud–Alexander Freud, June 22, 1938, *Letters*, p. 443, *448*.

515   "unwilling to believe": Freud–Nandor Fodor, quoted Nandor Fodor, "Freud and the Poltergeist," *Psychoanalysis: Journal of Psychoanalytic Psychology*, Vol. IV, No. 2 (Winter 1955–56).

516   "Even though Freud could speak": Robert A. Kann–Jones, May 29, 1956, Institute.

516   "While the motivation": Robert A. Kann–Jones, May 29, 1956, Institute.

516   "While I was crossing": Salvador Dali, *The Secret Life of Salvador Dali*, p. 24.

516   "The young Spaniard": Freud–Stefan Zweig, July 20, 1938, *Letters*, p. 444, *449*.

517   "I dared not show it to Freud": Stefan Zweig, *The World of Yesterday*, p. 423.

517   "When I talked": H. G. Wells, *Experiment in Autobiography*, Vol. I, p. 301.

517   "[Freud] gave the odd reply": Charles Singer–Jones, Dec. 22, 1954, Institute.

517   "so much uncertainty": Freud–H. G. Wells, Nov. 26, 1938, University of Illinois.

517   "They left a facsimile," and "reserved for Lords": Freud–Arnold Zweig, June 28, 1938, Zweig Letters, p. 162.

518   "to bring together": Outline of Psycho-Analysis, p. 144.

518   "The teachings of psychoanalysis": Outline of Psycho-Analysis, p. 144.

518   "His teachings have in their time": *The Lancet* (June 11, 1938), p. 1341.

518   "A remark of yours": Freud–Jelliffe, Feb. 1939, quoted *Psychoanalytic Pioneers*, p. 228.

519   "the legions of Freud" and "one of the most reactionary": quoted at Scientific and Theoretical Conference on Questions of Ideological Struggle with Contemporary Freudianism, Moscow, Nov. 1958.

page 519   "He pointed out that even now": Schur, p. 509.

519   "I am very glad": Anna Freud–Marie Bonaparte, quoted Schur, p. 510.

520   "the Hampstead War Nursery": Anna Freud in collaboration with Dorothy Burlingham, *Infants Without Families and Reports on the Hampstead Nurseries, 1939–1945*, p. xxiv.

520   "four old women": Freud–Marie Bonaparte, Nov. 12, 1938, *Letters*, p. 451, *455*.

520   "probably the main thing": Freud in Introduction to Hebrew translation of *Totem and Taboo*, quoted Aron, p. 293.

521   "If you do not let your son": Graf, p. 465.

521   "Emotionally, Jewishness": Freud–Arthur Schnitzler, quoted *Die Neue Rundschau* (1955), I Heft 100, 24/v/1926.

521   "I have always felt": Freud–editor of *Jüdische Pressen-Zentrale* (Feb. 26, 1925), quoted Aron, p. 292.

521   "You no doubt know": Freud–YIVO, June 8, 1938, *Jewish Frontier*, (Sept. 1951).

521   "Don't you think," "a certain growth" and "give rise to a wave": Freud–Lady Rhondda, editor of *Time and Tide*, Nov. 16, 1938, printed *Time and Tide* (Nov. 26, 1938).

521   *The Man Moses, a historical novel:* Freud–Arnold Zweig, Sept. 30, 1934, Zweig Letters, p. 91.

522   "Experts would find it easy": Freud–Eitingon, quoted Jones, III, p. 207, *194*.

522   "let us leave it aside": Freud–Arnold Zweig, Nov. 6, 1934, Zweig Letters, p. 96.

522   "it tormented [him]": Freud, *Moses and Monotheism: Three Essays* (1939 [1934–38]), *S. E.* Vol. XXIII, p. 103 (afterward referred to as "*Moses and Monotheism*").

522   "was really open to objection": *Moses and Monotheism*, p. 103.

522   "which reduces religion": *Moses and Monotheism*, p. 55.

522   "the new enemy": *Moses and Monotheism*, p. 55.

522   "preserved in concealment": *Moses and Monotheism*, p. 56.

522   "I had scarcely arrived": *Moses and Monotheism*, p. 103.

523   "Needless to say": Freud–Charles Singer, Oct. 31, 1938, *Letters*, p. 448, *453*.

523   "His voice showed signs of pain": Jacob Meitlis, *Jewish Frontier* (Sept. 1951).

523   "He had no preference": Jacob Meitlis, *Jewish Frontier* (Sept. 1951).

523   "The *Moses*, printed in German": Freud–Sachs, Mar. 12, 1939, Sachs, p. 182.

523   "now that everything": Freud–Stefan Zweig, *The World of Yesterday*, p. 424.

524   "Because of the active opposition": Freud–Jacob Meitlis, Aug. 19, 1939, *Jewish Frontier* (Sept. 1951).

524   "In his later years": Jones–A. A. Roback, A. A. Roback, *Freudiana*, p. 194.

524   "I am very well aware": *Moses and Monotheism*, p. 27.

525   "I have overcome" and "waiting for patients": Freud–Jelliffe, Oct. 1939, quoted *Psychoanalytic Pioneers*, p. 228.

525   "At first it looked like": Schur, p. 517.

page 525   "gives a kind of life insurance": Freud–Eitingon, Mar. 5, 1939, quoted Schur, p. 520.

525   "prepared for an onslaught": Freud–Eitingon, Mar. 5, 1939, quoted Schur, p. 520.

526   "be interested in any book" and "a recurrence": Freud–Arnold Zweig, Mar. 5, 1939, Zweig Letters, p. 178.

526   "Some kind of intervention": Freud–Marie Bonaparte, Apr. 28, 1939, *Letters*, p. 454, *458*.

526   "You won't see me": quoted Harry Freud, "My Uncle Sigmund," in Ruitenbeek, p. 313.

526   "My last war": quoted Schur, p. 527.

527   "My dear Schur," "Tell Anna about this" and "When he was again": Schur, p. 529.

528   "direct observation": D. W. Winnicott, *The Child, the Family, and the Outside World,* p. 149.

528   "should study analytically": Freud–Marie Bonaparte, quoted Ernest Jones, "Psychiatry Before and After Freud," read joint meeting of American Psychiatric Association and the American Psychoanalytic Association, Chicago, April 30, 1956, printed Jones, *Four Centenary Addresses,* p. 86.

528   "Let the biologists": quoted Oberndorf, p. 158.

529   "heard the mile-wide mutterings": Rudyard Kipling, "The Explorer."

530   "How good, dear Dr.": Martha Freud–Ludwig Binswanger, Nov. 7, 1939, quoted Martin Grotjahn, "Sigmund Freud and the Art of Letter Writing," *Journal of the American Medical Association,* Vol. CC, No. 1 (April 3, 1967), p. 18.

Index

408; early interest in psychoanalysis; wife's reaction against, 259; described by Jones, 262; as Freud's most influential supporter in U.S., 237, 277; comes to the aid of Jones; Jones quoted on, 236; on psychoanalysis, 259; at important psychoanalytical meeting in Boston, 261; effect on, of Freud's Clark Lectures, 270; his camp in the Adirondacks, 274–75; Jones to, on Freud's plans, 278; Freud analyzes when staying at Jung's home, 302–3; at the Weimar Congress, 302, 351; his "On the Aetiology and Treatment of the Psycho-Neuroses"; Freud on, 303–4; his paper at Weimar Congress, on "The Importance of Philosophy for the Further Development of Psychoanalysis"; Freud and Pfister on, 304–5; on Jung's Fordham Lectures, 323; and Starr's attack on Freud, 325; at the American Psychopathological Association, 384; correspondence with Freud, see Freud: Correspondence

Raimann, Emil, and psychoanalysis, 285; involved in the "Wagner-Jauregg Process," 405
Rank, Otto, 426, 442–43; member of the Wednesday Society; indispensable to Freud, 214; and "the Committee," 320, 321; joint editor of Imago, 349, 359; and mythology, 351; and prehistory, 357; trouble with Jones, 442–43; dissension with Freud and Jones, 448–57; joint editor with Jones of International Journal of Psychoanalysis, 449; director of International Psychoanalytic Publishing House, 449; and "The Trauma of Birth," 450–51, 453, 454, 456; collaborates with Ferenczi in "The Development of Psychoanalysis," 452; vi-

sits U.S.; finally settles there, 453, 456–57; circular letter to "the Committee," 455–56; Anaïs Nin reports him on psychoanalysis, 457; correspondence with Freud, see Freud: Correspondence
Rat Man, The, see Freud: Case Histories
Read, Major C. Stanford, on Freud and hysteria, 385
Reich, Wilhelm, joins Vienna branch of the International Association, 407, 460
Reichenhall: Freud visits, 199
Reik, Theodor, 92, 115, 194; on Freud, 84; lawsuit on lay analysis; Freud intervenes, 464
Reitler, Rudolf, and the Wednesday Society, 213; and "Leonardo," 348, 361
religion: Freud examines in "The Future of an Illusion"; discussion with Binswanger on, 468–69; Freud, and the Catholic Church "my true enemy," 491; Meitlis describes Freud's views on, 523
Remarque, Erich Maria: his books burned in Berlin, 489
repression, 24, 107; Freud quoted on, 27; and Johann Friedrich Herbart, 115; first use of term in "Preliminary Communication," 130; and the Oedipus complex, 169; and infantile sexuality (q.v.) under sexuality; and word association, 238; and the "Dora" case, 230–31; and "Little Hans," 235; "excuse" word in U.S., 408; New York Times and, 415
Revue Française de Psychanalyse: Marie Bonaparte helps found, 447
Revue Neurologique, and "Heredity and the Aetiology of the Neuroses," see Freud: Books, etc.
Rhondda, Lady, 521
Richards, I. A., on psychoanalysis and the artist's mind, 340–41

Richter, Johann Paul Friedrich ("Jean Paul"), 35
Rilke, Rainer Maria (a lover of Lou Andreas-Salomé), 313
Rivers, W.H.R., on Freudian method, 184; paper on "Freud's Psychology of the Unconscious" read to Edinburgh Pathological Club, 384; and war casualties in World War I, 385–86
Riviere, Joan, translator of Freud, 490
Roazen Paul, 400
Roback, Abraham: Jung writes to, on Freud, 494
Rolland, Romain, proposes Freud for Nobel Prize, 383; Freud to, on "Group Psychology," 433; Freud to, on religious belief, 496
Rome: Freud's obsession with, 200; Father Dempsey and Maryse Choisy quoted on Freud's obsession, 201; Freud's first visit to, 202, 358; Freud's subsequent visits to, 202, 336; and "The Moses of Michangelo," 357–58
Röntgen, Wilhelm, and X-rays, 190
Roosevelt, President Franklin Delano, and Freud's release from Austria, 504, 505, 506, 507, 509
Rosenfeld, Eva, (pupil of Freud), is rebuked by Freud, 123; and the "Committee" ring, 321
Rosenthal, Moritz, and male hysteria, 90
Royal Anthropological Institute: Jones reads paper to, on "Psychoanalysis and Anthropology," 452
Royal Army Medical Corps, and psychoneurosis in World War I, 384–85
Royal Society, The: Freud elected Foreign Member of, on his 80th birthday, 498; Charter Book brought to Freud for signing, 517
Royal Society of Medicine: psychiatric section's warm reception of Jones, 374

Grateful acknowledgment is made to the following for permission to reprint previously published material:

Basic Books, Inc., and The Hogarth Press Ltd: excerpts from *Free Association: Memories of a Psychoanalyst* by Ernest Jones. Copyright © Katherine Jones 1959, Basic Books, Inc., Publishers, New York. Excerpts from *The Life and Work of Sigmund Freud* by Ernest Jones. Copyright © 1953, 1955, 1957 (volumes 1, 2, and 3 respectively), by Basic Books, Inc., Publishers, New York. Excerpts from *The Origins of Psychoanalysis: Letters to Wilhelm Fliess.* Copyright © 1954 by Basic Books, Inc., Publishers, New York. Excerpts from *Psychoanalysis and Faith: The Letters of Sigmund Freud and Oskar Pfister.* Copyright © 1963 by Basic Books, Inc., Publishers, New York. Excerpts from *A Psychoanalytic Dialogue: The Letters of Sigmund Freud and Karl Abraham, 1907–1926*, edited by Hilda C. Abraham and Ernst L. Freud. Copyright © 1965 by Hilda C. Abraham and Ernst L. Freud, Basic Books, Inc., Publishers, New York. British rights administered by The Hogarth Press Ltd, London.

Basic Books, Inc., and George Allen & Unwin Ltd: excerpts from *The Interpretation of Dreams*, by Sigmund Freud, translated from the German and edited by James Stracey, published in the United States by Basic Books, Inc., Publishers, New York, by arrangement with George Allen & Unwin Ltd, and The Hogarth Press Ltd, London. British rights administered by George Allen & Unwin Ltd, London.

Grune & Stratton, Inc.: quote from *Reminiscences of a Friendship* by Ludwig Binswanger, 1957. Reprinted by permission of Grune & Stratton, Inc., New York and London.

Harcourt Brace Jovanovich, Inc., and The Hogarth Press Ltd: excerpts from *Sigmund Freud and Lou Andreas-Salomé: Letters*, edited by Ernst Pfeiffer, are reprinted by permission of Harcourt Brace Jovanovich, Inc. Letters of Lou Andreas-Salomé Copyright © 1966 by Ernst Pfeiffer, letters of Sigmund Freud Copyright © 1966 by Sigmund Freud Copyrights Ltd. British rights administered by The Hogarth Press Ltd, London.

International Universities Press, Inc., and The Hogarth Press Ltd: excerpts reprinted from *The Meaning of Illness* by Georg Groddeck and *Freud: Living and Dying* by Max Schur. By permission of International Universities Press, Inc. British rights administered by The Hogarth Press Ltd, London.

New Left Books: excerpts from *The Freudian Slip* by Sebastiano Timpanaro. Reproduced by permission of New Left Books Ltd., London.

Princeton University Press, The Hogarth Press Ltd and Routledge & Kegan Paul Ltd: excerpt from *The Freud/Jung Letters: The Correspondence Between Sigmund Freud and C. G. Jung*, edited by William McGuire, translated by Ralph Mannheim and R. G. C. Hull. Bollingen Series XCIV. Copyright © 1974 by Sigmund Freud Copyrights Ltd and Erbengemeinschaft Prof. Dr. C. G. Jung. British rights administered by The Hogarth Press Ltd and Routledge & Kegan Paul Ltd, London.

Sigmund Freud Copyrights Ltd: Approximately 7,000 words of unpublished material and 3,724 word of previously published material. Reprinted by permission of Sigmund Freud Copyrights Ltd.

Philosophy/Religion in Paladin Books

Mythologies   £2.95 ☐
Roland Barthes
An entertaining and elating introduction to the science of semiology
– the study of the signs and signals through which society expresses
itself – from the leading intellectual star.

Frames of Mind   £5.95 ☐
Howard Gardner
Gardner's controversial theory of multiple intelligences has major
implications for our view of intelligence and our view of education.

Infinity and the Mind   £3.50 ☐
Rudy Rucker
In the wake of *Gödel, Escher, Bach* comes this exceptional book
which draws from a staggering variety of source material to explore
the concept of infinity and its effect on our understanding of the
universe.

Confucius and Confucianism   £2.95 ☐
D. Howard Smith
A skillful and thoroughgoing study which illuminates the man and
his influence and the doctrines of Confucian thought.

Paladin Movements and Ideas Series Series editor Justin Wintle
The series aims to provide clear and stimulating surveys of the ideas
and cultural movements that have dominated history. The first six
volumes are:

Rationalism   £2.50 ☐
John Cottingham

Darwinian Evolution   £2.50 ☐
Antony Flew

Expressionism   £2.50 ☐
Roger Cardinal

The Psychoanalytic Movement   £3.50 ☐
Ernest Gellner

Western Marxism   £3.95 ☐
J. G. Merquior

Structuralism   £3.95 ☐
John Sturrock

To order direct from the publisher just tick the titles you want
and fill in the order form.   PAL13082

Sexual Politics in Paladin Books

The Female Eunuch   £3.95 ☐
Germaine Greer
The book that caused a revolution, the central focus of the Women's
Liberation movement.

Love, Sex, Marriage and Divorce   £2.95 ☐
Jonathan Gathorne-Hardy
Did sexual intercourse really begin in 1963? Can a feminist revolution ever succeed? Over the last decades our attitudes to sexual
behaviour have shifted dramatically. The whole complex of love,
sex, marriage and divorce has undergone a radical change. In this
entertaining and wide-ranging survey, Jonathan Gathorne-Hardy
questions where it all leads.

Female Desire   £2.95 ☐
Rosalind Coward
Vivid, genuinely thought-provoking essays on the symbols, emblems
and enigmatic codes – from romance to royalty, from food to fashion
– that still govern our perceptions of female sexuality.

What a Man's Gotta Do   £3.95 ☐
Antony Easthope
A stimulating analysis of a neglected aspect of contemporary sexuality – masculinity, and how it is portrayed and defined in contemporary culture. Illustrated.

Femininity   £2.95 ☐
Susan Brownmiller
An examination of femininity in all its complexities: its roots in
history, culture and religion; the points at which it mirrors biology,
and the points where the two diverge (and often conflict).

To order direct from the publisher just tick the titles you want
and fill in the order form.   PAL15082

Paladin Reference Books

A Dictionary of Drugs (New Edition)   £2.50 ☐
Richard B. Fisher and George A. Christie
From everyday aspirins and vitamins, to the powerful agents prescribed for heart disease and cancer, this is a revised reference guide to the gamut of drugs in today's pharmaceutical armoury.

A Dictionary of Symptoms   £3.95 ☐
Dr Joan Gomez
A thorough-going and authoritative guide to the interpretation of symptoms of human disease.

Dictionary for Dreamers   £2.95 ☐
Tom Chetwynd
A comprehensive key to the baffling language of dream symbolism. Over 500 archetypal symbols give essential clues to understanding the ingeniously disguised, life-enriching, ofen urgent messages to be found in dreams.

A Dictionary of Mental Health   £1.95 ☐
Richard B. Fisher
A useful, sensible guide around the confusing world of mental health, mental illness and its treatment.

A Dictionary of Diets, Slimming and Nutrition   £3.95 ☐
Richard B. Fisher
How do diets really work? Are the claims made for them justified? What does the body need to function properly? This is a comprehensive, up-to-date compendium packed with information vital for those concerned about the food they eat and what it does for them.

The Jazz Book   £4.95 ☐
Joachim E. Berendt
From New Orleans to Jazz Rock and beyond – simply the best modern companion to jazz available. Completely revised and updated.

To order direct from the publisher just tick the titles you want and fill in the order form.   PAL14082

Biography in Paladin Books

Mussolini £3.50 ☐
Denis Mack Smith
'Will be remembered . . . for the exceptional clarity and brilliance of the writing. His portrait of Mussolini the man is the best we have.'
Times Literary Supplement.

Karl Marx: His Life and Thought £3.95 ☐
David McLellan
A major biography by Britain's leading Marxist historian. Marx is shown in his private and family life as well as in his political contexts.

Miles Davis £3.95 ☐
Ian Carr
'For more than a quarter-century Miles Davis has personified the modern jazz artist. Mr Carr's biography is in a class by itself. He knows his music and his Miles.' *New York Times Book Review*.

Freud: The Man and the Cause £3.95 ☐
Ronald W. Clark
With great objectivity, Ronald Clark provides a new, human and revealing portrait of the physician who changed man's image of himself. He also gives a clear and balances account of the medical world of Freud's early professional years; the conception of psycho-analysis; Freud's struggle for recognition; and how his achievement can be viewed in the light of contemporary knowledge. Illustrated.

Chaplin: His Life and Art £8.95 ☐
David Robinson
In this definitive biography, the only one to be written with full access to the Chaplin archives, David Robinson provides a uniquely documented record of the working methods and extraordinary life of the mercurial genius of early cinema. Illustrated.

To order direct from the publisher just tick the titles you want and fill in the order form. PAL4182

Psychology/Life Sciences in Paladin Books

The Life Science £1.25 ☐
P. B. and J. S. Medawar
As the frontiers of biological knowledge continue to be extended this is a timely critical appraisal of the central thinking of biologists.

The Cosmic Clocks £1.50 ☐
Michel Gauquelin
The classic book which first established the links between the ancient art of astrology and the modern science of the rhythms of the universe and of all life, the time patterns that are etched into the personality of every living being.

The Great Extinction £2.95 ☐
Michael Allaby and James Lovelock
Until about 65 million years ago the huge reptiles known as dinosaurs flourished on Earth. Then – comparatively abruptly – they became extinct. This is the first book to reconstruct what might really have happened. Illustrated.

Infinity and the Mind £3.50 ☐
Rudy Rucker
In the wake of *Gödel, Escher, Bach* comes this exceptional book, which draws on a massive range of sources to explore our concepts of infinity and how they affect our understanding of the universe.

To order direct from the publisher just tick the titles you want and fill in the order form. PAL11082

All these books are available at your local bookshop or newsagent, or can be ordered direct from the publisher.

To order direct from the publishers just tick the titles you want and fill in the form below.

Name _____

Address _____

_____

Send to:
Paladin Cash Sales
PO Box 11, Falmouth, Cornwall TR10 9EN.

Please enclose remittance to the value of the cover price plus:

UK 60p for the first book, 25p for the second book plus 15p per copy for each additional book ordered to a maximum charge of £1.90.

BFPO 60p for the first book, 25p for the second book plus 15p per copy for the next 7 books, thereafter 9p per book.

Overseas including Eire £1.25 for the first book, 75p for second book and 28p for each additional book.

Paladin Books reserve the right to show new retail prices on covers, which may differ from those previously advertised in the text or elsewhere.

Psychology/Life Sciences in Paladin Books

Crime and Personality   £1.25 ☐
H. J. Eysenck
A revised edition of the controversial and classic study of intelligence, genetics and criminality.

The Myth of Mental Illness   £2.95 ☐
Thomas S. Szasz
'I submit that the traditional definition of psychiatry, which is still in vogue, places it alongside such things as alchemy and astrology and commits it to the category of pseudo-science.' *Thomas Szasz*. The book that rocked the psychiatric establishment.

Confessions of a Knife   £1.95 ☐
Richard Selzer
Richard Selzer attempts to find meaning in the ritual of surgery, a ritual 'at once murderous, painful, healing, and full of love'. In the careening, passionate language of a poet he speaks of mortality and medicine, of flesh and fever, and reveals something of the surgeon's thoughts and fears as he delves into the secret linings of our bodies.

The Freudian Fallacy   £3.95 ☐
E. M. Thornton
In this controversial and comprehensive attack on Freudian orthodoxy, E. M. Thornton substantiates an extraordinary claim that Freud was addicted to cocaine throughout the period when his central theories of the unconscious mind and child sexuality were formulated. Illustrated.

To order direct from the publisher just tick the titles you want and fill in the order form.
PAL11182